The Civilian Elite of Cairo in the Later Middle Ages

THE CIVILIAN ELITE OF CAIRO IN THE LATER MIDDLE AGES

CARL F. PETRY

PRINCETON UNIVERSITY PRESS PRINCETON, NEW JERSEY

Princeton Studies on the Near East

Published by Princeton University Press, Princeton, New Jersey
In the United Kingdom: Princeton University Press, Guildford, Surrey

Library of Congress Cataloging in Publication Data will be found on the last printed page of this book

Publication of this book has been aided by a grant from the Northwestern University Research Committee

This book has been composed in Linotron Aldus

Clothbound editions of Princeton University Press books are printed on acid-free paper, and binding materials are chosen for strength and durability

Printed in the United States of America by Princeton University Press, Princeton, New Jersey

To My Mother,
and My Father's Memory

Table of Contents

LIST OF TABLES AND CHART ix
LIST OF LISTS IN APPENDIX II x
LIST OF REGIONAL MAPS xi
LIST OF FIGURES (CAIRO AREA MAPS) xii
LIST OF ILLUSTRATIONS xv
LIST OF ABBREVIATIONS xvii

Note on Methodology and Transliteration xix

Preface xxi

Introduction 3
Collective Biography in the Islamic Historiographic Tradition 5
The Sources 8
I. The Fifteenth Century in the History of Cairo 15
The Mamluk Institution and Its Establishment in Egypt 15
The Administration of the Circassian Sultans 19
The Economic Condition of the Mamluk Empire 25
The International Scene throughout the Islamic World 34
II. Geographic Origins of the Civilian Elite 37
Migration to Cairo from the Delta 39
Migration to Cairo from the Nile Valley (al-Ṣaʿīd) 47
Migration to Cairo from Syria-Palestine 51
Migration to Cairo from Iran 61
Migration to Cairo from Anatolia (al-Rūm) 68
Sites of Origin in Iraq and the Arabian Peninsula 72
Migration to Cairo from North Africa (al-Maghrib) 74
Migration to Cairo from Other Areas of the Muslim World 77
Conclusions 77
Regional Maps 83
Tables 1 through 10 109
III. Residence Patterns of the Civilian Elite 128
Methodology 129
Cairo as City and Metropolis during the Circassian Period 131
The Institutional Types 138
The Distribution of Geographic Groups 143
The Metropolis of Cairo 145
The Nile Delta 148
The Nile Valley 151
Syria-Palestine 152
The Iranian Areas 154
Anatolia 156

Iraq 157
North Africa: the Maghrib 158
The Arabian Peninsula 159
Conclusions on the Distribution of Geographic Groups 160
Figures 1 through 8 165
IV. Occupational Patterns of the Civilian Elite 200
The Executive and Military Professions 202
The Bureaucratic (Secretarial-Financial) Professions 202
The Legal Professions 220
The Artisan and Commercial Professions 241
The Scholarly and Educational Professions 246
The Religious Functionaries 255
The Ṣūfī Mystics 269
The Copts 272
Figures 9 through 27 275
Table 11 307
V. A Tripartite Elite: Conclusions and Hypotheses 312

Appendix I. A Survey of Major Institutions 327
Appendix II. Positions Held by Individuals Engaged in the Twenty-one Occupations of the Major Group, and by Ṣūfīs and Copts 343
Appendix III. Glossary of Occupational Terms 390

Notes 403

Bibliography 436

Index 448

List of Tables and Chart

1. Geographic Distribution of Individuals Engaged in Military-Executive Occupations (Category I) 112
2. Geographic Distribution of Individuals Engaged in Bureaucratic Occupations (Category II) 114
3. Geographic Distribution of Individuals Engaged in Legal Occupations (Category III) 116
4. Geographic Distribution of Individuals Engaged in Artisan-Commercial Occupations (Category IV) 118
5. Geographic Distribution of Individuals Engaged in Scholarly-Educational Occupations (Category V) 120
6. Geographic Distribution of Individuals Engaged in Religious Occupations (Category VI) 122
7. Regional Influence on Occupations According to Nisbas in the Mamluk Empire 124
8. Regional Influence on Occupations According to Birthplaces in the Mamluk Empire 125
9. Regional Influence on Occupations According to Nisbas in All Regions 126
10. Regional Influence on Occupations According to Birthplaces in All Regions 127
11. Distribution of Positions Held by Individuals Engaged in Occupations of the Major Group 307

CHART. Genealogy of the Bulqīnī Family 236

List of Lists in Appendix II

List 1. Occupational Positions Held by Kātibs 344
List 2. Occupational Positions Held by Kātibs al-Sirr 346
List 3. Occupational Positions Held by Mubāshirs 348
List 4. Occupational Positions Held by Muwaqqi's 350
List 5. Occupational Positions Held by Nāẓirs 352
List 6. Occupational Positions Held by Nāẓirs Awqāf 354
List 7. Occupational Positions Held by Shaykhs 356
List 8. Occupational Positions Held by Muḥtasibs 358
List 9. Occupational Positions Held by Shāhids 360
List 10. Occupational Positions Held by Nā'ib Qādīs 362
List 11. Occupational Positions Held by Qāḍīs 364
List 12. Occupational Positions Held by Qāḍīs al-Quḍāt 366
List 13. Occupational Positions Held by Nāsikhs 368
List 14. Occupational Positions Held by Tājirs 370
List 15. Occupational Positions Held by Muʿīds 372
List 16. Occupational Positions Held by Mudarrises 374
List 17. Occupational Positions Held by Khāzins al-Kutub 376
List 18. Occupational Positions Held by Imāms 378
List 19. Occupational Positions Held by Khaṭībs 380
List 20. Occupational Positions Held by Muqri's 382
List 21. Occupational Positions Held by Muʿtaqads 384
List 22. Occupational Positions Held by Ṣūfīs 386
List 23. Occupational Positions Held by Copts (Qibṭīs) 388

List of Regional Maps

I-A.	Nile Delta, Sites	88
I-B.	Nile Delta, Migration throughout the Century	89
II-A.	Nile Valley, Sites	92
II-B.	Nile Valley, Migration throughout the Century	93
III-A.	Syria-Palestine and Anatolia, Sites	96
III-A	Enlargement. Aleppo and Damascus Provinces, Sites	97
III-B.	Syria-Palestine and Anatolia, Migration throughout the Century	98
IV-A.	Iran, Iraq, and the Arabian Peninsula, Sites	100
IV-B.	Iran, Iraq, and the Arabian Peninsula, Migration throughout the Century	101
IV-C.	Iran, Iraq, and the Arabian Peninsula, Migration during the First Half of the Century	102
IV-D.	Iran, Iraq, and the Arabian Peninsula, Migration during the Second Half of the Century	103
V-A.	North Africa and the Mediterranean, Sites	106
V-B.	North Africa and the Mediterranean, Migration throughout the Century	107

List of Figures

Fig. 1.	Cairo, Central City. Location of Religio-Academic Institutions. Based on J. Abu-Lughod's one-sheet rendition of W. Popper's four maps dividing the city into quadrants. Abu-Lughod, *Cairo, 1001 Years of the City Victorious* (Princeton, 1971), p. 45.	169
Fig. 2.	Cairo and Environs. Location of Religio-Academic Institutions. From W. Popper, *Egypt and Syria under the Circassian Sultans* (Berkeley, 1955), p. 61, Map 5.	170

Distribution of Individuals in Cairo by Geographical Groups

Fig. 3-A.	Central City, Individuals from Cairo, Educational Sites	171
Fig. 3-B.	Central City, Individuals from Cairo, Occupational Sites	172
Fig. 3-C.	Environs, Individuals from Cairo, Occupational Sites	173
Fig. 3-D.	Central City, Individuals from Cairo, Residential Sites	174
Fig. 3-E.	Environs, Individuals from Cairo, Residential Sites	175
Fig. 4-A.	Central City, Individuals from the Delta, Educational Sites	176
Fig. 4-B.	Environs, Individuals from the Delta, Educational Sites	177
Fig. 4-C.	Central City, Individuals from the Delta, Occupational Sites	178
Fig. 4-D.	Environs, Individuals from the Delta, Occupational Sites	179
Fig. 4-E.	Central City, Individuals from the Delta, Residential Sites	180
Fig. 4-F.	Environs, Individuals from the Delta, Residential Sites	181
Fig. 5-A.	Central City, Individuals from Upper Egypt, Educational Sites	182
Fig. 5-B.	Central City, Individuals from Upper Egypt, Occupational Sites	183
Fig. 5-C.	Environs, Individuals from Upper Egypt, Occupational Sites	184
Fig. 5-D.	Central City, Individuals from Upper Egypt, Residential Sites	185
Fig. 5-E.	Environs, Individuals from Upper Egypt, Residential Sites	186
Fig. 6-A.	Central City, Individuals from Syria and Iran, Educational Sites	187
Fig. 6-B.	Central City, Individuals from Syria, Occupational Sites	188
Fig. 6-C.	Central City, Individuals from Iran, Occupational Sites	189
Fig. 6-D.	Environs, Individuals from Syria and Iran, Occupational Sites	190
Fig. 6-E.	Central City, Individuals from Syria and Iran, Residential Sites	191

Fig. 6-F. Environs, Individuals from Syria and Iran, Residential Sites 192
Fig. 7-A. Central City, Individuals from Anatolia and Iraq, Educational Sites 193
Fig. 7-B. Central City, Individuals from Anatolia and Iraq, Occupational Sites 194
Fig. 7-C. Environs, Individuals from Anatolia and Iraq, Occupational Sites 195
Fig. 7-D. Central City, Individuals from Anatolia and Iraq, Residential Sites 196
Fig. 8-A. Central City, Individuals from North Africa and the Arabian Peninsula, Educational Sites 197
Fig. 8-B. Central City, Individuals from North Africa and the Arabian Peninsula, Occupational Sites 198
Fig. 8-C. Central City, Individuals from North Africa and the Arabian Peninsula, Residential Sites 199

Distribution of Individuals by Occupation

Fig. 9. Central City, Distribution of Kātibs (Secretaries) 277
Fig. 10-A. Central City, Distribution of Mubāshirs (Stewards) 278
Fig. 10-B. Environs, Distribution of Mubāshirs 279
Fig. 11. Central City, Distribution of Muwaqqiʿs (Clerks) 280
Fig. 12-A. Central City, Distribution of Nāẓirs (Controllers) 281
Fig. 12-B. Environs, Distribution of Nāẓirs 282
Fig. 13. Central City, Distribution of Nāẓirs al-Awqāf (Controllers of Endowments) 283
Fig. 14-A. Central City, Distribution of Shaykhs (Legal Authorities) 284
Fig. 14-B. Environs, Distribution of Shaykhs 285
Fig. 15-A. Central City, Distribution of Shāhids (Notaries) 286
Fig. 15-B. Environs, Distribution of Shāhids 287
Fig. 16-A. Distribution of Nā'ib Qāḍīs (Deputy Judges) 288
Fig. 16-B. Environs, Distribution of Nā'ib Qāḍīs 289
Fig. 17. Central City, Distribution of Qāḍīs (Judges) 290
Fig. 18. Central City, Distribution of Nāsikhs (Copyists) 291
Fig. 19. Central City, Distribution of Tājirs (Merchants) 292
Fig. 20. Central City, Distribution of Muʿīds (Repetitors) 293
Fig. 21-A. Central City, Distribution of Mudarrises (Professors) 294
Fig. 21-B. Environs, Distribution of Mudarrises 295
Fig. 22. Central City, Distribution of Khāzins al-Kutub (Librarians) 296
Fig. 23-A. Central City, Distribution of Imāms (Prayer Leaders) 297
Fig. 23-B. Environs, Distribution of Imāms 298
Fig. 24-A. Central City, Distribution of Khaṭībs (Friday Preachers) 299
Fig. 24-B. Environs, Distribution of Khaṭībs 300
Fig. 25-A. Central City, Distribution of Muqri's (Koran Readers) 301
Fig. 25-B. Environs, Distribution of Muqri's 302

Fig. 26-A. Central City, Distribution of Muʿtaqads (Revered Persons) 303
Fig. 26-B. Environs, Distribution of Muʿtaqads 304
Fig. 27-A. Central City, Distribution of Ṣūfīs (Mystics) 305
Fig. 27-B. Environs, Distribution of Ṣūfīs 306

List of Illustrations

Frontispiece. An Entrance to al-Azhar (fig. 1, no. 36) ii
Source: George M. Ebers, *Egypt: Descriptive, Historical and Picturesque* (London, 1884), II, p. 65.
1. Entrance to the Māristān al-Manṣūrī (fig. 1, no. 28). 137
Source: Ebers, *Egypt*, I, p. 247.
2. Interior of the Mausoleum of Qāytbāy (fig. 2, no. 121). 142
Source: Ebers, *Egypt*, I, p. 284.
3. From a Manuscript of the Koran Copied during the Reign of Sultan Sha'bān (764-778/1363-1376). 243
Source: Ebers, *Egypt*, II, p. 74.
4. Lecturing in al-Azhar (fig. 1, no. 36) 249
Source: Ebers, *Egypt*, II, p. 68.
5. A Night of Ramaḍān, Hour of Prayer 257
Source: Ebers, *Egypt*, II, p. 118.

List of Abbreviations

AFDSEB	*Annales de la Faculté de droit et des sciences économiques de Beyrouth* (Beirut)
AI	*Annales islamologiques* (Cairo)
ʿAlī Mubārak	*Al-Khiṭaṭ al-Tawfīqīya al-Jadīda li-Miṣr al-Qāhira*, 20 parts in 4 vols. (Cairo, 1888)
Berlin	W. Ahlwardt, *Verzeichnis der Arabischen Handschriften der Königlichen Bibliothek*, Vols. I-X (Berlin, 1887-1899)
BIE	*Bulletin de l'Institut d'Egypte* (Cairo)
BIFAO	*Bulletin de l'Institut français d'archéologie orientale du Caire* (Cairo)
BN, f.a.	*Paris, Bibliothèque nationale, fonds arabs*
BSOAS	*Bulletin of the School of Oriental and African Studies* (London)
CHE	*Cahiers de l'histoire égyptienne* (Cairo)
Chronology	K.A.C. Creswell, "A Brief Chronology of the Muḥammadan Monuments of Egypt to A.D. 1517," *BIFAO* XV (1918), 39-164
EI[1], *EI*[2]	*Encyclopedia of Islam*, first and second editions (Leiden)
EMPH	*Etudes orientales à la mémoire de Paul Hirschler*, O. Komlos, ed. (Budapest, 1950)
GAL	Carl Brockelmann, *Geschichte der Arabischen Litteratur*, 2 vols. (Leiden, 1949); three supplementary vols. (Leiden, 1936-1942)
IC	*Islamic Culture* (Hyderabad)
IGM	*Ignace Goldziher Memorial Volume* (Jerusalem, 1958)
IJMES	*International Journal of Middle East Studies* (Cambridge)
Index	G. Wiet, "Les biographies du Manhal Safi," *MIE*, XIX (1932).
Intiṣār	Ibn Duqmāq, *Kitāb al-Intiṣār li-Wāsiṭat ʿIqd al-Amṣār*, vols. IV and V (Cairo, 1309/1891-1892)
JAOS	*Journal of the American Oriental Society* (New Haven)
JESHO	*Journal of the Economic and Social History of the Orient* (Leiden)
JRAS	*Journal of the Royal Asiatic Society* (London)
Khiṭaṭ	Al-Maqrīzī, *Al-Muwāʿiẓ wa'l-Iʿtibār bi-Dhikr al-Khiṭaṭ wa'l-Āthār*, 2 vols. (Cairo, 1270/1853-1854)
Leiden, Or.	Oriental MS Collection of the University Library, Leiden
Map	K.A.C. Creswell, *Map of Cairo Showing Mohammedan*

	Monuments, Survey of Egypt, 2 sheets (Cairo, 1947, 1951)
MIE	*Mémoires de l'Institut d'Egypte* (Cairo)
MIFAO	*Mémoires de l'Institut français d'archéologie orientale du Caire* (Cairo)
MMAFC	*Mémoires de la mission archéologique française du Caire* (Cairo)
MRB	*Mélanges René Basset*, 2 vols. (Paris, 1925)
MSRGE	*Mémoires de la Société royale de géographie d'Egypte* (Cairo)
REI	*Revue des études islamiques* (Paris)
ROC	*Revue de l'Orient chrétienne* (Paris)
RSO	*Revista degli studii orientali* (Rome)
SI	*Studia Islamica* (Paris)
SO	*Studi orientalistici in onore di Georgio Levi Della Vida* (Rome, 1956)
ZA	*Zeitschrift für Assyriologie und Verwandte Gebiete* (Berlin)

Note on Methodology and Transliteration

Information from the combined total of 4,631 biographies was recorded in a computerized data retrieval system. The criterion for selection of cases was residence and/or professional activity in Cairo during the fifteenth century, based on nomenclature and references to occupations and residence. Both dictionaries were examined in their entirety during the coding process. Only the Arabic terminology employed by the two compilers was used in this procedure.

The purposes of the computer processing were to retrieve accurately all the elements of data recorded from the biographies relevant to specific subjects, and to compare these elements as variables. The first objective involved the retrieval of data to establish the statistical profile of a given type of information. All the details transcribed from the sources relating to a specific fact or person could be listed, together with all the information recorded in association with that item. The second objective involved counting variables and comparing them with others, thereby deriving a set of proportional relationships. Any variable could be contrasted with all the others that were recorded. For example, the degree to which professional activity was affected by religious identity, educational background, or political contacts could be explored. The system also presented the data with all the desired comparisons counted, referenced, and sorted in alphabetical order, thus simplifying the procedure of interpreting them.

The biographies were ultimately processed on some 45,000 cards that were read onto a computer tape. The actual data used represent only a small portion of the total information recorded.

Although the body of information from the biographical records is vast, it is uneven. Many items appeared irregularly, so that the resulting figures may not be regarded as "hard statistics." That is, they do not hold up uniformly well to tests of statistical validity, and the majority of patterns are to be interpreted as suggestive rather than absolute. The study thus makes no claim to being a definitive statistical analysis. The configurations we shall ponder are often highly illuminating, and entice the historian precisely because they call forth his intuitive powers. Nevertheless, the conclusions that can be drawn from these patterns in many cases remain speculative.

The Library of Congress system of transliterating Arabic terminology has been followed with the following modifications: Tā marbutā, signaling feminine singular endings, is written with a terminal "a." In general usage of Arabic terms, the anglicized plural of joining an "s" to the singular form has been used. These terms include: nisba, laqab, kunya, shuhra, madhhab, occupational titles, sectarian and legal affiliations, and so on. The terms aʿyan, ʿalim, ʿulamaʾ, and Mamluk, when they appear in the text, are written without elongation of vowels.

Preface

> I beheld in Cairo the garden of the Universe, the orchard of the world, the assemblage of the nations, the myriad flow of humanity, the portico of Islam, the seat of power. Palaces and arcades glimmer in her air. Monasteries and colleges blossom along her horizon. I beheld orbs and stars shining among her scholars. The shores of the Nile resembled the river of Paradise, the waters of Heaven. Its flow quenches the thirst of the Egyptians without cease, collecting for them fruits and riches. I walked through the streets of the city crowded with the masses of passers-by, their markets filled with luxuries. We continuously talked about this city, marveling at the extent of its buildings, the magnitude of its stature. Accounts of Cairo are frequent and varied from our savants and colleagues, returning from the Pilgrimage or commerce. I asked our colleague . . . Abū ʿAbd-Allah al-Muqriʾ . . . upon his return from the Pilgrimage . . . saying to him, "What is this city of Cairo like?" He replied, "Whoever has not seen it has not known the glory of Islam."
>
> Ibn Khaldūn, *Taʿrīf, Gharban wa-Sharqan*

The renowned scholar and philosopher of history Ibn Khaldūn rarely permitted himself such extravagance in responding to monuments of human civilization, regardless of their outward splendor. He most often confined his interpretations of the phenomena he observed to carefully measured analyses, based on a set of previously determined principles of evaluation. Yet, upon his arrival in Cairo in Dhū'l-Qaʿda 784/January 1382, Ibn Khaldūn was overwhelmed by the magnificence of the city, a metropolis larger and more grandiose than any urban center of the western Mediterranean.

The life and works of Ibn Khaldūn are well known to students of Islamic history. His significance for this study, however, involves his place of origin. Ibn Khaldūn was an immigrant to Cairo from North Africa. He moved when middle-aged, having abandoned his established, if controversial, position at the royal court of Tunis. He had lost his family during their sea voyage to Egypt. Ibn Khaldūn's fame as a scholar and jurisprudent had preceded him in Cairo, and he was assured of support from the sultan and the literary elite. Yet, final departure from his homeland suggests a fundamental decision to break with his past.

What motivated Ibn Khaldūn to leave his homeland for Cairo, a city he had never actually visited? It is true that he desired to escape from political embroilments in Tunis; but he might have resolved these without taking so drastic a step. Ibn Khaldūn was drawn to Cairo for more compelling reasons. During the later Middle Ages Cairo enjoyed a reputation as the supreme repository of Islamic culture in the central Muslim world. Most learned persons traveling east from North Africa, either on the Pilgrimage or business, passed through the Mamluk capital; and all returned with glowing reports of life in the city. Ibn Khaldūn realized that if the military and learned elites of Cairo were as munificent as he had heard, an individual of his academic reputation would be able to attract patrons with little difficulty. He could be supported on the basis of his scholarship alone, released once and for all from the burdensome administrative and legal tasks at which he had proved himself competent as well as controversial. As it turned out, Ibn Khaldūn was obliged to accept legal responsibilities during his Cairo years; but he also received the patronage he coveted and was able to devote himself to research, interrupted only by calls for his services in times of foreign crisis.

I have selected Ibn Khaldūn as a famous case, but his motives for moving to Cairo were shared by many other individuals throughout the Muslim world. Because Cairo was the major urban center of the central Islamic lands during the later Middle Ages, it attracted many of the most eminent literati from all over the Near East, who left their ancestral regions for a variety of reasons. These individuals constituted an appreciable percentage of the cases surveyed in the biographical sources I have examined in this study. Few of these people had a reputation even nearly as great as Ibn Khaldūn's, but their collective presence in Cairo made the city a cosmopolitan seat of orthodox Islamic civilization unequaled by any other during the later Middle Ages. The example of Ibn Khaldūn illustrates the most interesting characteristics of Cairo's foreign population, and also illustrates some of the qualities that defined the civilian elite as a social class during the period. These qualities are the object of the following analysis.

Cairo itself has received the attention of a wide array of travelers, historians, and urbanists, and my own debt to them will be seen in subsequent chapters. No other Islamic city has been so thoroughly investigated in such a variety of contexts. The diverse elements of Cairo's population during the Middle Ages, when the city was at the peak of its grandeur, certainly appear in these works—often quite vividly. But to date, no systematic study of their collective behavior as members of social groups has been attempted. Undertaken as a doctoral dissertation, this project began as an experiment to determine whether such an analysis for this time period was feasible. The tale grew in the telling, as the saying goes, or rather as the data base expanded along with my own sense of its potential. Although only a small fraction of that data has been used thus far, it is enough both to broaden our knowledge of the one group that is thoroughly documented, the civilian elite, and to modify certain prevailing interpretations of its activities.

Ibn Khaldūn was only one among the many illustrious scholars to fall under Cairo's spell, and yet in time he saw through the opulence of its ruling class to the more intriguing relationships between them and their civilian subordinates. His attitude toward the distinctly Near Eastern urban entity and its human components has been an inspiration to me as to many others.

I have been able to complete this book because of the encouragement and generous support of several agencies, whom I recognize here with pleasure. The research was carried out under the auspices of a grant from the American Research Center in Egypt in 1970-1971, which permitted me to examine source materials not only in Cairo but in the Netherlands, France, and England, as well. The dissertation committee of the National Science Foundation agreed to support the project at thesis stage and underwrote the cost of designing and implementing the computerized data retrieval system. The staff of the Center for Near Eastern and North African Studies at the University of Michigan, in addition to granting me a generous allotment of computer time, rendered many services to expedite various procedures of the analysis. The director of the center at this time, K. Allin Luther, had a sustained interest in the study and supported it enthusiastically. The Faculty Committee of the Office of Research and Sponsored Programs at Northwestern University provided both funds and computer time to implement the retrieval system at this campus. Upon completion of the final manuscript, the Committee offered me a subvention to offset cartographic expenses and overall production costs of the book. To all these agencies I express my gratitude. Without their support, the project could not have been completed.

I would also like to acknowledge the scholars and archivists in several countries who have shown me both courtesy and genuine interest concerning the sources I wished to consult. In Cairo the staff of the Egyptian National Library, headed by Dr. Maḥmūd al-Shinītī, granted me access to the collection and duplication facilities. A number of scholars who were engaged in their own research in the manuscript collection of the National Library assisted me during my work. I benefited repeatedly from the insights of: Professor Ḥasan Ḥabashī and Mr. Muṣṭafā Ṭāhir, then of ʿAyn Shams University; Professors Saʿīd ʿAbd al-Fattāḥ ʿĀshūr and Ḥasanayn Rabīʿ, Mssrs. ʿAbd al-ʿAzīz Maḥmūd ʿAbd al-Dāyim and Yahyā ʿAbd al-Ḥamīd al-Ḥadīnī, then of Cairo University. Finally, I must invoke the memory of Mr. Rashād ʿAbd al-Muṭṭalib of the Manuscript Institute of the Arab League. As for so many students of

Islamic culture in Cairo, he provided me with bibliographical assistance and access to the microfilm collection of the Institute. His store of knowledge and his unique personality will be sorely missed.

In Europe I was assisted by Mr. P. Sj. van Koningsveld, Keeper of the Oriental Manuscripts in the University Library, Leiden; and by Professor Georges Vajda and Dr. Jacqueline Sublet of the Bibliothèque nationale and the Institut de recherche et d'histoire des textes. I am especially indebted to Dr. Sublet for my initial exposure to a computer program collating Arabic biographical sources.

A researcher venturing into new territory can only gain from the observations and criticisms of interested colleagues. During the thesis phase, my mentors, Andrew S. Ehrenkreutz and Richard P. Mitchell of the University of Michigan, provided me with wise guidance throughout the preparation of the manuscript. Mr. Stanley Mendenhall transformed my rough ideas about the range of information hidden in the sources into a working retrieval system. While at Northwestern, I have profited from the comments and advice of my colleagues in the Department of History and at centers of Near Eastern studies elsewhere. Thanks are especially due to John E. Woods and Bruce D. Craig at The University of Chicago, who advised me of the problems I would face transforming a formidable mass of data into a manageable whole suitable for publication. George Makdisi at the University of Pennsylvania shared his unrivaled knowledge of medieval curricular terminology with me. At my home institution, Kenneth Janda of the Department of Political Science contributed to the refinement of my data presentation; Janet L. Abu-Lughod in Sociology and John R. McLane, Ivor G. Wilks, and Lacey Baldwin Smith in my own department challenged me to enlarge upon the broader implications raised by my data. Although I bear sole responsibility for any defects that still persist in the study, I owe the stimulus behind many of its arguments to conversations with these scholars and friends.

To conclude, the format of this book owes much to the skills of the editorial staff of Princeton University Press. Production of a monograph of this sort with its abundance of maps, tables, and technical phrases presents many organizational problems. The sound advice of Margaret Case in particular is apparent throughout the work.

Given the benefits I have reaped from my association with all of the above and others too numerous to mention, I am reminded that God is truly "al-Karīm."

Evanston, Illinois
December 1979

The Civilian Elite of Cairo in the Later Middle Ages

Introduction

The imperial state centered in Cairo during the later Middle Ages was, in the eyes of its own chroniclers, based on a threefold social division: a ruling military caste, the Mamluks; a civilian administrative elite, the majority of whom were designated ʿulamaʾ or "those learned in the law"; and the masses upon whose labor and obedience the ruling class depended. A scholar interested in the structure of traditional Muslim societies, the roles of their notables, and the effectiveness of their bureaucracies is fortunate in the case of Mamluk Egypt during the period because of the survival of a voluminous biographical literature. The vital statistics these sources provide on prominent figures enable the investigator to examine the higher ranks of medieval Egyptian society with some precision. This study focuses on the civilian elite of Cairo as they were described in two biographical dictionaries compiled during the ninth Hijrī / fifteenth Christian century. The elite warrant our attention because of their critical position between the military rulers and the civilian populace. They staffed the bureaucratic, legal, educational, and religious offices of the state, and determined the course of intellectual inquiry.

Because documents on them are readily available, the civilian elite have been extensively studied.[1] But no one has attempted a thorough analysis of this group, which is considered relatively homogenous. This study proposes to examine the civilian elite in terms of their ethnogeographic background and urban distribution in the metropolis of Cairo. Its quantitative methodology is a means not only of presenting a more detailed and accurate picture of this group but also of assessing the nature of professionalism in a premodern, pretechnical society, the distribution of power and influence in such a society, and finally the interplay of those factors that promoted social cohesion in a noncorporate state.

The general impression we have of the Mamluk epoch is rather negative. The defects of this era, which is depicted by medieval and modern authors alike as one of violence and instability, may have been exaggerated. But my aim is not to apologize for the defects but to explain how the civilian elite, inseparably bound to the Mamluk regime, managed to flourish. For the Mamluk age witnessed many positive cultural achievements, of which production of a rich legacy of sources is not the least significant. Throughout this period of extended domination by an arbitrary, often callous alien caste, certain elements of the civilian elite retained their autonomy. They developed survival strategies that would serve them well during the long centuries of Ottoman rule.

What bearing did these strategies have on the nature of bureaucratic procedures, theories of government, scholarly pursuits, or spiritual guidance? If service in this society entailed subordination, how can this subordination be weighed against the persistence of autonomy? The legacy of this epoch clearly depicts a high level of sophistication in the several spheres of professional activity. How does the prevailing view of the ʿulamaʾ as undifferentiated and multicompetent hold up to countless examples of specialized expertise?[2] Indeed, is this view consistent with the political realities of the period? We must inquire as to which components constituted the civilian elite and whether they regarded each other as kindred parts of a larger whole, sharing common options and goals. It is widely assumed that in traditional Islamic societies no occupational field below the military hierarchy was exclusive—closed to any other. The study will test this assumption against the data yielded by the biographical evidence. I shall argue that every professional category involved differing responsibilities and prerogatives.[3] Whether the same group could fulfill all of them at the same time is critical to our understanding of urban social organization in the Middle East during the medieval period.

The term ʿulamaʾ itself is often used interchangeably with aʿyan or "notables." The latter actually connoted a broader social stratum than the former, who were regarded as the literati of traditional Islamic cultures. The aʿyan included military personnel, and the biographers usually elected to use this term because their works were not restricted to civilians. To clarify possible ambiguities, I have coined the term "civilian elite" to embrace the nonmilitary personnel whom the biographers regarded as notables, but who may not be classified solely as ʿulamaʾ.

The research behind the study does not deal directly with the Mamluk elite per se, whose military organization has been exhaustively probed.[4] Only those Mamluks whose families had close ties with the ʿulamaʾ are considered.

The analysis is confined to the city of Cairo and its suburban districts, which formed a metropolis of several hundred thousand persons during the fifteenth century: Old Cairo (Miṣr), Fusṭāṭ, the Qarāfa and Ṣaḥrāʾ mortuary zones, Būlāq, Jīza (Giza), Minbaba, Raydanīya, Kawm al-Rīsh, and the Elephant Island Tract (Jazīrat al-Fīl). It is restricted to the ninth century A.H., and includes individuals who died from the years 800/1397-1398 to 900/1494-1495.

COLLECTIVE BIOGRAPHY IN THE ISLAMIC HISTORIOGRAPHIC TRADITION

The evolution of a genre so rich in the materials of Islamic social history—family background, educational and career profiles, and myriad glimpses into the political process—was no happenstance affair. The vast biographical dictionaries assembled by savants of the central Arab lands during the later Middle Ages represent the culmination of scholarly procedures extending back over centuries, rather than a dramatic innovation. Thus, both the plenitude and limitations of the works supporting this study may be regarded as the result of cumulative tendencies dating from the earliest stages of Muslim historiography. The compilation of biographical works is a phenomenon indigenous to the Islamic learned community.[5] The nature of their coverage, their extraordinary emphasis on certain kinds of data and virtual exclusion of others stem from the purposes these compendia were to serve, as interpreted by custodians of legal practice and spiritual guidance.

The origins of this historical genre may be discerned in an early, overriding concern for accurate depiction of the Prophet's life. Minute coverage of his words and deeds was essential in order to recapture the circumstances surrounding his personal conduct (the basis for Ḥadīth or Prophetic traditions), which, after the revelation itself (the Koran), constituted the second pillar of Islamic law. Selected as Allah's instrument for transmission of His word to the community of the faithful, Muḥammad was venerated as the prototypical Muslim, *the* exemplar for correct patterns of behavior. Accordingly, not only was the Prophet's life probed meticulously to establish the circumstances behind his statements, but also to define a model for both public and private behavior. Such, in brief, were the motives behind the compilation of the *Sīrat al-Nabī* or *Biography of the Prophet*. The term *sīra* itself invokes a sense of "conduct" or "manner of living."[6] In other words, from the very beginnings of Muslim biography, a precedent was established for stressing certain aspects of an individual's activities. Emphasis on these aspects promoted highly stylized accounts of individuals' careers, and set durable standards for professional and social advancement in traditional Muslim societies.

If it was essential to record the life of the Prophet so as to inspire the community of believers, it was equally important to preserve the history of his companions (aṣḥāb), for to them fell the task of implementing Muḥammad's message. The process of transmitting statements attributed to the Prophet by those who claimed to be firsthand witnesses was soon complicated by the insertion of blatantly false or at least highly suspect allegations. Among the techniques devised to sort out accurate statements from questionable claims was the arrangement of Ḥadīth referees in generational classes (ṭabaqāt).[7] These individuals were assessed, again according to criteria exemplified in the Prophet's *Sīra*, as to their reliability. Due to the numbers of referees, the accounts of their lives were adapted to fit highly standardized models. Of critical importance to the transmission process was the exact identity of the individual, his lineage and family circumstances, his major dates, his abilities as measured by learned attainment, and his moral qualities as measured by social esteem. As Gibb put it, "who, when, where, intellectual powers, reputation."[8] The model established for transmitters of Ḥadīth, influenced by the exemplary qualities of the Prophet as idealized in his *Sīra*, thus set a precedent at the origins of Muslim historiography for subsequent prosopographic writing.

From the tenth century on, a distinct genre emerged, based on an increasingly sophisticated system of collecting and collating information, and embracing ever-wider circles of individuals, but still adhering closely to the patterns established during the late eighth and early ninth centuries, the era of Ḥadīth proliferation and codification. The progression of biographical works may be traced through companions of the Prophet, subsequent transmitters of Ḥadīth, to early judges and pious figures who set the course of Islamic learning and spiritual observance during the classical period.[9] Compendia tended initially to be limited according to generations or to categories of individuals—that is, those grouped by common activities, affiliations, or contributions. However, compendia focusing on the notables of certain regions and in particular urban centers proliferated during the eleventh and twelfth centuries.

The biographical tradition culminated in efforts to record the collective achievement of an entire period for a broad region during the central and later Middle Ages. Following the precedent set by al-Dhahabī in the fourteenth century,[10] the major works tended to group prominent persons by centuries. The *Ḍaw'* of al-Sakhāwī, discussed below, constitutes an outstanding example of the centennial type of dictionary. These late works, in addition to incorporating a wide variety of notables, had greatly elaborated the range of information reported on them, especially in the second category mentioned by Gibb.[11] Acknowledgment of sources was also more evident in these later works, but the basic procedure of recording an individual's life did not go beyond the classical model. For this reason there is little progress in the analytical assessment of a person's character or motives for pursuing a particular calling in life to parallel the growing sophistication in collating accepted types of data.

But indirect assessments of character are certainly apparent in these compendia, usually through selection of anecdotes and evaluatory statements made by contemporaries.

The biographical style and tradition were well established and tested by our period, the fifteenth century. The perceived need for collated lists of traditionists that provided the impulse behind the prosopographic movement during the early period had been largely satisfied by the several canonical collections of Ḥadīth. Nonetheless, meticulous study of the early transmitters remained a venerated pillar of the formal curriculum. They were the exemplars of spiritual conviction during the heroic age of faith, on whose lives the learned classes of later periods sought to pattern their own. The early biographical works thus retained their centrality in the roster of texts absorbed by educated people throughout the Islamic world. Indeed, the early works were more widely distributed, especially in non-Arabic speaking regions, as a fundamental component of the curriculum than were the later compilations focusing on districts or chronological intervals. Savants dwelled lovingly over the lives of individuals described in these works as a means of spiritual attainment second only to contemplation of the *Sīra* itself.

The maturation of the Shāriʿ system of jurisprudence during the high Middle Ages effectively terminated controversy surrounding the issue of Ḥadīth transmission, but the evolution of the prosopographic method continued unabated. Once the procedure of collective consensus among the ʿulamaʾ was established by the acceptance of the four orthodox doctrines as canonical, the need for tracing the reliability of transmitters was replaced by a concern for weighing the moral fiber of the current custodians of Sunna—the tradition doctrines. Although the range of types to be considered broadened considerably during the high and later Middle Ages, the majority of cases were those with legal training. As noted below, several of the major authors, such as al-Sakhāwī, expressed anxiety over the quality of such training—"quality" being measured, of course, according to their perceptions of learning and its goals. The emphasis they placed on certain lines of study are subtle measures of the scholarly values of their age. The data they provided, along with their anecdotal comments, give us an insight into their conceptualization of the background necessary for maintaining the continuity of the Sunna.

But such emphasis did not preclude the inclusion of many persons not directly charged with preserving the Sunna. The final aim of these writers was to impart a historical legacy through the collective biography of all those who had an impact on the politics and culture of their times. This latter objective, so clearly evident in the *Manhal* of Ibn Taghrī-Birdī and the necrologies inserted at regular intervals in major chronicles, rests upon the fundamental assumptions that the civilization of a period is the sum of its participants' achievements,[12] and that political history may best be recorded by observing the behavior of individuals immersed in practical politics throughout their careers. This latter aspect has yet to receive the attention it merits by analysts of traditional Islamic societies—particularly since many literary works that reflect a sophisticated grasp of politics appeared during the later Middle Ages, an era widely regarded as one of cultural decline and intellectual stagnation. The political process during the period was highly innovative and well worth study through scrutiny of the sources compiled to trace it, especially since overt pamphleteering was discouraged.

Although restricted in the scope of data and critical analysis of the individuals surveyed, biographical sources in the central Arab lands during the medieval period reflected the development of systematic techniques of collating information. They served to encourage the accurate procurement and reporting of details, within the guidelines of idealized models formulated during the classical age.

Regardless of whether the biographer was inspired by pious respect for his subject or by a profound concern for demonstrating the integrity of the Muslim community through the lives of its guardians, he was pursuing a venerated task. Inaccuracy due to error or blatant dishonesty would defeat the very purposes of such a holy and laborious enterprise. This relationship between goals and accuracy is of critical importance. Although the authors of these works were subject to the frailties and biases that have plagued scholars in any age, their desire to record facts accurately was unswerving. For this reason, the reliability of data regarded as crucial to the genre may be assumed by the modern researcher.

THE SOURCES

Two biographical dictionaries form the base of this study: *Al-Ḍaw' al-Lāmiʿ fī Aʿyān al-Qarn al-Tāsiʿ (The Light that Illumines Notables of the Ninth Century)* by al-Sakhāwī,[13] and *Al-Manhal al-Ṣāfī wa'l-Mustawfī baʿd al-Wāfī (The Pure Spring of the Fulfillment after the Completion)* by Ibn Taghrī-Birdī (the last word in the title refers to the *Wāfī* of al-Ṣafadī).[14] The first dictionary was compiled over a number of years by a prominent Egyptian exponent of classical Ḥadīth scholarship during the later Middle Ages. Shams al-Dīn Abū'l-Khayr Muḥammad ibn ʿAbd al-Raḥmān al-Sakhāwī al-Shāfiʿī (born Rabīʿ I 830/January 1427, died Shawwāl 902/June 1497) was born in the Bahā' al-Dīn quarter of the old Fāṭimid district in Cairo to an established scholarly family that had moved to the capital from the central Delta town of Sakhā two generations earlier.[15] Al-Sakhāwī received a formal education typical for a student who planned to specialize in and teach the Islamic sciences. He was introduced to advanced scriptural and Ḥadīth studies by the famous exegete, Ibn Ḥajar al-ʿAsqalānī, whom al-Sakhāwī revered as the pivotal influence on the direction of his own career. Al-Sakhāwī demonstrated impressive energy and persistence throughout his life, and studied many texts dealing with Prophetic traditions and the individuals who transmitted them.

During the middle years of his career, al-Sakhāwī became critical of the state of contemporary studies in Prophetic traditions, convinced that they were declining in accuracy for three reasons: minimal training in the art of transmissions, inadequate knowledge of history and its applications to related disciplines, and parochial deviation from orthodox curricular norms.[16]

Al-Sakhāwī's concern over these problems motivated him to compile his enormous biographical work, which occupied much of his time during his last productive years. The dictionary was completed in Rabīʿ II 896/February-March 1491, during his sojourn in the holy cities of Makka and Madīna. He modeled his compilation on the format established by Ibn Ḥajar al-ʿAsqalānī, who confined his own work, *Al-Durar al-Kāmina*, to notables living during the eighth century A.H. Al-Sakhāwī's dictionary represents a survey of the notables of the central Muslim world during the ninth century A.H., and included individuals from Cairo, the Egyptian provinces (*al-Diyār al-Miṣrīya*), Syria-Palestine, and the Ḥijāz (western Arabia)—all provinces of the Mamluk empire. More rare were references to individuals from North Africa, Nubia and the Sudan, Anatolia, Iran, India, and Central Asia who never resided in Cairo or the major cities of the empire. Of the 11,860 biographies in this dictionary, 4,067 were selected for this study on the basis of information certifying residence and/or occupations in Cairo.

Al-Sakhāwī's main objective was to provide accurate information on the educational and legal backgrounds of the eminent ʿulamaʾ of his day. For this reason, the *Ḍawʾ* provides detailed coverage of the educational and occupational backgrounds of these people. However, al-Sakhāwī also wished to produce a work of historical biography, and, since he possessed an extraordinary capacity for details, the *Ḍawʾ* provides a wide variety of other facts about his subjects. Al-Sakhāwī's data on individuals from Cairo, Makka, and Madīna was most complete because he lived in these cities himself. His accounts of persons from Damascus, Aleppo, Tripoli, Ḥamā, and Jerusalem are also very detailed. He relied on his own notes and on notes provided him by his students and colleagues for his contemporaries (persons active from roughly A.H.

800 to 900), and on a number of earlier sources for persons active between A.H. 750 and 850.

Al-Sakhāwī's biographical dictionary may be regarded as a major prosopographic achievement during the final scholarly period of the Muslim Middle Ages. Its wealth of detail and the range of individuals surveyed render it an invaluable source for the social history of Cairo during its period. Nonetheless, al-Sakhāwī exhibited certain excesses of character that must be weighed in assessing his work. A highly tendentious individual, al-Sakhāwī clothed a propensity for personal vindictiveness against his rivals and those of his associates with the guise of a pious desire to evaluate his contemporaries' moral fiber in order to determine the validity of their opinions, both for interpretation of the Sharīʿa and transmission of Prophetic traditions or historical facts. Evaluation of moral fiber is a delicate business for even the most objective observer, and al-Sakhāwī was rarely objective about his contemporaries. His opinions of these people and accounts of their personal flaws make fascinating reading, but must be interpreted with extreme caution. Al-Sakhāwī's factual information is reliable, however, because he had little reason to distort it, especially since he realized that his rivals would immediately expose any errors or distortions he committed in return for his criticism of them and their works.

The author of the second dictionary, *Al-Manhal al-Ṣāfī*, is considered one of the two most important chroniclers for the Circassian Mamluk period, along with his teacher, al-Maqrīzī. Jamāl al-Dīn Abū'l-Maḥāsin Yūsuf ibn Taghrī-Birdī al-Atābakī (b. Shawwāl 813/February 1411, d. Dhū'l-Ḥijja 874/June 1470)[17] was the second son of a prominent Mamluk amir. His father had been purchased from Anatolia during Sultan Barqūq's program to expand his personal corps of troopers. Ibn Taghrī-Birdī's father died when he was a child, but the boy was raised in the household of a sister who had married within the Mamluk hierarchy. Ultimately, his several sisters' relations by marriage brought the young man into contact with the highest echelons of both the military and civilian elites in the capital.[18]

Ibn Taghrī-Birdī was provided with a substantial education, for which he showed a remarkable aptitude. He developed an interest in historical studies early, and this interest became an avocation when he studied with al-Maqrīzī. Ibn Taghrī-Birdī manifested the qualities of an individual firmly established in the literary elite of Cairo, but he continued to identify socially with the Mamluk ruling class. Indeed, he was able to lay claim successfully to some of his father's iqṭāʿ allotments, and received a permanent income from them, which relieved him of dependence on administrative, legal, or educational duties. No professional positions were reported in his biography. Ibn Taghrī-Birdī's contemporaries, including al-Sakhāwī, who recorded him in the *Ḍaw'*, were keenly aware of his social position. There was a degree of ambivalence toward this "Turk" who had adopted their calling for himself.

Ibn Taghrī-Birdī's historical works are noteworthy for their candor and objective reporting. He was ready to admit the possibility that he might have committed errors, especially in dating events. He was very interested in economic trends, and carefully tallied price changes on staple goods, crop yields, Nile fluctuations, and natural disasters or phenomena at the end of each year's events in his two large chronicles, *Al-Nujūm al-Zāhira* and *Al-Ḥawādith al-Duhūr*. Al-Sakhāwī accused him of factual errors, although there is some controversy over their significance in light of the overall validity of the events reported.[19] Ibn Taghrī-Birdī compiled the *Manhal* as his first substantial historical exercise, a collection based on the careers of important persons. He intended to pick up where al-Ṣafadī's biographical compendium, *Al-Wāfī bi'l-Wafīyāt*, had left off.

Ibn Taghrī-Birdī's work did not aim at a comprehensive survey of all the notables of the period, as did the *Ḍaw'* of al-Sakhāwī. Rather, its purpose was to identify individuals prominent in the Mamluk elite or civilians closely associated with these individuals, especially in the imperial court, the bureaucracy, and the courts of law. In short, Ibn Taghrī-Birdī described the people he knew best: persons involved with the processes of government and with the machinations of politics. Ibn Taghrī-Birdī attempted to demonstrate how power was wielded or manipulated to suit personal interests by assembling a collection of biographies depicting persons who had known power and authority, often as a right of caste or birth. Given this purpose, Ibn Taghrī-Birdī did not attempt to identify as many persons as al-Sakhāwī, and the entire work included only 2,822 biographies, of which 564 were selected for this study. Ibn Taghrī-Birdī emphasized first-generation Mamluks, and many of the individuals included in his work died prior to A.H. 800.

The *Manhal* differed to some extent from the *Ḍaw'* in the type of information recorded. Al-Sakhāwī concentrated on education and literary attainments, and included many of his personal opinions about moral qualities. Ibn Taghrī-Birdī provided many intimate details revealing personal and political relationships between Mamluks and their civilian clients or associates. This information, more accessible to Ibn Taghrī-Birdī than to al-Sakhāwī, constitutes the primary value of his work to the social historian. Ibn Taghrī-Birdī was fascinated by the processes of political maneuvering and infighting he observed. The ambiguous position of the civilian bureaucrat operating, often precariously, in a governmental system dominated by Mamluks is very clearly shown throughout the accounts in his biographical dictionary.

Both al-Sakhāwī and Ibn Taghrī-Birdī conformed to a standard method of portraying the individuals they described. The amount and quality of information varied widely according to the type of individuals involved, but the arrangement of details was invariable, and there are similarities between their accounts and those of a modern *Who's Who*. First, the individual's full title was listed, including his ism or personal name (rarely used in formal address), his kunyas (an agnomen consisting of Abū [father] or Umm [mother], followed by the name of the son), his laqabs (a title claiming religious piety or other personal attribute), his full genealogy as known to the compiler, all his family nisbas (attributes based on geographic origin, tribal ties, or a prominent ancestor), his madhhab (affiliation with one of four orthodox legal schools), and his shuhra (title of public address). This was done to render the individual readily identifiable and distinguishable from any other.

The statement of nomenclature was followed by date and place of birth, if either was known to the compiler. The occurrence of dates in the biographies was irregular. The most likely to appear was the death date, which was also apt to be the most exact. The death date was the most likely to provide both the day and the month (and on occasion even the hour of the day) in addition to the year. Birth dates more rarely included the day and month. Dates of important events in the individual's life, such as the receipt of diplomas, awards, professional appointments, dismissals, arrests, accidents, and political developments appeared often but irregularly. They were included if known to the compiler on sound authority.

All familial ties known to the compiler were reported. These included identification of children, parents, grandparents, brothers, sisters, wives, uncles, and other relatives. Details about the occupations of fathers, grandfathers, and uncles (both paternal and maternal) were often included, as were the names of women's husbands and male relatives. Women were likely to be included if they had important spouses who belonged to major families.

These preliminaries were followed by the first large body of information: a survey of education. Al-Sakhāwī provided many more details on this than did Ibn Taghrī-Birdī. The survey would begin with the acquisition of basic literacy through elementary Koranic instruction. It then proceeded into the secondary and advanced levels, if these had been attained. The formal curriculum and texts studied were listed with the instructors or professors who directed the individual's study. Public recitation and subsequent disputation were mentioned, along with a listing of those scholars who certified the individual's proficiency and granted his diplomas. On occasion, an assessment of performance and quality appeared, but this was given much less frequently than the other educational information. In general, al-Sakhāwī devoted more than fifty percent of a civilian ʿalim's biography to an account of his education. Ibn Taghrī-Birdī devoted less space to this aspect.

The second major body of information focused on professional appointments. It included details on the nature of the individual's occupation or positions held, the person who appointed the individual to office and subsequently dismissed him, places of occupation, dates and length of sojourn in office, and those who preceded or succeeded him in an office. Both al-Sakhāwī and Ibn Taghrī-Birdī devoted a considerable portion of each biography to these details.

Third, both compilers added miscellaneous items, such as: marriages and divorces; inheritances; political-social ties; literary works; charities and pious acts; arrests, crimes, punishments, and confiscations; residences; travels and pilgrimages; diseases and accidents; causes of death; and places of death, funeral, and burial. These items appeared irregularly but, viewed collectively, provide a critical insight to the civilian elite as a social class.

Finally, both compilers identified sources they had used for individuals with whom they were personally unfamiliar or who had been active before their own time. It is apparent that not all sources were acknowledged in every instance, but the roster of sources that did appear includes many of the important biographical and narrative works for the period.[20] In acknowledging his sources, al-Sakhāwī provided more references than did Ibn Taghrī-Birdī.

Their labors were immense, and both al-Sakhāwī and Ibn Taghrī-Birdī omitted certain items. For example, educational sites were reported more regularly than were occupational sites, and several major offices, such as judgeships and numerous dīwān posts, were given without location. Birthplaces appeared much less frequently than geographic nisbas. In general, the most accurate data were the rarest, thus placing limits on what can be conclusively stated in contrast with what can only be hypothesized.

Second, few details on fiscal matters other than fines or confiscations were reported. Accordingly, amounts of endowed institutional wealth, salary levels, fortunes inherited, fees paid, and so on, may only be surmised in a vague way. Information given on fines and confiscations, although specific, applied to individuals rather than to institutions or agencies. Therefore, unless we refer to other sources—such as waqf writs—we are in no position to determine precisely how the religio-academic network of Cairo fared financially under the vagaries of Mamluk rule. And the broader questions of income levels for the various components of the civilian elite and variations in institutional endowment remain open.

Finally, the biographical records provide few evaluative or qualitative statements about many of the items they mention. The great majority of attainments—social, professional, or other—were simply listed without comment, on the assumption of common knowledge among contemporary readers. This knowledge was often lost to subsequent generations. Thus, the analyst is left with the task of imposing some index of quality according to aggregate variations and comparisons with other sources.

These are the sources that constitute the foundation of the inquiry. On the basis of the evidence they yield, the study attempts to identify the major groupings within the civilian elite and to explain the reasons behind their differentiation. To pursue these goals, the analysis proceeds with chapters on the geographic origins of this elite, their distribution in the religious institutions of the capital, and their professional organization as measured by the relationships between their various occupational endeavors. To set the analysis in proper perspective, Chapter I will discuss the political turbulence and unsettled economy of Mamluk times: the behavior of the civilian elite was, in large measure, a creative response to adversity.

CHAPTER I

The Fifteenth Century in the History of Cairo

During the ninth Hijrī/fifteenth Christian century, Cairo displayed an imposing façade to foreign visitors such as Ibn Khaldūn. Over the almost five centuries of its evolution, unmarred by the pillage of foreign invaders,[1] Cairo had developed into a major cultural center of the Islamic world—a development that only such a prolonged state of security could have fostered. Before all else, however, fifteenth-century Cairo was the seat of the Burjī-Circassian sultans. The complexities and shortcomings of their rule cast a shadow over almost every aspect of life in the capital. Since the civilian elite were financially dependent upon and politically subordinate to the Mamluks, the social system in which they functioned was crucially affected by their rulers' policies.

THE MAMLUK INSTITUTION AND ITS ESTABLISHMENT IN EGYPT

The origin of the Mamluk system predates its foundation in Egypt by several centuries. Widely dispersed in the central Islamic lands during the Middle Ages, this type of regime should not be regarded as unique to any particular Muslim state, but rather as characteristic of the Islamic political tradition as a whole.[2] The term *Mamlūk* is a passive participle of the Arabic verb *malaka*: to own or possess, and means literally "one owned." It referred specifically to a white male slave imported for military service, primarily from Turkish-speaking regions of Central Asia, although slaves were purchased from several other areas at various times as well.[3] The Mamluk institution emerged as a consequence of the Arab penetration of Central Asia, when the need for a reliable professional army arose, to replace the Bedouin forces of the initial conquests, who began to settle and be assimilated by general society, thereby abandoning many of the traits that had rendered them such effective warriors.[4] Although the caliphs began sporadic use of Mamluks during the late Umayyad period (A.D. 715-750), reliance upon them as the critical element of a regime's military apparatus dates from only the first half of the ninth century during the reign of the ʿAbbāsid caliph, al-Muʿtaṣim (A.D. 833-842). The ʿAbbāsid empire was multinational and could not rely upon the support of some favored regional element, as the

Umayyads had relied on their Arab-Syrian elite. Instead, the ʿAbbāsids inaugurated a policy of developing a military machine, the core of which was composed of imported slaves.

Such slaves owed their status and power entirely to the ruler or dominant oligarchy responsible for their purchase. Highly impressionable adolescents, selected for their quick wit and physical prowess, would be trained not only to excel in the martial arts but also to bestow their undivided loyalty upon their benefactors. By such a strategy the rulers of several imperial states during the medieval period sought to secure their control over populations whose allegiance was often doubtful. Until the thirteenth century and the era of the great invasions, the success of this policy from a military perspective was outstanding. Mamluk armies, rarely larger than a few thousand troops, scored extraordinary victories against both external enemies and internal rebellions. Socially, however, the slaves' peculiar status created abiding tensions and laid the foundations for serious defects in the political and economic structures of the central Muslim zone.

The training procedures devised for the Mamluk corps were designed to emphasize their elite, alien status in whatever society they dominated. Their patrons sought to separate these troops from the indigenous population in order to prevent their assimilation, which would have led inevitably to divided loyalties and a breakdown in morale and group solidarity. Indeed, the earliest rationale behind these policies of forced isolation and virtual encapsulation within a society stemmed from the efforts of the first caliphs to preserve the fighting spirit of their Bedouin forces by stationing them in military camps away from the conquered peoples. Since the Bedouin Arabs were free men, this attempt was doomed to failure, but the ideal of their pristine valor, unsullied by contact with the masses, remained to haunt subsequent rulers and their advisors. Separation from the general society was achieved much more effectively with the corps of purchased slaves.

Yet the impact of separation on these slaves did not promote the total dependence and absolute reliability initially envisioned. The competitiveness instilled in Mamluk trainees combined with their sense of isolation to produce a peculiar blend of arrogance and insecurity. Rarely beloved by the masses that they were encouraged to despise, the Mamluks came to regard themselves as a privileged caste who could lay claim to the lion's share of their state's fiscal assets in return for the security they provided. They soon demonstrated that the exercise of a military monopoly must lead to political manipulation at the highest levels. Few regimes were able to restrict their Mamluks to solely military functions. Indeed, the histories of several regimes were characterized by the effective supplanting of the ruler's independent political authority.[5] In other words, he became the pawn of his own slaves, who maintained him as a figurehead. Over time, astute sovereigns sought to cope with this phenomenon by disenfranchising their predecessors' Mamluks, replacing them with their own recently imported troops. Thus, the Mamluk institution was riven with factionalism; internal strife was endemic to the system.

The resultant political milieu imbued the individual Mamluk trooper with a keen sense of his personal vulnerability. He responded to it with a narrow projection of loyalty to the barracks mates of his unit and his immediate patron; he trusted no one else. To all other elements in the society, the Mamluks exhibited scornful disdain marked by a degree of self-interest unfathomable even to many of their contemporaries. Restricted to a program of training in the use of arms, the Mamluks knew little of agriculture, commerce, or conditions promoting sound economic development. They were willing to delegate these matters to civilians who had the expertise to deal with them; but they always made it clear that their own demands were to be met, even if the economy suffered.

Thus, the balance sheet of the Mamluks exhibits a mixture of achievements and shortcomings. Without question, their military record was extraordinary. Indeed, the Mamluk institution was responsible for the capacity of the Islamic community to sustain itself militarily against a host of enemies during the Middle Ages. The Mamluks could lay claim to many splendid episodes in Islamic history.[6] They also remained the staunchest of orthodox Muslims. Although guilty of many personal excesses, over which contemporary chroniclers gloated in their works, the Mamluks uniformly supported the ʿulamaʾ in the latter's efforts to promote solidarity of belief.

Yet the vulnerability of their position, combined with the factionalism that was natural to such a system created an atmosphere of instability at the very zenith of the social hierarchy that took its toll at all levels below. This study will explore the Egyptian case as a specific illustration. At this juncture, we must be aware of the widespread cynicism and lack of public confidence in the body politic inspired by the Mamluk example, regardless of the impressive record of triumphs on the battlefield or the outward impression of security and communal cohesion.

The presence of Mamluks in the Nile valley on a regular basis began with the reign of Aḥmad ibn Ṭūlūn (A.D. 868-883), himself a Turk from Samarrā in the service of the ʿAbbāsids; but the Mamluk institution became entrenched in the country only as a consequence of policies implemented by the Ayyūbid conqueror, Ṣalāḥ al-Dīn (A.D. 1169-1193).

It was Ṣalāḥ al-Dīn who expanded and modified the system of land allotment (*iqṭā*ʿ) in Egypt by introducing techniques developed in the Saljūq East as a means of supporting a professional standing army without relying on taxation to pay salaries.[7] Subsequent Ayyūbids maintained Mamluk contingents, along with Kurds and other ethnic forces; but a regime actually controlled by a clique of military slaves emerged from a coup following the death of the last Ayyūbid sultan, al-Ṣāliḥ Najm al-Dīn, in A.D. 1249, and the assassination of his legitimate heir, Tūrān-Shāh, in A.D. 1250. Al-Ṣāliḥ's widow, Shajar al-Durr (Spray of Pearls), a woman of Armenian extraction, governed jointly with a grand amir by the name of Aybak. The new regime was torn by conflict from the start, however, and Shajar al-Durr, having instigated the dispatch of her partner in usurpation, survived him by only four days.[8] Thus the real architect of the Mamluk state in Egypt, al-Ẓāhir Baybars, did not assume the sultanate until 1260. His organizational programs, bolstered by a series of spectacular victories in Syria-Palestine, consolidated an empire and a system of government destined to last some 250 years.[9]

Medieval chroniclers divided the Mamluk epoch into two broad segments: the Baḥrīya (to A.D. 1382), so called after Mamluks purchased by al-Ṣāliḥ and housed in a fortress complex on the Nile (Arabic baḥr or river) island of Rawḍa; and the Burjīya (to A.D. 1517), after Mamluks housed in the Tower (burj) Barracks of the Citadel. The initial Baḥrī Corps and their successors were recruited primarily from Qipjak-speaking Turks, with sizable contingents of Mongols, while the majority of the Burjīya were imported from Circassian regions of the Caucasus. The Baḥrī period witnessed the solidification of the Mamluk institution in Egypt, the legitimization of its autocrat by the transferral of the ʿAbbāsid caliphate to Cairo for the express purpose of his enthronement, the elimination of residual Crusader elements in Palestine, and the centralization of the iqṭāʿ system.

The latter policy, rigorously pursued by Baybars and al-Manṣūr Qalā'ūn (A.D. 1279-1290), fulfilled its primary objective of supporting the Mamluk elite while preserving their isolation in the capital and regional administrative and defense centers. It also had momentous consequences for Egyptian agrarian history, and indeed for the very nature of Egyptian society. By concentrating the ruling caste in Cairo and blocking the alienation of holdings to individual amirs,[10] the Baḥrī sultans inhibited the growth of a rural aristocracy in Egypt during the later Middle Ages—that is, a gentry class familiar with the mass of peasantry and concerned in a positive way with the realities of agricultural production.[11] To the ruling elite, the iqṭāʿ system served to yield revenues—and that was all. Few Mamluks extended their interest beyond the fiscal potential of this system, which nonetheless remained the foundation of the economy.

By establishing the Mamluk institution in Egypt, the Baḥrī sultans formalized the separation of military and civilian spheres of influence. The consequences of this policy were to prove as fateful in shaping Egypt's future as was the centralization of the iqṭāʿ system; they are outlined below in conjunction with discussion of the Circassian administration of the fifteenth century.

Assessed as a whole, the Baḥrī period saw considerable progress in terms of commercial growth and sophistication of the artisan. Egypt attained its medieval zenith as an imperial power during the early decades of the fourteenth century. During the latter half of the century, however, the state was sapped by famines, plague, depressions, and social unrest. No autocrat of stature emerged to deal with these catastrophes, and the subsequent rise of the Circassian faction did little to ameliorate them.

THE ADMINISTRATION OF THE CIRCASSIAN SULTANS

It is widely recognized that the Circassian sultans never successfully imposed a dynastic principle of succession on the imperial throne.[12] Although al-Ẓāhir Barqūq (A.D. 1382-1399) designated his son, al-Nāṣir Faraj (A.D. 1399-1412), as his heir, the latter's unfortunate and tumultuous reign set no precedent for future successions.[13] Subsequent attempts of sons and their supporters to hold their fathers' thrones were doomed to failure. Such emphatic rejection of the dynastic principle by the upper echelons of the Mamluk oligarchy was characteristic of the Circassian period. This may well accord with the principle of primus inter pares that governed the status of the sultan vis-à-vis his colleagues, the great amirs of the realm, during the early Mamluk period, but it did little to promote the stability of the central government. During the fifteenth century, the throne became the ultimate goal of every ambitious amir, and the institution of the sultanate lost much of the respect it had accrued since the reigns of Ṣalāḥ al-Dīn and Baybars.

The great amirs of the fifteenth century regarded the office of sultan as a legitimate prize for their political machinations. Their attitude permeated the ranks of the entire Mamluk establishment from the viceroys, atabeks (field commanders), and provincial governors who were closest to the sultan, down to the lowest barracks trooper. Once in office, a sultan considered the security of his position the major responsibility of his administration, and took elaborate steps to confound and disrupt any possible alliances against his person.[14] No one could be more familiar with the possible tactics an amir might employ to overthrow his sovereign than the incumbent sultan himself, who had successfully employed such tactics to gain the throne. The highest levels of the Mamluk elite during the fifteenth century were thus engaged in an unceasing struggle between the sultan and his supporters on one side and the constantly shifting alliances among the amirs and their clients on the other.[15] This phenomenon permeated every aspect of government throughout the Mamluk empire. No official in the bureaucracy, wherever he might be, felt completely secure from its effects.

The civilian elite and the Mamluks whom they served functioned in a symbiotic relationship. Neither class tended to intrude upon the other's sphere of influence. Indeed, each regarded the other as naturally unsuited for its ordained function. During the Mamluk period, all military activities and most executive authority remained the exclusive prerogative of the Mamluk elite,[16] while the mundane staffing and operation of the administrative bureaucracy, as well as exclusive control over the civilian legal, religious, and educational establishments (although not necessarily the power of appointment), was reserved for the civilian learned or ʿulamaʾ. Given this state of mutual dependence, recognized by both classes, one might assume that mutual respect would automatically arise. Throughout their tenure of exclusive military and executive authority, however, the Mamluks maintained an ambivalent attitude toward the ʿulamaʾ.

In general, during the Baḥrī period the sultans who distinguished themselves as statesmen as well as soldiers did recognize the critical role of the learned man in society, beyond his specific duties in the bureaucracy.[17] Some of these sultans were illiterate, but they possessed a keen political acumen that noted the importance of a stable and respected educated class to maintain orderly government. The Circassian period did produce individual sultans endowed with political sagacity; but they largely failed to maintain the tradition of genuine respect for the ʿalim on his own terms, a tradition actively promoted during the Ayyūbid period and at least paid lip service under the Baḥrī rulers. The resulting situation seriously demoralized the varied elements of the civilian elite.

The ʿulamaʾ were exposed to political tension caused by the incessant feuds between volatile factions of the Mamluk elite. Indeed, they found themselves compelled to take sides in the complex tapestry of alliances among the great amirs. Such alliances affected the staffs of these amirs, who in turn demanded the loyalty of the men serving them. They expected their civilian clients to engage in certain activities and forms of intrigue not open to the Mamluks.

The pattern of alliances was ever changing because of the intricate ranking system of the military elite, a system established during the

Baḥrī period and adjusted to the tenure of each sultan in office. Mamluks acquired their basic identity from the sultan or amir who had commissioned their purchase. Those destined for the imperial court (al-mamālīk al-sulṭānīya) affixed their loyalty to the sultan and his associates, who supported and trained them for his particular service.[18] These men, upon their manumission at early maturity, were designated purchased royal Mamluks (mushtarawāt, ajlāb, julbān) and enjoyed a dominant position in the military hierarchy—but only as long as their patron occupied the throne. At the sultan's death or deposition, the majority of them immediately fell to a status reserved for those whose loyalties lay with a previous sultan (mamālīk al-salāṭīn al-mutaqaddima, qarānīṣ, qarāniṣa).[19] Since even the Mamluks who were most intimately associated with the former sultan (khāṣṣakīya), who had constituted his household and personal bodyguard, were subjected to this humiliating diminution of status, the position of even the highest offices of the realm was precarious at best.

Furthermore, the new sultan tended to view the Mamluks of his predecessor as a prime source of intrigue, if not open rebellion. In general, this attitude was fully justified. Political realities and experience within the Mamluk elite stressed the importance of securing one's own position by building up a body of troops who owed their preferred status to oneself.[20] If a sultan were to entertain any hopes of a stable reign, they would have to rest on his success in developing and augmenting his loyal body of mushtarawāt.

This volatile system was held to an equilibrium of sorts during the Baḥrī period by two circumstances: a partial system of dynastic succession, and the relatively long reigns of the major sultans. Neither of these conditions prevailed in the Circassian period, except during Qāytbāy's reign. As a result, the tendency toward anarchy now became the normative state of political life in the empire. Of the twenty-one individuals who ascended to the sultanate during the fifteenth century, only eight reigned for more than five years.[21] The political history of the empire during this century derives essentially from the activities and policies of these eight men, but it was the rapid turnover that produced the tension permeating the various Mamluk cliques. The system of formal dispossession outlined above, when applied to the pervasive phenomena of short reigns and subsequent struggles for succession, meant that individual Mamluks (mamālīk al-umarā'),[22] who had spent their adult lives and invested their talents in the service of an ambitious amir, aiding his rise in the hierarchy, could look forward to only a few years as the most favored of the realm (khushdashīya)—*if* their patron actually did attain the throne. The odds were, of course, that he would not.

The mushtarawāt who had been purchased by a sultan after his enthronement were often barely manumitted before they were out of royal service, facing an uncertain future. Many officials in the military hierarchy were dishonorably discharged from their positions and confined or exiled for indefinite periods. Indeed, many Mamluks at all levels were subjected to brutal torture or execution in order to rid the incumbent ruler of as many potential sources of insurrection as possible. This attitude of the sultans may appear callous, but it was pragmatic and based on personal experience. Every contender for the sultanate had to surround himself with troops of proven loyalty. All cadres of Mamluks who had served other masters or earlier rulers were suspect and viewed as potentially mutinous, and this assessment was basically sound.

The effect on the state as a whole of this constant need to replace Mamluks was of great consequence. Due to the depressed economic conditions prevalent during the fifteenth century, the sultans were unable to counteract the threat of mutiny by mass purchases of new Mamluks from abroad. Historians have assumed that the sultans of both the Baḥrī and Circassian periods purchased large numbers of youths every year from the Black Sea steppes, Central Asia, and the Caucasus.[23] This demand for the continuous importation of new Mamluks would have required enormous sums of money, however, sums that would have exceeded the capacity of the available tax base or yield from iqṭāʿ holdings throughout the empire.[24] Recent research suggests that the sultans of the Circassian period were either unwilling or unable to purchase more than four or five hundred youths per year, at a cost not exceeding 35,000 dīnārs.[25] This figure represents only a fraction of the annual revenues required by the sultans to maintain the courtly establishment and the military apparatus. The sultans could not expend vast revenues to import new Mamluks, regardless of the exigency of their own position, because of the related problems of shrinking receipts and rising overall expenses. To offset these expenses, they were forced to neglect the augmentation of their personal armies.

Furthermore, the sultans turned to systematic extortion of the general population at all levels to meet their expenses.[26] By doing so, they set an ominous precedent for the hordes of dispossessed Mamluks who, being out of service, were not permitted to draw revenue from the iqṭāʿ land allotments reserved for those who actually served the ruler during his reign.[27] Ultimately, these individuals turned on the general population of Cairo, robbing or extorting "protection" money, with the tacit approval of the sultan who was glad to be rid of their demands for support.

By the third decade of the fifteenth century, a large proportion of the

Mamluks in Cairo had served masters other than the incumbent sultan.[28] Their inferior status and lack of legitimate sources of revenue compelled them to realign themselves with promising new coalitions. Since the reigning sultan rarely welcomed them into the ranks of his own troops or personal associates, it was natural for these unemployed but experienced and capable soldiers to take sides with his personal enemies.[29] Of course, enemies of one day might well be royal allies the next, and thus previously sought-after clients might become serious liabilities within relatively brief periods of time. Even though the Circassian epoch produced competent rulers, these individuals were neither able nor willing to prevent a process of shifting alliances—a situation conducive to plotting, intrigue, and open strife often bordering on civil war. Indeed, capable sultans manipulated such strife according to their own purposes, hoping to nullify any serious threat to their position. This internal conflict inevitably inhibited the effective operation of the governmental bureaucracy. That this did not particularly concern those responsible for generating the discord only aggravated the situation, creating an atmosphere of crisis that became the standard condition of service within the bureaucracy.

Compounding the problem, Mamluk officers at all levels began to neglect their official executive responsibilities, and since no one else in the state could legally assume them, such responsibilities were increasingly left unfulfilled.[30] The most important of the functions that were neglected by these officers involved public security. The system of police networks both within the major cities and throughout the provinces was organized on the basis of professional Mamluk officers at the top supervising local units of militia. The administrative governors (*wālīs*) kept an eye on commerce within their provinces and enforced the decisions of their civil officials, such as the nā'ib muḥtasibs (deputy market inspectors), local qāḍīs (judges), and town or village headmen. In Cairo the heads of the guard corps (ra's nawbat al-nuwwāb) and their subordinate officers backed up the authority of the civil officials who directed the commercial life of the city.[31] Throughout the provinces, responsibility for maintaining open roads, irrigation systems, fortifications, and postal systems was assigned to the Mamluk provincial inspectors (kāshif, kashafa).[32] In theory, these officers were to guarantee a level of agrarian productivity commensurate with the fiscal requirements of the Mamluk elite. This is a crucial point. The Egyptian agrarian economy was not under civilian authority, but was reserved for Mamluk supervision, on the assumption that Mamluks should be responsible for the security of their primary source of revenue. If they failed to provide such supervision, no one else in the system could take their place. During the

Circassian period, the Mamluk officers and administrators paid attention to their executive offices only to the extent that they could extort money from them. This attitude especially characterized the administrators of the iqṭāʿ estates.[33]

A major cause for the neglect of official duties and executive responsibilities was the Mamluks' preoccupation with the discord among their own factions. This sapped their creative energies and encouraged them to ignore many significant developments in the outside world. The most important of these outside developments was the growth of the rival empire to the north, the Ottoman state. The fifteenth century witnessed the remarkable recovery of the Ottomans from the disasters of the Timurid invasion, and demonstrated the resiliency and pragmatism of their bureaucracy. The internal conditions of their bureaucracy compared quite favorably with those of the regime maintained by the Circassian Mamluks. The differences were to hasten the demise of the latter.

The impact of this internal conflict among the Mamluks on the ʿulamaʾ who staffed the Mamluk bureaucracy was profound. They were demoralized, and many of them corrupted, by the rampant factionalism.[34] They were forced to realign themselves continuously within the shifting patterns of Mamluk dissension, seeking thereby to strike a balance between the factions—a balance in reality unobtainable. Therefore, the nature of an ʿalim's bureaucratic career was rendered intrinsically unstable. In other words, the nature of the self-imposed political milieu that plagued the life of a Mamluk officer also warped and belittled the professional careers of the ʿulamaʾ in the bureaucracy. Deprived of security in their legitimate fields, civilians were virtually compelled to involve themselves in the corrupt dealings of the Mamluks who employed them.

This need for deception was not limited to individuals engaged in bureaucratic functions. The unstable nature of the Mamluk elite also affected the ʿulamaʾ who retained their traditional functions in the legal, educational, and religious establishments. The activities of the qāḍīs and their associates were the most obviously affected, since they took responsibility for the direction of litigation. Indeed, all the chief qāḍīs were appointed by the sultan directly and were therefore subject to the whims of his personal idiosyncracies, as well as his ambitions or intrigues. Furthermore, the sultans of the Circassian period tended to appoint judges according to the suggestions of key associates, who nominated members of their own staffs whom they regarded as pliable to their wishes. The power to influence if not to dictate juridical decisions was a sensitive issue during the Circassian period.[35]

Because the scholarly and religious establishments of Cairo administered vast waqf endowments, they too did not escape the oppression and coercion of the imperial bureaucracy. Wherever new sources of revenue could be detected, Mamluk amirs were likely to ascertain whether or not their confiscation were feasible. This was true even though, as the number and magnitude of surviving monuments attest, the Mamluks invested lavishly in religious and educational endowments. The Circassian Mamluks were not embarrassed by their eagerness to expropriate any source of invested funds, however, even if they sought to immortalize their own names later by making similar endowments at the end of their careers. In an age of financial insecurity, the great amirs who struck it rich were willing to make such gifts as a token of appreciation for their good fortune—and, perhaps, to appease a vengeful God, pledged to punish rapacity and sin in the next world. The majority of Mamluks from the Circassian period did not succeed financially, and recognized no debt to society or religion, however. They did not debate the morality of confiscating educational or religious funds if the opportunity occurred. The ʿulamaʾ administering these endowments therefore continually faced the grim task of maintaining themselves and their institutions in the face of imminent confiscation. The shaykhs in charge of colleges, monasteries (khānqāhs), hospitals, shrines, and orphanages joined the ranks of the great merchants in the status of the fiscally oppressed.[36] They spent much of their time concealing their wealth and confusing their accounts—or making payments to one faction of the Mamluk elite in order to ward off others.

The disturbance of these unsettled times went beyond the realm of finances, however, to stain the quality of intellectual life. The Circassian period did not witness any major flowering of new ideological activity, although it did produce an enormous encyclopedic synthesis of previous work. The reasons for this may be found in part in the uncertain nature of the times. Men who dared to disagree with established canons of belief, or who even dared to offer differing interpretations of established canons, were accused of heresy, a capital offense. The Mamluk elite demanded strict orthodoxy from the mass of their subject population. Thus, the learned civilians during the Circassian period presented an imposing façade, but they were caught up in an unstable political process that demoralized and corrupted their traditional position in Islamic society. This process was further complicated by the deteriorating economic situation throughout the fifteenth century.

THE ECONOMIC CONDITION OF THE MAMLUK EMPIRE

The economy during the fifteenth century exhibited few positive indications of growth or innovation. The chroniclers of the period concurred that the fiscal condition of the empire was deteriorating steadily, and that this process stemmed from numerous defects in the management of the state.[37] The hindsight of contemporary economic theory permits us to note one fundamental and apparently insoluble dilemma that drove the Mamluks and their major officials to unscrupulous procedures for raising revenues. This dilemma lurks behind the divergent views held by the chroniclers, but was not explicitly articulated in their works. Basically, shrinking returns from taxes and iqṭāʿ landholdings no longer yielded revenues equal to the rising fiscal demands of the regime. Precisely why the traditional sources of revenue diminished is open to debate.[38] Quite likely, the trend stemmed from causes beyond the control, and indeed the comprehension, of any premodern government. Whether the Mamluk elite could have tailored their demands to accord with these straitened circumstances and still survived is also unclear. It is important to consider the specifics of this issue here, since they bear on the question of ultimate responsibility for Egypt's precipitous decline as an economic power and the consequent impact of this decline on her civilian elite.

The demands of the Mamluk caste—and particularly of the sultan—for cash funds grew throughout the century for several reasons: the demand for new Mamluks; the increasing scale of pensions paid to unemployed, out-of-service, or retired Mamluk officers and troopers; the costs of military campaigns; the extravagant tastes and requirements of the imperial court and households of great amirs; and a general price inflation throughout the century. The first three of these merit further comment.

As previously mentioned, the financial straits of the Circassian regime can be detected in the declining numbers of new Mamluks imported annually. We can assume that the sultans of the fifteenth century would have liked to increase the number of youths purchased in order to secure their positions, replacing the extant cadres of Mamluks with their own men who owed them unquestioned loyalty. In practice, however, the level of importation declined until the latter part of the century, and increased moderately during the reigns of al-Ashraf Qāytbāy (1468-1495) and al-Ashraf al-Ghawrī (1501-1516). The majority of Mamluks imported during the fifteenth century were bought by the eight sultans who reigned long enough to gather the necessary funds.[39] These individuals managed to remain in power because of their personal ability and tenacity, and because they possessed more purchased Mamluks than their less fortunate competitors. From a fiscal point of view, these eight rulers did the worst damage to the country, and even their relatively diminished expenditures for new troops contributed to the depressed economy. This was so in part because of the rising cost of military slaves.

The trade in youths from Central Asia has a history beyond the scope of this study.[40] The important point here is that the various regimes in the Near East employing a Mamluk military system rarely controlled either the source of their manpower or the trade supplying it. During the Egyptian Mamluk period, merchants of varied backgrounds gathered adolescents from the Black Sea steppes, Turkish Central Asia, or the Caucasus, and transported them to Alexandria or Damietta. Those who operated this slave trade could set the price according to their own interests and requirements, for they realized that the Circassian regime in Egypt was dependent on them for their supply of new troops, regardless of numbers demanded. Rising prices contributed to the decrease in numbers of new Mamluks purchased.

The resultant shortage of mushtarawāt was temporarily compensated for by the charisma of the last great sultan of the Circassian period, Qāytbāy, whose ability to mitigate the intensity of strife among his subordinates for three decades and bring them together in his service may well have saved the regime from collapse.[41] But Qāytbāy could not escape the system of military pensions and special salaries to achieve this balance, and he placed a further strain on the economy.

The system of special salaries or pensions (murattab, rātib, khubz) for out-of-service or unemployed Mamluks originated with much earlier Mamluk military systems. It was established in Egypt by the late Ayyūbids, who employed Mamluks as their special elite force and bodyguard.[42] The purpose of the special salaries and pensions, added to income from assigned land allotments, was to encourage or reward loyalty and distinguished service, to enable an individual to save enough for his old age, and to support the inevitable percentage of those who were out of service or retired without adequate income. As was the case for other regimes in the Near East employing similar systems of payments, however, the procedure in Egypt fell into abuse during the Circassian period. Mamluks had always regarded it as their special leverage against the demands of the state. But when their financial position declined during the fifteenth century, due to the high percentage of their number who were unemployed, the Mamluk troops at all levels came to regard this special salary as their primary source of support from the sultan.[43] Indeed, this it was for those not in his service, since they were no longer entitled to an iqṭāʿ land allotment.

As the percentage of unemployed and out-of-service Mamluks grew during the century, the demands on the sultan for support became unbearable. If the sultan failed to pay off at least a large percentage of those demanding support, however, he faced the certainty of insurrection. I would argue that the majority of even the military elite of Egypt during the Circassian period did not enjoy financial security, although certain individuals did amass great fortunes. Since many of the members of this elite faced financial ruin, they became a dangerous and unpredictable faction within Egyptian society. They constituted a menace to both public order and the sultan's security, because they monopolized the military force available to the state, and had been trained to regard themselves as its pivotal element.

The sultans of the Circassian period responded to this menace with three courses of action: they attempted to eliminate or disperse the mass of out-of-service Mamluks by execution, imprisonment, or exile; they paid off at least some of them; and they turned others loose on the civilian population.[44] The sultans used all three policies whenever feasible. But even if they did support the many troops who rendered them no service, they realized that this did not bring them true loyalty. Throughout the century, the mass of Mamluks remained a latent threat to the sultan's personal security. Many of them entertained the hope of joining a successful insurrection that would topple the individual who stood between them and the power and wealth they expected as their right of class.

Finally, the Circassian regime inherited from its predecessors, the Ayyūbids and Baḥrīs, a reputation for the successful defense of Sunnī Islam against foreign invaders, specifically Franks from the west and Mongols from the east. The burden of maintaining this tradition became severe during the fifteenth century, however, when the cost of mounting military expeditions, always a major expense of the regime, had to be met in addition to the other expenses. Military campaigns had previously constituted the central, routine item of the imperial budget; but during the Circassian period, all campaigns constituted extraordinary items to be budgeted through extraordinary methods.[45] Sultan Qāytbāy spent some eight million dīnārs on his campaigns, and other major rulers spent vast sums on theirs.[46] Since the requirements of these expeditions could not be predicted, their costs could not be anticipated in even the best of circumstances. When there was no appreciable reserve in the treasury, they had to be funded by forced payments from the civilian population.[47]

The purchase and support of Mamluks and the cost of military campaigns represent the major areas of demand by the Mamluk regime on revenues generated within the state—demands that were inflating. Even during prosperous times they would have presented difficulties, but since the very foundations of the economy were declining, their impact was devastating. The fundamental cause of Egypt's long-range deterioration was the steady decrease in agrarian production. This production provided the basic revenues funding the activities of the Mamluk elite, and thus indirectly supported the religio-academic establishment. The reason for this decrease in production, as measured by diminishing tax receipts, remains an arguable subject.[48] Debate focuses on whether the decline evolved in response to natural phenomena, such as famines, plagues, and resultant demographic factors,[49] or derived primarily from governmental neglect and exploitation.[50] No regime functioning in a pretechnological age could effectively counteract the impact of plague and famine, of course. If Egypt's rural population was indeed drastically reduced during the fourteenth and fifteenth centuries, her agrarian output would reflect the effects. Population decline would also explain the progressive abandonment of large tracts of arable land, especially in Upper Egypt, and their return to waste or pastoral conditions. Even if there were severe natural disasters, however, the Mamluk regime did little to develop a policy of adjustment. No attempts were made to transfer populations and resettle underpopulated allotments.[51] Nor did the Mamluk muqṭā'sʿ (recipients of land allotments) reserve any portion of their income for reinvesting in their estates. From their point of view, they could no longer spare income for such purposes. The primary goal of the elite vis-à-vis their land holdings thus became little more than to wring out the maximum revenue, returning as little as possible to either the land or those who worked it. As a consequence, the economic position of the peasant tenants declined drastically during the century, even with the expanded opportunities for inheritance resulting from plague deaths. It is quite possible that the peasants saw little reason to improve their output, even if they had access to more land, since resulting increases would be taken by their landlords as dues. In any case, the number of units of land under cultivation did not increase during the Circassian period.

The prevalent Mamluk attitude toward maximizing profit was not confined to their iqṭāʿ holdings, but affected the mercantile systems of the state as well. The success of medieval Islamic merchants in the highly competitive world markets of the early and central Middle Ages had become proverbial even in their own day. This success was achieved because both the mercantile classes and their governments recognized that profitable trade required both a pragmatic interpretation of the laws of Sharīʿa governing business and contracts[52] and a keen awareness of conditions affecting foreign suppliers and consumers. From the Fāṭimid period to the late Baḥrī period, the ruling regimes in Egypt gave the merchant considerable freedom to do business.[53] Above all, the regimes sought in their foreign policies to maintain Egypt's role as the central relay station or emporium in the Oriental trade that supplied Europe with exotic products.[54] The major products in this trade were spices, and the spice merchants (tujjār al-kārim, kārimī) were at the core of the ascendant mercantile class in Egypt.

The kārimī merchants of Egypt during the central Middle Ages, when they exercised their maximum influence and created vast personal fortunes, stand as one of the brilliant commercial classes of Near Eastern history. They exhibited an abiding concern for the cultural aspects of their society and endowed it richly with waqfs in support of libraries; chairs for scholars, teachers, mystics, and poets; mosques that were magnificent architectural monuments; public fountains and baths; orphanages, hospitals, and rest homes.[55] With regard to the practical requirements of their profession, they endowed guest houses along trade routes, improved harbor facilities, and built up a system of warehouses, khāns (inns), and caravansarays in which business could be carried out efficiently.[56] They maintained contacts throughout the ports of the Indian Ocean, and kept themselves abreast of political developments from Europe to China.[57] The kārimī merchants were among the best-informed people of the Middle Ages and often served their governments as bankers, wazīrs, ambassadors, secretaries, and controllers of privy funds.[58]

During the Baḥrī period, a monopoly of political authority was held by the Mamluk elite, but the sultans retained the commercial pragmatism of earlier regimes. Thus, the kārimīs continued to thrive, maintaining their prosperity and independence because of the economic interests they shared with the regime rather than thanks to altruistic qualities of individual sultans.[59] The position of the kārimīs was not immune to shifts in trade routes and market conditions, of course. Their independence during the Baḥrī period can be explained in part by a diminution of their activities in Egypt during the fourteenth century.[60] When Egypt again regained her central position in the international spice trade during the fifteenth century, the regime was quick to take advantage of the opportunity for more thorough exploitation.

The first sultan who both recognized the inadequacies of his fiscal base and elected to intervene directly in the commercial process was al-Ashraf Barsbāy (825-841/1422-1437).[61] He inaugurated a policy of imposed state monopolies over the major forms of trade and production in the empire, which lasted, with temporary lapses, until the extinction of the regime in 1517. The details of this policy have been studied elsewhere and warrant only an outline here.[62] The policy of monopoly entailed establishing control over those engaged in trade in order to regulate buying and selling prices according to levels set by the sultan's bureaucracy. The sultan could then charge percentages of these prices as monopoly dues. Barsbāy did not wish to involve himself personally in the lucrative spice trade, but only to exploit its profits.[63] These profits, carefully and meticulously augmented by the kārimīs over a long period of manipulating suppliers and consumers, were interpreted by Barsbāy and his successors as a state asset. Thus from now on, the individuals who made the profits could no longer operate independently, but must act as state servants. The kārimī merchants and others who dealt in foreign traffic managed to survive the intermittent monopoly system for approximately fifty years before they disappeared from the scene.[64] During this half century, they were compelled to operate within an elaborate network of controls. Barsbāy took over the ports of the Red Sea and set up his own agents as regulators of prices and goods. He built up Jidda as the regime's major transit station, and forced merchants from his empire and the Indian Ocean to deal there rather than in Aden and Sawākin.[65] His agents set the selling prices for goods and, since no other ports were available, Indian and Egyptian merchants had to comply. Producers in India faced a difficult situation because Barsbāy forced down their profit margin to a level that, on occasion, did not merit loading the ships.[66]

Barsbāy also compelled merchants in his empire to deal with the Franks or Europeans in Alexandria. In this port his bureaucratic apparatus could supervise the trade and set its artificial price levels.[67] These exceeded normal market prices for Oriental goods, and to the disadvantage of European merchants buying goods to sell in their domestic markets. The system of state monopolies originating during Barsbāy's reign represents one of several stimuli that prompted European exploration for direct all-water routes to East Asia.[68]

The mercantile groups of the empire correctly perceived the negative potential of the monopoly policies and appealed to the imperial throne itself. Although respites were occasionally granted, the ultimate response of the sultans was to replace the independent merchants with state merchants (tujjār al-sulṭān), who represented an extension of the bureaucratic apparatus to commerce.[69] These state merchants received their positions as offices, as mercantile farms. They functioned mainly as bureaucrats who were out to provide their master with his required fiscal quotas while simultaneously fattening their own purses. The sultans were willing to permit this siphoning of funds, and indeed encouraged it, since such purses were ripe for confiscation.[70] The state merchants could prosper within the empire but were powerless outside it, and they exhibited little of the independent merchants' skill in analyzing external market conditions or building relations of mutual confidence with their foreign counterparts. Accordingly, the state merchants of the Circassian period contributed directly to the decline of Egyptian prestige in world trade.[71]

Furthermore, because these merchants were responsible for supplying the imperial household with its voluminous inventory of imported luxuries, they soon were subjected to retaliatory price-setting by foreign merchants.[72] The sultan's household continued to live in proverbial opulence, regardless of the burden on finances. The Mamluks had become accustomed to an abundant supply of foreign luxuries—silks, fine China wares, jewelry, ornamental weapons, foreign steel for armory and weaponry, building stone, mechanical instruments, and so forth—and they continued to demand these luxuries as a service from their merchants, even though the state merchants could not keep down their prices, as had the independent merchants in an atmosphere of open trade.

The consequences of the bureaucratization of commerce were far-reaching and have left their imprint on Egypt into modern times. The kārimī merchants have been discussed because of their relative significance to international commerce, but the monopolies over such commodities as sugar and textiles effectively crippled these industries as well.[73] The weakening of foreign and domestic commerce and home manufactures contributed to a decline in domestic buying power. Thus, the relatively high standard of living with its consequent demands for quality goods that had characterized the cities of the empire during the thirteenth and fourteenth centuries diminished throughout the fifteenth century. This diminution in buying power led to a corresponding decline in demand for high-quality manufactures, particularly textiles, which had always commanded high prices.[74] The general depression thus affected Egypt's internal market conditions and contributed to a deterioration in the quality of goods produced by local artisans.

On the question of responsibility for these complex problems of decline, we cannot deny the underlying reality of inexorable natural and social phenomena such as plagues and demographic shifts. But the Mamluk elite was psychologically ill-equipped to cope with these phenomena or even to venture an attempt to live within the means dictated by them. The fundamental cause of this inability may be traced in large part to the elite's conception of their raison d'être, their role in the state. During the Circassian period the elite failed to grasp the relationship between their immense executive authority and their state's economic interests. The Mamluks, with the sultan as their primary exponent, quite literally owned most of Egypt and Syria's assets in real estate.[75] They were steadily augmenting their control over the industrial and commercial capital of the empire.[76] Yet they failed to provide pragmatic leadership or encouragement to the individuals who managed their vast holdings, and were interested solely in the immediate revenue potential.[77] Again, the sultans appear as the most serious offenders, since they, by virtue of their office, held more capital assets than anyone else in the state.

The attitude of the Mamluks can be explained by the nature of their self-identity. As a military elite, they scorned the activities and life styles of their subjects, who were barred from sharing their prerogatives. Their training physically separated the first generation of Mamluks from the general population and deemphasized all but their own peer values. The Mamluks therefore embodied an extreme barracks mentality, which was responsible for the ultimate direction of the economy. The Mamluks, and especially the sultan, were aware of their economic self-interest only in the sense that when they saw their critical fiscal resources threatened they took action, but of the most negative sort. Programs of local internal improvements had been established by progressive rulers and governors from Ṭūlūnid times on, and had been maintained by the major Baḥrī sultans. But the level and intensity of the strife among the Mamluks during the fifteenth century compelled the rulers to neglect such policies.[78] The state monopolies were imposed on a self-sustaining but dependent and subservient bureaucracy, which allowed the ruler and his associates to pursue their political ambitions with no impediments. The monopolies yielded revenues, with no investment required. Thus, although the Mamluk elite was confronted by economic circumstances beyond their control, the policies they adopted ultimately intensified the negative effects of these circumstances.

Another aspect of the economic deterioration within the Egyptian state was the commercial revolution, one of several far-reaching consequences of the European Renaissance. The century from 1450 to 1550 witnessed a radical readjustment of world trade. Although the commercial revolution was possible because of the rapid development of new navigational techniques, European merchants and their patrons were motivated to search for new routes in part by a desire to circumvent Near Eastern middlemen. The increasingly arbitrary policies adopted by the Egyptian sultanate concerning east-west traffic in the Oriental commodities demanded by European consumers contributed to a European desire to discover routes granting direct access to sources of supply.[79] Prior to the commercial revolution, mercantile associations of the Italian city-states handled most of the goods transferred through Egypt. By the end of the fifteenth century, however, the governments of Spain, Portugal, and England had taken the lead in the search for new routes and spheres of commercial interest, followed by the French and Dutch somewhat later. The impact of their discoveries on the economy of the Near East, and particularly of Egypt, effectively diminished this part of the world as a force in world commerce. It did not prove to be a devastating blow to the region, especially after the Ottomans partially resurrected the trade network based on a new orientation of routes. From the sixteenth century on, however, transit trade to Europe through the Red Sea ports and the delta cities of Alexandria and Damietta never regained its medieval prominence.

THE INTERNATIONAL SCENE THROUGHOUT THE ISLAMIC WORLD

The largely negative economic picture sketched above produced a decline in many aspects of life throughout the Mamluk empire, but even in decline, the Mamluk state was an impressive edifice, the major Sunnī entity in the central Muslim world prior to the Ottoman expansion after 1453. It managed to repel the invasions from the east in the later Middle Ages, and acquired an international reputation for security and orthodoxy. As suggested in recent studies,[80] the state did not entirely warrant its prestigious reputation; but prestige did accrue to it, and the central Muslim world viewed Mamluk Egypt as a bastion against the disruptive and alien forces from both east and west that threatened to dissolve the Dār al-Islām and reduce it to impotence. Therefore, when the fourteenth century ended with the upheavals of the Timurid invasions, many individuals of diverse backgrounds elected to leave their homes in the east and journey elsewhere, settling at last in Cairo, which might offer the security denied them by the spoliations of Timur Lenk.

The Timurid invasions marked the final stages of an era of migration and upheaval that had intensified after the career of Jenghis Khān. The cumulative impact of the Timurid style of conquest was a weakening of urban institutions and of the control of established landed families throughout the conquered regions.[81] The undisciplined conquerors imposed an arbitrary system of taxation on the mass of peasantry, who often lost tenure over their land.[82] Many thousands of persons from all social classes lost their property and real estate because of either outright pillage or insupportable taxes. The upheavals accompanying the Timurid invasions also produced a shake-up within most bureaucratic institutions of the conquered regions.[83] Although the Iranian elite classes administering these bureaucracies ultimately adapted themselves to the conditions imposed by the Timurid hoards, many individuals lost their positions as well as their property. At the same time, the ʿulamaʾ of the eastern Islamic states did not remain immune to the devastations wrought by the invaders. Many college mosques lost their waqf endowments, since the conquerors did not uniformly respect documents drawn up prior to their arrival. When the ruling classes of the various Iranian regimes were dispossessed, a major source of endowment funds and protection lapsed temporarily. Although second- or third-generation Timurids tended to support the learned elite, as had the Iranian nobility, during the intervening period many individuals left their ancestral homes and migrated west, beyond the pale of the Timurid conquests. To these people, the reputation and legend surrounding Cairo seemed attractive. The city had never fallen to the conquerors of Timur's ilk, which impressed Muslims from the east who longed to settle in a society secure from foreign conquests. The immigration of these individuals and families from the east had a significant impact on the quality and breadth of Cairo's civilian elite.

A similar though less dramatic development was taking place in the far western regions of the Muslim world. Although no invader was devastating the cultures of North Africa, the area constituted something of an intellectual backwater in comparison to the heartlands to the east. Spain had been a great center of scholarly activity, but here the inroads of the Reconquista from the north threatened the future of the remaining Muslim community. As a result, many individuals from Spain and North Africa migrated to Cairo, where they hoped to take advantage of the wide variety of opportunities available in the city. The example of Ibn Khaldūn serves to illustrate this migration.[84]

The experience of Ibn Khaldūn in Cairo represents one individual contribution to an important social phenomenon. Regardless of misrule by its government, during the fifteenth century Cairo remained a great cosmopolitan city. In the next century, Istanbul would supersede Cairo as the major cultural center, but in the fifteenth century, Cairo offered more opportunities to the learned classes. The very fact of their presence in Cairo added a unique dimension to the city's cultural life. The range of opinion and debate over the state of the Islamic sciences and other established fields of learning was more comprehensive than in other cities, even under the restrictions of Mamluk orthodoxy. Representatives from most major schools of thought, localized in various regions of the Muslim world, were either established in Cairo permanently or resident temporarily during their travels. The city became famous as a center for public lectures and disputations by eminent scholars, and the madrasas often filled to capacity when a famous shaykh from abroad was scheduled to read or discourse on a text. These factors were sufficient to render Cairo a vital scholastic center, despite the negative conditions imposed by the Mamluks on the ʿulamaʾ during the fifteenth century.

It is possible to summarize the international status and position of Cairo during the fifteenth century as follows: ruled arbitrarily by a Turko-Circassian military elite and administered by an international community of Islamic literati bound together by a common language and educational background, Cairo was a forum for the scholarly activities of the central Muslim world. Although neither entirely Egyptian nor Arab, the city related to both Egypt and those regions that revered Arabic as the language of the revelation and of education. From the point of view of the scholar sensitive to the difficulties impinging upon his society and class, Cairo was not a perfect environment in which to live. But it was the best available, and the most exciting place to be for those who nurtured lofty ambitions in politics or wished to pursue a learned career.

CHAPTER II

Geographic Origins of the Civilian Elite

Medieval historians of the Near East allude repeatedly in their works to highly mobile classes of soldiers, administrators, merchants, scholars, and religious ascetics who established themselves in urban centers far from their birthplaces, often leaving even their homelands behind. The famous accounts of great travelers such as Ibn Jubayr and Ibn Baṭṭūṭa suggest how extensive such travel could be. But any analysis of the specific nature of travel and causes for migration from one distinct region or culture zone to another during the Middle Ages poses unique problems because of the lack of archival sources such as census lists, alien subsidies, record books of foreigners registering their arrival at ports, and so forth.[1]

The biographical sources examined in this study, however, do include numerous references to, if not statistics of, the geographic origins of the individuals they describe. It is therefore possible to formulate certain hypotheses, though not absolute conclusions, concerning the origins of individuals not born in Cairo, or born to families who had recently settled in the city. This study does not purport to plot out the general patterns of immigration to Cairo for two reasons: the nature of the class described in the biographical sources; and the nature of the data itself. First, the individuals described in the biographical sources belonged to a specific social class, the civilian elite, whose migratory and residence patterns did not parallel those of other social groups. And they had interests and needs not shared by the general population that dictated their choices of location in which to settle. Mercantile groups, for example, would tend to gather at centers of exchange—ports, markets, transferring stations—while military groups would be associated with administrative centers and garrison posts. The civilian elite, on the other hand, were associated with the religio-academic institutions that had trained them. Though they were involved with governmental administration, they were appointed to such posts primarily on the basis of reputations they had acquired as jurisprudents or scholars, and secondarily on the basis of personal connections with individuals wielding executive authority. Only an individual who had been able to acquire certain skills in his place of origin was able to make a successful transfer to a large metropolitan center such as Cairo with any hope of meeting success in advanced studies and securing placement in a position.

The second limiting factor in our study involves the scope of the information provided and the objectives of those who compiled the biographical sources. The compilers of these sources were not geographers but prosopographers interested in identifying as precisely as possible the individuals they described. Therefore, the geographic material that they provided was meant to identify persons by their location rather than trace their own or their families' private movements. The biographies did include all the nisbas for each individual as known to the compilers, but the nisbas were employed principally to distinguish one person from any other. Since so many individuals possessed common Koranic names such as Aḥmad or Muḥammad, the nisba, whether geographic or other, functioned as a surname or agnomen. Because nisbas, along with the shuhra, which might uniquely characterize one person and his offspring, were the titles passed down over generations as the "family name," the geographic nisba must be interpreted with caution; it may well be an indicator of an individual's own place of origin, but it may only reflect ancestral origins. And the practice of listing several nisbas for some individuals resulted in a multiplicity of place names, which might or might not reflect an actual pattern of migration.[2]

It must be stressed that many terminal nisbas mentioned in the biographies do represent an individual's place of birth, but unless a birthplace is specifically identified as such, it is impossible to be sure. Origins and sequences of successive residences of individuals or their ancestors may be determined by examining the sequences of nisbas as a group, but the birthplaces must be specified to be considered accurate. In general, it is possible to ascertain a general pattern of origins by comparing the large number of place names provided by the nisbas with the smaller numbers of birthplaces cited, and working out a proportional estimate. This is the procedure adhered to in the subsequent analysis.[3]

Given the limitations of the biographical sources, this chapter can claim four goals. First, it will plot the origins of the individuals described in the biographical dictionaries as far as possible, and then suggest the ancestral regions of these people or their families. The patterns revealed in the maps will quite accurately depict the families' origins, but be less accurate for individuals.[4] They are interrelated phenomena, however, and should be regarded as phases of an ongoing process.

Second, the analysis will examine the various regions or urban centers in which these individuals or their families originated. The purpose here is to establish hypotheses explaining why certain areas produced large numbers of civilian elite during various periods and why others did not. Some individuals adapted to conditions in Cairo with considerable success, due to their previous training and eminence elsewhere. Can we delineate zones or regions that produced more members of the elite than other areas? Is it possible to define the type of environment necessary to produce a viable class of literati capable of communicating with their peers throughout the Muslim world? What sorts of institutions were necessary to support this class, and where were they in abundance within the Near East? How would the types and number of such institutions vary according to region? These questions, based on "internal" stimuli or causes behind migration, may contribute to an interpretation of the patterns on the maps.

Third, certain political and economic stimuli behind decisions to migrate will be discussed. These can be classified as "external" causes, in contrast with those mentioned above. They would have included such phenomena as political upheavals, internecine wars, foreign invasions, and imposition of control by alien ruling groups. These external factors, unique to any given region, may well have influenced the political attitudes and even the psychological qualities of persons who traveled to Cairo to rebuild interrupted careers. Such contrasting attitudes could create a unique political milieu in the city that received these people.

Finally, this analysis aims to establish a general hypothetical pattern of migration to Cairo based on several broad categories of occupations and professional activities.

The feasibility, and indeed the credibility, of these analytical procedures and the resultant hypotheses depend on the quality of geographic evidence available. Accordingly, the regions most suitable for this type of inquiry lay within the frontiers of the Mamluk empire: the Nile Delta, Syria-Palestine, and the Nile Valley (in the order of quantity and quality of data). Beyond the Mamluk frontiers, we must rely increasingly on assumptions derived from more isolated cases. Since the Iranian regions yielded the most geographic data of any area outside the Mamluk empire, and were also the seat of an ancient historiographical tradition, our methodology may be applied more rigorously there than to the other zones of the Muslim world—Anatolia, Iraq, the Arabian Peninsula (technically, a part of the Mamluk empire), and North Africa. For these regions, the analytical procedures are not uniformly applicable.

MIGRATION TO CAIRO FROM THE DELTA
(Maps I-A, I-B)

The biographical sources indicate, predictably, that the majority of the individuals who themselves or whose families moved to Cairo had their place of origin within the valley of the Nile River. Furthermore, the sources indicate the greatest general concentrations of geographical nisbas and birthplaces for these Egyptians in the Delta region.[5] Because the integrity and security of the Nile Valley remained constant during the fourteenth and fifteenth centuries, this pattern of intraregional migration was not notably influenced by the external factors of war, foreign invasion, or confiscation of property by alien conquerors, as was true in other regions of the Near East.

The reasons for an individual or family to contemplate transfer to Cairo were substantial. Cairo had been the major urban center of Egypt from its foundation by the Fāṭimids. The older commercial city of Fusṭāṭ had developed rapidly after the Arab conquest. Only Alexandria could claim to rival the mercantile establishment of Fusṭāṭ during the early and central Middle Ages. Indeed, this urban site, located just above the cleavage of the river into its Delta branches, had represented the crucial strategic control center of the country from ancient times. During the Mamluk period, however, Cairo assumed a role disproportionate even to its status under previous regimes. Since the Mamluks divided most of the real estate, commercial, and productive assets of the country among themselves in a system of allotment and tenure, most revenues from rents charged on these assets accrued to them. And because the Mamluks tended to concentrate in Cairo, they did not distribute these enormous revenues back to the provinces but spent them maintaining themselves in the capital. The city was therefore receiving an extraordinarily large proportion of the state's revenues throughout the Mamluk period. The percentage of these revenues spent by the Mamluks on the foundation and endowment of religio-academic institutions or monuments varied considerably throughout the period, but the great majority of whatever was spent was concentrated in Cairo. As a result, the city offered more of the kinds of positions sought by the ʿulamaʾ than did any other site in Egypt.

We must recall that the civilian learned were confined to a limited number of professional options, even though their training was not very specialized and they could in theory fit equally well into a variety of bureaucratic, legal, scholarly, and educational positions. Regardless of the positions they ultimately attained, these people usually began their careers as petty salaried officials, legal adjutants, teachers, or religious custodians. They were employed in the bureaucratic staffs of great Mamluk amirs or of the central governmental authority beneath the sultan, or found their place within a substantial commercial class, or in an institution supported by endowments. Under the Mamluk regime, only Cairo constituted an environment providing these conditions of employment on a massive scale. An ambitious individual who sought to attain renown or to pursue a higher education would therefore be obliged to continue his studies and seek his fortune in the capital.

Given these motives behind a move to Cairo, we can discern a series of steps or phases in the resettlement of these Delta Egyptians. In general, an individual tended to transfer to Cairo after he had completed his initial studies in the Koran and the fundamental Islamic sciences. He might have already held a post in a local mosque or madrasa. More rarely, he had occupied some minor administrative post. Often, but not always, at the behest of a relative or friend of the family who was established in Cairo, he transferred to the capital to continue his studies in one or more of the collegiate madrasas of the city. At this time, the individual would begin to specialize in some aspect of the Islamic sciences. Following successful completion of such specialized study and appropriate licensing by groups of recognized scholars, the individual would be appointed to a post in the bureaucracy, the judiciary, or the religio-academic institutions.[6] It was usually at this time that the young man married. In the majority of cases, he selected a woman from a well-established family in Cairo rather than from his home town, thereby associating himself with his wife's family and the elite of the city. Thus, the individual tended to create a family within his new environment. His only significant relationship with his place of origin was to provide opportunities for education and positions to younger members of his family once he had established himself in the capital.

The concentrations of sites within the Delta mentioned in the biographical sources indicate a consistent flow of individuals to Cairo from the following areas: the two major Mediterranean ports of Alexandria (al-Iskandarīya) (1) and Damietta (Dumyāṭ) (318), the towns and villages of central Gharbīya and Minūfīya districts; and to a lesser degree, the towns and villages of Sharqīya, Qalyūbīya, and Buḥayra districts. Alexandria and Damietta were not the primary centers of migration, but they stood out as two of the major urban sites. Alexandria was exceeded only by al-Maḥallat al-Kubrā (99), in the heart of Gharbīya, in terms of frequency of reference in the sources. Damietta ranked behind Alexandria but also yielded a major concentration of references.[7] These two cities stood out in relative isolation, since their surrounding areas did not produce a consistent flow of immigrants to Cairo. Apparently, they did not function as local administrative and cultural centers, or relate to their hinterlands as regional capitals. In the sources there is repeated reference to travel between the three cities by Mamluks, bureaucrats, the judiciary, and particularly merchants. In addition, groups of foreigners were obliged to take up residence in the two ports in order to carry on their business. The range of activities, professions, and occupations engaged in by the Skandarīs and Dumyāṭīs differed to some degree from those of the sites in the central Delta, especially in terms of emphasis on artisanship and commerce as against education and religion, but all of the representative types did appear among the individuals originating in the port cities.[8] And one relationship to Cairo that remained constant for Alexandria and Damietta was their direct tie with the Mamluk military elite and the administrative-commercial bureaucracy.[9] During the early Mamluk period, the ruling regime built extensively in both cities. A significant proportion of the Mamluk elite was obliged to reside in those outposts (designated *thaghr*, or "frontier region") in order to oversee trading activities between Egyptians and foreigners, and guard against raids by potentially hostile naval powers. Alexandria also became famous as a center for exiled Mamluk amirs, relatives of deceased sultans, and political or religious prisoners. Therefore, these two cities appeared in the biographical sources as prominent but somewhat isolated ports, distinct from their surrounding districts and maintaining direct ties to Cairo.

The pattern of migration exhibited by the central Delta differed from that of Alexandria and Damietta. In the Gharbīya[10] and Minūfīya districts, several large towns yielding relatively high numbers of nisbas and birthplaces were complemented by dense clusters of villages throughout their hinterlands. The most prominent Egyptian provincial town, in terms of migration to Cairo, was al-Maḥallat al-Kubrā (99), located in one of two salient clustering patterns of the Delta. The second-ranked town in the Delta was Minūf (160), located in the midst of the second cluster.[11] The two districts yielded the majority of references to individuals moving to Cairo from the Delta. Individuals from these areas often transferred from a small village or town to one of these two cities prior to their final move to the capital. Unlike Alexandria and Damietta, therefore, the provinces of the Delta were made up of a series of interrelated centers through which individuals often moved in one or more phases before leaving the region permanently. It should be noted that the clustering patterns of sites in the districts of Gharbīya and Minūfīya followed the contours of the Damietta branch of the Nile, which constituted a focus for emigration. The regions mentioned most frequently in the sources lay to the immediate west of the Damietta branch.

The provinces of Buḥayra and Sharqīya possessed several noticeable centers of migration, but they did not reveal any such clustering patterns. Qalyūbīya district, although the closest in proximity to Cairo, was significant only in terms of four centers—Qalyūb (218), Siryāqūs (221), al-Khānqāh (222), and Ṭūkh (231). It too revealed no integrated cluster of sites. Al-Khānqāh and Siryāqūs supported a prominent monastic institution, and enjoyed the benefits of lavish endowments from the ruling elite in Cairo. The district of Jīza (Giza), immediately southwest of Cairo, revealed several distinct centers, but again no cluster, a trend that held throughout the Upper Valley. Jīza was unique; as the sultan's personal property, its estates and revenues were reserved exclusively for the requirements of the imperial court.[12] Here were located, for example, the tracts of grazing land reserved for the herds of horses belonging to the Mamluk cavalry.

There were substantial tracts of the Delta that were not represented in references to migration to Cairo, and the areas of highest representation can be sharply distinguished from them. Most apparent are the extreme northerly areas of the central Delta (modern Kafr al-Shaykh and western Daqhilīya), the eastern areas of Sharqīya, and the southwestern sections of Buḥayra. These vacant areas may have been underdeveloped agrarian zones of the Delta with large unirrigated tracts and undrained tidal swamps or marshes. During the later Mamluk period, relatively little progress toward land reclamation was made anywhere in Egypt, except perhaps in Jīza district. The profile of underdeveloped areas, therefore, held fairly constant throughout the fourteenth and fifteenth centuries.

The frequency of migration by the ʿulamaʾ from the Delta to Cairo varied only to a limited degree during the fifteenth century.[13] Any variations cannot be explained without detailed studies of the local histories of the various districts, for which there are few sources. It is unlikely, however, that the general economic and social conditions saw any improvement during this period. The general provincial neglect, mismanagement, and exploitation so characteristic of the central government during the Circassian period may well have resulted in a marked decline in agricultural production throughout the country. The various mechanisms for endowing religio-academic institutions were closely tied to the revenues that flowed from such production, so the generally depressed economic conditions of the provinces could stimulate individuals associated with the ʿulamaʾ to leave these areas for better prospects in Cairo.

We can perceive in the data on migration from the Delta to Cairo certain patterns that elucidate the cultural conditions of the various Delta districts and towns, the type of individual they tended to produce, and the activities that the individual was likely to pursue. In general, the regions and centers producing individuals who migrated to Cairo possessed certain institutions that could socialize and educate these people for their subsequent careers in the capital. In addition, those towns enjoying the status of regional administrative centers for the Mamluk bureaucracy possessed an environment conducive to training bureaucrats and jurisprudents. The more institutions there were in a center or region that corresponded to institutions in Cairo, the more likely it was for the area to produce individuals who made the transfer. Comparative figures for the various general categories of occupations engaged in by the individuals examined here (Tables 1-6) indicate dissimilar conditions throughout the Delta.

In general, the two port cities of Alexandria and Damietta generated far fewer representatives of all the various occupational categories than did the central delta districts, but among those that did appear, the commercial and judicial types appeared more frequently than the executive, secretarial, and scholarly types. This would accord with the roles of the port cities as entrepôts for transferring goods and as seats for district courts dealing with the constant stream of litigation arising from an active commercial establishment. The almost total absence of individuals who were successfully engaged in executive roles is striking, since the Mamluk elite maintained an elaborate administrative apparatus in both ports. Apparently, these cities did not serve as training grounds for future executives, since most decision-making officials, Mamluk or civilian, were sent directly from Cairo to supervise commercial and judicial activities.

The districts of Gharbīya and Minūfīya, and to a lesser degree Sharqīya and Buḥayra, were well represented in all six occupational categories, particularly the religious, scholarly, judicial, and bureaucratic fields. The high figures indicate that these areas supported major cultural establishments during the later Middle Ages. Since the classical Islamic period, these areas have been known throughout the central Muslim world as a "saints zone." Many revered and pious preachers, miracle workers, and holy hermits have been buried here in tombs endowed to their memory by successive regimes over the centuries. Even today, the city of Ṭanṭa (121) is famous for the mawlids (birthdays) and ʿīds (festivals) celebrating the memory of its great shaykh, al-Sayyid al-Badawī. We can postulate a large number of such endowed tombs (zāwiyas) and their associated mosques, madrasas, monastic houses, and libraries supporting a group of revered men (muʿtaqadūn), sayyids (saints), and sharīfs (descendants of the Prophet) who lent a special aura of distinction to the communities fortunate enough to maintain them. Many of these revered individuals, born to local families highly respected in their communities, moved to Cairo on their own volition to continue their educations and to join a Ṣūfī order, or came at the bidding of an associate or relative already established in one of the urban monastic houses or zāwiyas in the cemeteries to the east of the city.

Nūr al-Dīn ʿAlī ibn Muḥammad al-Haythamī al-Ṭibnāwī al-Qāhirī, who was born in Maḥallat Abū Haytham (96) in Gharbīya in the year 800/1397-1398 to a prominent family bearing the nisba al-Ashʿarī, pursued a career that exemplifies this phenomenon.[14] Journeying to Cairo at the encouragement of his mentors in Maḥallat Abū Haytham, al-Ṭibnāwī completed his studies in Koranic commentary and jurisprudence and then joined a Ṣūfī order. Through his influence over a Mamluk amir, he managed to gain access to the newly opened madrasa-khānqāh of al-Ashrafīya Barsbāy. He did not restrict himself to the Spartan environment of a monastic cell, however; he succeeded in persuading his Mamluk patron to purchase a house for him near Jannaq Lake. Al-Ṭibnāwī ultimately married his patron's wife after the latter's death, and lived an opulent life until Sultan Jaqmaq confiscated the house and imprisoned him. Influential associates secured his release, however, and al-Ṭibnāwī lived out the remainder of his life in the Ashrafīya complex. He died in Rabīʿ I 888/March-April 1483. The notable aspect of al-Ṭibnāwī's career is that he never held a remunerative post obliging him to perform a service in return for his income, nor did he receive a sinecure supported by a waqf endowment, except for his initial placement in al-Ashrafīya as a Ṣūfī. He managed, as a muʿtaqad, to gain first the attention and subsequently the reverence of a Mamluk amir who provided him with a lavish house and income for life. This illustrates that such individuals were able to take with them the prestige and lucrative status that they enjoyed in their places of origin when they transferred to Cairo. Their local reputation helped them to reestablish themselves in the capital. Indeed, this reputation was indispensable to them in seeking the respect and support of new patrons.

The districts of Gharbīya and Minūfīya produced a host of functionaries associated with the maintenance of the mosques. In particular, we note the incidence of Koran readers (muqriʾs), prayer leaders (imāms), Friday preachers (khaṭībs), and prayer callers (muʾadhdhins). The large numbers of these individuals in Cairo who were born either in these districts or to families who hailed from them indicates the extent and range of the zāwiya and local mosque-madrasa complexes in the central Delta. Many of the prominent scholarly and judicial families of Cairo also originated in these districts. In spite of competition from foreign scholars attracted to Cairo from all over the Muslim world, the Delta Egyptians held the edge, and some of the most eminent families of the later Middle Ages in Cairo descended from them.

Few families illustrate this phenomenon more clearly than the descendants of Sirāj al-Dīn ʿUmar ibn Raslān al-Bulqīnī[15] and Shihāb al-Dīn Aḥmad ibn Abū Bakr ibn Raslān al-Bulqīnī.[16] These two individuals, uncle and nephew, were born in the Gharbīya town of Bulqīna (98) in 724/1323-1324 and 767/1365-1366, respectively. ʿUmar, the more famous of the two, moved to Cairo in 738/1337-1338 at the age of fourteen, after successfully memorizing the Koran and completing his basic studies in Bulqīna. He studied jurisprudence and Prophetic traditions in Cairo with some of the most reputable specialists in those disciplines. ʿUmar then embarked upon an extremely successful teaching career, beginning in the mosque of ʿAmr ibn al-ʿĀṣ in Old Cairo, at the invitation of his father-in-law and former teacher, Bahāʾ al-Dīn ibn ʿAqīl, who had previously held the position. His teaching posts culminated with an endowed lectureship in Koranic exegesis in the collegiate mosque of Sultan Barqūq. ʿUmar was also appointed muftī of the Justice Palace in the Citadel, and in 769/1367-1368, was appointed Shāfiʿī chief justice of Damascus, a position he held for a year. He also received the Shāfiʿī chief justiceship of Old Cairo (Miṣr al-Qadīma). These positions outline an extremely successful academic and judicial career for an individual who arrived in Cairo as a youth of fourteen with little but the praise of his teachers to recommend him.

ʿUmar's nephew, Aḥmad, pursued his education in both Bulqīna and al-Maḥallat al-Kubrā before traveling to Cairo at the request of his eminent uncle to complete his education. Aḥmad then returned to al-Maḥalla and entered the local judiciary as a deputy judge. He later returned to Cairo as a deputy in the service of his cousin and uncle's son, Jalāl al-Dīn al-Bulqīnī. His career culminated in 810/1407-1408, when he was appointed Shāfiʿī justice of al-Maḥallat al-Kubrā, a post he held until his retirement from the bench twenty-eight years later.

Both ʿUmar and Aḥmad were industrious and ambitious men. The roster of the positions they held is noteworthy in its own right; but the eminence of the family only began with them. Both men fathered several sons, some of whose fame greatly exceeded that of their fathers, and they were part of the small group composing the summit of the academic and judicial elite of Cairo during the fifteenth century. They held deanships in the most prestigious collegiate madrasas, and occupied chief justiceships both in Cairo and abroad. We shall return to the career of this family in Chapter IV, but it is interesting to note here how the progenitors were able to establish themselves within the elite structure and prepare the way for their descendants.

The central Delta was also prominent as a source of individuals involved in the bureaucratic occupations (Table 2). These secretarial, administrative, and fiscal activities devolved upon a distinct secretarial class that tended to maintain its integrity over time. Bureaucrats were recruited principally from this class, and positions tended to be handed down over generations within related families. For any region to produce a large number of individuals engaged in this type of activity, it would have to maintain relatively complex local bureaucracies in which such individuals could receive their initial training. The great number of bureaucrats originating in the Delta region provides further evidence that especially Gharbīya and Minūfīya, and to a lesser degree Sharqīya and Qalyūbīya, possessed such administrative and fiscal institutions.

The majority of individuals in this secretarial class were involved in the lower or medial ranks of bureaucratic jobs, however—the notaries (shāhids), secretaries (kātibs), document clerks (muwaqqiʿs), superintendents (mubāshirs), controllers (nāzirs), and supervisors of waqf foundation properties and institutions. The major positions, approaching the major executive offices in rank and authority and therefore the highest open to civilians in the Mamluk empire, were apt to be restricted to established Cairo families (Table 2, references to individuals born in Cairo) and to non-Egyptians, particularly Syrians. For example, the office of secretary of the chancellery (kātib al-sirr), who functioned as minister of state under the wazīr and sultan, was only rarely held by individuals who were from the Delta or who had family ties there. From this we can surmise that the bureaucratic institutions in Gharbīya, Minūfīya, and Sharqīya handled procedural matters such as estate auditing, tax collection, recording of district court proceedings, and administration of the myriad waqf foundations associated with the zāwiyas, mosques, and madrasas scattered through these districts. The upper-level positions, demanding considerable experience and personal connections, were open almost exclusively to individuals who successfully penetrated the Mamluk elite and developed personal ties with some of its members. No distinct region of Egypt could be expected to monopolize this type of candidate, but other areas of the Mamluk state did tend to do so. On the basic administrative and procedural level, however, the central Delta provided Cairo with a significant portion of its bureaucratic cadres (see Tables 7-10).

MIGRATION TO CAIRO FROM THE NILE VALLEY (AL-ṢAʿĪD) (Maps II-A, II-B)

The biographical sources indicate that the Nile Valley between Cairo and Aswān produced approximately 20 percent of the Egyptians born outside Cairo who established themselves in the city. This general estimate was reflected in the relative paucity of Ṣaʿīdīs engaged in the occupations reported in the biographies. Middle and Upper Egypt did produce individuals who achieved renown, but they appeared as somewhat isolated, unpredictable cases. Consequently, it is more difficult to deduce what kinds of institutions existed in Middle and Upper Egypt that might have been conducive to generating distinguished members of the ʿulamaʾ. It is only possible to describe the figures as they stand and to pose certain hypotheses.

The majority of the Ṣaʿīdīs, some sixty percent, who moved to Cairo or whose families had transferred there came from Middle Egypt—the districts of Aṭfīḥīya and Bahnasawīya, and to a lesser extent, Ushmunayn-Ṭahawīya and Fayyūm. In these regions, particularly in the vicinity of the towns of Aṭfīḥ (9), Būsh (25) [near Banī Suwayf (28)], Qāy (33), Iqfahs (46), Ṭanbadī (49), Bahnasā (56), and Minyat Banī Khasīb (59), some indication of site clustering is discernible, although it never approaches the density of the central Delta districts. In Upper Egypt, which accounts for about 40 percent of the Ṣaʿīdīs in Cairo, we can discern little clustering, but there were several prominent centers, including Asyūṭ (77), which yielded more nisbas and birthplaces than any other site in the valley.[17] The four districts of Upper Egypt reflected the importance of their administrative towns: Manfalūṭ (74), Asyūṭ, Akhmīm (89), and Qūṣ (102). These four towns figured prominently in the biographical sources, as did Abū Tīj (79), Ṭahṭā (83), Jirjā (91), Balyanā (92), Qinā (101), Asnā (107), Idfū (109), and Aswān (112). These towns of Upper Egypt appear to have been somewhat isolated centers of cultural activity. They did not function as intermediate steps through which immigrants passed, as did the large towns in Gharbīya and Minūfīya, but rather seem to have been the only places of origin reported for the individuals who identified with them in Cairo.[18]

A phenomenon related to this pattern of isolated urban sites in Middle and Upper Egypt was the discrepancy between the numbers of nisbas reported and the numbers of actual birthplaces. The ratio of nisbas to birthplaces for the Delta and for much of Syria-Palestine was roughly three to one, with certain sites reporting a much higher proportion of birthplaces. For the Ṣaʿīd, however, the proportion was roughly four or five to one, and some areas did not report any birthplaces whatsoever. This implies substantial numbers of individuals whose families derived from the upper valley but who themselves were born in Cairo. The discrepancy may suggest a comparatively lower level of economic and therefore cultural development in the upper valley than in the Delta or Syria-Palestine. In certain respects, this does appear to have been the case, but there are other factors unique to the Ṣaʿīd that merit consideration.

Recent research on Upper Egypt during the later Middle Ages has detected a gradual decline in the general population.[19] Data from the biographical sources would not only corroborate this general decline but also suggest that it was reflected in the proportion of ʿulamaʾ migrating to Cairo from this region. Several local factors may have influenced the institutional base supporting the ʿulamaʾ class in the area. Although Middle and Upper Egypt were exposed to severe fiscal exploitation during the Circassian period, as a result of the thorough entrenchment of Mamluk infeudation and enlargement of iqṭāʿ holdings throughout the upper valley, yields from these holdings remained roughly stable at best.[20] This suggests a decrease in overall production, resulting from the population decline and diminution in the number of feddans cultivated. A decrease in yields for iqṭāʿs was almost certainly accompanied by diminishing yields for waqf properties, the primary source of support for the Muslim religious establishment.[21] Thus, it is unlikely that the religious establishment of the Nile Valley was comparable to that of the Delta, if measured by prominence and number of zāwiyas, madrasas, and similarly endowed institutions.

The problems of infeudation, decreasing agrarian production, and diminishing population levels did not fully account for the economic and social decline of the upper valley. From the Fāṭimid period to around 1400, several towns of Upper Egypt had become important entrepôts of the international carrying trade, particularly in spices. As a result of the increasingly elaborate monopolistic policies employed by the sultans of the Circassian period, these cities saw their lucrative trade wither away throughout the century. Indeed, such famous centers as Qūṣ and Qinā on the Nile and Quṣayr and ʿAydhāb (see Map IV-A:1, 2) on the Red Sea coast became virtual ghost towns. Their once affluent commercial and military aristocrats abandoned them, leaving behind empty mosques and caravansarays as mute testimony to an economy that had once flourished.[22] In general, the Nile Valley during the later Mamluk period became steadily more depressed and unproductive. This was reflected in both the quality of individuals who moved out of the area and the quantity of data describing them.

The occupations held by individuals who themselves or whose families had come from the upper valley suggest a lower level of development than that of the Delta. All the percentages of occupational categories in proportion to numbers of individuals settling in Cairo were lower for the upper valley than for the Delta and abroad (Tables 7-10). Variations among the categories of occupations also showed marked differences. Artisans and commercial types (Table 4) were extremely rare, and several highly specialized professions, such as medicine, jewelry, and gold inlaying, were not reported at all. Although the Ṣaʿīd supported an artisan-commercial class, the region does not appear to have exported its members to the capital in large numbers during the Circassian period. The bureaucratic occupations (Table 2) were also sparsely represented, indicating a paucity of procedural and administrative bureaucracies in the upper valley.

For the executive occupations (Table 1), theoretically the most exclusive, the pattern of birthplaces suggests that most Ṣaʿīdīs who attained executive office were actually born in Cairo (Tables 8, 10). The proportions here indicate very low numbers of individuals born in Upper Egypt, and the figures for nisbas (Tables 7, 9) raise the question of the large number of Copts who were frequently employed in bureaucratic and executive positions throughout medieval Egyptian history. The ancient Coptic establishment in Middle and Upper Egypt resisted conversion to Islam, and even today, Upper Egypt includes several areas that are populated by more Christians than Muslims. During the later Middle Ages, these areas were more extensive than at the present time.[23] The Coptic establishment was therefore able to tap more resources and real estate in the upper valley for its own support than could Muslims. The position of Copts is discussed in more detail in Chapter IV, but we can note here briefly that the majority of Copts who attained high office (most of whom were converts to Islam or their descendants) were born in Cairo, although often to families who had ties to Upper Egypt. Ṣaʿīdī Copts do not appear to have received any more training in Upper Egypt for high position than their Muslim counterparts. Only in Cairo did their representation in these positions loom large.

In the judicial, scholarly, and religious categories, the biographical sources indicated a more even balance between individuals deriving from the upper valley and those from the Delta (compare percentages, Tables 7-10), and the wide discrepancy between nisbas and birthplaces was less extreme for these categories. It still appears, however, that Middle and Upper Egypt produced fewer scholars, teachers, and judges than did the Delta; and many of the most eminent Ṣaʿīdīs to hold these posts were born in Cairo. The career of the famous polymath, Jalāl al-Dīn ʿAbd al-Raḥmān ibn Abū Bakr al-Suyūṭī serves to illustrate this situation.[24] Al-Suyūṭī's father[25] was born in Asyūṭ and attained the posts of Shāfiʿī deputy judge in both Asyūṭ and Cairo, and of instructor in Shāfiʿī jurisprudence in the Shaykhūnīya madrasa. He was later appointed imām to Caliph al-Mustaʿīn. Attainment of so prestigious an office was unusual for a person born in a provincial Upper Egyptian town. The son, raised in Cairo, actually never attained such a distinguished post himself, but he received a professorship at Shaykhūnīya, largely through his father's connections and reputation. Here he was free to spend the considerable time necessary to compile his encyclopedic works—compositions representing the apogee of eclectic encyclopedic writing so characteristic of later medieval Muslim historiography. It is doubtful whether al-Suyūṭī would have acquired the outlook or received the opportunities to compile such works had he grown up in Asyūṭ rather than Cairo.

Partly because some regional resources went into the endowments of Coptic institutions, and partly because of economic instability, the traditional Muslim establishment of Middle and Upper Egypt did not secure as broad a foundation as did that of Lower Egypt. The general trend emerging from the data therefore suggests that although a number of distinguished individuals were born in or derived from Middle and Upper Egypt, they never constituted an appreciable percentage of an occupational or social group in Cairo during the fifteenth century, and their collective activities evade accurate description.

MIGRATION TO CAIRO FROM SYRIA-PALESTINE (Maps III-A, III-B)

During the fifteenth century Palestine and Syria were integral parts of the Mamluk empire. Evidence yielded by the sources suggests a high degree of social and political integration between the elite of Egypt and that of her southwest Asian provinces. Palestine and Syria produced the largest number of individuals transferring to Cairo or claiming foreign ancestry of any region outside Egypt—some 30 percent of the total not native to Cairo (Tables 9 and 10). There was a constant flow of travelers moving back and forth between the major cities of this area and Cairo. The biographical sources provide hundreds of references to individuals initiating, continuing, or terminating their careers in these major cities. Indeed, the pattern of migration does appear to be largely a tale of cities.

During the Mamluk period, the political organization of the levant was based on its major urban centers, especially Damascus (66) and Aleppo (141), and secondarily Ṣafad (21), al-Karak (27), Tripoli (Ṭarābulus) (84), Ḥimṣ (88), and Ḥamā (104). These cities were the seats of political administration and of judicial and cultural activities. Damascus (Dimashq) and Aleppo (Ḥalab) were the two chief bases of Mamluk authority in the empire after Cairo. These large centers were complemented by clusters of villages, rather evenly distributed throughout Palestine and Syria. This grouping occurred in several areas that remain relatively underdeveloped today. It is possible to see how the economic and social backgrounds of several Levantine regions varied five centuries ago in comparison with the present. The terms *Filasṭīn* and *al-Shām* were employed in a geographic sense in the Levant by their medieval inhabitants and have acquired a national connotation only in modern times.

The city of Damascus yielded the greatest number of nisbas and birthplaces of any site outside Cairo, indicating a substantial rate of migration to the capital.[26] The reasons behind this move were both cultural and political. Damascus, more than any other city in the empire, and indeed in the entire Near East, paralleled Cairo as a social and cultural center. It duplicated the intellectual and political environment of the capital to such a degree that the Mamluks and the ʿulamaʾ of Cairo acknowledged it alone as a cultural seat fit for civilized social intercourse. From the Umayyad period on, with only temporary relapses, the city had developed one of the most sophisticated intellectual traditions of the Muslim world. It possessed a network of wealthy college mosques, libraries, monasteries, waqf properties, endowed chairs, and zāwiyas, plus a system of courts comparable to the judicial system of Cairo.[27] These institutions were staffed by many educators, scholars, and judges, accompanied by swarms of auxiliaries, and attended by throngs of students. Damascus thus produced a large number of individuals with the necessary background and training for a successful transfer to Cairene intellectual life. Many of the most eminent figures of Cairo had enjoyed equally high reputations in Damascus.

The cultural aspect of Damascus was not alone responsible for the high rate of migration, however. The strong Mamluk presence and influence over most economic assets, especially the receipt and distribution of revenues, is now widely recognized as a critical factor in the history of Damascus during the later Middle Ages.[28] Mamluk control over the distribution of income may have been even greater in Damascus than in Cairo, since Damascus' economic recovery from the misfortunes of the Crusader and Mongol periods was due primarily to its selection by the Mamluks as their second city. Especially during the fourteenth century, the Mamluk amirs and viceroys residing in Damascus endowed the city's religio-academic institutions lavishly, imitating their superiors in Cairo.

A more important consequence of the Mamluk presence in Damascus resulted from the nature of political and personal associations formed between military officers and their civilian bureaucrats. That the Mamluks relied on the ʿulamaʾ to supervise the various aspects of the state beyond the military sphere is widely recognized.[29] The great amirs who stood at the apex of Damascene society employed hosts of civilian officials to maintain their households, supply their troops, and organize their ceremonials. They were, of necessity, on familiar terms with all the civilian bureaucratic, judicial, and religious officials of the city, since their final authority enforced, and therefore influenced, the decisions made by everyone else who held an office. These amirs, and all the various lower grades of Mamluks who performed much of their service in Palestine and Syria, looked forward to culminating their careers in Cairo itself, where their class was concentrated. Especially if appointed to high office in Cairo, these men tended to transfer their Syrian civilian staffs with them. This accounted for a large portion of the Syrians who established themselves in Cairo during the fourteenth and fifteenth centuries. Amirs coming to Cairo not only from Damascus, but also from Aleppo and other administrative centers wished to maintain the relative efficiency and loyalty of their staffs and sought to preserve the benefits of associations built up over several years of duty in Palestine and Syria.

The city of Aleppo ranked second only to Damascus in terms of references to nisbas and birthplaces, and was well ahead of any Egyptian town.[30] This northern bastion of the Mamluk empire shared many of the characteristics of Damascus: religio-academic institutions, many supported by lavish endowments; a major judicial system; and one of the three largest Mamluk garrisons in the empire. Yet Aleppo differed from Damascus in a critical sense. Aleppo had known the devastation of war and the savagery of pillage at the hands of foreign invaders many times in its history. It had witnessed the destruction of its cultural institutions several times since the Umayyad period.[31] The city had always recovered some degree of its economic prosperity because of its crucial location at a confluence of trade routes, but no amount of trade and income could compensate for the spiritual and cultural losses inflicted by the wars and pillaging of centuries. The Mamluks reserved a special role for Aleppo, and organized their administration accordingly. The city became a huge fortified garrison with enormous walls and a citadel that inspires awe as a monument to military architecture even today. The amirs stationed in Aleppo did not attempt to create a replica of Cairo, as the governors of Damascus had attempted to do since the reign of Baybars. Rather, they applied themselves directly to military duties, and particularly to securing the unstable northern marches that extended deep into Anatolia and bordered the Armenian Knot.[32]

The history behind Aleppo's position as a bastion of defence was shared by all of Syria and Palestine in varying degrees. Even though the Levant belonged to the Mamluk empire, it did not enjoy the same security from foreign invasion that Egypt did. Indeed, the Mamluks regarded all of Syria-Palestine, particularly Aleppo, as a heavily garrisoned buffer zone, expected to absorb the initial thrust of invasions and allow the Mamluks time to prepare a counteroffensive from their power base in Cairo. This was the policy during both the Mongol and Timurid invasions, and Damascus itself did not escape the latter. The impact of this insecure environment on the ʿulamaʾ of Syria was profound. Even though they were residing within the borders of the Mamluk state, they tended to regard Cairo as a more stable alternative to their vulnerable location and were thus more emotionally prepared to abandon their ancestral homes for Egypt than they otherwise might have been. This willingness to leave contributed to the high rate of migration from Syria to Cairo during the later Mamluk period.

Both Aleppo and Damascus supported large learned classes. As seats of the Mamluk elite and bureaucracy, both cities witnessed the incorporation of many of these learned individuals into the personal staffs of the great amirs and viceroys. The Dimashqīs and Ḥalabīs thus formed a distinct group whose subsequent careers in Cairo were often adventurous. The occupations pursued by these individuals suggest that many of those who had cultivated ties with amirs in Syria attained political and social prominence in Cairo. Indeed, a large proportion of the highest offices in several of the occupational categories was occupied by Syrians. This was especially true in the judicial fields (Table 3). The several grades of qāḍīs and their subordinates were well represented by Syrians, particularly from Damascus, Aleppo, and Ḥamā, which were seats of high courts. Most of these qāḍīs had begun their judicial careers in their home cities prior to receiving an appointment to the bench in Cairo. The biographical sources indicate that Syria-Palestine actually produced about 30 percent of the qāḍīs appointed to the highest judicial posts in the capital. The Shāfiʿī chief justiceships of Cairo were dominated by individuals born in the city, but the Ḥanafī judgeships were equally distributed between Syrians and Egyptians. The influence of Mamluk amirs on the successful upward mobility of these jurisprudents was indirect, since the amirs were not empowered to make all judicial appointments. On occasion, judicial figures became associates of the amirs and moved with them to Cairo; but more often, it was the personal reputation or family connections of an individual that secured him a post in the capital.[33]

One qāḍī who did profit immensely from his connections with the great amirs was Muḥibb al-Dīn Muḥammad ibn Muḥammad al-Ḥalabī, known as Ibn al-Shiḥna, who was born in Aleppo in 749/1348-1349.[34] This judge became close to several amirs during his career, reaping the benefits and suffering the consequences of such connections. He was appointed Ḥanafī chief justice of Aleppo in 778/1376-1377 by Sultan al-Ashraf Shaʿbān, after studying in Damascus and Cairo as well as Aleppo. He was later dismissed from this post but regained it through the efforts of his associate, Grand Amir al-Nāṣir Faraj, Viceroy of Aleppo and the reigning sultan's son. He was again dismissed from the bench when

Sultan Barqūq discharged and imprisoned his son for the latter's alleged plotting of and participation in the coup that had exiled Barqūq temporarily to al-Karak. Sultan Barqūq imprisoned Ibn al-Shiḥna as well, although only briefly, for influential friends intervened on his behalf. After Barqūq's death, Ibn al-Shiḥna gained the Ḥanafī chief justiceship of Aleppo a third time in 800/1397-1398, by order of Sultan Faraj, who made a point of enfranchising many of his father's political prisoners or suspects who had befriended him. Ibn al-Shiḥna retained this position until offered the prestigious Ḥanafī chief justiceship of Damascus by another close associate, al-Mu'ayyad Shaykh, then Viceroy of Damascus. After his dismissal from this post when al-Mu'ayyad Shaykh was discharged by Faraj, he was offered and chose to accept a professorship in the Jamālīya madrasa in Cairo; the invitation was extended by Faraj and the secretary of the chancellery. Ibn al-Shiḥna had taught extensively before, but his reputation as a jurisconsult served to qualify him for lecturing on fiqh. He became very famous in this role, attracted notable students, engaged in juridical writing and commentary, and established al-Jamālīya as a major center for studies in Ḥanafī jurisprudence. Ultimately, he was appointed Ḥanafī qāḍī of Old Cairo by Sultan Faraj. He had always maintained ties with the sultan from their old Aleppo days, but these were strained repeatedly during the final chaotic years of Faraj's reign. An enemy of Ibn al-Shiḥna brought about his final deposition in 813/1410-1411, when several parties were angling for power. During the last two years of his life, Ibn al-Shiḥna traveled to Damascus and throughout Syria as a guest of the viceroy, Nawrūz, who, together with al-Mu'ayyad Shaykh, dominated Syria during Faraj's last years on the throne. He died in Cairo in Rabīʿ I 815/June-July 1412. The career of Ibn al-Shiḥna reveals the intricate interdependence between appointments to distinguished positions and associations with members of the power elite that was characteristic of the later Mamluk period. Such associations were even more important to the careers of the bureaucrats who received their appointments to offices directly from the amirs and the sultan.

The secretarial and financial occupations (Table 2) also drew a large percentage of their members from Palestine and Syria. One of the most important of these offices, that of secretary of the chancellery (*kātib al-sirr*), was held by more Syrians than Egyptians during the fifteenth century.[35] The office existed only in Cairo and the provincial capitals of Syria, and the high number of Syrians who held the position was due directly to the individuals' previous close associations with amirs who attained the office of viceroy or the sultanate itself and were entitled to appoint men they knew and trusted. In the case of the financial controllers (*nāẓirs*) of the various bureaus, and particularly those relating to the army, Syrians also predominated. However, the finance ministers or controllers of the mint, the waqfs, the trust properties (*aḥbās*), the state treasury (*bayt al-māl*), as distinct from the privy funds and special bureau, were primarily Cairenes, implying that such offices tended to remain under the aegis of both the financial cliques of Cairo and the amirs who were permanently based there. Many of the notaries, accountants, and clerks employed in the bureaus (but not necessarily in the local courts) had moved to Cairo from Syria, but there is less information on their connections with either Egyptian Mamluks or civilian notables.

The careers of this type of official, from the secretary of the chancellery on down, were tainted with corruption and embezzlement. The activities of Jamāl al-Dīn Yūsuf ibn Ṣafī al-Karakī al-Shawbakī provide an example.[36] His father a Christian convert to Islam, al-Karakī never managed to disassociate himself from the unsavory qualities associated with Christian officials, even those who professed Islam. Born in al-Karak (27), Jamāl al-Dīn Yūsuf entered professional life as a secretary in the service of ʿImād al-Dīn Aḥmad al-Muqayrī, qāḍī of the city. Al-Karakī's horizons broadened when he accompanied al-Muqayrī to Cairo. Following al-Muqayrī's death, he entered the service of Burhān al-Dīn al-Maḥallī, the eminent grand qāḍī, as a secretary, and prospered to the extent that he rode a donkey publicly, the noblest means of transport permissable to a second-generation Muslim in those times.

In 826/1422-1423, the first year of Barsbāy's reign, al-Karakī was appointed secretary of the chancellery to the sultan and immediately earned a reputation for swindling. He was dismissed in 827/1423-1424, but managed to avoid being mulcted of his fortune by the sultan.[37] His corrupt reputation did not prevent his appointment as controller of the army in 823/1428-1429 by Sultan Barsbāy. This was a fabulously lucrative post, and he held it for three years, a relatively long tenure in such an uncertain office. He was dismissed and returned to this office twice again by Barsbāy prior to being appointed secretary of the chancellery of Damascus. Then in 841/1437-1438, he regained the controllership of the army, his final position. He left office in 843/1437-1438 and retired comfortably in Damascus until his death thirteen years later.

His son, Mūsā, having modeled his ambitions after those of his father, also began his career as a secretary. He was appointed by Sultan al-Mu'ayyad Shaykh to the staff (*al-sirāfa*) of Mūsā's relative, ʿAlam al-Dīn ibn al-Kuwayz, controller of the army in Ṭarābulus (84), and managed to accumulate a considerable fortune. After succeeding to the controllership himself, and also inheriting his father's estate, Mūsā returned to Cairo a rich man. The story of al-Karakī and his son could be duplicated many times all over Syria. Indeed, Sultan Barqūq was so grateful to several officials in al-Karak who aided him in his successful return to the throne after his exile in 791/1389 that he brought them to Cairo and lavished honors on them.[38] The biographical sources report cases of individuals from all over the Levant ensconced in Cairo's judicial, executive, and bureaucratic offices.

Scholars and educators from Syria, many of whom had become eminent in their home cities, were also attracted to the capital (Table 5). With the possible exception of patronage by Sultan al-Mu'ayyad Shaykh, however, these academicians had relatively little to do with the Mamluk elite. They were invited to join the faculties of the collegiate madrasas because of their reputations as teachers and writers whose works received the avid attention of colleagues throughout the empire. Famous scholars and rhetors were often invited to Cairo to read and discourse in public upon scriptural texts and their own commentaries on them.

Syrians served less frequently as religious functionaries (with the exceptions of imāms and khaṭībs) (Table 6) and representatives of the artisan-commercial fields (Table 4), indicating that a majority of the individuals engaged in administering mosques or working at crafts were native to Egypt. The Syrians were quite evenly, if sparsely, represented in the crafts and commerce, although their distribution from sites within the Levant was uneven. Retailers of goods, merchants engaged in international commerce, and certain professionals such as copyists who successfully plied their trades in Cairo prior to pursuing scholarly activities, originated in the Levant more than in any other area outside Egypt. These individuals were concentrated primarily in the cities of Syria, however; Palestine was underrepresented and Jerusalem reported only four references to nisbas and only one, concerning a merchant, to a birthplace. The evidence would therefore suggest that the north and central Syrian cities maintained most of the commercial activities in the Levant during the later Middle Ages.

Jerusalem (al-Quds) (8) and Hebron (al-Khalīl) (7) held a special status among the provincial cities. As sites of two of Islam's most sacred shrines, they supported a host of religious functionaries and scholars. Since they did not administer provincial governments, however, they supported no complex civilian or military bureaucracies, nor did they maintain large Mamluk garrisons. Therefore relatively few executive, bureaucratic, or judicial officials derived from these two cities. This is not to claim that Jerusalem and Hebron failed to produce such individuals, but rather that the mechanisms for their successful transfer to Cairo did not exist there to the same extent that they did in the provincial capitals. Jerusalem was regarded as the place where God had first chosen to provide His revelation with a permanent shrine. He had called the Messenger Muḥammad to Him from the site of His temple built by David. Hebron, the site of the tomb of Abraham and Isaac, also received the veneration of the faithful, who came to view the shrine of God's first recipients of revelation. These two cities attracted pilgrims from the empire and the entire Muslim world who sought sanctuaries imbued with baraka (holy emanation). They functioned as places of residence for the pious and for those who wished to avoid the political turmoil so prevalent elsewhere in Mamluk society. They also became havens for exiled and out-of-service Mamluks who allegedly came to these apolitical sanctuaries to repent of their many excesses as Muslims against a Muslim society. A sizable group of these disenfranchised Mamluks lived in the Jerusalem area. Many left when they were able to return to active service, but a number stayed on and formed a class of peculiar recluses—pensioners, largely unschooled in theology, the Islamic sciences, or mysticism—who nonetheless clothed themselves in a guise of affected piety. Thus an individual who resided in the two holy cities of Syria-Palestine tended to be a religious scholar, pious ascetic, holy hermit, religious functionary, member of a mystic order, the pilgrim, or outcast from the ruling elite who found sanctuary here. In this sense, Jerusalem and Hebron did not resemble Cairo or the provincial capitals, and thus did not export the ʿulamaʾ in the same fashion.

The flow of individuals from the large cities of Syria to Cairo was supplemented by a secondary flow of individuals originating from relatively dense clusters of towns and villages in the immediate vicinity of these cities and throughout the provinces under their jurisdiction.[39] This clustering phenomenon, together with the sequences of nisbas reported by the biographical sources, suggests a pattern of primary and secondary stages of migration similar to that noted in Gharbīya and Minūfīya districts of the Delta.[40] Many individuals or their forebears who originated in a central Syrian or Palestinian town or village moved to one of the major cities, where they or their descendants established themselves in the elite structure. They or their descendants subsequently moved to Cairo, either temporarily or permanently, to take up any of a variety of positions. The birthplaces in the various Syrian and Palestinian zones mentioned in the sources indicate that this process applied to a large percentage of the total group of Syrians. This is to say that relatively fewer individuals from Syria or Palestine than from the Nile Delta moved directly to Cairo from small towns or villages. Rather, their parents or grandparents had moved to one of the major Levantine cities a generation or so before and retained the collective family memories and ties to the ancestral site.[41] Because fewer of the Syrians who were born in small towns and villages moved directly to Cairo, the biographical sources provided far more data for the cities of the Levant than for the sites in the hinterlands, which was not true of the data describing Delta sites.

The majority of the clustered sites in Syria-Palestine lay within the administrative jurisdiction and cultural influence of the major cities—Damascus, Aleppo, Ḥamā, Ṭarābulus, Ṣafad, Jerusalem, and al-Karak—and all occurred within fifty miles of one of these centers. References in the biographical sources to the sites within these clusters reveals considerable migration both from areas that are heavily populated today and from others that are rather sparsely populated and underdeveloped. According to the data, the concentration of sites lying between Aleppo and Damascus produced the greatest number of immigrants. This would suggest that the west central heartland of the Syrian steppe possessed the most highly developed agrarian and commercial economy of the area during the fifteenth century, since the institutions necessary for the maintenance of the civilian elite depended on this kind of an economic base. The Syrian littoral, west of this central zone, included most of modern Lebanon and all of the present-day Syrian coast. There was little evidence of site conglomeration here, but migration came from the coastal ports, especially al-Lādhqīya (121) and Ṭarābulus.[42]

A noteworthy concentration of sites appeared to the southeast, in what is now the east bank of Jordan. This area has recently experienced only modest population growth and economic development, but during the Mamluk period, according to evidence from the biographical sources, the region was moderately well developed. Its urban centers—al-Shawbak (24), al-Karak (27), al-Adhraʿāt (39), and Buṣrā al-Shām (40)—were cited frequently, and a number of eminent persons may be traced to them. Al-Karak was a provincial capital and major fortress of the Mamluk state. Important political prisoners, including Sultan Barqūq himself, were incarcerated in its citadel in order to isolate them from the seats of administration. These towns also possessed the cultural institutions that supported the ʿulamaʾ class.

West of the Trans-Jordanian area, in central Palestine, the number of sites referred to in the sources decreased; but there were a considerable number of nisba references to several Palestinian centers in addition to Jerusalem and Hebron. Ghazza (2) and ʿAsqalān (4) were particularly prominent. In general, however, evidence suggests a relatively low migration rate from southern Palestine to Cairo. To the east and north of the Syrian heartland—specifically, in the upper Euphrates and Tigris valleys and the intermediate Jazīra district (234)—there was also evidence of migration, although the sources provide relatively few details about the nature of the sites located there. All these zones are sparsely populated today. Since the number of birthplaces reported for these areas was rather meager, it is difficult to ascertain how many people actually originated there compared to those who just maintained some ancestral ties to them. Furthermore, with so few references to these areas in the biographical sources, hypotheses about their degree of economic and cultural development during the later Middle Ages are only tentative.

The rates of migration from all over the Levant appear to have remained relatively constant throughout the fifteenth century. The increase in references to sites from the mid-fifteenth century on was reflected in the numbers of both nisbas and birthplaces from the major cities. But whether this increase, weighed against the skewing factor of death dates, actually indicates that any real change in the rate of migration is indeterminable. The increase may indirectly reflect reactions of the elite classes to the Timurid invasions. The devastations wrought upon the Levant at the turn of the fifteenth century were aimed primarily at large cities. As repositories of currency, precious articles, and portable goods, these cities were the objects of Timur's campaigns wherever he went, though his horde's enormous forage requirements led to systematic looting and pillaging in the countryside as well. Because of its location, Aleppo bore the brunt of the Timurid thrust and therefore suffered more physical violence, although not necessarily more loss of material wealth, than any other Syrian city. Yet it is clear from the biographical sources that there was no significant augmentation in the flow of individuals from Syrian cities, even from Aleppo, to Cairo during the first half of the fifteenth century. Quite possibly, the option of moving to Cairo was open to only a limited group. Others may well have escaped to other Syrian towns or to those rural areas fortunate enough to have escaped Timur's invasion. Because of mass executions and widespread deaths resulting from disease and the ravages of war, many who might have left may also have died before reaching Cairo, to appear in the sources.

Another factor bearing on the possible increase in migration during the latter part of the century is proposed in an argument by Ira Lapidus.[43] He notes that since the Mamluk elite faced increasingly severe shortages in its own sources of revenue during the fifteenth century, it invested less money in the institutions that supported the ʿulamaʾ. This was particularly true in the Syrian cities, because the Mamluks permitted the provincial centers to decline first. The ʿulamaʾ were increasingly thrown on their own resources to support themselves and to maintain the essentials of religious and intellectual life in their society. Eminent academicians and theologians would suffer the most from this situation, since reliance on local resources would result in a decline in the founding or expansion of large, complex institutions with specialized programs, and an increase in smaller institutions that more directly served a local constituency. This provided an inducement for the specialists to transfer to the imperial capital itself, still the primary center of higher learning and concentrated (if diminishing) investment in specialized religio-academic institutions of the state.

MIGRATION TO CAIRO FROM IRAN
(Maps IV-A through IV-D)

Iran and its contiguous areas, supplying approximately 5 to 8 percent of the total number of elite immigrating to Cairo, represent the second most important source of these immigrants outside Egypt. To shift attention to Iran is to leave the confines of the Mamluk empire and the security it provided. The Iranian areas, a major locus of Islamic civilization and cultural progress, were exposed to one of the longest eras of foreign invasion and political-economic disruption in Near Eastern history. This disruption was most pronounced during the first Mongol invasions of the early thirteenth century, and lasted until the successful establishment of the Safavids at the turn of the sixteenth. The fifteenth century therefore coincided with the latter part of this era, and saw its social consequences. Although we can assume a constant flow of internally generated migration of the elite from Iran to major cultural centers such as Cairo, external causes added a dimension to the phenomenon. Before the Mongol invasions, all the internal conditions requisite to the existence of the ʿulamaʾ as a viable class were present in Iran; after 1200 the region was beset with unforeseen and initially insurmountable problems that introduced new stimuli to migration.

The initial impact of the Mongol invasions on the Iranian populace was shattering—at least in those regions bearing the brunt of the invasions. Local militarist-iqṭāʿ systems of government could not cope with such lethal force, and were eliminated. With the establishment of the Ilkhānid regime at mid-century, the new Mongol-Turkic elite had settled in to stay. This ruling class was alien to the type of government that had evolved in Iran over two millennia. As members of a highly specialized society of Central Asian warrior-nomads accustomed to vast expanses of grasslands, the Mongols knew little of the delicate ecological balance existing in the arid, irrigation-intensive, economy of Iran. Rarely a tolerant people, they regarded the complex agrarian system of Iran as a needless impediment to their pastoral cycle. During their first decades, they set about methodically destroying much of the qanāt irrigation network, and in doing so, reduced the affected peasantry to a state of economic ruin. They also dispossessed many members of the Turco-Persian ruling elite from their landed estates, and thus temporarily eliminated the old system of land tenure and peasant client rights.

The Ilkhānids ultimately incorporated many Persians into the governing bureaucracy when they belatedly recognized that they no longer lived in Central Asia and would have to adapt themselves to their new environment. But they retained the tradition of fiercely independent local chieftains responsible for maintaining themselves in their locale. This tradition impeded the reestablishment of a rational taxation policy in Iran. Early Ilkhānid chieftains extorted irregular sums from both the peasants and the Persian commercial classes. And although Ghazan Khān and his wazīr, Rashīd al-Dīn, imposed a set of reforms to correct this situation, the reforms were abandoned after his death.[44] Ghazan Khān also brought the Mongol elite of Iran into the pale of Islam when he himself converted. As time was to prove, however, Mongols who took the faith did not cease to behave as alien conquerors ruling over inferior peoples. The initial destruction of rich agrarian areas and urban centers was not compensated for by the Ilkhānids, even after the reign of Ghazan Khān; moreover, the control of the regime weakened steadily during the fourteenth century.

The devastations wrought by the Mongols damaged both the agrarian system and the urban network, both of which adversely affected the ʿulamaʾ. By damaging the irrigation-based agrarian system of Iran and abusing the peasantry that maintained it, the Mongols reduced the income base of the region. Since the types of institutions that supported the ʿulamaʾ were dependent on a consistently high and stable income level, these institutions were reduced in both number and stature throughout the region. The openly antischolastic stance assumed by many Mongols aggravated this situation, especially during the period preceding Ghazan's conversion to Islam. In general, the drastic decline in income, erratic taxation, and debasement of coinage accompanying the Mongol occupation meant that the traditional sources of revenue in support of religio-academic institutions declined well into the fourteenth century. This was exacerbated by the Mongol's attempts to disrupt the network of cities that had become foundations of Islamic high culture in Iran. Their hostility to urban life was not attributable to any senseless desire for destruction, but rather derived from their own economic and social structure, which required a pastoral environment.[45] Since the majority of the institutions important to the support of the ʿulamaʾ were urban-based, such disruption seriously affected Iranian Muslim culture and intellectual life.

In the late fourteenth century, Timur's invasions subjected Iran once again to a pattern of agrarian disruption, urban destruction, dispossession from land, and erratic taxation.[46] These developments directly affected the Iranian learned elite, many of whom, once they had lost their property and wealth, left their homeland. Great numbers of these individuals migrated east into India, and a smaller number went west. Some crossed the Mamluk frontiers and ultimately settled in Cairo. During the fifteenth century, Iran witnessed no such wholesale devastation again, but the area remained divided between the later Timurids in the east and two Turcoman federations in the central and western zones. The Black and White Sheep Turcomans proceeded to adapt their form of transhumant pastoralism to Iranian geography and ecology,[47] and therefore, tended not to disrupt the irrigated agrarian system, which had again begun to recover gradually, at least in certain areas.

Given the conditions, outlined above, one would guess that the externally stimulated migration of the ʿulamaʾ should have peaked around A.D. 1250 and again in A.D. 1400. The biographical sources bear out the latter date. Among the sites indicated as geographic nisbas and birthplaces, none of the major urban centers produced a high percentage of the total number of individuals migrating.[48] This was in marked contrast to the site configurations in Egypt or Syria-Palestine. The Iranian sites did conform to a clustering pattern that followed the broad concentrations of population in Iran during both the medieval and modern periods. The regions adjacent to eastern Syria and Anatolia and extending down along the Zagros mountain chain yielded numerous references, with the clustering pattern actually beginning in the Armenian Knot. During the Middle Ages the polyglot population of this area was dominated alternately by regimes based in Anatolia or Iran. Persian cultural influence reached everywhere in this northwestern section of Iran, but it coexisted with Turcoman, Kurdish, or Azerbayjānī traditions. The central and southern Zagros, however, had been the heartland of Persian civilization from ancient times, even though other ethnolinguistic groups retained their identity in those regions.

Three other concentrations of sites appeared: Fārs proper along the Persian Gulf to the Straits of Hormūz; the region of the Elburz Mountains immediately south of the Caspian Sea, including Jīlān (115) and Jurjān (114) and extending northeast to the Khwarazm steppe (116); and finally, the Khurāsānian regions (130), extending east into Afghanistan and north into Transoxiana. The cities of this latter province that were mentioned in the biographical sources were among Iran's most vital cultural centers. All the prominent centers of Persian civilization were reported among the geographic nisbas, although as previously noted, none dominated the overall configuration; nor did the cities supply more immigrants than the relatively small towns or villages. None of these cities—Tabrīz (56), Qazvīn (69), Rāy (78), Hamadān (80), Shīrāz (91), Kirmān (98), Bām (99), Mardān (101), Yazd (107), Iṣfahān (108),[49] Nīshabūr (120), Mashhad (121), Marw (122), Hirāt (Herat) (126)—or the two urban centers of Transoxiana—Samarqānd (124) and Bukhāra (125)—yielded more than eight to ten nisbas each. Most yielded fewer than eight. Yet some one hundred Iranian place names were mentioned.

Migration from Iran to the west was therefore much more random and evenly distributed than that from Egypt and Syria. Since all of the Iranian cities lay east of the Mamluk sphere of influence, none maintained the active relationship of mutual exchange with Cairo that appears to have been responsible for the high concentrations of nisba and birthplace references to a specific site.

The clusters of sites supplying immigrants from Iran occurred especially along the main routes of access to the Iranian Plateau from the northeast and from the plateau into Syria and Anatolia. These routes were followed by the Mongols in the thirteenth century, and again in the fourteenth century by Timur Lenk, who managed to apply his policies of systematic destruction to all the major areas of Iran except the province of Fārs south of Shīrāz.[50] The regions of Khurāsān, the Caspian Sea, and the Armenian Knot endured the most sustained pillaging.

The impact of this wave of invasions by Timur was reflected in the variation in migration rates from Iran to Cairo during the fifteenth century (Maps IV-C and IV-D). Even given the fact that more deaths occurred after 850/1446-1447 among the individuals surveyed, the number of nisbas and birthplaces indicated for Iran was greater for the first half of the century than for the second. Variations in the locations of the sites also reflected the major thrusts of the Timurid invasions. Sites for the first half of the century occurred in clusters, particularly in the Armenian Knot, the Caspian regions, and Khurāsān. The configurations for the second half of the century did not indicate any true clustering; rather, sites were distributed more randomly in the areas of concentration outlined above. This phenomenon of variation in both rate of migration and concentration of sites must be considered in relation to where the Iranians traveled when they departed their homeland. The majority went east to India, because the Muslim regimes of the north welcomed recruits to the cadres of Persian scholars and bureaucrats who staffed their governments. A minority moved west; and of this minority, many, such as the family of the famous mystic poet of the thirteenth century, Jalāl al-Dīn Rūmī, settled in Anatolia rather than Egypt or Syria. Therefore, the data we have from the biographical sources on Iranians who did transfer to Cairo can only suggest the dimensions of the mass exodus from Iran by the ʿulama' during the mid-thirteenth century and again after A.D. 1400.

The Iranians were not as widely distributed among the several categories of occupations as were the Egyptians and Syrians, but they did appear in all of them (Tables 1-6). Those who succeeded in establishing themselves in Cairo and in developing a sound reputation tended to pursue careers as scholars, jurists, bureaucrats, religious functionaries, and mystics, in that order. The scholars were primarily specialists in the Islamic sciences and in particular jurisprudence (Table 5). They tended to specialize in the tradition of their legal school and became prominent as authorities on the legal doctors. The natural sciences also constituted a field in which Iranian scholars excelled. It is significant that even at this late date the only instructor in alchemy (*kīmiyā'*) who was reported in the biographical sources traced his family's origin to the town of Īj (64).[51] Iranian scholars resident in Cairo were also prominent in literary fields both as poets and as specialists in Koranic exegesis and Arabic grammar. They maintained the long-standing tradition of Persian distinction in the Islamic literary fields.

One Persian who attained renown as a scholar and jurist in Cairo was Jalāl al-Dīn ʿUbayd-Allah ibn ʿAwḍ al-Ardabīlī al-Shirwānī, who was born in Ardabīl (59) during the mid-fourteenth century.[52] He was the son of a physician who practiced in Ardabīl and Shirwān (83). Al-Shirwānī arrived in Cairo prior to the Timurid invasions to continue his studies in fiqh at the Shaykhūnīya madrasa. He was appointed a repetitor at the madrasa of Ṣarghatmish, and was supported there by part of a waqf endowment granted to maintain study and recitation of Ḥadīth. He was subsequently appointed professor of jurisprudence in the madrasas of Aytmish, Abū Bakr, and Umm al-Sulṭān, all institutions maintained by lavish Mamluk endowments. Through his connections with several amirs, he later received an appointment to a military judgeship; no details on his tenure in office or its dates were provided in the sources. Al-Shirwānī was a partisan of the two famous viceroys, Minṭāsh and Nawrūz, the latter of whom studied under him. He journeyed to Syria with Minṭāsh when the amir broke openly with Barqūq, and was later arrested and tried by the sultan because of this; but he was soon released and returned to his teaching posts. Al-Shirwānī spent his final years free from political embroilments, and died in Rajab 807/January-February 1405.

An example of an individual who derived from an eminent family in eastern Iran and attained social prestige and judicial authority in Cairo is Shihāb al-Dīn Abū ʿAbd-Allah Muḥammad ibn ʿAṭāʾ-Allah al-Rāzī al-Hirawī, born in Hirāt (126) in 767/1365-1366.[53] After leaving Iran during the Timurid crisis, traveling to the Ottoman court, and teaching in Jerusalem in 814/1411-1412, al-Hirawī arrived in Cairo in 818/1415-1416. His fame as a jurist had caught the attention of al-Mu'ayyad Shaykh, who was then viceroy. In 821/1418-1419, as sultan, al-Mu'ayyad Shaykh appointed al-Hirawī Shāfiʿī chief justice of Cairo, as a replacement for Jalāl al-Dīn al-Bulqīnī. Al-Hirawī's sentiments remained with Jerusalem, however, and he returned there, with the sultan's permission, as controller of the Two Shrines and as professor in the Ṣalāḥīya Madrasa in 823/1420-1421, a year before Shaykh's death. In 827/1423-1424, he was appointed secretary of the chancellery to Sultan Barsbāy, in place of the previously mentioned al-Karakī, but he resigned the same year to accept for a second time the office of Shāfiʿī chief justice of Cairo. He resigned this post a year later because of his rapidly increasing infirmity. Al-Hirawī died in Dhūʿl-Ḥijja 829/October-November 1426.

Al-Hirawī was on close terms with several great amirs of Syria, especially Nawrūz and Shaykh, the latter of whom invited him to Cairo when he became sultan. He managed to develop a viable if not warm relationship with Sultan Barsbāy, who was not known for his personal cordiality toward the ʿulamaʾ. This ability to weather changes of regime smoothly became a characteristic of certain Persian notables, in contrast to many Syrians and Egyptians. Possibly, this was due in part to the relative infrequency with which corruption and greed were attributed to the Persians, although al-Hirawī was able to commission the foundation of a madrasa in Jerusalem with his assets and the contributions made by his Mamluk associates.

According to the biographical sources, even individual Persians who attained major posts as bureaucrats and who were therefore given the opportunity to build immense fortunes illicitly, rarely took advantage of their positions. The example of Ḥasan al-Dīn Ḥaydar ibn Aḥmad al-Rūmī al-ʿAjamī, known as Shaykh al-Tāj, is a case in point.[54] Born in Shīrāz (91) in 780/1378-1379, al-ʿAjamī began and terminated his career as a scholar and pious ascetic. He received a salaried honorarium from the sultan's treasuries (*murattab al-dhakhīra*) under Sultan Jaqmaq, and could have exploited his access to such a repository of wealth; but there is no evidence that he did. Instead, he accepted the respectable but modest post of shaykh in the zāwiya of the Qubbat al-Naṣr.

Individuals born in Iran or claiming Iranian ancestry often worked as silk merchants, calligraphers, and merchants in foreign commerce. Iranians also attained a prominence commensurate with their ancient reputation as scientists and physicians (Table 4). The chief physician, closely associated with the royal court, was highly respected as the leading medical authority of the state. And during the early fifteenth century, this post was held by a Persian who exemplified the highly cosmopolitan nature of the Iranian ʿulamaʾ during the later Middle Ages, Fatḥ al-Dīn Fatḥ-Allah ibn Mustaʿsim ibn Nafīs al-Israʾīlī al-Daūdī al-Tabrīzī,[55] born in Tabrīz (56) in 749/1348-1349. His grandfather had converted to Islam from Judaism and his family was associated with the line of David, in Jewish circles a status equal to that of the Muslim sayyids. Al-Tabrīzī's career falls into a pattern often repeated by his non-Iranian contemporaries. Leaving Iran with his father during the Timurid crisis, he journeyed to Cairo, where his grandfather had settled as an associate of the famous amir, Shaykhū. He established himself in the family medical practice and, on the retirement of his uncle (his grandfather's son), was appointed chief physician. Al-Tabrīzī met his nemesis when he chose to accept the post of secretary of the chancellery from Sultan Barqūq and entered the chaotic political milieu of the early fifteenth century in Cairo. He became deeply involved in the political factions that proliferated after Barqūq's death and managed to acquire a substantial fortune during the period prior to the enthronement of al-Muʾayyad Shaykh, whom he initially supported. He later plotted against al-Muʾayyad Shaykh with several amirs, however, and after several brief incarcerations, he was mulcted of 40,000 dīnārs by the sultan. He was ultimately strangled in the Prison of the Burnt Gate during Rabīʿ I 816/June-July 1413. Al-Tabrīzī was unusual, since relatively few Persians chose to involve themselves to such an extent in the politics of the court for material gain. His fame as a physician and Persian literateur was tarnished by his political ambition and greed, a fact his biographers did not overlook. Interestingly enough, none of this was attributed to his Jewish ancestry.

There are many other interesting examples of individual Iranians who successfully penetrated the elite structure of Cairo. The presence of famous poets and literateurs who attracted even semi-literate Mamluks to their recitations, of mystics who maintained classical traditions of personal deprivation to prove their faith and who therefore were revered widely in Cairo, contributed to the esteem enjoyed by Iranians in the city. The Iranians, in fact, attained a preeminence in the Cairene elite

note

disproportionate to their relatively limited numbers. They remained conscious exponents of the Persian intellectual tradition in Cairo and were respected for this by their contemporaries.

MIGRATION TO CAIRO FROM ANATOLIA (AL-RŪM)
(Maps III-A, III-B)

All the remaining areas of the Near East from which migration was discernible together made up no more than 10 to 15 percent of the total numbers of civilian elite originating outside Cairo and no more than 3 percent were from Anatolia. It is difficult to apply exact percentages to any of these vast regions, since the returns from the biographical sources were not comprehensive enough to permit an accurate estimate, but there is no question that they produced far fewer individuals than those heretofore discussed.

Since the Mamluks exercised suzerainty over a considerable portion of what is now southeastern Turkey, the nisba and birthplace references to sites in Anatolia must be subjected to further categorization in terms of political regime.[56] Even after 1450, when the certainty of eventual Ottoman rule over eastern Anatolia became apparent, the Mamluks retained their control over the Anatolian portions of Aleppo province.[57] Until the Mamluks were ousted from this area after 1500, the regions to the east centering at the Armenian Knot and the juncture between Anatolia and Iran remained semiautonomous, loosely administered by Turcoman tribal confederations. The political condition of this region between Anatolia and Iran is significant, because the majority of those referred to as Rūmīs (Anatolians) originated in this zone and the northern areas of Aleppo province. The evidence relevant to the areas west and north of Aleppo province is extremely sparse and scattered.[58]

The areas east of the Mamluk frontier fell within the Persian cultural sphere, but were populated largely by Turcomans, Kurds, and Armenians with Turkish, Arab, and Iranian elements scattered through their learned elite. The major centers mentioned in the sources were ʿAynṭāb (modern Gaziantep) (159), Marʿash (160), Bahasna (161), Kakhtā (162), Malaṭya (164), Adana (166), Amida (Diyār Bakīr) (212), Ḥiṣn Kayfa (213), Mardīn (216), and Urmā (Urmia) (232). To the west of the Mamluk frontier, in Rūm proper, prominent sites and regions were Qunīya (Konya) (171), Ṣarukhān (176), Qaṭrān (179), Burṣā (183), Iṣtanbūl (186), Aqsarāy (193), Sīwās (197), and Irzinjān (203). None of these sites yielded more than five nisba references each.

Why such a prominent and relatively close region as central and western Anatolia contributed so few members to the civilian elite of

Cairo during the later Middle Ages is difficult to explain on the basis of our minimal evidence. Two hypotheses come to mind. First, the political or external causes of migration so prevalent in Iran did not apply to Anatolia in the same way. Although this area experienced invasions, including those of the dreaded hordes of Timur, it was largely spared the devastation experienced by Iran and northern Syria. And though the *beyliks* (principalities) of Anatolia warred among themselves, this intermittent strife did relatively little damage to the economy or to urban institutions. Furthermore, as the Ottomans increased their authority from the mid-fourteenth century on, the area was increasingly stabilized under a central government. Timur's invasions temporarily disrupted this authority, but it was rapidly restored. Therefore, the ʿulamaʾ of central and western Anatolia had less incentive to leave their homelands because of insecurity and threats to life and property.

A second possibility is that the Anatolian learned establishment may have been numerically smaller at this time than that in other major zones of the Islamic world. Several of the Anatolian sites remain small rural towns even today, and it would be misleading to regard all Anatolians as highly urbanized, or having access to sophisticated institutions. It is widely known that the early Ottoman sultans attracted many prominent ʿulamaʾ from the eastern Islamic lands, especially when they enlarged their bureaucratic apparatus and founded new religio-academic institutions. This may indicate that there was only a relatively small ʿulamaʾ class established locally in western Anatolia prior to the heyday of the Ottoman state. Also, the individuals who did establish themselves in Cairo tended to exhibit a markedly regional outlook, reflected in the activities they pursued and the classes of Cairene society with which they identified—at least initially—when they settled there.

The Anatolians who can be traced to a birthplace tended to fall into the judicial, academic, and religious categories of occupations (Tables 3, 5, and 6), while nisba references occurred quite evenly in all categories except the artisan-commercial group. Since the nisbas referred to individuals of a particular ancestry, not necessarily to a specific origin, their even distribution implies that over time the Anatolians tended to be assimilated into the general framework of the ʿulamaʾ class. In addition, the academicians and jurists who were definitely born in Anatolia exhibited characteristics shared by their contemporaries throughout the Muslim world. Indeed, individuals from the cities of Aleppo province identified with Arabic civilization as much as they did with Turkish culture.

The career of the famous historian al-ʿAynī shows what an advantage it was to be familiar with both. His diverse cultural background served his interests well. Badr al-Dīn Maḥmūd ibn Aḥmad al-ʿAynṭābī al-Ḥalabī, known to students of Islamic history as al-ʿAynī,[59] was born in the city of ʿAynṭāb, north of Aleppo, in Rajab 762/May-June 1361. His activities are widely known, and only one aspect of his erudition concerns us here: his fluency in Turkish. Al-ʿAynī's education, pursued both in ʿAynṭāb and Aleppo, did not differ appreciably from the studies of his contemporaries. There was no reference in his biography to any formal study of Turkish, and therefore it is evident that he used Turkish interchangeably with Arabic as a language that he had learned in his youth. Upon his arrival and settlement in Cairo in 788/1386-1387, al-ʿAynī entered into a long and varied career that ultimately elevated him to the presence of the sultan and great amirs. There is no question that his knowledge of Turkish aided him in his rise to prominence within the Mamluk elite. Indeed, his widely publicized competition with his great rival, al-Maqrīzī, over the informal but esteemed status of court historian was ultimately decided in his favor due to his fluency in both spoken and written Turkish.

That al-ʿAynī's facility in Turkish stood him in good stead with the Mamluk ruling class helps us understand the unique status occupied by many of the ʿulamaʾ who came from Anatolia and spoke Turkish. These individuals did not consider themselves a part of the Mamluk elite, nor would the Mamluks have accepted them as such. But the Mamluks regarded Turkish as their caste's vehicle of communication, even though they themselves spoke Central Asian dialects such as Qipjak, or Circassian, a Caucasic language. They rarely made an effort to develop genuine fluency in Arabic—particularly in its literary form, since their own training was hardly academic. For many of them, ignorance of Arabic acted as a barrier between themselves and the mass of population.[60] The Mamluks therefore regarded native Turkish-speaking individuals as a special segment of the ʿulamaʾ. They tended to seek out such individuals and draw them into their personal circles to a greater degree than the Arabic speakers. This was particularly true of revered holy men (*muʿtaqadūn*) who came from Anatolia. The pious ascetic, regardless of ethnic background, played an important role in the Mamluk elite, as we shall see. But those who were Turkish-speaking who were descended from Mamluks, or who derived from Anatolia were particularly respected as qualified to minister to the spiritual needs of the ruling elite. Actually, these individuals are somewhat difficult to trace, since they came from diverse and often illiterate backgrounds with little genealogy to support their social status. In addition, they did not identify with the main body of the ʿulamaʾ, since their concerns were focused on mystic communication with God rather than bureaucratic or academic matters. The biographers included them in the compendia of notables because of their influence over the society in general and over the Mamluks in particular, who took care to provide for their material needs.

Aḥmad ibn Ibrahīm al-Yamanī al-Burṣāwī al-Miṣrī al-Ṣūfī, known as Ibn ʿArab, and born in the old Ottoman capital of Burṣā during the late fourteenth century, was one of these Turkish-speaking pious ascetics.[61] His father had moved to Burṣā from the Yemen and had married there, so Ibn ʿArab benefited from both Yemeni Arabic and Anatolian Turkish backgrounds. After receiving his basic education in Burṣā, Ibn ʿArab came to Cairo as a youth and settled in the Shaykhūnīya khānqāh to devote himself to the pursuit of knowledge in an atmosphere of pious abstinence. Possessing virtually no material assets, he first supported himself as a copyist, a skilled trade that permitted him considerable time for study. He was able to resign from his duties as a copyist when he was admitted to the Ṣūfī community of Shaykhūnīya, where he received the stipend of thirty dirhams per month. For the next thirty years, Ibn ʿArab patterned his daily existence around intensive scholarship and extreme piety and prayer. His reputation as a muʿtaqad spread throughout Cairo, attracting the attention of the sultan himself. Ibn Taghrī-Birdī came to know and revere him, and recounted various anecdotes about his behavior and attitudes. During his later years, Ibn ʿArab became an institution in his own right and was offered a comfortable income by the sultan and other amirs; but he declined to accept, claiming that thirty dirhams a month was enough for any believer whose nourishment came, after all, from faith in God rather than material wealth. He died in Rabīʿ I 830/April-May 1426 and was given a state funeral in the Citadel by Sultan Barsbāy. Another Anatolian, Ḥanafī chief justice Badr al-Dīn Maḥmūd al-ʿAynṭābī (none other than the historian, al-ʿAynī) led the prayer service, which was attended by a host of notables. Ibn ʿArab was buried in the yard of the Shaykhūnīya, where he had devoted himself to perfecting a state of pious abstinence.

A second class of Anatolians occupying a unique position in the Mamluk state was a group of Turkish-speaking militarists who were granted a semi-Mamluk status. These individuals rarely appear in the sources, because they did not identify with the ʿulamaʾ at all. Their numbers in Cairo may have been considerable, but if so, the biographers did not comment on them. These people, often renegades from their own governments, took service with the sultan, who provided them sanctuary and an income in return. They appear in the sources as a shadowy, rather ill-defined group. They were recognized as an influential and cosmopolitan body of individuals, however, who, widely traveled and familiar with a variety of political environments, formed a circle of informants and advisers at the royal court and in the households of the great amirs. They came from exceedingly diverse backgrounds—some may even have been Europeans—but they all used Turkish as a common language.

The extreme paucity of individuals from Anatolia in the artisan-commercial category of occupations must be noted (Table 4). Only one birthplace was reported for an Anatolian immigrant in this category. The only group within this category that had any notable number of Anatolian nisbas was the group of merchants, who belonged to the class that staffed the sultan's commercial bureaucracy and managed the state monopolies. Some of the merchants were also involved in the slave trade and received the title *khawājā*. This latter group dealt with the foreigners who transferred the future Mamluks to Cairo from Central Asia and the Caucasus. As such, they did not identify with the free mercantile classes of the Near East, who dealt with foreign goods from south and east Asia.

In contrast, nisba references to Anatolia appeared frequently for individuals in the executive class (Table 1). This suggests that descendants of the immigrants from Asia Minor, over an indefinite period of time, were able to penetrate the exclusive executive offices reserved primarily for Mamluks and their immediate descendants. The Rūmīs or "Turks" again seemed to occupy a status unique among the civilian population with regard to their capacity to intermingle with the Mamluk elite.

SITES OF ORIGIN IN IRAQ AND THE ARABIAN PENINSULA
(Maps IV-A through IV-D)

Iraq and the Arabian Peninsula yielded only a small number of nisbas and birthplaces, except for three urban centers—Madīna (11), Makka (14), and Baghdād (41)—which ranked among the most frequently quoted sites in this study.[62]

During the fifteenth century, Iraq came under the rather amorphous control of several Turcoman confederations. Throughout this period Baghdād did not play an active role in Near Eastern politics. Since foreign invasions had affected Iraq as much as they did Iran, much of the population had moved west from this region. Iraq's cities, particularly Baghdād, never fully recovered from the Mongol invasions of the thirteenth century. Only a remnant of the former ʿAbbāsid capital's bureaucratic and scholarly institutions survived into the later Middle Ages, and these were largely stripped of their previous eminence in the Islamic world. This decline was reflected by the Iraqis who themselves or whose families resettled in Cairo. As a group, they attained only modest positions in the Egyptian capital; they did not rise to major offices, as individuals from other regions of the Near East tended to do. They appeared in all the occupational categories except the executive, from which they were virtually absent. General migration from Iraq stemmed from relatively few sites other than Baghdād: Baṣra (34), Makhlaf (35), Wāsiṭ (38), Kūfa (39), al-Jaʿfarīya (40), Takrīt (42), Sinjār (44), and Mawṣil (Mosul) (45), among the prominent towns. None of these yielded more than six references in the biographical sources.

The individuals from the Arabian Peninsula were so overwhelmingly Makkans or Madīnans that migration from the peninsula might be interpreted in terms of these cities alone. During the Mamluk period, the Ḥijāz and its holy cities were ruled from Cairo. The Red Sea remained under the control of the Mamluks until the end of the fifteenth century, when the Portuguese, gaining access to the Indian Ocean, penetrated the area. Therefore, through the fifteenth century, the inhabitants of the holy cities were subjects of the sultan in Cairo and enjoyed the relative security provided by the empire. They also identified with Arabic culture, although many claimed ancestry from all over the Muslim world. Makka and Madīna had long been sanctuaries for Muslims who wished to spend their last years on holy ground and for those who wished to devote themselves to meditation in the cities where the Prophet had received his revelation. The variety of backgrounds of individuals born in Makka and Madīna, whose forebears had come from all over the Dār al-Islām, makes it impossible to distinguish their regional or ethnic characteristics in the biographical sources. These people moved back and forth between the holy cities, Cairo, Damascus, and Jerusalem rather than settling in Cairo. Predictably, Makkans and Madīnans were represented in all the occupational categories of the sources except the executive.

Apart from the holy cities, only one other region of the Arabian Peninsula was represented in the biographical sources—the Yemen. Relatively few individuals came from this area themselves, but a larger number traced their ancestry there or to south Arabian tribes. Several merchants and artisans derived from the Yemen, a center of commerce since ancient times. From the reign of Barsbāy on, the Ḥijāzī and Yamanī ports were controlled by the sultanate, and a class of merchants commissioned by the government settled in these cities to administer the monopolies over international trade passing through the Red Sea. Sites located along the Persian Gulf did not appear as either nisbas or birthplaces, although there were scattered references to them as places visited in the course of an individual's travel.

MIGRATION TO CAIRO FROM NORTH AFRICA (AL-MAGHRIB)
(Maps V-A, V-B)

The Maghrib supplied no more than 3 to 4 percent of the total number of individuals described in our sources. The regions of North Africa where the sites of origin tended to cluster were predictable: Ifriqīya (modern Tunisia) and al-Maghrib al-Aqṣā (modern Morocco), the vicinity of Fās (Fez) (10) in the north, and Marrākish (27) in the south. Only three important towns—Tilimsān (Tlemcen) (31), Bijāya (Boujie) (32), and Qusṭanṭīna (Constantine) (33)—were located outside these two regions.[63] References to these sites in the context of travel through North Africa suggest that because of their location in the areas between the more densely populated zones of the extreme Maghrib, Tūnis (36), and the Nile Valley, these towns functioned as way stations and transit entrepôts along the trade routes of North Africa. They were also the northern termini of caravan routes extending across the Sahara to the states of central and western Africa.

The individuals who came to Cairo from the Maghrib appeared in all the occupational categories; but since their numbers were few, it is not possible to discern general trends. One trait of the Maghribīs becomes obvious in studying the sources, however. Many of their contemporaries in Cairo regarded them as rustic when they arrived, aloof and austere in character.

North Africans had developed their own cultural qualities by the central Middle Ages, and Maghribīs who settled in Cairo or whose families had done so were regarded as a distinct group that tended to retain its own traditions. Nevertheless, many individual Maghribīs rose to positions of prominence. They became famous not only in Egypt but throughout the Muslim world. The career of Ibn Khaldūn[64] is an outstanding case in point: he was known even to Timur Lenk.

Maghribīs distinguished themselves in Cairo as teachers, scholars, theologians, jurists, merchants, and physicians. One basis of identity that they shared was the adherence of the majority of them to the Mālikī madhhab, and several of Cairo's eminent Mālikī qāḍīs, including Ibn Khaldūn, came from North Africa. And two physicians from North Africa, erudite in several fields, became eminent in Cairo. Aḥmad ibn Ḥātim al-Basaṭī al-Sanhājī al-Fāsī, known in Cairo as Ḥātim al-Fāsī, was born in Fez in 751/1350-1351.[65] His education completed in Qusṭanṭīna and Tūnis, Ḥātim al-Fāsī journeyed to Egypt while making the Ḥajj; he arrived in Cairo in 773/1371-1372. Once in Cairo, he made the acquaintance of prominent scholars and Mamluk amirs alike. Upon his return to Cairo in 805/1402-1403, after a prolonged sojourn in the Ḥijāz and Syria, he gained access to the imperial court. Sultan Faraj was so taken with him that he had him spend a week at a time in the palace. Whether Ḥātim al-Fāsī actually treated the sultan is unclear from the account in the sources, but there is no question that he impressed the entire court with his erudite stance, regardless of whether his knowledge was real or assumed. Al-Fāsī continued to travel the rest of his life, but the imperial court and elite circles of Cairo remained his home base.

The other individual who combined medicine and scholarship was Abū'l-Faḍl Muḥammad ibn Muḥammad al-Mashdālī al-Zawāwī al-Bijā'ī, known as Ibn Abū Qāsim.[66] He was born in the coastal city of Bijāya (now in modern Algeria) in Rajab 821/August-September 1418, and received an extensive education in all the standard literary texts of his age while growing up in Bijāya and Tilimsān. Al-Sakhāwī made specific reference in his biographical sketch of Ibn Abū Qāsim to subjects rarely included in a standard late medieval curriculum: philosophy, medicine, geometry (handasa), "ancient sciences" (ʿulūm qadīma), and Ṣūfī theology. Ibn Abū Qāsim traveled widely in the Near East before settling in Cairo, where his fame as a physician and scholar had preceded him. He befriended Ibn Ḥajar al-ʿAsqalānī during that savant's last years, and was summoned to his deathbed as a trusted friend to attempt treatment. That Ibn Abū Qāsim was chosen over native Egyptians to serve the most eminent Egyptian ʿālim of the age suggests the reputation he enjoyed. He was appointed professor of jurisprudence in al-Azhar during 852/1448-1449, and subsequently received an endowed lectureship in Koranic exegesis at the madrasa of the Manṣūrī mausoleum complex. In 864/1459-1460 he died in ʿAynṭāb (III-A:159) during a trip through Aleppo Province. He was only 43 years old at the time.

This reference to travel is noteworthy. Many of the Maghribīs who appeared in Cairo were seasoned travelers. Most came to the capital on their way to the holy cities or on business. Ibn Khaldūn used his desire to make the Ḥajj as an excuse to escape from Tūnis. The travels of Ibn Baṭṭūṭa during the fourteenth century have immortalized the adventures of North Africans, who, originating in the westernmost corner of the Islamic lands, seem to have been obsessed with a desire to see the world.

Persons of North African origin or descent attained considerable economic stature in Cairo. The careers of two cousins who became royal merchants (tujjār al sulṭān) serve to illustrate such stature. Ibrāhīm ibn ʿAbd al-Malik al-Barantīshī al-Maghribī al-Judhamī,[67] born in 800/1397-1398, and Shams al-Dīn Muḥammad ibn Abū Qāsim al-Murtadī al-Barantīshī al-Maghribī al-Judhamī, known as al-Barantīshī[68] and born in 859/1454-1455, belonged to a family established in al-Andalus. Al-Sakhāwī—who knew al-Barantīshī personally, having lectured to him on the *Alfīya* of al-ʿIrāqī—mentioned that he was actually born in al-Andalus and pursued his education in Malaga. He came to Egypt in order to claim his cousin Ibrāhīm's property after the latter's death in Alexandria, and succeeded to his position as a royal merchant. Al-Judhamī had launched his lucrative career as a state merchant when he became an associate of the amir and future sultan, al-Ashraf Qāytbāy. Al-Sakhāwī noted that prior to his death, al-Judhamī arranged for the division of his estate among his family back in al-Andalus. The noteworthy development involves the cousin's successful accession to al-Judhamī's position after the latter's death. Al-Barantīshī was apparently highly recommended to Sultan Qāytbāy by his cousin and thereby managed to take over the post. He acquired a considerable fortune before his own death in Shaʿbān 892/June-July 1487, but there was no reference to any provision for his family back in al-Andalus.

Maghribī prominence in the realm of religious activities is attested to by the career of Abū ʿAbd-Allah Muḥammad ibn Muḥammad al-Andalusī al-Maghribī, known as al-Rāʿī.[69] Born in the famous Spanish city of Granada (2) in 782/1380-1381, al-Rāʿī received a thorough grounding in jurisprudence during his youth in Spain and was exposed to a wide variety of exegetical texts and primers on proper recitation of scripture. He left his home city to travel through the Near East, studying and reciting before famous literateurs "from the west and the east," as al-Sakhāwī phrased it. He ultimately settled in Cairo in 825/1421-1422 where he attained renown as a Koran reader, poet, and author of commentaries on several texts, including the *Alfīya* of al-ʿIrāqī. He was appointed an imām in the Mu'ayyadīya madrasa. At his death in Dhū'l-Ḥijja 853/January-February 1450, al-Rāʿī was given a funeral in al-Azhar because of his fame as a Koran reciter. He was also granted a posthumous honor more significant than any he had known during his life by being buried adjacent to the tomb of Zayn al-Dīn al-ʿIrāqī, the author of the *Alfīya,* which al-Rāʿī considered the most inspirational work he had studied.

The careers of these persons, so successfully consummated in Cairo, suggest a high level of competence among the Maghribīs who settled in the capital of the Mamluk Empire. Individual excellence, however, must be weighed against the infrequency with which Maghribīs appeared in the sources. Why was an area as prominent in Islamic history as the Maghrib represented by so small a percentage of the persons migrating to Cairo? North Africa appears to have been something of a cultural backwater in comparison with the central and eastern Islamic lands. None of its cities could compare with Cairo or centers further east in terms of wealth or population. So sophisticated and keen an observer as Ibn Khaldūn was overwhelmed by the sheer magnitude of Cairo when he first saw it. Because of the lower percentage of urbanized population in North Africa, the overall incidence of institutions requisite to the maintenance of the ʿulama' was lower than in other major regions of the Near East. The religio-academic institutions of North Africa do not appear to have been inferior to those of other regions, but there were fewer of them; thus North Africa tended to produce fewer highly specialized members of the ʿulama' class than regions further east. Those it did produce were likely to fall under the spell cast by the central and eastern cities, which offered many opportunities to the talented and ambitious.

MIGRATION TO CAIRO FROM OTHER AREAS OF THE MUSLIM WORLD

Only a minute percentage of the total number of geographical references in the biographical sources applied to the more peripheral regions of the Muslim world. These regions included sub-Saharan Africa, the Indian subcontinent, and Central Asia north and east of Transoxiana. The references were so scattered and infrequent that no generalizations about the individuals from these regions can be made. One special class, however, was very evident in the sources and originated in Nubia, Somalia, or Ethiopia; this class was identified as Ḥabashī. The term probably denoted any person who was black, but the sites mentioned do point to East Africa and the Upper Nile Valley. These Ḥabashīs formed an integral part of the Mamluk social system, since they were imported as slaves and personal servants to the ruling elite. Several of them attained high political office after their emancipation, and demonstrated a keen political acumen. This group cannot be classified as part of the ʿulama', although certain individuals chose to adopt a scholarly life style after amassing a personal fortune.

CONCLUSIONS

The geographical data provided by the biographical sources relevant to individuals who came from regions outside Cairo do not suggest a random pattern of migration by the ʿulama'. The migration of these individuals or their ancestors was influenced by specific internal and external stimuli. The internal stimuli involved the urban and cultural conditions of an individual's homeland in comparison with those of Cairo. Since the institutions supporting the ʿulama' were essentially urban, the majority of the immigrants originated in cities or towns. In certain areas, there was a long-standing tradition of these institutions functioning in a rural environment, but such cases did not occur often in the Near East. In general, the greater the proportion of the population living in urban areas, the larger the ʿulamaʾ class was likely to be. Accordingly, individuals from highly urbanized regions would be more likely to appear in the biographical sources. Furthermore, the more complex and specialized the urban centers and institutions in a region, the greater its propensity was to produce individuals capable of making the transfer to Cairo and adjusting to the rigors of life there. Finally, the more similar in organization, function, and attitudes the ʿulamaʾ of a specific city were in comparison with Cairo, the more likely these persons were to possess the talents and social skills necessary for a successful career in their adopted city. One particular aspect of certain citys' relationships to Cairo that gave their ʿulamaʾ a decided advantage over others was the presence of the Mamluk ruling elite. The more pervasive the Mamluks, the more extensive their contacts with and influence over the ʿulamaʾ would be, as was the case in Cairo. And the ʿulamaʾ who had acquired their professional training and social skills under the aegis of Mamluks were the most likely to make a successful transfer to Cairo. Individuals holding bureaucratic or service positions tended to maintain the closest personal ties with the Mamluks. In the urban centers of Syria, these individuals served in the staffs of Mamluk executive officers, and were well suited to assuming bureaucratic offices in Cairo, especially if their employers were relocated in the capital.

Externally stimulated migration to Cairo varied from region to region. Migration from certain areas, such as the Delta or the Ḥijāz, was virtually unaffected by outside events. They did not experience the civil strife, foreign invasion, or other related phenomena endured in varying degrees by other parts of the Muslim world during the fifteenth century. In such areas as Syria-Palestine, external factors prompted some increase in numbers of people leaving for Cairo. But the eastern Islamic lands experienced a series of disasters that caused many members of the ʿulamaʾ to leave their homeland in search of more stable political conditions.

As measured by the geographic references in the sources, the rate of migration varied only slightly, if at all, throughout the course of the fifteenth century. And given the skewing factor resulting from the majority of deaths occurring during the second half of the century, migration appears to have been a relatively stable process for the entire century. There were several exceptions to this profile, however. Iran and the three somewhat isolated cities of Baghdād, Makka, and Madīna appeared more often in references to individuals departing for Cairo during the first half of the century, implying a higher rate of migration at this time. The reason for this increase was evident in the cases of Iran and Iraq, which experienced the Timurid invasions. But the apparently higher rate of migration from the two holy cities of the Ḥijāz cannot be explained in terms of known external events.

Certain regions or urban centers of the Islamic world cited in the biographical sources seemed to produce individuals inclined to engage in specific kinds of occupational activities. The statistics for occupations are organized according to regions and degrees of concentration in Tables 7 through 10 and suggest that patterns of migration were broadly influenced by the type of professional endeavors pursued by the individuals who established themselves in Cairo. The occupations attracting individuals from the least disparate backgrounds are the small craftsmen and laborers, most of whom came from Cairo and the Delta. But merchants and certain elite service professions such as manuscript copying and medicine had a highly cosmopolitan background. Individuals involved in these occupations were among the most geographically diverse of any group appearing in the biographical sources. Their backgrounds are responsible for the unusual profile of the artisan-commercial category as a whole.

The majority of individuals engaged in religious occupations in Cairo derived from either Cairo or the Delta (Table 8: 81 percent; Table 10: 79 percent). This general pattern was mirrored by the distribution of specific occupations (Table 6). The concentration is significant, since it emphasizes a distinct difference between religious service occupations and the legal-scholarly professions. These latter, together with the bureaucratic fields, drew their members in more equal proportions from throughout the Near East; the Cairo-Delta area was less dominant a source. This pattern, although varying among the three occupations, suggests that the requisite training, especially for the legal and scholarly fields, was relatively uniform throughout the central Islamic world. It also suggests that these professions were primarily responsible for the cosmopolitan nature of the civilian elite in Cairo. The extent to which this cosmopolitanism influenced the mass of the city's population remains unclear, however, because of a distinction between the functions of the upper and lower levels of the civil judiciary.

The distribution of sites depicting the backgrounds of individuals engaged in bureaucratic occupations differed from the patterns for the legal and scholarly groups—many came from Syria and Palestine. That is, the cosmopolitanism of the bureaucratic class reflected the bureaucratic procedures refined in the urban network of the Mamluk state and in the central Arabic lands it ruled. In comparison, the origins of individuals in the legal and scholarly fields were more evenly distributed throughout the Islamic world. This broad dispersion would lend support to the belief that there was a uniform process of higher learning and legal training among the orthodox ʿulamaʾ during the later Middle Ages, regardless of their geographic origin or ethnic background. In general, the levels of the judiciary above the level of court notary (*shāhid*) appear to have been staffed by a highly cosmopolitan group. Accordingly, Cairo seems to have maintained a major component of the consciously international judiciary extant throughout orthodox Islam during the period.

However, the notaries did not follow this cosmopolitan trend. The shāhids derived primarily from Cairo and the Delta (Table 3). Although we classified the court notaries with the other legal professions, many of their characteristics as well as their distribution more closely paralleled those of individuals in the bureaucratic fields.[70] The localism of the notaries suggests that the lower levels of the judiciary—those affecting the majority of the civilian litigants in Cairo—were staffed primarily by long-term residents in the district or quarter they served. Much litigation considered by judges and chief justices was appellate, having been first heard by a neighborhood court. More significant, this distinction between the two levels of the judiciary highlights the difference between litigation actually practiced in the popular courts and the more abstract quality of the cases decided by the higher judiciary—and of the Sharīʿa itself. This issue transcends the scope of the present study. But it raises several questions, the most important of which involve the role of the shāhids in litigation at the popular level.[71]

The pattern yielded by individuals holding scholarly positions closely paralleled that of persons in the judicial fields because of the primacy of the Sharīʿa in higher learning. In general, the geographic background of the scholarly establishment in Cairo, as distinguished from the religious functionaries, indicates that a standardized curriculum had evolved for the Sunnī Islamic sciences and was uniformly acquired by orthodox scholars throughout the Muslim world. Reputations established in a particular region could be attested according to procedures and documentation recognized in other orthodox areas, thus enabling—and even encouraging—geographic mobility among proven scholars. However, the cosmopolitan pattern established by eminent scholars did not apply to individuals involved mainly in elementary pedagogy. Persons who taught basic literacy at the *kuttābs* or who functioned primarily as repetitors (*muʿīds*) (Table 5) tended to originate in Lower Egypt. Thus, the less prestigious teaching positions appear to have been staffed from the local population.

The military-executive category (Table 1) also reflected a broad geographic spectrum, although the prominence of Cairo, the Mamluk capital, was obvious (Tables 8 and 10). The apparent distribution of geographic origins must also be qualified by the nature of the source. Only individuals from civilian or second-generation Mamluk origins were included in the sample. The precise geographic background of first-generation Mamluks or individuals deriving from a military elite in other regions would be difficult to determine in any case, because of peculiarities inherent in their reported nomenclature, as well as a paucity of birthplaces. But given this intrinsic flaw in the biographical sources, the overall pattern suggested a broad distribution, itself implying a highly cosmopolitan executive class. Of course, many individuals who inaugurated their careers as bureaucrats were promoted—or even coerced into accepting—executive offices. This phenomenon, to be considered further in Chapter IV, explains the prominence of Cairo and to a lesser extent the Syrian provincial capitals as places of origin. Many of these people were Muslims with Coptic Christian backgrounds, who were based primarily in the Cairo area. The pattern depicted in Tables 7 through 10 thus suggests that those executive positions open to civilians were mainly staffed by Cairenes and Syrians of urban background. Several regions outside the Mamluk empire were also prominently represented, however, (Tables 9 and 10). The highest percentages of Iranians were in the executive category. Thus, although there was a symbiotic relationship between civilian bureaucrats native to Cairo or derivative from the Syrian provincial capitals and their military patrons, the executive apparatus was on the whole geographically diverse. Of all the occupational categories staffed by civilians, the executive was the most thoroughly integrated into the Mamluk elite which, because of its own traditions, recruited its members from the periphery of the Muslim world.

In general, the evidence available from the biographical sources did not depict widespread transferral of regional traditions and skills to Cairo. Rather, those individuals whose biographies clearly indicated a non-Cairene or non-Egyptian background tended to pursue careers in professions widely practiced throughout the Islamic Near East during the later Middle Ages. Activities affecting the mass of local population, however, tended to recruit individuals of parochial backgrounds. Persons involved in such activities appear to have been less geographically mobile than individuals whose biographies listed no such involvement. Yet most regions represented by the geographic indicators did produce individuals engaged in every occupational category, suggesting that geographic mobility was not absolutely restricted to any broad occupational field.

Regional Maps

The maps use a set of symbols arranged according to a scale in order to indicate the proportions of migration from various sites of origin to Cairo. The maps appear as follows:

I. The Nile Delta (Lower Egypt)
II. The Nile Valley (Upper Egypt)
III. Syria-Palestine and Anatolia
IV. Iran, Iraq and the Arabian Peninsula
V. North Africa and the Mediterranean.

Each map is duplicated in the following fashion:

A. Name of sites and definition of political boundaries
B. Overall migration throughout the late fourteenth and the fifteenth centuries.

In addition, Map IV includes:

C. Migration during the first and second quarters of the fifteenth century
D. Migration during the third and fourth quarters of the fifteenth century.

Maps I, II, III, and V omit the C and D patterns because of a skewing factor in the data. Since the dictionaries focused on individuals active during the ninth/fifteenth century, the majority of death dates occurred during its last two quarters. Accordingly, the configurations reported for all regions, with the exception of Iran and western Arabia, were uniformly weighted in favor of the latter period—and are thus of questionable accuracy as indicators of migration. But even given this skewing factor, Map IV reported a majority of cases during the first two quarters, warranting the inclusion of the quarter-century breakdown for these regions.

Symbols

Map B uses circular symbols for the geographic nisbas and "×"s for birthplaces. Maps C and D use circular symbols for the geographic nisbas reported during the first and third quarters of the century, and triangular symbols for the second and fourth quarters. Birthplaces reported for the first and third quarters are represented by crosses (+) and by ×s, in the same proportionate sizes as the circles and triangles, for the second and fourth quarters. The four types of symbols appearing on each map are directly superimposed on the site, with the exception of very small symbols, which are arranged immediately adjacent to each other. In such cases, the circular symbols and crosses are always on the left, the triangles and ×s on the right. The sites are numbered on the maps and in the text for ease of identification.

The assignment of nisbas and birthplaces to quarters was done on the basis of death dates, which were the most frequently recurring dates available from the biographical sources. The actual date of migration was rarely provided in the sources, and the specific time of migration should be moved back some twenty to thirty years on the average. At this time, however, a more precise means of dating the migratory movements of these individuals is not available.

SCALE

× and + symbols are in proportion to circles and triangles

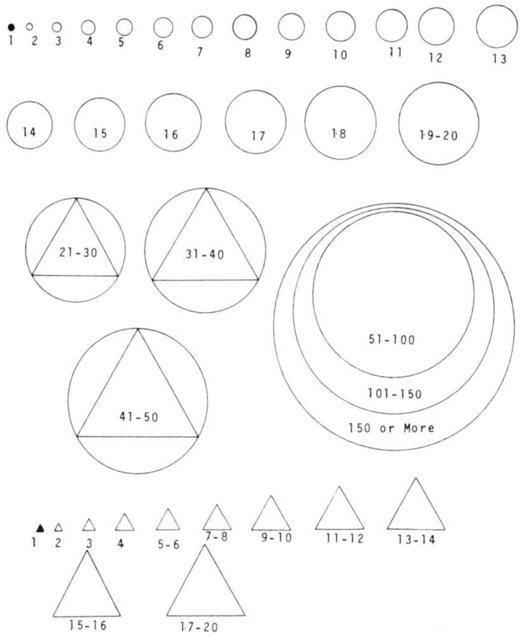

Key to Sites on Map I-A

1. al-Iskandarīya (Alexandria)
2. al-Maʿmūra
3. Raslān
4. Idkū (Itkū)
5. Rashīd (Rosetta)
6. Dayrūt
7. Bardala
8. Bilāl
9. Lūqīn
10. Khiḍr
11. Batūka
12. Fākhūr
13. Birkat Ghitās
14. Qāfil
15. Tarūja
16. Qabīl
17. Samādīs
18. Damanhūr
19. Qaraqīs
20. Hawwāra
21. Shanhūr
22. Sharnūb
23. Laqāna
24. Abū Durra
25. Farnawā
26. Zubayda
27. Qilīshān
28. Bibān
29. Salamūn
30. Khirbitā
31. Dist
32. Dayr al-Barāmūs
33. Minyat al-Murshid
34. Mīt al-Gharrāqa
35. Dumays
36. Nastarāwa
37. Shūra
38. Balṭīm
39. Būn
40. al-Burullus
41. Kawm al-Abyaḍ
42. Qamāṣ
43. Kawm al-Zilāʿ
44. Nimrā
45. Fuwwa
46. Shabās al-Milḥ
47. Nuṭūbis
48. Sanhūr
49. Maḥallat ʿAbd al-Raḥmān
50. Ṣandalā
51. Nashart
52. Sakhā
53. Ṭā'if
54. Isḥāqa
55. Matbūl
56. Maṣīr
57. Birkat al-Sabāʿ
58. Bishbīsh
59. Buhūt
60. Bilqās
61. Barnabār
62. Shirbīn
63. Bisāṭ
64. Diyāsṭ
65. Sharinqāsh
66. Ṭalkhā
67. Damīra
68. Rutama al-Sharqīya
69. Nishā
70. Ṭabānūhā
71. Ṭayyiba
72. Nabarūh
73. Tannīkh
74. Minyat Sirāj
75. Bānūb
76. Afnīsh
77. Maḥallat Zayyād
78. Jawjar
79. Ṭurayna
80. Abshīṭ (Ibshīṭ)
81. Nawāj
82. Shushayn
83. Simirbay
84. Bushbīsh
85. Quṭūr
86. Amyūṭ
87. Ṣurad
88. Janāj
89. Armānīya
90. Basyūn
91. Mashāl
92. Dumāṭ
93. Simillā'
94. Dhirwa
95. Sijīn
96. Maḥallat Abū Haytham
97. Zubār
98. Bulqīna
99. al-Maḥallat al-Kubrā
100. Maḥallat al-Burj
101. Buṭayna
102. Saḥīn
103. Samannūd
104. Minyat ʿAssās
105. Dawākhil
106. Dijwa
107. Minyat Badrān
108. Kafr Kilā
109. Mīt al-Mubāshirīn
110. Baqlūl
111. Damshīt
112. Difra
113. Bīrat al-ʿAjūz
114. Rutāma
115. Shifā'
116. Maḥallat Bār
117. Birmā
118. Naḥrārīya
119. Abyār
120. Maḥallat Marḥūm
121. Ṭanṭa
122. Ikhnā
123. Nifyā
124. Jawharīya
125. Baṭīm
126. Sanṭā
127. Sunbāṭ
128. Dahtūra
129. Ziftā
130. Sindbasṭ
131. Farsīs
132. Ziyād
133. Bandarīya
134. ʿUrjān
135. Ẓunūb
136. Dinshaway
137. Sirsinā
138. Ṭablūhā
139. Batanūn
140. Janān
141. Kalbishū
142. Diyama
143. Hūrayn
144. Minyat al-Rakhā'
145. Ṭanān
146. Tafahnā
147. Ṭahat al-Marj
148. Ṭambishā
149. Mustay
150. Ibnāhs
151. Malīj
152. Ṭanbidī
153. Kamshīsh
154. ʿAshmā
155. Shubrā Basyūn

156. Barnasht
157. Dakamā
158. Ghamrīn
159. Titā
160. Minūf
161. Sudūd
162. Bihwāsh
163. Shunūfa
164. Shanwān
165. Samān
166. Sirs
167. Manāwahla
168. Mīt Masʿūd
169. Mīt Sirāj
170. Ashlīm
171. Qusayna
172. Damhūj
173. Bayjūr
174. Minshat Damallū
175. Minyat al-Ḥūfīyīn
176. Damallū
177. Umm Khunān
178. Abshīsh
179. Minyat Wahla
180. Ibkhāṣ
181. Subk al-Daḥḥāk
182. Abū Sunayṭa
183. Bahnay
184. Fīshā
185. Tilwān
186. Hayt
187. Qalatā
188. Naṣṣār
189. Wardān
190. Ashmūn
191. Subk al-Aḥad
192. Shaṭānūf
193. Sarawa
194. Shinbār
195. Nahiyā
196. Sharānīs
197. Minbāba
198. al-Jīza (Giza)
199. Minyat ʿUqba
200. Tirsa
201. Abū Ṣīr
202. Badrashayn
203. Dahshūr
204. Shawbak al-Gharbī
205. Ḥulwān
206. Ṭūra
207. al-Maʿādī
208. Dayr al-Ṭīn
209. Dimirdāsh
210. al-ʿAbbāsīya
211. Shubrā
212. Kawm al-Rīsh
213. Minyat al-Sirīj
214. Bulāq
215. al-Maṭarīya
216. al-Marj
217. Bilqās
218. Qalyūb
219. Ṣanāfīr
220. Nāy
221. Siryāqūs
222. al-Khānqāh
223. Kirbat Ṭaha
224. Nawā
225. Janā'in
226. Sindbīs
227. Shanaway
228. Ajhūr
229. Barshūm
230. Mashtūl
231. Ṭūkh
232. Nabtīt
233. Damrā
234. Mujūl
235. Marṣafa
236. Minyat Suhayl
237. Quwaysinā
238. Binha
239. Shubrā al-Nakhla
240. Bilbays
241. Sanhūt
242. Nashwa
243. Minyat al-Qamḥ
244. Ṣufayṭa
245. Burdayn
246. Sunayka
247. ʿAmrīṭ
248. al-ʿAbbāsa
249. Ẓāhirīya al-Muʿajama
250. Banī ʿĀmir
251. Zankalūn
252. Ṣaḥraja
253. Shimbār
254. Banāyūs
255. Safṭ al-Ḥannā
256. Salamūn
257. al-ʿAlāqima
258. Kafr Hirbīṭ
259. Manzil Hayyān
260. Karadīs
261. Farghān
262. Minyat Ghamr
263. Daqādūs
264. Bashālūsh
265. Itmīd
266. Ṭahat Būsh
267. Sarnajā
268. Sanafā
269. Damāṣ
270. Ṣafūr
271. Baramkīn
272. Shawbak Ikrāsh
273. Barhamtūsh
274. Ṣuwayn
275. Ikhṭāb
276. Minyat Abū Ḥusayn
277. Minyat ʿAmīl
278. Quṭayf
279. Barqīn
280. Ghazāla
281. Nāṭūra
282. Minyat al-ʿIzz
283. Fāqūs
284. Malkīyīn al-Sharq
285. Sammakīn al-Gharb
286. al-Jabbāra
287. Ṣān
288. Mīt Jarrāḥ
289. Ṭanāḥ
290. Mīt Fāris
291. Qibāb
292. Maḥallat Dimna
293. Shāwa
294. Salaka
295. Jarrāḥ
296. Bandar
297. Barq al-ʿIzz
298. al-Manṣūra
299. Buwayt
300. Dikirnis
301. Ashmūn al-Ruhmān
302. Mīt Ḥadīd
303. Dinjaway
304. Maḥallat Isḥāq
305. Shārimsāḥ
306. Ṣarāwa
307. Mit al-Qamaṣ
308. Daqahla
309. Mīt Salsīl
310. Judhām
311. al-Manzala
312. al-Duḥayr
313. Maṭarīya
314. Atrīb
315. Fāriskūr
316. ʿAṭīya
317. Hawf
318. Dumyāṭ (Damietta)

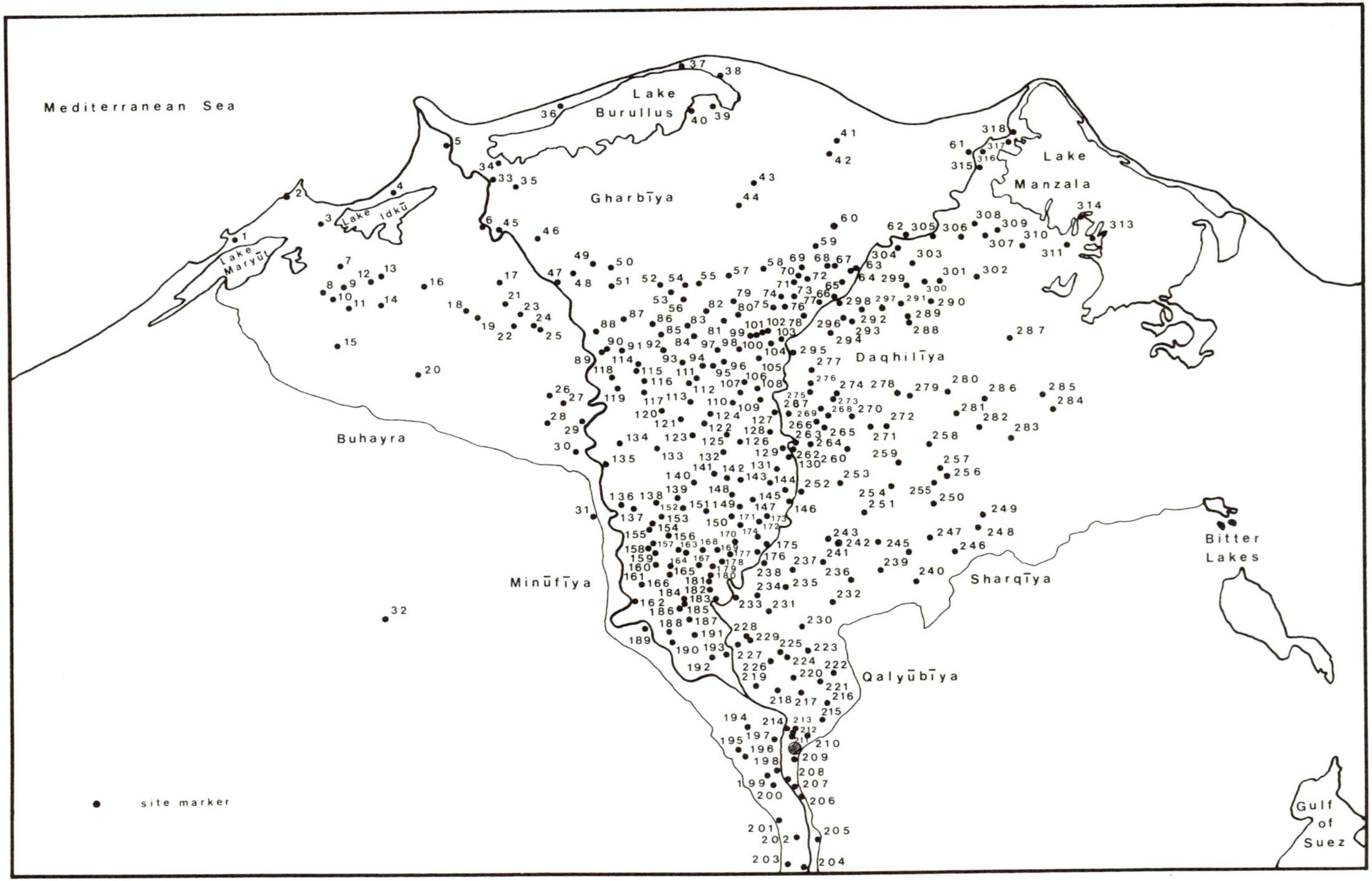

I-A. Nile Delta, Sites

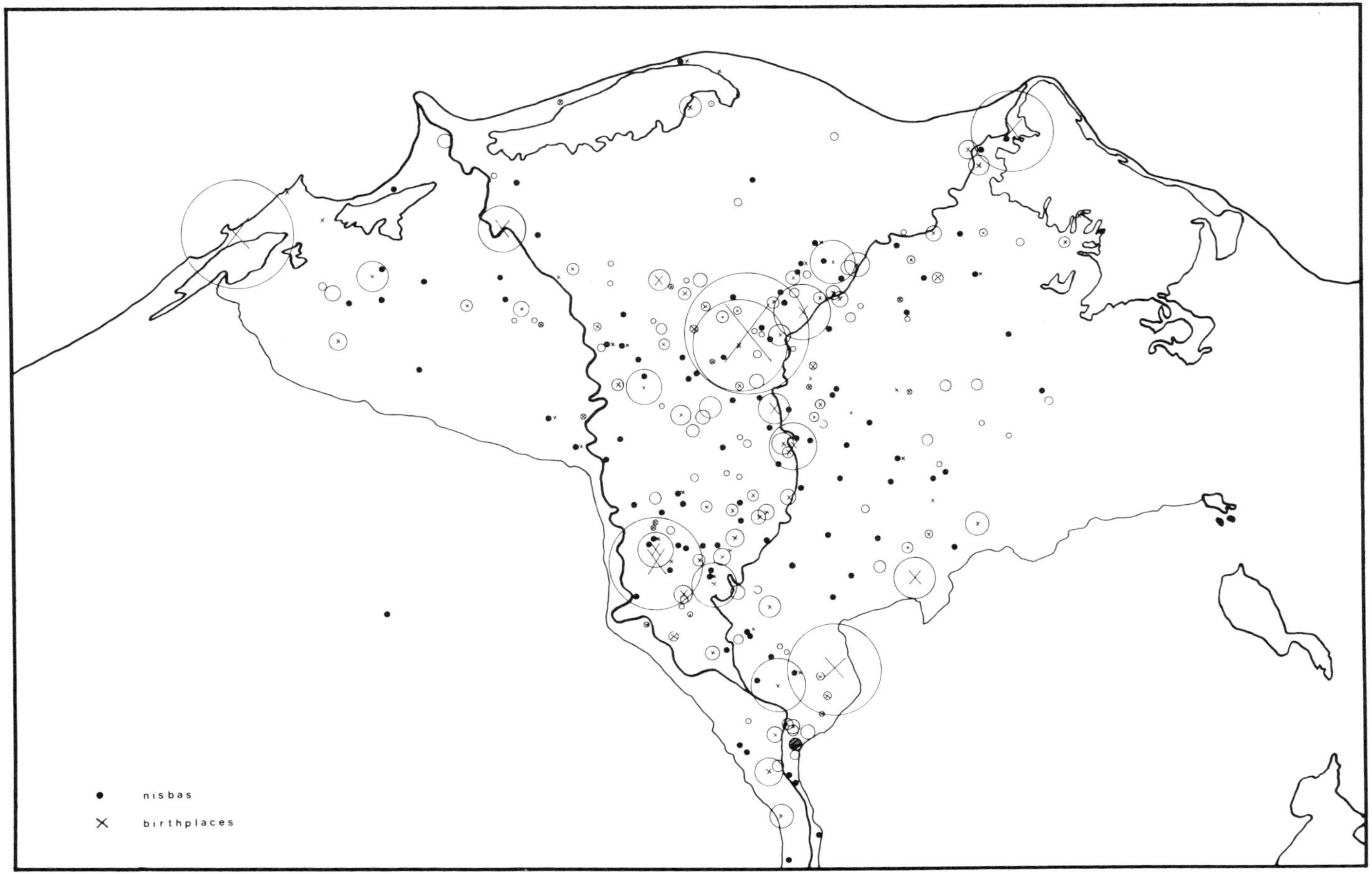

I-B. Nile Delta, Migration throughout the Century

Key to Sites on Map II-A

1. Barnasht
2. Shawbak al-Sharqī
3. Zarzār
4. Shawrā'
5. Bamhā
6. Minyat al-Qā'id
7. Muḥarraqa
8. Ṣaf
9. Aṭfīḥ
10. Maydūm
11. Wasṭa
12. Wanā al-Qis
13. Dimwa
14. al-Lāhūn
15. Sirsinā
16. al-ʿIdwa
17. al-Fayyūm
18. Maltūt
19. Hawwāra
20. Nawwāra
21. Nāy
22. Shirā'ij
23. Dandīl
24. Tansā
25. Būsh
26. Dalāṣ
27. Manqarīsh
28. Banī Suwayf
29. Bāhā'
30. Bilifyā
31. Banī Mūsa
32. Tizmant
33. Qāy
34. Ihnās
35. Nāmusīya
36. Qilla
37. Ṭūwa
38. Qanbush
39. Ṣīmūn
40. Ninā
41. Saft Rashīn
42. Bibā
43. Huwwāra
44. Saft Hannā
45. al-Fashn
46. Iqfahṣ
47. Dahmarū
48. Malaṭīya
49. Ṭanbadī
50. Jalāla
51. Ashnīn
52. Dahrūṭ
53. ʿAbbād Sharūna
54. Shulqām
55. Ṣandafā
56. Bahnasā
57. Sanqūrīya
58. Maṭay
59. Minyat Banī Khasīb
60. Tallās
61. Māqūsa
62. Sharāra
63. Makayn
64. Naway
65. Ashmunayn
66. Itqā
67. Mallawī
68. Dhirwa
69. Ṭūkh
70. Dalja
71. Zurzūr
72. Dayrūṭ
73. Minshat al-Kubrā
74. Manfalūṭ
75. Sarāwa
76. Sallām
77. Asyūṭ
78. Badrān
79. Abū Tīj
80. Banī Sumayʿ
81. Salamūn
82. Fazāra
83. Ṭahṭā
84. Bihtā
85. Marāgha
86. Iqṣāṣ
87. Wannīna
88. Suhāj
89. Akhmīm
90. Bindār
91. Jirjā
92. Balyanā
93. Samhūd
94. Abū Tisht
95. Yaʿqūba
96. Bakhānis
97. Farshūṭ
98. Hiww
99. Hīsh
100. Fāwa
101. Qinā
102. Qūṣ
103. Ṭūkh
104. Damāmīn
105. Qamūl
106. al-'Uqsur (Luxor)
107. Asnā
108. Shanshan
109. Idfū
110. Sarrāj
111. Salwa
112. Aswān
113. Suhayl

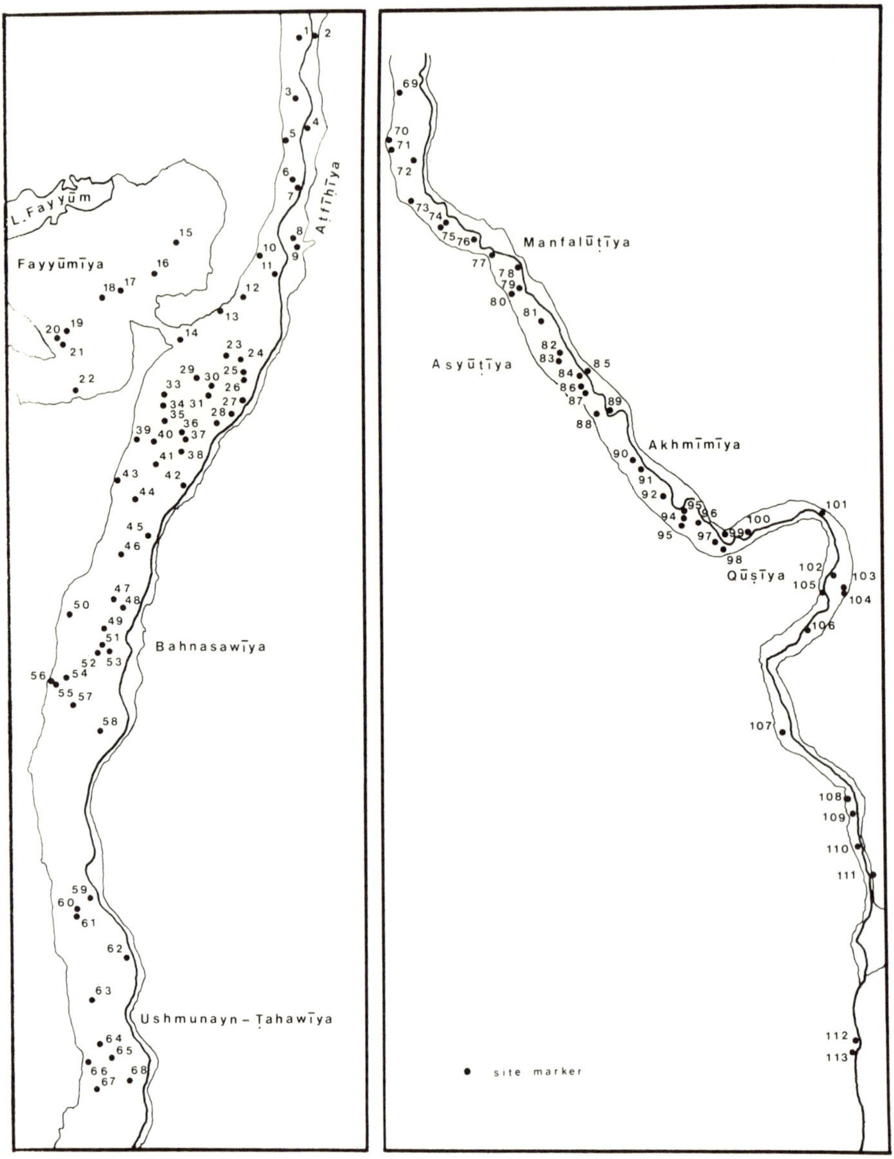

II-A. Nile Valley, Sites

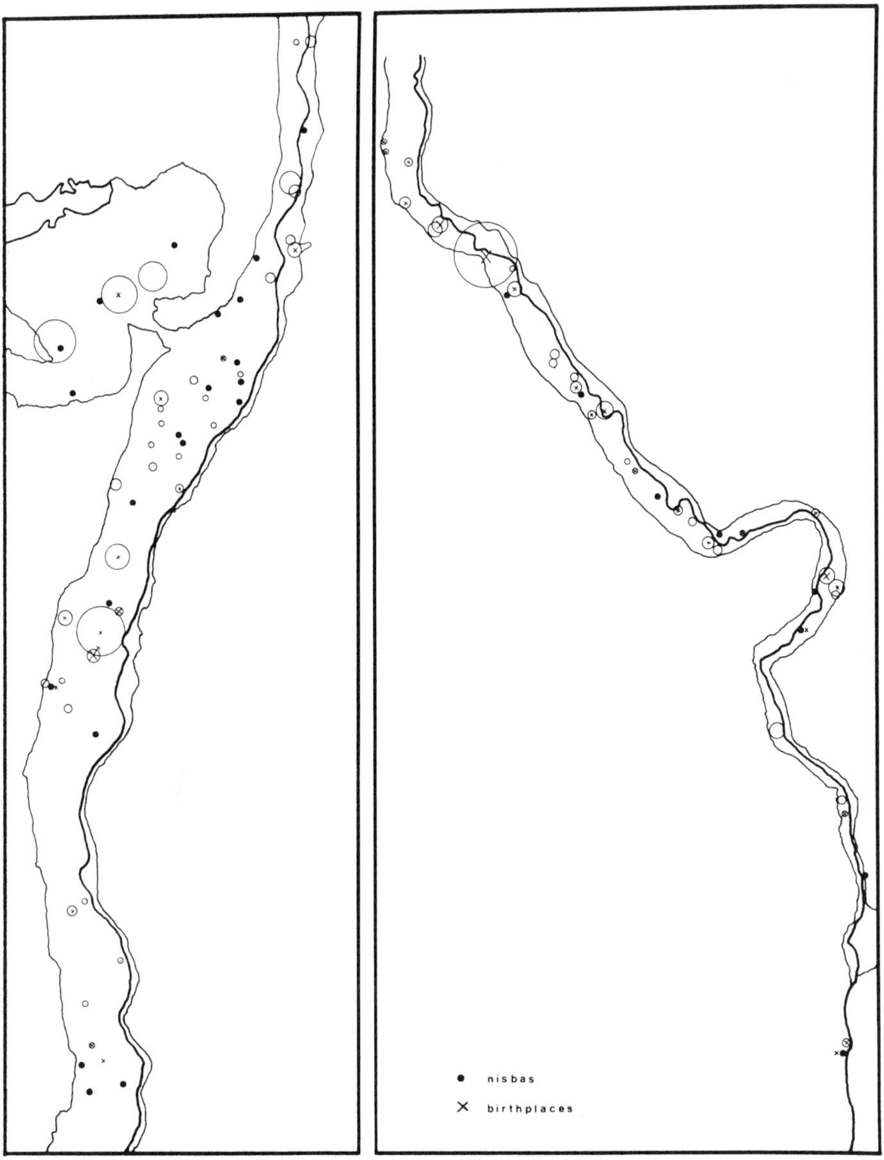

II-B. Nile Valley, Migration throughout the Century

Key to Sites on Map III-A

1. al-ʿArīsh
2. Ghazza (Gaza)
3. Jibrīn
4. ʿAsqalān (Ashqelon)
5. Ramla
6. Lidda (Lod)
7. al-Khalīl (Hebron)
8. al-Quds (Jerusalem)
9. Nātūt
10. Qalqilīya
11. Mardā
12. Balāṭa
13. Qiṭṭ
14. Nābulus
15. ʿAyzarīya
16. Qānā
17. Qalansāwa
18. Qayṣarīya
19. al-Nāṣira (Nazareth)
20. Shāghūr
21. Ṣafad
22. al-Naḥrīya
23. Maqbara
24. al-Shawbak
25. Tafila
26. ʿAynāʾ
27. al-Karak
28. Natl
29. Sudda
30. Hisbān
31. Adam
32. Nāʿūr
33. al-Zarrāʿa
34. Naṣīb
35. ʿAjlūn
36. Bāʿūn
37. Irbid
38. Saḥāmīya
39. al-Adhraʿāt
40. Buṣrā al-Shām
41. al-Kafr
42. Sumarīya
43. al-Raḥā
44. Taymā
45. al-Suwaydā
46. al-Lajā
47. Bazūk
48. Ghadīr
49. Ṣūrmān
50. Kafr Baṭnā
51. al-Dakka
52. Says
53. Surayt
54. Sāssa
55. Khazrajīya
56. Dalwān
57. Bāniyās
58. Barāmika
59. al-Mazza
60. Sūbayna
61. Marrār
62. Musaḥarā
63. Bāriza
64. Dumayr
65. Nīn
66. Dimashq (Damascus)
67. al-Qābūn
68. Zamalkān
69. Ḥurayra
70. Hasīb
71. Qamūn
72. Qasṭal
73. Jayrūd
74. Saṭḥ
75. Ḥumayr
76. Qārā
77. al-Dayr
78. Ṣūr (Tyre)
79. al-Nabaṭīya
80. Bayrūt (Beirut)
81. al-Biqāʿ (rgn)
82. Baʿlabakk (Baalbak)
83. ʿAshāsh
84. Ṭarābulus (Tripoli)
85. Darmīna
86. Naḥrīya
87. Balḥa
88. Ḥimṣ (Homs)
89. Nawfalīya
90. Tadmur (Palmyra)
91. Maḥlabīya
92. al-Sūsa
93. Ḥaṣrat
94. Buqrus
95. Farwān
96. Shanbār
97. Salamīya
98. Qarāmish
99. Qubaybat
100. al-Tīzīn
101. al-Sijn
102. Tall ʿAfar
103. Jibrīn
104. Ḥamā
105. Saskūn
106. al-Musallā
107. Maʿarrat al-Nuʿmān
108. Ḥabīta
109. Qirāta
110. Qulayla
111. Ṣakr
112. Juhann
113. Suṭūḥ al-Dayr
114. Biklifūn
115. ʿAmūrīn
116. Fāsān
117. Rahibīya
118. Ḥubayt
119. Qammīn
120. Arshūq
121. al-Ladhqīya
122. Balāṭ
123. Fīlīk
124. Shaghir Bāzār
125. Farka
126. Ghanī
127. Bashīr
128. Bayāḍīya
129. Bālis
130. Buṣaylīya
131. Idlīb
132. Ṣarmūn
133. Dumāṭ
134. Makhlaf
135. Baṭḥā
136. Saqila
137. Ḥādar
138. Diman
139. ʿAbṭīn
140. Qasṭalān
141. Ḥalab (Aleppo)
142. Azraq
143. Tādif
144. Rummāna
145. Mārīt
146. Ṣal
147. Rahabīya
148. Qabājiq
149. Ḥarrān
150. Anās
151. Urfa
152. Bīra
153. Sanjak

154. Aʿzāz
155. Hawār al-Naḥr
156. Ṭuranṭā (Turanda)
157. Sinbuk
158. Saylak
159. ʿAynṭāb (Gaziantep)
160. Marʿash (Maras)
161. Bahasna
162. Kakhtā (Kahta)
163. Kaykān
164. Malaṭya (Malatya)
165. Qudmir (Kotimir)
166. Adana
167. Sīs
168. Qilimṭā
169. Laranda
170. Karamān
171. Qunīya (Konya)
172. Bayt Shahīr (Beyshehir)
173. Ṭāz (Tazi)
174. Dunarsa
175. Lama
176. Ṣarukhān (Saruhan) (rgn)
177. Ājaq
178. ʿUryān (Uryan)
179. Qaṭrān (Katran)
180. Thīra (Tire)
181. Manisa
182. Bikādīs
183. Burṣā
184. Aqfisīya (Afisia)
185. Bahz (Bahsi)
186. Iṣtanbūl
187. Alwāh (Alva)
188. Dunaysa
189. Ṭukuṣlār
190. Ṭarhān
191. Qirim (Kirim)
192. Bābur
193. Aqṣarāʾ (Aksaray)
194. Qayṣarīya (Keysari)
195. Malāḥas (Malahaci)
196. Tūrīza (Turisa)
197. Sīwās (Sivas)
198. Tūqāt (Tokat)
199. Kakja Kuy (Kökçeköy)
200. Sīs
201. Aksar
202. Ṭuquṣ
203. Arzinkān (Erzinjan)
204. Khartbart (Hert)
205. Bāburt
206. Qalimṭā
207. Ṣūr
208. Urumān
209. Ṭāgh (Tag)
210. Mayyāfāriqīn (Miyafarqin)
211. Milḥa
212. Amida (Diyār Bakīr)
213. Ḥiṣn Kayfa (Hasankeyf)
214. Bajās
215. Hirbiṭa (Hirbeta)
216. Mārdīn
217. Masaltān
218. Marīn
219. Shāshir
220. Nawfalīya
221. Surkha
222. Kaʿka
223. Ṭāww
224. Ṣakir
225. ʿAlwa
226. Sharwān
227. Jīl
228. Qirim
229. Hakkārīya
230. Babān (Babanis)
231. Wān (Van)
232. Urmā (Urmia)
233. Kurdistān (rgn)
234. al-Jazīra (rgn)

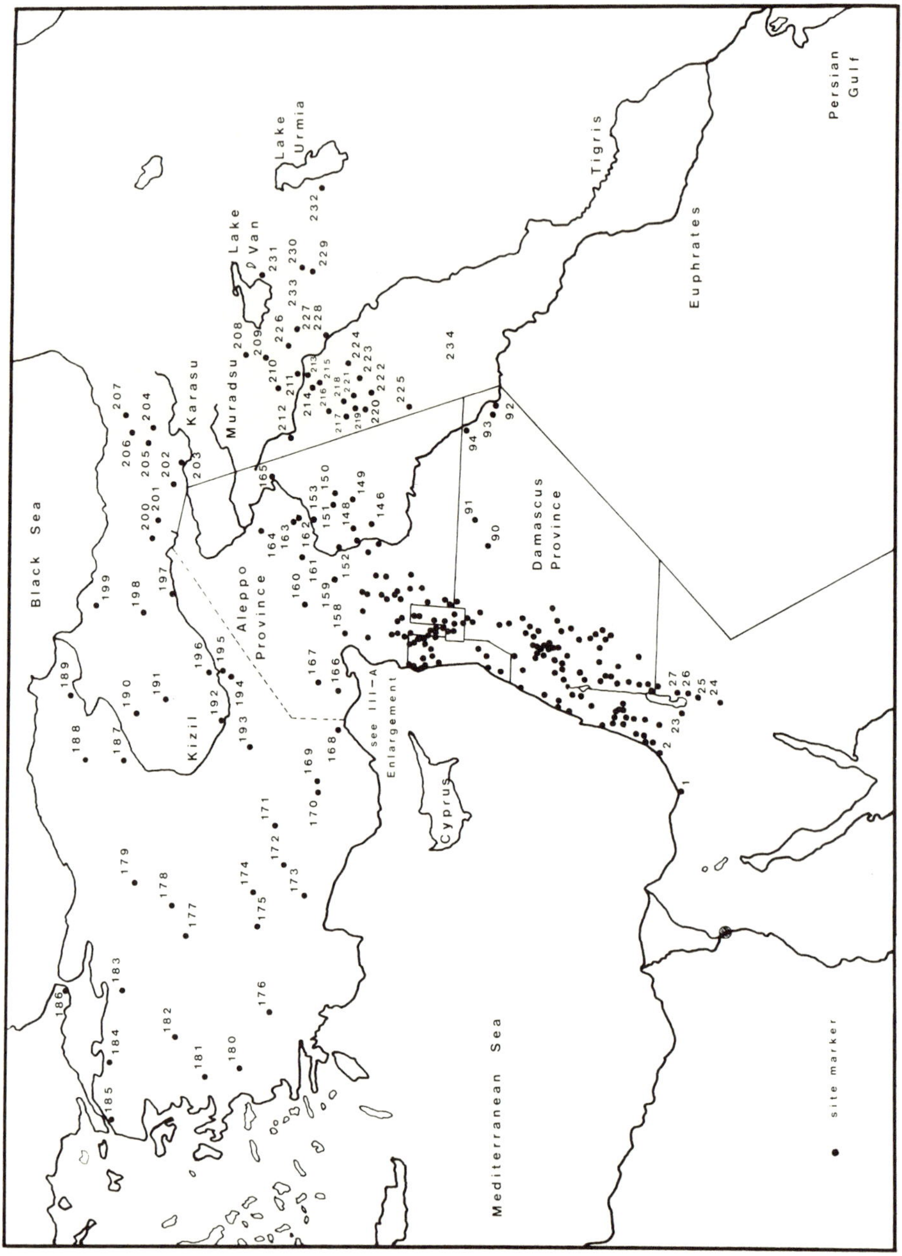

III-A. Syria-Palestine and Anatolia, Sites

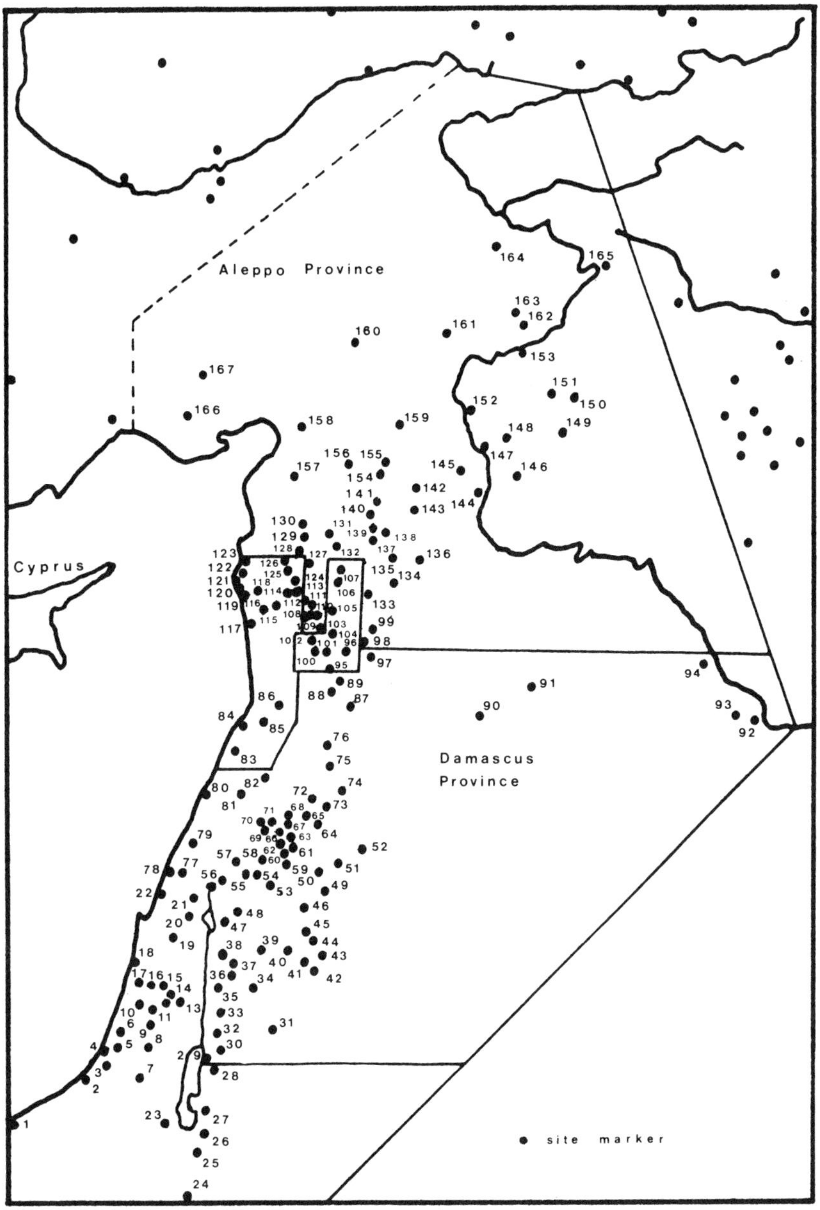

III-A. Enlargement. Aleppo and Damascus Provinces, Sites

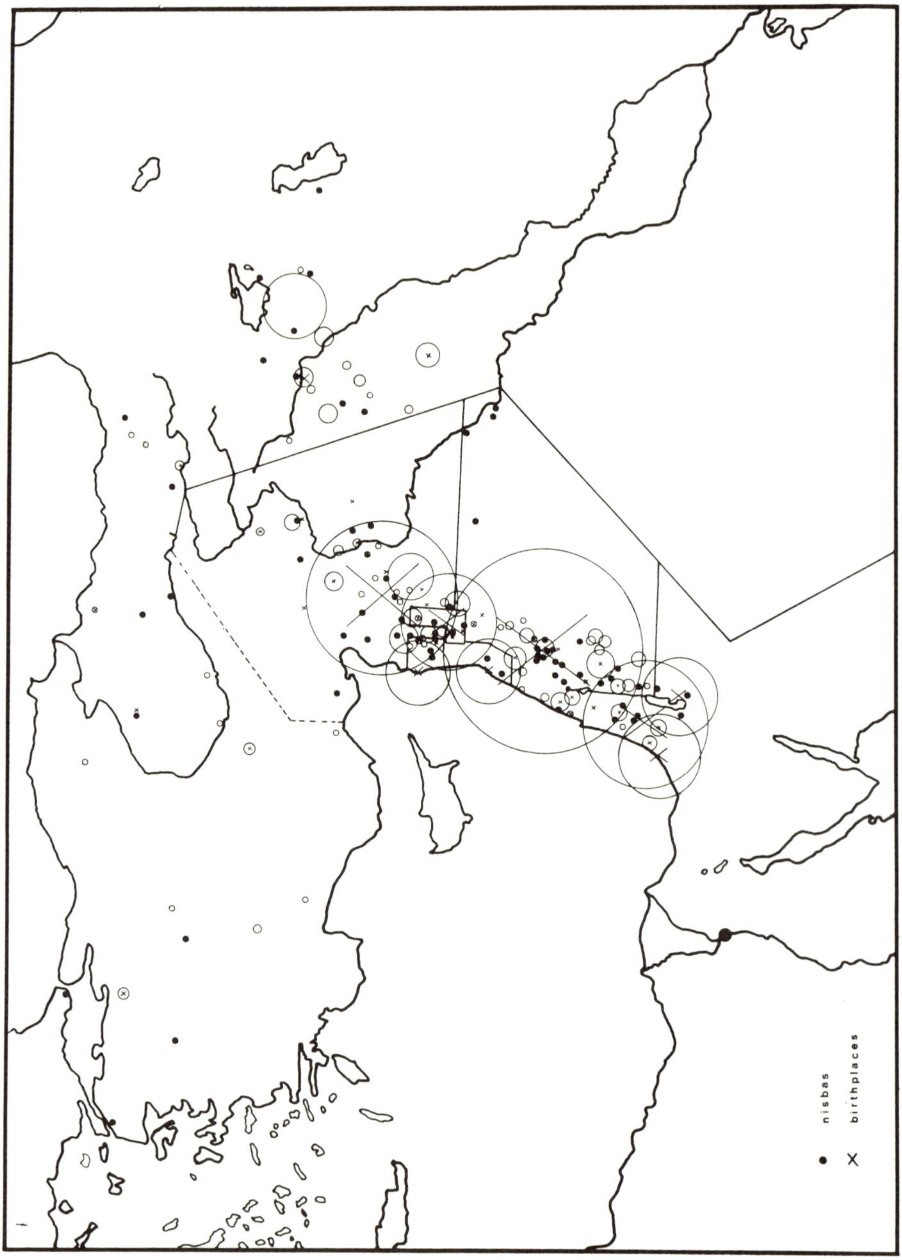

III-B. Syria-Palestine and Anatolia, Migration throughout the Century

Key to Sites on Map IV-A

1. Quṣayr
2. ʿAydhāb
3. Suwākin
4. Tabūk
5. Taymā
6. Nawf
7. al-Muwayliḥa
8. Ghamr
9. Abraq
10. Yanbuʿ
11. al-Madīna (Medina)
12. ʿAwf (rgn)
13. Jidda
14. Makka (Mecca)
15. Ṭāʾif
16. Sharab
17. Bajīla
18. Layth (rgn)
19. Wusaym
20. Saʿīda
21. Ṣanʿā
22. Zabīd
23. al-Kadrāʾ
24. Muhjam
25. Taʿiz
26. Zubayd
27. ʿAdan (Aden)
28. al-Miqdār
29. Yāfiʿ
30. Shirāʿ
31. al-Ḥaḍramawt (rgn)
32. al-Yamāma
33. Dahrān
34. Baṣra
35. Makhlaf
36. Batāʾih
37. Yaʿqūba
38. Wāsiṭ
39. Kūfa
40. al-Jaʿfarīya
41. Baghdād
42. Takrīt
43. Ḥīt
44. Sinjār
45. Mawṣil (Mosul)
46. Arbīl
47. Ṭufān
48. Sulaymānīya
49. ʿĀfān (Āfān)
50. ʿAmadīya
51. Tiflīs
52. Basṭām
53. Ghulistān (rgn)
54. Marand
55. Kafī
56. Tabrīz
57. Barzandīq
58. Bulāgh
59. Ardabīl
60. Rāsht
61. Kāzirūn
62. Amad
63. Walāysh (Valaysh)
64. Īj
65. Bijār
66. Kujūr (Qojūr)
67. Qatwānd (Qatvānd)
68. Kulām
69. Qazwīn (Qazvīn)
70. Kakajīn
71. Rūdbār
72. Sīrām
73. Daylam (rgn)
74. Tuwān (Tovān)
75. Shahrāsār
76. Mardābād
77. Shirīn
78. Rāy
79. Alwān (Alvān)
80. Hamadān
81. Bahādur
82. Bābāzayd
83. Shirwān (Shervān)
84. Ṣaranja
85. Malyān
86. Manār
87. Shūshtār
88. Qayṣarīya (Qeyṣariyeh)
89. Ṭabara
90. Dīl
91. Shīrāz
92. Tafihān
93. Tabīn
94. Nīrīz (Neyrīz)
95. Marwās (Marvas)
96. Bāshtak
97. Faryān
98. Kirmān (Kermān)
99. Bām
100. Sabzāwārān
101. Mardān
102. Nisāʾ (Neyseh)
103. Zurrāt (Zorratū)
104. Sijistān (rgn)
105. Sahāmīya
106. Kajān
107. Yazd
108. Iṣfahān
109. Shaydān
110. Kurand
111. Samandīl
112. Habla
113. Rūyān
114. Jurjān
115. Jīlān (rgn)
116. Khwarazm (rgn)
117. Kūrān
118. Khākiān
119. Kafkī
120. Nīshabūr
121. Mashhad
122. Marw (Mary)
123. Fārāb
124. Samarqand
125. Bukhāra
126. Hirāt (Herāt)
127. Ghazna
128. ʿAnbārī
129. Dahān
130. Khurāsān (rgn)
131. Mazanabād
132. Zarkish (Zar Kesh)
133. Rāz
134. Idinān
135. Birjānd
136. Murtawānd (Murtavand)
137. Fāl
138. Takhtijān
139. Jīt (Gīt)
140. Bādāmistān

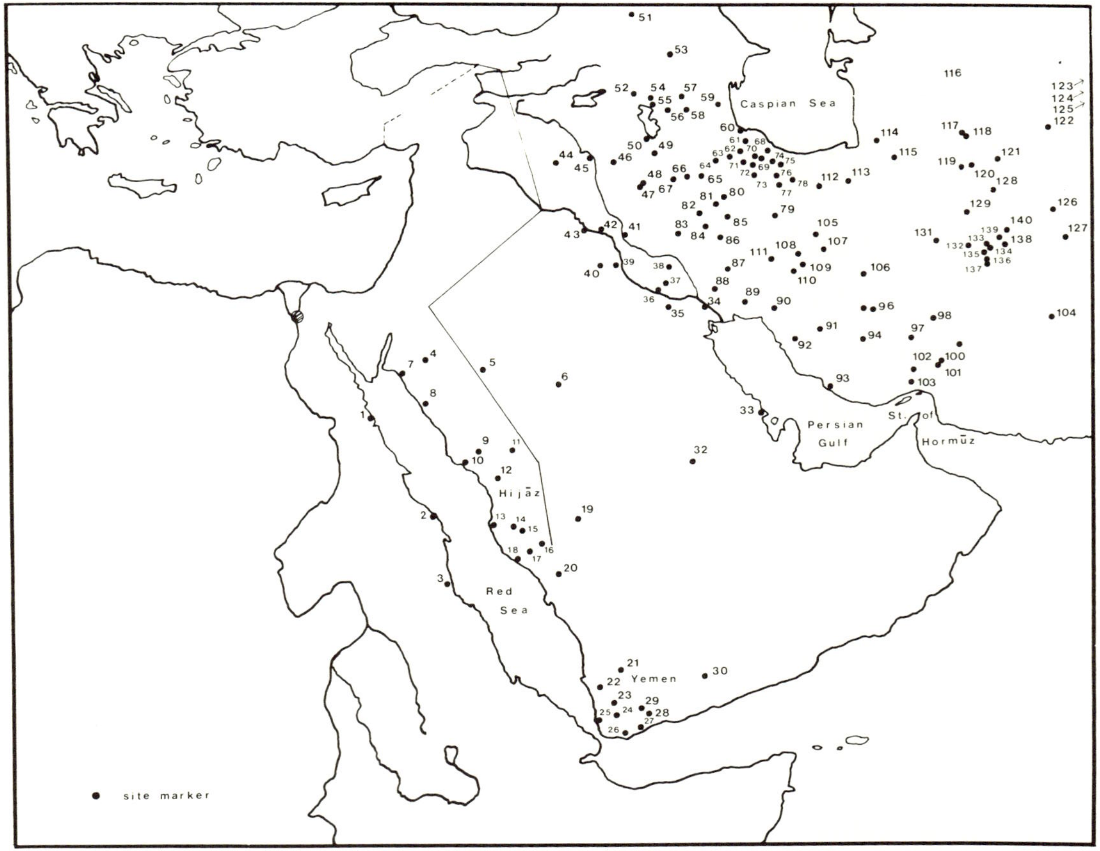

IV-A. Iran, Iraq, and the Arabian Peninsula, Sites

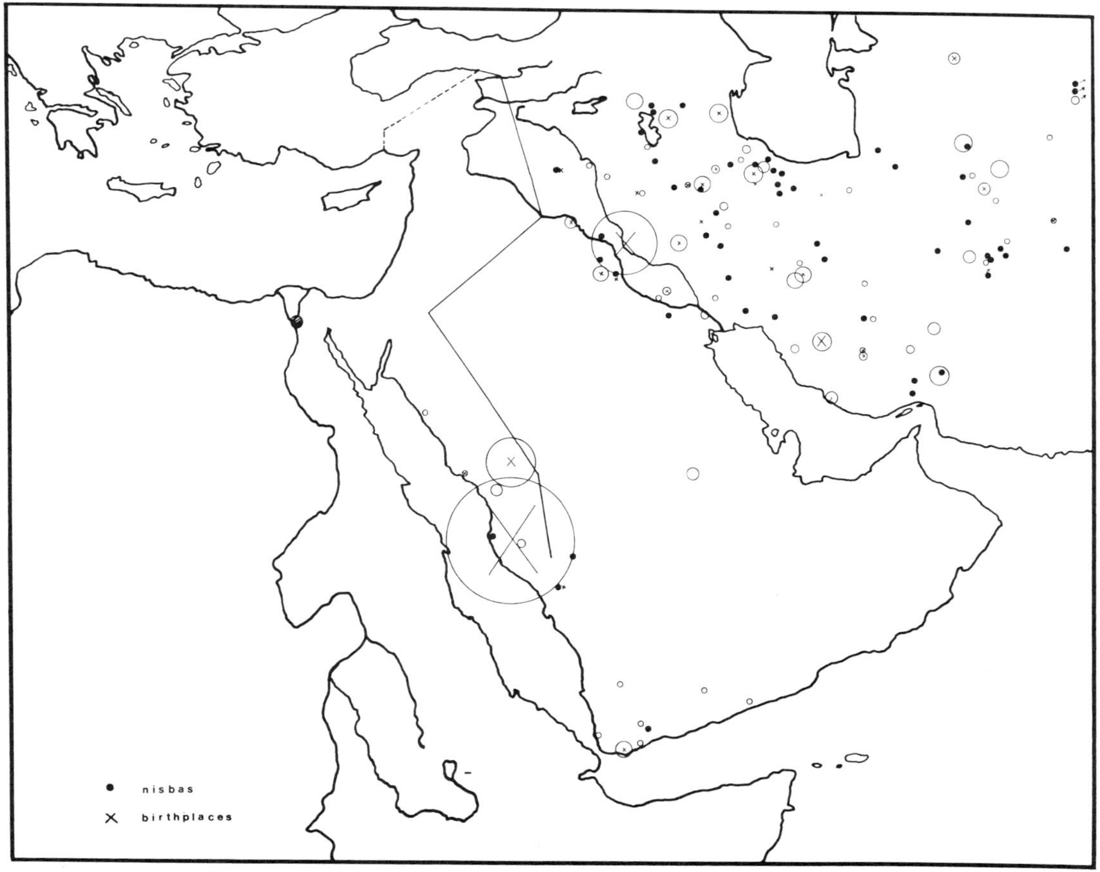

IV-B. Iran, Iraq, and the Arabian Peninsula, Migration throughout the Century

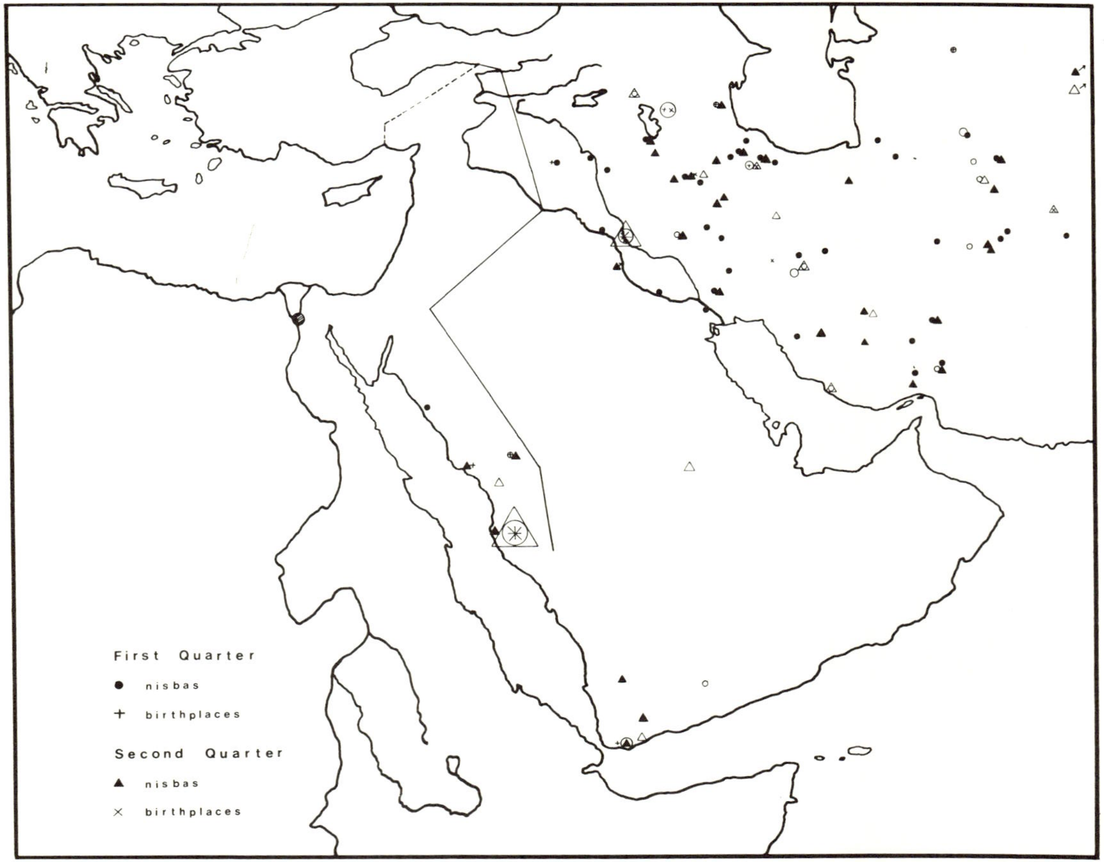

IV-C. Iran, Iraq, and the Arabian Peninsula, Migration during the First Half of the Century

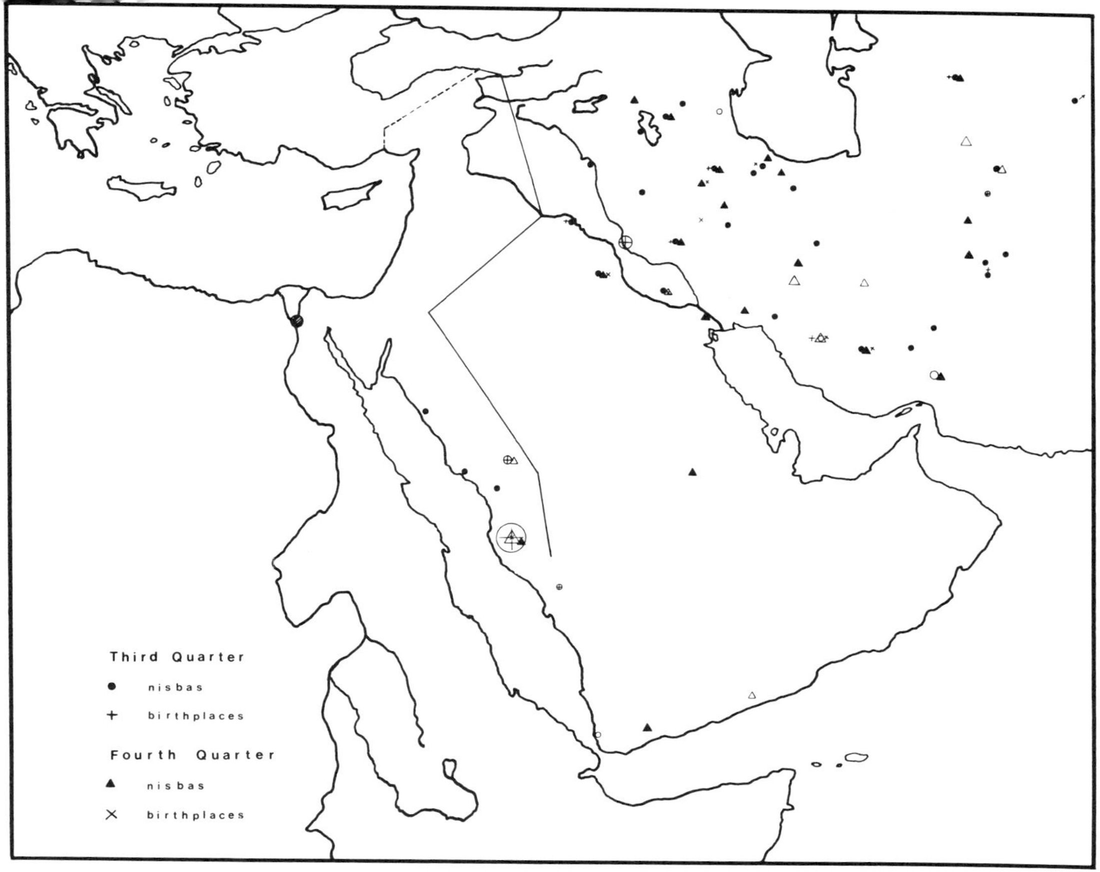

IV-D. Iran, Iraq, and the Arabian Peninsula, Migration during the Second Half of the Century

Key to Sites on Map V-A

1. Ashbīl (Seville)
2. Gharnāṭa (Granada)
3. Wajla (Ouagla)
4. Khirārka
5. Dukkala
6. Mijjāṭ
7. al-Hanatā
8. Zanāta (rgn)
9. ʿInāb
10. Fās (Fez)
11. Kifīfāt
12. Baskara
13. Mazūz
14. Liyāna
15. Zawāwa (rgn)
16. Tawzirt
17. Tāza
18. Zarāʿa
19. Musūn
20. Rabāṭ
21. Kahla
22. Miskala (rgn)
23. ʿĀṣṣif
24. Miḥāṣ
25. Kharkha
26. Ghimāra
27. Marrākish
28. Fuzāra (rgn)
29. Ṣanhāja (rgn)
30. Sijilmāssa
31. Tilimsān (Tlemcen)
32. Bijāya (Boujie)
33. Qusṭanṭīna (Constantine)
34. Majāz
35. Maksīn
36. Tūnis
37. Būna (Bone)
38. Qayrawān
39. Jarīr
40. Furrīyāna
41. Tawzar
42. Ṣafāqis (Sfāqs)
43. Ṭarābulus (al-Maghrib)
44. Mazzūn
45. Ṣiqilīya (Sicily)

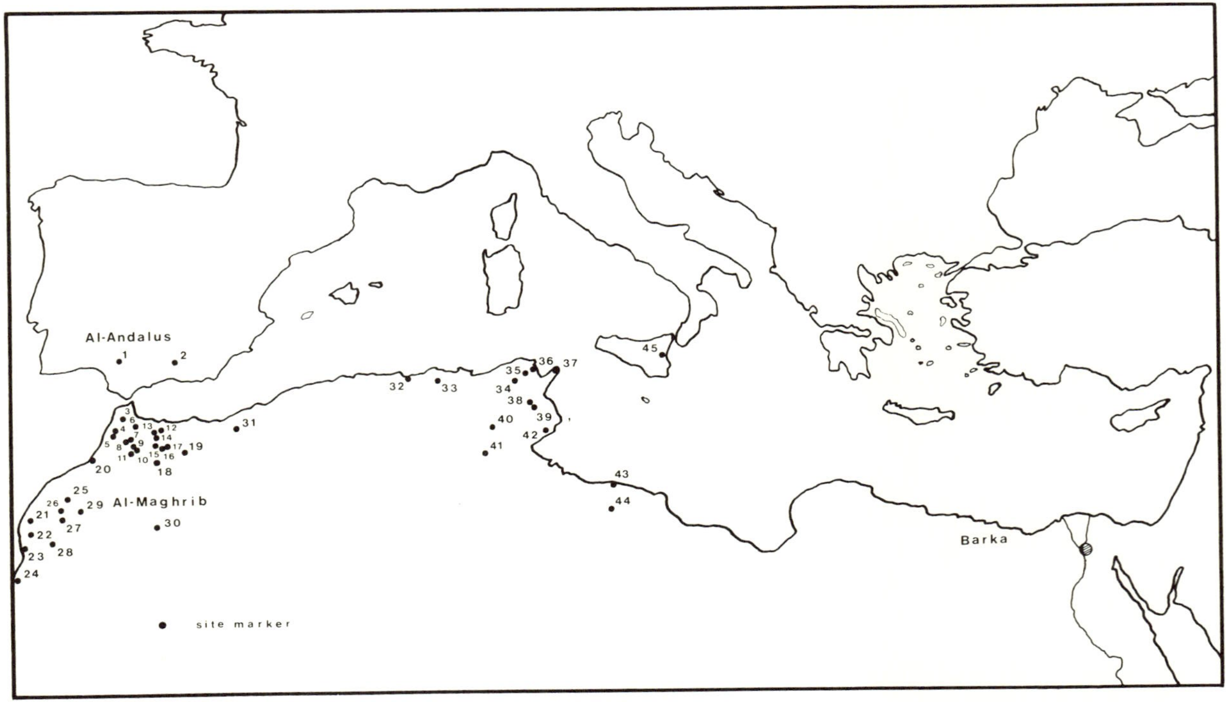

V-A. North Africa and the Mediterranean, Sites

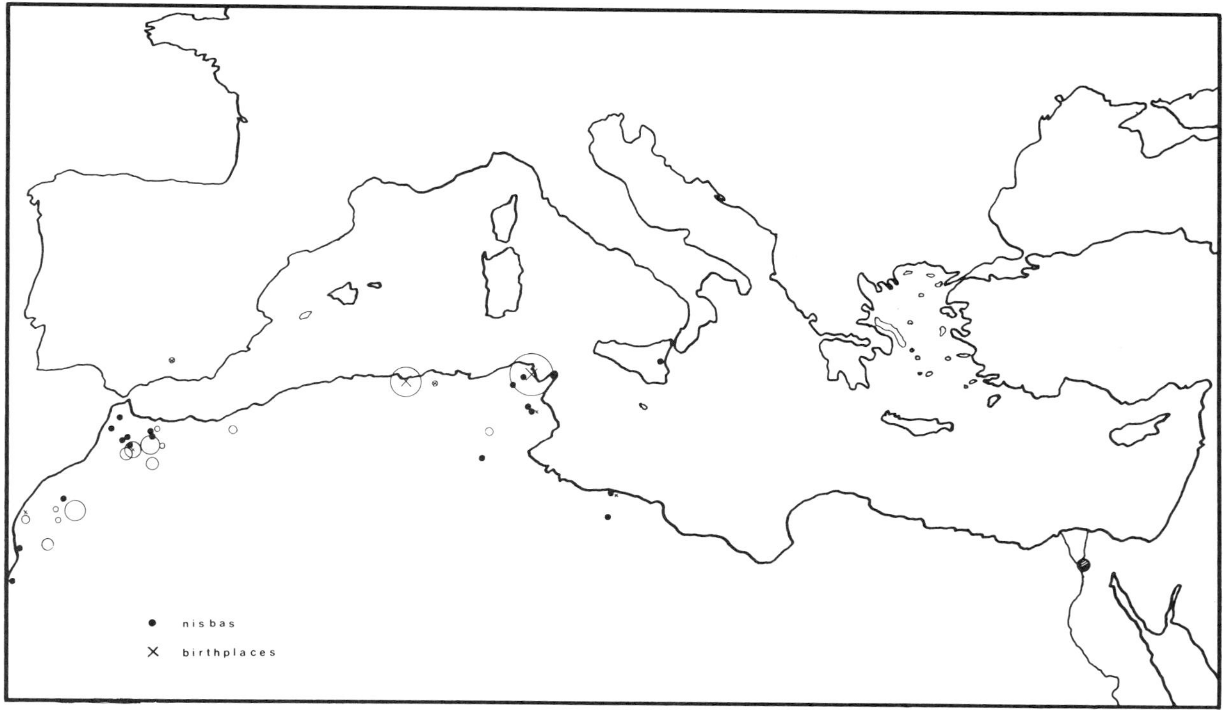

V-B. North Africa and the Mediterranean, Migration throughout the Century

Tables 1 through 10

Tables 1-10 show the relationships between occupations and geographic nisbas and birthplaces. The six occupational categories are:

I. Military-Executive
II. Bureaucratic (secretarial-financial)
III. Judicial
IV. Artisan-Commercial
V. Scholarly-Educational
VI. Religious (those occupations associated with religious service and the administration of mosques).

The classifications come from the system devised by William Popper in *Egypt and Syria under the Circassian Sultans*, pp. 111-20, although I have included occupations not indexed in his notes. The military-executive category lists only those occupations in which civilians were engaged; several of the various grades of amirs and military offices were monopolized by Mamluks and did not qualify for inclusion in these tables.

Tables 1-6 show the distribution of individuals according to regions and occupational categories. Tables 7-10 summarize regional totals of positions according to occupational categories for all surveyed regions, facilitating comparisons within the empire (which generated the majority of references, among which proportions are more statistically valid) and throughout the Near East (where proportions are less valid statistically due to sample size). These tables compare percentages and coefficients measuring degrees of concentration. This coefficient (CC) is computed according to the following equation:

$$CC = \frac{\Sigma P^2 - \frac{1}{n}}{1 - \frac{1}{n}}$$

where P = regional percentages, n = the number of categories. The larger the coefficient, the more concentrated were occupational references to persons from a specific region. Conversely, the lower the coefficient, the more even was the distribution of references. Note that nisbas referring to Cairo itself were not listed because of their wide use and basic inaccuracy as a geographic indicator. Tables 7 and 9 therefore do not include Cairo. In order to provide parallel opportunities for comparison, percentages and concentration coefficients in Tables 8 and 10 have been computed twice: excluding and including birthplaces reported for Cairo.

Tables 8 and 10 also provide ratios of nisbas to birthplaces, based on the total number of references to individuals holding positions. These ratios indicate the discrepancy between nisbas and birthplaces according to region. Since the birthplace is a more accurate indicator of geographic origin, the correlation between it and the nisba provides a general check on the latter's accuracy. The widest discrepancies occurred for Upper Egypt and regions outside the Mamluk empire. The ratios reported for Syria-Palestine were slightly lower than for the Delta, underscoring not only the close ties between the Syrian provincial capitals and Cairo but also the relative accuracy of nomenclature listed in the biographies of Syrians.

KEY TO TABLES 1-6

Figures listed under regional totals refer to all sites reported in a region and are not restricted to figures appearing under specific sites in these tables.

GHZ:	Ghazza (city)
DM:	Dumyāṭ (Damietta, city)
DQ:	Daqhilīya province
SH:	Sharqīya province
QAL:	Qalyūbīya province
MN:	Minūfīya province
GHR:	Gharbīya province
BUH:	Buḥayra province
Alex:	Alexandria (city)
Jīza:	Jīza (Gīza) province
FAY:	Fayyūmīya province
AT-B:	Aṭfiḥīya-Bahnasawīya provinces
USH:	Ushmunayn-Ṭahawīya provinces
MN-AS:	Manfalūṭīya-Asyūṭīya provinces
AKH:	Akhmīmīya province
QUS:	Qūṣīya province
Jeru:	Jerusalem (city)
East Bank:	Regions east of the Jordan River
Dmshq:	Damascus (city)
Ḥalab:	Aleppo (city)
ṬARĀB-BIQĀʿ:	Ṭarābulus-Biqāʿ province (modern Lebanon)
ANATOL:	Anatolia
IRAN:	Iranian Plateau
IRAQ:	Tigris-Euphrates regions
ARAB:	Arabian Peninsula
MGRB:	North Africa
AFR:	Nubia and the Sudan

TABLE 1. Geographic Distribution of Individuals Engaged in Military-Executive Occupations (Category I)
Figures without ( ) refer to nisbas Figures within ( ) refer to birthplaces

		LOWER EGYPT					(Nile Delta)					UPPER EGYPT			
Occupations	Cairo	GHZ	DM	DQ	SH	QAL	MN	GHR	BUH	Alex	TOTAL	Jīza	FAY	AT-B	USH
Shādd	(1)						2	1			3				
Shādd (variants)	(4)	1					1(1)		2		4(1)	1			
Ustādār	(18)				2		4(2)	1(3)	5		12(5)	1		2	
Dawādār	(6)		1					5		1	7				
Ḥājib	(2)						2	2(1)	1		5(1)			1(1)	1
Jāmdār				1							1				
Kāshif	(1)	1					2(1)				3(1)				1
Nā'ib	(2)	1	3(1)	1	1		1(1)	4(1)	3(1)		14(4)				2
Naqīb	(9)			1	1		1(1)	6(1)			9(2)		1	1	
" Jaysh	(2)						1				1				
Murattib	(9)	1(1)		1			1(1)	1			4(2)	2(1)	1		
Wakīl	(3)	1						1			2		1		
" Bayt Māl	(7)						5(1)	3(2)		1(1)	9(4)	2		1(1)	
Khāzindār	(1)		1	1							2				
Zimām	(1)		1								1				
TOTAL	(66)										77(20)				

TABLE 1 (cont.)

(Nile Valley)				PALESTINE			SYRIA									
MN-AS	AKH	QUS	TOTAL	Jeru	East Bank	TOTAL	Dmshq	Ḥalab	Tarab Biqa	TOTAL	ANATOL	IRAN	IRAQ	ARAB	MGRB	AFR
										2	2			2(2)		
						1					1					3
1			4(1)	1	2	3	5(1)	3(1)	2	14(2)		2			1	
					4	4			1	6	4				2	
			2(1)	(2)		(2)				6(1)		3				
											1					1
						2		2	1	3	5	1(1)			2(1)	
1(1)			5(1)	(1)	3	4(2)	1	3	1	7(1)	3	1(1)	1		2(1)	1
			3(1)				1	2(1)		3(1)		2				1
											1	1				
1			4(1)				1(1)		1(1)	3(2)	1	5(3)	(1)		3	
			1				1			3						
			4(1)				5(2)	1		6(2)		3	1(1)			1
											6	1(1)				5
									1(1)	2(1)	5					8
			23(6)			14(4)				55(10)	29	19(6)	2(2)	2(2)	10(2)	20

TABLE 2. Geographic Distribution of Individuals Engaged in Bureaucratic Occupations (Category II)
Figures without ( ) refer to nisbas Figures within ( ) refer to birthplaces

		LOWER EGYPT		(Nile Delta)								UPPER EGYPT			
Occupations	Cairo	GHZ	DM	DQ	SH	QAL	MN	GHR	BUH	Alex	TOTAL	Jīza	FAY	AT-B	USH
Shāhid (bur. variants)	(16)			1			1	9(3)	1		12(3)				1
" Awqāf	(4)							1	2		4				
Ṣāḥib					2			1		2	5				
" (variants)	(1)			1			1(1)	3			5(1)			1	
Jāb	(1)							1			1				
Kātib	(12)			(1)	2(2)	1(1)	4	8	1	1(2)	17(8)	1		1	1
" (variants)	(12)				2	5	3(1)	4	1		15(1)				
" Sirr	(14)			1	1		1	5(4)	1	(1)	9(5)			1	5
Mubāshir	(14)	1	2		2(1)		3(2)	4(2)		(1)	12(6)	1	1	2(1)	
" (variants)	(10)				2		2	4(1)		1(1)	9(2)	1	1		
" Awqāf	(1)								1		1			1	
Mustawfī															
Ṣayrafī	(1)					1					1				
Mutaṣarrif								2			2				
Mutakallim	(11)			1	2		1(1)	5(2)			9(3)			1	1
" Awqāf	(3)					1	2	1			4				
Muwaqqiʿ	(26)			4	2(2)	3	5(1)	13(3)	1	1(1)	29(7)	1		3	1
" Dast	(10)				1			4(2)			5(2)				1
" Dīwān	(5)							1(1)			1(1)		1		1
" Ḥukm	(2)			1		1		4(1)			6(1)				1
" (variants)	(9)							1			1				1
Mudīr	(3)							1			1				
Nāẓir	(30)	2	2(2)		4	1(1)	5	21(8)		2(1)	37(12)	1		6(1)	1(1)
" Aḥbās	(3)							5(3)			5(3)				
" Dār Ḍarb	(2)						1	2(1)			3(1)				1
" Dawla	(2)					1		1			2			1(1)	
" Dīwān	(11)							3		1	4				
" Jawālī	(6)						1(1)	2			3(1)				
" Jaysh	(9)	2					1(1)	3(3)		1(1)	7(5)			1	
" Awqāf	(14)	1(1)			3(1)	1(1)	1	10(3)			16(6)	2	1	2	
" Iṣṭabl	(8)							3(1)			3(1)				
" Aswāq										1	1				
" Bayt Māl							2			1	3				
" Ḥaramayn					1			1(1)			2(1)				
" Kiswa	(4)				1		2(1)	3(2)		1(1)	7(4)	2		1	
" Khāṣṣ	(11)				1		3(2)	2(2)		2(2)	8(6)			1	
Wazīr	(19)						3(1)	5(2)	3	1(1)	12(4)			2	1
TOTAL	(274)										262(84)				

TABLE 2 (cont.)

(Nile Valley)				PALESTINE			SYRIA									
MN-AS	AKH	QUS	TOTAL	Jeru	East Bank	TOTAL	Dmshq	Halab	Tarab Biqa	TOTAL	ANATOL	IRAN	IRAQ	ARAB	MGRB	AFR
2	1		4(1)		1(1)	1(1)				1	1				2	
1			1						1	1				1	2	
									2	2	1(1)	2		1(2)		
						1					1					1
1		1	5		4(2)	7(2)						3				
2	1		3		3	3	1	5(2)	1	12(4)	1	1		3	4	
1		1	8	1(1)	6(2)	13(3)	15(8)	10(7)	2	43(22)	3	13(4)			2(2)	
	1	1	8(1)		1(1)	2(1)		1(1)	1	5(1)	1		2	2(1)		
2			4				1(1)	1(1)		2(2)	1			2		
			1		1	1		2		3		1	1			1
1			1	1	1	2	1(1)		1	2(1)	1					
		1	1		1	1										
		1	3			1	1(1)		1	2(2)		1	1			1
			1		1	1	1			1						
4(3)			9(3)		1(1)	3(1)	3(2)	12(9)		22(12)	1	3	3(2)	2		
			1		2(1)	3(1)	1	3(2)		4(2)		1				
			2			1		3(1)		5(2)		1				
	1	1	4							1						
			1					1		1						
2	2(2)		4(2)	2		3				1				3		
2		3(1)	14(3)	3(2)	2	7(4)	5(1)	2	3(1)	17(5)	8(1)	8(2)	4	5(1)	1	1
						1	3(1)			5(1)	1(2)	4				
			1	(2)		(2)					2			1(1)		
			1(1)			2										
3		1	4		2(1)	2(1)		2(2)		3(2)		1(1)	2			
1			1				1		1	3(1)	1	1				
		3(1)	5(1)	1(1)	9(2)	11(3)	9(5)	4(2)	1	23(11)	4	3				
		3(1)	4(1)		1	1	1	1		3	1	1				
				(1)		1(1)	4(2)		1	5(2)	1		1		1	
		1	1													
				1		1			1	1	1	3(1)				
		2	5								3					
		3(1)	4(1)		1	1	1	1		3	1	1				
			4			1(2)	1	1		4					1	
			105(14)			71(22)				175(70)	34(4)	48(8)	14(2)	20(5)	13(2)	4

TABLE 3. Geographic Distribution of Individuals Engaged in Legal Occupations (Category III)
Figures without ( ) refer to nisbas Figures within ( ) refer to birthplaces

		LOWER EGYPT			(Nile Delta)							UPPER EGYPT			
Occupations	Cairo	GHZ	DM	DQ	SH	QAL	MN	GHR	BUH	Alex	TOTAL	Jīza	FAY	AT-B	USH
ʿAdl	(1)							3(2)	2		5(2)				
ʿAqd	(3)	1(1)				2	1(1)	4(2)			8(4)	1	1		1
Sharūṭī	(2)							2			2				
Shaykh	(54)	3	2(1)	2(2)	6(1)	6	16(7)	29(11)	4	2(2)	70(26)	3(1)		8(2)	3(1)
" Shuyūkh															
" Shāfiʿi	(1)								1(1)	1	2(1)				
" Islām					1						1				
" Āthār	(1)			1							1			1	
" Balad														1	
" Ṣūfī	(11)						2	4(3)		1	7(3)			4(2)	
" Fuqarā'	(1)														
" Ḥanbalī															
" Ḥanafī									1		1				
" Mālikī									1(1)	1	2(1)				
" Muwaqqiʿīn	(1)						1				1				
" Khuddām								3(1)			3(1)	1(1)			
Amīn															
" Ḥukm	(7)			1	2	1(1)		1			5(1)			1	
Faqīh	(8)			2(1)	1		5(2)	12(3)			20(7)		1	1	
Muftī	(9)	1		3(1)	1		5	8(4)			18(5)	2			
" Dār ʿAdl	(13)					1		5(1)			6(1)	1			
Muḥtasib	(11)			1	1	1(1)	2	10(4)	1	2(1)	28(8)	2		1	1
Shāhid	(94)	1	6(3)	15(3)	8(2)	17(1)	30(9)	59(15)	15(1)	3(1)	154(37)	5	4	16(4)	6(1)
Nā'ib Qāḍī	(129)		6(5)	6(2)	8(4)	5(1)	29(12)	58(19)	10(1)	2(3)	124(47)	7(1)	4	10(2)	6(6)
Naqīb Ashrāf	(2)													1	
" Ḥukm	(3)														
Qāḍī	(44)	3(1)	3(2)	6(1)	3(1)	1(2)	5(4)	21(9)	9	4(2)	55(22)	3	3	7(2)	4
" ʿAskar	(11)						1	4			5				
" Rakb	(1)														1
" Quḍāt	(10)						1(1)	5(1)	1	2	9(2)			1	
" Shāfiʿī	(5)				1		1(1)	1	1		4(1)		1	2(2)	
" Ḥanbalī	(3)														
" Ḥanafī	(4)	1(1)			2	1		3(1)			7(2)				
" Ḥanafī	(2)			1				3(2)	3	2(1)	9(3)			1	
" Maḥmal	(3)			1	1(1)	1	2	5(1)			10(2)				1
Rasūl	(1)						1	1			2	1			1(1)
TOTAL	(435)										559(176)				

TABLE 3 (cont.)

(Nile Valley)				PALESTINE			SYRIA									
MN-AS	AKH	QUS	TOTAL	Jeru	East Bank	TOTAL	Dmshq	Halab	Ṭarab Biqaᶜ	TOTAL	ANATOL	IRAN	IRAQ	ARAB	MGRB	AFR
						1				1						
			3	1(1)	1	3(1)	1			2(1)						
6(2)	1(2)	4(1)	25(9)	6(6)	1(1)	17(9)	7(5)	9(4)	3	29(10)	24(4)	38(13)	6(3)	5	4(1)	
										1		1	1			
1		1	2						1	1						
			1													
			1													
1			5(2)						1(1)	2(1)	1	2	1(1)		1	
1			1													
									1(1)	1(1)						
			1(1)								1					1
													1		1(1)	
2	1(1)		4(1)													
2		3(1)	7(1)	2(1)	1	6(1)	5(3)	6(1)	2	13(4)	6(1)	9(1)	1	8	5(1)	1
1(1)		1(1)	4(2)	2		6(1)	3(1)	2(2)	1(1)	10(4)	1	3	5(3)		3	
			1				2(1)			5(1)		2	2(2)			
		5	9		1	2	3		1	6(1)	5(2)	8(2)		3		
11(2)	2	6	51(7)	3(1)		9(2)	3(1)	2(1)	3	22(4)	4	10(1)	3(1)	5(3)	6	
7(3)	1	6(1)	41(13)	7(3)	1(1)	10(9)	9(4)	9(6)	5	36(18)	8	8(1)	3	9(1)	6(1)	
			1				2(1)			3(2)	2					
1			1				1			1		1	1			
5(3)	3(1)	4(1)	30(7)	4(1)	3(3)	17(7)	12(6)	13(8)	2(1)	54(27)	10(2)	8(1)	6(5)	4(1)	4	
				1		2	3(1)	3(3)	1	10(4)	5	8(1)				
2(1)	1(1)		4(2)				1			2						
1		1	3			2	2(1)	1(1)		8(4)		2			2	
			3(2)		2(2)	3(2)	5(1)	2		13(1)		3(1)			2(1)	
1			1	2	1	4				2(1)			3(3)	1		
1			1	5(2)	2	7(2)	11(3)	11(1)	5(1)	38(7)	8(4)	3			1	
2(2)	1	1	4(2)	2		2	1			3			1	(1)	9(2)	
			1				1(1)			2(1)		1			1	
			2(1)					3(2)		4(2)	3(2)	3(1)			1(1)	
			207(50)			91(34)				269(94)	78(15)	1[illegible]0(22)	34(18)	35(6)	46(8)	2

TABLE 4. Geographic Distribution of Individuals Engaged in Artisan-Commercial Occupations (Category IV)
Figures without ( ) refer to nisbas Figures within ( ) refer to birthplaces

		LOWER EGYPT		(Nile Delta)							UPPER EGYPT			
Occupations	Cairo	GHZ	DM	DQ	SH	QAL	MN	GHR	BUH	Alex	TOTAL	Jīza	FAY	AT-B	USH
ᶜAṭṭār							1(1)	5(3)			6(4)				
Ṭabīb	(3)							3(1)			3(1)				
Bawwāb	(3)				1	1		2(1)		2(1)	6(2)				
Bayyāᶜ	(6)			1(1)	3(1)	1					5(2)				
Bazzāz	(1)			1	2(2)			5(1)	1(1)		9(4)				
Ṣanāʼiᶜī	(7)							5(2)	2(1)	1	8(3)			1(1)	
Dallāl	(1)			1				3			4	1			
Farrāsh							1				1				
Ḥāʼik	(1)			1(1)			1(1)				2(2)				
Ḥabbāk	(2)														
Ḥaddād															
Ḥajjār															
Ḥakīm															
Ḥalwāʼī															
Ḥammāmī	(1)							1			1				
Ḥarīrī	(2)			2			1	3		2(1)	8(1)		1		1
Jarrāḥ	(1)														
Jawharī			1					1(1)			2(1)				
Kutubī	(5)			2(1)				5(1)			7(2)				
Muhandis															
Nāsikh	(16)		2(2)	4(3)	6(3)	1	6(3)	10(4)	1(1)	1	31(16)	3(1)	1	1	5(1)
Najjār	(2)		1								1				
Qabbānī	(3)				1	1					2				
Qazzāz								1			1				
Simsar	(1)		1					1			2				
Tājir	(22)	5(1)	1(1)	3	7(2)	3	5(3)	22(6)	5	10(1)	61(14)	4(2)	3	2	4
" (variants)	(3)				2(1)	2		3(1)	1		8(2)	1			
Kārimī		1									1				
Mujallid	(3)							1			1				
Warrāq	(1)			1(1)				1			2(1)				
Khaṭṭāṭ								1			1				
Khawājā								2			2				
Khayyāṭ	(5)	1(1)	1		2		1		1(1)		6(2)			3(1)	1(1)
Zarrāᶜ						1	1	1			3		1	1	1
Zayyāt	(2)						2(1)				2(1)	1			
TOTAL	(91)										186(58)				

TABLE 4 (cont.)

(Nile Valley)				PALESTINE			SYRIA									
MN-AS	AKH	QUS	TOTAL	Jeru	East Bank	TOTAL	Dmshq	Halab	Tarab Biqa	TOTAL	ANATOL	IRAN	IRAQ	ARAB	MGRB	AFR
							1		1	2						
											1	3(1)	1		11(3)	
		1	1									1				1
		1	1				1	1	2	4(2)	1					
1			1									3(1)	1(1)	1		
			1(1)							3		2	2(1)	2(1)	2	
			1											1(1)		
							1			1						
							1(1)			1(1)						
								1(1)		1(1)						
							1		1	2	1					
												1				
									1	1						
										1						
			2	1		1	2(1)			3(1)		1	1(1)			
												1				
										1				1		
						1	1			6	1	2		1		
													1			
	1(1)		14(3)	2		3	3(2)	1	2(1)	12(5)	1(1)		1(2)			
														1(1)		
											1		2		1	
			1											1(1)		
1(1)		5(1)	19(4)	1(1)		2	8(3)	2(2)	1	14(6)	14	6(1)	4(1)	12(6)	7	3
1			2		2(1)	5(2)	2			4	3	2			1	1
											1					
															1	
					1	1				1						
								2(1)		2(1)		4(1)	1	1		
							3(1)			4(1)	4	2				
			6(2)							3	2	3			2	
			3													
			1			1										
			53(10)			14(2)				66(18)	30(1)	31(4)	14(6)	21(10)	25(3)	5

TABLE 5. Geographic Distribution of Individuals Engaged in Scholarly-Educational Occupations (Category V)
Figures without ( ) refer to nisbas Figures within ( ) refer to birthplaces

		LOWER EGYPT			(Nile Delta)							UPPER EGYPT			
Occupations	Cairo	GHZ	DM	DQ	SH	QAL	MN	GHR	BUH	Alex	TOTAL	Jīza	FAY	AT-B	USH
Shā^{c}ir	(47)	2(1)	2(1)	2(1)	4(1)	4(2)	7(3)	21(10)	2(1)	8(5)	52(26)			4	2(1)
Shaykh Iqrā'													1	(1)	
" Ismā'												1(1)			
" Ḥadīth	(3)						1				1				
" Mī^{c}ād	(1)						1				1				
" Qirā'āt	(1)							2			2				
" Taṣawwuf	(11)				2(2)	2	4(1)	3			11(4)	1			
I^{c}āda	(2)							3(2)			3(2)		1		
Adīb	(4)		1(1)			1		3(1)	(1)		5(3)				1(1)
Ismā^{c}	(3)							1			1				1
Mu^{c}īd	(34)	1	1(1)		1		3	10(3)	3		19(4)	1	1	1	1
Mudarris	(95)	5(3)	4(4)	8(5)	8	6(2)	19(6)	44(18)	3	2(3)	99(41)	12	1	10(2)	2(2)
" ^{c}Arabī							1(1)				1(1)				
" Shāfi^{c}ī	(6)				1		1	1			3			1(1)	1
" Dār al-Ḥadīth	(1)														
" Fiqh	(49)			1(1)	1(1)		4(2)	12(5)	1	1(1)	18(10)	2	2	5(3)	1
" Farā'iḍ	(2)						1(1)	1			2(1)	1			
" Ḥadīth	(32)			1(1)		1(2)	2(1)	7(2)	3	2(2)	16(8)			1(1)	
" Ḥanbalī	(3)							2			2			1	
" Ḥanafī	(1)									1	1				
" Kashshāf	(2)														
" Kīmiyā'															
" Mālikī	(2)		1						1		2				
" Mī^{c}ād	(4)								1		1				
" Naḥw															
" Qirā'āt	(2)				1		1	2(1)	1		5(1)		1		
" Taṣawwuf	(2)			1(1)							1(1)				
" Tafsīr	(16)					1	1	4(2)	1		7(2)				
Muḥaddith	(9)		1		2		4(2)	5(4)	1	1(2)	14(8)	2			
Mukattib	(1)					2		3			5				
Muqrī-Aṭfāl	(7)			2(2)	4(1)		6(2)	7(4)	4		23(9)	2	1(1)	2(1)	1
" Mamālīk	(2)				1(1)						1(1)				
Mu'addib	(7)			2(1)	2(2)	2		8(4)	3		17(7)			1	
Mu'arrikh	(3)							1(1)			1(1)				
Naḥwī	(1)					1	1(1)	1			3(1)				
Khāzin Kutub	(17)			1(1)	2(1)		1(1)	5	(1)		9(4)				1
Mutaṣaddir	(19)			1		2	2(1)	6(1)	1		12(2)			1	
TOTAL	(389)										338(137)				

TABLE 5 (cont.)

(Nile Valley)				PALESTINE			SYRIA									
MN-AS	AKH	QUS	TOTAL	Jeru	East Bank	TOTAL	Dmshq	Ḥalab	Tarab Biqa	TOTAL	ANATOL	IRAN	IRAQ	ARAB	MGRB	AFR
3(3)	1	6(2)	18(7)	4(5)	3(2)	11(9)	7(5)	10(4)	2(1)	43(18)	8(2)	12(4)	2	1(1)		
		(1)	1													
			1(1)													
										1		1				
											1	1		2		
1(1)			3(1)		1	1	1(1)	2	(1)	6(2)	2	3(1)				
		(1)	2				2(1)		1	3(1)	1	1	1(1)	3(1)	2	
			1(1)		1(1)	1(1)	2(1)			4(2)	2	1	1		1	
			1			1								1		
1			5	4(2)	1(1)	6(3)	2(1)	1(1)	2(1)	9(4)	3	5(1)	3(2)	2(2)	4(1)	
4(4)	1	3	33(8)	14(3)	5(3)	31(7)	13(6)	14(6)	4(2)	46(18)	19(2)	32(6)	11(7)	7(1)	13(3)	
			2(1)			1	1			2						
												2(1)				
1			13(3)	2(2)	1	6(4)	1		1(1)	5(1)	5(3)	9(3)	4(2)	1	12(3)	
1			2								1				(1)	
2(1)			3(2)	1	1	3	3(2)	2(1)	1(1)	9(4)	2(1)	4		3(1)	5(2)	
			1							2	1	3	2(2)			
		1	1		1	1			1(1)	1(1)	1	3				
											1					
												1				
1(1)			1(1)			1									2	
				1(1)		4(1)						1				
							1(1)			1(1)			2			
			1		1(1)	1(1)			1(1)	1(1)		1				
1(1)			1(1)					1(1)	1	3(1)						
				1		2	1(1)	1(1)	1	3(2)	3(1)	3(1)			8(2)	
			2		(1)	2(1)	2(2)	2(1)		8(3)	1	3			3	
	(1)	1(2)	1(2)													
			7(3)		1(1)	1(1)	1			3	2	3		1		
					1(1)	1(1)		1		2						1
			1(1)			1				1				1	2(1)	
1			1			1	1	2(2)		3(2)	2(3)			1		
	1(1)		1(1)					3(1)		4(1)				2		
		1	2		1(1)	2(1)			1	5(1)	1					
			1	1		1	1(1)	1		3(1)		3	1	1	2	
			106(33)			79(30)				168(64)	56(12)	92(17)	27(14)	26(6)	54(13)	1

TABLE 6. Geographic Distribution of Individuals Engaged in Religious Occupations (Category VI)
Figures without ( ) refer to nisbas   Figures within ( ) refer to birthplaces

		LOWER EGYPT (Nile Delta)										UPPER EGYPT			
Occupations	Cairo	GHZ	DM	DQ	SH	QAL	MN	GHR	BUH	Alex	TOTAL	Jīza	FAY	AT-B	USH
Imām	(50)	2(2)	2	10(7)	10(3)	6(2)	15(2)	24(6)	2(1)	3(4)	74(27)	4(1)	4(2)	3	4(1)
Mu^ctaqad	(9)		2	2	4	2	1	10(2)	3(1)	4(1)	28(4)	1	1	2	4
Majdhūb				2				1			3	2			
Muqri'	(36)	3	2(2)	7(2)	8(2)	3(2)	13(5)	34(9)	2	3(3)	75(25)	2(1)	1	4(1)	3(1)
Muqri' Ṭibāq			1				1(1)				2(1)				
Muqri' Jawq	(11)			4(2)	1			6(1)	1		12(2)				1
Mu'adhdhin	(2)			1(1)				5	1	2(1)	9(2)			1	1(1)
Mu'aqqit				1	1(1)					1(1)	3(2)				
Mīqātī	(7)			1					2	1	4	1			
Wā^ciẓ	(9)		1(1)		1		2	5(1)			9(2)	1		1	
Khaṭīb	(65)	12	7(2)	12(7)	12(4)	7	17(7)	33(15)	4	1	105(41)	2	7(1)	1	4(2)
TOTAL	(189)										324(106)				

TABLE 6 (cont.)

(Nile Valley)				PALESTINE			SYRIA									
MN-AS	AKH	QUS	TOTAL	Jeru	East Bank	TOTAL	Dmshq	Ḥalab	Ṭarab Biqa	TOTAL	ANATOL	IRAN	IRAQ	ARAB	MGRB	AFR
5(2)		3(1)	25(7)	4(2)	2(2)	8(4)	7(1)	5(3)	2(1)	23(11)	8	6	3(1)	1	5	
1			14	2(1)		9(1)	1(1)	1		12(1)	9(1)	10	2(1)	9	10	
		1	3							1	2	1				
1(1)	1	1(1)	14(5)			2	2(2)			5(3)	8(1)	10(1)	5(2)	4	7	1
			1													
			2									4	1	2		
		1	4(1)				1			3	1	2		1(2)		
				1		2(1)	1			1						
			1							1		2		(1)		
1(1)	(1)	1	4(2)			1		1(1)		4(5)	1	2				
2(1)	1(1)	1	20(6)	7(5)	3(2)	15(8)	3(3)	4(2)	3(1)	28(12)	5	4	2	9(1)	2	
			88(21)			37(14)				78(32)	34(2)	41(1)	13(4)	26(4)	24	1

TABLE 7. Regional Influence on Occupations According to Nisbas in the Mamluk Empire

	Delta		*Valley*		*Pal*		*Syria*		*Occup.*	
	RT	*%*	*RT*	*%*	*RT*	*%*	*RT*	*%*	*Totals*	*CC*
Mil.	77	(46)	23	(14)	14	(8)	55	(33)	169	.12
Bur.	262	(43)	105	(17)	71	(12)	175	(29)	613	.07
Leg.	559	(50)	207	(18)	91	(8)	269	(24)	1126	.13
Art.	186	(58)	53	(17)	14	(4)	66	(21)	319	.21
Sch.	338	(49)	106	(15)	79	(11)	168	(24)	691	.11
Rel.	324	(61)	88	(17)	37	(7)	78	(15)	527	.23
RT	1746	(51)	582	(17)	306	(9)	811	(24)	3445	
	Percentages According to Regional Totals									
Mil.	4		4		5		7			
Bur.	15		18		23		22			
Leg.	32		36		30		33			
Art.	11		9		5		8			
Sch.	19		18		26		21			
Rel.	19		15		12		10			
	100% of 1746		100% of 582		100% of 306		100% of 811			
CC	.05		.06		.06		.06			

NOTE: RT = regional totals of positions
CC = concentration coefficient

TABLE 8. Regional Influence on Occupations According to Birthplaces in the Mamluk Empire

	Cairo	Delta	Valley	Pal	Syria	Occup. Totals	CC
	RT %	RT %ex %in	RT %ex %in	RT %ex %in	RT %ex %in	ex in	ex in
Mil.	66 (62)	20 (50) (19)	6 (15) (6)	4 (10) (4)	10 (25) (9)	40 106	.12 .28
Bur.	274 (59)	84 (44) (18)	14 (7) (3)	22 (12) (12)	70 (37) (15)	190 464	.12 .24
Leg.	435 (55)	176 (50) (22)	50 (14) (6)	34 (10) (4)	94 (27) (12)	354 789	.13 .20
Art.	91 (51)	58 (66) (32)	10 (11) (6)	2 (2) (1)	18 (20) (10)	88 179	.32 .21
Sch.	389 (60)	137 (52) (21)	33 (13) (5)	30 (11) (5)	64 (24) (10)	264 653	.11 .26
Rel.	189 (52)	106 (61) (29)	21 (12) (6)	14 (8) (4)	32 (18) (9)	173 362	.23 .20
RT	1444 (57)	581 (52) (23)	134 (12) (5)	106 (10) (4)	288 (26) (11)	1109 2553	
Ratio Nis/Bp	—	3/1	4.3/1	2.9/1	2.8/1	3.1/1 —	
	Percentages According to Regional Totals						
Mil.	5	3	4	4	3		
Bur.	19	14	10	21	24		
Leg.	30	30	37	32	33		
Art.	6	10	7	2	6		
Sch.	27	24	25	28	22		
Rel.	13	18	16	13	11		
	100% of 1444	100% of 581	100% of 134	100% of 106	100% of 288		
CC	.06	.05	.08	.08	.07		

NOTE: RT = regional totals of positions
CC = concentration coefficient
ex = excluding Cairo
in = including Cairo

TABLE 9. Regional Influence on Occupations According to Nisbas in All Regions

	Delta *RT %*	*Valley* *RT %*	*Pal* *RT %*	*Syria* *RT %*	*Iran* *RT %*	*Other* *RT %*	*Occup. Totals*	*CC*
Mil.	77 (31)	23 (9)	14 (6)	55 (22)	19 (8)	63 (25)	251	.07
Bur.	262 (35)	105 (14)	71 (10)	175 (23)	48 (6)	85 (11)	746	.05
Leg.	559 (39)	207 (14)	91 (6)	269 (19)	110 (8)	195 (14)	1431	.08
Art.	186 (42)	53 (13)	14 (4)	66 (17)	31 (7)	95 (21)	445	.10
Sch.	338 (36)	106 (11)	79 (8)	168 (18)	92 (10)	164 (17)	947	.06
Rel.	324 (49)	83 (13)	37 (6)	78 (12)	41 (6)	98 (15)	666	.14
RT	1746 (39)	582 (13)	306 (7)	811 (18)	341 (8)	700 (16)	4486	
				Percentages According to Regional Totals				
Mil.	4	4	5	7	6	9		
Bur.	15	18	23	22	14	12		
Leg.	32	36	30	33	32	28		
Art.	11	9	5	8	9	14		
Sch.	19	18	26	21	27	23		
Rel.	19	15	12	10	12	14		
	100% of 1746	100% of 582	100% of 306	100% of 811	100% of 341	100% of 700		
CC	.05	.06	.06	.06	.05	.02		

Note: RT = regional totals of positions
CC = concentration coefficient

TABLE 10. Regional Influence on Occupations According to Birthplaces in All Regions

	Cairo		*Delta*			*Valley*			*Pal*			*Syria*			*Iran*			*Other*			*Occup. Totals*		*CC*	
	RT	*%*	*RT*	*% ex*	*% in*	*RT*	*% ex*	*% in*	*RT*	*% ex*	*% in*	*RT*	*% ex*	*% in*	*RT*	*% ex*	*% in*	*RT*	*% ex*	*% in*	*% ex*	*% in*	*% ex*	*% in*
Mil.	66	(56)	20	(38)	(17)	6	(12)	(5)	4	(8)	(3)	10	(19)	(8)	6	(12)	(5)	6	(12)	(5)	52	118	.06	.24
Bur.	274	(56)	84	(40)	(17)	14	(7)	(3)	22	(10)	(5)	70	(33)	(14)	8	(4)	(2)	13	(6)	(3)	211	485	.13	.26
Leg.	435	(51)	176	(42)	(21)	50	(12)	(6)	34	(8)	(4)	94	(22)	(11)	22	(5)	(3)	47	(11)	(5)	423	858	.10	.20
Art.	91	(45)	58	(52)	(29)	10	(9)	(5)	2	(2)	(1)	18	(16)	(9)	4	(4)	(2)	20	(18)	(10)	112	203	.20	.19
Sch.	389	(54)	137	(42)	(19)	33	(10)	(5)	30	(9)	(4)	64	(20)	(9)	17	(5)	(2)	45	(14)	(6)	326	715	.11	.23
Rel.	189	(51)	106	(58)	(28)	21	(11)	(6)	14	(8)	(4)	32	(17)	(9)	1	(1)	(0)	10	(5)	(3)	184	373	.24	.24
RT	1444	(52)	581	(44)	(21)	134	(10)	(5)	106	(8)	(4)	288	(22)	(10)	58	(4)	(2)	141	(11)	(5)	1308	2752		
Ratio Nis/Bp		—	3/1			4.3/1			2.9/1			2.8/1			5.9/1			5/1			3.4/1	—		

Percentages According to Regional Totals

	Cairo	Delta	Valley	Pal	Syria	Iran	Other
Mil.	5	3	4	4	3	10	4
Bur.	19	14	10	21	24	14	9
Leg.	30	30	37	32	33	38	33
Art.	6	10	7	2	6	7	14
Sch.	27	24	25	28	22	29	32
Rel.	13	18	16	13	11	2	7
	100% of 1444	100% of 581	100% of 134	100% of 106	100% of 288	100% of 58	100% of 141
CC	.06	.05	.08	.08	.07	.10	.08

NOTE: RT = regional totals of positions
CC = concentration coefficient
ex = excluding Cairo
in = including Cairo

CHAPTER III

Residence Patterns of the Civilian Elite

The existence of numerous religio-academic institutions flourishing in Cairo during the central and later Middle Ages has been recognized by scholars familiar with Egyptian narrative sources for many years. Few inquiries, however, have been made into the specific nature of these institutions or their interrelationship as part of an academic system. One exception, the august mosque of al-Azhar, has received detailed study by both Egyptian and western scholars, but as an isolated case rather than in the context of a larger institutional network.[1] This chapter examines one dimension of this system: the distribution of the civilian elite in Cairo as documented by biographical sources, within the context of institutional relationships—a context influenced by the internal dynamics of ideological exchange, academic competition, religious ferment, and political manipulation. By examining in detail where the various groups tended to locate within the metropolis, it is possible to distinguish those institutions most or least preferred by them as occupational sites and residences. From the resulting patterns, it is possible to rank the specific institutions according to the status of persons associated with them. Such a procedure is possible because the biographical compilers in many cases provided a detailed list of the institutions in which an individual received his formal education and where he subsequently pursued his career. By analyzing the patterns that locate these people in Cairo, one may also perceive them as a social class. To date, it has not been possible to work with such a concept because no study has been made of the class on the basis of data describing a large sample of individuals in their professional settings. Only eminent figures have been studied, and these as examples isolated from their less eminent colleagues.

The present study only depicts the residential and occupational patterns of the civilian elite during the fifteenth century. No claims are made for other social groups treated by the biographical sources in less detail, although it may be possible after subsequent research to relate the results of this inquiry to other elements of the medieval population of Cairo and to Islamic society in general.

Another limitation of the present study is the static quality of the picture we have. Information provided by the biographical sources on geographic origins of the individuals, their occupations, and places of occupation and residence was available for more than 4,600 persons resident in one city during a century. It has thus been possible to make composite maps of locations where individuals tended to congregate, according to these variables. It would also be possible to plot out the various stages of careers according to where individuals moved, and, in fact, I discuss some of the data on these movements, and suggest reasons behind them.

This analysis examines the distribution of the civilian elite in Cairo from three perspectives. First, in this chapter, their distribution according to geographic origin is plotted through a comparison of geographic nisbas and birthplaces with places of education, occupation, and residence. Second, in Chapter IV, the major fields pursued by the elite are compared with occupational and residential sites.[2] This reveals patterns suggesting both the nature and purpose of religio-academic institutions, evolving and altering over time, and the goals of the individuals who were either employed or resident in them. Of equal importance, the interests and aspirations of the professional and political associates of these individuals, particularly influential Mamluks who supported them and their institutions as patrons, can be detected. Finally, residential and occupational distribution can be related to spiritual orientations, for which only the most prominent, Sufism, provided a sample size large enough to permit mapping.[3]

METHODOLOGY

In this analysis, schematic maps of Cairo depict the following comparisons of biographical data: geographic origins (nisbas and birthplaces) with educational, occupational, and residential sites (Figs. 3-8); twenty-one occupations with occupational and residential sites (Figs. 9-26); and individuals identified as Ṣūfīs with occupational sites and residences (Fig. 27). These schematic maps are preceded by two maps that label all sites mentioned in the biographical sources for immediate reference (Figs. 1 and 2). The geographic areas outside Cairo discussed in these comparisons are those defined in the preceding chapter: the Nile Delta (Lower Egypt); the Nile Valley (Upper Egypt); Syria-Palestine and Iran; Anatolia and Iraq; and North Africa and the Arabian Peninsula.

The classifications devised by William Popper constitute the basis for the following arrangement of prominent fields. Popper's classifications were checked against the examples and commentaries provided by al-Qalqashandī in his manual.[4] The final decision as to location in a professional category, however, was taken after initial cross tabulation of data to reveal concentrations of positions. On the whole, Popper's judgments proved to be sound, based as they were on his own thorough examination of Ibn Taghrī-Birdī's works and those of his contemporaries. Nevertheless, certain offices—particularly that of shaykh—overlapped heavily with others, thus calling into question any decision as to their placement in a professional category. Nevertheless, the following classifications are the most accurate representation I could achieve to reflect both secondary professional preferences and related qualities intimately associated with professional success in this society. Problems emerging from pronounced cases of crossover are discussed when appropriate.

The twenty-one occupations studied in the comparisons were selected on the basis of frequency of reference in the sources and significance in their respective categories. The military-executive fields were not used because no single occupation in this category provided a substantial number of cases. Also, these fields were somewhat ancillary to the activities of the elite. The financial-secretarial professions were represented by secretaries (kātibs) of various ranks and bureaus including the office of secretary of the chancellery (kātib al-sirr), steward or superintendant (mubāshir), bureau and court clerk (muwaqqiʿ), supervisor or controller (nāẓir) including supervisor of waqf endowments (nāẓir al-awqāf). The legal professions were represented by shaykhs, who were involved primarily with the legal affairs of religious communities, market inspectors (muḥtasibs), court notaries (shāhids), deputy judges (nāʾib qāḍīs), judges (qāḍīs), and chief justices (qāḍīs al-quḍāt) of the several legal schools. The artisan and commercial professions were represented by copyists (nāsikhs) and merchants (tājirs). The scholarly and educational professions were represented by repetitors or drill masters (muʿīds), professors (mudarrises)[5] and librarians (khāzins al-kutub). Finally, the religious functionaries were represented by leaders of prayer service (imāms), preachers of the Friday prayer and sermon (khaṭībs), Koran readers (muqriʾs), and pious ascetics (muʿtaqads).

The biographical sources yielded information on hundreds of other occupations, many of which may be closely associated with the ones selected here (Appendix II, Lists 1-21). Although they did not occur frequently enough to warrant plotting on the maps, they do shed light on the overall patterns of location and distribution, and were considered together with the basic groups they tended to parallel. This study will discuss the movements of individuals between different institutions at various stages of their careers, but the process is not depicted on the maps, each set of which indicates only one occupation.

Approximately 200 places of occupation or residence were cited in the biographical sources in relation to another variable, and about 150 of these were mentioned several times. Of these, 130 were located at least approximately on historical maps of Cairo during the later Middle Ages (Figs. 1-2). The maps are derivations from those drawn by Popper and Creswell, who both owe their initial introduction to the topography of Cairo to the works of Max Herz.[6] The primary sources used to aid in identifying, locating, and analyzing the institutions are, above all, Maqrīzī, and somewhat less, Ibn Duqmāq and ʿAlī Mubārak.[7] The secondary sources, largely produced by scholars associated with the Institut français d'archéologie orientale du Caire, deal primarily with the topography of Cairo prior to the Mamluk period. They are the works of Ravaisse, Casanova, Salmon, and Clerget.[8] Creswell's monumental accounts of medieval Egyptian architecture constitute the major secondary source for a number of institutions during the Mamluk period.[9] Unfortunately, even his works do not record every institution. More recently, Abu-Lughod and Staffa have completed studies of Cairo as an evolving urban society that contain valuable chapters on the medieval city, supported by interpretive maps.[10] A survey of sources dealing with education in Egypt from the Mamluk period to the early twentieth century has been compiled by Salama.[11] It includes summaries of a number of waqf documents concerning institutions of the Mamluk period. Appendix I gives descriptions of the major religio-academic institutions mentioned in this chapter.

CAIRO AS CITY AND METROPOLIS DURING THE CIRCASSIAN PERIOD

During the later Middle Ages Cairo was more than a city. It was a group of distinct urban centers, all related to one another, but each retaining traits from its own past. Although Fusṭāṭ and Old Cairo (Miṣr al-Qadīma) (198) represented the earliest centers of population, they had ceased to represent the focus of Cairene political and intellectual life for centuries prior to the Circassian Mamluk period. Rather, the metropolis of Cairo still exhibited the influence of the Fāṭimid city, as implied by the application of its title to the entire area in modern times. In contrast, the sources of the Mamluk period applied the name "al-Qāhira" specifically to the Fāṭimid rectangle that had developed into the northeastern section of the city (Fig. 1, NE). This rectangle, roughly a square mile in area, was originally restricted in access and reserved for the residences of the Fāṭimid court elite. It remained the center of both commercial and intellectual life in the Mamluk metropolis and retained elements of the plan imposed on its construction by its founders in the tenth century. The "Main Avenue," (145) which took its name from the royal square it had once bisected, the Bayn al-Qaṣrayn, still divided the rectangle.

By the fifteenth century, many of the Fāṭimid structures had disappeared and the orderly network of streets had been blurred by crowded alleys, dead-end covered streets, markets, and courts. During the Fāṭimid period the rectangle was the seat of both the administrative apparatus of the empire and the famous but somewhat mysterious shadow government of the Ismāʿīlī Dāʿīs. The two enormous palaces, the state mosques of al-Azhar and al-Ḥākim, the ceremonial squares, and the palaces and gardens of the wazīrs and court functionaries literally filled the area between the walls.[12]

After Ṣalāḥ al-Dīn's nephew, al-Malik al-Kāmil, transferred the executive and judicial apparatus of the state to the Citadel of the Mountain (172),[13] the rectangle ceased to be the political nerve center of the government, and the Fāṭimid structures were replaced, largely by commercial establishments and religio-academic institutions.[14] The early Ayyūbid sultans inaugurated this transition by founding several of these. Because the Fāṭimids were not regarded as liturgically legitimate by Sunnīs, the ʿulamaʾ of subsequent periods regarded Ṣalāḥ al-Dīn and his dynasty as the true founders of the scholarly tradition of Cairo. Religio-academic institutions that dated from his reign on into the height of the Baḥrī Mamluk period were regarded as bastions of religious orthodoxy and seats of untarnished Sunnī scholarship. Scholars and historians of later periods, keenly aware of their less favorable intellectual environments, were to look back at this age with considerable nostalgia and admiration. As a result, academic institutions established in the former Fāṭimid rectangle and dating from the Ayyūbid period attracted more respect and reverence than any others in Cairo or elsewhere in the Mamluk empire. The institutions in the rectangle that dated from the later Mamluk period did not enjoy the same status, but they were immensely wealthy. Their founders, primarily sultans and grand amirs, seem to have wished to equal instantly the glorious reputations of their predecessors by lavishing enormous sums both on the construction of their mosques, madrasas, and khānqāhs, and on the waqf endowments that maintained them. By the fifteenth century, the institutions dating from the Ayyūbid, Baḥrī, and early Circassian periods were gradually coalescing into a collegiate system. The former Fāṭimid rectangle had become a university town.

This northeast rectangle also included other social and economic activities, however. It remained the heart of a large city, and was not as dependent on its academic institutions for survival as were medieval Oxford or Cambridge. The seat of the highest civil judicial authority in Egypt was located in this rectangle, for example. The chief justices of the empire heard cases in several of the madrasas located here, and the majority of lower courts, although not based in any one particular institution, operated in this section. Also, during the Ayyūbid period, many of the major streets were transformed into markets and covered bazaars (called the Qaṣaba district). Caravansarays and khāns were founded in former gardens and squares. This formerly elite sector, reserved for government and administration, now maintained the highest concentration of mercantile and industrial enterprises in the metropolis.[15] The dominant position of the former Fāṭimid capital within the larger city was reflected in all the contemporary sources. Historians meant this district when they used the term "al-Qāhira." They referred to other urban districts by their own titles or as a part of the capital district. Institutions were designated as either inside (*dākhil*) or outside (*khārij*) al-Qāhira, and especially as within or without the walls and gates that defined the rectangle. So deeply imbedded in the popular mind were these walls and gates that the local population of modern Cairo still refer to them as locators, even though several of them no longer exist.

The southeastern section of the city (Fig. 1) developed into a truly urban area largely during mid-Ayyūbid times on into the Mamluk period. During the Fāṭimid period, this zone, lying between the rectangle and Aḥmad ibn Ṭūlūn's center of al-Qaṭā'i', contained vacant waste and rubbish heaps, interspersed with cemeteries and individual estates or parks. The central event stimulating the transformation of this zone into an urban area was the construction of the Citadel at the base of the Muqaṭṭam escarpment during the late twelfth and early thirteenth centuries. The Citadel was designed to accommodate the imperial court and the central bureaucracy, and fulfilled this function from its foundation into the nineteenth century. The areas lying between the Citadel and the Bāb Zuwayla, the southern entrance into the rectangle, were rapidly settled, and former roads and tracks became streets. An active commercial establishment grew up here, although it did not supplant or even rival the northeast rectangle until after the Mamluk period. This section differed from the rectangle in one important aspect. It owed its growth to the relatively dense settlement of Mamluk amirs along its streets, by the shores of the Elephant Lake (*Birkat al-Fīl*) and in the Qaṭā'i' and Qaṣr al-Kabsh districts (173). The amirs of both the Baḥrī and Circassian periods lavished their enormous incomes on great town houses, palaces in their own right. The proliferation of these houses supported an entire class of servants, civilian clients, and merchants who catered to the needs of the military elite.[16] The Mamluks' investment in huge building programs could be considered wanton squandering of essential cash revenues, but this section of the city did benefit. The southeastern zone attained its height of development during the third and final reign of al-Nāṣir Muḥammad ibn Qalā'ūn, 709-741/1309-

1340.[17] After his reign, a series of plagues and commercial depressions weakened the demographic and economic bases of the city, and this area, rapidly settled, now rapidly declined. It began to recover during the reign of Barqūq and was densely populated once again by the mid-fifteenth century. This southeastern section was never completely encircled by walls. The cemetery-like qualities of the areas near the Muqaṭṭam Hills and Desert Plain, and the plantation setting of the shores of the Birkat al-Fīl were never forgotten and were often recalled in textual references.

The Mamluk amirs did not confine their lavish spending to town houses, stables, and polo fields. Many built and endowed madrasas and khānqāhs—some in the northeastern, but most in the southeastern section of the city, close to their founders' palaces. The southeastern section thus became a center of religio-academic institutions second only to the former Fāṭimid rectangle. Most of these institutions dated from the reign of al-Nāṣir Muḥammad on, and were regarded as relative newcomers to the academic establishment. Although several were immensely wealthy, the nature of their influence on the ʿulamaʾ is unclear, as will be seen below.

The southwestern and northwestern sections of the city (Fig. 1), as defined by Popper, only partially developed into urban areas. They, along with the Ḥusaynīya quarter north of the Bāb al-Naṣr (142), remained primarily suburban-residential districts, plantations, and orchards. Indeed, these two sections had been reclaimed from the Nile swamps only during the preceding century, and several reservoir lakes testified to the high water level. Population in these sections tended to accumulate along the major roads traversing them between the northeast and southeast centers and the Nile shore ports. Only one distinct part of these sections is significant to this study. The Qaṭāʾiʿ and Qaṣr al-Kabsh districts (173) extended into the lower southwestern section. This included the ancient Ṭūlūnid mosque and several other madrasas founded by Mamluk amirs, the most prominent of which was the madrasa of Ṣarghatmish. Several palaces were built here, including that of Jaqmaq prior to his enthronement. The Ṭūlūnid mosque and madrasa of Ṣarghatmish are included in the discussion dealing with the southeast district, because of the contiguity and functional similarity of institutions.

The port of Būlāq and the Nile shore districts (Fig. 2:190-192), including Rawḏa Island, were somewhat removed from the city proper during the Middle Ages. The Nile shore districts were almost entirely residential and agricultural. Although several religio-academic institutions were founded there, they did not compare with those of the inner city in terms of prestige, scholarship, or numbers of students. Būlāq, however, was a highly developed commercial zone, its pulse attuned to trade and transferral of goods to and from the inner city. As the port of the capital, Būlāq maintained a bustling cosmopolitan atmosphere heightened by the mercantile and foreign population, both oriental and occidental, that took up residence there during the later Middle Ages. In terms of the individuals described in the biographical sources, however, Būlāq played an insignificant role in the intellectual or political culture of Cairo. Only seven institutions were mentioned there, and these infrequently.

The southernmost conglomeration of population in the metropolis was the center of Old Cairo (198), as it is called today. In late medieval times, this center was called Miṣr or Miṣr al-Qadīma; the biographical and narrative sources did not consider it a part of Cairo proper, but recognized it as a separate entity. Miṣr had its own courts; its markets were regulated by its own muḥtasib, who exercised his authority independently of his counterpart in Cairo.[18] This urban center had experienced an extremely varied, indeed turbulent, history over the centuries. The later medieval town represented only a remnant of the once-flourishing commercial city of Fusṭāṭ.[19] The abrupt termination of that city's existence in the final years of the Fāṭimid period is well known. By A.D. 1400, the sites of central and southern Fusṭāṭ remained an area of waste and rubbish heaps, as they do today, but the western district along the river, centering around the Mosque of ʿAmr ibn al-ʿĀṣ, had recovered elements of its former vitality. In general, this town maintained its concentration of Copts, the highest of any district in the metropolis. Several important Muslim religio-academic institutions were maintained here also, especially the ancient mosque of ʿAmr, which enjoyed the status of the oldest Muslim place of worship in Egypt. Several Ayyūbid and Mamluk amirs had contributed funds for the renovation of ʿAmr's mosque and for the foundation of others, but very few elected to settle in Miṣr themselves. This section of the metropolis did not constitute a primary center of ʿulamaʾ activity, according to the biographical sources.

The final district of the metropolis possessed yet a different character. It was composed of two areas, similar in function: the great cemetery or Qarāfa to the southwest of the Citadel (200), and the Desert Plain or Ṣaḥrāʾ to the east of the city proper (202). Here the notables of Cairo had been buried for centuries, their tombs forming a city in its own right. Such an extensive mortuary zone was unparalleled elsewhere in the Muslim world. The Qarāfa was filled with the tombs of notables from the Fāṭimid period on; the Desert Plain had been developed from the late Ayyūbid period, and primarily contained tombs of Mamluk amirs and sultans. This latter zone was, indeed, selected by most of the

Circassian sultans for their burial. The minarets and domes of their monuments still create a spectacular skyline.

These mortuary zones supported a class of tomb guards and custodians, who maintained and protected the monuments and were supported from waqfs endowed for this purpose. These people lived in the mortuary areas and formed their own social groupings, somewhat apart from the population of the other districts. Also, many of the tombs and all the great shrines of saints and revered scholars possessed munificent endowments to support pious ascetics and holy hermits. Some of the mortuary mosques (zāwiyas) supported the descendants of the saints buried there. Such individuals were revered by both the local population and the great Mamluks at the pinnacle of society. The sources provided many glimpses into the lives of these revered persons, but rarely on a sustained basis, since not all of them were regarded as truly learned, even if they were endowed with baraka.

In summary, the zones of the city that will constitute the primary foci of the study are the northeast rectangle and the southeastern districts, including the Citadel and Cross Street areas. Within these areas, the religio-academic institutions were very close to each other. In the northeast, most lay within walking distance of the others (one mile or less). The group of madrasas along the Bayn al-Qaṣrayn, for example, were built adjacent to one another. It would be quite possible to walk from hospice cell to the īwān class area for lectures and then on to a library, all of which were within a few hundred feet of each other. This proximity created an environment conducive to a continuous interchange of persons, ideas, methods, political discussion, and academic gossip—all essential to collegiate life in any age. The concentration of famous libraries here was very important, since books were rare and expensive, and relatively few institutions could afford to develop major book collections. The existence of so many libraries located in these collegiate clusters provided an unparalleled environment for study.

This concentration of religio-academic institutions in the northeast and southeast sections must be seen, however, in the context of the city as a whole. Cairo was no academic cloister. Beyond the gates of the madrasas and khānqāhs was the teeming bustle of a commercial and political universe, and, indeed, markets were often interspersed among the madrasas. Political life was not distant from the life of the scholars: the hand of the sultan or great amir was always involved in the affairs of major institutions, even though the Mamluks were anything but learned and publicly disdained the academician's career as effete. However, the Mamluks recruited many of their civilian cadres from these institutions. And they possessed enough political acumen to recognize

1. Entrance to the Māristān al-Manṣūrī

that politics were discussed by students and teachers, although the extent of significance the Mamluks attached to such elite civilian opinion remains an unresolved question.

The influence of the Mamluks was particularly apparent in the institutions they had founded and endowed themselves. These were expected to glorify the memory of their founders, usually buried there, and to serve the interests of their descendants, if any, who often used part of the endowment for their personal expenses. We shall examine the relative prestige of these institutions, mostly in the southeast quadrant, in relation to their counterparts in the northeast rectangle.

THE INSTITUTIONAL TYPES

The prominent institutions in the biographical texts fall into categories that are familiar to the student of Islamic culture, and their counterparts could be found throughout the Muslim world.[20] The most common was the mosque (*jāmiʿ*), literally a house of prayer or meeting. The great mosques of Muslim cities were traditionally centers of political and commercial activity as well as prayer, and were theoretically large enough to accommodate the entire adult male population of the community. During Friday prayer services at such great mosques, political events and governmental edicts were publicly announced. The male population of Cairo had, obviously, exceeded the capacity of any single building centuries prior to the late Mamluk period. By A.D. 1400 no single mosque could claim primacy, although al-Azhar still exhibited more characteristics of the cathedral mosque than any of its contemporaries. Indeed, mosques serving the community solely as a meeting place for worshipers were mentioned in the biographical sources, but not as often as more specialized institutions. These mosques, consistently listed as *jawāmiʿ* to distinguish them from other types, were probably not noted for any educational activities.

The seat of higher education during the central and later Middle Ages was the madrasa or collegiate mosque. The orthodox madrasa owed its prevalence in the East to the policy of the famous Saljūq wazīr, Niẓām al-Mulk, who founded the college named for him in Baghdād. The establishment of such institutions, dedicated to Sunnī learning, dates in Egypt from the reign of Ṣalāḥ al-Dīn; prior to the Ayyūbids, the academies (*diyār al-ʿilm*) had been centers of Ismāʿīlī teaching.[21] By the later Middle Ages, the madrasas of Cairo had evolved into elaborate institutions, supporting specialized staffs who taught advanced students. The curricula of these institutions centered around the orthodox Islamic sciences of jurisprudence; Koranic exegesis, recitation, and readings; Prophetic traditions; theology; and logic. All these basic areas were subdivided into numerous fields in which the specialist developed a recognized expertise. In addition to these sacred fields, the more secular disciplines, such as grammar and rhetoric, poetics and literature, history, secular philosophy, calligraphy, mathematics (arithmetics, geometry, and algebra), medicine, chemistry and alchemy, astronomy and chronometry (extremely important in a society using several calendars and time-keeping systems simultaneously) were taught, although not as part of the official curriculum.[22] In addition to its scholastic and educational activities, the madrasa remained a functioning mosque. Elementary schools for orphans (that is, orphanages, complete with dormitories and kitchens), hostels, poor houses, and public fountains were often attached to the wealthy madrasas. Therefore, even the most elite institutions were linked to the most humble elements of the society.

An institution in theory dedicated more directly to the care of the poor and needy and to those who sought to communicate with God by associating with a spiritual fraternity was the convent or khānqāh.[23] Ṣūfī khānqāhs did not exist in Egypt prior to the reign of Ṣalāḥ al-Dīn, although the Ismāʿīlī dāʿīs formed a restricted community in al-Azhar during the Fāṭimid period, and the ancient tradition of Coptic Christian monasticism and individual asceticism was highly respected by Egyptian Muslims as well as Christians. When Ṣalāḥ al-Dīn assumed power, the time was auspicious for the foundation of retreats for mystics seeking to perfect themselves in seclusion from the temporal world. The khānqāh, an institution borrowed from the cultures of eastern Islam, particularly Iran and Anatolia, rapidly became a revered and prestigious institution after the reign of Ṣalāḥ al-Dīn.

By the fifteenth century, Cairo maintained several prominent Ṣūfī khānqāhs. These institutions had acquired such a level of spiritual influence that many more eminent individuals wished to establish residence in them than could be accommodated. Access to them became competitive and political. Indeed, the great khānqāhs exercised a considerable influence over the Mamluk elite, which, like other military castes throughout the Muslim world, held groups of individuals dedicated to asceticism in great esteem. Sultans and grand amirs lavished substantial sums to endow the khānqāhs, and subsequently arranged to place members of their own families there. Due to the prestige and attractive living conditions offered by the wealthy khānqāhs,[24] many of the most distinguished members of the civilian elite sought to gain admission to them, at least temporarily. Sharing in a communal life, a rather heterogeneous group of notables—including pious ascetics, worldly scholars, and even a number of militarists—lived together for a period of their lives. The dynamic tension produced by such a dissimilar group held together by a commitment (taken for a variety of reasons) to communal self-perfection was very stimulating. The khānqāhs of Cairo therefore became centers of both intellectual and political ferment, often more significant than either the madrasas or the Palace itself.[25]

The khānqāhs of Cairo at the beginning of the Circassian period, with rich endowments from their founders and from subsequent rulers, amirs, and merchants, were expensive enterprises which, of course, produced no material assets in return. The standard of living enjoyed by their residents and expectations concerning the maintenance of such a standard were high, even though communal asceticism remained a primary goal. Teaching and scholarship took place in the khānqāhs, and a variety of charitable institutions were associated with them: libraries, orphanages, kitchens, public fountains, baths, and public oratories for continuous recitation of the Koran during festivals. This last institution was usually set up in galleries (shabābīk) around the tomb of the founder, if he were buried in the convent. The khānqāhs thus absorbed a substantial amount of capital, and provided support for a variety of specialized groups that were associated with them.

Finally, it must be stressed that, with one exception,[26] the khānqāhs of Cairo were urban institutions. They provided a degree of seclusion from temporal society and mundane affairs, but never total separation. The Ṣūfīs who resided in them never intended to withdraw completely from active involvement with life in their city.

A fourth type of institution was the hospital or māristān, which in later medieval Islam was confined to large cities. The māristān was primarily a center for medical treatment, but it served several other social functions. It was a convalescent home for both the aged and for patients recovering from disease or accidents. And it was a retirement home for elderly infirm persons who lacked a family to support them in their old age. Most of the individuals discussed in the sources who lived out their final years in the māristān and died there had achieved renown and were recognized as ʿulama', but had no children or fiscal assets to support them. The biographical sources do not tell us whether the infirm and aged common people could gain access to the hospital in their final years.

The māristān was a complex organization maintaining, first of all, a staff of physicians who specialized in various categories of disease and who also taught students. Students learned in an apprenticeship system, and were expected to aid the physician in administering treatment. The physicians were assisted by a host of nonprofessional stewards and aids (mubāshirūn). It is likely that these individuals functioned as orderlies and agents for the professional staff. Male and female patients were cared for by special servants (farrāshūn), both men and women. Direction of the māristān's bureaucracy lay in the hands of the supervisor or controller (nāẓir), who did not, according to the biographical sources, receive any particular training in medicine. The post appears to have been lucrative, since the nāẓir had access to the waqf funds supporting the institution, and could draw up the budget according to his own purposes. Appointment to the office of nāẓir al-māristān seems to have been based primarily on political connections. This would raise the question of how well the hospital was administered over time.

The māristān represented a substantial expense, particularly since most founders wished to defray the patients' fees for treatment. Individual physicians might have charged fees, but the hospital was a charity in God's sight and, theoretically, no charges were to be assessed patients.[27] To support the cost of such a diverse facility and staff, an array of waqfs were set up from all over the state. The maintenance of the waqfs in their original form, secure from manipulation and transfer, remained a controversial issue, because without them even the elites might be denied medical care.

A fifth kind of institution in Cairo was built around the tombs of notables. There were two types: the shrine of a revered person (zāwiya), and the burial place of a powerful and wealthy politician. The first of these types, a saint's burial place, had its counterparts throughout the Muslim world. The more ancient shrines tended to accumulate both veneration and endowments. Various regimes rebuilt and gave gifts to famous shrines continuously, until vast complexes grew up around an originally humble edifice. Individuals attached to these shrines not only benefited from the endowments, but also absorbed some of the baraka emanating from the saint buried there. Such shrines attracted individuals who, possessing their own baraka, tended to congregate around the complexes as communities of revered persons.

The tombs of powerful politicians—primarily the great Mamluks during our period—could never attain the reputations enjoyed by the shrines; too many sultans and amirs had earned unsavory reputations in the popular mind. However, these men were immensely rich and sought to lure ascetics to settle in their tombs, recite prayers over their graves, and be buried there. These tombs were often associated with madrasas and khānqāhs. The ʿulamaʾ attached to them often read prayers over the sarcophagi of the founders. The tombs of sultans and amirs therefore usually formed a part of the religio-academic network, while the shrines and zāwiyas were less likely to belong to an associated madrasa or Ṣūfī hospice. Revered persons were more likely to congregate

2. Interior of the Mausoleum of Qāytbāy

voluntarily in the latter institutions, although the Mamluk tombs offered them substantial fiscal benefits.

The sixth category of institutions reflected in the biographies is unrelated to those discussed above, as they served no religious or educational functions. These were the bureaucracies of the imperial court, both local and in other countries. The major organizations to be considered here were the ministries (dīwāns), which supported the majority of individuals engaged in secretarial and financial occupations. The dīwāns of the imperial court were housed in the Citadel complex and in royal residences throughout Egypt and Syria. The staffs of amirs were housed in their residences, rural estates, and urban properties. The sources were far less precise about the location of these secular activities than for the religio-academic ones, since the biographers were primarily concerned with legal, scholarly, and spiritual figures. They often mentioned the secular fields, but rarely located or described them in detail.[28]

Finally, the wide range of commercial enterprises must be mentioned. A great variety of shops (ḥawānīt), markets, caravansarays, baths, and khāns were mentioned in the biographical sources. These were rarely located, but other sources, particularly Maqrīzī, have provided topographical details for many of them. These centers of trade were also the seats of local courts, notaries, currency changers, and service occupations such as barbers, food and drink venders, bath attendants, and so on. Since this study focuses on the civilian elite, these occupations are somewhat marginal for us, as they are in the sources.[29] One must keep in mind, however, that the religio-academic institutions were scattered among myriad commercial establishments, whose presence is felt continually in the biographical literature.

THE DISTRIBUTION OF GEOGRAPHIC GROUPS

Just as the geographic origins of the Cairo ʿulamaʾ can be seen to follow certain patterns, so distribution of the ʿulamaʾ in the city reveals trends that contribute to our understanding of the urban religio-academic network. While analyzing the nature of this network, I shall be attempting to define the city's cosmopolitanism, to pinpoint where it applied, and to detect both continuities and variations that may relate to geographic origins. The broader questions of the impact of cosmopolitanism on civilian politics and legal practice, on the quality of higher learning, and on the perspectives of students—and whether the students' contact with foreign scholars and jurists served to widen or restrict their outlook—are all difficult issues, requiring consultation of a wider variety of sources than biographical literature. But the foundation for such a study consists of the geographic data this literature yields.

From the narrower perspective of this analysis, two questions must be considered: first, where was there a genuinely cosmopolitan intellectual establishment, that is, institutions appointing individuals of non-Cairene birth or attested derivation to their staffs? And, conversely, which elements of the religio-academic network seem to have played no appreciable role in this international legal-academic milieu? We shall see that the majority of institutions endowed for higher learning do not appear to have played an active role in the international scholarly network of the central Muslim world. Indeed, affinity with this network would seem to constitute one of the factors determining a limited group of elite institutions that were prominent in all aspects of scholarship and legal training in Cairo.

The limitations on the data that applied to the analysis of geographic origins also apply here. The methodology provides the most accurate results for those regions for which there are extensive data: provinces of the Mamluk Empire. But even the limited data from the other areas may be interpreted as indicating the actual foreign presence in the religio-academic network of Cairo. Since the compilers of the biographical sources, especially al-Sakhāwī, wished to be comprehensive, one may assume that the patterns appearing for the several geographic groups are as complete as possible. Therefore, even when arguments are based on the minimal evidence available for the smaller foreign elements of the civilian elite, one can be reasonably sure of accurate proportional representation. There is no indication that either compiler tried to limit coverage of any ethno-geographic group, or even that either was sensitive to national distinctions. They reported geographic data in order to distinguish individual persons as precisely as possible.

Before proceeding with a survey of the geographic groups, a word on the three variables is in order. The terms "educational," "occupational," and "residential" sites are based on rather specific usages in the texts. The first refers to formal enrollment in an institution of higher learning, usually a madrasa but on occasion another type, almost invariably reported together with the instructor supervising or certifying progress in a specific discipline or curriculum item.[30] The educational pattern revealed important distinctions between institutions and institutional types, even though the pattern was most complete for native-born Cairenes and Lower Egyptians, and was based on progressively less information for persons from Syria-Palestine, Upper Egypt, Iran, the Maghrib, Anatolia, the Arabian Peninsula, and Iraq (no ranking variations were discernible for the last three). Clearly, most individuals outside the

Cairo-Delta heartland had inaugurated or even completed their educations prior to their arrival in the capital.

The second variable, occupational sites, refers to remunerative appointed positions in an institution or a governmental bureaucracy. The information for this variable was the most complete for all the geographic groups, and the pattern based on it therefore most accurately depicts their distribution in the religio-academic network of the city.[31] However, it is important to stress the distinction between positions held within this network, which were specifically located, and bureaucratic offices, the majority of which were not.[32] Thus, the occupational pattern is primarily illuminating for positions associated with institutions founded and endowed for higher learning.

The third variable, residence, is the most specialized and limited. It refers almost exclusively to extended habitation in an endowed institution which, we may presume, supported the individual's housing and food requirements during his tenure there. This pattern emphasized the khānqāhs and is most accurate for individuals associated with Ṣūfī communities. However, residence in these communities did not require exclusive identification with a mystic order. Indeed, the array of backgrounds revealed in the biographies of persons involved with khānqāhs is so varied that the residence pattern remains a useful indicator, provided that its limitations are recognized. The residence pattern was not, in fact, restricted to khānqāhs, but it was confined within the religio-academic network. There were very few cases of residence in private households reported, and for this reason the biographical sources contribute little to our knowledge of where most of the ʿulamaʾ—those who maintained private homes and belonged to extended families—lived.

Finally, since the same geographic indicators as in Chapter II—nisbas and birthplaces—constitute the basis for the three surveys discussed above, the same problems of nisba overlap apply. Accordingly, all maps supporting the following discussion (Figs. 3-8) depict both nisbas and birthplaces.

THE METROPOLIS OF CAIRO
(Figs. 3-A through 3-E)

Those individuals born in the city or its environs predictably constituted the largest group reported in the biographical sources. Nevertheless, they did not always constitute the largest element in the comparative surveys. That non-Cairene groups were substantially represented in several of the surveys suggests the cosmopolitan nature of the Mamluk capital. On the basis of the information available, the individuals born in Cairo tended to pursue their studies in a limited set of institutions, a trend that also holds for other geographic groups. The noticeable concentration in the Ẓāhirīya madrasa (23)[33] was supplemented by representation in Kāmilīya (19), Barqūqīya (20), Nāṣirīya (21), and Ṣāliḥīya (26)—all part of the Bayn al-Qaṣrayn cluster. The second concentration appeared at the Baybarsīya khānqāh (13), but the representations for Saʿīd al-Suʿadāʾ (15) and other major Ṣūfī hospices (84) were small, suggesting that the student communities of these institutions included many individuals from outside the city. Such a hypothesis is further supported by the relatively low representation reported for al-Azhar (36)—nine in all—which sustains the hypothesis that al-Azhar was a center of study for non-Cairenes and foreigners. Even so, the high status of the institution and the esteem in which it was held by all inhabitants of the city make this low figure paradoxical.

Outside the Fāṭimid district, there were only three noteworthy concentrations of Cairenes at educational institutions: Shaykhūnīya (84), the Ṭūlūnid Mosque (91) and the Citadel (135).[34] What may we deduce from this pattern? In general, there is no question that madrasas dominated the educational configuration. Yet, although representation for the khānqāhs was lower, the fact that some individuals studied the Sunnī Islamic sciences at houses ostensibly dedicated to mysticism would suggest that these institutions were integrated into the orthodox religio-academic network, and that they served to some degree in the formal training of the ʿulamaʾ. It is also true that both types of institution belonged to an exclusive group: the Festival Gate and Bayn al-Qaṣrayn clusters and the cathedral mosque—all in the northeast—and that al-Azhar combined the two in one complex. The only institution in the southeast of equivalent prominence was Shaykhūnīya, a college-hospice complex. It is well known that madrasas were seats of higher learning during the medieval period, and less well known that certain Ṣūfī communal houses functioned within the formal educational system. But the predominance of a few institutions of both types permit speculation on the actual composition of the hierarchies that governed both scholastic activity and entry into the upper echelons of the ʿulamaʾ class. The educational survey reveals little about scores of other institutions, all in theory dedicated and endowed to the same purpose. A phenomenon of preferential ranking would seem apparent.

The distribution of occupations (Figs. 3-B, 3-C) involved the largest number of cases for any survey, and Cairenes appear to have been the most thoroughly dispersed of the geographic groups. Their representation in the prominent institutions, such as the two collegiate clusters, al-Azhar (36) and the two royal Circassian madrasas (30, 51), was proportionally lower than for any other geographic group, although the pattern for persons from the Delta was closely parallel. Also, their representation in these institutions was relatively uniform, indicating a broad dispersion of indigenous Cairenes professionally engaged in both the major and minor institutions of the Fāṭimid district. The parallel between their configuration and that of individuals from the Delta suggests that these two groups shared more common characteristics in terms of distribution, education pursued, occupations, and legal-religious identities than either did with any other group. This occupational configuration for the native-born of the capital can be regarded as a model against which all the other occupational patterns can be compared.

Occupational representation of these groups in the other districts of the city was more limited, also establishing a model. In the southeast, there were more Cairenes than any other group, but the trend was similar. Even this largest geographic element failed to appear at the Mamluk foundations of the district in proportions equivalent to their representation in the northeast. There were several obvious exceptions, the same as those in the educational pattern—Shaykhūnīya (83-84), the Ṭūlūnid mosque (91), the Citadel—with one addition, the mosque of Sultan Ḥasan (74). The large concentration at Shaykhūnīya was predictable: this khānqāh ranked among the most prestigious institutions in the city, the only one of such high status outside the northeast. The concentration of Cairenes at the Ṭūlūnid mosque, the Ḥasanīya madrasa, and the Citadel (including the imperial court [131-132, 135-136], the Nāṣirī mosque [68] and the Mamluk barracks [134]) was not matched by any other group, suggesting that Cairenes were more visible in these institutions. The cases of the Ṭūlūnid mosque and the Ḥasanīya madrasa may reflect local interests and contacts, but the concentration in the Citadel complex implied association with the royal household—the administrative center of the empire and ultimate seat of political authority. Other concentrations appeared in other sections of Cairo, especially in the mosque of ʿAmr ibn al-ʿĀṣ (113) in Old Cairo, indicating that this mosque was staffed primarily by local residents. Representation of Cairenes was apparent in the two mortuary zones of the Qarāfa and Ṣaḥrāʾ, but it was not noticeably greater than for other geographic groups that were numerically much smaller. These other groups, particularly the Anatolians, in other words, produced proportionately more individuals who sought out the specialized environment of the mortuary zones than did the native-born Cairenes. In the northwest and southwest districts and the Būlāq port area, there were more Cairenes reported than anyone else, but in proportion to the size of the total group from which they were drawn, their proportion was again relatively low.

The occupational pattern raises questions about the nature of the religio-academic network. The sparse distribution of the majority group indicates that many Cairene jurist-scholars were employed in institutions not mentioned in the educational survey. It is possible to hypothesize that the majority of the less prominent institutions of the city were staffed primarily by Cairenes, perhaps by less eminent persons, as measured by qualifications, family background, and political connections. This issue becomes significant when one contemplates the low number of students reported for the majority of endowed institutions, especially the wealthy amirate madrasas of the southeast.

The residence pattern (Figs. 3-D, 3-E) shows the majority of individuals established in the two Festival Gate khānqāhs: Saʿīd al-Suʿadāʾ (15) and Baybarsīya (13). These two sites accounted for about 60 percent of the total references. Although aggregations appeared for several other major institutions, none compared with these two hospices. Such a concentration implies a pervasive identification with Saʿīd al-Suʿadāʾ and Baybarsīya, an identification shared by many Lower Egyptians. What this signifies in terms of spiritual outlook, affiliation with mystic organizations (but not necessarily formal membership in a Ṣūfī order), and the political activities of the civilian elite in a setting providing some degree of sanctuary awaits further study. But the extraordinary concentration of persons whose birthplace was Cairo or the Delta was clearly shown, and underscores the prominence of the Festival Gate khānqāhs. It may be that the smaller aggregates at Shaykhūnīya (84) and Siryāqūs (130) imply that they attracted a larger percentage of outsiders than did the Festival Gate houses. The social and political implications of these variations will be discussed in Chapter V.

THE NILE DELTA
(Figs. 4-A through 4-F)

As previously noted, the largest number of individuals originating in or maintaining ties with regions outside Cairo came from the Delta districts, and their influence transcended even their numerical preponderance. The numbers and widespread dispersion of individuals from the Delta may be explained partly in terms of proximity. Cairo was their capital city, and moving there meant no long and difficult journey or change of state and culture for them. However, the concentrations of these individuals cannot be explained solely by proximity and common ethnicity. Individuals from the Delta tended to study, work, and reside in distinct sets of institutions—the same as those in which Cairenes gathered. The prominence of these institutions attests to the influence of Delta people among the civilian elite. Indeed, so interrelated were the Cairo and Delta people that they should be interpreted as a single geographic group and their region should be considered a core zone.

The educational pattern (Figs. 4-A, 4-B) was similar to the profile for indigenous Cairenes, revealing the same set of institutions. Several madrasas of the northeast predominated; Ẓāhirīya (23) and al-Azhar (36) accounted for more than 50 percent of all references.[35] The majority of the remaining references were to the institutions of the two collegiate clusters. Only the madrasa-khānqāh complex of Shaykhūnīya (83-84) in the southeast exhibited a concentration outside the Fāṭimid district. The high proportionate representation for al-Azhar constitutes the major difference between the patterns for indigenous Cairenes and those from the Delta, and we will see the prominence of al-Azhar for all ethnogeographic groups originating outside the capital. Ẓāhirīya had only a slightly lower concentration than al-Azhar. This suggests, first, that both institutions were regarded as major centers of study in both the Ḥanafī and Shāfiʿī madhhabs; and second, that both institutions may well have maintained ties with institutions in the provincial towns of the Delta. The biographical sources repeatedly mentioned that an individual was encouraged to study at a certain madrasa because his local teacher had contacts there. Since individuals from the Delta were very influential in the dominant Shāfiʿī school of the Egyptian legal community, the prominence of these institutions would imply their critical role in the training of the ruling judicial establishment. Entry into and promotion within this establishment would depend in large part on admission to one of these institutions, and al-Azhar, of course, functioned as a center for students who had no family in the city. Shaykhūnīya, very prominent for Ḥanafī jurisprudence, would also seem to have had a highly cosmopolitan student community, similar to that of al-Azhar. The pronounced concentration of the Delta people in the two collegiate clusters, al-Azhar and Shaykhūnīya indicates that these institutions constituted the points of entry into the judicial establishment and thus into the ʿulamaʾ of Cairo. The core of Cairo's learned community, originating either in the city or the Delta, was trained in them.[36]

The pattern of occupational sites for Delta people (Figs. 4-C, 4-D) paralleled that for indigenous Cairenes, but a tendency toward concentration in the major institutions of the northeast is noticeable. The Festival Gate and Bayn al-Qaṣrayn clusters revealed the largest collective concentrations, although al-Azhar (36) and Muʾayyadīya (51) represented the largest single conglomerates.[37] The concentration at al-Azhar is significant; given the sustained representation of other non-Egyptian groups at this institution (which combined mosque, madrasa, and khānqāh in a single structure), it stands out as a major locus of interaction between ʿulamaʾ from all over the Muslim world, and was possibly the most cosmopolitan and standardized institution in the capital. All these foundations, in fact, produced similar training in scholarship, teaching, religious service, medicine, and administration. It is not surprising that individuals from the Delta, trained in these institutions, were widely active in these fields. The one important occupational category in which Cairene and Delta persons from these foundations did not predominate involved bureaucratic activities of the government. Here, certain non-Egyptian groups figured equally.

The striking decrease in numbers of Delta people in all other districts of the city should be compared with the proportionate representation of Cairenes and certain other geographic groups. Some Delta people held positions in the southeast, particularly at Shaykhūnīya (83-84), but no large concentrations appeared. The southeast quarter was primarily the seat of institutions founded by Mamluk amirs and sultans, and of the royal bureaucracy housed in the Citadel. Individuals from the Delta did not predominate in these institutions, even though they were more numerous than any other non-Cairene element. Although the biographical sources failed to locate precisely most bureaucratic offices, the location of amirate madrasas is certain, and the low proportion of Delta people in them is noteworthy.

In the northwest and southwest, only the madrasa of Ṣarghatmish (92) and the Ṭūlūnid mosque (91) had concentrations of individuals from the Delta. The Qarāfa and Ṣaḥrāʾ districts did reveal aggregates of these people, but they were not significant. The pious ascetics and holy hermits, so many of whom came from the Delta, seem to have identified more with the great mystic hospices than with the rather isolated sites in the mortuary zones.

The residence pattern (Figs. 4-E, 4-F) was so extremely concentrated that most ʿulamaʾ of Deltaic origin seem to have been associated with three institutions: Saʿīd al-Suʿadāʾ (15), al-Azhar (36), and Baybarsīya (13), in ranked order.[38] Since the first and third functioned primarily as hospices for Ṣūfīs, the pattern suggests not only that a high percentage of the Lower Egyptians tended to seek membership in a spiritual community, but that they preferred these two houses to either Shaykhūnīya (84) or Siryāqūs (130). This should be compared to the patterns reported for non-Egyptians, in which Shaykhūnīya predominates. In general, the pattern would accord with the hypothesis that the central districts of Gharbīya and Minūfīya constituted a regional "saints zone" with a highly developed network of local khānqāhs and zāwiyas, in which individuals transferring to Cairo received their initiation into taṣawwuf (mystic principles). The concentration for al-Azhar confirms its function as a hospice for students and scholars from outside the city. The Azhar complex certainly attracted many Ṣūfīs, although not as many as went to the two major khānqāhs.

THE NILE VALLEY
(Figs. 5-A through 5-E)

Many fewer Upper Egyptians lived in Cairo than did people from the Delta. The overall numbers for the Ṣaʿīdīs throughout the metropolis were smaller than for those from Syria-Palestine, and only slightly larger than those for Iranians. Moreover, there was a more even balance in their distribution between the northeastern and southeastern districts. Their proportionate representation in the northeast, an indicator of relative status within the civilian elite, was less pronounced. This would suggest their lack of influence as a group in the religio-academic establishment. However, any such generalization must be qualified both by their consistent representation in the major institutions and by the modest size of the sample. Although data on educational sites (Fig. 5-A) were sparse, all three concentrations—at al-Azhar (36), Ẓāhirīya (23), and Ṣarghatmishīya (92)—were within the network of core institutions, which reflects the degree of successful entry by individuals from this group into the major training centers. Even though the sample is very small, it probably does represent the Upper Egyptian presence within the ʿulamaʾ class of the city because the compilers tried to be comprehensive. Upper Egyptians were clearly able to gain access to the restricted circle of institutions providing entry into the upper echelons of the learned community.

How did they fare once they arrived? The distribution of occupational sites (Figs. 5-B, 5-C) confirmed the placement of Upper Egyptians in the core group: the two collegiate clusters, al-Azhar, Ashrafīya (30), Muʾayyadīya (51), and Shaykhūnīya (83). Yet the relatively even balance between the northeast and southeast may suggest that Upper Egyptians tended to accept more positions in the more recent and less exclusive amirate madrasas than did their counterparts from the Delta, who managed more readily to penetrate the institutions of the rectangle (though there were, of course, individuals, such as al-Suyūṭī and his father, who were able to ascend to the highest levels).

Upper Egyptians were virtually absent from the northwest and southwest districts and Būlāq. In the Desert Plain and the southern cemetery there were more of them, implying that the Ṣaʿīd did produce ascetics who settled in the mortuary zones.

The residence pattern (Figs. 5-D, 5-E) exhibited the only substantial concentrations of the group. Many Upper Egyptians congregated in Saʿīd al-Suʿadāʾ (15) during this period.[39] Al-Azhar, however, did not exceed several other sites in the district. A second concentration occurred in Shaykhūnīya (83-84) in the southeast.[40] The concentration at Saʿīd al-Suʿadāʾ suggests the geographically diverse character of that khānqāh's community, a trend paralleled but not surpassed by al-Azhar and the other major hospices. The representation of Upper Egyptians in these institutions confirms the existence of mystics from Upper Egypt, and it should be compared with the Ṣaʿīdīs in the Ṣaḥrāʾ and Qarāfa, who lived withdrawn from society.

One of the few cases of an individual resident in the wilderness of the Muqaṭṭam (201) was a Ṣaʿīdī.[41] He or his family came from the area of Minyat Banī Khaṣīb in Ushmunayn district. He was regarded as both a muʿtaqad and a majdhūb, or one who, as an elect communicant with the divine, was subject to trances and spells of holy sickness or convulsions. Such individuals were respected by the Ṣūfī orders but appeared highly eccentric to the general population. These individuals tended to live alone in remote forbidding areas under conditions of extreme privation. They followed the tradition of Christian holy hermits, many native to the Upper Valley, from the pre-Islamic period.

SYRIA-PALESTINE

(Figs. 6-A, 6-B, 6-D through 6-E)

This group, the largest from a non-Egyptian region, was prominently represented throughout the religio-academic establishment. The pattern for educational sites (Fig. 6-A) reflects a trend repeated for all the remaining geographic groups. The majority of individuals from Syria-Palestine had completed their formal studies before transferring to Cairo, but the data available indicate that those who elected to continue their studies in Cairo were concentrated in the major centers of legal scholarship and mystic discipline. The institutions cited belonged to the elite core, with the exception of Ṣarghatmishīya (92), the only amirate madrasa included. References to the hospices were to be expected, since they had been founded in part to provide foreign students with living accommodations. The Syrians seem to have been less inclined toward identification with Ṣūfī institutions than any other ethno-geographic element in the city. But there was an even balance between Shaykhūnīya (84) and the khānqāhs of the Festival Gate complex (13, 15). The latter two outweighed Shaykhūnīya in proportionate representation of persons from the Cairo-Delta zone. Shaykhūnīya was clearly more prominent for foreigners, and particularly Syrians engaged in formal study. Yet the one striking concentration appeared at Ẓāhirīya (23), that paramount center of Shāfiʿī and Ḥanafī jurisprudence.[42] Syrians were attracted to this college specifically to train themselves in advanced treatises on the Sharīʿa and to prepare for legal careers in the capital. Down the street, they could observe the four chief justices in the Ṣāliḥīya court at work. This high concentration at Ẓāhirīya suggests its reputation within the Mamluk state as the prime center of advanced juridical study in the capital.

Although the pattern of occupational distribution (Figs. 6-B, 6-D) revealed a variety of fields, it did not do justice to the Syrian presence in several professional categories. The Syrians were very active in both the executive and the bureaucracy, and since we rarely have information on the location of institutions in these fields, this critical dimension of the Syrian presence eludes us. Were we to possess better data, the configuration might well reveal a majority of Syrians based in the southeast or Mamluk zone—the only probable case of a preponderance of some group in a district other than the northeast. The pattern that we do have depicts appointments within the religio-academic network, including those bureaucratic offices related to its administration. Even given the concentration in the Fāṭimid district, there are deviations from the model established by the Cairo-Delta group. Although the two collegiate clusters were predictably prominent, the two royal madrasas, Ashrafīya (30) and Mu'ayyadīya (51), figured large in the distribution. Most of those who received appointments to chairs in the major institutions had already attained considerable renown in their own country, but the individuals invited to the two royal madrasas came initially at the behest of the founders themselves. The concentration at Mu'ayyadīya attests to its founder's close ties with his Syrian clients.[43]

There were two distinct aggregates of Syrians in the southeast: at Shaykhūnīya (83) and the Ṭūlūnid mosque (91). The former reconfirms the pronounced Syrian association with this madrasa-khānqāh complex, a respected center of Ḥanafī jurisprudence, along with Ṣarghatmishīya (92) just down the street.[44] For the Ṭūlūnid mosque, in the same quarter, Syrians constituted the largest foreign representation. The Ṭūlūnid mosque was not a major center of fiqh scholarship during the period, let alone of Ḥanafī studies, so the reason for this concentration of Syrians is not clear. In contrast, Syrians were only modestly represented in the amirate madrasas of the district, despite their close association with Mamluks. Surprisingly, the Iranians outnumbered the Syrians in these institutions.

The residence pattern (Figs. 6-E, 6-F) reveals a modest aggregate of

Syrians in the khānqāhs and hospices belonging to the elite group in the northeast. The sites paralleled those in the occupational distribution: Baybarsīya (13), Saʿīd al-Suʿadā' (15), Barqūqīya (20), Ashrafīya (30), and Mu'ayyadīya (51). Only one individual was reported for al-Azhar (36). The extraordinary paucity of Syrians in the southeast reflects the type of evidence reported in the biographical sources, but it may also indirectly clarify our concept of their presence in the city. Syrians maintained proportionately closer ties with the military elite than any other civilian group except the Copts. Yet in the southeast zone of high Mamluk concentration, there do not seem to have been many Syrians entrenched in institutions founded by those who may be assumed to have been their patrons. This pattern may confirm the proclivity of Syrians to penetrate the bureaucratic apparatus of the state. Those who pursued scholarly and judicial careers in Cairo, quite possibly a minority of the total Syrian presence, would not have migrated to Cairo unless they were eminent enough to establish themselves in the elite institutions. The Syrians who came to the capital as clients of Mamluks, possibly a majority, pursued careers that were not associated directly with the religio-academic network, and thus do not appear in these surveys.

There were few Syrians in all other districts of the metropolis. The figures for the Būlāq area suggest that only a few were engaged in trade or commerce in the port district. The minimal numbers reported for the two mortuary zones support the evidence in Chapter II that few Syrians were muʿtaqads or majdhūbs. This reinforces the impression that the Syrian presence in Cairo was pronouncedly bureaucratic. Because only the people actively involved with the religio-academic network of the city were well depicted in the biographical sources, the majority of Syrians, whose careers were probably spent in the service of their Mamluk patrons, was not adequately described there. Accordingly, the impression we have of the Syrian distribution in the capital is incomplete.

THE IRANIAN AREAS
(Figs. 6-A, 6-C through 6-F)

Unlike the Syrians, the Iranians in Cairo were primarily scholar-teachers and religious functionaries. Since they were tied to the religio-academic network of the city, the Iranians can be located more accurately than the Syrians, despite the smaller size of their sample. The educational pattern (Fig. 6-A) was very sparse, indicating that few Iranians who could be identified as such studied in Cairo. Most arrived after completing their educations.[45] No concentrations of them appeared, and the few institutions that had as many as a handful were Baybarsīya (13), Jamālīya

(16), Ẓāhirīya (23), al-Azhar (36), and Ṭaybarsīya (37) in the northeast; Maḥmūdīya (57), the madrasa of Aṣlam (54), and Shaykhūnīya (83) in the southeast. All these Iranians were pursuing advanced studies under noted scholars. Indeed, except for two people, one at each of the amirate madrasas, all Iranians doing advanced study in Cairo were at the elite institutions.[46]

The occupational pattern (Figs. 6-C, 6-D) reflected more of the Iranian presence. There was a relatively even balance between the numbers of individuals at the elite institutions and those at the amirate madrasas; the contrast with the Delta pattern is quite striking. There were between five and ten nisba references connected with several institutions, although references to birthplaces remained relatively infrequent. Concentrations appeared in the two collegiate clusters, Bāsiṭīya (11), al-Azhar (36), Mu'ayyadīya (51), and Abū Bakrīya (48) in the northeast; in Maḥmūdīya (57), Ṣūdūn min Zāda (70), Aljayhīya (69), Ḥasanīya (74), Aytmishīya (62), the Citadel mosque (68), and Ṣarghatmishīya (92) in the southeast; and Siryāqūs (130) north of the city. The prominence of Iranians in both the prestigious institutions of the old Fāṭimid district and the amirate colleges suggests that they were highly regarded by both their Egyptian peers and by the Mamluk elite, which tended to appoint at least the initial staffs of their foundations. The Mamluk emphasis on the Ḥanafī madhhab in the curricula of their foundations may also have influenced the appointment of large numbers of Iranians to their staffs: many of the Iranian ʿulama' in Cairo were connected with this school. Moreover, the Iranians had been less exposed to the hostile polarization between the ʿulama' and the Mamluks in the empire. They and their descendants appear to have remained somewhat aloof from the mutual antagonism that often complicated relationships between the literary and military elites of Egypt and Syria. Indeed, the Iranians seem to have had a facility for accepting a condition of authority and adjusting to it in a profitable way. Many had developed such a facility of necessity after the Mongol invasions. They thus may have been more inclined, proportionately, to accept posts in the amirate madrasas than were their Egyptian colleagues—who may, conversely, have been treated with greater antipathy by the Mamluk founders.

The residence pattern (Figs. 6-E, 6-F) showed settlement of Iranians to have been confined largely to the northeast.[47] The concentrations appeared in all the large khānqāhs except Shaykhūnīya (13, 15, 130) (in contrast, note that no references to Syrians were reported for Siryāqūs), in the collegiate clusters, al-Azhar (36), and the two royal Circassian madrasa-hospices (30, 51). The individuals resident in the khānqāhs were uniformly Ṣūfīs. Only a few Iranians lived in other sections of the city, including the two mortuary zones. Even though Iran produced famous mystics throughout the Middle Ages, Ṣūfī shaykhs, pious ascetics, and holy hermits did not necessarily all follow the same type of life, and the Iranians tended not to locate in the isolated and austere environment of the cemeteries. The Iranians resident in the Qarāfa lived in the complex surrounding Imām al-Shāfiʿī's tomb (115). Several Iranians were teaching in the mausoleum madrasa of Yashbak and the Succor Dome (Qubbat al-Naṣr) (6-D: 127, 126).

ANATOLIA
(Figs. 7-A through 7-D)

The remaining non-Egyptians did not appear frequently enough to produce many concentrations. However, a few clusters did emerge, suggesting several trends.

The Anatolians or Rūmīs contrasted with the Iranians because many of them were not scholars, and with the Syrians because relatively few of them were bureaucrats. Their pattern of educational sites (Fig. 7-A) was sparse, and can only indicate that relatively few Anatolians completed their formal studies in Cairo. Those who did appear attended a few madrasas of the northeast and southeast. Only Shaykhūnīya (83) had as many as two cases. Outside the inner city, there was one case in Siryāqūs (130).

The distribution of occupations (Figs. 7-B, 7-C) was more illuminating. Due to the one discernible concentration at Shaykhūnīya,[48] the distribution between the northeast and southeast was fairly even. Anatolians were only minimally represented in the Festival Gate group. However, there were definitely Ṣūfīs among them, who were admitted to monastic houses; they appeared in the Shaykhūnīya and Siryāqūs (130) khānqāhs as well as in the two royal madrasas of Ashrafīya (30) and Mu'ayyadīya (51). Anatolians were represented in the Bayn al-Qaṣrayn colleges, where they taught jurisprudence. Their most prominent concentration here was in the Manṣūrīya madrasa and tomb (22).

The biographical sources indicated that individual scholars of Anatolian origin were not at all regarded as Mamluks or unlettered *Atrāk*, but rather as Rūmīs who had achieved scholarly renown. However, there were fewer of them than there were Syrians or Persians. Most tended to specialize in legal subjects—as indicated as by their presence in the Bayn al-Qaṣrayn group, famous for jurisprudence. The Anatolian representation at Ashrafīya and Mu'ayyadīya bespeaks the relative wealth of these institutions and their receptivity to foreign scholars. This was a policy established by Sultan al-Mu'ayyad Shaykh, in particular. Indeed, the Mamluk elite did identify with the Turkish-speaking ʿulamaʾ from Anatolia, even though this cordiality was not fully reciprocated. Such an attitude may explain their proportionately large representation in the royal madrasas, both founded during the Circassian period. Except for Ṣarghatmishīya (92) and Aytmishīya (62), the data were too sparse for the amirate madrasas of the southeast to guess whether this sense of fellow-feeling by Mamluks influenced the appointment of Rūmīs to their institutions.[49] Ṣarghatmishīya seems to have constituted a unique case among these foundations, as is discussed below. There were several cases of Rūmīs who served the royal family personally rather than as bureaucrats, perhaps because of the bond of a common language. These Anatolians were employed in the Sultan's palace (135-136) itself, and belonged to the imperial household.

The Anatolians were prominent in the two mortuary zones, although the map does not represent their number accurately. This was primarily because most of them were resident in zāwiyas that were not positioned by the topographical sources.[50] Those in institutions whose location is specified in these works taught in the madrasas associated with the tombs of Imām al-Shāfiʿī (115) and three great Mamluks (120, 121, 123). It is certain that there were many other Anatolian muʿtaqads and majdhūbs living or teaching in Mamluk tombs, since the biographical texts constantly referred to this situation, albeit imprecisely.

Anatolians were sparsely represented in the other districts of the metropolis, though there were two references to the Mosque of ʿAmr ibn al-ʿĀṣ (113) in Old Cairo. The evidence therefore indicates that the majority of Anatolians were based in the inner city and the two mortuary zones.

IRAQ
(Figs. 7-A through 7-D)

As noted earlier, Iraqis tended not to attain the prominence achieved by other foreign groups in Cairo, although, of course, there were several eminent individuals. Fewer of them were associated with recognized institutions, so their actual numbers are not reflected in the maps. The educational and residential patterns (Figs. 7-A, 7-D) were too limited to indicate anything except that those Iraqis who did appear were associated with institutions of the northeast. Al-Azhar (36), the haven for foreign students, had a grand total of two. The distribution of occupational sites (Figs. 7-B, 7-C) was somewhat better. The only true cluster was at the Bayn al-Qaṣrayn group, although there were three cases reported for the Festival Gate group. No single institution accounted for more than three cases. A few scattered cases were reported for the southeast section and Cross Street area. Iraqis were virtually absent from other districts, including the two mortuary zones. In general, these figures do confirm that Iraqis were living in Cairo, but the data were too sparse to be compared with the profiles for other groups.

NORTH AFRICA: THE MAGHRIB
(Figs. 8-A through 8-C)

Although individuals from North Africa did not constitute a large element, they were more prominent than either the Iraqis or Peninsular Arabians. This may be explained by their conspicuous role in the judiciary of Cairo. Persons of North African origin or descent were very influential in the Mālikī courts of Egypt. Since Cairo possessed a large community identifying with the Mālikī madhhab, these people were well represented in the biographical sources. The situation is reflected by the pattern of educational sites (Fig. 8-A), which reveals a concentration of Maghribīs in the Ẓāhirīya madrasa (23). Although Sultan Baybars had originally endowed it for instruction in Shāfiʿī and Ḥanafī jurisprudence, the other two madhhabs were also taught; we find Mālikī North Africans there as well as Ḥanbalīs from the east.[51] Elsewhere, North Africans were represented, in token numbers: at al-Azhar (36), Saʿīd al-Suʿadāʾ (15), and the Basiṭīya madrasa (11) in the northeast; and at Shaykhūnīya (83) in the southeast. In other words, the institutions that tended to attract other foreign groups also drew Maghribīs. The overall number of cases was too low, however, to provide an adequate picture of the distribution of North Africans studying in Cairo.[52]

The occupational and residential patterns (Figs. 8-B, 8-C) indicated a North African presence in both collegiate clusters, al-Azhar (36) and Mu'ayyadīya (51) in the northeast; and in Shaykhūnīya (83-84), the Ṭūlūnid mosque (91), and several amirate colleges in the southeast. The lack of individuals teaching at Ẓāhirīya, in contrast with the concentration of students there, may be explained by the fact that very few occupational sites were quoted for judges of all four schools. Al-Azhar exhibited the largest concentrations of North Africans for both configurations.[53] This reinforces the general hypothesis that al-Azhar had already developed its international character and reputation throughout the Muslim world. In more recent periods, North Africans have formed an established student community within al-Azhar, and there may have been a similar situation during the later Middle Ages. Instruction in Mālikī jurisprudence was maintained consistently at al-Azhar, attracting Maghribīs who were expert in their madhhab. Only a few North Africans were actually appointed to posts in the khānqāhs and madrasas of the Festival Gate, but several were resident in the hospices as Ṣūfīs. This was also true for the Shaykhūnīya khānqāh in the southeast, but not for Siryāqūs (130). In proportion to the total number of cases reported for residence, which was low, the concentration in the hospices indicated that the North African group tended to produce roughly the same percentage of individuals as the Iranians or Anatolians. The complete absence of these people from the two mortuary zones again implies that Ṣūfī mystics were not the same as pious ascetics or recluses. North Africa is well known for its individuals endowed with holy emanation, but this type of individual does not seem to have migrated to Cairo from North Africa to any great extent.

The overall representation of North Africans in mosques and the amirate madrasas of the southeast was very sparse. The cases occurring for Shaykhūnīya (83), Ṣarghatmishīya (92), and the Ṭūlūnid mosque (91) were to be expected, since these three institutions consistently attracted individuals of foreign background. There were no cases at all reported for the Citadel complex, implying that relatively few North Africans managed to gain access to the Imperial Court, in contrast to the Syrians or Anatolians. Except for token representation in the mosque of ʿAmr ibn al-ʿĀṣ (113) in Old Cairo, North Africans were absent from the other districts of the metropolis.

THE ARABIAN PENINSULA
(Figs. 8-A through 8-C)

Chapter II suggested that many individuals in Cairo were of Peninsular origin or derivation. Large concentrations were reported for the two holy cities, and there were representatives from areas throughout the Ḥijāz and the Yemen. These people were all living in Cairo, but little data was provided by the biographical sources on exactly where they lived. One must therefore regard the patterns that did appear as suggestive rather than definitive. Only three modest concentrations emerged. There were several Arabians studying at the Ẓāhirīya madrasa (23) or residing at Saʿīd al-Suʿadāʾ (15) and in the Ṣaḥrāʾ mortuary zone during the century (202). There were other references to individuals scattered throughout the northeast and southeast districts, but these merely confirmed the presence of people from the Peninsula in the city. Not a single case was reported for al-Azhar, which is quite extraordinary. Every other foreign group was represented there. Since no cause can be determined to explain this phenomenon, we should be cautious about drawing conclusions from it. The concentration of students at Ẓāhirīya may be attributed to its status as a center of legal scholarship; the Ḥanafī madhhab was and remains prominent in the Arabian Peninsula. The concentration of residents in Saʿīd al-Suʿadāʾ shows that Ṣūfī mystics of Peninsular origin or descent were present in Cairo. The appearance of several Arabians in the two mortuary zones may imply a tendency toward asceticism and seclusion, although the sources did not attest to it elsewhere.

CONCLUSIONS ON THE DISTRIBUTION OF GEOGRAPHIC GROUPS

A basic pattern revealed by the data shows that a limited number of religio-academic institutions, a minority of the total, seem to have played a dominant role as seats of learning, professional activity, promotion, and residence for the civilian elite of Cairo, irrespective of ethno-geographic background.

The educational pattern varied least among the geographic groups. Predictably, madrasas dominated all the educational configurations, although the prominence of several khānqāhs suggests that the madrasas did not exercise a monopoly over higher learning or even formal training in the Islamic sciences. But certain madrasas trained the majority of those persons who became entrenched within the civilian elite, most prominently the two collegiate clusters and, in particular, Ẓāhirīya. The elite institutions were confined primarily to the northeast quarter of the city. Only two institutions in the southeast, a zone of Mamluk influence (Shaykhūnīya and Ṣarghatmishīya), and one outside the city (Siryāqūs) can be included among them. The primacy of the old Fāṭimid city, formalized during the Ayyūbid and Baḥrī periods, would seem to have persisted undiminished to the end of the Mamluk era, regardless of munificent donations to found and maintain similar institutions elsewhere.

That the patterns produced by the several ethno-geographic elements repeatedly emphasized the same institutions implies that these institutions established their reputations throughout the cities and towns of the Mamluk empire, as well as in regions beyond its borders. Traditions of scholarly interchange, consciously sustained on behalf of universal orthodoxy, would promote the growth of their stature, and also explain in part why renowned savants from abroad elected to join these institutions, especially if they intended to settle in the Mamluk capital.

A second possible explanation for the dominance of a few houses is related to the issue of professional entry and reaffirmation of credentials. Upon their arrival in the capital, individuals seeking to penetrate the civilian elite or to duplicate ʿalim status attained elsewhere sought admission to these institutions as the best means of realizing their objective. These institutions produced the candidates who received the bulk of the legal and scholarly positions in the city. Admission to this elite group and receipt of diplomas from their staffs would therefore seem to constitute an initial stage of entry into the upper echelons of the civilian elite.

Third, it is possible that certain ethno-geographic elements had built up "interests" within the religio-academic network of the Mamluk capital. This would be very likely in the case of the Syrians, but might apply to the Iranians, Anatolians, and Maghribīs, as well. The presence and influence of such hypothetical interests would vary according to specific institutions. One might speculate on a pronounced Cairo-Delta interest in the khānqāhs of Saʿīd al-Suʿadāʾ and Baybarsīya, a Syrian sphere of influence at Shaykhūnīya and Ṣarghatmishīya, a Maghribī presence at the Azhar. What such interests might provide for newcomers beyond an avenue of admission to a course of study at a certain institution remains subject to conjecture, because of the lack of direct evidence. The possibility of interests established within the religio-academic network is most discernible in the residential survey.

Finally, because of their backgrounds or the intentions of their benefactors, not all or even a majority of the institutions in the capital may have drawn students and staff from beyond the Cairo-Delta zone. There is little evidence in the descriptive literature on these institutions to suggest that any madrasa or hospice was consciously closed to persons viewed as foreign, but the circumstances of their funding and the outlooks of their staffs may have encouraged recruitment of local personnel. The parochialism of the majority of the religio-academic establishment seems to be a fact. Although the curriculum of the Sunnī madrasa during the later Middle Ages was supposedly standardized—and clearly was for the highly cosmopolitan elite group—the curricula of more parochial institutions may have varied according to local practice, and probably provided the training ground for individuals composing the lower strata of the civilian elite.[54] These hypothetical observations are not mutually exclusive. Indeed, they may be interrelated in explaining the cosmopolitan clientele associated with the elite institutions. The widespread reputations of these institutions and the professional opportunities associated with them would appear to be the most plausible explanations in terms of available evidence.

The occupational pattern, limited as it was to institutional positions, varied more widely than the educational one. Although the same institutional core prevailed in each survey, individuals, particularly Cairenes, were employed in a broader spectrum of institutional settings. The religio-academic establishment functioned as a network and, therefore, the general impression is of social cohesiveness, with no absolute exclusion of a specific group from any one institution. Nonetheless, there are differences between the patterns, suggesting that integration into the ʿulamaʾ class varied according to ethno-geographic origin—either because of circumstance, subtle exclusion, or self-imposed distinctions.

The occupational pattern may be interpreted as a measure of two factors: cosmopolitanism versus parochialism, and relative prestige. The first involves the degree of assimilation into the civilian elite. Of all the ethno-geographic groups, only indigenous Cairenes and Lower Egyptians were broadly established at the local level. All other groups, including Upper Egyptians, tended to be employed in either the elite institutions or the amirate madrasas. The cosmopolitan elements of the ʿulamaʾ were thus confined primarily to the institutional core. In certain cases, these elements were represented at the amirate colleges of the southeast, which may suggest diversity of function and attainment of prestige. This tendency toward confinement to the major institutions does not imply isolation from the ʿulamaʾ class in general since, with the possible exceptions of Shaykhūnīya and Ṣarghatmishīya, individuals from the Cairo-Delta zone were numerically dominant in them. But these institutions seem to have constituted the milieu in which the genuinely universal aspects of the orthodox curriculum were refined and taught. They were the locus of ideological exchange, and cosmopolitan elements were consistently restricted to them. The majority of foundations, rarely mentioned in the biographical sources, probably served the mass of local population primarily, including the lower echelons of the civilian elite. Whether the curricula of these institutions differed appreciably from those of the elite group is unclear, but their absence from the biographical sources, compiled in large part to bolster the orthodox curriculum, is very interesting. Although they appear to have played no discernible role in higher scholarship, they were staffed by Cairenes and Lower Egyptians, like those who rubbed shoulders with the international elements in the elite core.

Indigenous Cairenes were present throughout the religio-academic network and would seem to have constituted the matrix within which all other groups functioned. In comparison, Lower Egyptians, although very similar to the majority group, tended to be connected with a more restricted range of institutions. The contrast indicated by their representation outside the elite core is apparent, suggesting that even the Delta people did not function at the local level to the same extent as those native to the city. Moreover, the Delta people collected so markedly at certain institutions that the existence of a Lower Egyptian identity with them is probable. Since all the remaining geographic groups also seem to have been concentrated at specific institutions, we are not left with an impression of uniform or routine assimilation of foreigners at all levels of the religio-academic network of the capital. Yet the biographical sources depict no systematic process of exclusion.

The second factor, that of prestige, must be considered in light of the status and background of the foreign ʿulamaʾ. We can probably assume that positions within the major institutions were the most prestigious and professionally beneficial in terms of mobility, influence, and remuneration, and that appointment to institutions outside this group carried less prestige and fewer professional options. Accordingly, the larger the percentage of positions held by an ethno-geographic element within the elite group, the more indication there is of that element's identity with and successful penetration of the upper echelons of the civilian elite. It is very likely that the majority of individuals originating outside the Mamluk state who achieved eminence in Cairo transferred there because they had already attained qualifications sufficient to position themselves within the cosmopolitan level of the ʿulamaʾ class throughout the Sunnī Islamic world.

The few Upper Egyptians mentioned constitute a case in point, as they were evenly divided between the elite group and less prestigious amirate colleges. The minimal influence of Ṣaʿīdīs on the ʿulamaʾ class is quite clear from the tables in Chapter II. The Syrians, on the other hand, with perhaps the most complex pattern, were substantially represented within institutions dominated by the Cairo-Delta element, while also forming concentrations at the two most prominent amirate foundations in the southeast. Indeed, Syrians may have numerically dominated the faculties of both Shaykhūnīya and Ṣarghatmishīya, which were famous for scholarship in Ḥanafī jurisprudence. Their representation in other amirate madrasas, as well as in institutions located elsewhere in the metropolis, would suggest the high degree of Syrian integration into the upper strata of the Cairo ʿulamaʾ, but the close ties between this group and the ruling Mamluk oligarchy, inadequately depicted in the survey, must also be recalled. Iranians seem to have been somewhat less well integrated into the elite group. They appear to have been more evenly divided between the elite institutions and the amirate colleges than any other foreign element in Cairo. There is no evidence that Iranians faced any barriers to assimilation into the civilian elite, and therefore the peculiarities of their distribution may imply a predisposition toward accepting positions at Mamluk foundations, a tendency influenced in part by their affiliation with the Ḥanafī school. The remaining ethno-geographic groups provided less data, but also tended to associate with the elite institutions. However, there were so few cases even at these institutions that they would seem to have had little influence at any level of the civilian elite. The Anatolians and Maghribīs, however, figured more prominently than some others in the patterns: the former in the mortuary zones, the latter at al-Azhar. And individual Anatolians and North Africans achieved such fame as to qualify our generalizations on prestige as measured solely according to group aggregation rather than by individual distinction.

The residence pattern, restricted primarily to Ṣūfī khānqāhs and hospices, indicates a highly specific type of institutional association. Yet the concentrations were suggestive in that they most clearly signal the existence of organized ethno-geographic interests. The residential configurations, like the educational ones, centered overwhelmingly on the elite institutions. But in this case the salient exceptions involved institutions established in the mortuary zones rather than the amirate madrasas. The pattern clearly isolated those institutions in which the cosmopolitan elements of the ʿulamaʾ class congregated. They defined the limited milieu in which the international dimensions of mysticism and fraternal communal activity occurred in the Mamluk capital. Viewed collectively with the preceding surveys, they identify, rather definitively, the restricted group of institutions constituting the seat of ʿulamaʾ cosmopolitanism in Cairo. In Chapter II, cosmopolitanism emerged as most evident in the judicial and scholarly fields. Here, this is confirmed by the overwhelming primacy of a distinct set of colleges and hospices.

It is now clear that cosmopolitan influences on the quality of intellectual life, methods of scholarship, practice of law, civilian politics, and mystic communal association were confined primarily to this set. It is also probable that ethno-geographic groups maintained a sense of common identity, an awareness of their regional heritage, while simultaneously functioning within the ʿulamaʾ class. Such a phenomenon was possible because of the nature of Sunnism, which at once maintained tenets common to all the orthodox learned and reflected the dominant culture of the local majority from the Cairo-Delta heartland.

Figures 1 through 8

SCALE

× and + symbols are in proportion to circles and triangles

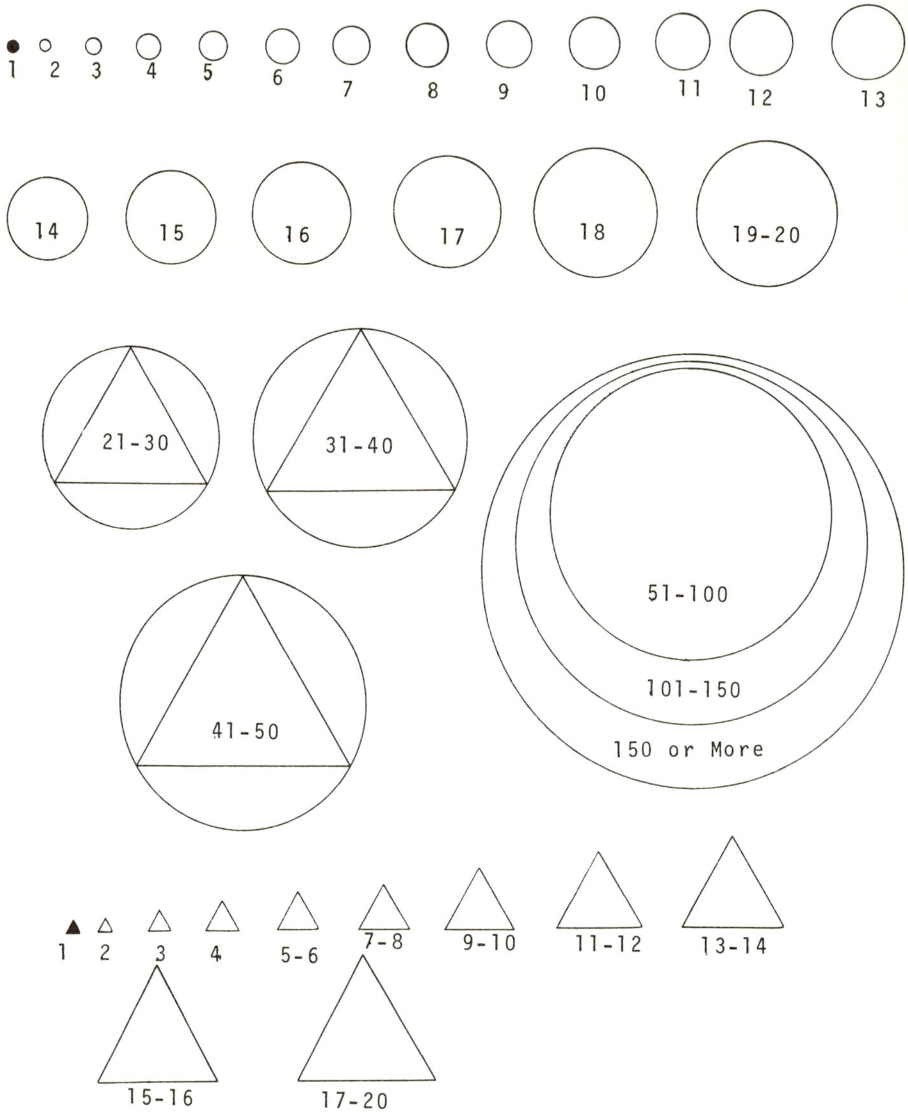

Key to Sites in Figures 1 and 2

Religio-Academic Institutions

Northeast

1. Mosque of al-Ẓāhir Baybars
2. Mazharīya madrasa
3. Mosque of al-Ḥākim
4. Bāb al-Naṣr oratory
5. Mosque of al-Bulqīnī
6. Mankūtamurīya madrasa
7. Mosque of Ibn Ḥajar
8. Qūṣūnīya madrasa
9. Mosque of Ibn Mazhar
10. Ṭarābulusīya madrasa
11. Mosque of ʿAbd al-Bāsiṭ
12. Mosque of Aqmar
13. Baybarsīya khānqāh
14. Qarāsanqurīya madrasa
15. Saʿīd al-Suʿadāʾ khānqāh
16. Jamālīya madrasa
17. Ḥijāzīya madrasa
18. Sābiqīya madrasa
19. Kāmilīya madrasa
20. Barqūqīya madrasa
21. Nāṣirīya madrasa
22. Manṣūrīya madrasa and tomb
23. Ẓāhirīya madrasa
24. al-Ṣāliḥ tomb
25. Badrīya hospice
26. Ṣāliḥīya madrasa
27. Ṣāliḥīya hospice
28. Māristān al-Manṣūrī
29. Suyūfīya hospice
30. Ashrafīya madrasa
31. Jamālīya al-Qadīma madrasa
32. Bardibakīya madrasa
33. Mosque and shrine of Ḥusayn
34. Aqbughāwīya chapel
35. Jawharīya chapel
36. al-Azhar
37. Ṭaybarsīya chapel
38. ʿAynīya madrasa
39. Zimāmīya (Kāfūr al-) madrasa
40. Mosque of al-Fākihiyīn
41. Mosque of Ibn Naṣr-Allah
42. Sharīfīya madrasa
43. Mosque of Yaḥyā al-Zaynī
44. Fakhrīya madrasa
45. Ṣāḥibīya madrasa
46. Mosque of al-Fakhrī
47. Ḥusāmīya madrasa
48. Abū Bakrīya madrasa
49. Jarkasīya madrasa
50. Jawdarīya madrasa
51. Muʾayyadīya madrasa

Southeast

52. Mosque of al-Ṣāliḥ Ṭalāʾiʿ
53. Qajmāsīya madrasa
54. Mosque of Aṣlam
55. Mihmandārīya madrasa
56. Māridānīya madrasa
57. Maḥmūdīya madrasa
58. Īnāl Yūsufīya madrasa
59. Jawbakīya madrasa
60. Umm al-Sulṭān madrasa
61. Aq Sunqūrīya madrasa
62. Aytmishīya madrasa
63. Qūṣūnīya khanqāh
64. Mosque of Manjak
65. Mosque of Yūnus
66. Qalamtāʾī tomb
67. Māristān al-Muʾayyadī
68. Nāṣirī (Citadel) mosque
69. Aljayhīya madrasa
70. Ṣūdūn min Zāda madrasa
71. Jawharīya Julbānī madrasa
72. Qānibayhīya madrasa
73. Jānibakīya madrasa
74. Mosque of Sulṭān Ḥasan
75. al-Muʾminī oratory
76. Qānibayhīya al-Jarkasī madrasa
77. Qūṣūnī tomb and mosque
78. Jānibak tomb
79. Zayn Yūsuf al-Dawādār tomb
80. Nāfisī shrine
81. al-Ruqāya
82. Mosque of Ibn Taghrī-Birdī al-Muʾdhī
83. Shaykhūnīya madrasa
84. Shaykhūnīya khānqāh
85. Qānibayhīya al-Maḥmūdī madrasa
86. Mosque of al-Fariqānī
87. Bunduqdārīya madrasa
88. Mosque of Almāṣ
89. Mosque of Yaḥyā al-Zaynī
90. Mosque of Qūṣūn
91. Mosque of Ibn Ṭūlūn
92. Ṣarghatmishīya madrasa

Southwest

93. Azbakīya al-Yūsufī madrasa
94. Jāwalīya madrasa
95. Mosque of Jaqmaq
96. Mosque of Bardibak
97. Mosque of Qarākhūj
98. Mosque of Bashtak
99. Mosque of Ghurāb

Northwest

100. Mosque of Amīr Ḥusayn
101. Mosque of al-Zāhid
102. Shaykh Madyan hospice
103. Mosque of Jawhar al-Ṭawāshī
104. Mosque of al-Maqs

Būlāq

105. Jīʿānīya madrasa
106. Mosque of al-Bārizī
107. Mosque of al-Wāsiṭī
108. Mosque of al-Khāṭirī
109. Mosque of Abū ʿAlā
110. Mosque of Ṭaybars

Environs

111. New Nāṣirī mosque
112. al-Kharūbīya madrasa
113. Mosque of Amr ibn al-ʿĀṣ
114. Ribāṭ (shrine) Āthār al-Nabawīya
115. Imām al-Shāfiʿī tomb complex
116. Layth tomb
117. Uqba tomb
118. Tombs of Joseph's brothers
119. Juyūshī mosque
120. Tankiz tomb
121. Qāytbāy tomb
122. Yūnus tomb
123. Barqūq and Faraj tomb
124. Anas tomb

125. Ināl tomb
126. Qubbat al-Naṣr (Succor Dome)
127. Yashbak min Mahdī tomb
128. Yashbak tomb
129. Mosque of Qaydān
130. Siryāqūs khānqāh

Governmental Institutions (Citadel)

131. Justice palace
132. State treasury
133. Chain Gate (Bāb al-Silsila)
134. Stables and stable barracks
135. Striped castle
136. Sultan's palaces (including the Duhaysha)
137. Vestibule and treasury of Privy Funds
138. N.E. Citadel barracks and Sārīya Gate
139. The ramp and gate of the Steps
140. The park and the pit barracks

Streets, Quarters, Districts

Northeast

141. Cairo canal
142. Ḥusaynīya district
143. Sha'rīya Gate
144. Victory Gate (Bāb al-Futūḥ)
145. Main Avenue (Qaṣaba)
146. Succor Gate (Bāb al-Naṣr)
147. Succor Gate street
148. Festival Fate square
149. Bahā' al-Dīn street
150. al-Juyūshī street
151. Bridge Gate
152. Kāfūrī street
153. Zuwayla quarter
154. Tent Makers' bazaar
155. Khān al-Khalīlī
156. Saqā'iba street
157. Muskī Bridge Gate
158. Ṣāḥib market
159. Crossbow Dealers' street
160. Book Dealers' market
161. Amīr Ḥusayn Bridge Gate
162. Kharq Gate
163. Jawdarīya quarter
164. Daylam street
165. Beneath the Apartments street
166. Burnt Gate
167. Zuwayla Gate

Southeast

168. Red street—Tabbāna street
169. Wazīr Gate street
170. Elephant Lake Shore (Birkat al-Fīl)
171. Rumayla square
172. Citadel (al-Qal'a)
173. Cross street (al-Qaṭā'i' and Qaṣr al-Kabsh districts)
174. Muqaṭṭam escarpment
175. Qarāfa Gate street
176. Qarāfa Gate
177. Qarāfa cemetary

Southwest

178. Kharq Gate street
179. Lūq Gate
180. Aq Sunqūr bridge
181. Mihrānī district

Northwest

182. Nāṣirī canal
183. Raṭlī Lake
184. al-Maqs district
185. Maqs/Nile Gate (to Būlāq)
186. Nile Gate bridge
187. Kawm Aljakī district (al-Uzbakīya)
188. Sha'rīya street
189. Little Sha'rīya street

Environs

190. Būlāq (Nile) port
191. Sabtīya street (to Nile Gate)
192. Khawr district
193. Minbaba
194. Elephant Island tract
195. Kawm al-Rīsh
196. Minyat al-Sirīj
197. Rawḍa Island
198. Old Cairo (al-Fusṭāṭ)
199. Dayr al-Ṭīn
200. Qarāfa cemetery
201. Muqaṭṭam hills
202. Desert Plain cemetery
203. Ba'l tract
204. Maṭarīya

Fig. 1 is based on Abu-Lughod's one-sheet rendition of Popper's four maps dividing the city into quadrants (Map—"The Built-up area of Cairo ca. 1460" in Janet L. Abu-Lughod, *Cairo, 1001 Years of the City Victorious* (Princeton: Princeton University Press, 1971), p. 45. Reprinted by permission of Princeton University Press). Fig. 2 duplicates Popper's Map 5, p. 61 (Published by the Regents of the University of California; reprinted by permission of the University of California Press).

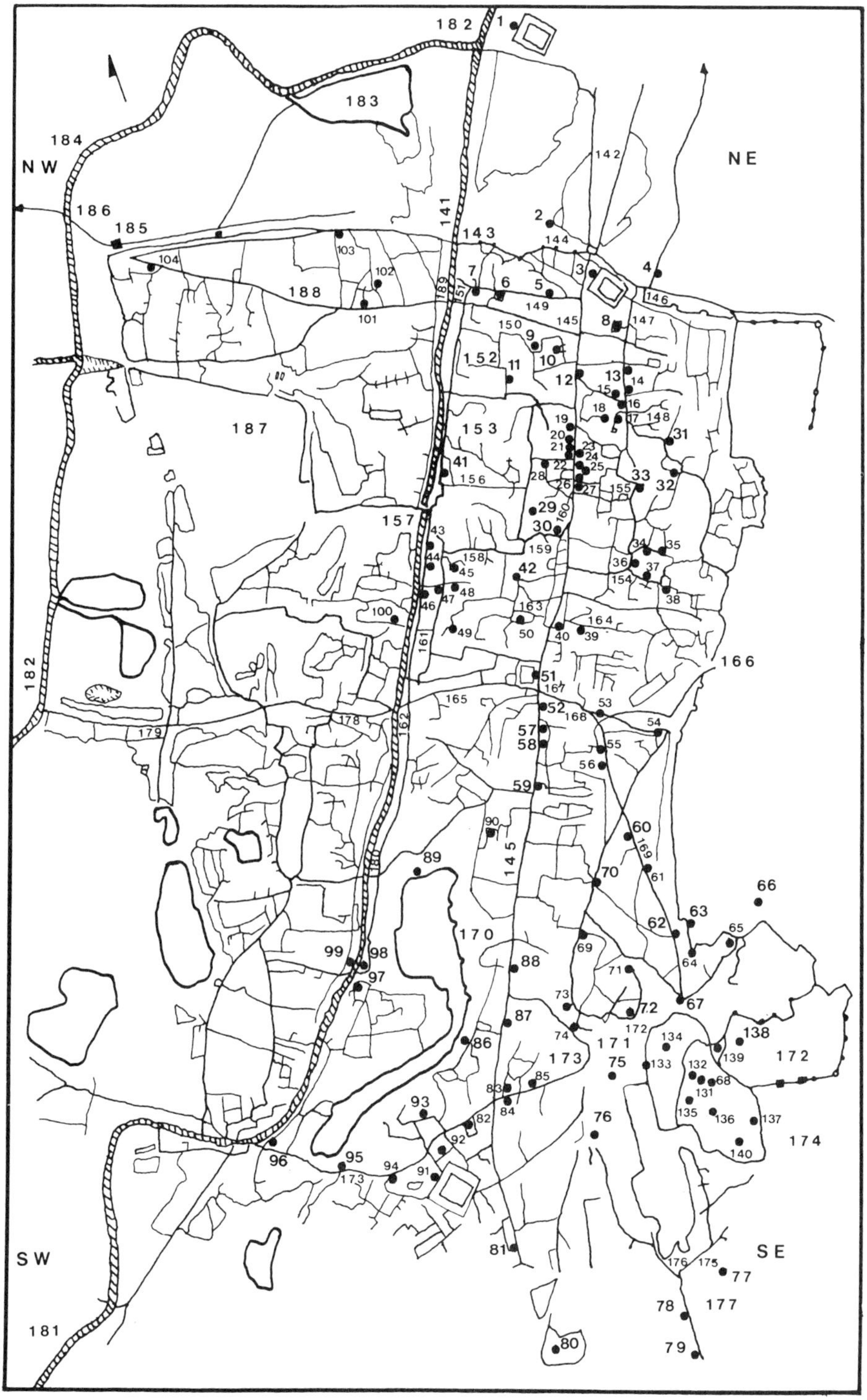

Fig. 1. Cairo, Central City. Location of Religio-Academic Institutions

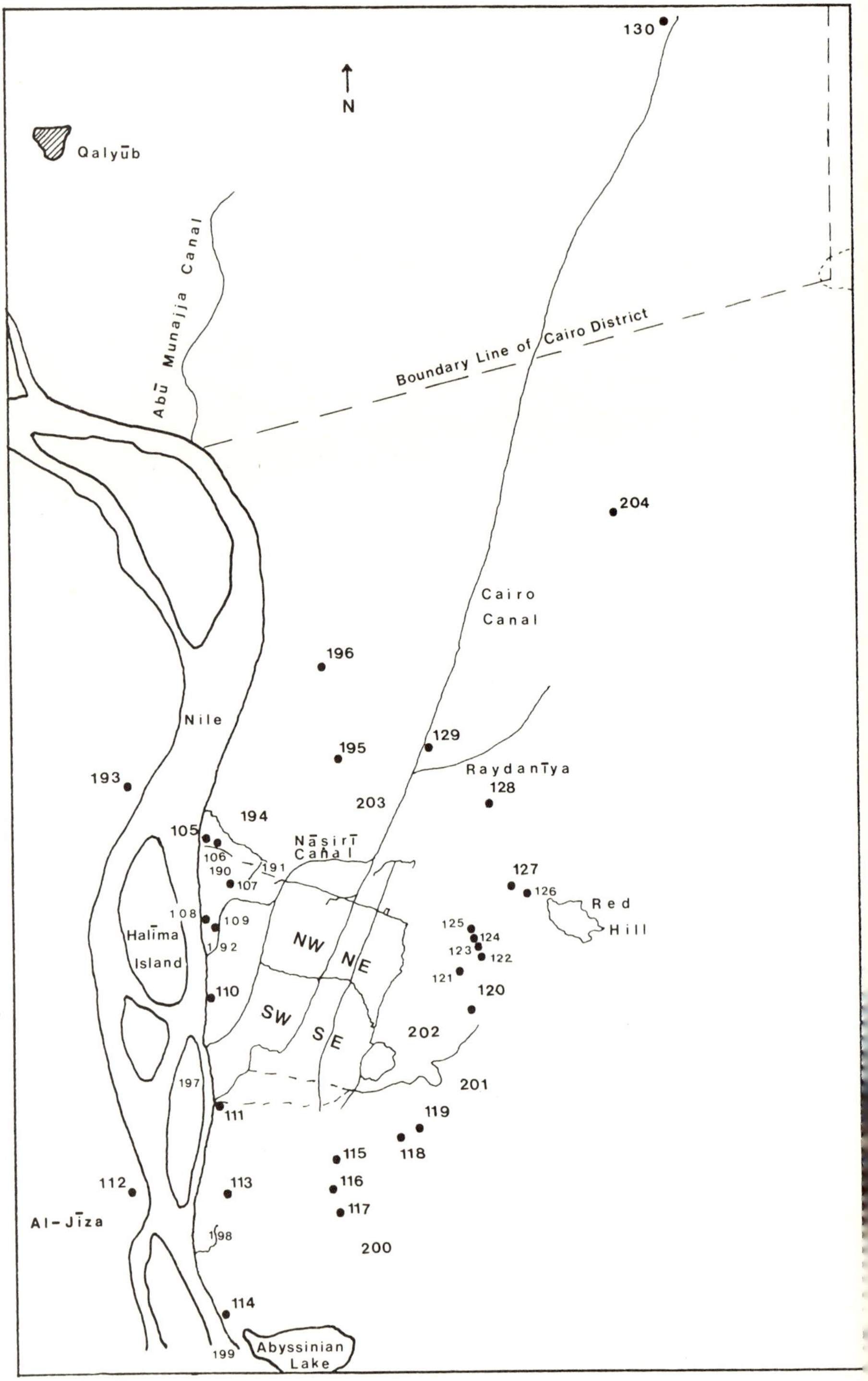

Fig. 2. Cairo and Environs. Location of Religio-Academic Institutions

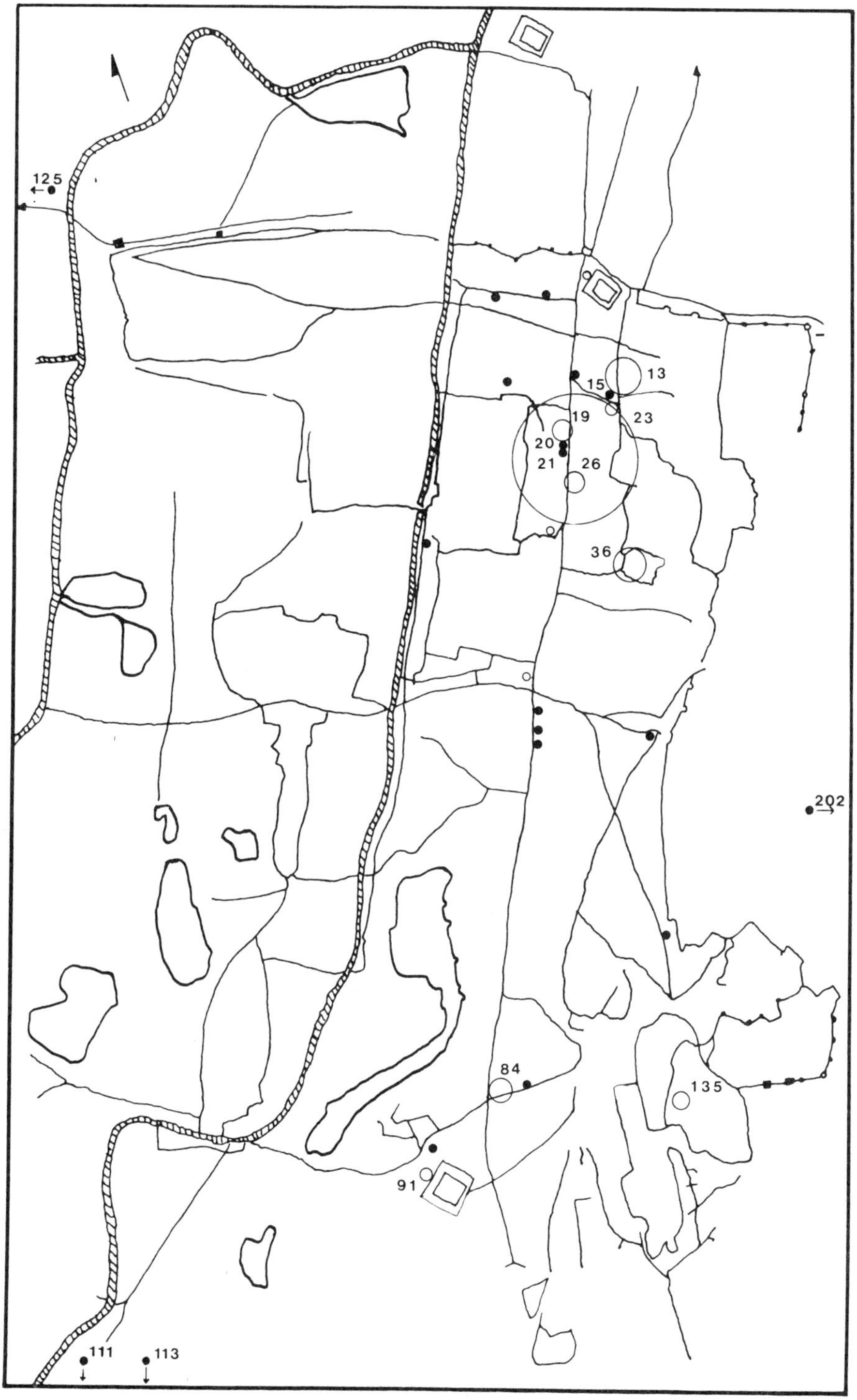

Fig. 3. Individuals from Cairo

3-A. Central City, Educational Sites
• birthplaces

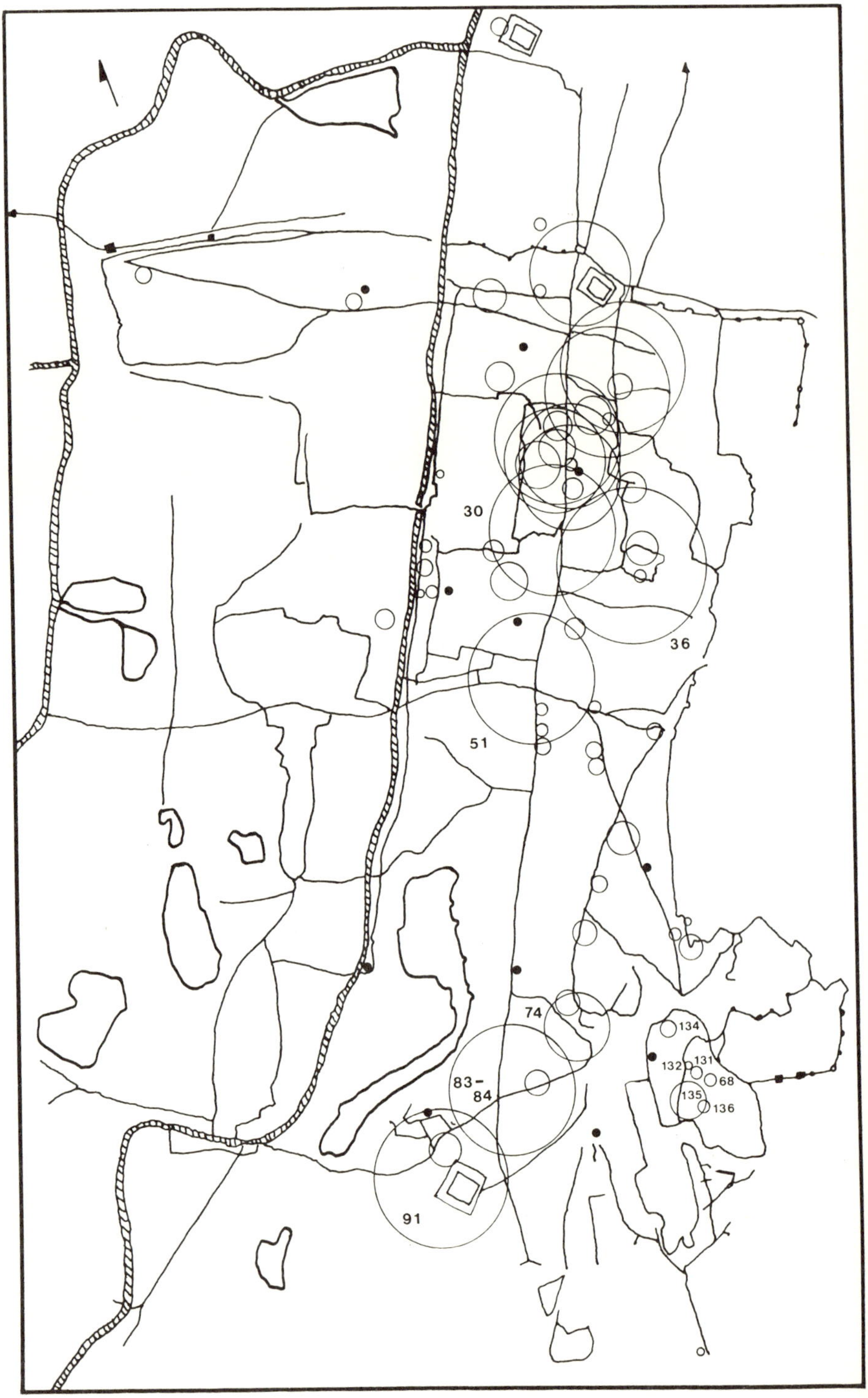

3-B. Central City, Occupational Sites
• birthplaces

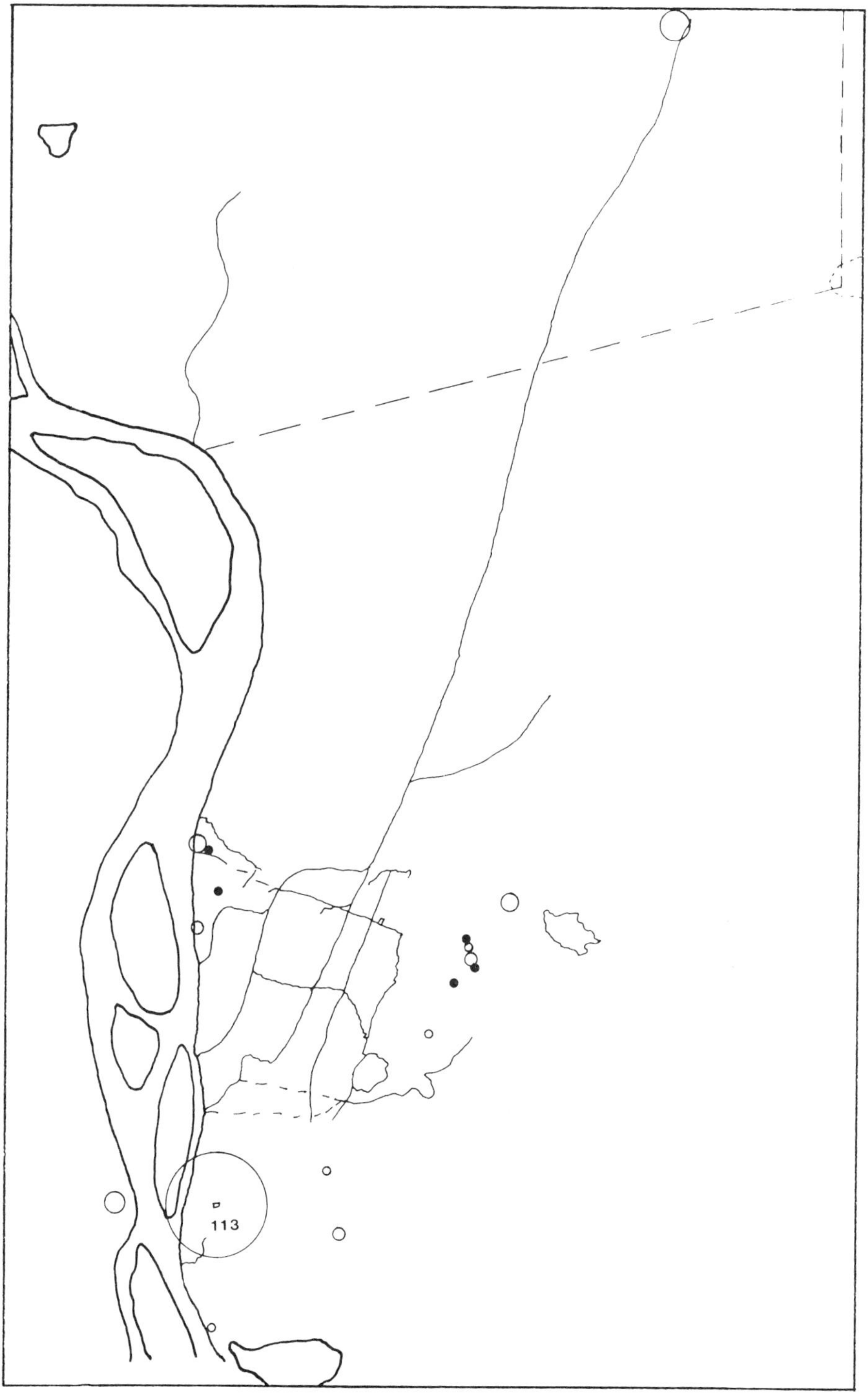

3-C. Environs, Occupational Sites
• birthplaces

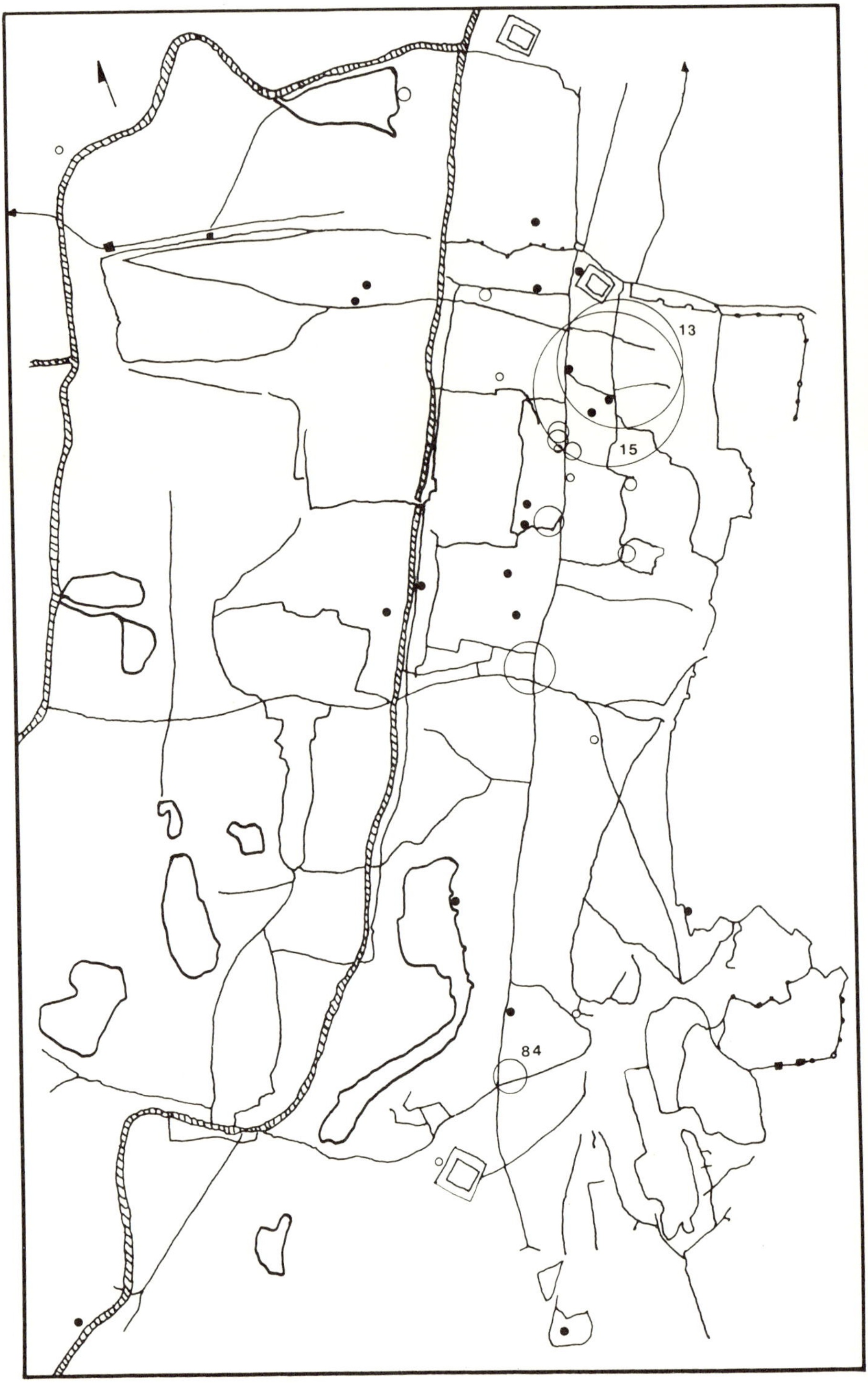

3-D. Central City, Residential Sites
• birthplaces

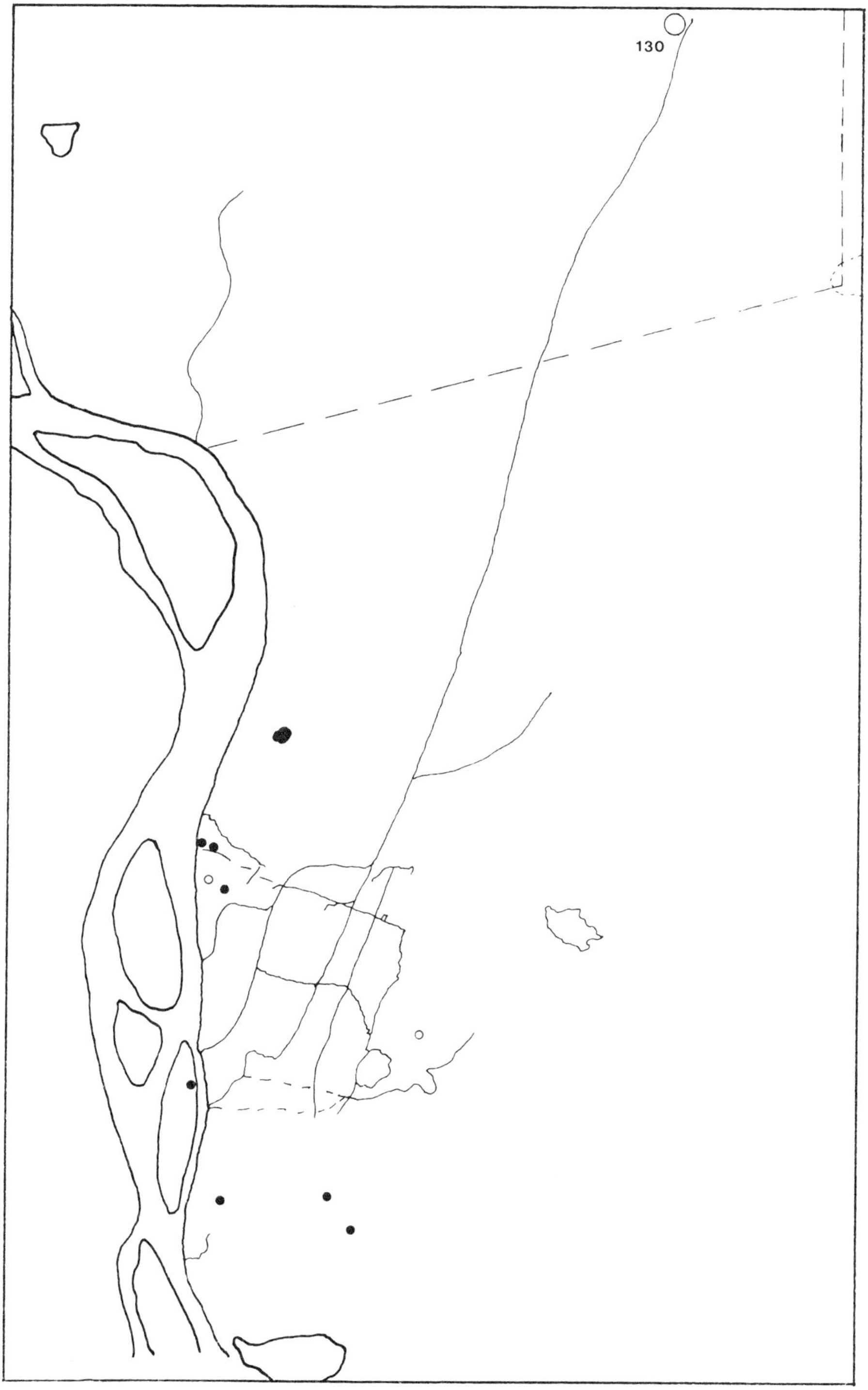

3-E. Environs, Residential Sites
• birthplaces

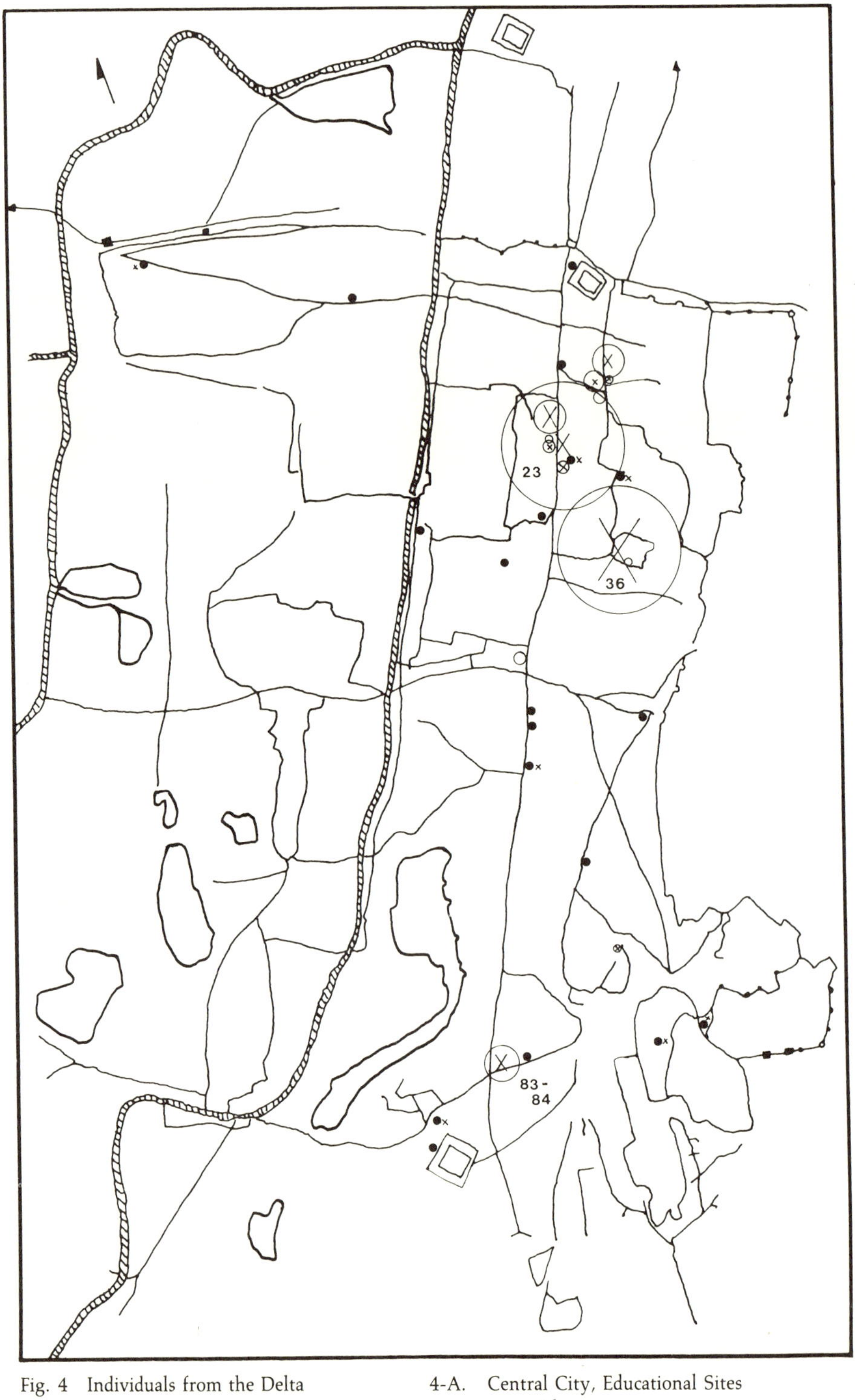

Fig. 4 Individuals from the Delta

4-A. Central City, Educational Sites
• nisbas
× birthplaces

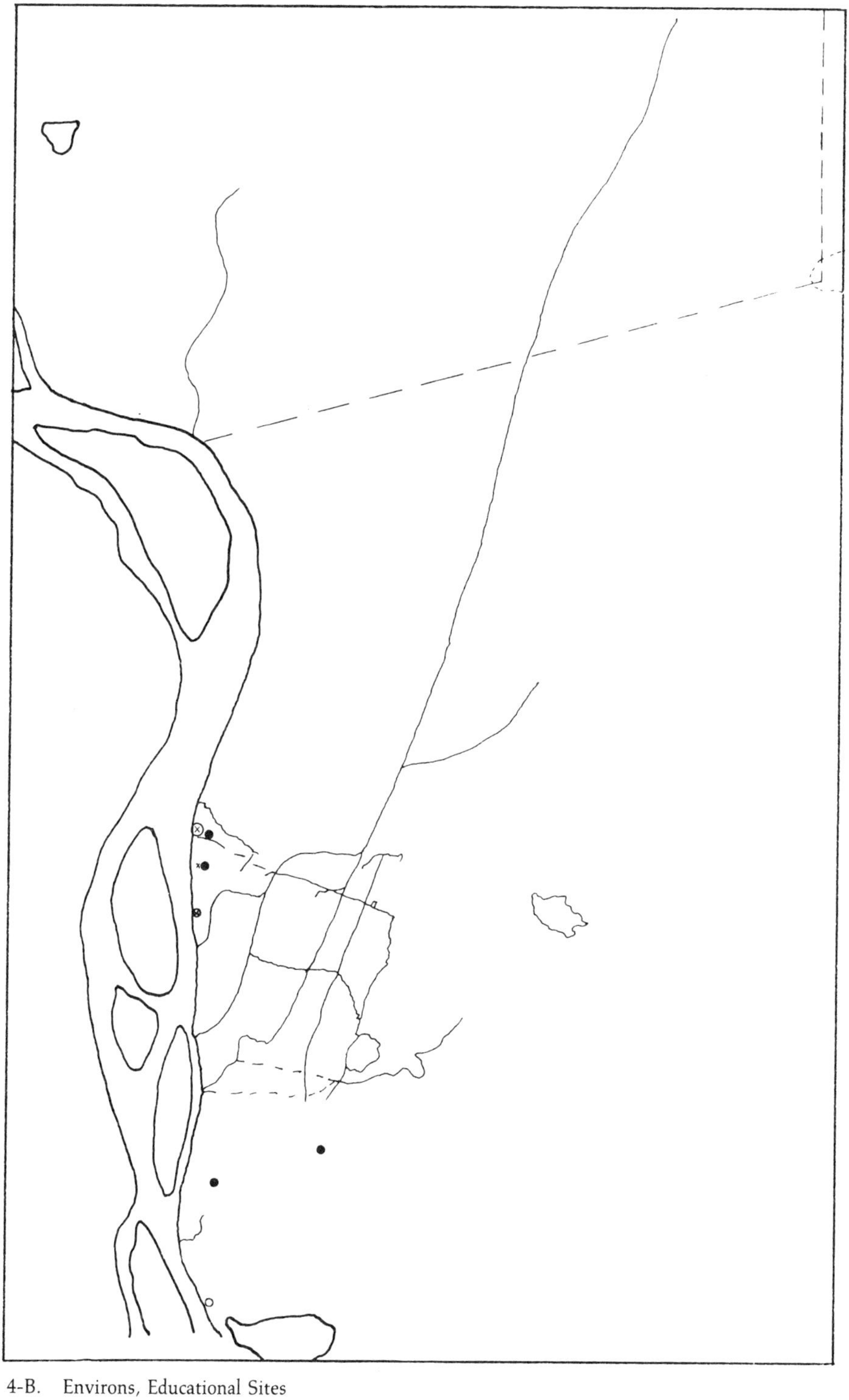

4-B. Environs, Educational Sites
• nisbas
× birthplaces

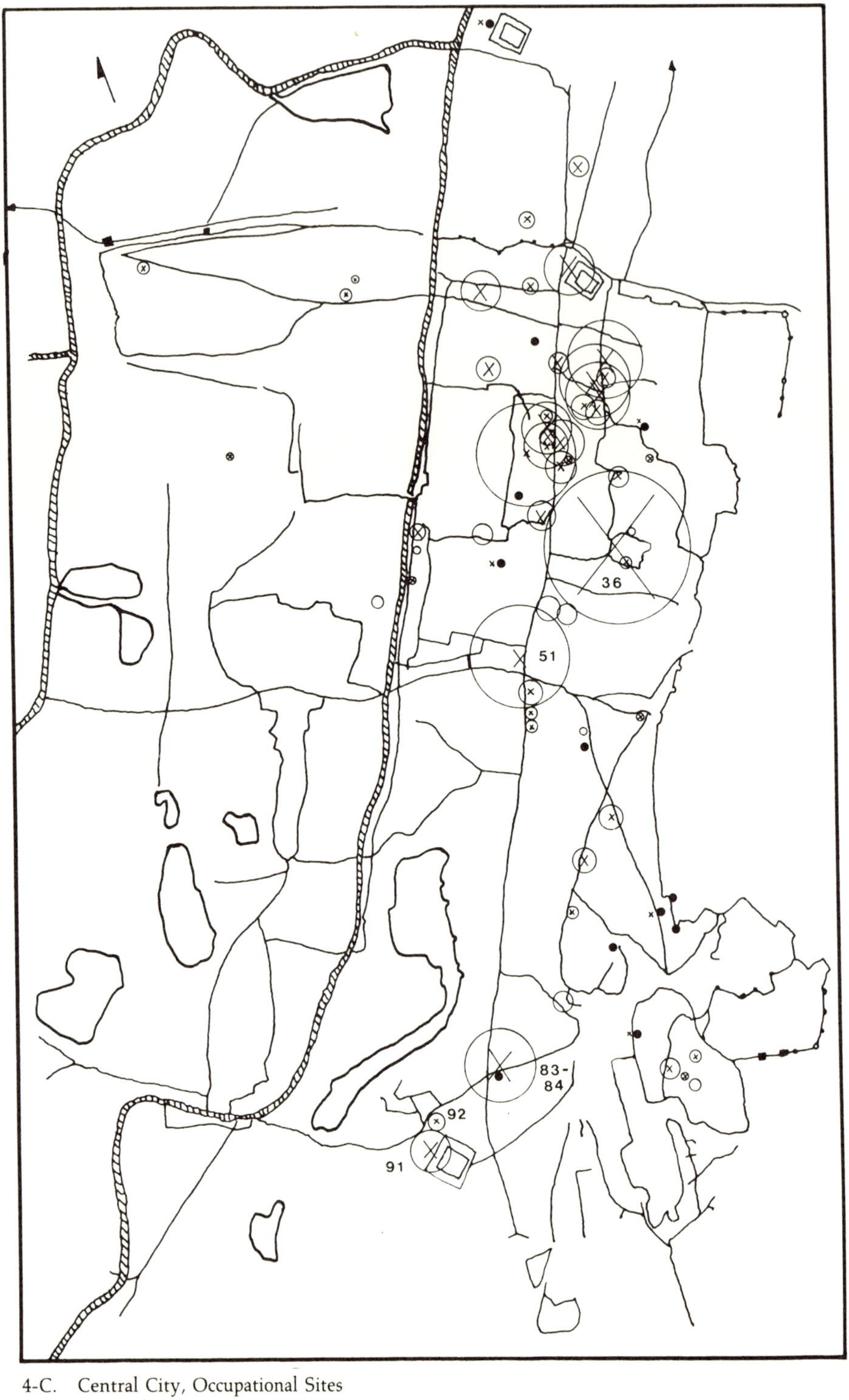

4-C. Central City, Occupational Sites
• nisbas
× birthplaces

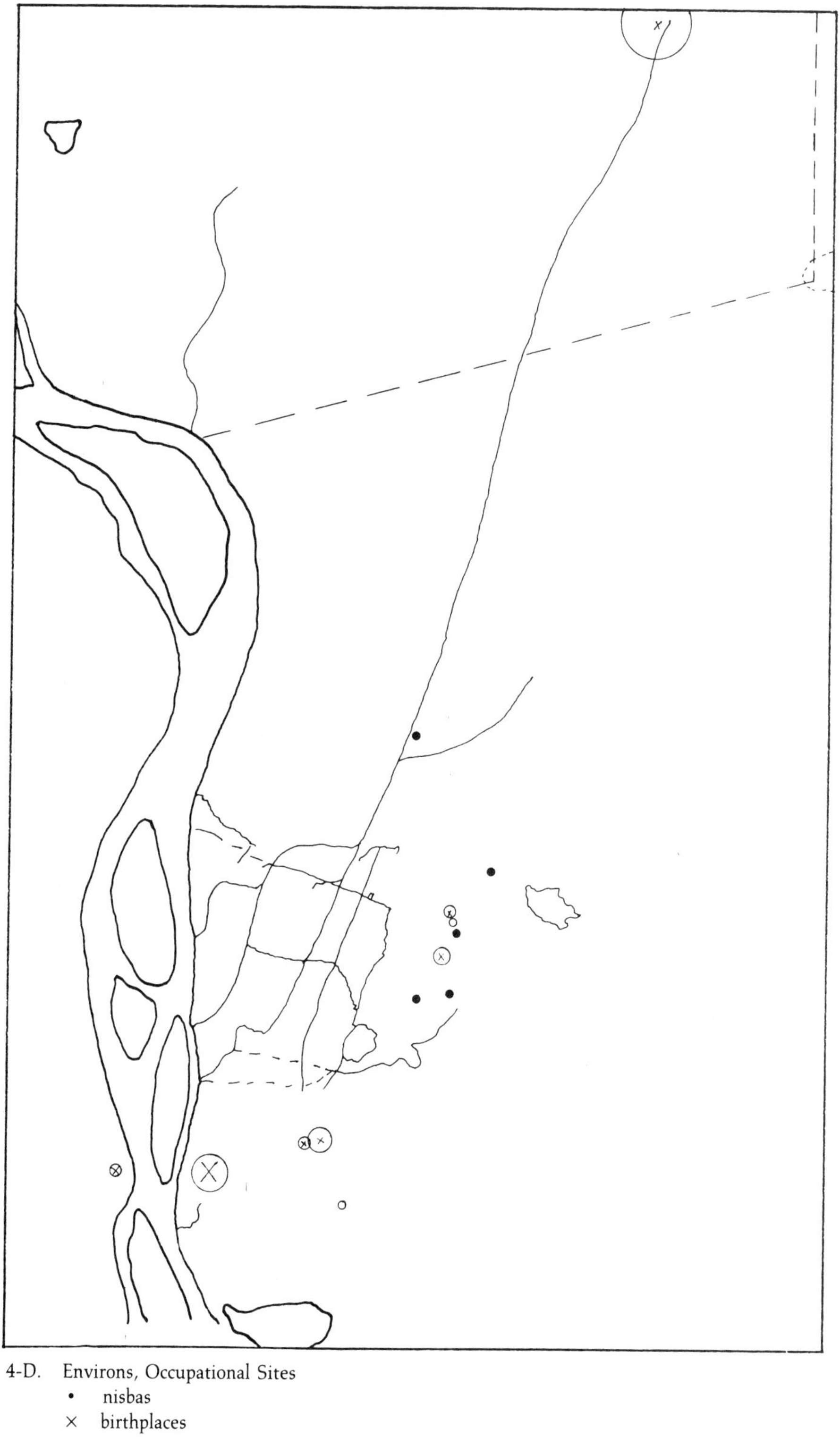

4-D. Environs, Occupational Sites
• nisbas
× birthplaces

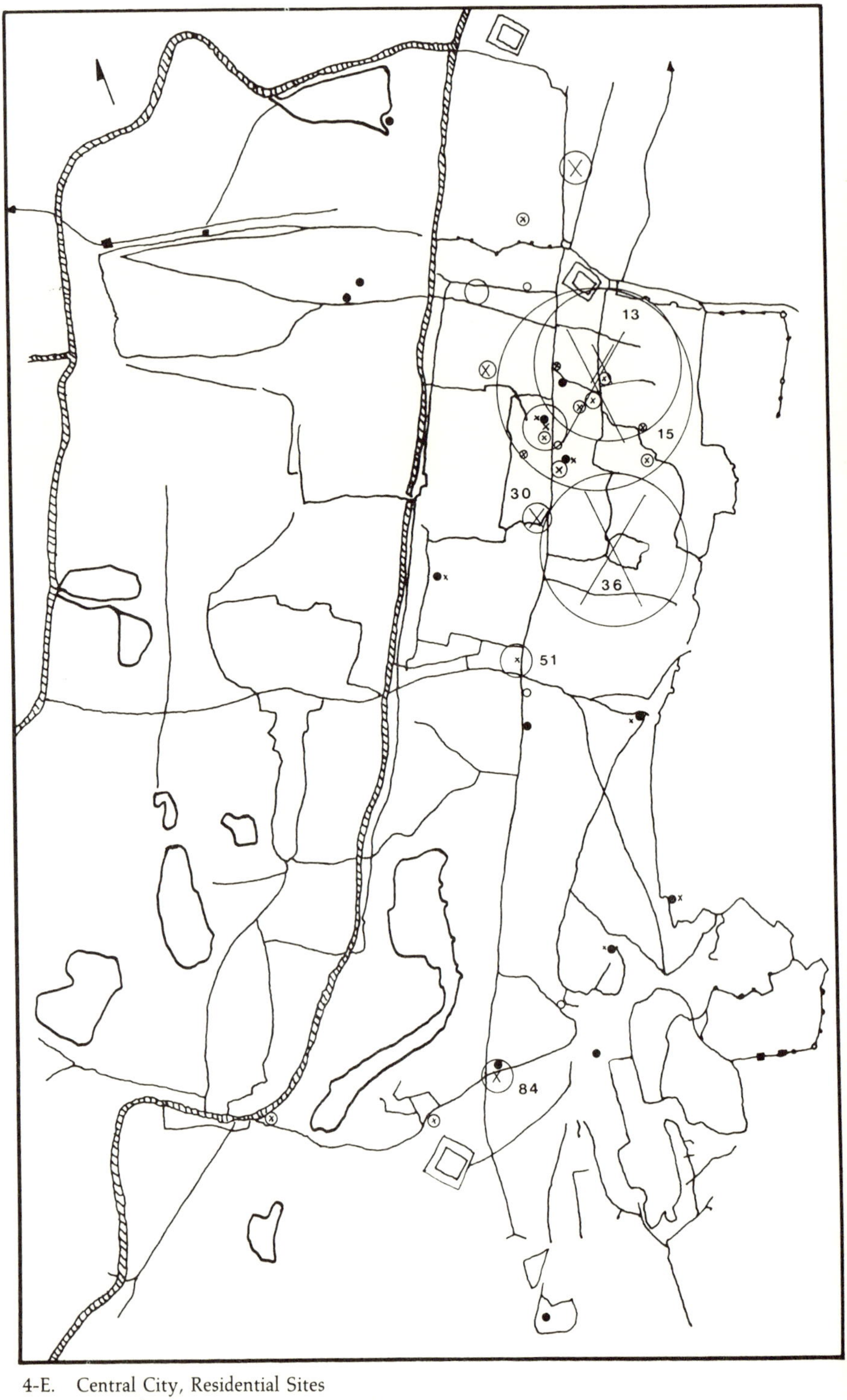

4-E. Central City, Residential Sites
• nisbas
× birthplaces

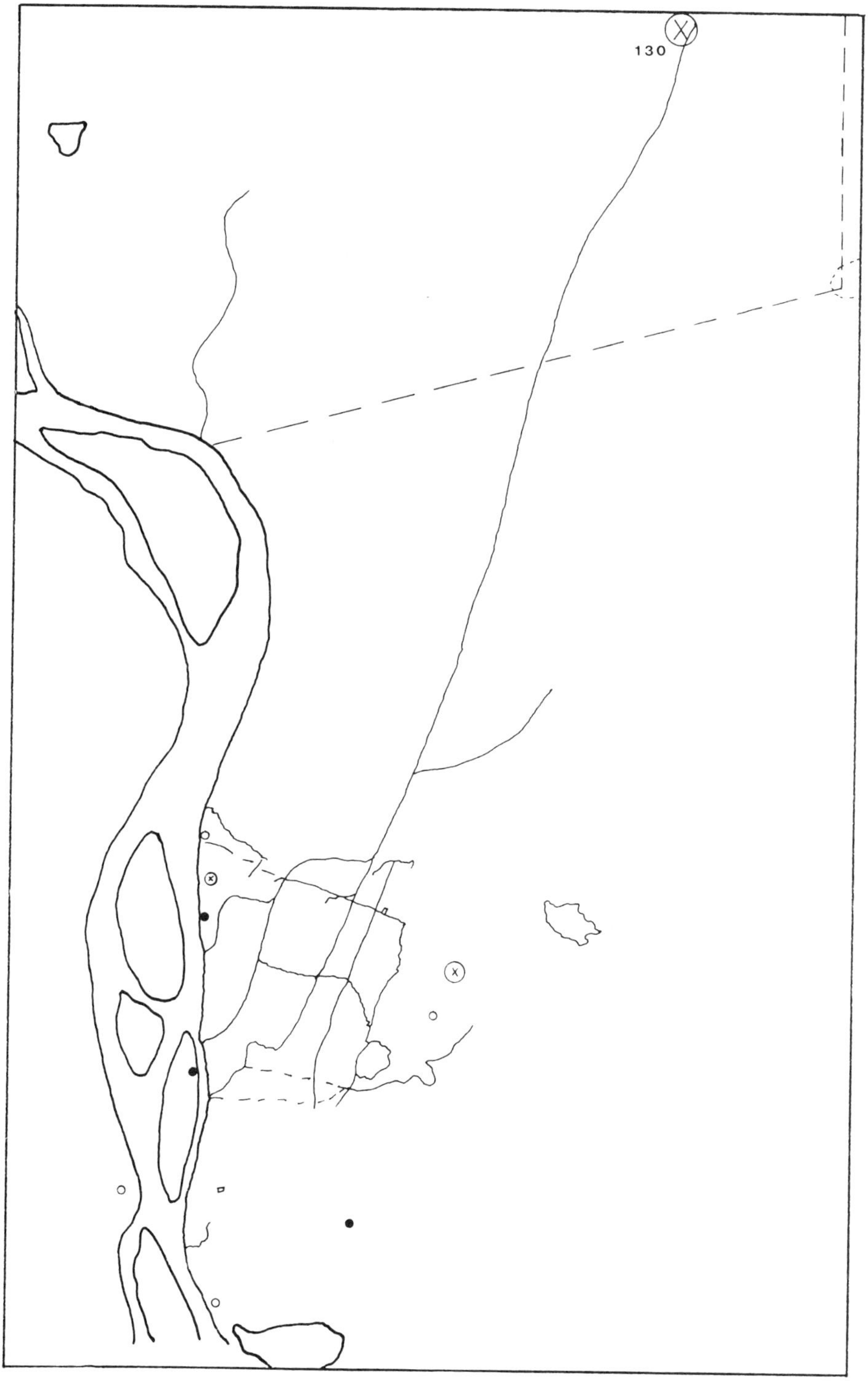

4-F. Environs, Residential Sites
• nisbas
× birthplaces

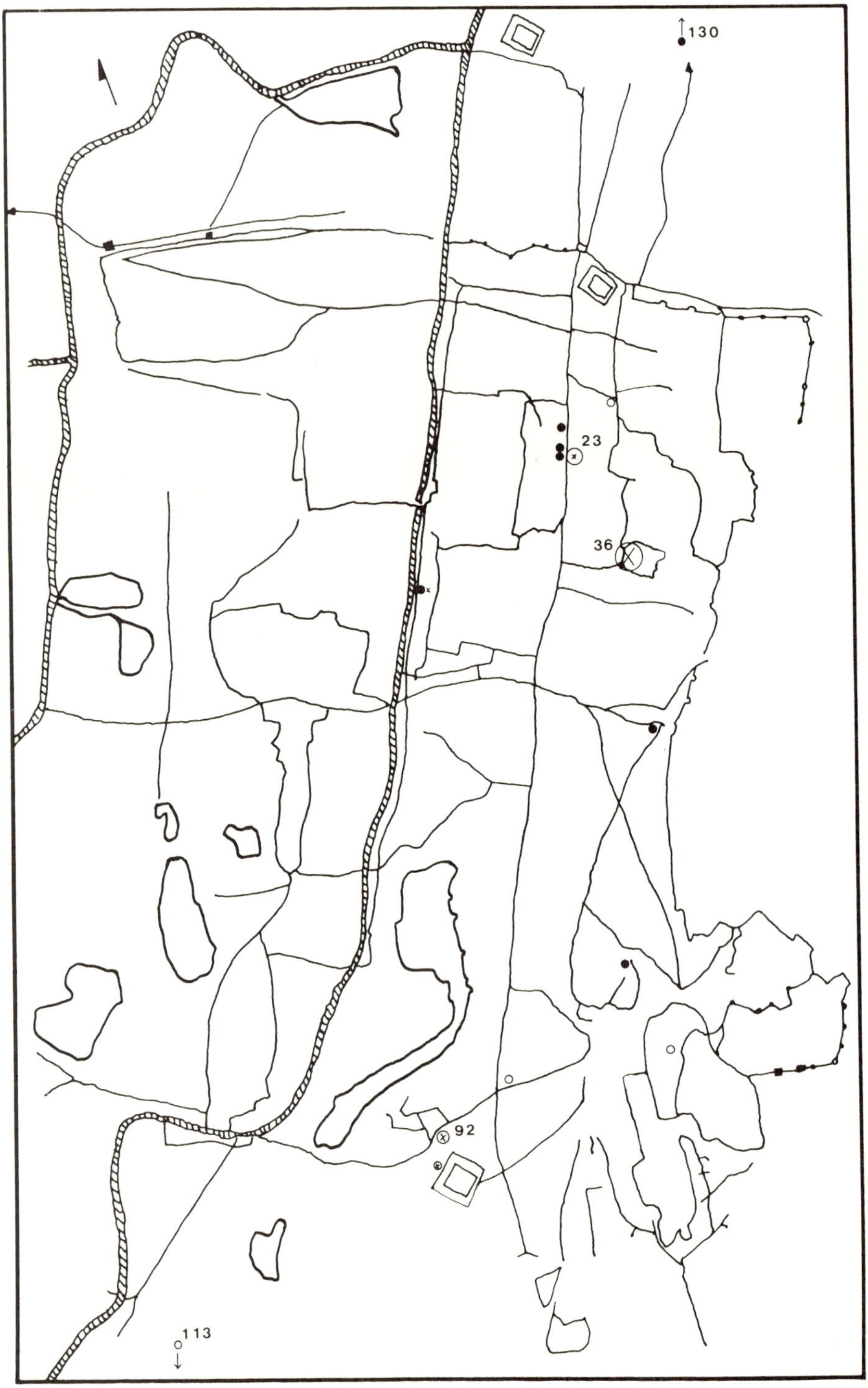

Fig. 5. Individuals from Upper Egypt

5-A. Central City, Educational Sites
• nisbas
× birthplaces

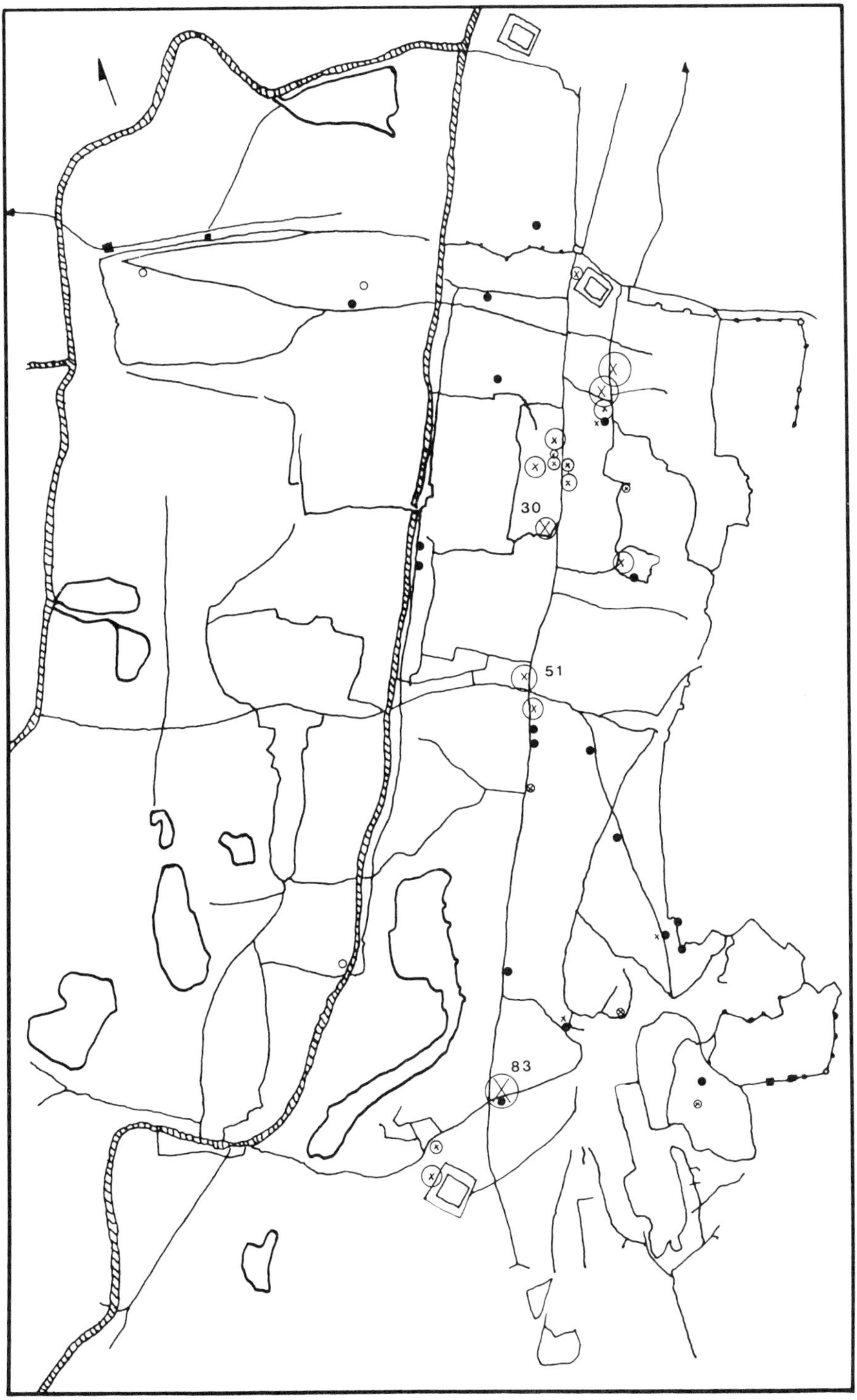

5-B. Central City, Occupational Sites
• nisbas
× birthplaces

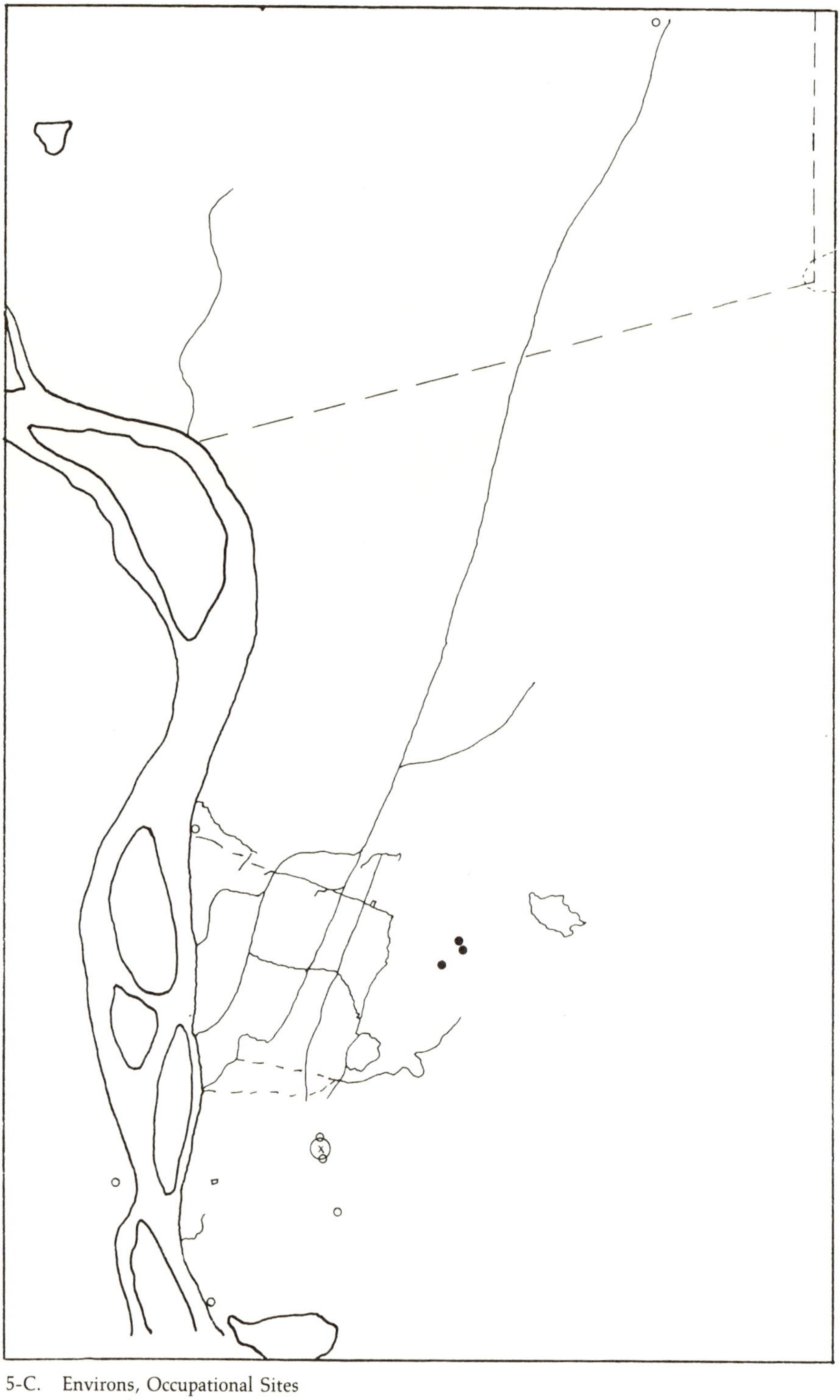

5-C. Environs, Occupational Sites
• nisbas
× birthplaces

5-D. Central City, Residential Sites
• nisbas
× birthplaces

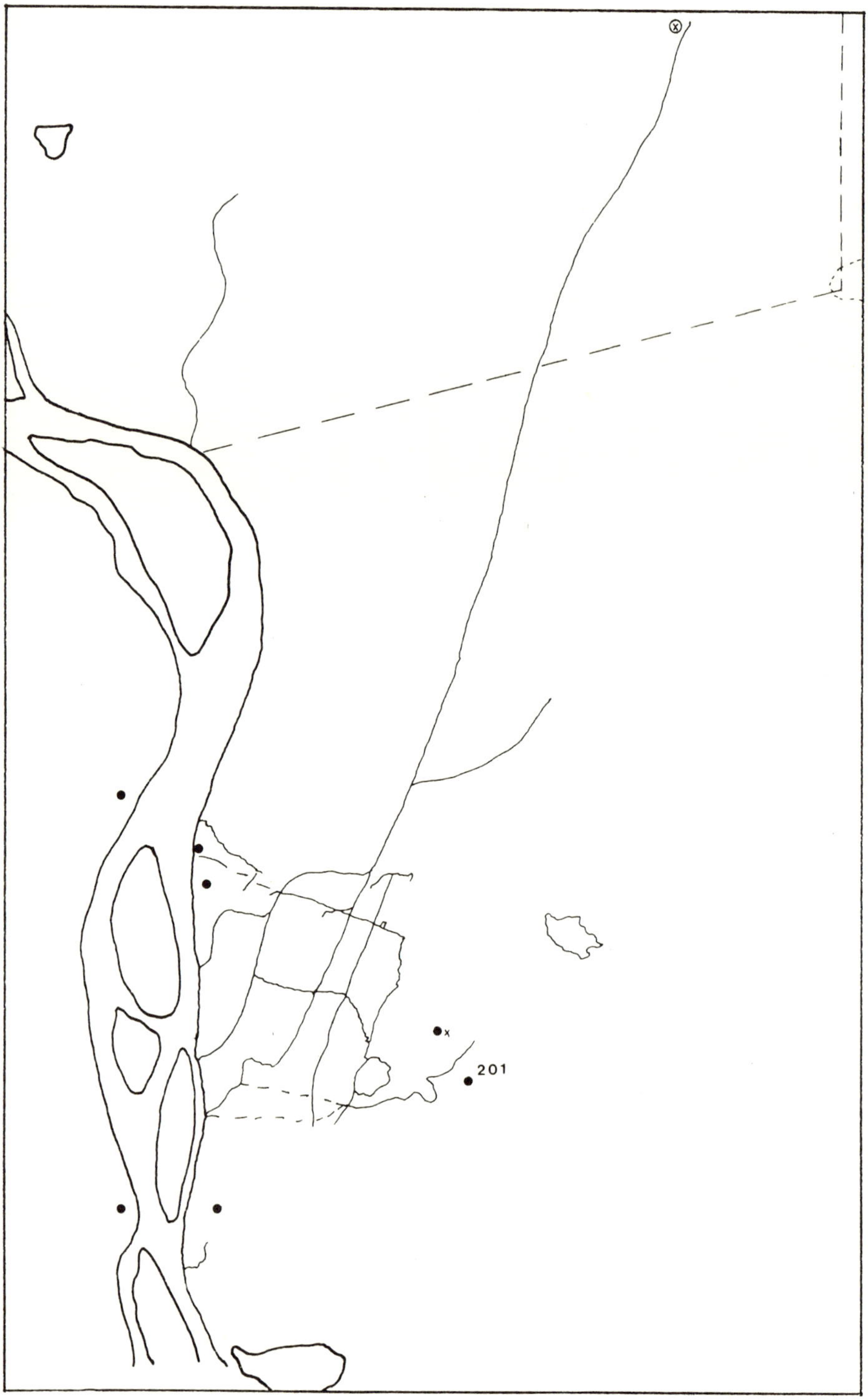

5-E. Environs, Residential Sites
• nisbas
× birthplaces

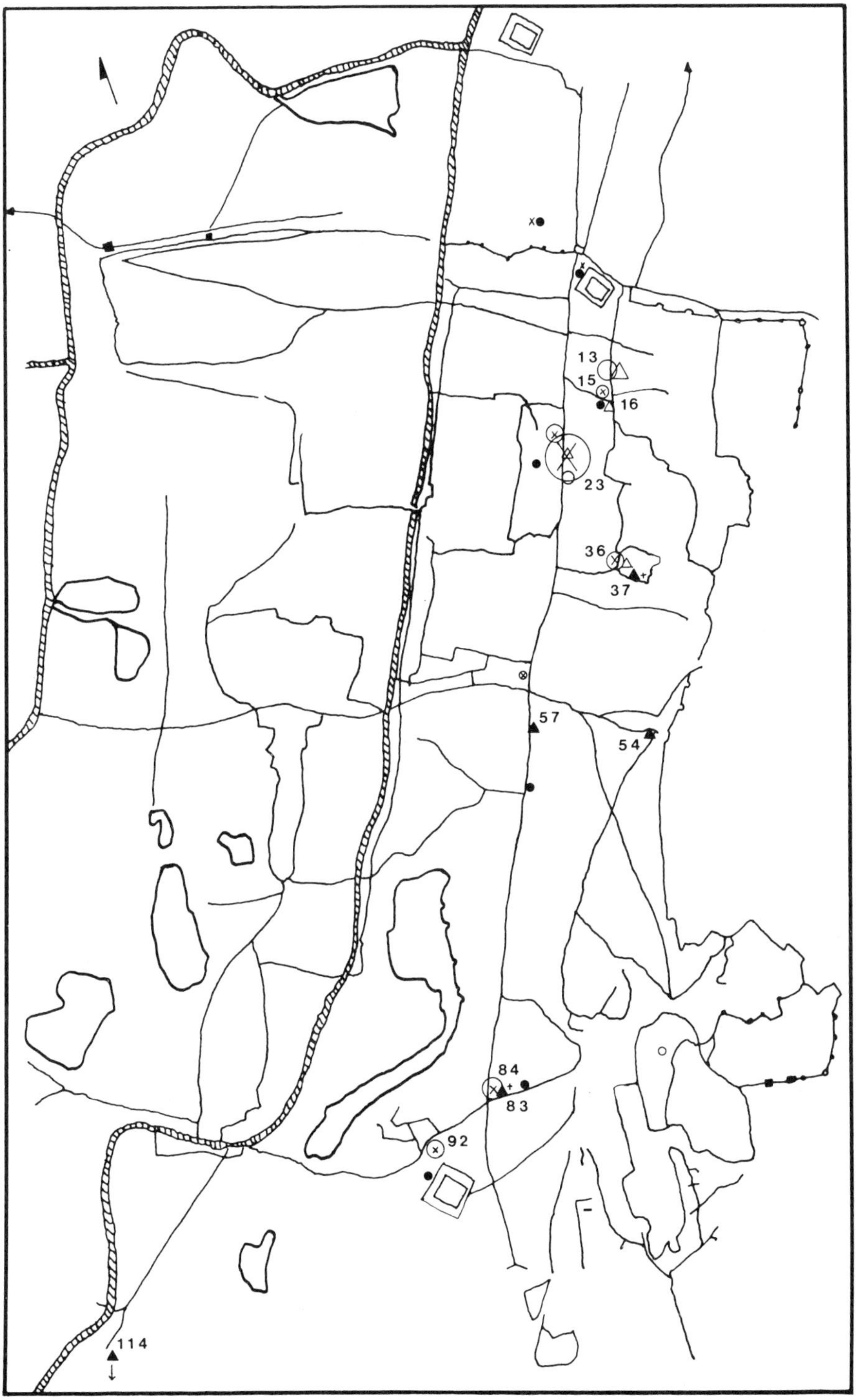

Fig. 6. Individuals from Syria and Iran
6-A. Central City, Educational Sites
• Syrian nisbas
× Syrian birthplaces
▲ Iranian nisbas
+ Iranian birthplaces

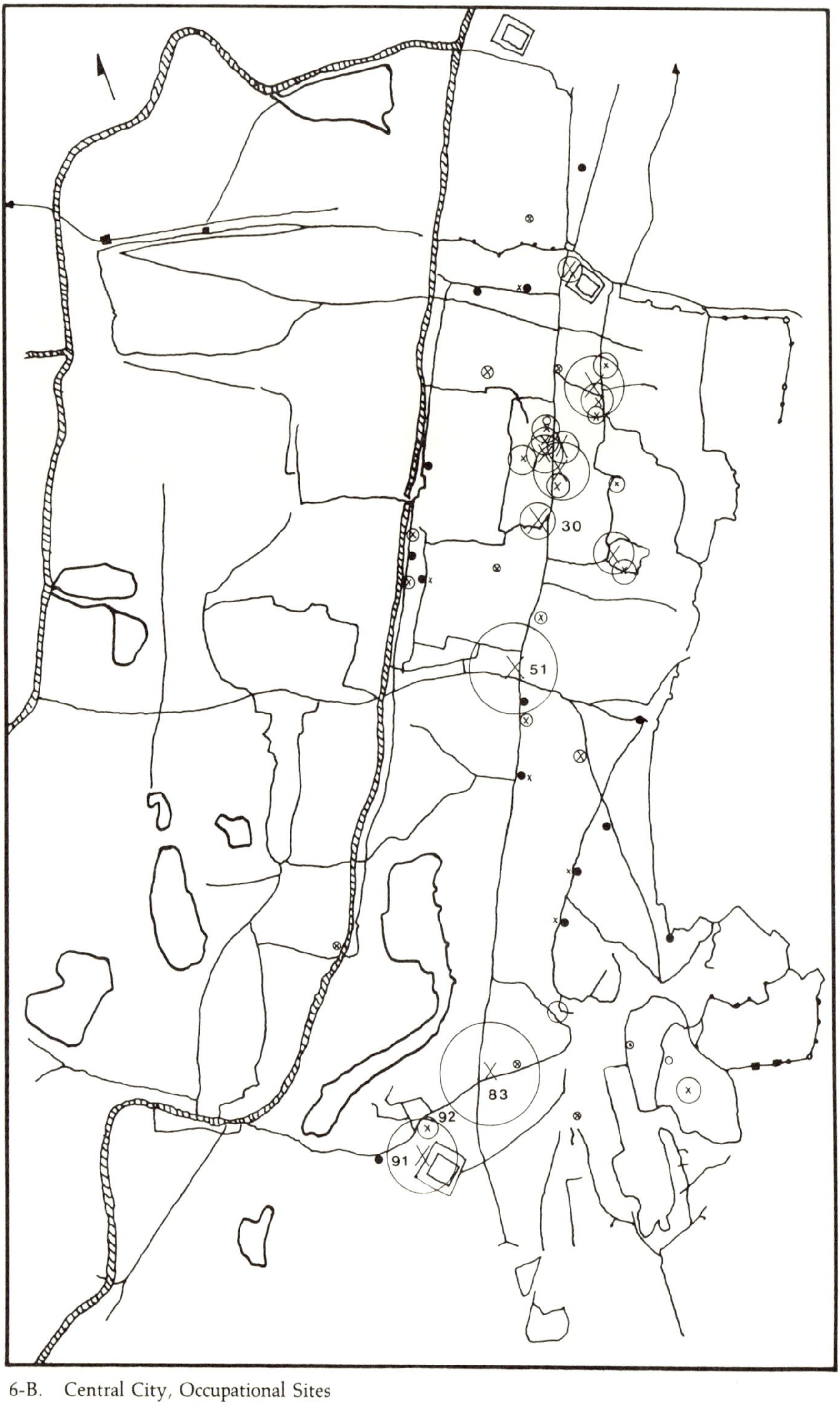

6-B. Central City, Occupational Sites
- • Syrian nisbas
- × Syrian birthplaces

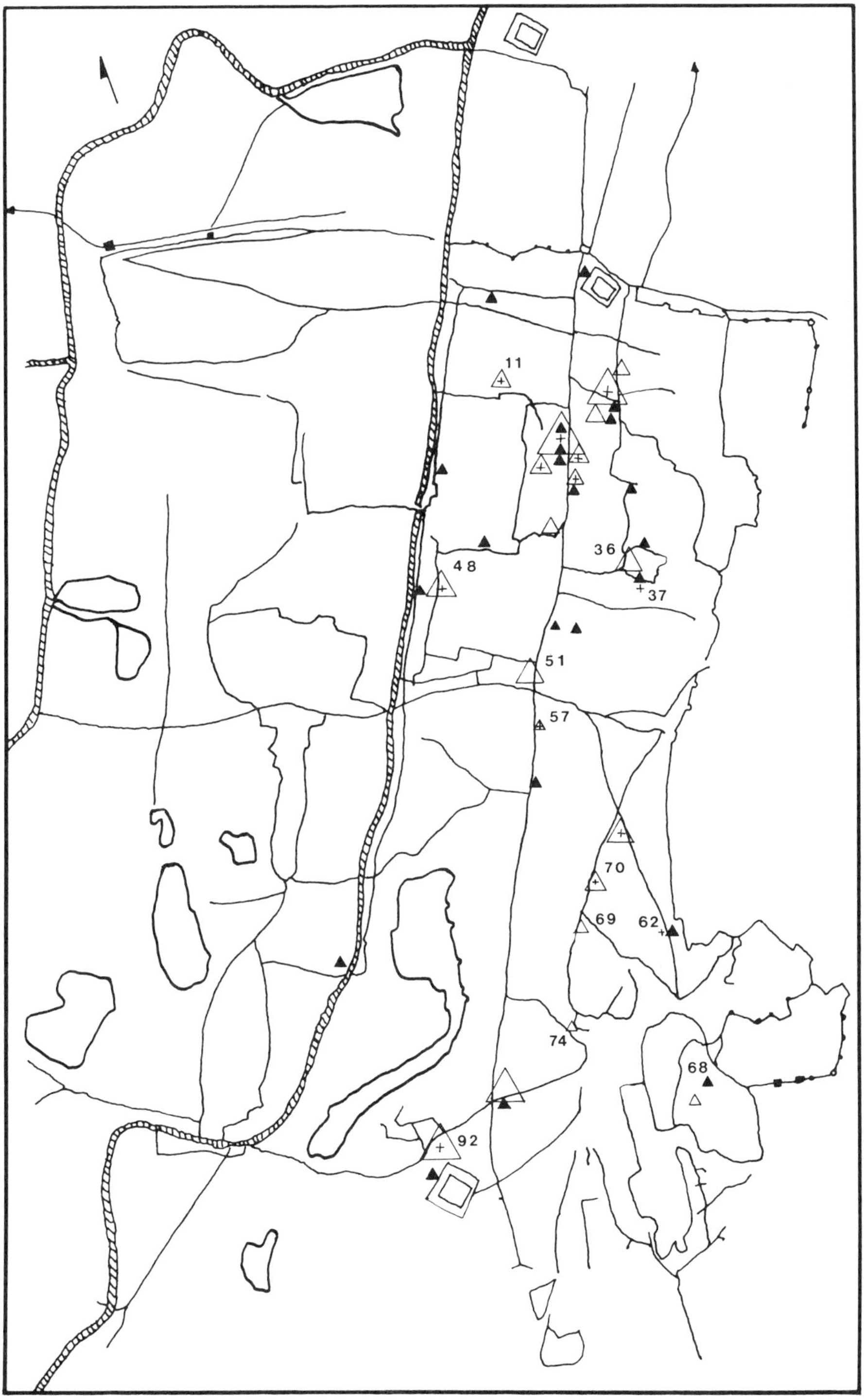

6-C. Central City, Occupational Sites
▲ Iranian nisbas
+ Iranian birthplaces

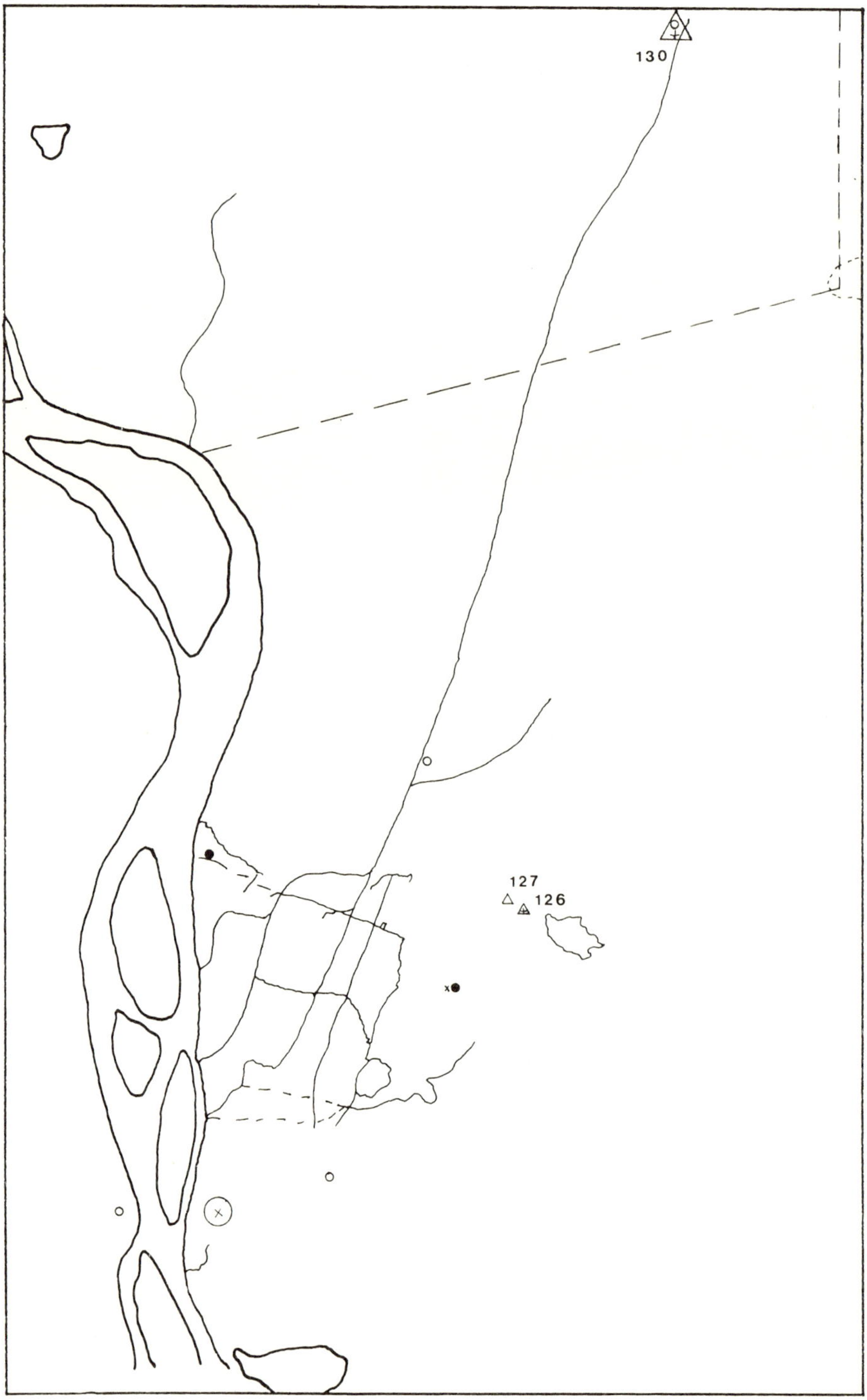

6-D. Environs, Occupational Sites
• Syrian nisbas
× Syrian birthplaces
▲ Iranian nisbas
+ Iranian birthplaces

6-E. Central City, Residential Sites
• Syrian nisbas
× Syrian birthplaces
▲ Iranian nisbas
+ Iranian birthplaces

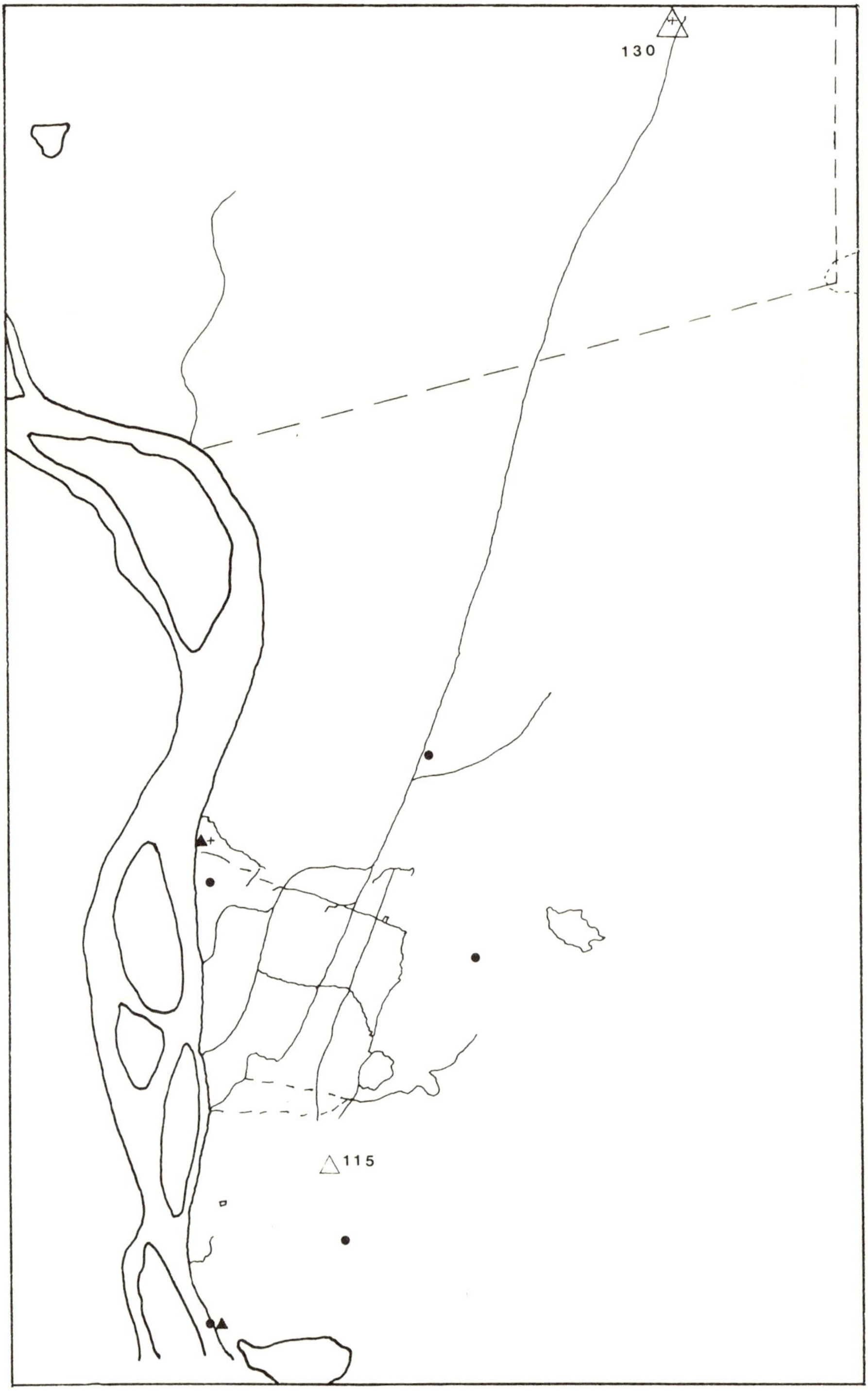

6-F. Environs, Residential Sites

- • Syrian nisbas
- × Syrian birthplaces
- ▲ Iranian nisbas
- + Iranian birthplaces

Fig. 7. Individuals from Anatolia and Iraq
7-A. Central City, Educational Sites
• Anatolian nisbas
× Anatolian birthplaces
▲ Iraqi nisbas
+ Iraqi birthplaces

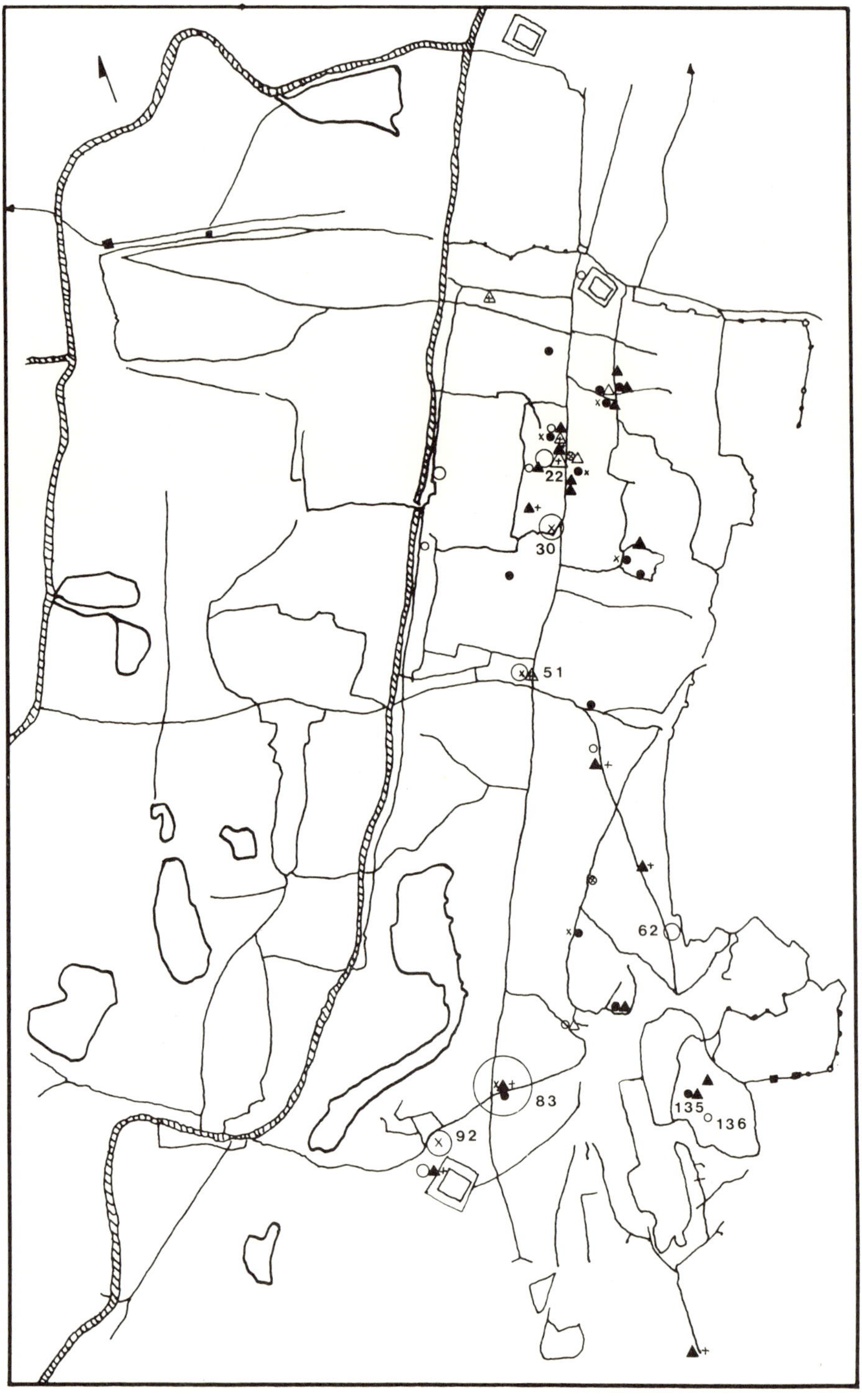

7-B. Central City, Occupational Sites

- • Anatolian nisbas
- × Anatolian birthplaces
- ▲ Iraqi nisbas
- + Iraqi birthplaces

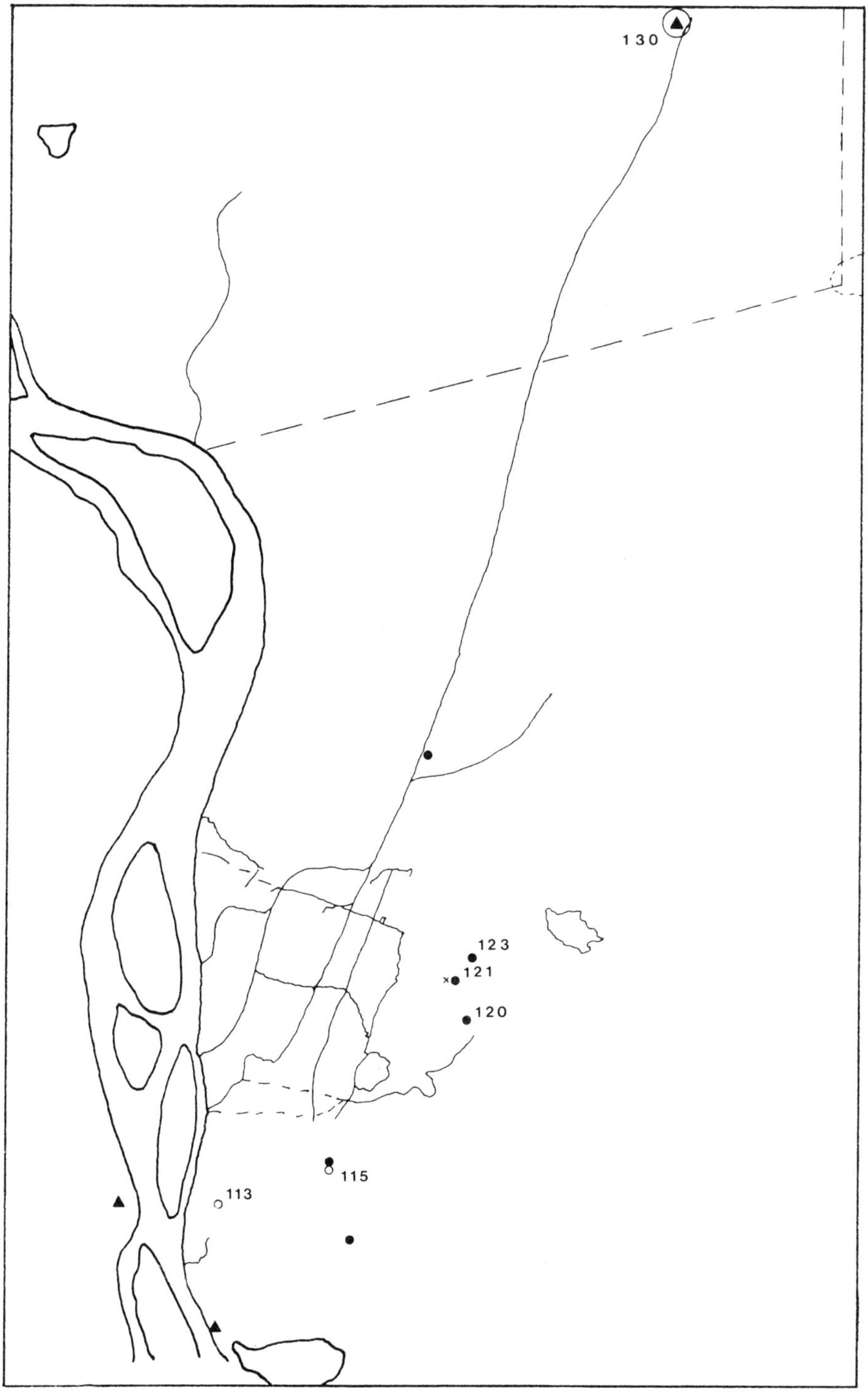

7-C. Environs, Occupational Sites

- • Anatolian nisbas
- × Anatolian birthplaces
- ▲ Iraqi nisbas
- + Iraqi birthplaces

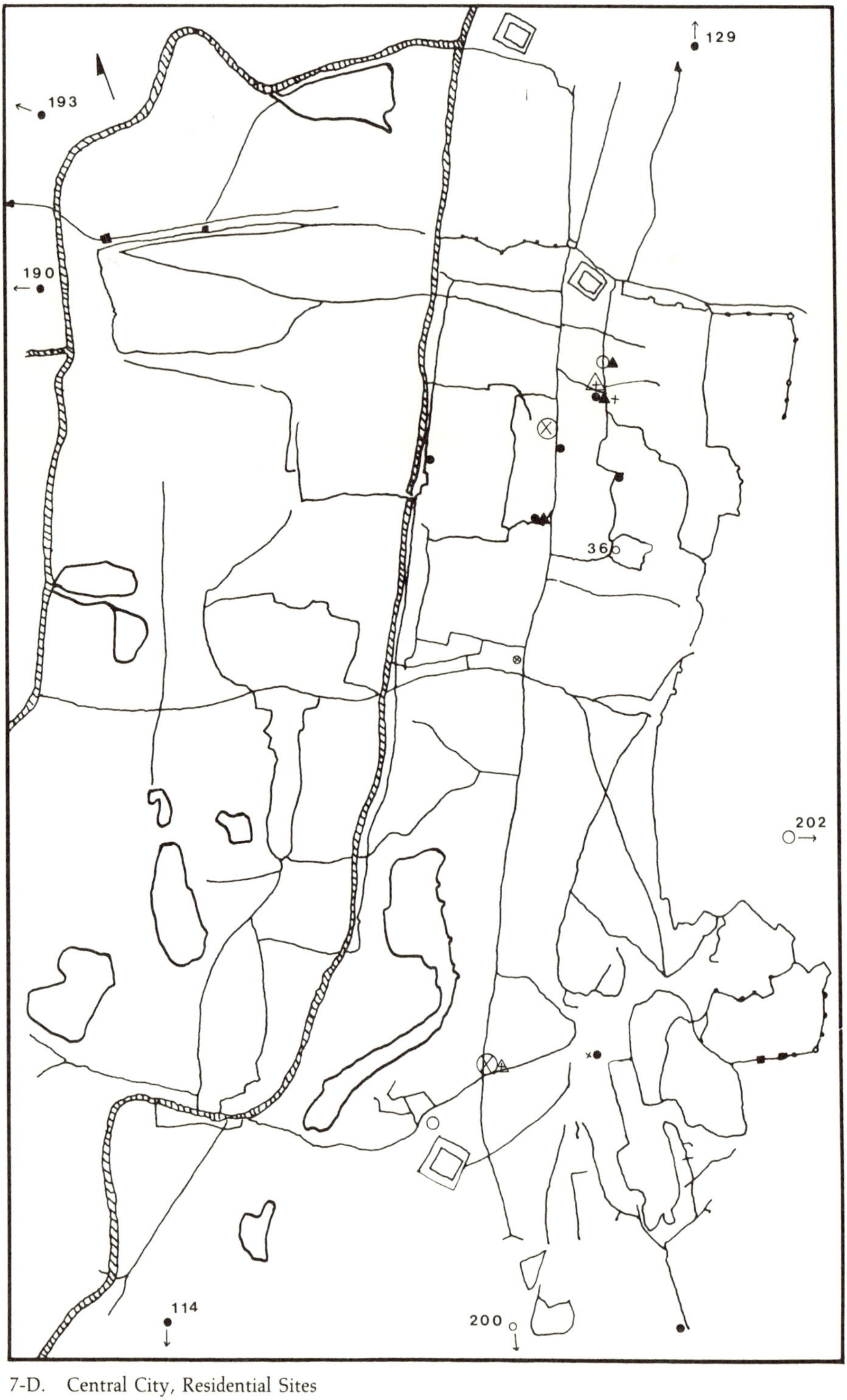

7-D. Central City, Residential Sites

- • Anatolian nisbas
- × Anatolian birthplaces
- ▲ Iraqi nisbas
- + Iraqi birthplaces

Fig. 8. Individuals from North Africa and the Arabian Peninsula
8-A. Central City, Educational Sites
• North African nisbas
▲ Arabian nisbas
× North African birthplaces
+ Arabian birthplaces

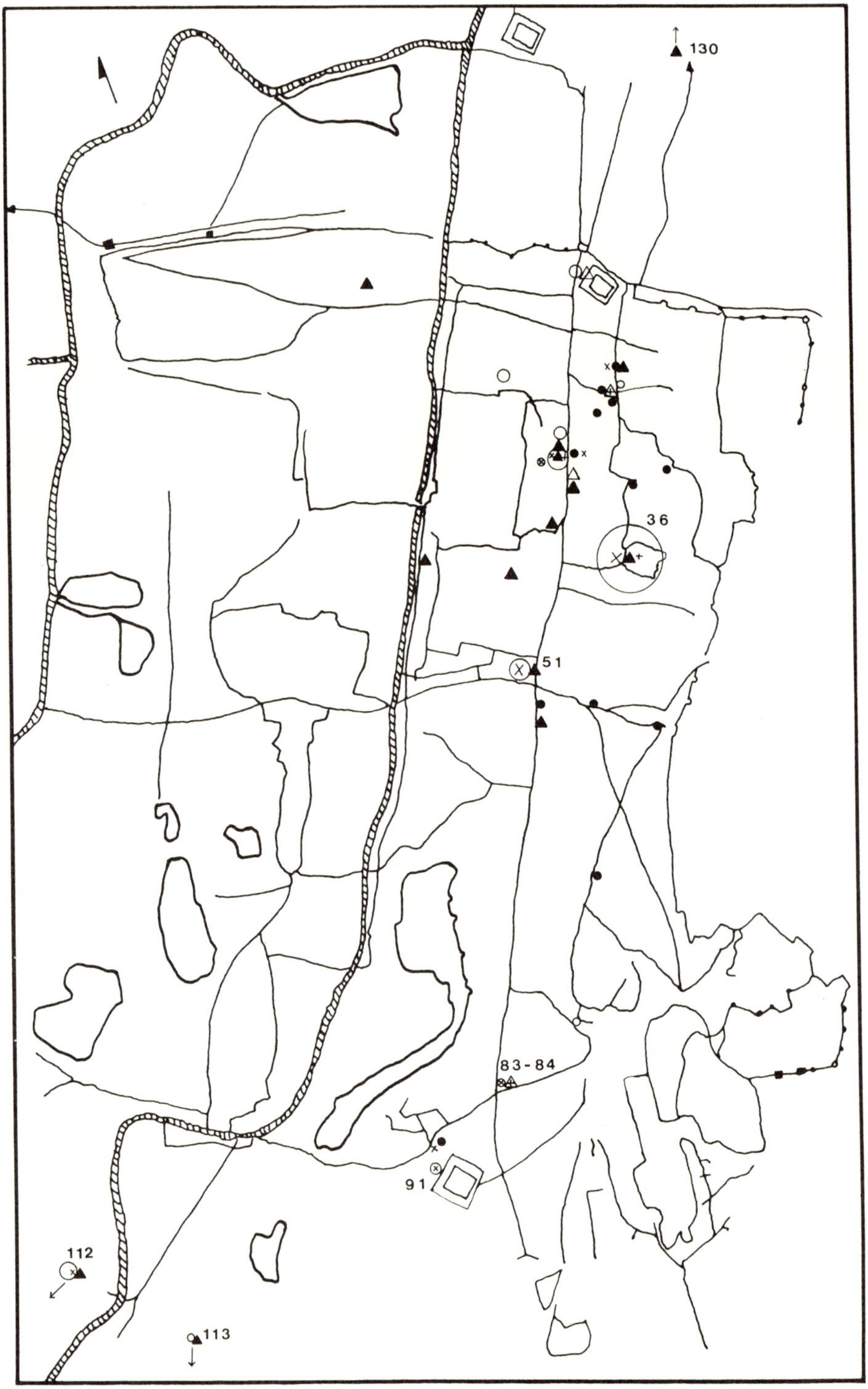

8-B. Central City, Occupational Sites

• North African nisbas
× North African birthplaces
▲ Arabian nisbas
+ Arabian birthplaces

8-C. Central City, Residential Sites
• North African nisbas
× North African birthplaces
▲ Arabian nisbas
+ Arabian birthplaces

CHAPTER IV

Occupational Patterns of the Civilian Elite

TWENTY-ONE major occupations of the civilian elite, together with their variants, from among the hundreds of occupations mentioned in the biographical sources will be discussed here. The objectives are to classify the occupations according to categories, and to form an impression of the civilian elite as a social class in the context of their professional endeavors.

The first objective implies that a categorization of these occupations is justified by the configurations of data yielded by the biographies. In fact, distinctions between occupations, with no evidence of crossover between fields, rarely occurred. There are exceptions to every generalization discussed below. But it is possible to establish general categories, and thus to provide tentative answers to some fundamental questions: did the civilian elite constitute a multicompetent unspecialized social class? That is, did the same individuals, undergoing similar training in a common intellectual milieu, staff the administrative, judicial, scholastic, and religious apparatuses? Did they transfer from one office to another with relative ease, encountering little opposition from vested interests in the several spheres of professional activity? Were there, in fact, vested interests, or did the same persons appear in all the spheres? This study will argue the case not only for distinct occupational categories, but also for a modification of the idea of an unspecialized civilian elite, simultaneously staffing the various professional settings open to civilians. It will thus test whether the terms *aʿyan* and *ʿulamaʾ* were, in reality, interchangeable.

The analysis of occupational distribution is also intended to create a rounded picture of this group. Who were these people? What were the political, economic, social, and even psychological conditions of their existence? Can special characteristics of individuals serving in certain of the occupational categories be discerned? Were the prerogatives, benefits, and liabilities of such service similarly balanced in all of them? If any imbalance seems likely, what motivated individuals to accept vulnerable, even dangerous offices? In a political system that theoretically excluded civilians from executive authority, were civilians able to influence, directly or indirectly, either the mass of society or even the military elite? Were all elements of the civilian elite equally exposed to both the benefits and liabilities of close association with the Mamluk ruling caste? Did various components of the elite interact socially or professionally, or are there signs of vested interests that maintained some degree of exclusiveness? These questions will also stir up an old controversy: did the ʿulama' serve primarily as mediators between the Mamluks and the general population, who were compelled to support the entire system? Or does the concept of mediation fail to do justice to the complexities of civilian elite status during this period? Doubtlessly, the following discussion will not resolve such a broad issue. But it will add some new perspectives to the debate.

One characteristic of all elements comprising the civilian elite is so prominent that it merits comment at the outset: multiple officeholding. This phenomenon has led analysts of medieval social organization in the Middle East to assume a similarity of competence that derived from uniform training.[1] There is no question that the majority of individuals examined here held more than one office simultaneously. But whether this suggests multicompetence and, if so, whether such multicompetence was due to the supposedly unspecialized nature of the offices held by these people needs to be examined. This study will suggest that some degree of specialization was, in fact, apparent, and that it varied according to the broad professional categories. But the issue of multiple officeholding raises several other questions about the nature of civilian professional activity in the Mamluk state, questions that also address realities of service in a closed political system. It is quite possible, for example, that certain positions held by an individual may not have been actively served by him. He may have drawn the pay for the post, while delegating its duties to a subordinate—or to a colleague as a favor, if illicit fees or personal connections resulted from it. The extent of sinecurism is exceedingly difficult to measure from the biographical records, which list positions with very little comment on performance of duties. But there are so many references to associates or subordinates whose careers were advanced by the individuals in return for assuming their responsibilities in an office that its widespread occurrence was probable.

In discussing each occupational category, I will first briefly describe the occupations, and then compare the range of activities engaged in by persons involved with these occupations during their careers. This comparison is depicted in Table 11, which lists the relative proportions of the several types of professional activity according to the twenty-one occupations in the major group. This table indicates the degree of concentration of people in several professions within their own and other categories. The concentrations differed quite markedly according to the specific occupations, and even within the categories configurations varied noticeably. Such variations are related to the occupation and residence patterns depicted on the city maps (cf. Figs. 9-27).

THE EXECUTIVE AND MILITARY PROFESSIONS
(Table 11, Category I)

These occupations, although dominant in the social and political hierarchy of Egypt during the Mamluk period, could not be analyzed here because of their infrequent mention in the texts, and our inability to establish specific occupational or residential sites for them. Mamluks and their civilian clients almost exclusively staffed this category. They monopolized most of the revenues produced in the society, and were able to afford luxurious accommodations. If they were not housed at court, these people tended to purchase or build homes in the city or suburbs. Unfortunately, only a small number of these survived into the nineteenth century to be located by Herz and Creswell.[2] Occupational sites were rarely reported for this class, and these people were not attached to the same institutions as the ʿulamaʾ. In general, this class tended not to gather in the northeast districts of the city. The Mamluks and their clients congregated in the vicinity of the Citadel, in the Cross Street-Qaṣr al-Kabsh area (Fig. 1: 173), along the shores of the Elephant and Raṭlī Lakes (Fig. 1: 170, 183), in the plantation districts of the northwest and southwest sections, and along the Nile shore (Fig. 2: 190-192).

THE BUREAUCRATIC (SECRETARIAL-FINANCIAL) PROFESSIONS
(Table 11, Category II)

This category appears so frequently and vividly in the narrative sources that its activities are considered a quintessential aspect of medieval Islamic civilization, and rightly so. Evolving over long centuries, the bureaucracies of premodern Near Eastern states were rich in personalities, character types, and intrigue. For better or worse, their traditions defined the quality of administrative practice. Although the individuals who staffed these bureaucracies clearly belonged to the civilian elite, controversy has persisted from the writings of contemporary observers to the present over the status of these people in relation to the ʿulamaʾ. Were the individuals imbedded in the bureaucratic network, for example, the same as those who practiced law, taught in the kuttāb and madrasas, and administered religious service to the populace at large? Were their family backgrounds, training, political circumstances, and, above all, relations with the military the same? To explore these problems, we must examine the several occupational components of the bureaucratic category, keeping two things in mind. First, these occupations were linked by common functions and services, outlined below. In other respects, especially in their popular esteem, they might differ radically. These occupations thus differed among themselves in the degree of their identity with fields generally acknowledged to be the province of the ʿulamaʾ. Second, the extent of interrelationship with other fields, both inside and outside the bureaucratic category, varied widely according to specific office. Such variation provides a rough measure of the integration of an office with other elements of the civilian elite.

The offices in this category all involved processing documents or balancing accounts (cf. Appendix II, Lists 1-6). Yet the official duties of their formal appointment rarely encompassed the full roster of their activities. Indeed, success in these positions, both for the bureaucrat and his sponsor, usually involved aggrandizement through gaining broad access to political authority and funds. These occupations differed widely with respect to nature of official duties, collateral activities, quality of the position, and degree of influence gained by holding it. But they shared one characteristic: individuals engaged in the bureaucracy had access to information from all levels of society. They often procured information for persons wielding immense political authority, but who could not themselves gain access to such information because of their status. In this environment, therefore, the bureaucrat was immersed in the politics of his employer, who used him as his personal agent in areas closed to him. Since Islamic society remained essentially uncorporate, its rulers had to deal with each of its many elements on a one-to-one basis, and thus required a pragmatic bureaucratic class. Since this class had access to information from all the elements and institutions of the society, it possessed a mechanism for manipulation and exploitation of various socio-political groups unequalled by any other professional category. We shall see that the bureaucrat tended to be located close to the scene of procurement of information, although not necessarily at the scene of highest political authority.

The Kātib or Secretary
(Appendix II, List 1)

> Every secretary is condemned to perpetual loyalty and at the same time expected to tolerate adversity; that is the contradictory situation imposed on him and the dilemma that lies in wait for him.[3]

Throughout the Middle Ages, historians, political theorists, and satirists commented on the role of the bureaucrat, but few writers assessed his qualities more keenly than al-Jāḥiẓ. Even though several centuries had elapsed since the heyday of ʿAbbāsid Baṣrā and Baghdād, his observations apply directly to conditions in Mamluk Egypt, as depicted by the biographical sources. The office of secretary (kātib) had evolved into a broad archival and administrative profession during the classical Islamic period.[4] The secretary dealt in the processing of records. Accuracy in transmission and political acumen were required for accomplishment in this field, but an education in the Islamic sciences was not.[5]

During the fifteenth century, the kātibs depicted in the biographical sources were entrenched primarily in the governmental bureaus. In this setting, secretaries were confined to archival and administrative tasks. But in their own sphere of information gathering, including military intelligence and local spy networks, they reigned supreme, and were thus able to gain considerable influence. The large bureaus, and particularly the dīwān al-inshāʾ, which combined the functions of a documents repository, foreign ministry, and intelligence office, constituted the ultimate goals for holders of secretaryships.[6] Those individuals who attained the highest positions were men of proven ability and learning, but they rarely came up from the lower secretarial levels. Members of the secretarial class, although skilled in bureaucratic procedures, remained objects of scorn and belittlement in the eyes of the learned, because of the alleged mediocrity of the class's scholarly attainments.

Al-Jāḥiẓ referred to the lack of adequate training in an offhand manner. Indeed, the occupations reported for the dīwān secretary, as contrasted with those of his more illustrious superior, the secretary of the chancellery, indicated that he was rarely employed in the legal, scholarly-educational, and religious fields (Categories III, V, and VI, respectively)—all of which required an orthodox education. No more than 4 percent of the total positions held by secretaries were in these areas. Even in the bureaucratic category (II), secretaries were largely confined to their own occupation. Multiple officeholding was thus less evident among secretaries than among any other profession. Few occupants of the office were documents clerks (muwaqqiʿs) or secretaries of the chancellery. Many members of the kātib class were Copts, the majority of whom were converts to Islam. Few of these converts or their descendants were credited with sound grounding in the Islamic sciences.[7] Their presence reinforced the image of this class as relatively uneducated and of low status. The lack of esteem—even hostility—toward holders of this office may, in fact, be traced in part to the presence of suspect Muslims who staffed it. Because of these stigmas, the secretarial class as depicted in the biographical sources appeared less professionally mobile than other occupations in its own category. The evidence points to a quasi-caste of information procurers.

There were two notable concentrations of kātibs, however, indicating two critical realms the secretarial class managed to penetrate. These were the administration of revenues and revenue-collecting bureaus (nāẓirs), and certain executive offices within the Mamluk sphere of influence (Appendix II, List 1, Categories II and I, respectively). No other professional types except the nāẓirs themselves, secretaries of the chancellery, and muḥtasibs in the legal category were represented in such large numbers there. These concentrations reveal the core of the secretarial class's influence within the bureaucracy. Although their formal duties did not grant them access to political authority or manipulation of funds, they managed to gain simultaneous appointments that did grant such access. The secretarial class thus managed to acquire a powerful position in the areas of information and revenue. They succeeded in doing so, of course, at the suffrage of their Mamluk overlords with whom they maintained close ties. There were thirteen references among them to the office of wazīr (List 1, Category II), the largest proportion to be found in any occupation in the survey. To the Mamluks, the secretarial class constituted an ideal base for recruitment to personal service. The Copts in particular were dependent on patrons to rise in the bureaucracy since their background would otherwise impede their upward mobility.

The social and professional qualities of the secretaries during the Circassian period shed light on the views so skillfully summarized by al-Jāḥiẓ. This class obviously was not fully established within the learned elite of Cairo. Although kātibs exercised considerable authority, it was not based on attainments sanctioned by the learned. The fact that secretaries exercised authority at the suffrage of the Mamluk elite, who exploited them as instruments of their own greed, goes far to explain the hostility exhibited by the ʿulamaʾ toward them.

The Kātib al-Sirr or Secretary of the Chancellery
(Appendix II, List 2)

This office, literally the "secretary of the (royal) confidence," differed in both official duties and level of prestige from the general secretaryship. The title implied a close advisory relationship with the sultan or his provincial governors.[8] The secretary of the chancellery belonged to the intimate inner circle of the royal court, along with the wazīr (whom he gradually supplanted) and nāẓirs of the royal bureaus, because he was head of the dīwān al-inshāʾ.[9] He supplied the ruler with confidential information and directed the various intelligence networks in Cairo and throughout the empire.[10] The sultans personally appointed their secretaries of the chancellery, and tended not to select them from the ranks of the secretarial class but from among men of proven ability in the financial bureaus and the courts, the nāẓirs and qāḍīs. These individuals were often men of considerable renown within the learned elite. There was no question about their established position within the ranks of the ʿulamaʾ; in this they differed from the secretarial class. Relatively few Copts attained this office (Table 11); the biographical sources reported only three cases, each of whom had been born a Muslim.[11]

Having access to more confidential information than any other imperial official brought the secretary of the chancellery both benefits and liabilities. Sultans relied heavily on their intelligence chiefs, but also distrusted them and often dismissed or imprisoned them without notice—especially if an individual showed more aptitude or skill in the office than was thought safe. The sultan was suspicious of individuals who knew too much and who mastered every facet of the chancellery. Such persons were often approached by the sultan's open or secret rivals and promised power and wealth in return for divulging court secrets. The office of kātib al-sirr tended to be dominated by powerful bureaucrats and legal figures, and the men who held it often possessed a substantial education. Yet the office also had great dangers as did all the civilian posts of the inner court circles.

Although kātibs al-sirr were appointed to executive offices, they did not exceed the percentage of dīwān secretaries (Table 11, Category I). However, more secretaries of the chancellery were represented in the legal and scholarly categories than were their subordinates (Categories III and V). Most of the kātibs al-sirr, indeed, were appointed to the office only after service in other areas of the bureaucracy or the courts.

Few of the secretaries of the chancellery were enlisted from the ranks of their subordinates (Table 11, Category II). This office was reserved for those whose position in the learned elite was unquestioned, but an unusually large number derived from Syria.[12] In fact, this was one of the few offices held more frequently by foreigners than by Egyptians. This may be explained in terms of the Mamluk provincial governors' practice of bringing with them their staffs when they transferred to Cairo. Many of the Syrians who ultimately became secretaries of the chancellery first held the position in one of the provincial capitals under a viceroy, or rose to the position when their patron gained the throne. We have noted that sultans required individuals of proven loyalty as well as ability. They turned to their own staffs to find them.

The Syrians seem to have combined two qualities as directors of intelligence. First, they identified with the ʿulamaʾ of the Mamluk state.

As such, they were granted access to the myriad activities of the learned elite in Cairo and throughout the empire. Most of them had seen previous service in other branches of the bureaucracy, the judiciary, and the scholarly establishment. Many belonged to prominent Syrian families that maintained ties with relatives in Cairo. These people were among the most cosmopolitan in the state, more familiar with diplomacy and statecraft than any other civilian group in the empire.

Second, as Syrians, most of these individuals owed their positions in Cairo to their Mamluk patrons. In an intensely competitive environment in which many qualified persons sought limited offices, this client relationship remained important throughout an individual's career. Appointment to all these dīwān posts was at the discretion of the military elite. The Mamluks maintained their dominant position and controlled the civilian elements of the state by manipulating their clients, binding them ever more tightly to their own interests. Syrians who attained high office in Egypt owed their status to their sponsors, and to secure their status, they were obliged to accept the role of chief spies and secret agents when the occasion arose. Syrians were more suitable for this role than Egyptians because of their foreign origin and dependence on Mamluk sponsors. Their patrons were keenly aware of this when they chose their confidential secretaries.

The character of the kātib al-sirr may be discerned by examining careers of individuals appointed to the office. The four examples examined here, all of Syrian background, were drawn from cases in which the office was held several times along with other positions. The first two cases involve a father and son, both born in Ḥamā: Nāṣir al-Dīn Abū ʿAbd-Allah Muḥammad ibn Muḥammad ibn ʿUthmān al-Ḥamawī al-Shāfiʿī, known as Ibn al-Bārizī,[13] and his son, Kamāl al-Dīn Abū'l-Maʿālī Muḥammad, who was known as Kamāl ibn al-Bārizī.[14] They were among the most famous and influential civilian politicians in Cairo during the fifteenth century. The senior Ibn al-Bārizī, born in Shawwāl 769/May-June 1368, belonged to an established judicial family in Ḥamā that traced its origins to Baghdād. He received his first judgeship in 796/1393-1394. He was subsequently appointed secretary of the chancellery for Ḥamā province and controller of the army in Aleppo in 809/1406-1407. He became an associate of the viceroy of Damascus and future sultan, Grand Amir al-Mu'ayyad Shaykh, who appointed him khaṭīb in the Umayyad mosque. His last office in Syria was very distinguished: he was appointed Shāfiʿī chief justice of Aleppo by Sultan Faraj. He transferred to Cairo at the request of al-Mu'ayyad Shaykh after the latter's enthronement, and was ultimately appointed kātib al-sirr of Egypt in 815/1412-1413. He resigned from the office in his last years and became the first librarian of his patron's new mosque (cf. Appendix I, Mu'ayyadīya). Al-Sakhāwī noted that Ibn al-Bārizī was a prolific poet in addition to his professional duties. He died in Shawwāl 823/October-November 1420.

The career of the son outshone that of the father. Kamāl ibn al-Bārizī, born in Dhū'l-Ḥijja 796/September-October 1394, entered professional life in Ḥamā as an assistant to his father in the dīwān al-inshā' after completing an impressive education. He accompanied his father to Cairo and succeeded him as kātib al-sirr in 823/1420-1421. Throughout his career he maintained close ties with Sultans al-Mu'ayyad Shaykh, Barsbāy, and Jaqmaq, who appointed him to the offices of controller of the army, secretary of the chancellery of Syria, two Shāfiʿī judgeships in Damascus, khaṭīb of the Umayyad mosque, secretary of the chancellery in Egypt a second and third time, and Shāfiʿī chief justice of Damietta, where he ended his career. He died in Ṣafar 856/February-March 1452. The list of political involvements in Kamāl's biography was enormous, indicating that he used his office as head of the chancellery to supply his employers, and particularly Sultan Jaqmaq, with secret details about amirs suspected of treason or bureaucrats who were becoming excessively rich and, therefore, ripe for mulcting.

The third case involved an individual who held the office four times prior to assuming four Mālikī judgeships in succession. He was ʿAlā' al-Dīn ʿAlī ibn Yūsuf ibn Ibrāhīm al-Ḥalabī al-Mālikī al-Qāhirī, born in Cairo in 781/1379-1380 and educated in Aleppo.[15] He received his first post as kātib al-sirr in Ḥamā at the behest of the caliph-sultan al-Mustaʿīn in 815/1412-1413. He was subsequently appointed to the office twice in Ṭarābulus and once in Cairo. He received the first of his judgeships from Sultan Barsbāy in Ṭarābulus and, after an interlude as controller of the army in Aleppo, from which he resigned, he went on to the chief justiceships of Ḥamā, Aleppo, and Damascus, the last at the request of Sultan Jaqmaq. Born in Cairo of Syrian parents, this individual developed most of his career in his family's ancestral region and acted as an agent of the great amirs who had promoted him.

The fourth example followed an opposite course. Born in Aleppo in 772/1370-1371, he terminated his career in Cairo as an associate of Sultan Barsbāy. He was Burhān (Shihāb) al-Dīn Abū'l-ʿAbbās Aḥmad ibn Ṣāliḥ al-Ḥalabī.[16] He did not practice law, but inaugurated his career as a legal documents clerk in Aleppo. He became controller of legal documentation in that city prior to his appointment as archivist to the atābek al-ʿasākir, Grand Amir Yashbak, in place of his own brother, Muḥammad. He was subsequently appointed secretary of the chancellery in Ṣafad and Aleppo before he was noted by Grand Amir Barsbāy, who made him his archivist and, after his enthronement, his confidential secretary in Cairo. His last office was the controllership of the documents bureau (nāẓir dīwān al-inshā'), at his patron's request, although he was dismissed from the office in his old age. He died in Cairo in Rajab 835/ October-November 1431. The sultan attended his funeral, and the caliph led the prayer service. These four examples suggest the type of background requisite to attainment of the office: considerable legal or bureaucratic experience and personal connections with the men most likely to win the sultanate.

DISTRIBUTION OF KĀTIBS (Fig. 9)

Due to the source bias toward positions within the religio-academic network, the occupational and residential survey for the secretarial group, including kātibs al-sirr, cannot be regarded as accurate. Few individuals engaged in secretarial activities were associated with institutions of higher learning. Not many Muslim Copts would maintain any affiliation with them, for instance. And the majority of occupational sites in the biographical accounts designated governmental bureaus not specifically located. Many references to residence were to private accommodation in the city, also of indeterminant location. The residual hardly provides a definitive pattern, but it does suggest the kātibs' lack of identity with the religious institutions, and especially the Ṣūfī khānqāhs.[17] Certainly the presence of Copts among the secretaries is a factor contributing to this small showing, but secretaries of the chancellery, few of whom were from this minority, were also conspicuously absent from the Ṣūfī establishments. This provides a negative confirmation of the secretarial class's segregation from the juridical, scholastic, and religious components of the civilian elite. Whether such a phenomenon was due primarily to self-imposed isolation, Mamluk pressure, or conscious exclusion by the ʿulamaʾ remains unclear from the biographical records. Nonetheless, the absence of civilian elements publicly regarded as minions of the ruling regime from the religio-academic network stands as a pattern repeated throughout the study.

The Mubāshir or Steward-Intendant
(Appendix II, List 3; Figs. 10-A, 10-B)

Mubāshirs served as stewards in a wide range of institutional settings.[18] The stewards reported in the biographical sources were attached to the religio-academic network of the city. These people worked under the authority of shaykhs, nāẓirs, and kātibs to process accounts and generally maintain institutional functions. They also appeared on occasion as couriers and precursors who cleared the streets for important officials, announcing their arrival at destinations. It might seem that their calling did not fit into the range of activities defining the learned elite, and yet they held a higher percentage of offices in the legal and scholarly categories (Table 11, Categories III and V) than the secretaries, and exceeded all other occupations in their class in the proportion of religious positions held (Category VI).

All factors considered, stewardship emerges in the accounts of individual lives as a rather shadowy and ill-defined post, mentioned in almost an off-handed manner in the texts. The stewardship usually inaugurated a career, and its occupants often aspired to more lucrative or prestigious posts in either the dīwāns or the religio-academic network. Indeed, the occupational pattern suggests that stewards managed to secure a degree of upward professional mobility and demonstrated a much broader occupational span than the secretarial class. Nonetheless, these individuals rarely advanced beyond the lower or medial echelons of the ʿulamaʾ, particularly its juridical-scholastic component. Few stewards managed to penetrate the civil judiciary. Thus the impression we have of the person initiating his career with this office contrasts sharply with that of his secretarial counterpart, places him within the institutional foundation of the learned elite, and still defines him as a bureaucrat. Stewards clearly belonged to the ranks of the orthodox faithful. Few representatives of the Coptic minority were permitted to administer the procedural affairs of the religio-academic establishment.

DISTRIBUTION OF MUBĀSHIRS (Figs. 10-A, 10-B)

The occupational pattern confirms the steward's involvement with institutional maintenance. The majority of sites referred to were prominent establishments in the religio-academic network. Concentrations of mubāshirs would imply both wealth and complexity in an institution. The two largest aggregates of stewards appeared in the mosque of al-Ḥākim (3) and the Manṣūrī hospital (28).[19] The former was one of the largest religious structures in Cairo and, after its repairs and renewal of waqf endowments during the Baḥrī period, it employed a sufficiently substantial body of stewards to be recorded in the biographical sources. The latter employed the largest operations staff of any civil institution in the city because of its manifold social services. Other concentrations or clusterings were reported for both the Festival Gate and Bayn al-Qaṣrayn groups, al-Azhar (36), Ashrafīya (30), and Mu'ayyadīya (51), in the northeast; Shaykhūnīya (83-84), the Ṭūlūnid mosque (91) (another large complex renovated during the Mamluk period), Ṣarghatmishīya (92), and Aljayhīya (69) in the southeast. Stewards also appeared in other districts of the metropolis, especially at the Khaṭīrī mosque (108) on the Nile shore in Būlāq. They were represented in the two mortuary zones, denoting the maintenance of waqf-supported staffs here as well.

The residence pattern, sparse as it is, conforms to the general trend of small Ṣūfī representation in all bureaucratic fields. Unlike the secretarial class, the stewards were professionally associated with the religio-academic establishment.[20] But the sparse data imply that few stewards were deeply immersed in the Ṣūfī community in Cairo. Whether they were denied access or chose not to affiliate is unknown. But the absence in the major khānqāhs of an office so symbiotically associated with the religious institution may point to subtle differences within the cadres staffing it.

The Muwaqqiʿ or Documents Clerk (Appendix II, List 4)

This official was responsible for copying court orders and judgments, and for transcribing state edicts both for public pronouncement and for archives.[21] The highest offices to which such a clerk or scribe could aspire were the muwaqqiʿ al-dast—clerk of the royal council bench in the Palace of Justice—and the muwaqqiʿ al-darj, or clerk of the scroll in the chancellery (dīwān al-inshā').[22] The muwaqqiʿ al-dast copied proceedings on petitions heard by the sultan in his capacity as final arbiter. Since decisions taken by the sultan (reflecting opinions of his close advisors) set precedents above the level of the four chief justices, maintaining accurate transcription of such proceedings was a prerogative of the throne over the civil judiciary. The muwaqqiʿ al-darj manned the documents bureau, preparing official statements of the imperial court and processing correspondence. Clerks in both offices were trained to inscribe the royal insignia in a manner that could not be forged. Although both were subordinate to the kātib al-sirr, the clerks alone were responsible for writing the final copies of diplomatic instruments and for processing the documents, receipts, and registers deposited in the state archives. The secretary of the chancellery might draft such instruments, but his clerks gave them the force of law.

Like the office of kātib, a clerkship tended to be a career-length post but unlike the former, it was clearly identified as a calling appropriate for a true believer. Indeed, it is important to distinguish this office from that of both the secretary and the notary, discussed subsequently. Although a relatively high percentage of the secretarial class were Copts, few of the clerks belonged to this minority.[23] The great majority were Muslims, from proven Muslim lineages. They identified with and were accepted as members of the Islamic learned elite. This relationship between religion (with its alleged traits) and office was important. Although

Copts were credited with possessing administrative skills, they were not generally permitted to write the final word on state policy. Official documentation remained a prerogative of proven Muslims in the imperial court.

The muwaqqiʿs appeared rather evenly distributed between the civil courts and the governmental bureaus. In the higher courts, muwaqqiʿs worked closely with notaries, who prepared statements but were allowed to draft neither final proceedings nor the ruling itself. The relative percentages on Table 11 (especially the ex. column) indicate that clerks and notaries held each others' positions in roughly the same proportion. In the dīwāns, then, the offices of clerk and secretary tended to overlap to some extent (compare Appendix II, Lists 1 and 4). There was a pronounced difference between the routine processing of documentation and the preparation of final copies for legal and archival purposes however. The clerks considered this latter duty their exclusive prerogative in government, and the Mamluk elite did not attempt to bypass or denigrate the role of the muwaqqiʿ. This implies both the significance attributed to official documentation by the society, a significance deriving from traditions established millennia earlier, and the obsession of the Mamluks for adhering to outward forms. The Mamluks also did not subject the clerks to the pressures or coercion they exerted so ruthlessly on the kātibs, nāẓirs, wazīrs, and members of their own caste.

The range of occupations pursued by the clerks during their careers paralleled those of individuals in other bureaucratic fields. They tended to remain within their category, although their representation in the legal (III) and scholarly (V) areas reinforces their status within the ʿulamaʾ. Their representation in the artisan (IV) and religious (VI) categories was relatively minor. Like the kātibs, many clerks followed the calling of their fathers, and formed a professional class handing techniques of transcription down through generations. The only noticeable group of them that appeared in the artisan category were nāsikhs or copyists. The relationship between this craft and that of the documents clerks is obvious. Few of the copyists came from among the secretaries. Dīwān kātibs do not seem to have been widely sought as reliable transmitters of the written instrument, especially since most books dealt with the Islamic sciences.

DISTRIBUTION OF MUWAQQIʿS (Fig. 11)

The occupational pattern for holders of clerkships was sparse because of the office's location in the dīwāns and courts rather than in religio-academic institutions. Accordingly, only three isolated occupational sites were reported. But the residential configuration is quite suggestive. In proportion to the total number of cases, affiliation with Ṣūfī hospices (13, 15, 30, 51) was greater for clerks than for any other bureaucratic field. The identification of clerks with Sufism, with its connotations of popularly acknowledged piety, that is implied by this pattern contrasts markedly with the image of all bureaucratic agents as arms of the state. In fact, the clerks enjoyed a special position in the bureaucracy, as indicated by their relative immunity from Mamluk harrassment. The prerogative of tawqīʿ or certification seems to have been granted only to individuals acknowledged as legitimate believers. Firmly grounded within the ʿulamaʾ, many of these people maintained simultaneous ties with the Ṣūfī network—perhaps the community most immune to Mamluk tampering of any civilian establishment in the city. The correlation between association with this community and professional independence does not seem coincidental.

The Nāẓir or Controller-Supervisor (Appendix II, Lists 5 and 6)

The fiscal officer of the traditional Muslim state had acquired a wide array of powers during the Mamluk period, and may be considered the epitome of the bureaucratic class.[24] The range of duties the nāẓir performed invariably dealt with budgeting and revenue management. All of the governmental bureaus and the major religio-academic institutions of Cairo were administered by controllers. Those placed in charge of bureaus served as the sultan's agents—of this there is no doubt. The status of nāẓirs appointed to religio-academic institutions, which were theoretically independent of royal control because their endowments were inviolate, is less clear, and far more varied.[25] The final decision over the selection of candidates was a perennial controversy between the military and civilian elites. In general, the staffs of religio-academic institutions sought to nominate candidates for controllerships from among their own ranks, while the sultan wished to appoint a trusted client. This was the case particularly when the institution was wealthy. The evidence points to an increasing encroachment of the sultans upon the waqf endowments in Cairo through placement of their own men as fiscal controllers.[26] Since these individuals were also the chief administrative officers in an institution, such appointments affected all the other staff. If the nāẓirs were men of no proven scholarly aptitude or interest, but rather were concerned with their own and their master's gain, the impact of their administration would bode ill for the faculties subordinate to them.

Indeed, the biographies of those who held controllerships would certainly suggest that the regime made its influence felt. Fewer of them limited their careers to bureaucratic occupations than did any other element in the bureaucratic category. Many came from the military-executive fields (I), as did the secretaries, but the similarity between the two ended here. Secretaries pursued a fixed set of tasks, most very subordinate. They could become royal stewards, butlers, intendants, and agents, but rarely military officers who formulated state policy. Nāẓirs, however, were often appointed from among these officers, and controllerships were held by the largest assemblage of Mamluks in the study.[27]

Yet the regime does not seem to have had the last word in this struggle. By no means all of the persons appointed to controllerships were Mamluks or their clients. The large numbers of shaykhs, judges, and professors (Categories III and V) who received fiscal controllerships implies that they still maintained a measure of authority over both the financial status and operational policies of their institutions. It is highly unlikely that staffs dared to risk an open confrontation with the regime over an appointment, with the possible exception of staffs in the large Ṣūfī hospices. Rather, they developed subtle means of influencing the nomination process—through bribes or a variety of favors and services, not the least of which was prayer and public praise for the reigning sultan. And sultans themselves were not uniformly committed to placing members of their own caste in this vital office. Thus, the individuals incumbent in the office were drawn from two basic sources: Mamluk officers and ʿulamaʾ of recognized standing.

Nāẓirs were appointed to either governmental or institutional posts. Those in charge of religio-academic foundations operated within the sphere of the learned elite; their activities were discussed continually in the biographies. Those in the governmental bureaus dealt with payment of troops and officials; building programs; troop and staff provisioning; maintenance of roads, ports, and sanctuaries; royal privy funds; royal commercial ventures; and, above all, with taxation.[28] The biographies rarely described these activities, although they named them repeatedly. What did emerge was a predominance of ʿulamaʾ in many of these posts. For example, the controller of the army (nāẓir al-jaysh) was usually a civilian rather than a Mamluk—a circumstance probably not unconnected with the high rate of resignation from these jobs, even though they were lucrative and opportunities for embezzlement almost unlimited. The officials who held these positions were frequently subjected to a horrifying array of public humiliations, confiscations, punishments, and tortures.[29] This appears to have been the result of a deliberate policy. If civilians with no military or even defensive options were appointed to these positions, they could offer little resistance to premeditated harassment and confiscation, and thus the sultan retained free access to the revenues of the civilian elite establishments. By accusing these relatively dependent and defenseless clients of crimes and corruption, induced by situations from which they could not escape, the sultan and amirs were able to collect substantial sums and simultaneously avoid accusations of having violated the Sharīʿa: the violators were those unfortunates who held the offices. The sultan could pose as the arm of divine law and collect the monetary benefits. This cycle appears to have been fundamental to the sultans' fiscal schemes throughout the fifteenth century.

A pronounced Coptic presence within the group of nāẓirs (Table 11),[30] similar to that in the secretarial class, reinforces this pattern and supports the hypothesis that the Mamluk elite did not act without foresight when they appointed men to these vital positions. Given the declining economic health of the state and decades of erratic fiscal policies, the legitimate sources of available revenue could no longer meet the sultans' and amirs' requirements, which were inflating. Those in power responded to this situation by creating a class of dependent extorters who held their positions at the sultan's sanction and were otherwise vulnerable to public hostility as members of a minority. These individuals could be dismissed and their immense fortunes confiscated whenever the need arose. They could not look to the general population, and especially the ʿulamaʾ class, for support.

There is little doubt that the controllership combined the highest stakes with the greatest risk of any office open to civilians. Several examples of persons whose careers culminated with the office may illuminate its nature, conditions of tenure, and the prerogatives that motivated acceptance. The cases were selected to indicate the variety of individuals holding the office, willingly or not. The first was ʿAlāʾ al-Dīn ʿAlī ibn ʿAbd-Allah al-Ṭablāwī al-Qāhirī, known as al-Ṭablāwī.[31] He came from a prominent mercantile family from the Delta, but elected to enter the fiscal bureaus at an early age. No education was reported in his biography. Al-Ṭablāwī managed to gain access to the executive establishment and became famous as a supervisor of the Manṣūrī hospital and of the fiscal bureaus. He received the governorship of Cairo in 792/1389-1390, an extremely high executive office for a civilian. He attracted the attention of Sultan Barqūq, who appreciated his ability to acquire wealth from taxes and endowments. He ultimately received an honorary amirate of forty (ṭabalkhānah) in return for his lavish contributions to the sultan's privy funds. Barqūq appointed him muḥtasib of Cairo in 796/1393-1394, and then made him a court chamberlain.

From this point, al-Sakhāwī related that al-Ṭablāwī's fortunes soared with the blessing of royal favor. He was appointed controller of the sultan's mercantile activities and subsequently of the royal mint. Since the regime was issuing debased currency regularly, opportunities to embezzle gold stores would be frequent. Al-Ṭablāwī received his most lucrative position during the late 790s, when he was appointed ustādār or overseer in charge of the royal treasuries (including clothing and furniture), estates, and privy funds. He proceeded to amass an immense store of valuable possessions that he collected as "gifts" for his services to the sultan, and adorned his home lavishly with royal or confiscated furnishings. Al-Ṭablāwī's final offices were controller of the Kaʿba mantle, largely an honorarium, and controller of the Manṣūrī hospital, where he had first entered public life. This post was extremely lucrative, since the budget of the hospital was the largest of any public institution in Cairo. Often the post was held by a high military officer. When a civilian held it, his appointment was a sign of his favor at court.

However, al-Ṭablāwī's fortunes were soon shattered, apparently as planned by the sultan and several of his grand amirs. Accused of extortion and usury, he was placed under arrest. His home and possessions were confiscated, and he was mulcted of 160,000 dīnārs, 500,000 dirhams, and 600,000 fulūs or small coins. His former master dealt him a cruel turn by imprisoning him in the dungeons of the imperial treasury, the scene of his recent successes. Ultimately, he was exiled to al-Karak and then permitted to return to Cairo in the first years of Faraj's sultanate. He proceeded to engage in his former pursuits until his death by assassination in Ghazza in Rajab 803/February-March 1401.

The case of al-Ṭablāwī provides an insight to the sultan's attitude toward the office. Al-Ṭablāwī did not win the opportunity to amass his wealth on his own. He was granted the opportunity as a matter of policy. He was placed in the legal position of blame for extortion and embezzlement, and therefore provided the sultan with the occasion to seize a large sum of money when the time was ripe. The sultan confiscated his wealth legally, as the sword arm enforcing the Sharīʿa.

The second case involved the career of a Copt, Saʿd al-Dīn Ibrāhīm ibn ʿAbd al-Rizzāq ibn Ghurrāb al-Skandarī al-Miṣrī al-Qibṭī al-Muslimī, known as Ibn Ghurrāb.[32] He was an associate of al-Ṭablāwī, and received his first post as secretary to the latter's brother, Maḥmūd. He rose rapidly through several posts, and was appointed controller of the army and of the privy funds by Sultan Faraj. His career culminated with his receipt of the vizierate under Faraj and an honorary amirate. He was also appointed major-domo or chief steward of the palace. Like al-Ṭablāwī, he was suddenly arrested, stripped of his offices, and mulcted of his wealth by the sultan who had raised him to prominence. Al-Sakhāwī did not dwell on subsequent humiliations or torture, but did state that Ibn Ghurrāb lived out his last years in seclusion and was granted a state funeral when he died in 808/1405-1406.

Only one subject of Ibn Ghurrāb's formal education was mentioned, but it was noteworthy. He learned Turkish in order to penetrate the imperial court. Many of his colleagues followed a similar course.

The third case involved a judge and professor of Shāfiʿī jurisprudence, Walī al-Dīn Abū ʿAbd-Allah Muḥammad ibn Aḥmad al-Safaṭī al-Qāhirī.[33] He inaugurated his legal activities apprenticed to the famous qāḍī, Jalāl al-Dīn al-Bulqīnī, as a deputy judge, and subsequently succeeded him. In 852/1448-1449, he was appointed controller of the Kaʿba mantle and agent of the exchequer (wakīl bayt al-māl), his first exposure to high finance in government. Upon his dismissal from these two related offices, he joined the faculty of the Jamālīya madrasa as its rector (shaykh), and soon thereafter was appointed controller of the Manṣūrī hospital. Al-Safaṭī also accepted a chair in jurisprudence in the mausoleum of Imām al-Shāfiʿī himself. He attained the zenith of his career, however, when he succeeded ʿAlam al-Dīn al-Bulqīnī as Shāfiʿī chief justice of Egypt in 851/1447-1448, and received the chair in Shāfiʿī jurisprudence at the Ṣāliḥīya madrasa, one of the most esteemed teaching posts in the empire. He also became controller of its waqfs. Like the other examples al-Safaṭī did not enjoy the fruits of his rise to fame. He was arrested by Sultan Jaqmaq and imprisoned as an arch criminal (min arbāb al-jarāʾim); even a respected jurist in this vulnerable position was subject to the rapacity of the ruler. He was mulcted of 60,000 dīnārs and then released to spend his final years in seclusion. He died in 854/1450-1451. The aging Ibn Ḥajar al-ʿAsqalānī followed him as Shāfiʿī chief justice.

The final person considered here was a merchant, ʿAlāʾ al-Dīn ʿAlī ibn Aḥmad al-Bakrī al-Dimashqī al-Qāhirī, known as Ibn al-Ṣābūnī.[34] He was born into a great mercantile family; his father had attained the status of khawājā. Ibn al-Ṣābūnī and his father first entered the royal entourage as sulṭānī merchants, but the son elected to accept the controllership of the royal stables from Sultan Khushqadam in 866/1461-1462. He resigned from this post to accept appointment as agent of the exchequer and controller of the Kaʿba mantle. He subsequently became controller of the hospitals and of pious trust foundations, even though holders of the latter had usually been trained in inheritance law, which Ibn al-Ṣābūnī conspicuously had not. This deficiency apparently did not disturb his patron either, since Sultan Khushqadam appointed him Shāfiʿī qāḍī of Damascus in 870/1465-1466. At the same time, he also made Ibn al-Ṣābūnī controller of the army in that city, and therefore one individual occupied the highest legal and fiscal posts in Syria. Ibn al-Ṣābūnī's last benefice from his munificent patron was the controllership of the privy funds in Cairo. Khushqadam died soon after and his successor, Qāytbāy, immediately arrested Ibn al-Ṣābūnī, subjected him to a brutal public flogging, and mulcted him of 100,000 dīnārs. This act reflected both a new sultan's suspicions of all his predecessor's henchmen and the degree of wealth Ibn al-Ṣābūnī managed to gain from his service to Khushqadam, who also had received a share of his client's income.

These four examples serve to indicate the lucrative nature of the controllership and the jeopardy that accompanied it. A question basic to our assessment of the ʿulama' during this period is whether they sought the office on their own initiative in order to amass a fortune, or whether they were coerced into doing so by their overlords. Most cases seem to fall between the two possibilities. Service in the fiscal bureaucracies was one of the few remaining avenues to wealth open to a civilian. Evading a royal appointment could be dangerous to oneself and one's family. The result of the two stimuli was the same, in any case.

DISTRIBUTION OF NĀẒIRS (Figs. 12-A, 12-B, 13)

The pattern of occupational locations for holders of this office included a large number of sites, but did not embrace several celebrated and wealthy institutions. (The data, of course, do not provide information on the large numbers employed in the dīwāns during the century.) Our working hypothesis was that the pattern would confirm either the continued existence or lapse of endowment funds throughout the system, and, in fact, it did attest to the importance of several specialized foundations. It also confirmed the modest levels of endowment at the majority of the amirate madrasas, none of which exhibited a concentration. Yet the near absence of references to the two royal madrasas (Mu'ayyadīya and Ashrafīya) cannot be explained by lack of endowment, since both were extremely wealthy. A possible alternative explanation may involve the status of the monastic houses, all prominently represented (13,15, 84, 130), which might have been obliged to submit to the installation of a nāẓir in charge of their accounts. Both Ashrafīya and Mu'ayyadīya enjoyed continual favor and support from the imperial court, and perhaps their accounts were supervised by persons less likely to appear in the biographical records. The khānqāhs seem to have maintained a more independent existence and operational policy than the royal madrasas. Sultans may have elected to place a personal appointee, very likely a civilian to moderate apprehension from members of the order, to watch over internal activities in these communities as well as to manipulate the endowment. Again, the presence of controllers in these monastic houses provides further evidence that they functioned as something more than a collection of mystics in search of divine harmony.

One major concentration of controllers occurred at the Manṣūrī hospital (28).[35] This provided the most conclusive proof in the study that the budget of the hospital was among the most fully regulated of any civil institution in the city. The individuals who managed the hospital's budget were rarely trained in medicine. Many were Mamluk officers, and the others civilian clients of the current sultan. The concentration of controllers at the hospital does not necessarily imply that its waqfs were large, since the hospital received annual appropriations from the regime and gifts from individuals of personal means; and the occupational configuration for controllers of waqfs did not reveal a single reference to the māristān (Fig. 13). It should be recalled that the initial foundation money so lavishly granted by Sultan Qalā'ūn dated from the late thirteenth century. Successive rulers and their agents had less reason to tamper with it than with any other donation in the capital, since they might find themselves in need of the hospital's services. However, the steady process of inflation plus occasional inroads on capital were inevitable. The evidence thus points to an administrative staff supported by substantial funding from various sources rather than from endowments alone.

There were several occupational references to nāẓirs in the southeast, notably at Shaykhūnīya and in the Citadel. However, the Citadel figures represented only a small portion of the hundreds of controllers active there during the century. The references reported did identify major centers of budgeting and accounting in the Citadel complex: the barracks (138), the Striped Palace (135), the privy treasury, and the vestibule area (137), where the storehouses were located. The only other areas of noteworthy aggregations were the mortuary zones of the Qarāfa and Ṣaḥrā'. A cluster was reported for the foundations surrounding the tomb of Imām al-Shāfiʿī (115). There were two separate references to the Qāytbāy mausoleum (121) and three for the tomb of Amir Yashbak (128). In Old Cairo only the mosque of ʿAmr ibn al-ʿĀṣ (113) was mentioned. All references pointed to institutions with recent or sustained endowments.

The residence pattern of nāẓirs was thin and scattered, indicating both the diversity of backgrounds from which controllers were drawn and their relative wealth. The sites were almost evenly balanced between Ṣūfī hospices and private homes. The representation in the khānqāhs confirms the evidence in Appendix II, List 22 of a clear identification with the Ṣūfī establishment by one element from which controllers were appointed: piety-minded civilians. Many controllers obviously maintained no such association, coming from social groups that were excluded or that abstained from participation in the mystic community. The number who lived in private houses, although small, was greater than for any other field of the major group, corroborating the vast resources available to these people. House sites were rather evenly scattered throughout the inner and suburban districts of the capital.

Assessment of the Bureaucrats

What image do we get of the individuals implanted in the bureaucratic apparatus? Above all, they played for high stakes. They might wield great power—rarely matched by moral influence—and manipulate vast sums, but they could never forget who elevated them. If they did, they were certain to suffer disastrous consequences. The bureaucrats who served the state enjoyed the benefits and endured the liabilities of the most intimate association with the ruling elite of any civilian group, and there is no question that those who survived possessed considerable political acumen in dealing with powerful and erratic patrons. The insecurity of their positions undoubtedly nurtured unsavory qualities—no other occupational category revealed such frequency of extortion and embezzlement—but the capacity of these people to devise new varieties of corruption, so disturbing to chroniclers of the period, may be more attributable to their patrons' expectations than to random circumstance or negative traits intrinsic to the bureaucratic class. A fiscal official succeeded to the extent that he generated revenue for his sponsors. Despite the biographers' bias against civilian bureaucrats and their delight in recounting evil practices and well-earned punishment, these bureaucrats rate serious consideration as the inevitable products of a long process of governmental evolution. And these offices were not so dangerous that they lacked for candidates to accept them. For the Coptic minority, at least, no equivalent avenue to advancement in society was open. How justified, then, were contemporary writers in their incessant, if indirect, censure of these officials? And were the legitimate ʿulamaʾ, whose exemplary character was consistently contrasted with that of the bureaucrats, able to remain untarnished by the policies of the military elite?

THE LEGAL PROFESSIONS
(Table 11, Category III)

No social element more clearly personified the legitimate ʿulamaʾ than the orthodox legal establishment. In premodern Islamic societies, the term "legal" automatically denoted the Sharīʿa. But although the civil judiciary, composed of those professionally involved with Sharīʿa practice, constitutes the main subject of the following discussion, not all legal fields may be interpreted as juridical. Indeed, the first two occupations considered here were quite distinct not only from the judiciary but from each other. They are included because they demonstrate that those dominating the court establishment did not control all litigious procedures in Cairene society during the later Middle Ages.

The Shaykh
(Appendix II, List 7)

This term denotes many functions in Islam.[36] Men bearing the title *shaykh* were represented in every category, although fewest were to be found in the executive and bureaucratic fields. When the office was designated specifically in the texts, however, it invariably related to religio-academic institutions, especially to the Ṣūfī khānqāhs and hospices. Most shaykhs exercised legal responsibility for a spiritual community, but those entrusted with primarily educational duties (Category V) were listed in the appropriate field.[37] The highest offices to which these individuals could aspire was a rectorship (*shaykh al-shuyūkh*) of a worshiping body or teaching faculty in a religio-academic foundation.[38] Persons appointed as chief justice also received the title *shaykh al-Islām* for life, whether incumbent or retired, because of the respect granted to their position.[39] The backgrounds of individuals holding shaykhships attest to the broad diffusion of those identified with the Ṣūfīs throughout the civilian elite. Yet the legal and scholarly fields (III and V) clearly dominated the configuration, rather than positions related directly to popular religious service (VI). This implies, at the very least, that training in the orthodox Islamic sciences was not incompatible with mysticism. Several Shāriʿ judges were appointed to shaykhships during their careers, proving that an orthodox judge or professor could maintain a simultaneous commitment to a Ṣūfī calling without compromising his beliefs. The reason for this most probably involves the lack of rigid dogma observed among Ṣūfī communities in the central Islamic lands during the period. Indeed, Sufism as manifested in a region or urban center should be interpreted primarily as a localized social system providing its eminent adherents with considerable moral influence and even political advantages.

The limited number of shaykhs in religious service occupations (VI) paralleled the modest involvement of all the higher echelons of the civilian elite with religious service at the mass level—indicating that holders of this office, as it emerged from the biographical sources, did not maintain extensive social contact with the broad popular dimensions of Sufism in Cairene society. This is further supported by the fact that few shaykhs were in artisan and commercial positions (IV), even though Ṣūfī movements had thoroughly penetrated these fields throughout the Muslim world during the medieval period. It is quite likely, of course, that the biographical accounts do not provide a complete picture of the Ṣūfī community in Cairo, since they focus on the ʿulamaʾ and other notables. Sufism's "grass-roots" dimensions are conspicuously absent, but the impression these sources provide about the men who rose to positions of moral guidance over the Ṣūfī community is probably accurate, and clearly depicts dominance by persons of ʿulamaʾ background.

Shaykhs were confined almost entirely to traditional activities of the civilian elite, and only seventeen positions were reported in the military-executive category (I). Several of these were held by Mamluks who carried the title of shaykh, which was not unusual. Indeed, al-Malik al-Muʾayyad, one of the most interesting of the Circassian sultans, used the title as his personal name. But none of the individuals appointed to a rectorship was of Mamluk origin.

DISTRIBUTION OF SHAYKHS (Figs. 14-A, 14-B)

The occupational and residential patterns of shaykhs were complementary, reinforcing a general impression of where this office was concentrated. The configuration was dominated by several foundations in the major group, but they were not overwhelmingly concentrated in the Fāṭimid district. The pattern suggests a close relationship between this office and a staff, congregation, or community attached to religio-academic institutions. It certainly highlights the status of the four major khānqāhs (13, 15, 84, 130), as well as hospices in the two collegiate clusters, the royal madrasas (30, 51), the Fakhrī mosque (46), and the Bāsiṭīya madrasa (11).[40] Many references to the khānqāhs were due to the rectorships over Ṣūfī orders resident there. Aside from the large concentration at Shaykhūnīya, shaykhs were modestly represented among several amirate madrasas. The cluster at the Vizier Gate (169), one of the entrances to the tombs of the Desert Plain, was created by small hospices built there by several grand amirs. The only noteworthy concentration in an amirate foundation appeared at Ṣarghatmishīya. In general, aggregates of shaykhs denoted a large faculty, spiritual community, and body of students or wards, such as orphans under the care of the religious establishment. That there were few shaykhs in the amirate colleges is yet another indication of those institutions' relative lack of prestige.

A fairly large number of shaykhs were employed in the two mortuary zones (200, 202). These individuals were associated mainly with the shrines of saints, such as that of Imām al-Shāfiʿī (115), and the royal tombs (121-123). The shrines, including many small zāwiyas, attracted a floating population who revered the local shaykh. The royal tombs, commissioned by individuals widely regarded as oppressors, rarely aroused such popular esteem; but their builders had provided for large resident communities and staffs to care for their graves and pray for their souls. Consequently, the appearance of shaykhs in these vast complexes was predictable. In Old Cairo there were no references at all to the mosque of ʿAmr, but two cases were reported for the Shrine of the Prophet's Relics (114).

The residence pattern, more restricted than the occupational sites, complemented the ʿulamaʾ background of individuals appointed to rectorships. Again, concentrations appeared in the four khānqāhs, paralleling the occupational configuration and reinforcing the tie between this office and a Ṣūfī community. Similarly, the two collegiate clusters, the royal madrasas and al-Azhar (36), figured prominently. But references to private residences were also scattered throughout the Bahāʾ al-Dīn (149), Juyūshī (150), and Zuwayla quarters (167) of the Fāṭimid district, all zones in which the civilian elite tended to live during this period. Indeed, these sites are similar to the location of private homes reported for the juridical-scholarly bloc (see Figs. 17 and 21).

The Muḥtasib or Market Inspector
(Appendix II, List 8)

The office of muḥtasib has inspired considerable research and discussion among western Islamists, who have often wished to read into it the rudiments of a corporate approach to urban commerce and regulation.[41] To contemporary Muslims, the muḥtasib was not the object of elaborate theories, although essayists and historians often commented wryly on the disparity between his ideal role and his actual performance, which was frequently tainted by corruption. Ideally, the muḥtasib was to act as an impersonal agent of equity, enforcing standards of weights and measures and fair business practices.[42] In reality, during the later Mamluk period he was increasingly entangled in the web of price controls and forced purchasing that the imperial monopolies necessitated. The muḥtasib was virtually powerless against the hordes of marauding out-of-service Mamluks who terrorized the markets of Cairo sporadically during the period. The office cannot have increased in prestige as a reliable defender of commercial equity under the economic conditions of the Circassian epoch.

The muḥtasib's duties were clearly legal. He was an arbiter whose judgments could be enforced by the state. Yet the incumbents of the office usually had backgrounds in the bureaucratic and executive spheres, unlike any others in the legal professions. The previous experience most frequently reported was the office of nāẓir (II), implying that at least during this period connections in the fiscal bureaus were more important to securing the office than formal training in the Sharīʿa. This trend touches upon a basic issue: the contrast between the Sharīʿa (orthodox law) as a moral code and practical applied law. The former stood above the state; the latter was increasingly dominated by it. The evolution of state control over many applied aspects of the legal system, of which commerce was only one, had begun long before the late medieval period. Under the Mamluks, however, the inspectorship itself fell increasingly within the regime's sphere of influence, and the preponderance of bureaucratic positions directly related to collecting revenues in the muḥtasibs' backgrounds indicates that they were manipulators, an arm of the royal extortion network. This is particularly indicated by the large percentage of executive offices held by muḥtasibs. Note also that there were seventeen cases of Mamluks holding the office, the highest such figure for any occupation in the legal category.

The proportion of muḥtasibs in the scholarly and religious categories (V and VI) was low in comparison with the other legal fields. One may conclude that a distinct cleavage in personnel separated muḥtasibs from the ranks of the civil judiciary, which implies that individuals from the core of the learned elite tended neither to seek nor to attain the office. The biographical evidence suggests that the market inspectors of Cairo did not derive from the prominent ʿulamaʾ families, although there were certainly exceptions, al-Maqrīzī being one of the more famous. Most muḥtasibs tended to be self-made men who had succeeded in bureaucratic posts, or individuals belonging to families associated with the imperial court, often of Mamluk derivation by marriage or blood. It is important to note that there was no report of a Copt holding the position, and only one secretary is reported to have held it. It therefore seems that although market inspectors did not belong to the inner circles of the learned elite, they were identified as genuine believers. The regime may have dominated this office and influenced its functions, but it did not install non-Muslims or converts to sit in judgment over the commercial classes.

References to occupational and residential sites occurred too infrequently to justify mapping them for this group. The muḥtasib was responsible for supervising a region encompassing many market and commercial zones, and was not tied to specific sites. The lack of data on residence indicates that few persons appointed to inspectorships appear to have developed formal ties with the khānqāh network.[43] Indeed, these people do not seem to have identified with either the religio-academic establishment or the ʿulamaʾ class. So, once more, even within the legal category, where we detect the direct influence of the regime, we see few cases of individuals integrated within the learned elite.

The Shāhid or Notary
(Appendix II, List 9)

The first level of the civil judiciary, this office was both one of the most vital and most enigmatic components of the Shāriʿ legal system. The notaries of civil courts were official witnesses of cases. They performed the role, unique to Muslim litigation, of weighing the validity of statements made by claimants and submitting their opinions to aid a judge's decision.[44] In the absence of written evidence, the act of certifying the accuracy of testimony heard by the qāḍī was a crucial service. The shāhid was selected on the basis of his rationality (*ʿaql*) and proven long-term residence in the district of the local court to insure that he had personal knowledge of the litigants. Obviously, holders of the office were often tempted to certify dubious testimony in return for remuneration. This temptation was augmented by the notaries' function as previewers of cases. In practice, they largely determined the roster of litigation a judge would hear, and did much of the preliminary interrogation.[45]

During the later Middle Ages, shāhids were employed as notaries in the fiscal and customs bureaus (II). Here they were responsible for certifying the accuracy of receipts accounted for by the administrative staff. They acted as legal agents, as did the muḥtasibs, but were directly involved in the financial mechanism of the state, often taking advantage of their positions to extract bribes in exchange for certification of false accounts. Just as in the courts, the favorable attitude of these notaries was anxiously sought by individuals, and agencies also called upon them to assess their accounts.

In general, individuals in both the bureaucratic and legal professions who were notaries held this post at the beginning of their career. The notaryship was therefore the point of entry for a lawyer into either the courts or bureaus, and appointment to the office often marked the beginning of a successful rise through a series of higher positions.[46] Nonetheless, some 25 percent of the citations for notarial positions referred to individuals who never attained any other office (Table 11). This was the largest fraction for any of the legal fields, suggesting that although shāhids were widely represented in the higher juridical and scholarly fields, not all sought or managed to attain a higher position. The frequency of positions reported in comparison to the number of judgeships suggests that there were more shāhids than higher legal or bureaucratic positions available.

The legal category clearly dominated the activities engaged in by notaries, and the most frequently cited office was the deputy judgeship. This supports a hypothesis that the successful individual proceeded from the position of notary to a judgeship in several steps. It is significant to note, however, that the higher offices of senior judge and chief justice represented only 5 and 1 percent, respectively, in Table 11 (ex), 3 and 0.4 percent (in), of the total positions held by notaries. These figures depict rather dramatically the exclusive nature of the upper judiciary. A modicum of training in the Sharīʿa provided no sure route to the civil bench.

Professorships (in Category V) ranked as the second most frequent specific occupation of the shāhids. This corresponded to the educational requirements for lawyers, although by no means did all notaries distinguish themselves scholastically. Most of the shāhids who became professors taught various aspects of jurisprudence, specializing in several legal texts.

There was a large number of shāhids represented in the religious (VI) and artisan (IV) fields. The prominence of both these fields complements the pronounced dispersion of the notaries, in contrast with concentration of the higher judiciary in a few centers. All elements of the judiciary maintained ties with the religio-academic network of Cairo, but the proportion of notaries who were religious functionaries in comparison with those in scholarly positions was greater than for others in this category. Participation in artisan-commercial occupations was even more striking: 11 percent of the total (Table 11, ex) had once pursued or continued to pursue jobs in this area, which did not fall within the sphere of the ʿulamaʾ.[47] Many notaries entered their legal/bureaucratic careers after experience as artisans or merchants, and if we view the religious and artisan percentages together, we can conclude that many notaries neither originated within the ʿulamaʾ class nor sought entry to it. Thus, although the office could be an entry position, many shāhids seem to have risen no further. The notaryship thus appears as the link between the judges, who tended to derive from the civilian elite, and the masses of population. Indeed, notaries may have constituted the critical element in the system of Sharīʿa courts. Fixed in their local districts, in contrast with judges who moved between them, the notaries were indispensable to the established procedure of litigation. Their responsibility for previewing cases becomes all the more comprehensible in the light of their backgrounds.

DISTRIBUTION OF SHĀHIDS (Figs. 15-A, 15-B)

Although the occupational and residential patterns differ markedly from one another, they support the conclusions drawn above. Occupational sites were highly dispersed, scattered throughout the northeast and other sections of the metropolis. These sites tended not to be located in close proximity to the major religio-academic institutions of the city, with two exceptions: the Ṣāliḥīya madrasa (26) in the Bayn al-Qaṣrayn cluster, and the mosque of al-Ṣāliḥ Ṭalā'iʿ (52), immediately south of the Zuwayla Gate.[48] The first concentration can be interpreted as a token of the myriad notaries who inaugurated their careers at al-Ṣāliḥīya, seat of the highest civil court in Egypt, during the fifteenth century. The second aggregate, in the Ṭalā'iʿ mosque, corresponds to the institution's function as a busy court located at a convergence of streets and mercantile establishments. Other than these sites, the configuration revealed no more than one or two individuals at each site, most near large streets, markets, and especially the city gates. These would seem to have been the locations of lower courts, convened when a qāḍī and his subordinates sat to hear cases. Here also agents of the fiscal bureaus assessed the value of properties and goods, particularly those of merchants entering or leaving the inner city, in order to collect taxes, tariffs, and customs duties.

The residential pattern, in contrast with the dispersion of occupational sites, showed a high concentration within the religio-academic network. Two institutions stood out: the khānqāhs of Baybars (13) and Saʿīd al-Suʿadā' (15).[49] It is evident from this pattern that a large percentage of notaries mentioned in the biographical texts were Ṣūfīs.[50] This relationship between occupation and spiritual outlook is not widely noted in the secondary literature, but the configuration is a fact and was not paralleled by other elements of the judiciary. Of course, a notary was not necessarily associated with a Ṣūfī community while he was professionally active, but there is no reason to assume that he was not. Thus, this pattern suggests that the Ṣūfī orders of Cairo were deeply imbedded in the local grass-roots level of the judiciary. Maintenance of some type of connection with the Ṣūfī community may have been requisite to the notarial office if this community were widespread among the civilian masses, as is commonly assumed.

The Judgeships

The formal arbiter of disputes in Muslim society since its classical age, the judge has been the object of voluminous study, and no general description of his office is required here.[51] There is little doubt that judges stood at the zenith of civilian society. Although scholars continue to debate the nature of his actual powers, the judge's moral authority was considerable, and the office carried heavy responsibilities as well as obvious prestige. The orthodox judiciary was clearly limited in jurisdiction, but the ruling military elite was extremely sensitive to its procedures. The sultanate never delegated its power of appointment over the higher judicial offices to any other agency. Judicial incumbents nominated candidates from among their own peers and advised the autocrat on their qualifications, but the choice remained his own.

What factors motivated individuals to accept or deny a summons to the most influential calling open to members of the civilian elite? Did the judges manage to retain their autonomy from Mamluk pressure, and if so, what devices could they employ? And the process of advancement also merits consideration. We shall examine three stages of the judgeship: the nā'ib qāḍī or deputy judge, the qāḍī or full judge, and the qāḍī al-quḍāt or chief justice. Evidence from the biographical sources indicates that these offices constituted a related series, each more exclusive than the preceding. What factors seem to have contributed to an individual's successful promotion to the top?

The Nā'ib Qāḍī or Deputy Judge
(Appendix II, List 10)

The sources provided many examples of individuals born into prominent legal families inaugurating their own careers as deputy judges, often in the service of fathers, grandfathers, or uncles who were themselves judges. The deputy, who was a trained lawyer, acted primarily in a subordinate capacity. Although he might attend court sessions presided over by a judge, he did not share in the final decision. His chief function was to preside over seats of litigation that were not independent, but under the jurisdiction of a qāḍī. Litigants whose case was decided by a deputy could, in theory, appeal his decision to the qāḍī under whose authority the local court lay. These local courts did not occupy a fixed site in the capital and its environs, but could be convened in shops (ḥawānīt), market streets, by the city gates, or in virtually any public place where tradespeople congregated. Rural towns often did not possess their own courts but were under the jurisdiction of a provincial court. The biographical records reported many cases of deputies sent to rural areas on their first assignment.

Deputy judges came from all the various levels of the civilian elite. In his study of the judiciary in Damascus during the final decades of the Mamluk period, Jon Mandaville argued that deputies did not necessarily come from the same social milieu as did judges and chief justices, nor did their office guarantee them upward mobility in the legal profession.[52] His observations on the position of deputies in Damascus were not paralleled by the evidence for their counterparts in Cairo during the same period. It is true that many deputies were unable to secure full judgeships, but a high proportion did. It is also true that professorships (mudarrisūn) constituted the largest bloc of positions held by the deputies. Indeed, more were employed in the scholarly-educational category (V) than in the legal group (III) (Table 11, ex). This confirms the symbiotic relationship between the two categories, justifying introduction of the term "jurist-scholars."

Some deputies ultimately became chief justices. Only thirteen chief justices were reported in the survey to have been deputies, and the full judges exceeded this figure by only one case. Although the office of chief justice was open primarily to individuals belonging to prominent legal families and to persons with recognized academic credentials and political contacts, it would be misleading to view either the judgeships or chief justiceships as closed to deputies. Members of the most eminent ʿulamaʾ families, in fact, had begun their careers as deputies. One further point of evidence suggesting that deputy judges were relatively mobile professionally was that 87 percent of the total positions reported (Table 11) were held in sequence. This was lower than for the full judges, but higher than for the notaries, shaykhs, and muḥtasibs. The proportion confirms that the office of deputy judge was often the initial phase of a legal career.

DISTRIBUTION OF DEPUTY JUDGES (Figs. 16-A, 16-B)

As the level of jurisdiction and prestige increased in the judicial offices, the yield of occupational sites diminished. Indeed, genuine patterns emerged only for the notaries and deputies: these patterns are similar, and provide an indication of where district and ward courts were located.[53] The fact that several madrasas were designated as courts suggests why there are fewer references to occupational sites for the higher judiciary. The colleges may have served a dual function: training in the Islamic sciences and seats of litigation. Since judges often held simultaneous professorships, it is possible that both activities occurred in the same setting, although the biographical accounts made no explicit reference to such a coincidence. Other circumstantial factors strengthen this hypothesis: the emphasis on jurisprudence in the curriculum; the practical experience to be gained by students observing cases; and the cementing of student-teacher ties indispensable to placement and promotion in the judicial establishment. It is unlikely, however, that this hypothesis applies to litigation beyond the scope of the Sharīʿa. There were no references for Būlāq or Old Cairo, both major port facilities in the capital. Commercial law, applying to most litigation in both districts, would not figure in patterns relative to Sharīʿa jurists.

The residence pattern revealed concentrations at several institutions of the major group (13, 15, 20, 30, 36, 51). These suggest that there were many Ṣūfīs among holders of deputyships (a hypothesis reinforced by List 22), but not quite so many as among the notaries. No judicial office, in fact, seems to have excluded persons identifying with the Ṣūfī community of Cairo, but as an individual progressed through the several levels of the legal establishment, the likelihood of such identification diminished. Already at the deputy level, the Ṣūfī presence appears to decline. But the presence of Ṣūfīs remains more characteristic of the legal establishment at this level than of the bureaucratic establishment or market inspectors.

The Qāḍī or Judge
(Appendix II, List 11)

The range of occupations pursued by judges paralleled the activities of deputies, although it was slightly more restricted to Categories III and V. In general, the pattern of activities implies that a judgeship ranked as the highest office within the ʿulamaʾ class, more prestigious even than a professorship. These figures, as well as family histories, also point to a large percentage of judgeships transferred from father to son or from uncle to nephew. Many of the deputies who did secure judgeships belonged to one of the judicial houses of Cairo, and served their apprenticeships under the aegis of their relatives. Deputies not fortunate enough to come from a major family were less successful in securing a judgeship. A large proportion of the juridical positions available in the capital during the fifteenth century were thus controlled by several prominent ʿalim families. The Mamluk rulers who made the formal appointments do not seem to have opposed this situation, but acquiesced so long as their final authority remained unchallenged.

Judges rarely held positions in the military-executive category (I). This was also true of the chief justices (Appendix II, List 12). These proportions lend credibility to the theory that judges came almost entirely from the civilian sector, and neither sought nor were recruited for positions within the Mamluk sphere. This seems to have been true even to the military judges (qāḍī al-ʿaskar) who presided over the special courts dealing with litigation involving Mamluk troopers. However, many judges also held bureaucratic posts (Category II), particularly fiscal controllerships. These offices were fairly evenly distributed between bureaus and institutions. The controllerships that the judges held, often simultaneously with their legal offices, may have provided a substantial portion of their income.[54]

That judges were represented, although sparsely, in the religious category (VI) was predictable. Judges were certainly offered honorary imamates and Friday preacherships in the major mosques. They were able to discharge these pious duties without taking much time away from their legal, scholarly, or bureaucratic affairs. Less predictable were the thirty positions in the artisan category (IV), covering many occupations. There was even one farmer, who presumably belonged to a wealthy landholding family.[55] These individuals often abandoned their trades when they had amassed some wealth and pursued a formal education. Their numbers were few but their very presence proves that it was possible for individuals who had originated outside the civilian elite to penetrate at least the lower and middle judicial levels.

The Qāḍī al-Quḍāt or Chief Justice (Appendix II, List 12)

Selection by the throne as a "judge of judges" granted the individual the prerogative of defining jurisdiction in one of the four orthodox schools. The four chief justices served as the final appellate judges of the Shārīʿ legal system. Although denied genuine executive authority, they exercised great moral influence in the society. If the holders of any one office can be considered the voice of the ʿulamaʾ and the articulate representatives of the civilian sector, the chief justices can.

Appointment depended on family background, scholarly reputation, political connections, or a combination of the three.[56] Especially in the three minority madhhabs, it was possible to achieve this office without family connections: both of the famous historians, Ibn Khaldūn and al-ʿAynī, were immigrants, and yet they became so famous that they were appointed to chief justiceships without a long apprenticeship in the lower courts. However, the major judicial families maintained a long-term influence over these positions.

Chief justices engaged in other activities, just as did deputies and full judges—with one exception. There were none at all reported in the artisan group (IV). Individuals who attained the chief justiceships were, without exception, noted scholars, politicians, or gifted members of famous houses. The social mobility of individuals originating outside the civilian elite thus seems not to have extended to the highest judicial level.

This office, with its universally acknowledged status, the crowning achievement of a learned career, was not an unmixed blessing. As the most salient representatives of the class that mediated between the ruling caste and the mass of the population, chief justices were placed squarely under the gaze of the regime. Their pressures came from above and below, from the Mamluks and from their peers, who looked to them as guarantors of pious orthodoxy at a time of widespread corruption and political upheaval. The regime fully recognized the significance of this office, and drew it into the inner circle of the imperial court. Even as the judiciary as a whole was subject to Mamluk influence, the chief justices were compelled to involve themselves in the maelstrom of Mamluk politics. In practice, most judges were insulated from direct intervention by the regime in litigation. But the chief justices, as members of the imperial hierarchy without official powers, had to be adroit in their relationship with their overlords, who controlled their tenure.[57] The nature of this relationship was ambivalent. Most chief justices developed a personal relationship with one or more sultans. They and the muftīs were often called upon to formulate legal pronouncements as the autocrat required. They were also expected to clothe even the most arbitrary of his political decisions with appropriate legal justifications, artfully culled from the Koran and Ḥadīth. Few chief justices resisted this pressure on their integrity, since the penalty for doing so was at best immediate dismissal. At worst, the individual might face arrest, confiscation of his assets, and physical humiliation or torture. However, there were cases of scholars who did refuse to accept the office because it required submission to the will and whim of the ruler, who in theory was beneath the Sharīʿa. Such refusal itself was a calculated hazard, since sultans looked askance at those who refused their summons to serve in high office.

Given the liabilities of the position, what motivated persons to accept it? Perhaps this question is best explored through the example of specific cases. Indeed, the integration of the various levels of the legal establishment may be seen by examining the most brilliant judicial family in Egypt during the later Middle Ages, the Bulqīnīs.

Prior to its rise to prominence in Cairo during the latter half of the fourteenth century, this family enjoyed renown in the central Delta province of Gharbīya. We have already noted the careers of two of its members, Sirāj ʿUmar[58] and Shihāb Aḥmad ibn Abū Bakr,[59] who represented the two lines of the family. ʿUmar was the progenitor of the Cairo branch, whose descendants were among the luminaries of the ʿulamaʾ. Aḥmad remained in Gharbīya, and built his career in al-Maḥallat al-Kubrā. The descendants of Abū Bakr and Muẓaffar continued the Gharbīya branch of the family. They established themselves in the local judicial posts that their ancestors had held, and were eminent enough to be included in the biographical surveys. It is significant to note that Sirāj ʿUmar's older brother, Nāṣir Muḥammad,[60] remained in the village of Bulqīna as a farmer. He presumably retained direction of the family's agrarian properties. It is possible that the younger brother, Abū Bakr, followed a similar course, but his career was not included in the sources. The two elder brothers kept in touch with each other throughout their lives, and died only a year apart. Subsequent biographies indicated that the illustrious descendants of Sirāj ʿUmar maintained some ties to the family landholding, possibly deriving income from it. Young and ambitious members of the Gharbīya branches could expect support and appointments if they elected to seek their fortunes in the capital.

Sirāj ʿUmar was so successful in Cairo as a professor and judge that he attracted the notice of the imperial court. His descendants over six generations never lost that attention, retaining their high position, if not their primacy, to the end of the Mamluk regime.[61] ʿUmar fathered five sons over the course of forty-three years. All five were included in the biographical accounts, and four held legal or scholarly offices. The oldest, Badr Muḥammad,[62] was not the most famous. He attained a military judgeship and wrote poetry that Ibn Taghrī-Birdī held to be worthy of mention. He might have achieved more, had he lived longer: he died at the age of thirty-five. His son and grandson were notable members of the family, but not as distinguished as their first cousins. Badr Muḥammad was the first of his family to be buried in the madrasa founded by his father on Bahāʾ al-Dīn Street in the Fāṭimid district. ʿUmar led the funeral prayer service for his oldest son.

ʿUmar's next two sons became very famous as scholars, jurists, and politicians: Jalāl ʿAbd al-Raḥmān[63] and ʿAlam Ṣāliḥ.[64] Both individuals took advantage of their father's status to acquire a thorough education, specializing in jurisprudence and Koranic exegesis. Collectively, the two held some fifteen professorships, most in institutions of the two collegiate clusters in the northeast. In the judiciary, they outshone their father who, although appointed Shāfiʿī chief justice of Damascus, never received the equivalent office in the capital. Both ʿAbd al-Raḥmān and Ṣāliḥ were appointed Shāfiʿī grand qāḍī of Cairo. Ṣāliḥ held the post five times. Neither of the two automatically achieved this position; both served long apprenticeships as deputies and judges.

The two brothers were quite distinct in terms of personalities and professional interests. Jalāl ʿAbd al-Raḥmān maintained an abiding interest in politics, occupying the office of military judge seven times. During his close dealings with the Mamluks, he established many personal associations and contacts that were to benefit his children, nephews, and nieces. He used his Mamluk connections to gain several appoint-

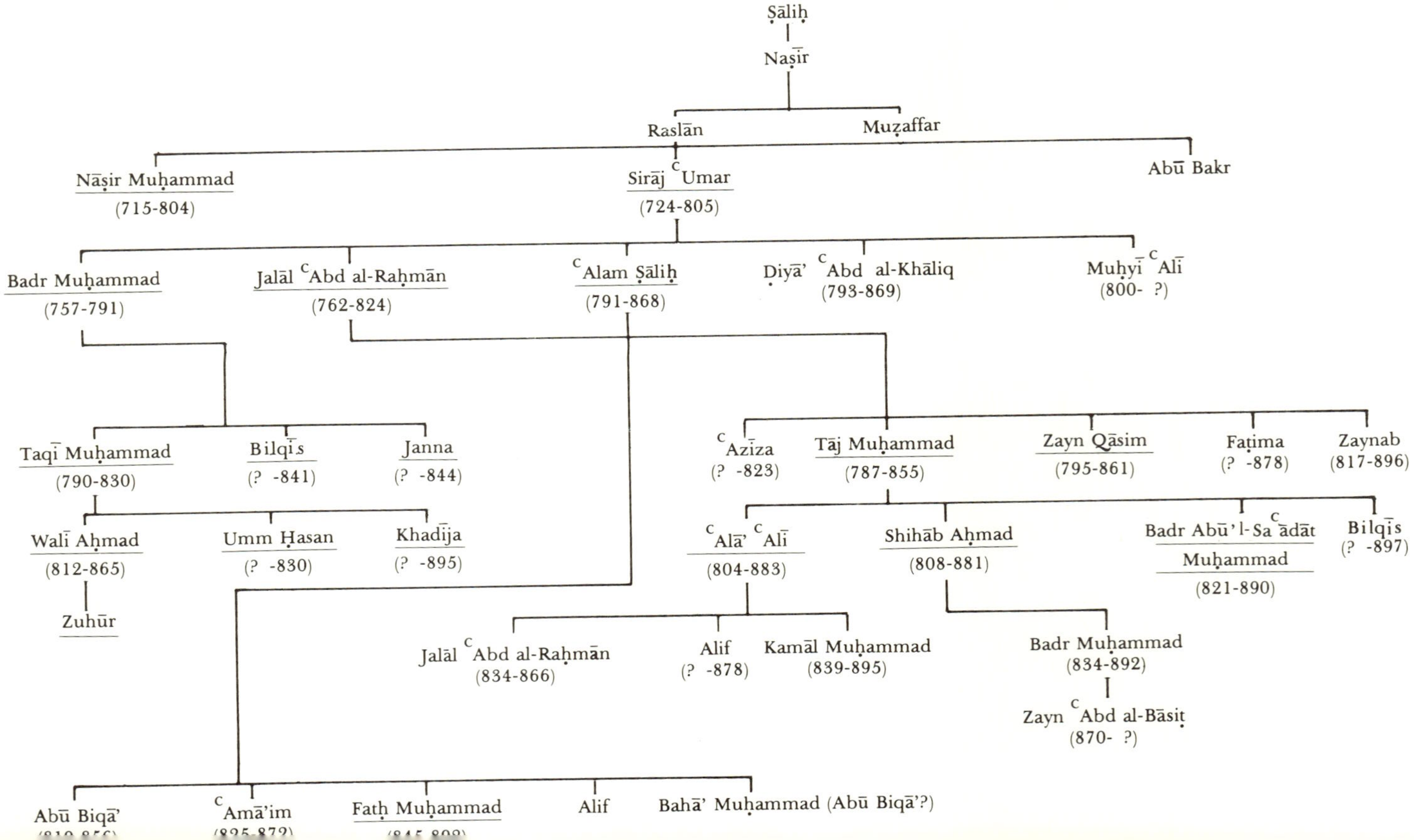
Ṣāliḥ
Naṣīr
Raslān
Muẓaffar
Nāṣir Muḥammad (715-804)
Sirāj ᶜUmar (724-805)
Abū Bakr
Badr Muḥammad (757-791)
Jalāl ᶜAbd al-Raḥmān (762-824)
ᶜAlam Ṣāliḥ (791-868)
Diyā' ᶜAbd al-Khāliq (793-869)
Muḥyī ᶜAlī (800- ?)
Taqī Muḥammad (790-830)
Bilqīs (? -841)
Janna (? -844)
ᶜAzīza (? -823)
Tāj Muḥammad (787-855)
Zayn Qāsim (795-861)
Fatima (? -878)
Zaynab (817-896)
Walī Aḥmad (812-865)
Umm Ḥasan (? -830)
Khadīja (? -895)
ᶜAlā' ᶜAlī (804-883)
Shihāb Aḥmad (808-881)
Badr Abū'l-Saᶜādāt Muḥammad (821-890)
Bilqīs (? -897)
Zuhūr
Jalāl ᶜAbd al-Raḥmān (834-866)
Alif (? -878)
Kamāl Muḥammad (839-895)
Badr Muḥammad (834-892)
Zayn ᶜAbd al-Bāsiṭ (870- ?)
Abū Biqā'
ᶜAmā'im
Fatḥ Muḥammad
Alif
Bahā' Muḥammad (Abū Biqā'?)

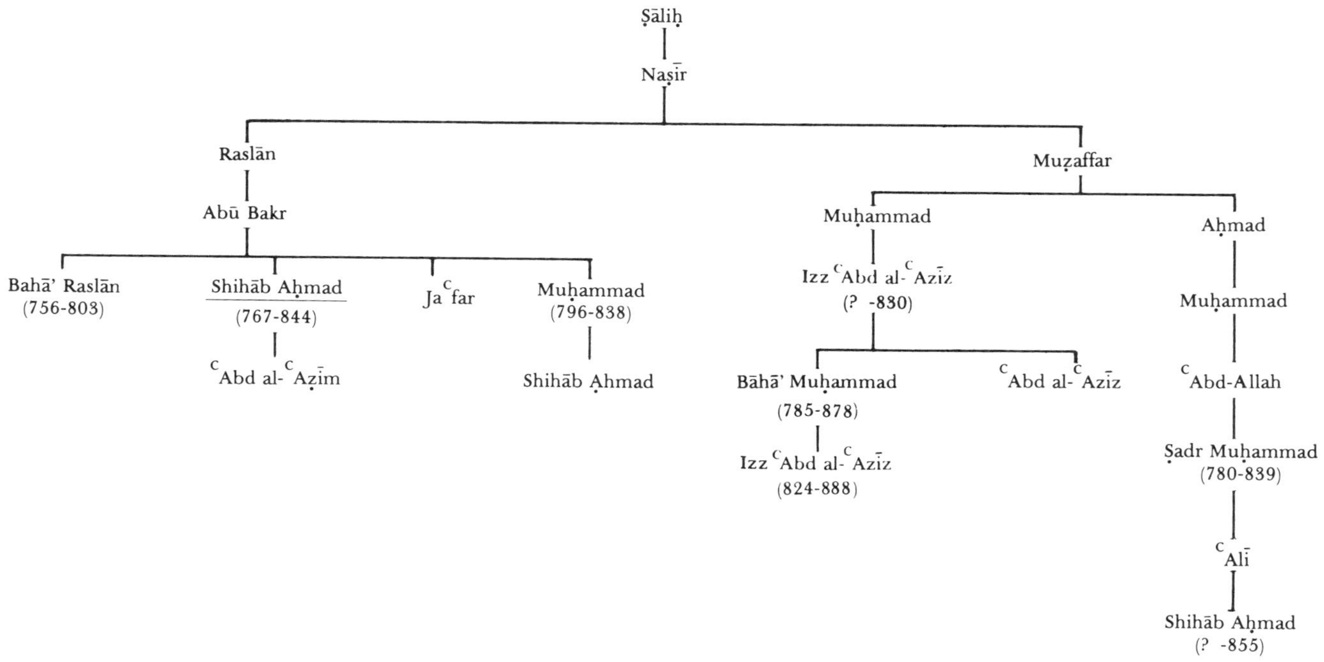

CHART. Genealogy of the Bulqīnī Family

ments to lucrative controllerships of waqf funds set up by amirs who wanted a reliable civilian to manage and safeguard their endowments. There is no evidence that ʿAbd al-Raḥmān embezzled anything from the endowments placed under his supervision, but he presumably paid himself a handsome fee for his services.

ʿAlam Ṣāliḥ became a noted scholar in jurisprudence and exegesis. He was sought as a textual expert by hundreds of students who valued his opinions and his formal certification of their qualifications. He owed his tenures as chief justice primarily to his scholarly reputation. He was a personal friend of the exegetes, Walī al-Dīn al-ʿIrāqī and Ibn Ḥajar al-ʿAsqalānī, and succeeded them at their recommendation. As was the case with a number of his eminent colleagues, Ṣāliḥ was invited into the court circle of Sultan al-Mu'ayyad Shaykh, a patron of scholars. Ṣāliḥ was also appointed to several controllerships but, unlike his brother, who presumably gained his positions through personal contacts, Ṣāliḥ's posts were to old endowments, and were granted directly by the sultan. The most important of these was the controllership of the Baybarsīya khānqāh, involving one of the largest waqfs in Cairo. Ṣāliḥ remained aloof from political embroilments, but his presence was repeatedly requested at court to lead ceremonials. He was selected to preach the khuṭba of the Lesser Festival (ʿĪd al-Ṣaghīr) by Sultan Ṭaṭar, and thus he presided over the imperial court's formal observation of the close of Ramaḍān.

The third generation of the Cairo branch continued to augment the family's position. Of the five male representatives of this generation, the two sons of ʿAbd al-Raḥmān, Tāj Muḥammad[65] and Zayn Qāsim,[66] succeeded to the highest offices primarily because of their father's and grandfather's political connections. After completing their educations, both sons were apprenticed to their father as deputy judges. Both held teaching positions, but concentrated their efforts on securing judicial and bureaucratic posts. Muḥammad succeeded his grandfather in one tenure as a military judge. After teaching Koranic exegesis in the Ṭūlūnid mosque, a position provided him by his father, he succeeded to his father's lucrative controllerships and was confirmed in them by the families of their Mamluk founders. In addition, he befriended Mamluk amirs on his own and supervised the funds they set aside for pious endowments. Finally, he was appointed chief justice by Sultan al-Mu'ayyad Shaykh after his father, but refused the post, thus straining his relationship with the aging ruler. Apparently, his financial dealings provided a more reliable and secure avenue to success and wealth than the chief justiceship, which inevitably made numerous powerful enemies for its incumbent.

Muḥammad's brother, Zayn Qāsim, also served as a deputy and taught exegesis in the Ṭūlūnid mosque, but spent several years away from Cairo as a provincial judge in Samannūd (I-A: 103) and as a deputy in Jīza. His greatest personal achievement was his appointment to the chairs of jurisprudence in the Nāṣirīya and Zimāmīya madrasas. These two professorships he attained on his own academic reputation, supported by his uncle, Ṣāliḥ. Many of the prominent lawyers of the fifteenth century were certified as competent in the requisite texts by Zayn Qāsim. He also served as a traditionist in the family madrasa. However, he did not decline the post of controller of minority taxes (nāẓir al-jawālī), and he managed to build a comfortable source of revenue from it.

The three cousins of these two brothers, Taqī Muḥammad ibn Muḥammad,[67] Bahā' Abū Biqā' Muḥammad,[68] and Fatḥ Muḥammad,[69] the latter two of whom were sons of Ṣāliḥ, developed respectable careers, but did not attain the prominence of the two sons of ʿAbd al-Raḥmān. They all served as deputy judges, but only Fatḥ Muḥammad became a military judge, in which office he succeeded his younger cousin, Abū'l-Saʿādāt.

The two daughters of Badr Muḥammad, Bilqīs[70] and Janna,[71] were discussed in the biographical records in terms of their marriages, as were all other women in the family. Bilqīs married permanently into an elite house, but Janna entered into three marriages. Among her husbands were the son of a Mamluk and her own nephew, Walī Aḥmad, discussed below. Marriage between collateral cousins, especially in the case of a first husband's death, was a typical solution to the personal and financial problems of a widow. It also kept inherited assets within the lineage. Few details were supplied on Janna's character or activities, but the facts that her funeral in the mosque of al-Ḥākim attracted throngs of notables and that she was buried in the family madrasa suggest that she commanded a measure of public respect.

The daughter of Ṣāliḥ, Alif,[72] also married three times, the third to the highest ranking civilian in the Mamluk state, the ʿAbbāsid Caliph al-Mustanjid Yūsuf. Although he wielded little personal power, the caliph remained the head of the orthodox Islamic community. This marriage indicates that the Bulqīnī house had established itself among the leading families of Cairene society within three generations.

The fourth generation produced the first reverses, the most prolific scholar, and further interesting marriages. Walī Aḥmad ibn Muḥammad[73] developed into a respected repetitor and scholar of jurisprudence. His appointment as a wāʿiẓ or preacher in the august Umayyad mosque of Damascus was an honor for an Egyptian, although it was understandable, given the prestige of his forebears in that city. His daughter, Zuhūr,[74] went through five marriages. Her first husband, Fatḥ Muḥammad ibn Ṣāliḥ, was her distant cousin. Although the son of her great grandfather's brother, he was not greatly her senior in age. Zuhūr's third marriage was to a Mamluk chief of the guards (*raʿs al-nawba*). Since other members of her family were married to second and third-generation Mamluks, this marriage revealed a trend toward consolidation of civilian and Mamluk familial interests, an elusive process to trace in the narrative sources. The frequency of marriages strongly implied divorces rather than deaths, although al-Sakhāwī did not comment on any tumultuous relationships.

Zuhūr's two aunts, Umm Ḥasan[75] and Khadīja,[76] also married collateral cousins and descendants of Mamluks. They each were linked to several husbands. Umm Ḥasan was married first to one Ibn Qubbān, a second-generation Mamluk trooper or Jundī. Since, in traditional Islamic society, arranging the first match was the responsibility of the parents, this deliberate choice of a Mamluk suggests that members of the military elite represented an attractive, even advantageous match to notable civilian families. The willingness of the groom's family to accept the approaches of the Bulqīnīs suggests that such a match was mutually beneficial. Umm Ḥasan's second and sixth marriages were also to Mamluks, but her third was to a descendant of Ibn Ḥajar al-ʿAsqalānī. The bare statistics of these unions reinforce the hypothesis that there was fusion between the two elites of Cairene society during this period. This fusion further suggests that both sides saw mutual social and economic advantages to be gained and, possibly, that caste differences between civilians and Mamluks were gradually blurring. Umm Ḥasan's sister, Khadīja, never married a Mamluk, but married two of her cousins.

The oldest son of Tāj Muḥammad, ʿAlāʾ al-Dīn ʿAlī,[77] became famous for both his great personal piety and his unusual memory. He learned by rote many texts on fiqh and Ḥadīth, and was appointed professor of jurisprudence and repetitor in several madrasas, including the tomb of Sultan Qalāʾūn in the Bayn al-Qaṣrayn group and the Baybarsīya khānqāh near the Festival Gate. He served Ibn Ḥajar al-ʿAsqalānī as a deputy judge, but did not pursue a legal career further, unlike his more ambitious relatives. Also, he accepted no lucrative administrative office, and died a poor man, fondly remembered by the local populace. Whether his own family held his poverty in such high esteem is unclear, but none of his children attained high office.

The second son, Shihāb Aḥmad,[78] demonstrated a pronounced inclination toward mysticism even in his early education, and became one of the few members of his house to join a Ṣūfī order. He became a specialist in Prophetic traditions and held several posts, including one at the Hospice of the Prophet's Relics in Old Cairo, before retiring to Baybarsīya. He was significant in the history of the lineage because his offspring can be traced to the end of the century.

The third son, Badr Abū'l-Sa'ādāt Muḥammad,[79] was the most prominent scion of the family during the second half of the fifteenth century. His career is an illustration of late medieval scholarship in the central Islamic lands. Abū'l-Sa'ādāt shared his older brother's aptitude for memorization, but evidently possessed an insatiable desire for encyclopedic mastery of a subject, for he examined a prodigious body of texts and studied a great number of subjects. He exhibited many characteristics of the polymath, al-Suyūṭī; that is, he developed a formidable general erudition, but pursued no discipline in depth. In contrast to al-Suyūṭī, however, he produced no major treatises or commentaries, but became one of the most famous professors of the day. Like his ancestors, Abū'l-Sa'ādāt specialized in jurisprudence and Prophetic traditions, and he taught these subjects at some eight madrasas during his career, including the Manṣūrī mausoleum and Barqūqīya in the Bayn al-Qaṣrayn group. Unlike his older brother, Abū'l-Sa'ādāt developed a parallel career in the judiciary, apparently as a deputy to his grandfather's brother, Ṣāliḥ. He held several provincial judgeships and was appointed a military judge for one term, but never attained a chief justiceship. This may have been due to his inability to establish close personal contact with the imperial court and especially with Sultan Qāytbāy. However, he carried on the family tradition of succeeding to several lucrative controllerships. He was appointed to no fewer than four of these, including that of Sa'īd al-Su'adā' itself, an office that he purchased with family backing and possibly with an agreement to share future proceeds. Abū'l-Sa'ādāt amassed a comfortable personal fortune and was a credit to his house, but he left no children who were recorded in the biographical accounts, even though he married into both his own family and the house of a Mamluk officer, Saburbāy.

Only the careers of the most eminent members of the Bulqīnī family have been outlined here. Their examples point out qualities shared by other leading families of the civilian elite. The success of this family in Cairo was not limited to its founder, nor passed routinely along over several generations. Appointment to the highest judicial offices was normally subject to intense competition among those eligible for them, although occasionally individuals were pressured into accepting the post by sultans who wanted to exploit the chief justiceship for their own purposes. All the individuals in the Bulqīnī family who succeeded as judges and professors did so because of their own intellectual gifts and political skills as well as their family connections. By no means were all members equally successful, nor did all share an inclination for judicial affairs. Nor did the Bulqīnīs monopolize the judicial offices, but were only the most prominent among a number of ʿulamaʾ families in Cairo, whose education, reputation, political connections, and wealth put them in a position to control the offices.

The attractiveness of the Bulqīnī women and their eligibility for marriage to both their own class and the Mamluk elite constituted a measure of the family's prestige and capacity to secure its position. Three generations after its initial transfer from the Delta, this family was marrying into both the civilian and military elites of Cairo. It is to be noted that the Bulqīnī women—and the men, for that matter—were married to second and third-generation descendants of Mamluks who were not regarded by their own caste as pure, but rather as culturally Egyptian and thus unfit for the highest executive and military offices. Yet the very occurrence of these marriages reveals a process of merging between the two classes. Why prominent civilian houses were regarded as desirable sources of spouses by Mamluk families is unclear. Sons and grandsons of first-generation Mamluks may have required incomes, since they were theoretically shut out from the iqṭāʿ system. However, in traditional Islam the groom must present the dower to the bride. It is unlikely that, in practice, these individuals were completely cut off from the revenues flowing to their ancestors. In any case, the Bulqīnīs were prosperous but not immensely rich. There was not a single case of fining or confiscation of assets by the sultan—the surest sign of accumulated wealth—reported for any of them. Indeed, the Bulqīnīs elected to avoid the fiscal offices of the imperial dīwān, so lucrative and so dangerous. They concentrated their ambitions on the judiciary, but were supported largely by their waqf-endowed professorial chairs. Did the marriage alliances provide the house greater security? Quite probably, since, as class distinctions lessened and lineage ties grew, the risks so typical of civilian contacts with the military elite would decline correspondingly.

DISTRIBUTION OF THE JUDGES (Fig. 17)

There were no occupational sites reported at all for judges, which is consistent with the nature of the office. The institutions appearing in the residence pattern may actually designate seats of litigation as well as professorial chairs. If this hypothesis is valid, then the residence pattern would indicate that the court system was centered in the northeast.[80] There is no question that this zone was the seat of the learned class, and the judges' concentration in this district complements previous surveys. Few judges held military-executive positions based in the Citadel, or service positions in the employ of Mamluks in the southeast or suburbs. Ṣarghatmishīya (92) was the only amirate madrasa in this area to be mentioned. This institution was unusual: many individuals there were foreigners who were able to penetrate the legal establishment.[81]

Concentrations of judges at the khānqāhs—Baybarsīya (13), Saʿīd al-Suʿadāʾ (15) and Siryāqūs (130)—were not nearly as dense as those of notaries. Thus, as mentioned previously, association with the khānqāh network appears to have dropped as one moved up the scale. However, not all Ṣūfīs were resident in hospices, nor were all pensioners in monastic houses Ṣūfīs.[82] These trends must thus be compared with other information before reliable conclusions about a Ṣūfī identity—or its lack—within the judiciary may be offered. The institutions that did dominate the pattern, as might be expected, were madrasas of the elite group. All of them were famous or wealthy enough to attract the most eminent legal minds in the Mamluk state and from abroad, and many of the judges resident in them belonged to their faculties.

THE ARTISAN AND COMMERCIAL PROFESSIONS
(Table 11, Category IV)

This rather motley category might be more readily defined by what it was not than by what it was. Medieval chroniclers tended to exclude these occupations from activities commonly associated with the ʿulamaʾ, although several of them demanded a high degree of specialized training. The significant point here is that such occupations were often mentioned in the biographical sources, suggesting that many among the ʿulamaʾ were not born into the class but gained access to it. Some had parents who succeeded at a trade or in business and provided their children with educational and social opportunities. The varieties of trade, skill, or commerce appearing in the accounts reflected most aspects of economic life in Egypt during the period, but only two fields, copyists and merchants, occurred frequently enough to warrant inclusion in the major group. But even while considering them, we should remember that there were many others, and that they were very diverse. Any study of social mobility concerning the ʿulamaʾ during this period would necessarily take them into account.

The Nāsikh or Copyist
(Appendix II, List 13)

Manuscript copyists performed a service that could not really be appreciated by generations living after the introduction of printing. According to educational and occupational data in the biographical records, copying seems to have been a relatively specialized profession. Youths with an obvious talent for accurate transcription and legible script were detected early, and gravitated toward the craft. Calligraphy (khaṭṭ), a recognized discipline, emerged frequently in the curricula of these individuals. They were trained to develop a sharp eye for detecting errors. Proofreading of copy assumed an importance second only to the art of transcription itself.

As indicated by collateral positions, copyists were quite distinct from secretaries and clerks associated with the dīwāns and courts. Copyists were tied to the religio-academic network, where the demand for written materials was focused. Those copyists who actually became instructors tended to specialize in teaching the various accepted styles of script, their appropriate uses, and the art of accurate proofreading. The case of the nāsikhs is significant because it represents a highly specialized craft closely associated with the institutional establishment, whose practitioners shared the social background of the ʿulamaʾ and yet were not integrated into it. Copying remained a trade. Few nāsikhs had positions among the juridical-scholarly fields, but a substantial proportion were in religious service (VI), much of which involved pedagogical duties.

Although no occupational sites were reported (Fig. 18), one may assume that copyists worked in the major libraries or in their vicinity, since books were to be read in situ and did not circulate. The limited residence pattern related this group to institutions wealthy enough to maintain libraries. Three khānqāhs: Baybarsīya (13), Saʿīd al-Suʿadāʾ (15), and Shaykhūnīya (84), plus Ṣāliḥīya (26) (the high court), al-Azhar (36), and the royal madrasas (30, 51) were represented. The clusters of residences in the three hospices coincides with the fifteen positions reported for Ṣūfīs (Table 11), and accords with the general background of individuals pursuing this craft. They were uniformly Muslims whose ties with the Ṣūfī community were parallel to those of the lower echelons of the civilian elite.

The Tājir or Merchant
(Appendix II, List 14)

Merchants who built their careers primarily around commerce were not included in the dictionaries. Many merchants, but by no means all, engaged in literary activities, and only those who did and had attained some degree of renown as learned men were included. Individuals most likely to appear had actually ceased to be involved in commerce. They had amassed revenues enabling them to pursue a formal education and to enter the ranks of the ʿulamaʾ on a full-time basis. Therefore, the

3. From a Manuscript of the Koran Copied during the Reign of Sultan Shaʿbān

following information from the biographies cannot be viewed as accurate for the entire mercantile class of Egypt during this period.

The merchants who were described engaged in legal, artisanal, bureaucratic, academic, and executive activities, in that order. Few elected to pursue careers as religious functionaries in mosques. But merchants were represented in every major legal office (III). Their predilection for the law may be explained in part by their commercial background. Although commercial law in practice did not fall within the province of the orthodox judiciary, the configuration suggests that the mercantile ethical system was governed by the precepts and prevailing interpretations of the Sharīʿa. That 5 and 3 percent of positions held by these individuals were judgeships compares favorably with all the other occupational groups. Only certain legal and scholarly fields yielded a higher percentage.

Among bureaucratic jobs, the merchants were unevenly distributed. Some merchants became dīwān notaries and fiscal controllers, and again, their affinity to law and monetary affairs was apparent. None held secretaryships of any sort (although this may reflect a bias in the sources); their representation among the stewards and clerks was only token. There were only two reported cases of Coptic merchants, even though this minority's alleged inclination toward business and financial affairs has become proverbial in more recent times.[83] Because of the prevailing prejudice toward minority converts to Islam, the absence of Copts from the mercantile survey may not adequately reflect their role.

The range of artisan activities (IV) pursued by the merchants was, predictably, one of the broadest of any field in the major group (see List 14). Merchants were involved in the preparation of cloth, confections, and spices; in metallurgy, book dealing, and aromatics. Only one of them had been a sulṭānī merchant dealing in the controversial royal monopolies.[84] There were many of these royal merchants active in Cairo during the fifteenth century, when the monopolies were imposed, but there were virtually no individuals who supervised them in this sampling. Whether this reflected on the type of individual disposed toward working for the regime against the interests of his class, or even indicated some degree of hostility on the part of the compilers toward them is unclear.

In the scholarly category (V), merchants tended to become professors. The individuals who taught were rather evenly distributed among the various traditional disciplines. The number of merchants who attained teaching posts suggests that the group as a whole received a fairly broad and comprehensive education. This characteristic has sometimes been attributed to Islamic mercantile classes as a whole, but the evidence here can be related only to those persons described in the biographical records.

The proportion of positions held by merchants in the military-executive fields (I) ranked only higher than that of the religious fields (VI), but this was due in part to my placement of khawājās in the executive group. Khawājā was a title applied almost exclusively to merchants who dealt in commodities of critical importance to the Mamluk regime—slaves, for example.[85] These merchants were not necessarily designated as royal agents—they might well retain their independence. Nor were all sulṭānī merchants entitled khawājā. But khawājās almost invariably attained some executive offices during their careers.[86] Many obviously purchased them since all khawājās were rich men. In general, merchants seem to have possessed more opportunities to acquire executive positions than any other element in the artisan-commercial group. Even under the adverse economic conditions of the fifteenth century, their political skills and capital assets were considerable, and provided them with connections among the Mamluk elite.

DISTRIBUTION OF MERCHANTS (Fig. 19)

The mapping of occupational sites is based on a relatively limited sampling. Nonetheless, some unexpected trends were revealed. Occupational sites, like residences, were concentrated in the northeast, along the Qaṣaba or central market district (145). But this zone did not encompass all the commercial districts of the metropolis. The extension of the Main Avenue from the Zuwayla Gate to the Cross Street was lined with bazaars and sūqs, as was the "Beneath the Apartments" Street between the Zuwayla and Kharq gates. Also, the port of Būlāq was the focus of international trade. Commodities destined for Europe arrived here from Upper Egypt and the Red Sea for processing and transferral to Alexandria or Damietta. Yet no references were reported for any of these districts. There were references to the Bāsiṭīya caravansaray area (163) of the Main Avenue, the Book Dealers' markets (160) along the Bayn al-Qaṣrayn, in the vicinity of the ʿAbd al-Bāsiṭ madrasa (11), and especially in the Juyūshī Street market district (150). These aggregates implied the presence of commercial activity in these districts, but they cannot be considered to give a complete picture of the commercial community.

The residence pattern was based on more data. No large concentrations appeared, but the majority of references were to institutions in the northeast. There was only one citation for the wealthy Raṭlī Lake section (183), and only one for Būlāq port (190). We cannot assume the cases provided by the biographical sources included the most prosperous merchants in Cairo, since these would presumably appear in the lakeside residential zones. However, since the pattern may be considered indicative of individuals identifying with the civilian elite, it does correspond to the cumulative impression provided by other artisan fields with a high rate of crossover into ʿulamaʾ-related activities: a solid Muslim background with little evidence of minority infiltration, but representation in the Ṣūfī community of the capital. The pattern thus does not permit speculation on the identities of the mercantile establishment as a whole, but does link this one section of it with the religio-academic network.

THE SCHOLARLY AND EDUCATIONAL PROFESSIONS
(Table 11, Category V)

This vast category, or at least its scholastic component, should be considered the alter ego of the legal establishment. The profile of the scholarly group was shaped by the same individuals who composed the juridical hierarchy. Together, these two occupational spheres made up the foundation of the ʿulamaʾ class, as distinct from other segments of the civilian elite. A person who penetrated neither area might be regarded as a notable but not an ʿalim.

Specific occupations within the category were all related, and were tied directly to religio-academic institutions. Yet each occupation, or groups thereof, were rendered distinct by differing educational requirements, teaching duties, and faculty contacts. And the various specialists dealt with different student clienteles. An elementary teacher (muʿallim), instilling basic literacy, did not function at the same level as a professor of Koranic exegesis (mudarris tafsīr). The former was primarily a pedagogue, the latter a jurist-scholar. The two tended to come from dissimilar backgrounds. The social stratification delineating the several echelons of this category were very real, but also very subtle, and no in-depth probe of it is ventured here.

For the purposes of this study, two fields were selected: the muʿīd and the mudarris. Not only did these two occur most frequently, but they represent the pedagogical and scholastic poles of the category as a whole. A third field, the khāzin al-kutub, was chosen primarily because of the light it sheds on academic honoraria.

The Muʿīd or Repetitor
(Appendix II, List 15)

This individual was involved with the drill and stylized repetition of texts required in a basic education or for competence in a special field.[87]

The preponderate role of memorization in traditional Muslim education is widely known.[88] The beginning student memorized the Koran, and he was considered to show promise for future work if he was able to commit it to memory at an early age. Repetitors were not necessarily involved with drill at the Koranic level; this was the responsibility of the muʿallim. They dealt with students at both the secondary and advanced levels, striving to instill in them an ability to commit to memory vast portions of difficult texts in the various disciplines. Rigorous drill followed by equally rigorous examinations were considered the necessary means of guaranteeing accurate rendition and transmission of basic materials. During the later Middle Ages, the basic corpus of knowledge, either revealed by God or interpreted by guided reason, was regarded as extant and complete. This corpus was formidable, and no single person could hope to attain mastery over all the texts of even a subdiscipline in a lifetime, although the achievements of some who possessed photographic memories were extraordinary.

The repetitor's role in the educational system may be grasped if the nature of what was sought and prized is kept in mind. Accurate rendition and transmission meant not merely comprehension of a work's ideas, but literal reproduction of its contents. In theory, this reproduction must duplicate the original work without errors of grammar or pronunciation. In practice, of course, these standards were met by few, even the repetitors, but the ideal was held up as the ultimate goal of learned excellence. A student was to concentrate on absorbing the corpus of the Islamic sciences and their acceptable interpretations lest he go astray and blunder into error. Independent interpretation of legal and theological texts was forbidden in any case, and excessive conceptualization and application of ideas to improper questions could lead to dangerous, even heretical, attitudes. A repetitor had to be on guard against this possibility. He was a student's murshid, his guide to a correct approach to the scholarly corpus of the faith. If he did his job properly, the students who came under his tutelage would possess the training to carry on after him in their own generation.

Repetitors shared a common educational background in the standardized madrasa curriculum. Most had been certified at least once in public and in writing by an appropriate collegium of scholars who testified that they could transmit a text of a certain level of difficulty. This certification was required before an individual could be considered for a position in an institution of learning. In general, a muʿīd's duties emphasized rote technique rather than explication. The office thus ranked below the mudarris in prestige and, presumably, remuneration. Yet the occupational ranges were quite similar for both, suggesting frequent promotion of muʿīds to professorships. Accordingly, the repetitorship differed from other essentially pedagogical posts, such as the muʿallim, which tended not to provide opportunities for equivalent mobility into the scholastic hierarchy.

The representation of repetitors in the military-executive category (I) was extremely low, as it was for all scholarly-educational fields. Nowhere was the cleavage between the military and civilian elites more clearly shown than by this uniformly minimal representation of scholars and teachers in governing circles. The high percentage of positions in the legal fields (III) at once reinforced the close relationship between judges and scholars, and confirmed the crossover between repetitors and professors. The proportion of muʿīds in the artisan-commercial category (IV) was quite low. The implications of this are discussed below in relation to the office of professor, since it applied to the entire scholarly group. That there were only a few repetitors among religious functionaries (VI) highlights the distinction between the scholarly and service aspects of the religio-academic network, while confirming the tie between muʿīd and mudarris. Other pedagogical jobs included a larger percentage of religious functionaries.

DISTRIBUTION OF MUʿĪDS (Fig. 20)

We have enough information on the muʿīds, who were involved directly with the religio-academic network, to plot the distribution of their occupational sites. The most notable aggregates were reported for major institutions of the northeast: the Festival Gate and Bayn al-Qaṣrayn groups, al-Azhar (36), and the two royal madrasas (30, 51). The pattern showed them to be present at other less eminent institutions, as well, such as the mosque of al-Ḥākim (3), the Ṭūlūnid mosque (91), and several of the amirate colleges of the southeast, particularly Ṣarghatmishīya (92) and Aljayhīya (69). Their presence in the Ḥākim and Ṭūlūnid mosques confirms the sustained maintenance of these institutions, which because of their age could not be assumed, as their endowments could have lapsed or been transferred. And the fact that specialized staff were being employed at the amirate madrasas is interesting: these institutions were obviously enrolling students, although their graduates are virtually ignored in the biographical texts. There was only one reference to an institution located in the mortuary zones, the tomb of Imām al-Shāfiʿī (115). Again, the specialized nature of these two districts was indicated by the scarcity of instructors associated with their foundations.

The residence pattern clearly placed holders of repetitorships within

4. Lecturing in al-Azhar

the khānqāh network. In general, this pattern parallels the configuration for professors and, more broadly, for the civil judiciary.

The Mudarris or Professor
(Appendix II, List 16)

Individuals in the sample held this office more often than any other position. Professors directed formal study at the advanced level,[89] and the range of their collective erudition was quite wide. They lectured to students on the several branches of the Islamic sciences and, unofficially, on certain disciplines outside the orthodox curriculum. They exposed students to basic texts of the Islamic corpus, and recited them aloud in order to set examples of grammatical rules and pronunciation. They examined students who presented themselves as candidates for certification, and who thus sought to enter the legal-academic establishment. Many devoted much of their time to study and writing both scholarly works and literary compositions in elaborately contrived styles. Professors were both generalists and specialists. All had been nurtured on the same basic subjects. But the luminaries concentrated on certain aspects of one or two disciplines and attained an encyclopedic level of expertise. Renowned professors formed a closely knit community throughout the central Arab lands. The faculties of the major institutions of Cairo, Damascus, and Aleppo knew one another on a personal basis and periodically exchanged their positions.

The numbers of individuals holding chairs in specific disciplines exceeded those designated simply as mudarris, although there were more of the latter than of specialists in any one field. The major specialties included the standard Islamic sciences; the secular sciences such as history or mathematics did not occur frequently enough to permit statistical analysis.[90] The most eminent professors held chairs in specific disciplines, particularly jurisprudence. All of them had advanced from the status of assistant, in which an individual was responsible for teaching several subjects under a master. A person became famous in a field according to his erudition in the texts, the popularity of his lectures, and the frequency of his commentaries or, more rarely, treatises. During this period commentaries on earlier standard texts greatly outnumbered creative scholarship in the form of new treatises.

The qualities of the mudarris group, indicated by the range of their activities, and their distributive patterns closely paralleled those of the more specialized professors. The generalists were thus selected for analysis. The occupational survey exhibited a superficially wide span of subjects taught, but closer inspection reveals a marked concentration in the legal category and, more specifically, the judicial fields. This configuration duplicates the occupational profile of the judges, although instructional offices outnumbered court posts. The collegiate network effectively monopolized instruction in the Islamic sciences, that is, the standard legal curriculum requisite to recognition as an ʿalim. Such recognition was formally certified by completion of a series of durūs or courses, testified to by a council of professors. Incumbents of both judicial and scholastic positions chose those who would follow them from among their own students. This personal contact was of the utmost importance for both entry to and promotion within the juridical-scholarly class. Certainly the quality of a student's performance in his dars counted heavily in a master's evaluation; his ijāza certificate dwelled on his control of a text and of the discipline treated by it. However, the concentrations at the elite institutions have repeatedly shown us that the prominent jurist-scholars dominating the civil sphere of Cairo studied and subsequently taught in these establishments. A student in an obscure amirate college was allegedly exposed to a program identical to instruction at Ṣāliḥīya or Ẓāhirīya, but did not have the contact with those in power that resulted from successful entry into the major institutions. This contact was more important for his advancement than the quality of his performance in the standard curriculum.

Formal study and cementing of collegiate ties in this network became all the more important for the students there because these foundations also housed the Sharīʿa court system, providing their students with opportunities for first-hand observation and experience in civil litigation. The Sharīʿa courts retained some measure of autonomy from the regime, and stood as the one major decision-making forum supervised independently by civilians. This is of paramount importance. In practice, the Sharīʿa rarely influenced the regime's practical policies, at least overtly. But since the Sharīʿa transcended any temporal power as a moral force, those who were recognized as its interpreters by the society never completely surrendered to the state. The court system may thus be viewed as a haven for civilian politics in an otherwise authoritarian world.

Not only was the judicial establishment somewhat independent of the regime, but the individuals who were filling temporary and insecure positions as judges were simultaneously holding relatively secure and stable academic positions. A judgeship was subject to termination at any time, but a professorship involved indefinite remunerative appointment. Thus, the interrelationship of these two positions explains in part how the ʿulamaʾ managed to endure the hazards of high office in Mamluk society, and the wider implications of the legal concentration in the occupational survey become apparent.

Although there were some professors in the bureaucratic category, almost all of them were clerks or controllers. We have noted that the secretarial profession was staffed by a particular class that included a large minority element ineligible for status as ʿulamaʾ. Among all the Muslim Copts who appeared in the sources, only one held a professorship—a specialist in taṣawwuf.[91] Most stewards were Muslims, but did not belong to the jurist-scholars. There were a few religious functionaries among the professors, but these figures must be compared with the figures for category VI to develop an impression of the relationship between the two groups. The absence of revered persons (muʿtaqads) from the professorial group is worthy of note. This distinct type of ascetic did not identify with the learned establishment of Cairo.

Few individuals from a nonliterary background appear to have been able to acquire the requisite education for academic life. It would be misleading to suggest that the learned establishment was closed to persons engaged in skilled trades or commerce, since there were some cases of such individuals who did attain professorships. Their numbers were limited, however, and few of them attained prestigious chairs.

DISTRIBUTION OF PROFESSORS (Figs. 21-A, 21-B)

Professorships were the most widely dispersed occupation in the major group. The pattern of occupational sites attests to the primacy of the elite institutions in the old Fāṭimid district (Fig. 21-A). The multiple concentrations for the Bayn al-Qaṣrayn madrasas point to their high status in legal studies.[92] But the pattern extended well beyond the northeast. Professors were active in many of the amirate madrasas of the southeast, as well as Shaykhūnīya (83) and the Ṭūlūnid mosque (91). Salient among these were the colleges of Ṣarghatmish (92), Umm al-Sulṭān (60), Ṣūdūn min Zāda (70), and Aytmish (62). The large number of professors teaching in these foundations contrasts with the insignificant role of these places as training centers of the jurist-scholars, raising a question of who actually studied there. It also leads us to ask whether individuals holding chairs at these institutions spent much time in them. Many probably held sinecures, and the subordinate staff (*nuwwāb*) apprenticing in these colleges of secondary rank taught most of the courses. That highly specialized faculty taught less often in these institutions than in the elite madrasas lends support to this hypothesis. It is also likely that the students at the amirate colleges catered to the Mamluk elite and its clients. Many of these people were not included in the biographical sources as members of the learned class, and thus were not widely represented in these surveys. But regardless of the clientele at these colleges, there is no doubt over their activity. And their faculties included, at least nominally, many luminaries from among the established professors.

There were scattered references to institutions outside the inner city (Fig. 21-B). The suburbs of the northwest and southwest had almost no cases, but concentrations appeared at the mosque of ʿAmr ibn al-ʿĀs (113) in Old Cairo, the Hospice of the Prophet's Relics (114) on the Nile shore, and the Kharrūbīya madrasa (112) in Jīza.[93] There were scattered cases in the port of Būlāq, indicating the activity of local colleges there. Finally, a cluster occurred at the complex surrounding the tomb of Imām al-Shāfiʿī (115) in the Qarāfa. This was the only noteworthy center of higher learning in either of the two mortuary zones.

Whereas the residence pattern for shāhids complemented the larger number of notarial positions held by Ṣūfīs (Table 11, Category III), the professors—some of whom clearly identified with Sufism—do not appear to have been closely associated with the khānqāhs. Aggregates certainly emerged in Saʿīd al-Suʿadāʾ (15) and al-Azhar (36). But the prominent monastic houses, the cathedral mosque, and the two royal madrasas, which were the primary seats of Ṣūfī orders in Cairo, did not seem to house many professors. If the residence pattern is compared with occupational sites, the relative position of the khānqāhs is diminished still further. In general, the juridical-scholarly class found its focus in the madrasa rather than the khānqāh. Legal training was not the ostensible function of khānqāhs, which were founded to promote an environment conducive to contemplation of divinity and spiritual self-perfection. Yet jurist-scholars were certainly represented within the mystic community.[94] Conversely, inmates of the major hospices were not completely withdrawn from active participation in the larger society, including the orthodox legal system and the policies of the ruling regime. The intricacies of the ʿulama's seemingly ambiguous identity with the Ṣūfī community thus await further analysis.

The Khāzin al-Kutub or Librarian (Appendix II, List 17)

The librarian, literally a "treasurer of books," did not appear frequently in the texts, and the nature of his duties do not suggest that the office was widespread. The term "honorarium" may more accurately depict the nature of the position rather than "office." A librarianship was rarely included among the positions specified in a waqf writ. Yet the status of this honorarium attests to the significance of libraries, even if these surveys did not reveal all of them. The importance attached to encyclopedic absorption of a fixed literary and ideological corpus rendered the maintenance of that corpus crucial. Since all textual materials had to be duplicated by hand, they were in limited supply and very expensive. Few scholars could afford to purchase many books for themselves, and a private library represented a substantial capital asset. If a scholar were obliged to sell even part of his library because of financial straits, this was viewed as a personal tragedy and a sign of his professional degradation.

Since few individuals could themselves acquire the textual materials indispensable to their function, the responsibility for doing so fell to religio-academic institutions and their benefactors. There was considerable prestige attached to maintaining a library; Maqrīzī often pointed to the presence or lack of a library in his evaluations of institutions (cf. Appendix I), and dwelled glowingly on the physical qualities of the major collections, describing the luxurious bindings and fine paper. The Mamluks who were moved to provide their institutions with vast sums of money and munificent endowments were eager to assemble book collections, even though few of them could understand the texts. On occasion, they were prepared to buy off, by underhanded means, a whole faculty in order to transfer a collection to their own institution, even if the collection was supported by a waqf and had been dedicated to a specific madrasa.

The position of librarian seems to have been awarded under two possible circumstances: to recognize outstanding service or accomplishment in the learned community, often by the institution's founder; and to provide a sinecure in return for donation of a personal collection. In other words, a lifetime stipend was offered as an incentive to contribute valuable textual materials. A librarianship thus rarely constituted an initial position, but usually signified the culmination of an individual's career. Some extremely eminent persons were made honorary book treasurers of madrasas, particularly when their patrons were involved with the foundation or augmentation of those institutions.

DISTRIBUTION OF LIBRARIANS (Fig. 22)

The data available on occupational sites identify some but not all institutions that possessed libraries during the fifteenth century. For example, the famous collection housed in the Manṣūrīya madrasa (the tomb of Sultan Qalā'ūn; cf. Appendix I) did not have a librarian mentioned in the sources. Also, the largest concentrations, if such they may be called, did not conform to the order of rank and quality of institutions so evident in the other surveys. For example, the Festival Gate group revealed only a small cluster. In the Bayn al-Qaṣrayn group, only the

Ẓāhirīya madrasa (23) was represented. Most institutions of these two groups possessed libraries, and yet the evidence here did not indicate a large number of librarians. Of the major foundations in the northeast, only the Ashrafīya madrasa (30) had a concentration. There were no references whatever to al-Azhar. Among institutions of secondary rank, the Bāsiṭīya college (11) yielded the only other noteworthy concentration in the northeast. In the southeast, among the amirate colleges, only Maḥmūdīya (57) stood out. Shaykhūnīya (83), Ṣarghatmishīya (92), and three other foundations (53, 60, 93) were mentioned. In summary, the data available did establish the Fāṭimid district as the primary repository of book collections, since the majority of references to librarians were located there. All the institutions so designated enjoyed sufficient endowment to maintain holdings, and most of them were so mentioned by Maqrīzī (Appendix I).

THE RELIGIOUS FUNCTIONARIES
(Table 11, Category VI)

The final group in this study consisted of individuals dedicated to religious service or observation. In premodern Muslim societies, the entire population, from those at the apex of power to the most humble elements of the masses, were willing, indeed felt compelled, to honor and support persons endowed with revered qualities, a sign of God's blessing. The forms that manifestation of piety could assume were almost infinite. They varied considerably even between the four fields examined here; but the objective—confirming God's ongoing concern for people in this life, his willingness to touch at least some of them directly—was the same.

The data configurations discussed here and in Chapter II suggest that individuals committed to religious service or public piety were distinguishable geographically (by pronounced localism) and professionally (by some degree of separation from the mainstream of civilian literary and political life) from other components of the civilian elite, particularly the jurist-scholars. Yet those who staffed the mosque and presided over its services were regarded as ʿulamaʾ, and did not exhibit the signs of social isolation so evident in several bureaucratic fields. Predictably, almost all were Muslims. Three of these offices (imām, khaṭīb, and muqriʾ) ministered directly to the local populace. Holders of these posts were responsible for whatever personal impact religion had on the people. In addition, religious functionaries performed the vital service of elementary education. This service they shared with the scholarly-educational group, although the evidence points to a larger contribution from them than from professors (compare Lists 16, 18, and 20, Categories V and VI). The individuals who taught beginners their basic literacy and fundamental religious principles did not attract the attention that famous authorities in jurisprudence did by their lectures and writings. Yet a variety of activities associated with elementary education were mentioned in the biographical accounts, suggesting that these fields were accepted as a legitimate calling of the ʿulamaʾ.

Only the most prominent of the religious functionaries shared the characteristics of the jurist-scholars. Professorships constituted the largest group of collateral occupations held by the imāms, khaṭībs, and muqriʾs. Yet those who were not professors tended not to participate in activities of the legal-academic establishment, but were confined more to mosque-related duties. Viewed collectively, the religious functionaries came from a lower social level than the jurist-scholars, so many members of which were born into famous ʿulamaʾ houses. The imāms and khaṭībs may be excepted from this trend, since they were clearly represented among the jurist-scholars, but their origins tended to be restricted to the Cairo-Delta zone.

Holy men and pious ascetics constituted a social type rather than a true profession. They were included in this last group because of their association with centers of worship and their impact on the popular mind. Otherwise, they were a unique element distinct from all the other occupations examined in the study.

Consideration of the selection process used by the biographical compilers is particularly important with respect to the religious functionaries. The compilers sought to describe individual notables, and did not explicitly attempt to define a social class. Their stress on prominence and status as requisites for inclusion would tend to emphasize the executive, bureaucratic, legal, and scholarly fields, since people in these professions were firmly entrenched in the military or civilian elites. The artisan-commercial group was considered only if someone from that field moved into the civilian elite. However, individuals in the group of religious functionaries were to be found at every level of Cairene society, as they were throughout the Muslim world. The compilers, naturally, tended to describe primarily those in the upper class. The majority of religious functionaries below the luminaries staffing major institutions were not included, and thus remain unknown to us. This is particularly true of imāms and khaṭībs, somewhat less so of muqriʾs. The muʿtaqads do not seem to have adhered to the general social trends and class lines characterizing the other fields. Included because of their unique spiritual qualities, they must be considered on their own terms.

5. A Night of Ramaḍān, Hour of Prayer

The Imām or Prayer Leader
(Appendix II, List 18)

The prayer leaders mentioned by al-Sakhāwī and Ibn Taghrī-Birdī presided over religious service in the prominent institutions of the capital. Many held their offices as honoraria, in addition to several other positions. As they resigned, retired, or were dismissed from such positions, these individuals tended to confine themselves increasingly to their spiritual office, and terminated their careers as leaders of a congregation. The imām served two types of clientele: the community of a mosque, madrasa, or khānqāh; or a household. The households retaining an imām to minister to them personally belonged to the highest levels of society, and the most important of them was the imperial court itself. Here the imām ministered to members and retinue of the current royal family as a chaplain, and led prayer service in the Citadel mosque. Many of the great Mamluk houses also retained an imām to guide prayer services and invoke supplication for their spiritual welfare. Maintenance of such a person in the home implied a show of conspicuous piety that only an aristocracy could afford.

Due to the honorary nature of higher imāmates, their incumbents held positions throughout the bureaucratic, legal, and scholarly categories. As was true for persons in all religious fields, imāms were rarely associated with the executive sphere. Conversely, there was no appreciable Mamluk presence, even of the second and third generations, among the group of imāms. Once again, the mutual phenomena of exclusion by the regime and conscious abstinence on the part of the ʿulamaʾ were implicit in this occupational profile. Nonetheless, although the religious and executive fields exhibited few signs of crossover, one should not assume a similar degree of isolation at the social level. Religious functionaries, and especially imāms, were closely associated with the Mamluk oligarchy. But the nature of their contact differed radically from that between Mamluks and their bureaucratic clients. An imām widely respected for his pious life style was held in awe by the military caste. A famous spiritual figure could exercise considerable influence over members of this caste, including the sultan himself, without wielding executive authority. Above all, he did not surrender his autonomy. His spiritual services were offered at his own discretion, unlike the substantial but subordinate powers of civilian bureaucrats. Note that overall representation of imāms in the bureaucratic category was lower than in the three ʿalim-related areas. The pattern was dominated by clerkships and controllerships rather than dīwān offices. Not a single secretary was reported.

Among the legal professions (III), holders of imāmates were more likely to occupy shaykhships rather than judgeships (compare Lists 7 and 18). The shaykh and imām played complementary roles. The former interpreted the law within the spiritual community; the latter presided over its prayer service. That the same person often held both positions seems natural. The proportions of court offices suggest that individuals who ultimately became imāms were fairly active in the lower ranks of the judiciary. Even given the source bias toward eminent persons, these figures may point to a connection between local litigation and local religious practice, although we may assume that less famous imāms would have held fewer judgeships than did this elite sample.

The figures for positions in the scholarly category confirm this group's status. The majority of professorships were in specialized disciplines, a measure of scholarly prestige, but whether the level of attainment exhibited by this sample was characteristic of the office as a whole throughout the central Islamic lands we do not know. We possess no information equivalent to the records available for the lower clergy of Europe, many of whom matched their congregations' ignorance. The cases examined here certainly compared well with high church officials, who often possessed minimal theological training—especially when they attained their positions through political and social connections.

DISTRIBUTION OF IMĀMS (Figs. 23-A, 23-B)

Occupational sites were widely distributed throughout the metropolis. This phenomenon would accord with both the popular role of the office and the local background of the majority of individuals. The concentrations confirm the elite status of this particular group, since they occurred at major institutions, several of which were not dedicated primarily to public worship.[95] But the pattern was not limited to foundations catering to specialized clienteles. Note that al-Azhar (36), the symbolic forum of the capital's inhabitants, was referred to more often than any other institution. Many foundations of secondary rank in the northeast and elsewhere were represented, including the western suburbs, Būlāq, Old Cairo, the two mortuary zones, and Siryāqūs. Overall, the pattern, especially if considered together with the distribution of preachers (khaṭībs), broadly outlined the zones of religious service.

The residence pattern revealed two notable concentrations at the khānqāhs of Baybarsīya (13) and Saʿīd al-Suʿadāʾ (15). Smaller aggregates were reported for Ashrafīya (30), Muʿayyadīya (51), and Shaykhūnīya (84). All five were hospices for Ṣūfī mystics, and we may assume that there were many Ṣūfīs among individuals appointed to imāmates. Indeed, the mappings showed a pronounced association with the mystic community among all the religious functionaries. In the case of the imāms there was a functional relationship, since organized prayer sessions were fundamental to the daily ritual of Ṣūfī orders. But this identity also serves to reinforce the distinction of the religious category from the juridical-scholarly group which was less inclined toward affiliation with the mystic community.

The Khaṭīb or Preacher
(Appendix II, List 19)

This official, whose chief responsibility was delivery of the Friday sermon, the khuṭba, was mentioned the most frequently of any occupation in the religious category.[96] Like the imāms, the khaṭībs often held their posts in addition to other activities. The office was not necessarily a full-time calling, since sermons and orations did not accompany all prayer sessions, but only the Friday service. Few of the individuals holding this office would consider themselves a khaṭīb first. They tended to regard it as acknowledgement of success in other fields and, indeed, this seems to have been the basis of appointment. Khaṭībs of the major religio-academic institutions in the capital were always eminent men. Many had proven their ability to lecture in the madrasas. To warrant the responsibility for publicly reminding the congregation of its obligation to follow the path God had revealed, the khaṭīb had to exemplify adherence to such a path himself. He must be an erudite scholar learned in scripture and the Islamic sciences.

The preachership involved certain temporal functions, foremost among which was invocation of the secular authority's titulary at the commencement of the khuṭba. The general public was thereby informed as to the continuity or disruption of the regime under which they lived. Moreover, the Friday sermon could reveal by inference and guarded phrases a wide range of political information concerning the regime's policies. Major events affecting the public interest were announced outright. The khuṭba therefore served as a semiofficial news medium. As such, it was eagerly attended in the great centers of worship in the city, especially during times of momentous political developments, internal upheaval, or foreign events. To blend political information with moral exhortation, a khaṭīb had to possess political acumen along with his scholarly and religious attainment. He would presumably enjoy social connections with high officials who could keep him abreast of the regime's policies. For these reasons, more individuals appointed to preacherships appear to have been firmly entrenched in the upper echelons of the civilian elite than any of the other religious functionaries.

Khaṭībs engaged in a range of activities appropriate to their social status. Their occupational profile paralleled that of jurist-scholars more closely than did that of any other religious office. Nonetheless, this office retained the independence characteristic of the religious category. Although well informed of the regime's machinations, the jurist-scholars themselves rarely functioned as its blatant instrument of implementation. Yet their presence in bureaucratic fields (especially controllerships, but also dīwān offices) provides further evidence of the khaṭībs' worldly orientation. Conversely, holders of preacherships tended to be less directly involved with mundane religious procedures than were other religious functionaries.

DISTRIBUTION OF KHAṬĪBS (Figs. 24-A, 24-B)

These configurations were broadly similar to those of the preceding office. But the occupational distribution was the most widely dispersed throughout the metropolis of any field in the major group, regardless of category. The concentrations help to identify those mosques (as distinct from khānqāhs) that acted as both centers of worship and disseminators of information. These aggregates, as well as the foundations lacking concentrations, merit attention, since they imply a separation of roles. Two striking concentrations appeared, one at al-Azhar (36), and the other at the mosque of ʿAmr ibn al-ʿĀṣ (113) in Old Cairo.[97] These institutions dominated the map, but others were also prominent: the mosque of al-Ḥākim (3); Ḥijāzīya Madrasa (17) near the Festival Gate; the mosque of Aqmar (12); Bāsiṭīya madrasa (11); Barqūqīya (20) and Ṣāliḥīya (26) colleges along the Bayn al-Qaṣrayn; Ashrafīya (30) and Muʿayyadīya (51); the Zaynī mosque (43) in the Bayn al-Sūrayn, all in the northeast. In the southeast several amirate colleges were mentioned. The salient institutions were the mosques of Aṣlam (54), Sultan Ḥasan (74), and the Citadel (68). In the southwest the Ṭūlūnid mosque (91) was frequently mentioned, as were the mosques of al-Zāhid (101)[98] and al-Maqs (104)[99] in the northwest, and the Jīʿānī (105)[100] and Khaṭīrī (108)[101] mosques in Būlāq. Several districts of the city were thus represented substantially for the first time in this study. The largest concentrations were located at the cathedral mosques of Fusṭāṭ (113) and al-Qāhira (36). All the others served specific quarters of the city; there were no cases of appreciable clustering. These institutions may well have defined local population conglomerates. Many of them did not appear significantly in the surveys for other occupations, implying that they were primarily social centers, rather than supporting the more specialized functions of the elite group. Although not all the wards or quarters of

Cairo contained such centers, if the occupational sites for imāms and khaṭībs are compared, one may develop an impression of where foundations dedicated to popular worship were located.

Lacunae in the pattern of occupational sites were filled by references to residence. In general, among the major centers of higher learning only al-Azhar (36) figured prominently, although several others were represented. But the pattern was dominated by the two khānqāhs so important not only for the Ṣūfī community but the Cairo-Delta zone: Baybarsīya (13) and Saʿīd al-Suʿadāʾ (15).[102] This residence profile fully conforms to the general patterns of the entire religious category: identification with the khānqāh network and derivation from the hinterland of the capital. Thus, this office, as an honorarium carrying great prestige, would seem to have been recruited within the ʿulamaʾ hierarchy—but primarily from those elements involved with the Ṣūfī community and born into the Egyptian component of the civilian elite. This is in marked contrast with the backgrounds of the highest officials of the imperial dīwāns, infiltrated by indigenous minorities and foreign Muslims. The khaṭībs were also familiar with state policies because of their position, and yet they belonged to the most firmly established Cairo families.

The absence of the Ṣūfī network from the occupational pattern of the khaṭībs suggests that khānqāhs maintained some degree of autonomy from the regime. These institutions are not generally interpreted as seats of public orthodox worship, and it is clear that khānqāhs, at least ostensibly, did not function as centers for disseminating public information, particularly governmental decrees.

The Muqriʾ or Koran Reader
(Appendix II, List 20)

The muqriʾ recited the Koran during annual festivals of the Muslim calendar, prayer services, and major familial events such as circumcisions, marriages, and funerals. Recitation of scripture was desirable on all these occasions, but it was considered indispensable for a funeral and subsequent wakes over the grave. Recitation of the Koran over the recently deceased bolstered his soul and, it was hoped, aided its transition to Paradise. Mamluk sultans and amirs lavishly endowed hosts of muqriʾs to recite the Koran in their tombs (cf. Appendix I). Muqriʾs were maintained by many religio-academic foundations for these purposes, and also to instruct the young in basic scriptural reading. Several wealthy institutions, such as al-Azhar and Baybarsīya, were equipped with special galleries in which muqriʾs sat reciting the Koran day and night during festivals or momentous occasions. The scene of these ritual recitations during a major feast day or national crisis in a mosque like al-Azhar must have stirred the imagination of the worshipers, inspiring them with a sense of divine presence.

Muqri's were a distinct professional type. Many derived from families long attached to a religio-academic institution, and inherited their positions from their fathers. Many were born into humble circumstances, and attained renown by virtue of their extraordinary retentive powers. Few muqri's belonged to the prominent learned families of Cairo. They all pursued an education that stressed memorization of scripture and Prophetic traditions, which often built upon their proven ability to recite several texts from memory. A photographic memory and a dramatic sense of poetry were prerequisites to a successful career and to the acquisition of fame that attracted patrons. Muqri's were often dependent on wealthy patrons, since maintenance of a muqri' in a great house, like supporting an imām, was a sign of conspicuous piety.

Muqri's often exhibited a physical handicap associated with their profession: blindness.[103] Not all muqri's were without sight, but individuals who had suffered the misfortune and who had retentive powers were often encouraged to find their vocation in the recitation of scripture.

Muqri's were more closely associated with the mundane functions of religious institutions than were either imāms or khaṭībs. Fewer were involved with bureaucratic and legal activities (II and III), and practically none were in executive fields (I), although, conversely, a number of readerships were held by Mamluks or their descendants.[104] More muqri's held positions in the scholarly and religious categories (V and VI), the former partly because of the large numbers engaged in elementary teaching, although a substantial number of professors also appeared, particularly in specialties relating to the Koran, Ḥadīth, and the art of public recitation. It must be stressed again, however, that few muqri's belonged to the famous ʿulama' families of the capital. They attained their positions largely due to their renown as masters of recitation, and as those who were the best qualified to train their successors. The characteristics of muqri's may best be seen in specific examples.

Muḥayy al-Dīn Yaḥyā ibn Yaḥyā al-Qibābī al-Qāhirī al-Shāfiʿī[105] was born in 761/1359-1360 in the Delta town of Qibāb (I-A: 291). How al-Qibābī lost his parents or moved to Cairo was not mentioned, but he began his elementary studies in the school for orphans attached to the mosque of Sultan Ḥasan, where his aptitude for memorization was first noticed. In 785/1383-1384 he traveled to Damascus, and was appointed a preacher (wāʿiẓ) and repetitor at the Citadel mosque by the Mamluk amir Nāṣir al-Dīn Muḥammad ibn Manjak. Al-Qibābī remained in Damascus the rest of his life, concluding his career as a professor in the Rawāḥīya madrasa and as a deputy judge. He died in Ṣafar 844/July

1440. His biography is noteworthy because from birth he suffered from nearsightedness, and went totally blind during his early adulthood.

One of the most famous muqri's of the fifteenth century hailed from Baghdād. He was Muḥibb al-Dīn Aḥmad ibn Naṣr-Allah al-Tustarī al-Baghdādī al-Ḥanbalī, born in that city in Rajab 765/April-May 1364.[106] He was known as Muḥibb ibn Naṣr-Allah al-Baghdādī. The son of a shaykh in the mosque of al-Mustanṣir in Baghdād, Ibn Naṣr-Allah was a cloth merchant (bazzāz) before turning to recitation. He memorized the Koran and attained proficiency in several traditional, exegetical, and legal texts. Before traveling west, he became an imām in the caliphal mosque of Baghdād, a muʿīd in Mustanṣirīya, and a copyist. After his departure, he recited in Syria and Alexandria, and finally settled in Cairo. His fame had preceded him, and he was immediately befriended by Ibn Ḥajar al-ʿAsqalānī and Sultan Barqūq. In 795/1392-1393 he was appointed a professor of jurisprudence and Prophetic traditions in Barqūqīya (20) soon after its opening. He subsequently held professorships in Mu'ayyadīya (51), Manṣūrīya (22), and Shaykhūnīya (83). He apprenticed as a deputy judge twice before his appointment to the Ḥanbalī chief justiceship of Egypt. He died in Jumādā I 844/September-October 1440.

Successful muqri's often enjoyed the favor of great Mamluks. A case in point was Badr al-Dīn Ḥasan ibn Aḥmad al-Ṭanṭadā'ī al-Qāhirī al-Shāfiʿī, born in the Delta town of Ṭanṭa (I-A:121) in 802/1399-1400.[107] He memorized the Koran in his native city before moving to Cairo. Although he never attained wide recognition as a master reciter, he won the favor of Sultan Jaqmaq, who appointed him a muqri' at court. The sultan provided his favorite with a lucrative controllership of minority tax receipts (the poll tax from Christians and Jews), which yielded a comfortable income for its incumbent. Jaqmaq thus supported his client in high style at no cost to himself.

A muqri' descended from a humble family attached to the service of a large khānqāh was Shams al-Dīn Muḥammad ibn ʿAlī al-Qāhirī al-Ṣūfī al-Shāfiʿī,[108] born at Saʿīd al-Suʿadā' in 809/1406-1407. His father was a gatekeeper (bawwāb) at the hospice, and Shams Muḥammad succeeded to the post. The family's social status did not prevent Muḥammad from studying texts in the community. He exhibited such talent that he was accepted as a student by the exegete, Ibn Ḥajar al-ʿAsqalānī, and was presumably certified by him, since he met the standards set by several other famous scholars. Muḥammad may have been obliged to develop his retentive powers, since he suffered severely from ophthalmia (ramad) at an early age, and could only distinguish light from darkness. He was appointed a muqri' in al-Azhar and Saʿīd al-Suʿadā' and a khaṭīb in the mosque of Ibn Sharaf al-Dīn. We may assume that Shams

Muḥammad prospered at least moderately from his recitations, since al-Sakhāwī mentioned that he owned a private house, which was pilfered of valuable possessions by thieves. He certainly improved upon his father's status as a gatekeeper.

One individual who never became famous at his vocation is interesting because of his social background. This muqri' was designated only by his personal name, ʿAlī.[109] Originally a baker (khabbāz), he was obliged to recite the Koran because of his blindness. No details on his whereabouts were given. He may have chanted Sūras in the streets or public squares, depending on the charity of the local populace for support.

The final example was a venerated master of recitation. He was Zayn al-Dīn Jaʿfar ibn Ibrāhīm al-Qurashī al-Sanhūrī al-Qāhirī al-Azharī al-Shāfiʿī,[110] born in the west Delta town of Sanhūr (I-A: 48) in 810/1407-1408. He pursued his early studies and memorized the Koran in his home town and al-Maḥallat al-Kubrā before being sent off to the colleges of Cairo for advanced work. More than sixty items were listed in his formal curriculum, and he was certified to recite and lecture on many of them. Al-Sakhāwī admired al-Sanhūrī, and provided a detailed account of his erudition as testimony to his astonishing capacity for accurate absorption of material. Al-Sanhūrī was appointed a muqri' and professor of Koranic recitation in the Mu'ayyadīya madrasa (51) and al-Azhar (36), where he established his permanent residence. Subsequently, he received the controllership of the Ṣarūjā mosque.[111] He enjoyed the respect of a wide circle of colleagues and scholarly associates, and the support of the Mamluk elite. He received a stipend of five dīnārs a month from the famous grand amir Yashbak min Mahdī al-Dawādār, who was inspired by his flawless command of the Sūras. He died in Cairo in Dhū'l-Ḥijja 894/October-November 1489.

DISTRIBUTION OF MUQRI'S (Figs. 25-A, 25-B)

The distribution of occupational and residential sites for the Koran readers, like the general configurations for imāms and khaṭībs, revealed a majority of cases in the northeast, but substantial numbers in other districts as well. Unlike the khaṭībs, the muqri's were not dispersed among local district mosques, but tended to be limited to several elite foundations. The largest aggregate was reported at al-Azhar (36), which was famous throughout the Muslim world, as Maqrīzī noted, for the host of muqri's it supported (cf. Appendix I). Smaller concentrations were reported for the khānqāhs of Baybarsīya (13) and Saʿīd al-Suʿadā' (15), and for the Jamālīya madrasa (16), all in the Festival Gate group. Occupational sites were clustered here and at the Bayn al-Qaṣrayn group, although no major concentrations at any specific institution were reported for the latter. This was to be expected because of the emphasis on legal training at madrasas.

In the southeast, several amirate colleges were represented, and a concentration was reported for Shaykhūnīya (83-84). However, numerous positions were based at institutions of the Citadel, although none at the Nāṣirī mosque. The royal (Striped) Palace (135), the harem (136), and two barracks for household troops or guards (134, 138) all maintained Koran readers. Muqri's were the only religious functionaries to be seen in such a close relationship with the imperial court. The Mamluk elite evidently revered scriptural oratory and held those who attained its mastery in great esteem. The Mamluk's attitude toward Koranic chanting may perhaps be explained by the high degree of illiteracy in Arabic among their ranks. Many could never hope to read the Koran themselves, and depended on others to quote it. This wide respect among the military caste for Koran readers was evident in their high degree of support through endowment or patronage, and the muqri' thus set an example of the practical benefits resulting from manifesting an aura of devoutness. The very capacity to memorize scripture was viewed as a sign of divine favor—especially to the Mamluk elite, who stood in awe of such a feat.

References to muqri's were scattered throughout other districts of the capital. Only two appeared at the Ṭūlūnid mosque (91). Their visibility in the two mortuary zones is attributable to the role assigned the muqri' in the tombs of notables—chanting Sūras over the grave to bear witness to (or compensate for the lack of) the deceased's faith, and to ensure a satisfactory transition to the Hereafter. One would expect to find muqri's established in the monuments of great Mamluks (121, 123, 124), since these individuals had reason to desire the reading of scripture over their graves.

The residence pattern was consistent with the vocation of the muqri's. Aggregates appeared at Sa'īd al-Su'adā' (15), Baybarsīya (13), and al-Azhar (36). Ashrafīya (30), Mu'ayyadīya (51), and Shaykhūnīya (84) ranked somewhat below these three. All six were bastions of the Ṣūfī community in the capital. A comparison of spiritual orientation and occupations also reveals a large Ṣūfī presence.[112] The connection between overt piety and affiliation with this community is again implied, and is strengthened in this case by the numbers of muqri's employed in Ṣūfī establishments. The khānqāhs and al-Azhar appear to have been forums of scriptural recitation. The hospices sponsored almost continuous prayer cycles to produce an ecstatic state of communication with divinity among their members. Al-Azhar was oriented more to public recitation before large throngs, particularly during major festivals and momentous occasions. These foundations, plus the vast court establishment in the Citadel, maintained the large assemblages of eminent Koran readers.

The Muʿtaqad or Revered Person
(Appendix II, List 21)

Traditional Muslim societies have recognized a variety of personal and behavioral traits combined with certain attitudes toward society and the self as indicating a pious character. Individuals possessing such traits have been revered as being in harmony with the divine. Indeed, in certain regions these persons are considered to be endowed with baraka, Godly emanation, which renders them holy men or women. The biographical sources described many such persons, but in general, they were not considered to possess baraka as if it were almost a physical quality, as is true in the Maghrib in recent times or Iran during the Ilkhānid and Timūrid periods. Rather, individuals noted in the sources were venerated because they deviated sharply from accepted norms of behavior. God had selected them to work His unfathomable will. These people differed so widely from one another that it is impossible to describe them as having a common profession. A better term for their condition in common would be vocation, although each attained it through a unique set of experiences. It is thus possible to define them as a social type, since they shared distinct qualities.

First, muʿtaqads encountered in the biographical accounts rejected for themselves a high material standard of living—not in principle or for society as a whole, but as inconsistent with the state of piety they wished to achieve. Second, the majority of these people were considered peculiar. Their unusual, even deviate, behavioral traits were often complemented by physical abnormalities, due either to accidents or deformities. Finally, several individuals had undergone extreme emotional crises that caused them to abandon their former way of life. Their contemporaries chose to interpret these phenomena as signs of God's intervention in the normal state of the human condition; He had elected to isolate certain individuals for transformation of their character. Such individuals diverged from social norms because He wished to demonstrate His omnipotence. Such individuals thus exemplified extreme holiness. The general society could not follow the path of the muʿtaqad, but could venerate him and support his physical needs.

Muʿtaqads came from all walks of life, but few could claim identification with a family of the ʿulamaʾ. These people were included in the biographical sources because of their revered status and extraordinary behavior. They rarely moved within the civilian elite, nor were many related to those who did. The range of occupations pursued by muʿtaqads indicated their token presence, at least, in every professional category, but there was a larger percentage of them in the artisan category (IV) than of representatives of any other field in the major group, with the exception of copyists and merchants. Few muʿtaqads seem to have been associated with either the bureaucracy or the juridical-scholarly establishment. The proportion for the legal fields was augmented by eleven positions referring to shaykhs, an office not directly involved with the civil courts. Few muʿtaqads staffed the administrative posts of religio-academic institutions, but the percentage for the religious category (VI) was raised by the group of majdhūbs or holy ecstatics.

Among the Ṣūfīs a majdhūb was the elect of God, an individual who attained a state of blessed harmony without having undergone a long and arduous preparation of the mind. In general, the term applied to a person prone to fits, trances, and prolonged states of ecstasy. The presence of majdhūbs among muʿtaqads is not surprising, given the similarity of the two types.

In the list of occupations held by muʿtaqads, there was a striking variety of humble livelihoods. Category IV yielded references to a broad beans seller (fawwāl), water carrier, greengrocer, oil dealer, servants, and so on. But there was also a Sulṭānī Mamluk[113] and a Mālikī professor,[114] indicating the wide range in social status of those who could become muʿtaqads. The majority of revered persons, however, originated outside the military or civilian elites.

Civilians in general, and Mamluks in particular, were acutely aware of the muʿtaqads. The revered person, as the ward of God, brought favor and good fortune to the neighborhood or district in which he settled. Muʿtaqads who remained in one place, often a shrine or zāwiya, for many years were regarded as sages by the local populace, who sought their advice and blessings for a wide assortment of problems. Support of ascetics constituted a supremely pious act. A neighborhood counted itself fortunate to have induced a muʿtaqad to remain by providing for his needs. And Mamluks showed an inordinate respect for the revered person, which may perhaps be traced to shamanistic tendencies surviving from the pagan culture of the Turkish peoples prior to their conversion. Veneration and even fear of the holy man has characterized conquering peoples from Central Asia in other parts of the Middle East. In any case, Mamluks of all ranks contributed openly to the support of muʿtaqads. Muʿtaqads who originated in Turkish-speaking regions were especially sought after as court attendants and personal associates, since the Mamluks could understand them easily, without interpreters. But the Mamluks courted the favor of all muʿtaqads, regardless of language or ethnic background.[115] Sultans proudly pointed to personal association with several revered persons during their reigns as a sign of God's personal endorsement of their rule. When a famous muʿtaqad died, the sultan was likely to attend the funeral. Amirs encouraged muʿtaqads to settle in their madrasas, although few accepted such invitations, preferring the monastic communities, great mosques, small zāwiyas, and tombs in the mortuary zones. Many of these latter sites were not listed in the topographical sources.

DISTRIBUTION OF MUʿTAQADS (Figs. 26-A, 26-B)

The spatial analysis of the muʿtaqads rests on the residence pattern alone. The lack of occupational sites was predictable, since work was not expected of revered persons. The three "occupational sites" given were at mosques or zāwiyas, which complemented the residence pattern. But this pattern was itself limited because the majority of host institutions were obscure. Three aggregates appeared: at Saʿīd al-Suʿadāʾ (15), al-Azhar (36), and the mosque-shrine of the martyr, Ḥusayn (33). These serve only to identify several ascetics who were also Ṣūfīs attached to a mystic community.[116] The other locations suggest a tendency to live in or near the great mosques, the imperial court, or the two mortuary zones, but the problem of locating minor zāwiyas and tombs resulted in many lacunae on the maps. The Desert Plain and Qarāfa (200, 202) were the muʿtaqad's special domain, where they settled along with the guards, caretakers, and their families—none of whom were included in the biographies. Their presence lent a holy, even exotic atmosphere to the mortuary zones. Families who came to visit their ancestors' monuments brought offerings of food and clothing for the local revered person. A family considered itself favored if he chose to honor its tomb with his presence. However, certain muʿtaqads withdrew almost entirely from society and retired to secluded areas, such as the desert wilderness of the Muqaṭṭam Hills (201). These holy hermits would leave their solitude only to accept food and clothing from their patrons.

In summary, information on the muʿtaqad in the biographical sources depicted a special group which, although humble, commanded the awe of the greatest in the state. Their social role in the traditional society of Cairo merits more attention than it has received.

THE ṢŪFĪ MYSTICS
(Appendix II; List 22)

Although individuals joined a mystic community to enter an environment conducive to contemplation, self-perfection, and spiritual harmony with God, they rarely withdrew permanently from society. Members of an order could engage in numerous temporal activities and still retain their identification with it; Ṣūfīs rarely spent the majority of their mature years confined to a hospice. A resident in a khānqāh was not barred from involvement with the world. If he chose to seclude himself from it, this was his own decision. The activities of Ṣūfī communities were not open to the public, but members could leave the house and return to it at stipulated times.

Two Ṣūfī orders, the Shādhilī and the Qādirī, were mentioned frequently in the biographical accounts, but not all individuals identified as mystics were designated as members in one of these. Since the references to Ṣūfīs in general greatly outnumbered specific citation of either order, and since the data on members of these orders closely paralleled the information on Ṣūfīs as a whole, only the general group was subjected to analysis.

The broad dispersion of popular Sufism throughout Islamic societies during the later Middle Ages is widely assumed.[117] And indeed, the range of occupations pursued by individuals claiming some tie with the Ṣūfī community was very extensive. Nonetheless, we may not assume that Sufism was uniformly dispersed throughout the civilian elite. Although the bias of the sources would tend to minimize the number of Ṣūfīs in executive fields,[118] it was also true that there were few citations in dīwān-related fields (II). Allowing for exceptional cases, individuals holding executive office or embedded in the regime's bureaucratic apparatus tended neither to claim a tie with the Ṣūfī community nor to reside in its institutions. This tendency may appear paradoxical, given the intense concern of the Mamluk caste about Sufism. But we have already suggested that the Mamluks, despite their own military and political preoccupations, tended to respect, even to fear individuals exhibiting a special relationship with the divine. Did such awe provide persons associated with Sufism with a buffer, or even a lever, against Mamluk incursion? If it did, then such leverage would constitute a powerful incentive for civilians to develop ties with the Ṣūfī establishment—and to guarantee that the military caste did not. This is all speculation, but it is a fact that individuals who were regarded as minions of the regime cemented few ties with the Ṣūfī community. Those elements of the civilian elite seeking to maintain their autonomy from Mamluk influence dominated the Ṣūfī configuration.

The number of Ṣūfīs in legal fields (III) constitutes something of an anomaly, as we have seen. Shaykhs, of course, were intimately involved with Ṣūfī communities. But no level of the judiciary was closed to persons claiming some tie with Sufism, although there were fewer of them in each higher rung of the judicial ladder. The implications of widespread identity with the Ṣūfī community among the lower judiciary have been discussed, and the steady diminution of such identity in the upper judiciary would seem to be in accord with the standard view of at least latent antipathy between the ʿulamaʾ and the principles of taṣawwuf. But the existence of Ṣūfīs even at the summit implies that there was no absolute break. Indeed, the pronounced representation of scholastic fields (V) is a caveat against drawing clean distinctions between the jurist-scholars and the Ṣūfī establishment. Of all civilian elements, the ʿulamaʾ were the most determined to ensure their autonomy under the Mamluk yoke. Identification with Sufism may well have provided a means to that end.

There was a strong connection between people in religious fields (VI) and the Ṣūfī community—not unexpectedly, if one assumes that personal piety was a prerequisite to leading public worship. The figures, at the very least, show that there were Ṣūfīs in the staffs of foundations dedicated to Sunnī religious service. The pattern of occupational sites reveals these people to have been quite widely distributed across the city, largely outside the khānqāh network. None of these configurations negated the hypothesis of a relationship between Sufism and public piety; it was quite possibly essential to be a mystic to gain popular acceptance as a spiritual guide.

Finally, the concentration of Ṣūfīs in artisan-commercial fields (IV) suggests that the social origins of many lay below the civilian elite. The list of artisanal occupations reported for the Ṣūfīs, although the largest in the study, only hints at the range of activities engaged in by Ṣūfīs who never penetrated the civilian elite. Yet, though our data do not allow us to analyze popular Sufism on its own terms, it does suggest that identification with the Ṣūfīs was requisite for persons dealing extensively with the masses, among whom Ṣūfī beliefs were deeply planted. Does it also suggest that, as an ʿalim's commitment to orthodoxy intensified, his propensity to associate himself with Ṣūfī beliefs diminished? Both possibilities may well be true, although neither can be tested with solid evidence here.

DISTRIBUTION OF ṢŪFĪS (Figs. 27-A, 27-B)

The distribution of Ṣūfīs throughout the capital confirmed the predominance of several large khānqāhs, all belonging to the elite group. The occupational survey, less focused than the residential, both complemented the primacy of the major institutions and confirmed the prominence of scholastic positions in List 22. The residential pattern showed pronounced aggregation in several institutions. The two khānqāhs of Saʿīd al-Suʿadāʾ (15) and Baybarsīya (13) together accounted for half of all references.[119] Shaykhūnīya in the southeast also housed a major concentration, but Siryāqūs (130) to the north of the city fell well below the levels reported for several madrasa complexes in the Fāṭimid district. Al-Azhar (36), the multifunctional cathedral mosque, ranked below the two royal madrasas: Ashrafīya (30) and Muʿayyadīya (51).[120] This pattern is important, since it depicts the institutional foundation of the Ṣūfī community in Cairo. The figures for the two Festival Gate hospices indicate their dominant status in this community. The prominence of Shaykhūnīya (83-84) and the royal madrasas, however, suggests both the abiding interest of the Mamluk elite in the Ṣūfī establishment and the vital nature of their support. All of these bases of the Ṣūfī network should be studied to probe their role in the professional and political life of the civilian elite, and to see whether, in fact, Ṣufism gave these people leverage in civilian politics.[121]

THE COPTS
(Appendix II, List 23)

Individuals identified by the word *qibṭ* figured prominently in the biographical sources. The term referred to persons descended from Coptic lineages. Virtually all the cases in this study were themselves practicing Muslims, as were their fathers and often their grandfathers. Yet they were still regarded as "of the Coptic people" (min ahl al-Aqbāṭ). They were depicted as having a natural aptitude for accounting and administration, but also an inclination toward treachery, dishonesty, guile, and above all, spiritual ambiguity. Several writers of the period claimed that a Muslim of Coptic descent was potentially a false Muslim.[122] Even worse, he was accused of converting to the majority faith, admittedly often under pressure or duress, in order to aggrandize his own position at the expense of his genuine Muslim colleagues. Indeed, this person was frequently accused of converting in order to blaspheme against Islam and to lead true believers astray. Such a false Muslim was always, it was alleged, on the verge of retrogressing to Christian practices.[123]

The Copts who succeeded in Cairo during the late Mamluk period unquestionably found themselves in a delicate situation. They professed Islam, and yet were not widely accepted as true believers. How many of them were actually backsliders is difficult to assess. Most did retain some ties with their religious past, and many continued to associate with Coptic social groups. This association was the subject of wide discussion, and was viewed as a sign of indifferent adherence to the true faith. Yet Muslim Copts apparently had little choice in the levels of society open to them, since all the indicators point to a state of partial segregation from the various elements of the orthodox ʿulamaʾ class. Had they been willingly accepted, these people might have been assimilated into its ranks.

They were not accepted, however, and the range of activities they pursued implies the limited extent to which their contemporaries were disposed to allow their penetration into the Mamluk power structure—or their participation in the Islamic establishment. The Mamluks were ready to recruit Muslim Copts to their service, and it is likely that they promoted propaganda hostile to Copts in order to bind them more tightly. Indeed, only the Mamluks stood between the Copts and the potentially dangerous masses of the population: no acts of persecution could occur without their acquiescence. Individual Copts who realized that they stood to lose in any contest on their own with a legitimate Muslim were ready to accept the unattractive conditions of service imposed by their Mamluk overlords, since the latter alone opened the doors of influence and wealth. That Mamluks provided security to Copts largely because they were of use to them did not instill feelings of mutual affection. But whatever the motives, security in return for service was better than none at all.

The Mamluks appointed Muslim Copts to several of the highest executive offices of the state, where they often administered the fiscal and procedural affairs of the imperial court and the households of the great amirs. Copts were occasionally rewarded for exceptional assistance in times of crisis with the honorary rank of amir (List 23, Category I). But they were never permitted to engage in any military activities, which remained the exclusive prerogative of the Mamluks, especially those of the first generation. Copts were allowed to infiltrate several levels of the governmental bureaucracy (II). They staffed many segments of the secretarial class. They were appointed to financial controllerships expressly to amass substantial fortunes that they were to share, perforce, with their patrons. Yet only one individual held the post of controller of waqfs in a religio-academic institution, and his social status deviated considerably from the usual.[124] In general, Copts appeared consistently in controllerships directly associated with dīwāns of the government, and did not administer the funds of Muslim institutions, even though they professed the faith. The evidence points, in fact, to the general exclusion of the Copts from offices involved with the functions of the Islamic community. They were rarely recruited as official clerks (muwaqqiʿs) in either the civil courts or the governmental bureaus, and few ever attained the pivotal office of secretary of the chancellery.

During this period, the Muslim Copts do not seem to have gained access to offices endowed with the authority to make decisions affecting the spiritual lives of legitimate Muslims. Their role in the bureaucracy was primarily financial and procedural. Few appeared among the stewards (mubāshirs) who managed the mundane operation of mosques, colleges, and hospitals. There were no cases of Muslim Copts who were court notaries, because the shāhid was first a lawyer trained in the Sharīʿa and second a bureaucrat. Persons of Christian ancestry were not widely regarded as suited for studies in Islamic Law. Above all, they were not considered legitimate arbiters in legal questions concerning Muslims. Copts were absent from all legal offices (III); not a single case was reported for the entire judiciary. Since the legal profession was a fundamental constituent of the ʿulamaʾ class and its most authoritative element, the absence of Muslim Copts from its ranks implies their marginal status.

This hypothesis of marginality is reinforced by the virtual absence of Muslim Copts from the scholarly and religious categories (V and VI). They tended neither to pursue advanced studies in the Islamic sciences nor to minister to the spiritual needs of the Islamic community. Since they were Muslims, many of them would presumably have wished to do so, and one must conclude that they were denied the opportunity. Al-Sakhāwī and Ibn Taghrī-Birdī did not say why Muslim Copts pursued no studies in the Islamic curriculum. They simply did not record any such studies, as they did so meticulously for persons they considered true believers.

In summary, the Muslim Copts emerge from the biographical accounts as a highly specialized group, channeled by both the military and civilian elites into fiscal and administrative activities. There they were useful to the Mamluks who, although rarely adverse to extorting money by any available means, nonetheless displayed little interest—or finesse—in the bureaucratic techniques required by a dīwān post. Moreover, a Mamluk could not justify his doings to the extent that his clients could, especially if they were not held accountable to Islamic principles, as he was. The Mamluks proclaimed themselves defenders of the faith, pledged to protect the community of believers from its enemies. In practice, they found the Copts ideal agents for unobtrusive infiltration into the revenue-yielding processes. The notables of the ʿulamaʾ were not as subject to control, and thus were less useful as clients. The picture of the Muslim Copts that emerges from the data thus depicts little justice or fair play, but does suggest skillful adjustment to difficult conditions.

Figures 9 through 27

SCALE

× and + symbols are in proportion to circles and triangles

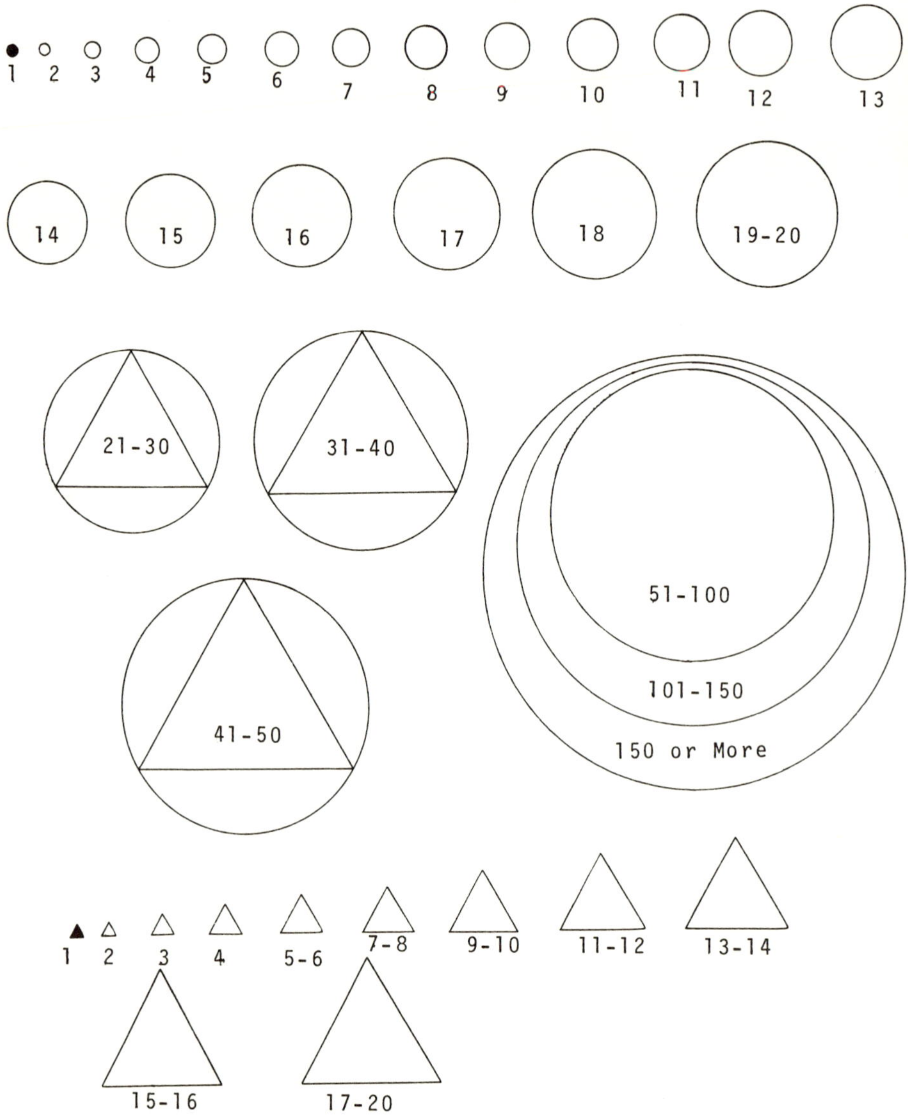

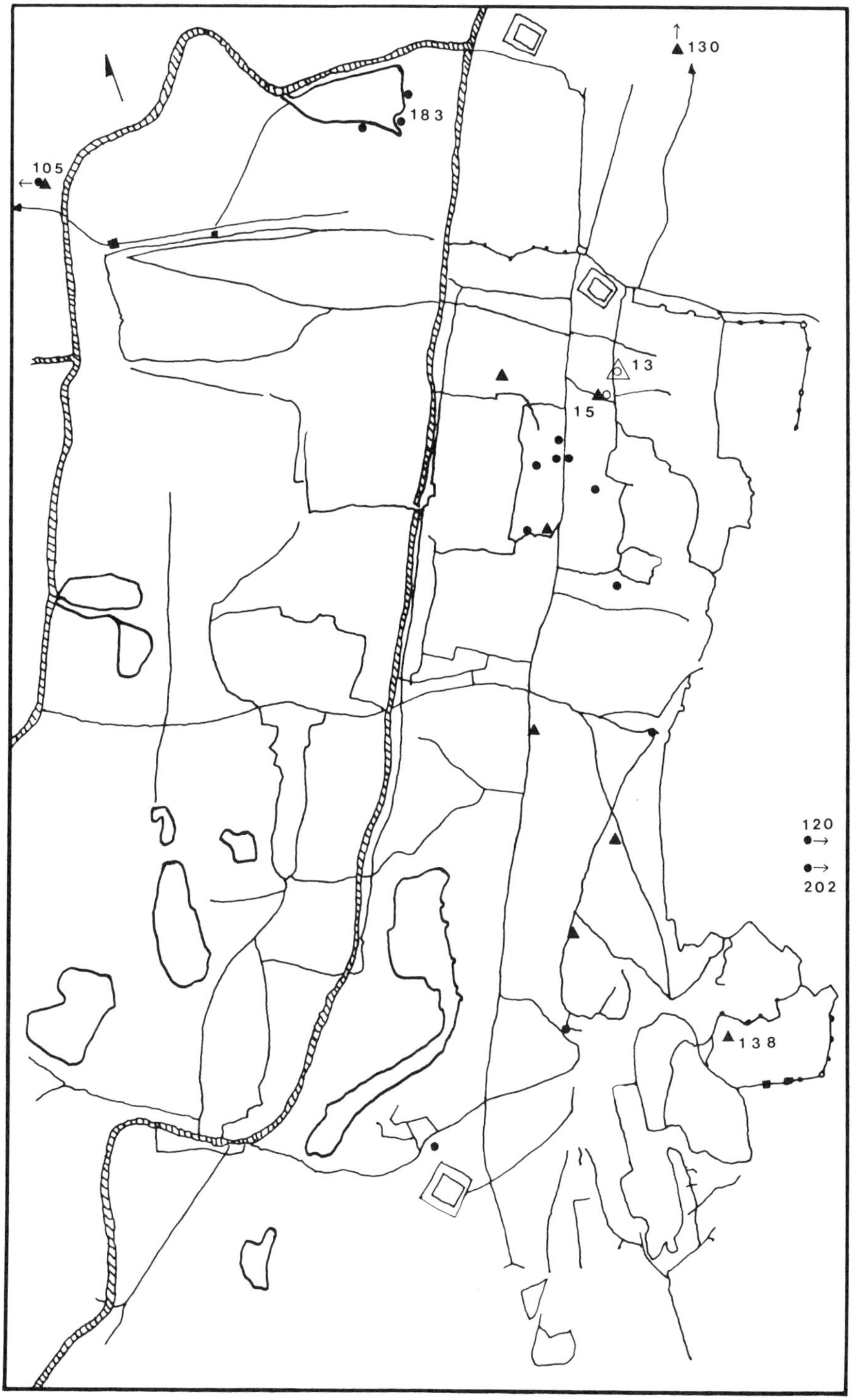

Fig. 9. Central City, Distribution of Kātibs (Secretaries)
• residential sites
▲ occupational sites

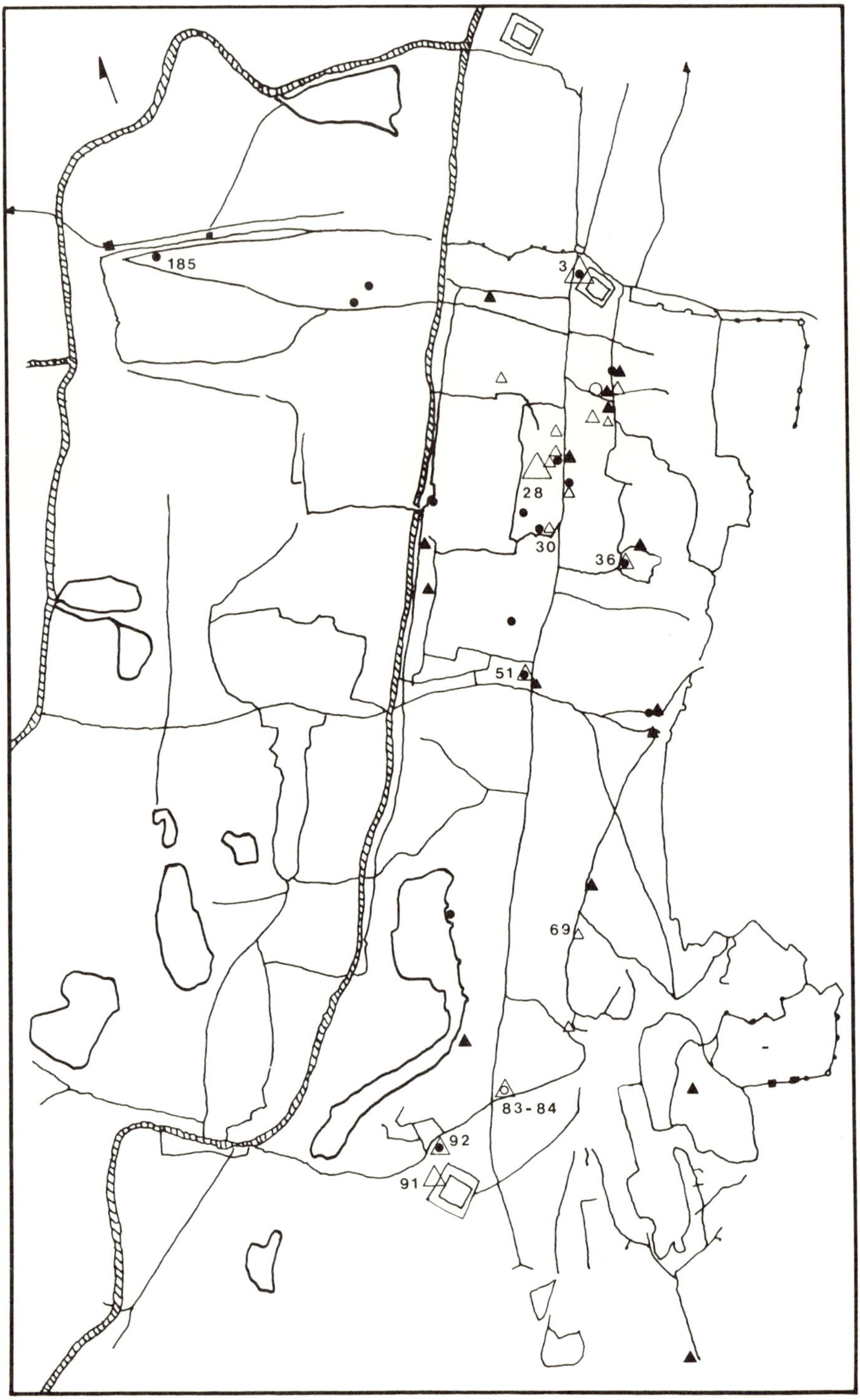

Fig. 10-A. Central City, Distribution of Mubāshirs (Stewards)
• residential sites
▲ occupational sites

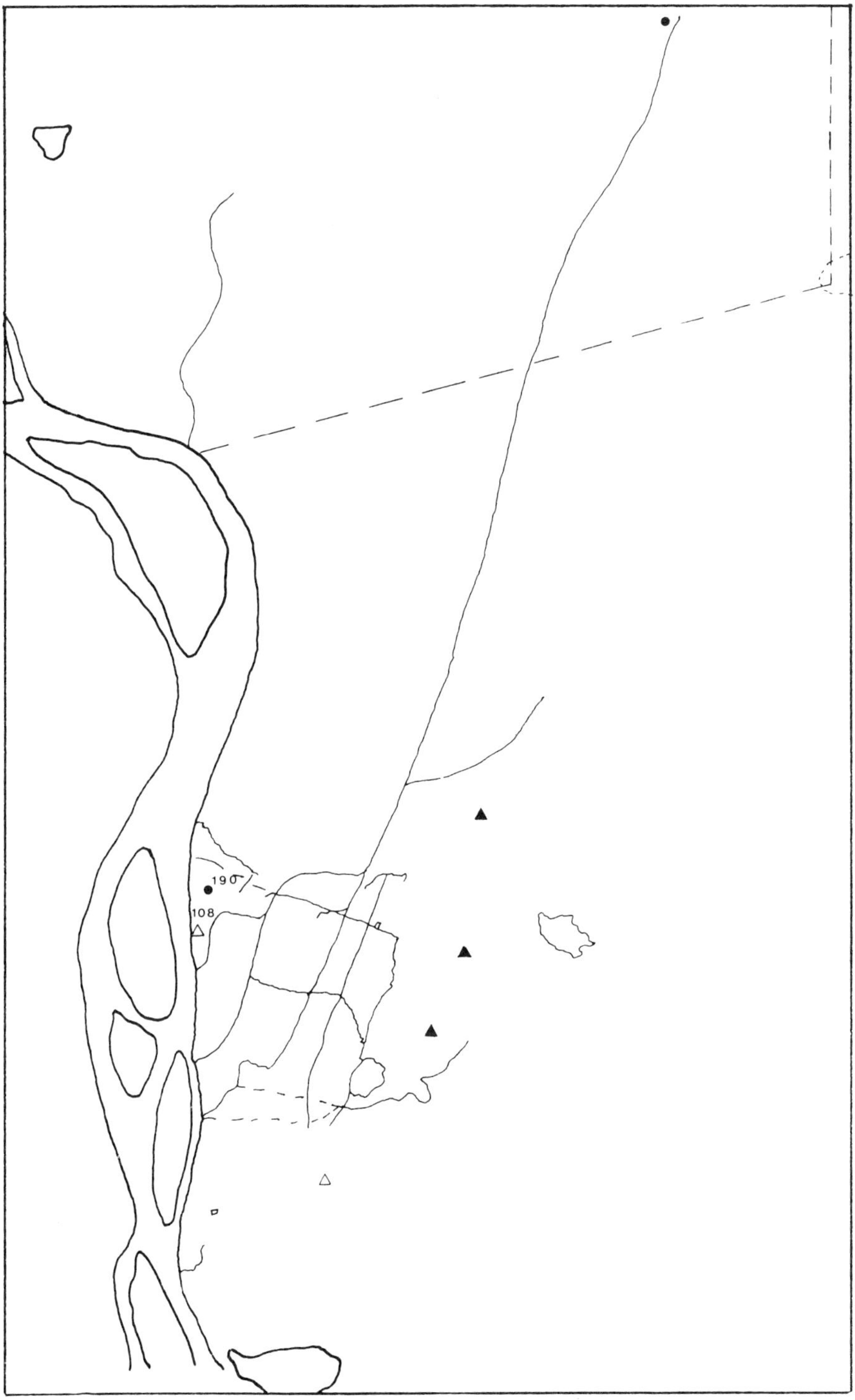

Fig. 10-B. Environs, Distribution of Mubāshirs
• residential sites
▲ occupational sites

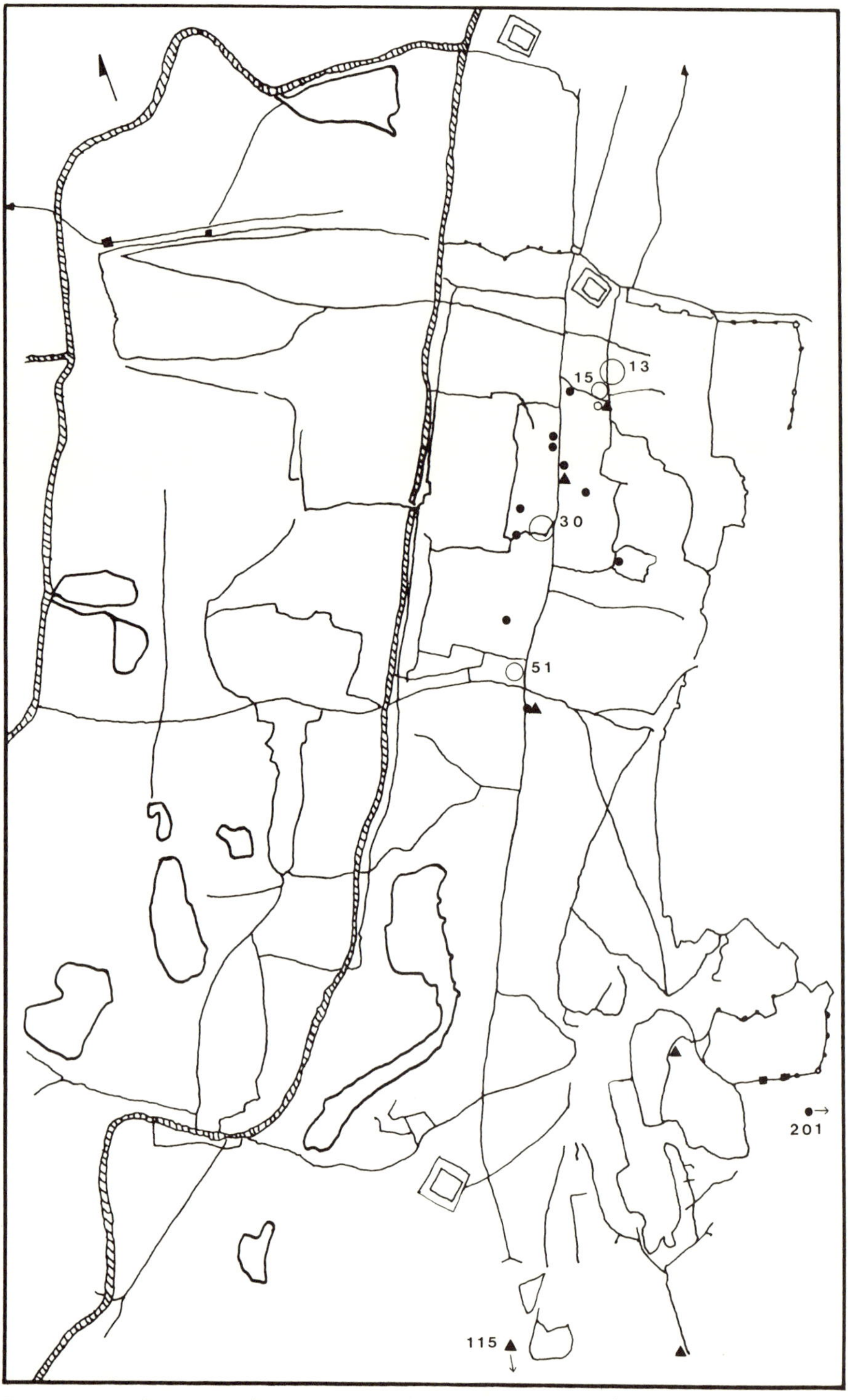

Fig. 11. Central City, Distribution of Muwaqqiʿs (Clerks)
• residential sites
▲ occupational sites

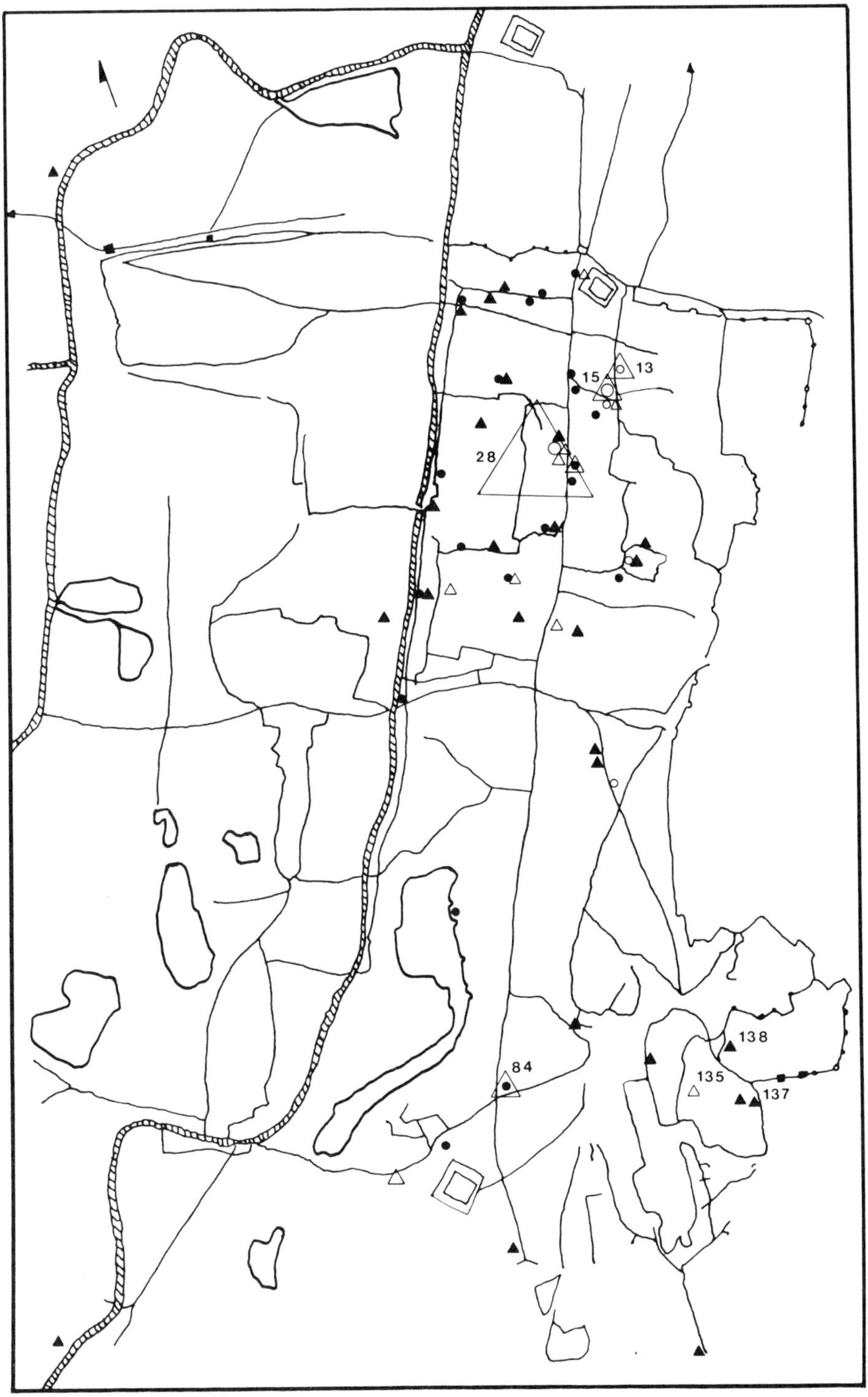

Fig. 12-A. Central City, Distribution of Nāẓirs (Controllers)
• residential sites
▲ occupational sites

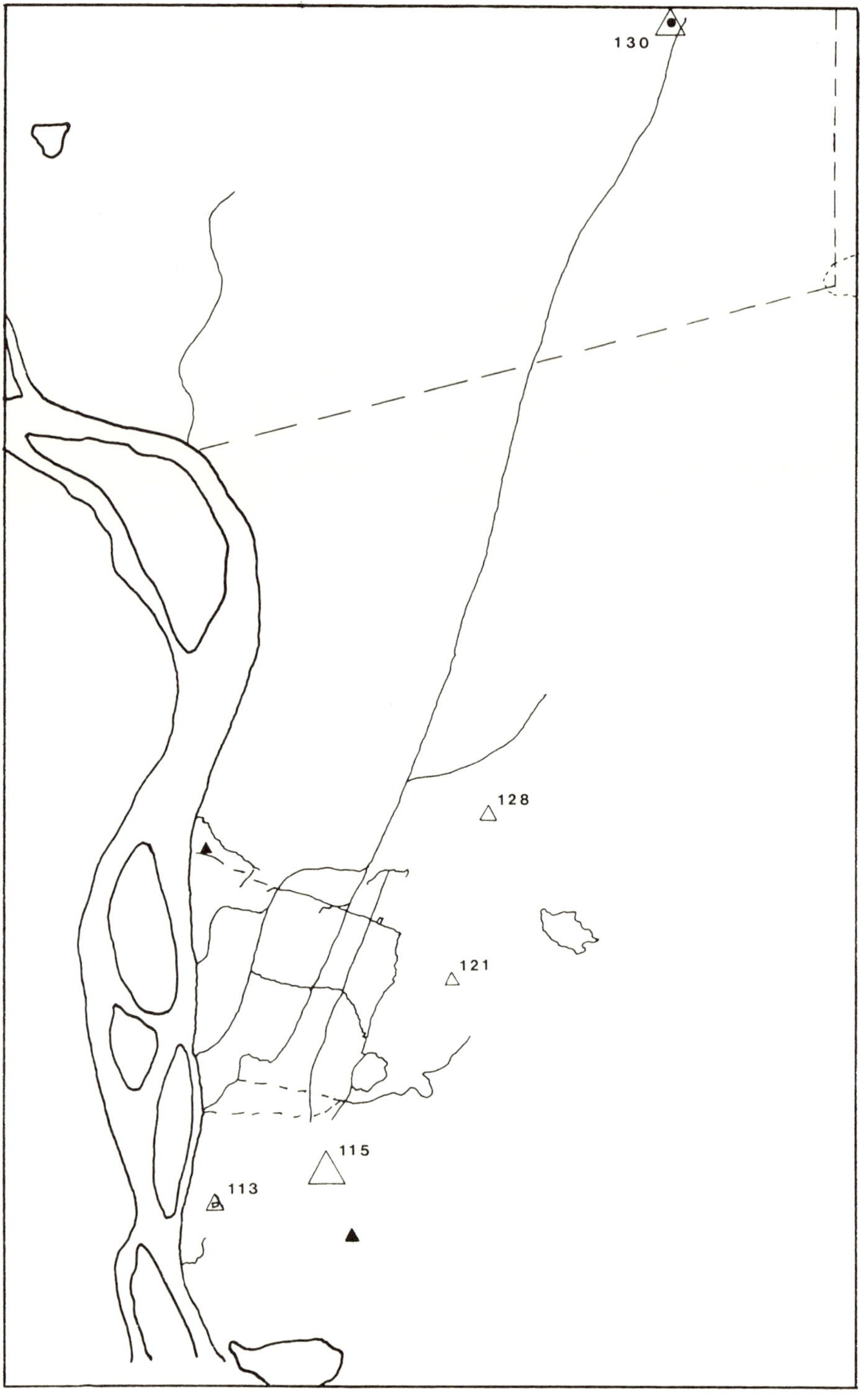

Fig. 12-B. Environs, Distribution of Nāẓirs
• residential sites
▲ occupational sites

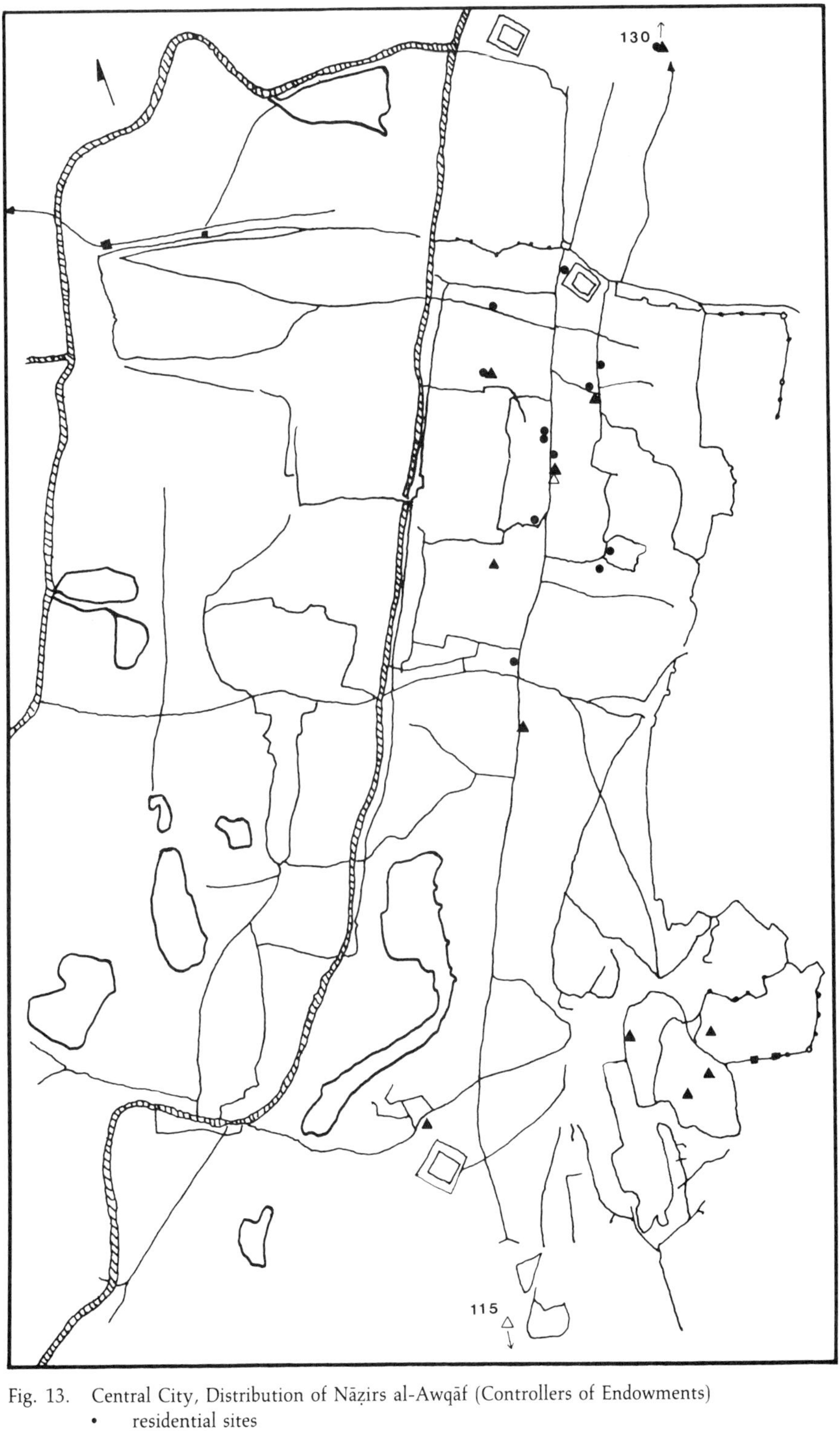

Fig. 13. Central City, Distribution of Nāẓirs al-Awqāf (Controllers of Endowments)
• residential sites
▲ occupational sites

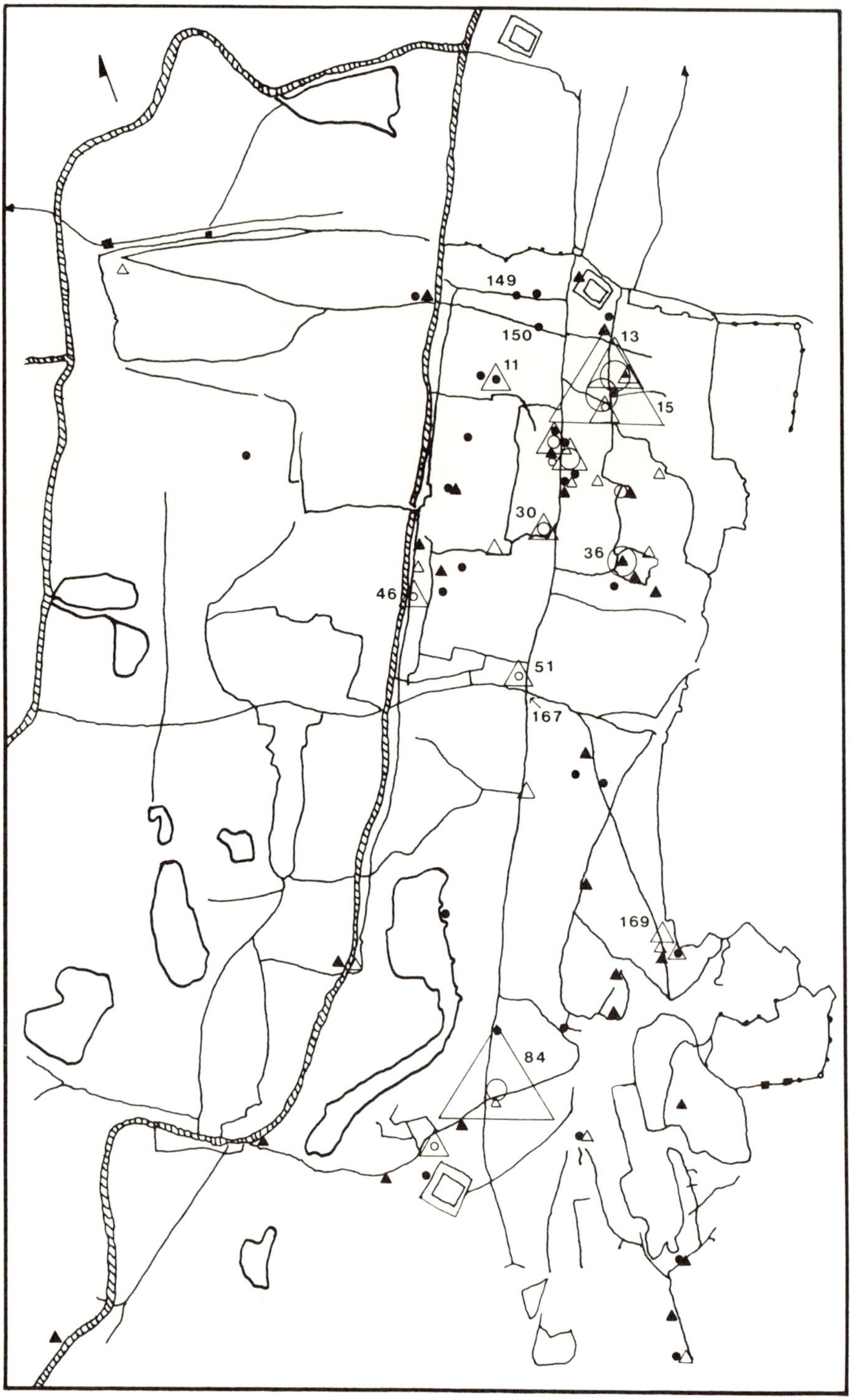

Fig. 14-A. Central City, Distribution of Shaykhs (Legal Authorities)
• residential sites
▲ occupational sites

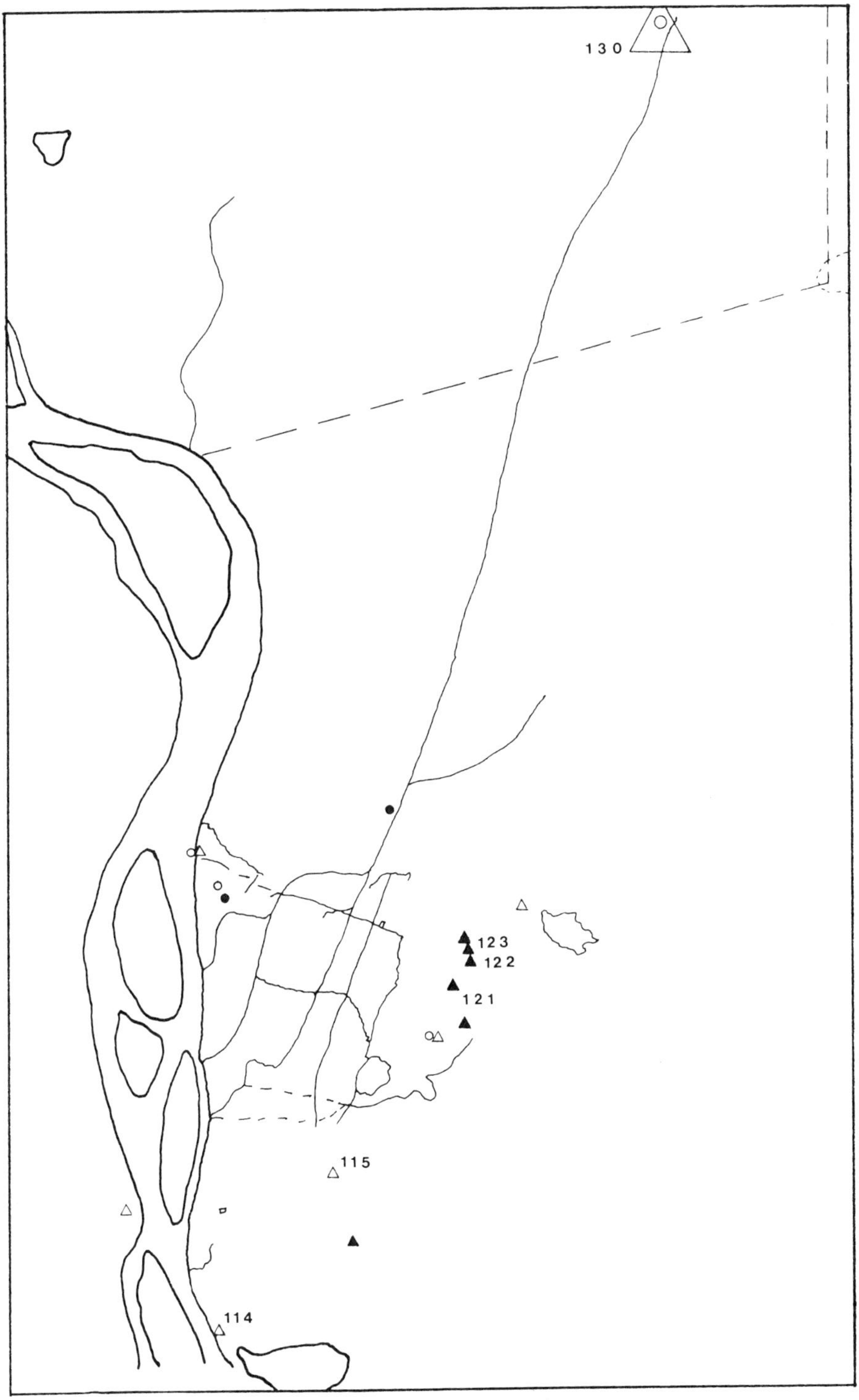

Fig. 14-B. Environs, Distribution of Shaykhs
• residential sites
▲ occupational sites

Fig. 15-A. Central City, Distribution of Shāhids (Notaries)
• residential sites
▲ occupational sites

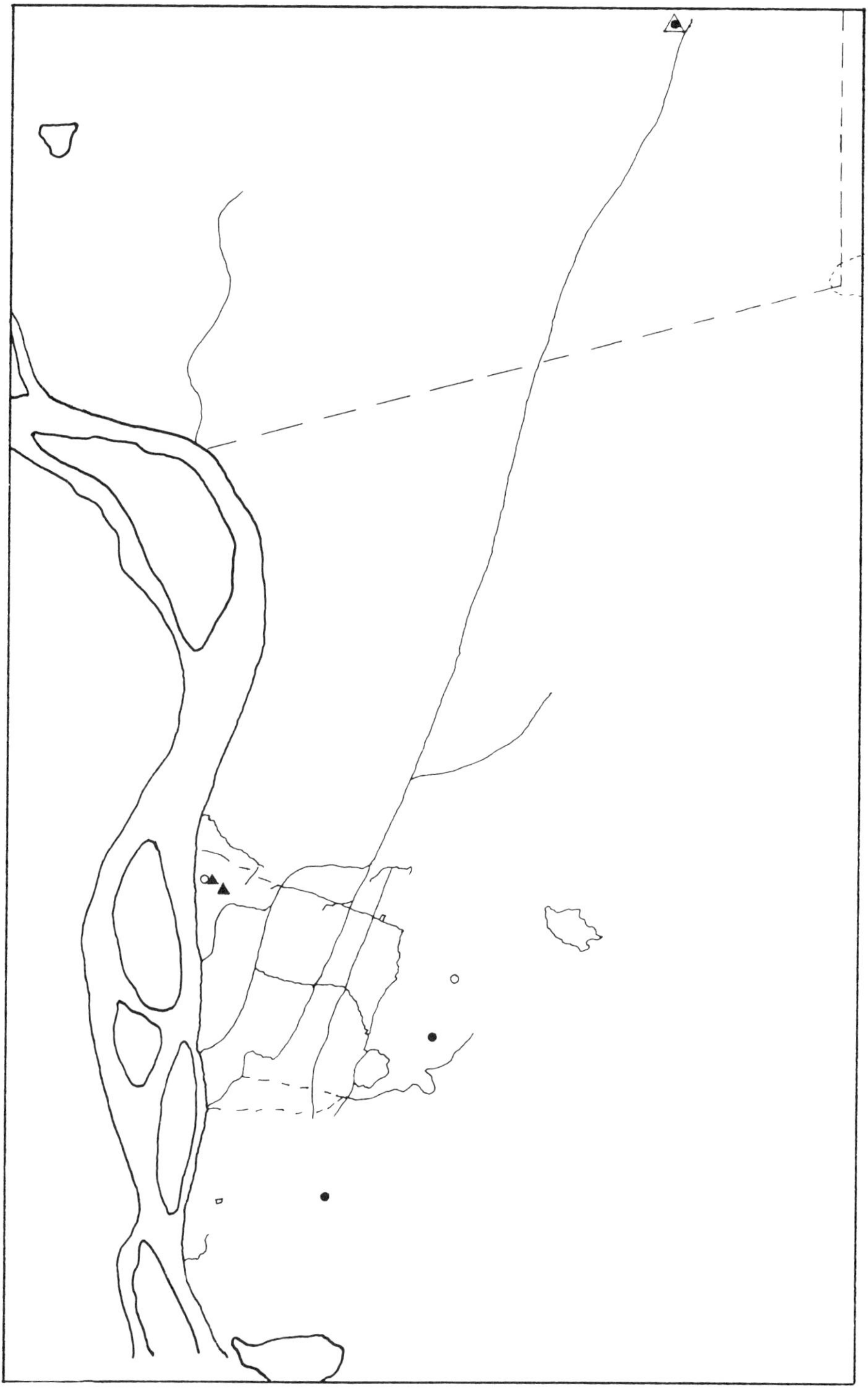

Fig. 15-B. Environs, Distribution of Shāhids
• residential sites
▲ occupational sites

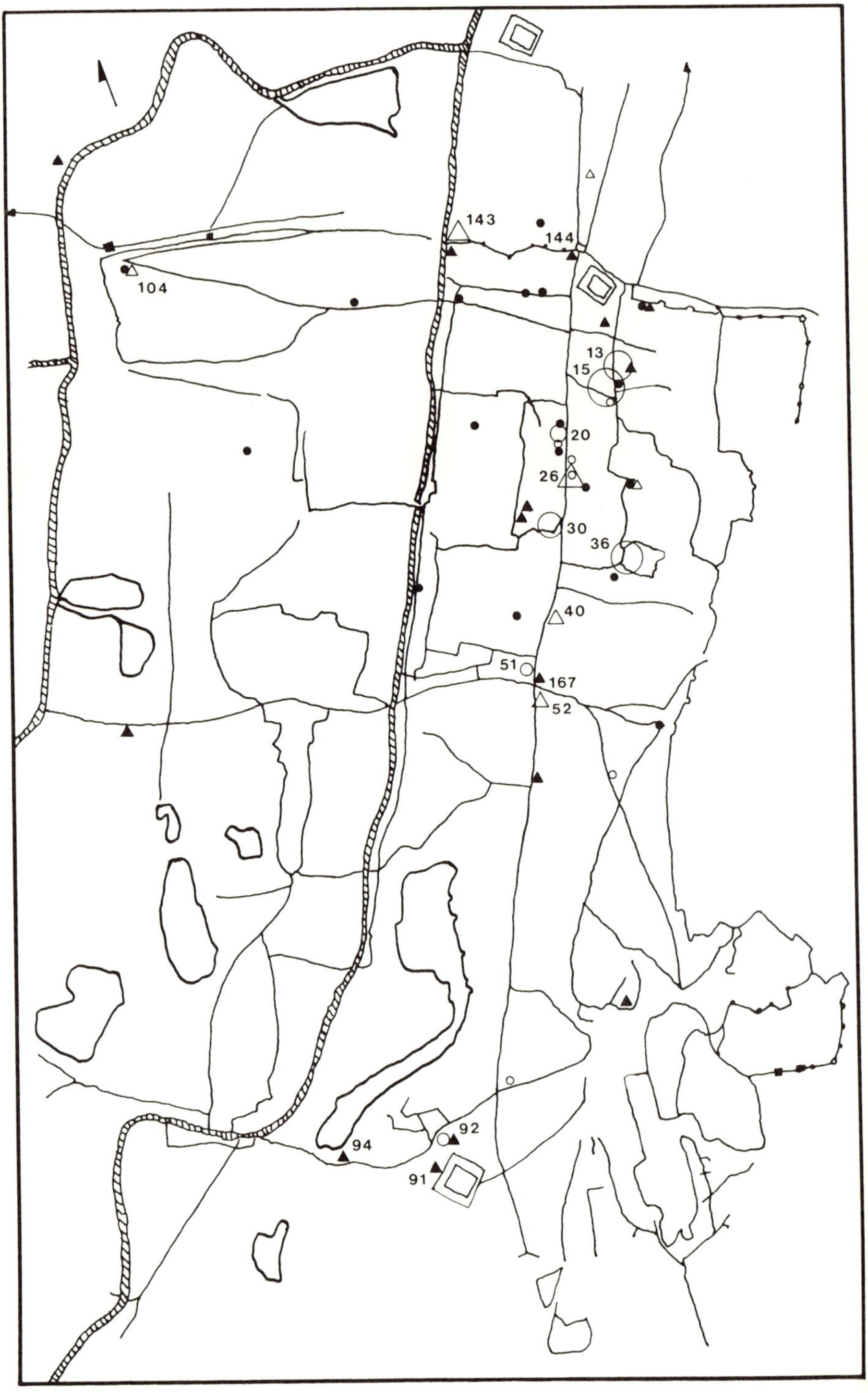

Fig. 16-A. Distribution of Nā'ib Qāḍīs (Deputy Judges)
• residential sites
▲ occupational sites

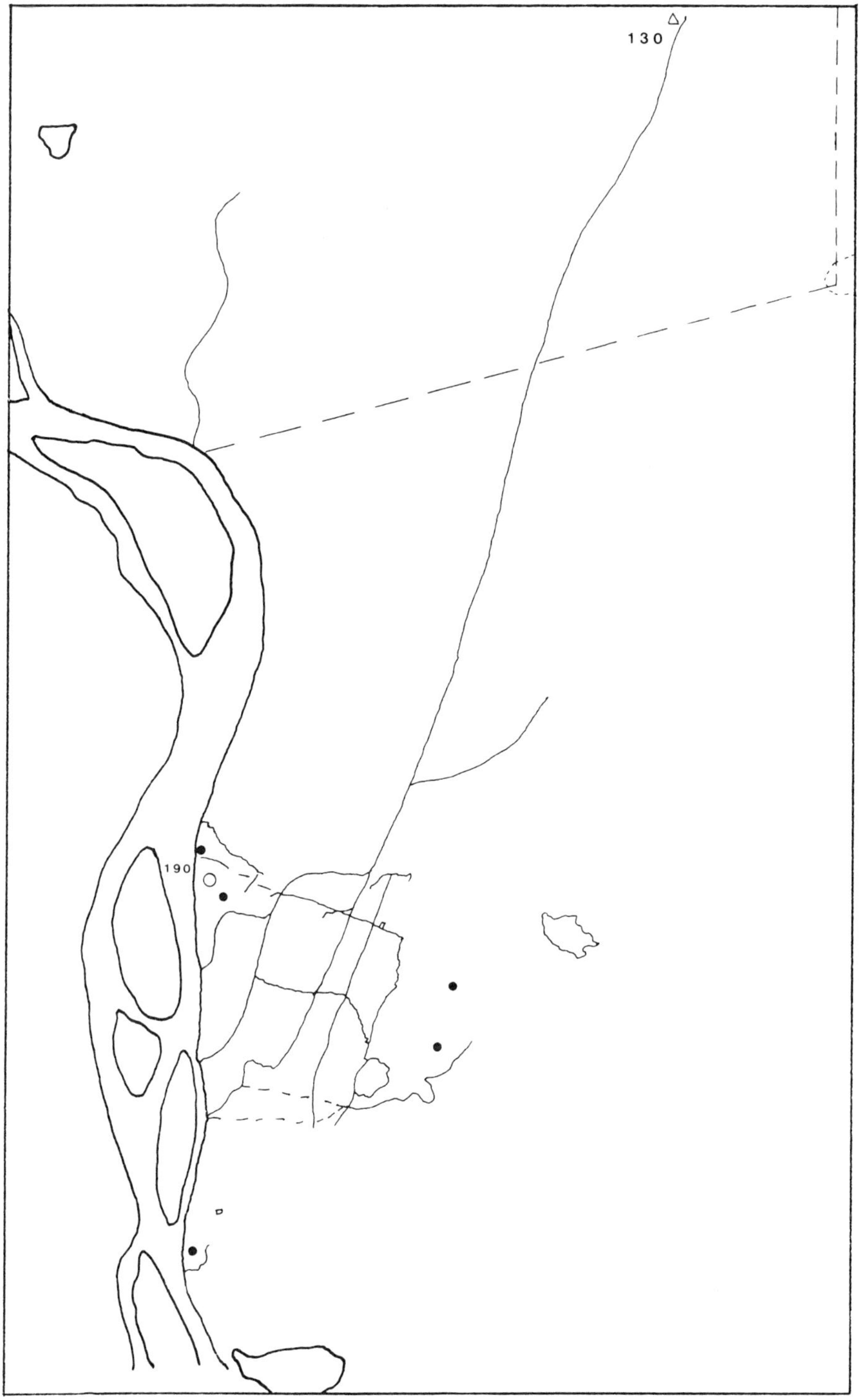

Fig. 16-B. Environs, Distributions of Nā'ib Qāḍīs
• residential sites
▲ occupational sites

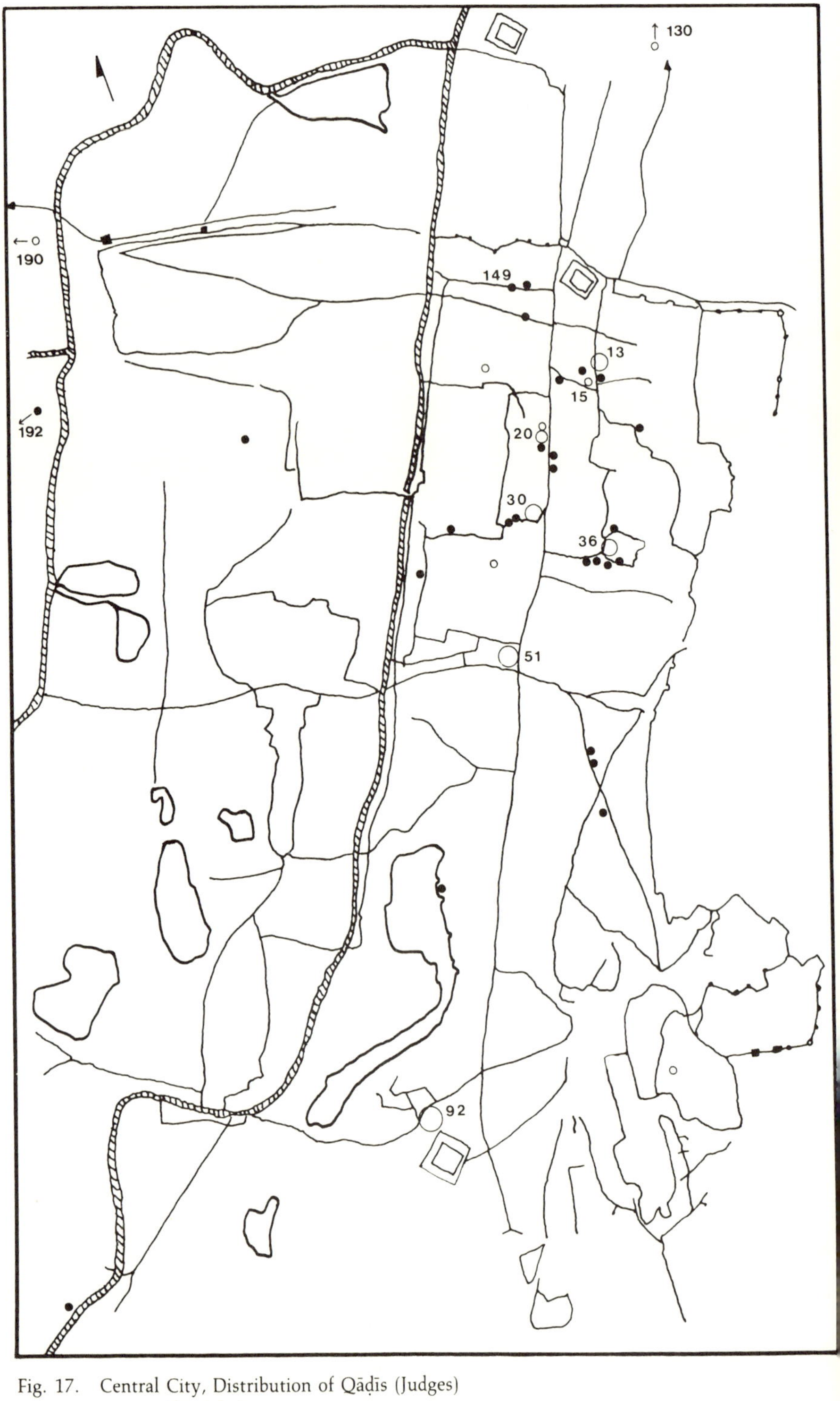

Fig. 17. Central City, Distribution of Qāḍīs (Judges)
• residential sites

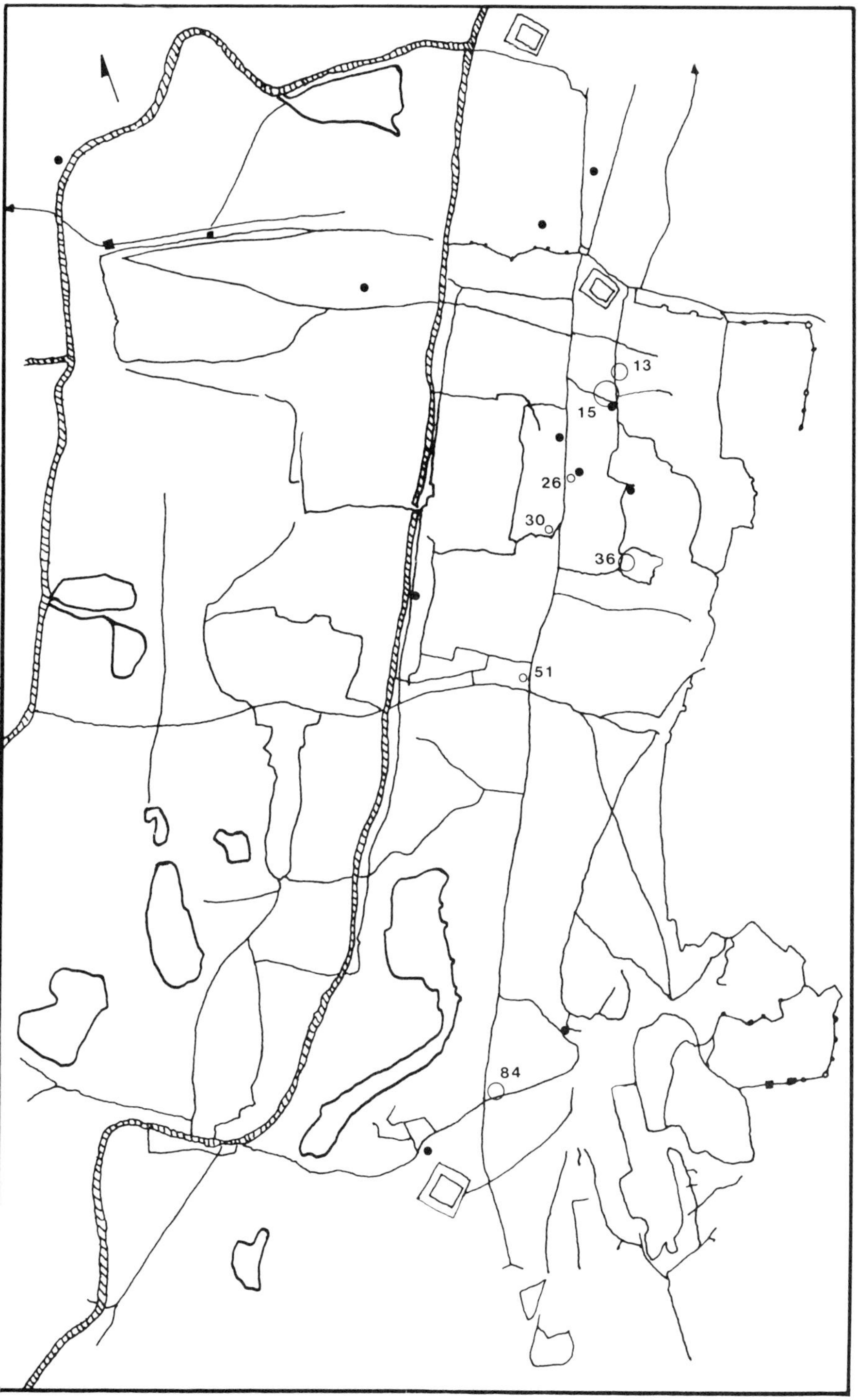

'ig. 18. Central City, Distribution of Nāsikhs (Copyists)
• residential sites

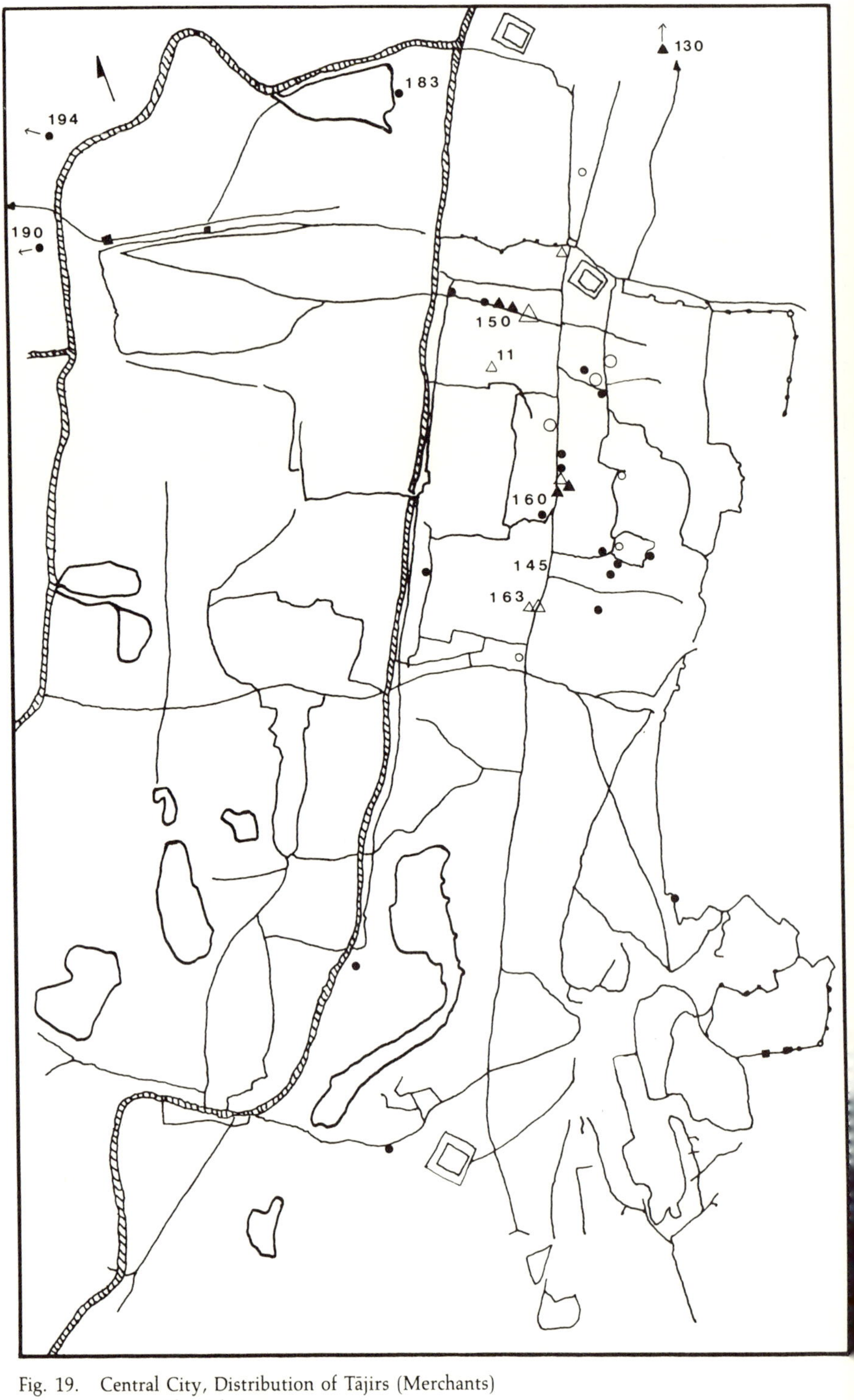

Fig. 19. Central City, Distribution of Tājirs (Merchants)
• residential sites
▲ occupational sites

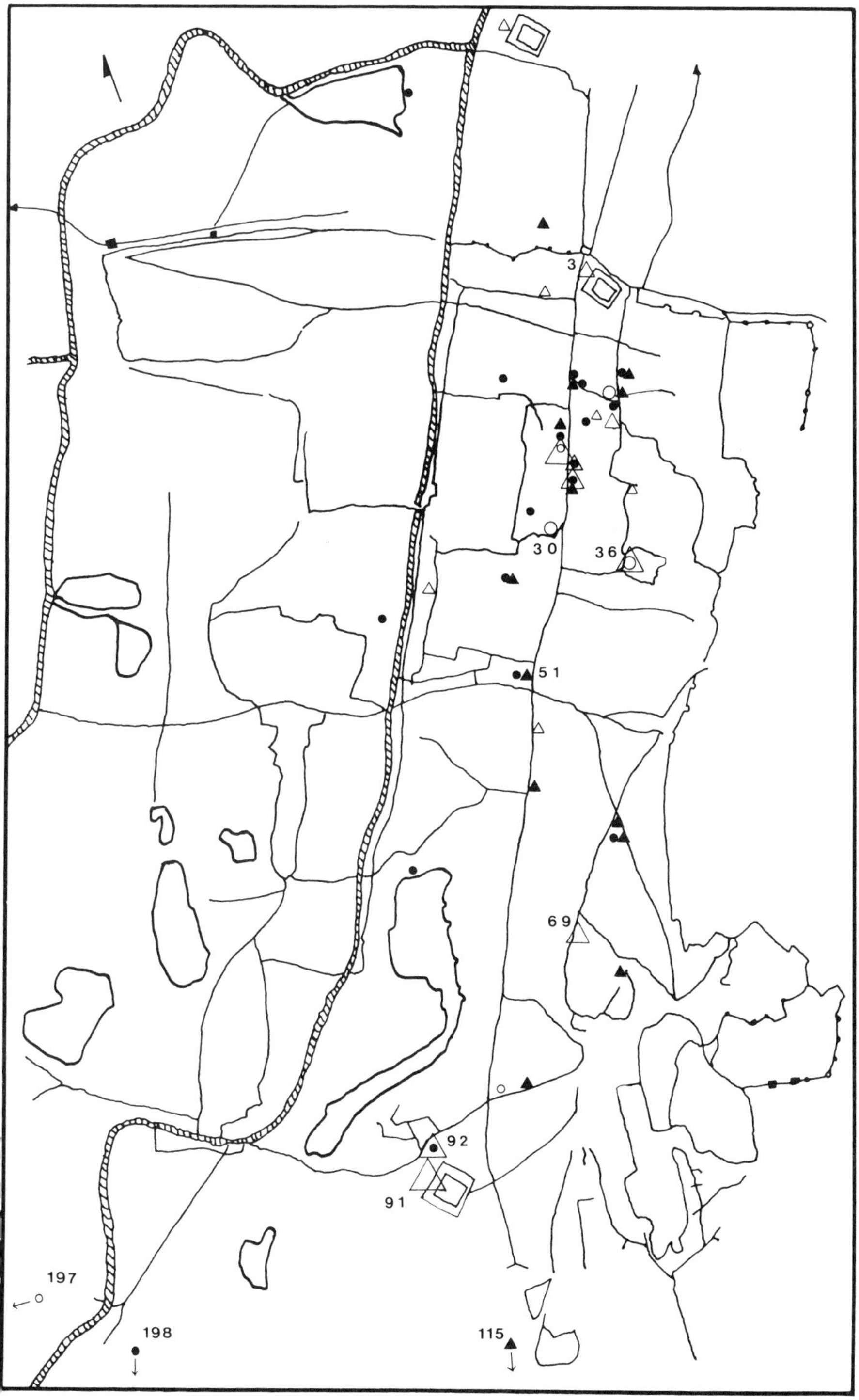

Fig. 20. Central City, Distribution of Muʿīds (Repetitors)
• residential sites
▲ occupational sites

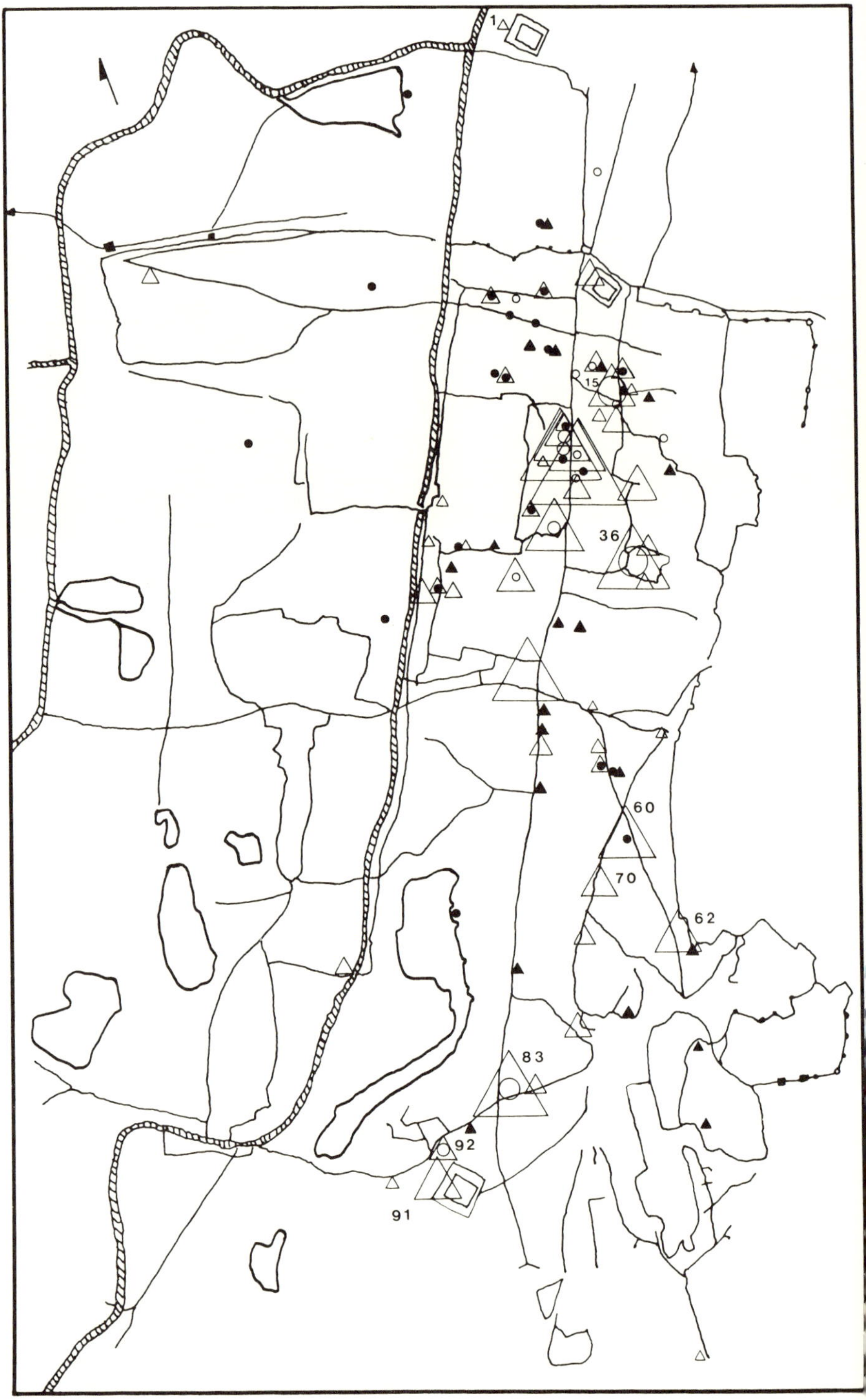

Fig. 21-A. Central City, Distribution of Mudarrises (Professors)
• residential sites
▲ occupational sites

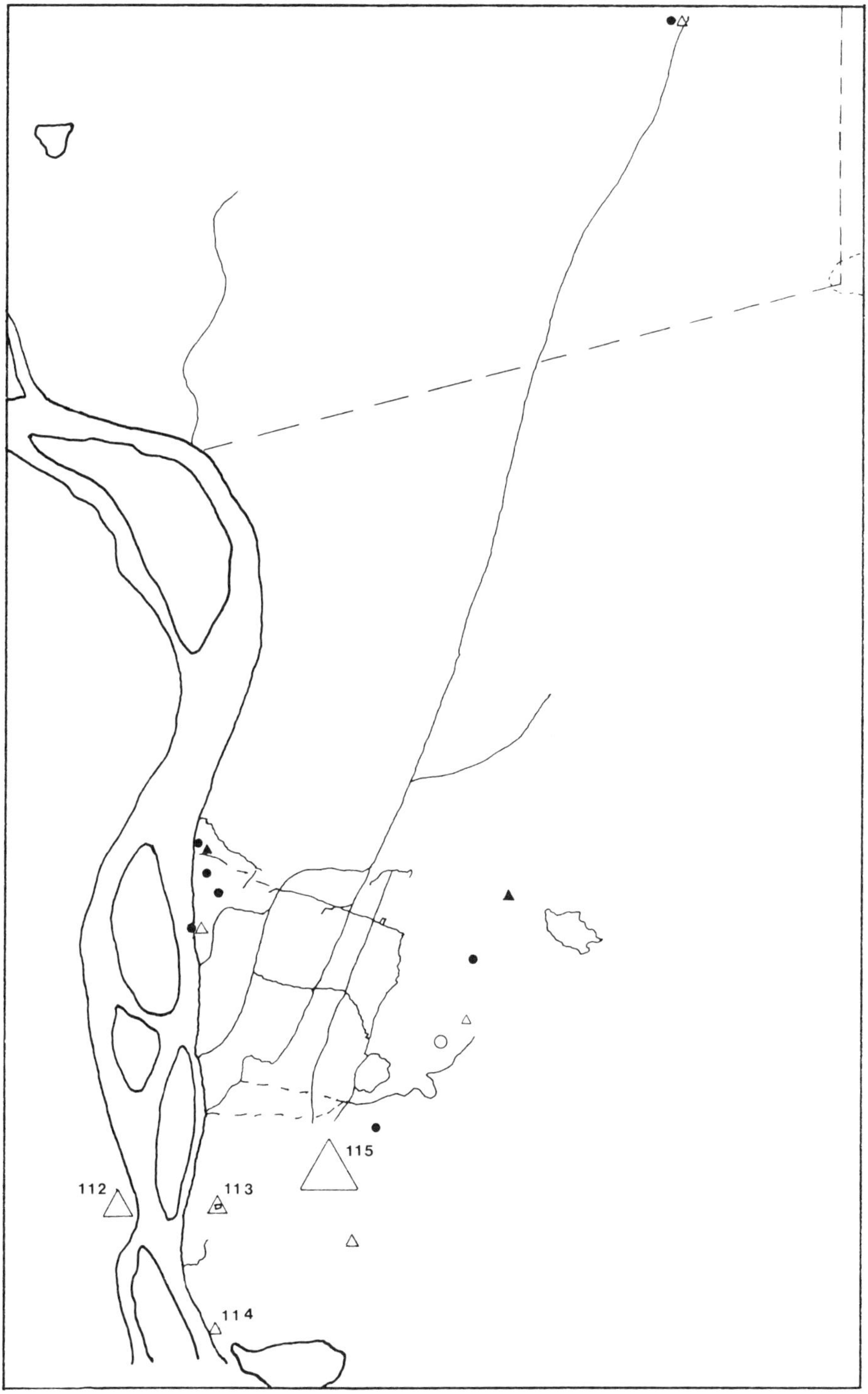

Fig. 21-B. Environs, Distribution of Mudarrises
• residential sites
▲ occupational sites

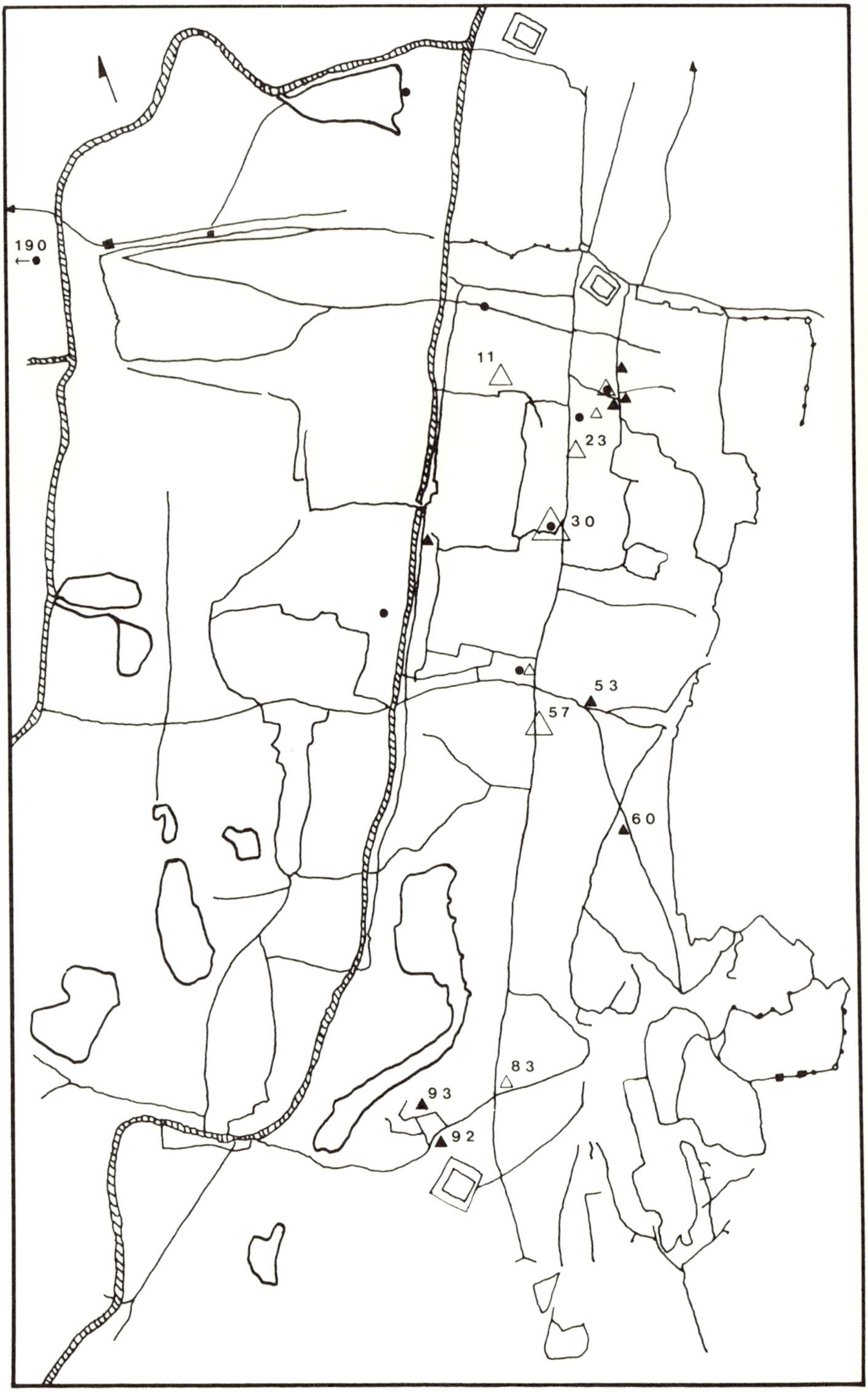

Fig. 22. Central City, Distribution of Khāzins al-Kutub (Librarians)
• residential sites
▲ occupational sites

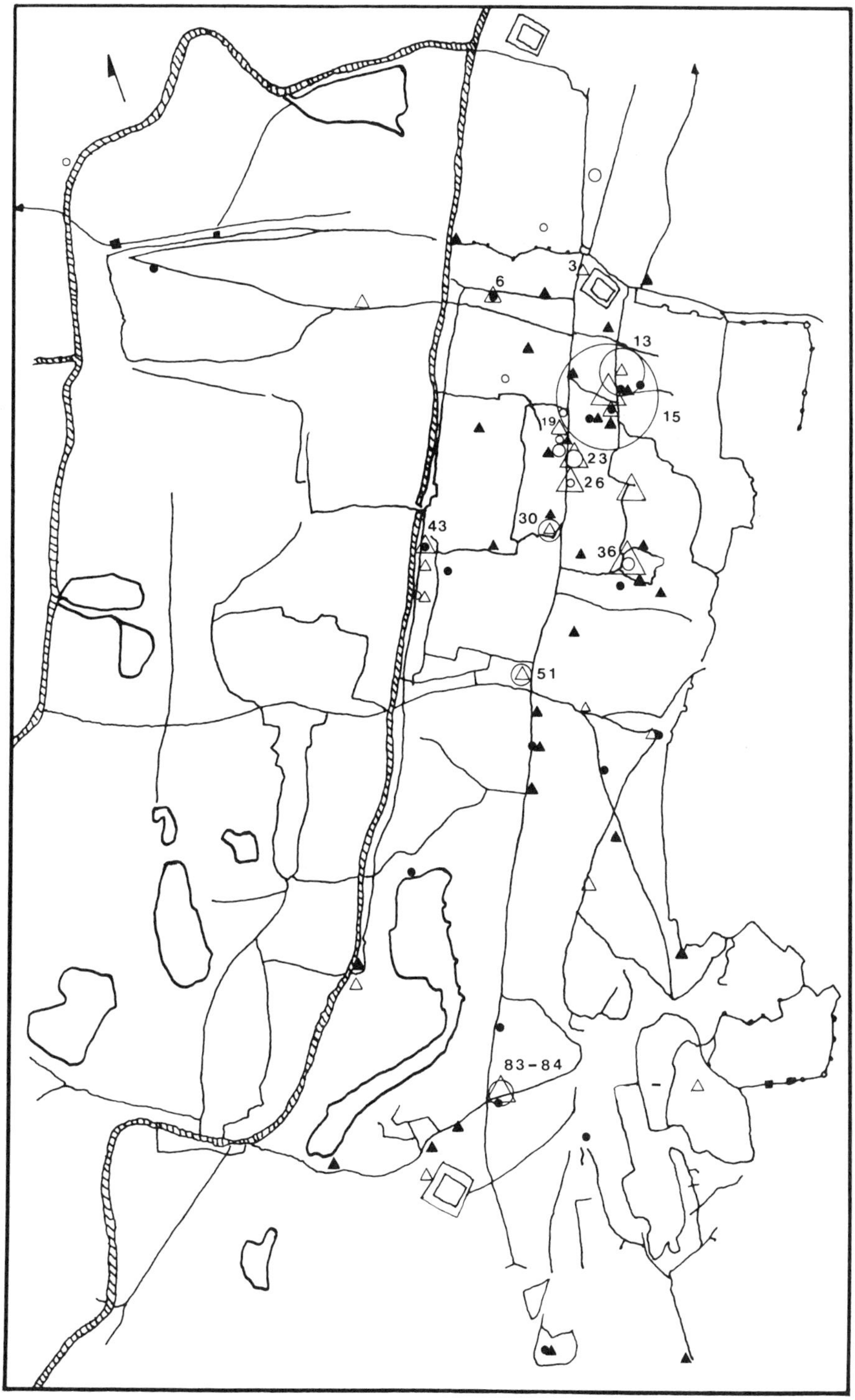

Fig. 23-A. Central City, Distribution of Imāms (Prayer Leaders)
• residential sites
▲ occupational sites

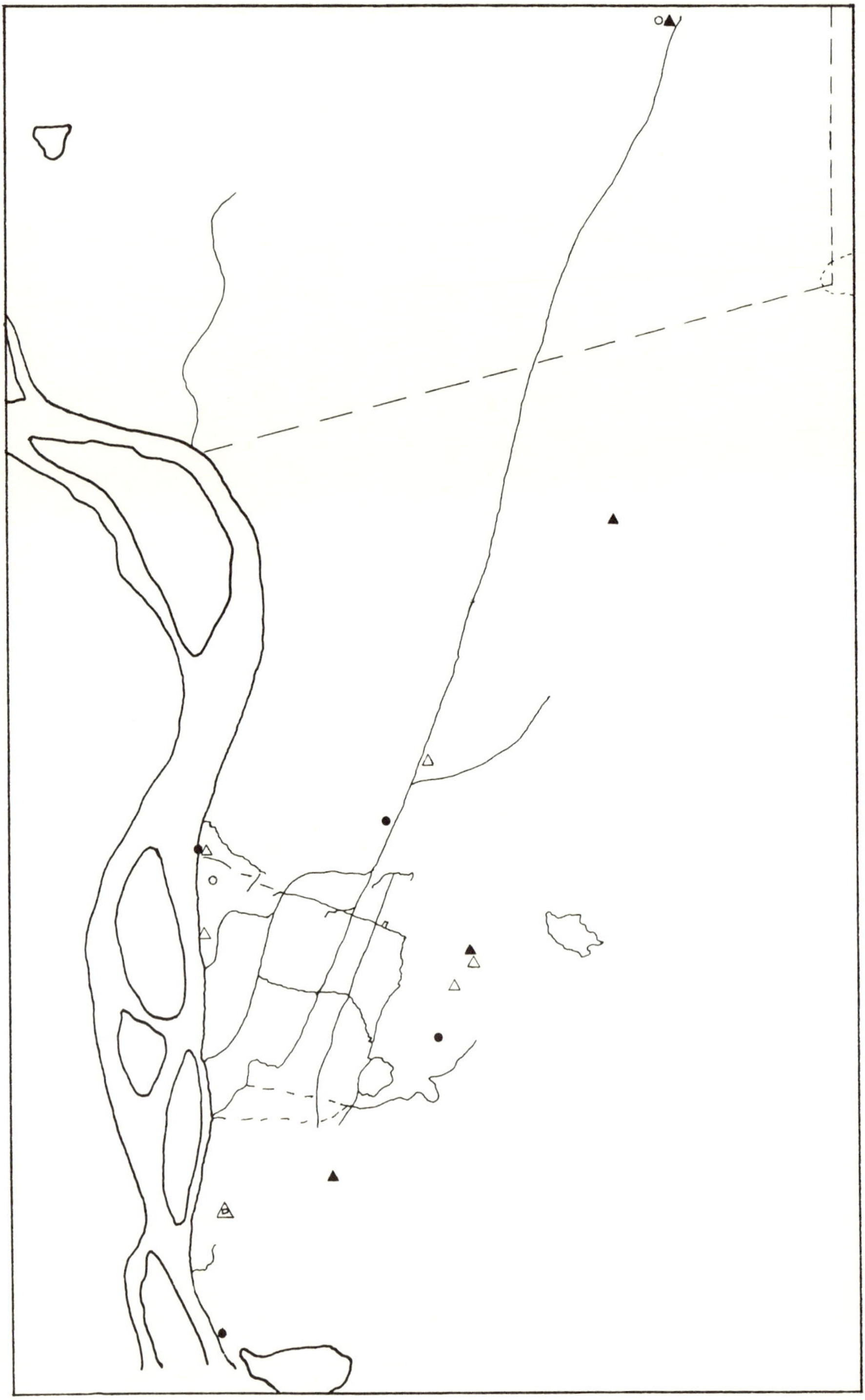

Fig. 23-B. Environs, Distribution of Imāms
• residential sites
▲ occupational sites

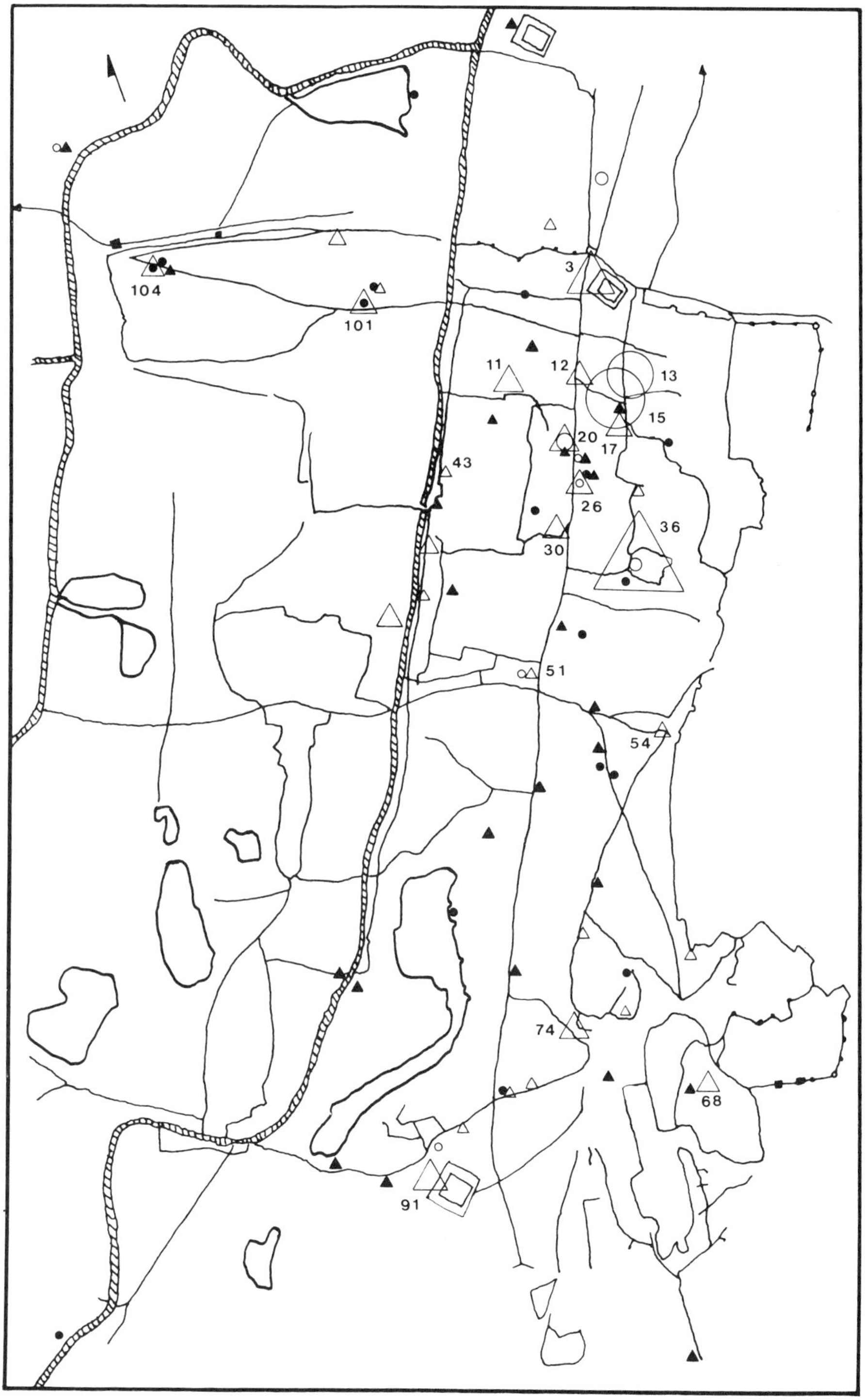

Fig. 24-A. Central City, Distribution of Khaṭībs (Friday Preachers)
• residential sites
▲ occupational sites

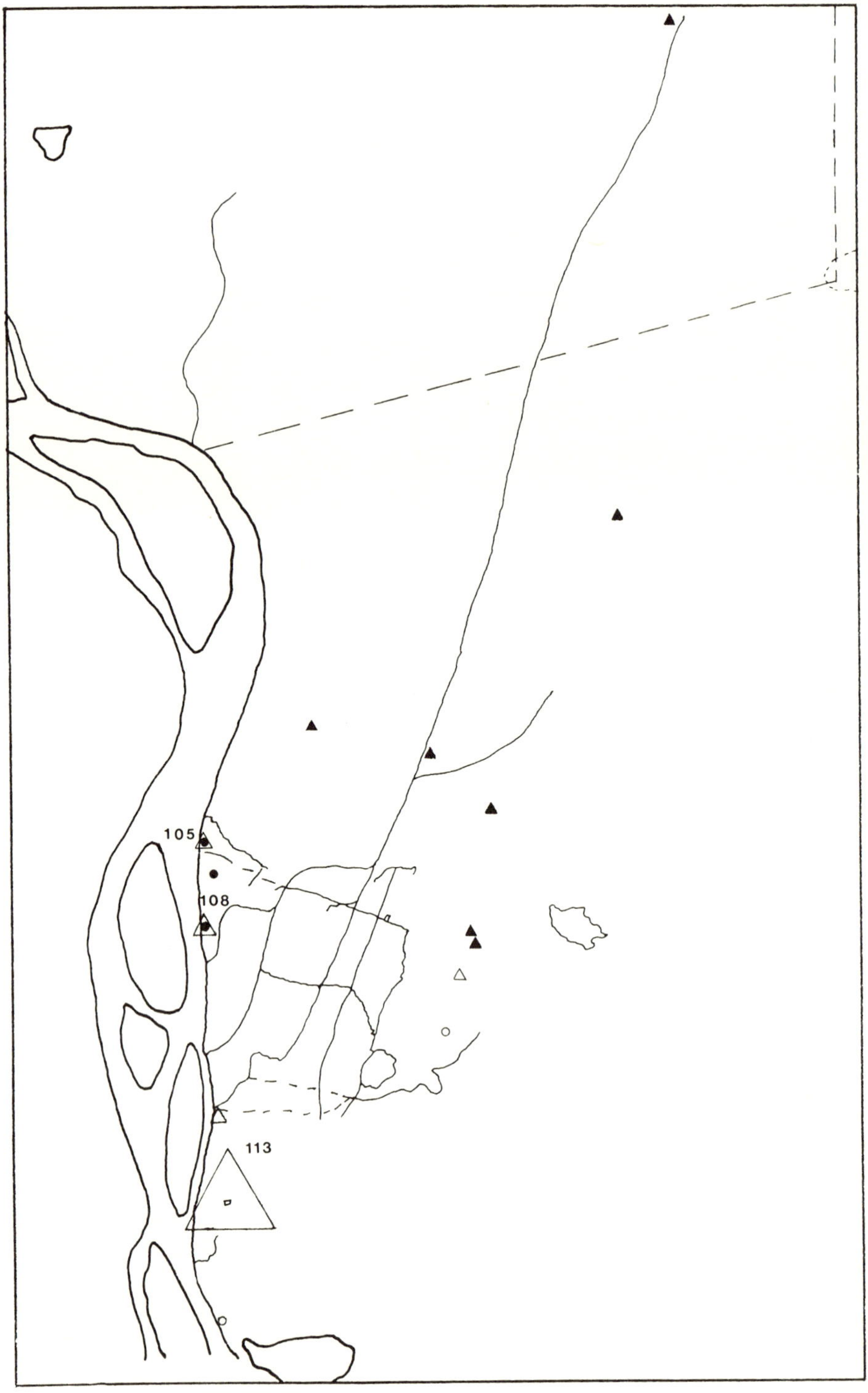

Fig. 24-B. Environs, Distribution of Khaṭībs
• residential sites
▲ occupational sites

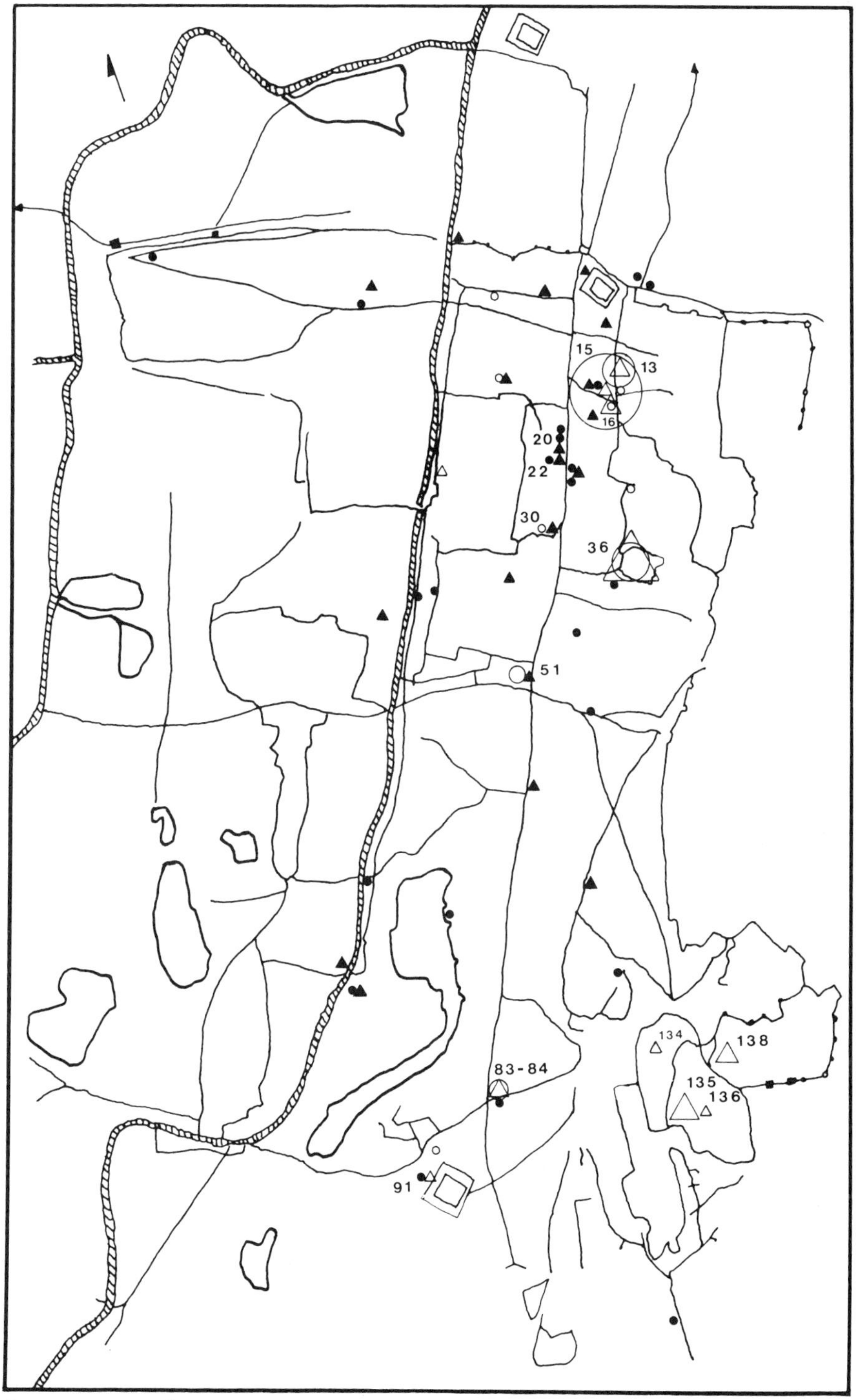

Fig. 25-A. Central City, Distribution of Muqri's (Koran Readers)
• residential sites
▲ occupational sites

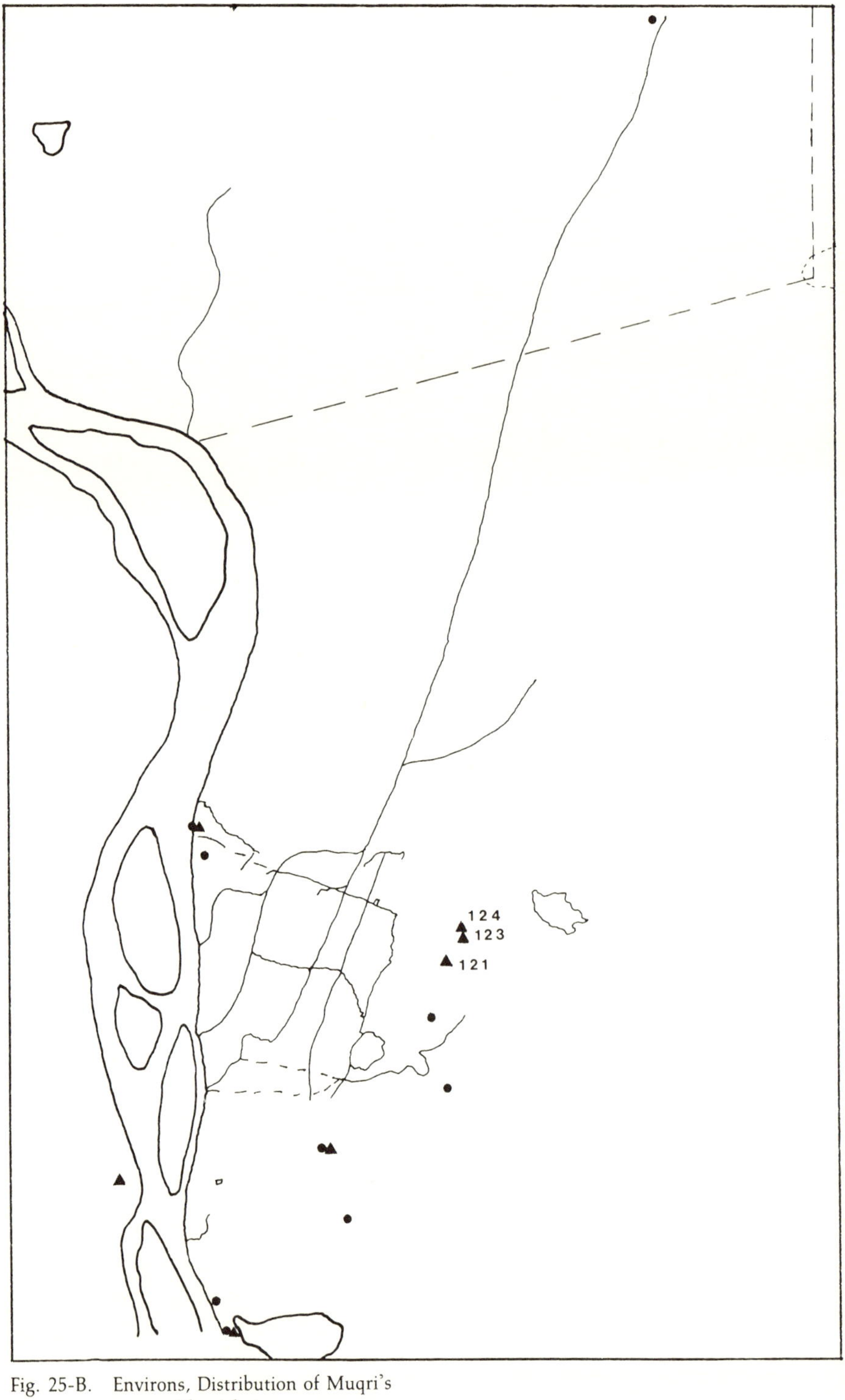

Fig. 25-B. Environs, Distribution of Muqri's
• residential sites
▲ occupational sites

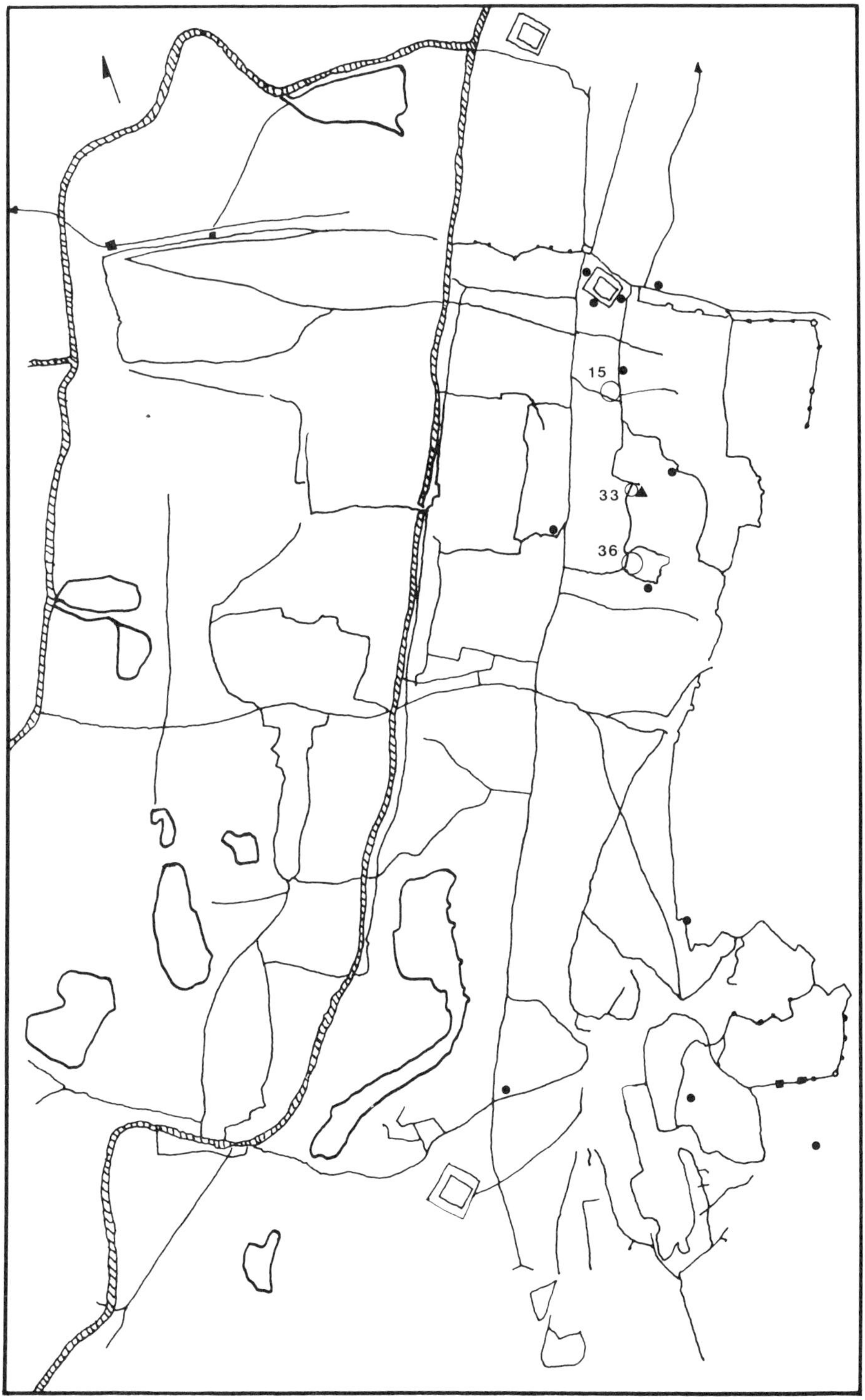

Fig. 26-A. Central City, Distribution of Muʿtaqads (Revered Persons)
• residential sites
▲ occupational sites

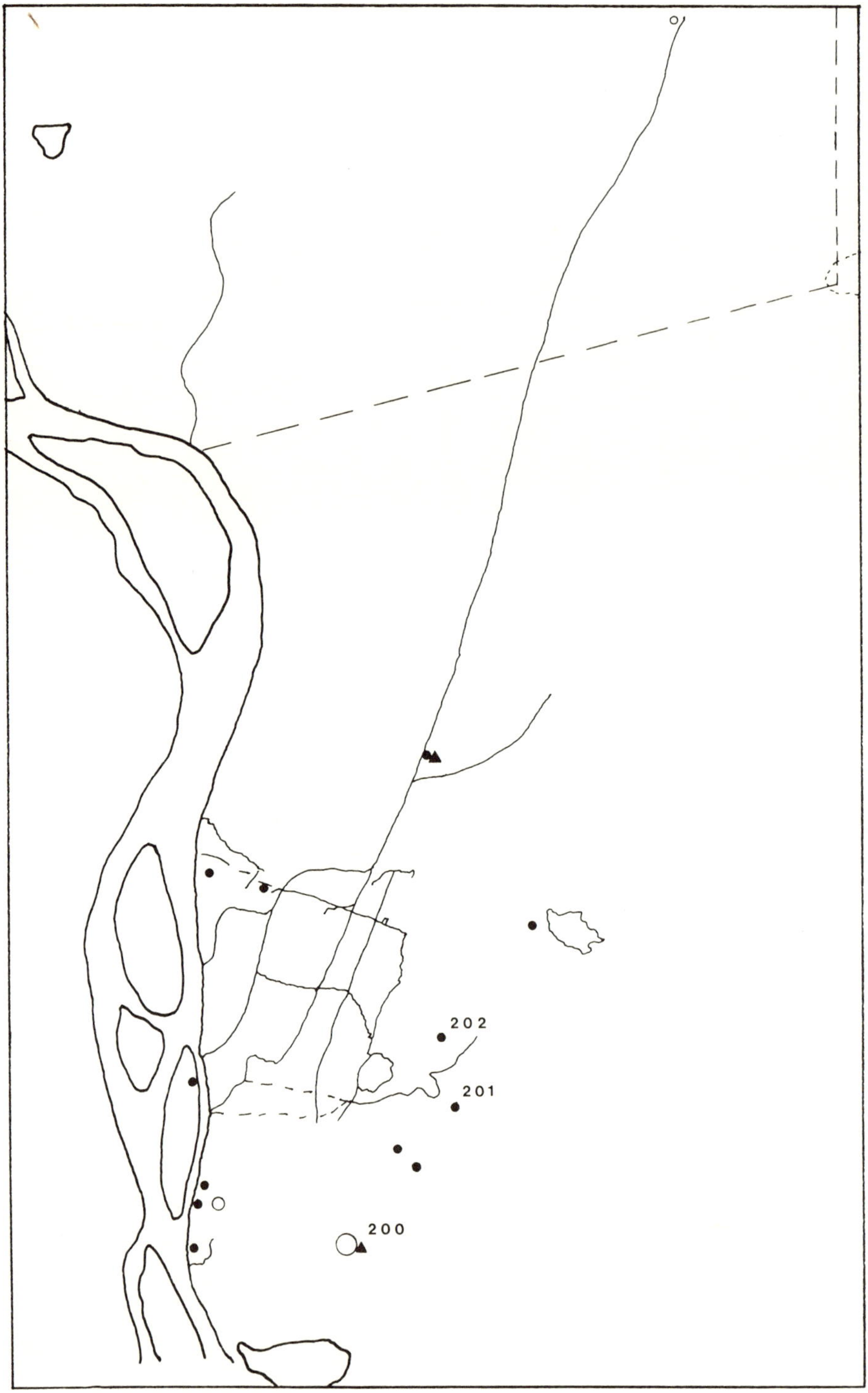

Fig. 26-B. Environs, Distribution of Muʿtaqads
• residential sites
▲ occupational sites

Fig. 27-A. Central City, Distribution of Ṣūfīs (Mystics)
• residential sites
▲ occupational sites

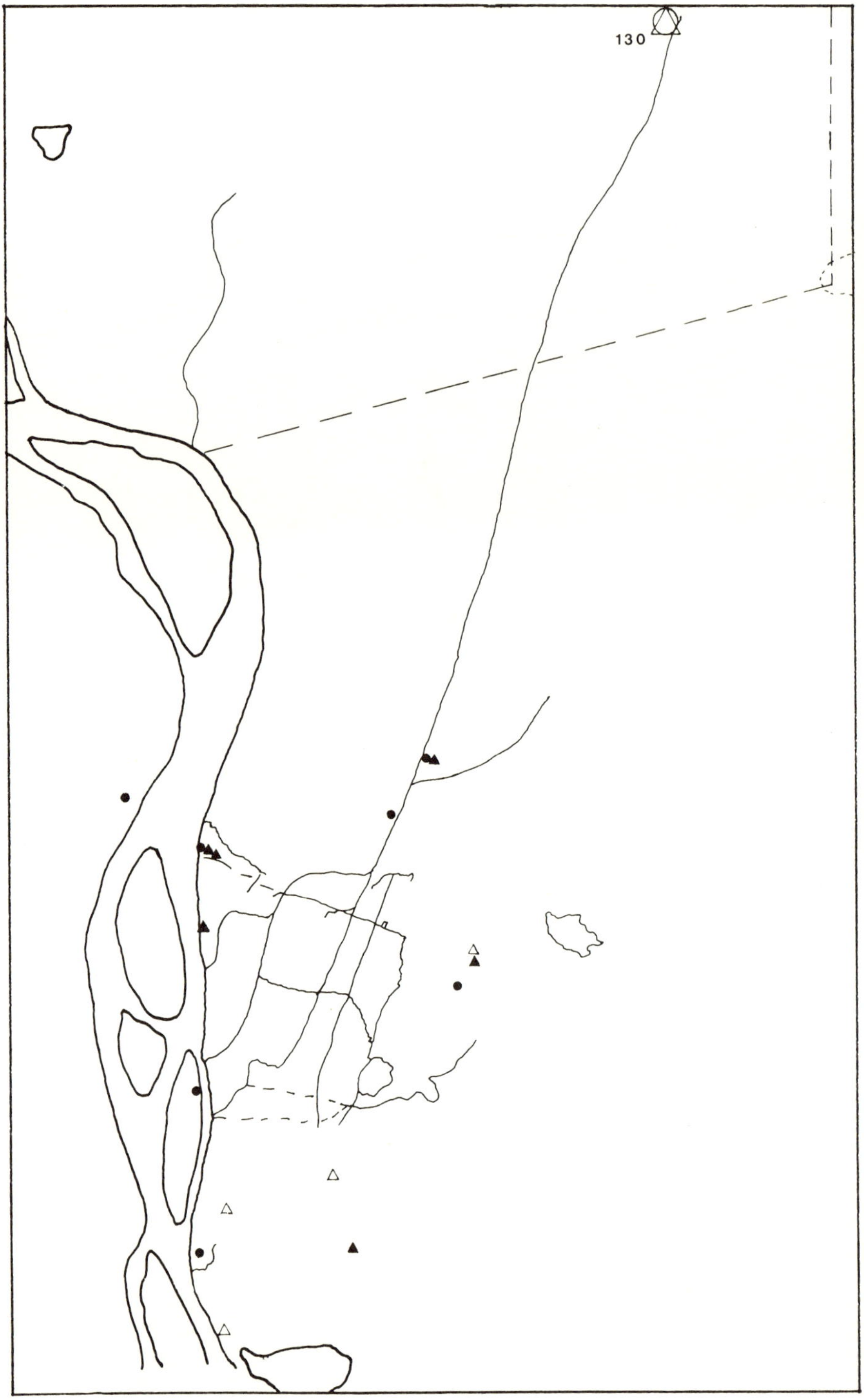

Fig. 27-B. Environs, Distribution of Ṣūfīs
• residential sites
▲ occupational sites

Table 11

Table 11 shows numbers of positions held according to occupations and professional categories rather than numbers of individuals holding them. The number of persons holding two or more posts during their careers in each occupation of the major group is provided, but all other figures refer to positions. The table lists both figures and rounded percentages for specific occupations, and provides total figures and percentages for each category, including all occupations within the category, not just the ones specified here. The totals for each category, therefore, always exceed the aggregate total from the occupations listed in the table: refer to the complete lists of activities reported for each of the twenty-one major occupations in Appendix II.

Within categories, percentages and totals have been computed twice, including and excluding the major occupations when compared with themselves (italicized). This procedure distinguishes the other activities engaged in by individuals in each of the major fields, thereby defining the contrasts in figures and percentages more clearly. No column totals have been computed, since this would result in duplication of many positions. Although broad shifts in concentration according to categories may be detected by column comparisons, the table should be read horizontally to trace specific proportional variations.

NOTE: % = percentage of total positions

ex, in = excluding, including positions in occupations of the major group

Ditto marks refer to numbers immediately to the left.

TABLE 11. Distribution of Positions held by Individuals Engaged in Occupations of the Major Group

	Category I		Category II														
	Mil. Exec.	% ex in	Kātib	% ex in	Kātib Sirr	% ex in	Mubāshir	% ex in	Muwaqqi'	% ex in	Nāẓir	% ex in	Nāẓir Awqāf	% ex in	Total-II % ex	Total-II % in	% ex in
Kātib	14	(9) (6)	*90*	(36)	9	(6) (4)	9	(6)(4)	8	(5) (3)	42	(26)(17)	1	(1)(0)	95	185	(59)(73)
Kātib Sirr	30	(10) (4)	17	(6) (4)	*100*	(25)	3	(1)(1)	25	(8) (6)	77	(25)(19)	1	(0)(0)	145	245	(48)(61)
Mubāshir	3	(2) (1)	5	(3) (2)	1	(1) (0)	*66*	(29)	4	(2) (2)	16	(10) (7)	2	(1)(1)	45	111	(28)(49)
Muwaqqi'	15	(5) (4)	11	(4) (3)	17	(6) (4)	6	(2)(1)	*130*	(32)	35	(13) (9)	7	(3)(2)	93	223	(33)(55)
Nāẓir	62	(10) (7)	6	(1) (1)	9	(1) (1)	12	(2)(1)	9	(1) (1)	*235*	(27)	23	(4)(3)	87	322	(14)(37)
Nāẓir Awqāf	8	(3) (2)	4	(1) (1)	1	(0) (0)	3	(1)(1)	10	(4) (3)	59	(22)(18)	52	(16)	83	135	(31)(42)
Shaykh	19	(2) (2)	2	(0) (0)	8	(1) (1)	6	(1)(1)	5	(1) (0)	64	(8) (6)	6	(1)(1)	106	"	(13) (9)
Muḥtasib	43	(16)(11)	1	(0) (0)	8	(3) (2)	8	(3)(2)	7	(3) (2)	52	(19)(14)	9	(3)(2)	97	"	(35)(26)
Shāhid	37	(5) (3)	10	(1) (1)	1	(0) (0)	20	(3)(2)	38	(5) (3)	28	(4) (2)	6	(1)(1)	133	"	(18)(11)
Nā'ib Qāḍī	31	(3) (2)	6	(1) (0)	8	(1) (0)	16	(1)(1)	35	(3) (2)	62	(5) (4)	12	(1)(1)	169	"	(14)(10)
Qāḍī	5	(1) (1)	3	(0) (0)	22	(3) (2)	8	(1)(1)	13	(2) (1)	49	(8) (5)	7	(1)(1)	112	"	(18)(12)
Qāḍī Quḍāt					4	(3) (3)			5	(4) (3)	12	(11) (8)	6	(5)(4)	27	"	(22)(17)
Nāsikh	6	(3) (2)	3	(2) (1)					8	(4) (3)	3	(2) (2)			18	"	(9) (6)
Tājir	17	(6) (4)					2	(1) (0)	2	(1) (0)	22	(8) (5)	2	(1) (0)	42	"	(15) (9)
Mu'īd	6	(2) (1)	1	(0) (0)	2	(1) (0)	3	(1) (1)	10	(3) (2)	21	(6) (5)	5	(1) (1)	51	"	(15)(12)
Mudarris	12	(1) (1)	6	(1) (0)	8	(1) (0)	9	(1) (1)	17	(2) (1)	73	(7) (4)	17	(2) (1)	149	"	(14) (9)
Khāzin Kutub	2	(1) (1)	1	(1) (1)	2	(1) (1)	2	(1) (1)	3	(2) (2)	3	(2) (2)	1	(1) (1)	15	"	(11) (8)
Imām	7	(1) (1)	5	(1) (1)	1	(0) (0)	6	(1) (1)	15	(2) (2)	32	(5) (4)	7	(1) (1)	77	"	(12) (9)
Khaṭīb	12	(2) (1)	4	(1) (0)	7	(1) (1)	16	(2) (2)	11	(1) (1)	40	(5) (4)	9	(1) (1)	104	"	(13)(10)
Muqri'	3	(1) (1)	2	(1) (0)	1	(0) (0)	4	(1) (1)			16	(5) (3)	3	(1) (1)	29	"	(8) (5)
Mu'taqad	3	(3) (1)					2	(2) (1)							7	"	(7) (3)
Ṣūfī	12	(2)	4	(1)	2	(0)	7	(1)	17	(2)	34	(4)	6	(1)	93		(12)
Qibṭī	42	(14)	38	(13)	3	(1)	6	(2)	5	(2)	100	(34)	1	(0)	228		(77)

TABLE 11. (*continued*)

	Category III							
	Shaykh % ex in	*Muḥtasib* % ex in	*Shāhid* % ex in	*Nā'ib Qāḍī* % ex in	*Qāḍī* % ex in	*Qāḍī Quḍāt* % ex in	*Total III* ex	in / % ex in
Kātib	1 (1) (0)	1 (1) (0)	7 (4) (3)	7 (4) (3)	1 (1) (0)	1 (1) (0)	22	" (14) (9)
Kātib Sirr	9 (3) (2)	8 (3) (2)	1 (0) (0)	12 (4) (3)	22 (7) (5)	18 (6) (4)	81	" (27)(20)
Mubāshir	9 (6) (4)	3 (2) (1)	8 (5) (4)	8 (5) (4)	3 (2) (1)	3 (2) (1)	44	" (27)(19)
Muwaqqiʿ	2 (1) (0)	5 (2) (1)	23 (8) (6)	36 (13) (9)	13 (5) (3)	6 (2) (1)	97	" (35)(24)
Nāẓir	46 (7) (5)	12 (2) (1)	12 (2) (1)	37 (6) (4)	36 (6) (4)	17 (3) (2)	196	" (31)(22)
Nāẓir Awqāf	8 (3) (2)	8 (3) (2)	7 (3) (2)	14 (5) (4)	13 (5) (4)	12 (4) (4)	79	" (29)(25)
Shaykh	*336* (30)	19 (2) (2)	18 (2) (2)	56 (7) (5)	43 (5) (4)	35 (4) (3)	211	547 (27)(49)
Muḥtasib	13 (5) (3)	*105* (28)	6 (2) (2)	14 (5) (4)	16 (6) (4)	6 (2) (2)	71	176 (26)(46)
Shāhid	22 (3) (2)	5 (1) (0)	*427* (36)	94 (12) (8)	39 (5) (3)	5 (1) (1)	201	628 (27)(53)
Nā'ib Qāḍī	54 (5) (3)	9 (1) (1)	81 (7) (5)	*461* (28)	125 (11) (8)	28 (2) (2)	377	838 (32)(51)
Qāḍī	31 (5) (3)	9 (1) (1)	25 (4) (3)	110 (17)(12)	*262* (29)	26 (4) (3)	239	501 (38)(56)
Qāḍī Quḍāt	5 (4) (3)		1 (1) (1)	13 (11) (8)	14 (11) (9)	*35* (22)	45	80 (37)(51)
Nāsikh	4 (2) (1)		29 (15)(10)	14 (7) (5)	5 (3) (2)	2 (1) (1)	62	" (31)(22)
Tājir	16 (6) (3)	4 (1) (1)	16 (6) (3)	15 (6) (3)	13 (5) (3)	9 (3) (2)	88	" (32)(19)
Muʿīd	17 (5) (4)		8 (2) (2)	39 (11) (9)	19 (5) (5)	13 (4) (3)	115	" (33)(27)
Mudarris	111 (10) (7)	7 (1) (0)	31 (3) (2)	149 (14) (9)	93 (9) (6)	60 (6) (4)	543	" (52)(32)
Khāzin Kutub	10 (7) (6)		4 (3) (2)	10 (7) (6)	4 (3) (2)	2 (1) (1)	35	" (25)(19)
Imām	38 (6) (4)	5 (1) (1)	39 (6) (4)	46 (7) (5)	17 (3) (2)	7 (1) (1)	174	" (27)(20)
Khaṭīb	42 (5) (4)	5 (1) (0)	55 (7) (5)	73 (9) (7)	41 (5) (4)	18 (2) (2)	272	" (35)(26)
Muqri'	24 (7) (4)	4 (1) (1)	20 (6) (4)	20 (6) (4)	7 (2) (1)	4 (1) (1)	95	" (27)(17)
Muʿtaqad	11 (11) (5)		1 (1) (0)				16	" (16) (7)
Ṣūfī	57 (7)	17 (2)	47 (6)	40 (5)	17 (2)	15 (2)	216	(28)
Qibṭī								

TABLE 11. *(continued)*

	Category IV				*Category V*				
	Nāsikh % *ex in*	*Tājir* % *ex in*	*Total-IV* *ex in*	% *ex in*	*Muʿīd* % *ex in*	*Mudarris* % *ex in*	*Khāzin Kutub* % *ex in*	*Total V* *ex in*	% *ex in*
Kātib	1 (1) (0)		11 "	(7) (4)	1 (1) (0)	3 (2) (1)	1 (1) (0)	13 "	(8) (5)
Kātib Sirr			11 "	(4) (3)	2 (1) (0)	14 (5) (3)	1 (0) (0)	28 "	(9) (7)
Mubāshir		3 (2) (1)	11 "	(7) (5)	4 (2) (2)	21 (13) (9)	1 (1) (0)	33 "	(20)(15)
Muwaqqiʿ	4 (1) (1)	2 (1) (0)	10 "	(4) (2)	2 (1) (0)	11 (4) (3)	1 (0) (0)	41 "	(15)(10)
Nāẓir	3 (0) (0)	7 (1) (1)	40 "	(6) (5)	12 (2) (1)	139 (32)(16)	2 (0) (0)	193 "	(30)(22)
Nāẓir Awqāf		2 (1) (1)	10 "	(4) (3)	3 (1) (1)	50 (19)(16)	1 (0) (0)	72 "	(27)(22)
Shaykh	3 (0) (0)	13 (2) (1)	42 "	(5) (4)	16 (2) (1)	225 (28)(20)	7 (1) (1)	316 "	(40)(28)
Muḥtasib		4 (1) (1)	19 "	(7) (5)		15 (5) (4)		30 "	(11) (8)
Shāhid	27 (4) (2)	20 (3) (2)	86 "	(11) (7)	8 (1) (1)	82 (11) (7)	4 (1) (0)	157 "	(21)(13)
Nā'ib Qāḍī	7 (1) (0)	14 (1) (1)	57 "	(5) (3)	31 (3) (2)	282 (24)(17)	7 (1) (0)	414 "	(35)(25)
Qāḍī	2 (0) (0)	23 (3) (2)	32 "	(5) (4)	11 (2) (1)	138 (22)(15)	3 (0) (0)	203 "	(32)(23)
Qāḍī Quḍāt					3 (2) (2)	27 (22)(17)		42 "	(34)(27)
Nāsikh	*91* (32)	4 (2) (1)	17 108	(9)(38)	7 (4) (2)	16 (8) (6)	4 (2) (1)	57 "	(29)(20)
Tājir	3 (1) (1)	*199* (42)	61 260	(22)(55)		23 (8) (5)		41 "	(15) (9)
Muʿīd	6 (2) (1)		11 "	(3) (3)	*73* (17)	102 (29)(24)	2 (1) (0)	127 200	(36)(48)
Mudarris	5 (0) (0)	12 (1) (1)	54 "	(5) (3)	48 (5) (3)	*639* (38)	11 (1) (1)	157 796	(15)(47)
Khāzin Kutub	4 (3) (2)		7 "	(5) (4)	5 (4) (3)	34 (24)(19)	*38* (21)	59 97	(42)(54)
Imām	10 (2) (1)	8 (1) (1)	48 "	(8) (5)	11 (2) (1)	87 (14)(10)	7 (1) (1)	200 "	(32)(23)
Khaṭīb	15 (2) (1)	9 (1) (1)	53 "	(7) (5)	15 (2) (1)	139 (18)(13)	8 (1) (1)	246 "	(31)(23)
Muqri'	3 (1) (1)	5 (1) (1)	28 "	(8) (5)	6 (2) (1)	60 (17)(11)	1 (0) (0)	123 "	(35)(23)
Muʿtaqad		3 (3) (1)	31 "	(32)(13)		1 (1) (0)		8 "	(8) (3)
Ṣūfī	15 (2)	13 (2)	103	(13)	12 (2)	92 (12)	5 (1)	208	(26)
Qibṭī		2 (1)	18	(6)		1 (0)		7	(2)

TABLE 11. (*continued*)

	Category VI: *Imām* % *ex in*	*Khaṭīb* % *ex in*	*Muqri'* % *ex in*	*Muʿtaqad* % *ex in*	*Total VI* *ex in*	*Total VI* % *ex in*	*Total Positions* *ex*	*Total Positions* *in*	*Total Individuals*	*Total Individuals with Other Positions*	*Percentage of Individuals with Other Positions*
Kātib	4 (2) (2)	1 (1) (0)	2 (1) (1)		7 ″	(4) (3)	162	252	82	67	(82)
Kātib Sirr	1 (0) (0)	5 (2) (1)	1 (0) (0)		8 ″	(3) (2)	303	403	100	92	(92)
Mubāshir	3 (2) (1)	13 (8) (6)	7 (4) (3)	1 (1) (0)	25 ″	(16)(11)	161	227	59	50	(85)
Muwaqqiʿ	9 (3) (2)	9 (3) (2)	2 (1) (0)		23 ″	(8) (6)	279	409	116	98	(84)
Nāẓir	17 (3) (2)	24 (4) (3)	11 (2) (1)		59 ″	(9) (7)	637	872	169	162	(96)
Nāẓir Awqāf	5 (2) (2)	8 (3) (2)	2 (1) (1)		17 ″	(6) (5)	269	321	56	52	(93)
Shaykh	28 (4) (2)	30 (4) (3)	17 (2) (2)	9 (1) (1)	96 ″	(12) (9)	790	1126	322	263	(82)
Muḥtasib	5 (2) (1)	5 (2) (1)	4 (1) (1)		14 ″	(5) (4)	274	379	105	81	(77)
Shāhid	39 (5) (3)	55 (7) (5)	29 (4) (2)	1 (0) (0)	142 ″	(19)(12)	756	1183	424	317	(75)
Nā'ib Qāḍī	39 (3) (2)	59 (5) (4)	23 (2) (1)		133 ″	(11) (8)	1181	1642	461	400	(87)
Qāḍī	11 (2) (1)	28 (4) (3)	5 (1) (1)		46 ″	(7) (5)	637	899	250	234	(94)
Qāḍī Quḍāt	1 (1) (1)	5 (4) (3)	1 (1) (1)		8 ″	(7) (5)	122	157	34	33	(97)
Nāsikh	12 (6) (4)	14 (7) (5)	7 (4) (2)		37 ″	(19)(13)	197	288	91	73	(80)
Tājir	7 (3) (1)	5 (2) (1)	7 (3) (1)	2 (1) (0)	23 ″	(8) (5)	272	471	197	119	(60)
Muʿīd	10 (3) (2)	14 (4) (3)	6 (2) (1)		38 ″	(11) (9)	348	421	73	70	(96)
Mudarris	28 (3) (2)	51 (5) (3)	31 (3) (2)		122 ″	(12) (7)	1037	1676	496	451	(91)
Khāzin Kutub	9 (6) (5)	10 (7) (6)	3 (2) (2)		24 ″	(17)(13)	142	180	38	32	(84)
Imām	*239* (27)	60 (9) (7)	43 (7) (5)	1 (0) (0)	128 367	(20)(42)	634	873	238	203	(85)
Khaṭīb	54 (7) (5)	*279* (36)	23 (3) (2)		100 379	(13)(36)	787	1066	279	252	(90)
Muqri'	39(11) (7)	20 (6) (4)	*196* (36)	6 (2) (1)	74 270	(21)(49)	352	548	187	142	(76)
Muʿtaqad	1 (1) (0)		6 (6) (3)	*136* (58)	32 168	(33)(72)	97	233	136	80	(59)
Ṣūfī	40 (5)	34 (4)	38 (5)	19 (2)	153	(19)	785				
Qibṭī			1 (0)		1	(0)	296				

CHAPTER V

A Tripartite Elite: Conclusions and Hypotheses

The preceding study has explored the nature of the element that linked ruler and ruled within the greater urban society of Mamluk Egypt. Specifically, the inquiry examined the civilian elite of Cairo from two perspectives: its ethno-geographic composition and its professional organization. A picture emerged of a learned class with common values deriving from the religious consensus and uniform training of its members, but of a class nevertheless internally differentiated by its various degrees of cosmopolitanism and its occupational diversity.

The members of the civilian elite derived from no single class or restricted stratum of the populace. Social mobility remained a reality as well as an ideal even during the later medieval period. It stemmed in large measure from the egalitarian principles of the faith—orthodox Islam—which were inculcated by the education that most of the elite had received. In theory at least, an individual's status within the civilian elite was determined by the extent of his formal training in the law of Islam, regardless of his personal background. The literary skills he acquired qualified him for a wide range of careers, and one of the characteristic features of the man of learning was his multicompetence—his ability to hold positions in diverse occupational fields at the same time.

Yet the analysis of the biographical data revealed clear evidence of professional specialization. Numerous cases were found of individuals educated in the common Islamic foundation, but whose subsequent careers followed tracks which diverged so markedly that a person in one office might have no access to another attained by a different route. Such specialization reflected the wide variety of backgrounds revealed in the biographical records, but it also resulted from the fact that many positions required specific skills that only experience of a relevant kind could provide. Yet although certain offices were closed to those who had not followed the appropriate career track, the exclusivity of office must not be exaggerated. The analysis yielded evidence of many professional men who did indeed cross over into other fields. The matter of differentiation and exclusivity was therefore only one of degree.

From the myriad patterns of officeholding yielded by the analysis, three broad occupational categories can be identified: bureaucrats, jurist-scholars, and religious functionaries.[1] The proportion of foreigners (those not native to the Cairo-Delta zone) in each category varied markedly. Bureaucrats tended to originate in the major cities of the Mamluk empire, although some came from farther afield. The chancellery and higher dīwāns were staffed almost exclusively with personnel of urban background, well versed in diplomacy and finance. Foreigners were deliberately placed in key positions throughout those bureaus that processed domestic information or correspondence from other states. The jurist-scholars were recruited even more widely. The analysis suggested that regional identity was less important than their similar training and cosmopolitan outlook as a condition of their employment. In sharp contrast with both preceding groups, however, the religious functionaries came mostly from the Cairo-Delta zone, and their relative parochialism appears to have related directly to their calling.

The variations in the geographic origins of individuals in each category can be correlated with their contrasting activities. The multifaceted pursuits of the three groups fit into a logical schema if official duties are distinguished from practical functions. The former were overt, the latter often covert. Yet these practical services often assumed the most importance to an individual holding a set of offices and coping with the vagaries of an erratic political environment.

Bureaucrats were formally employed as administrators and archivists. They translated the regime's will, often expressed as capricious edicts, into a feasible policy. Dīwān officials maintained time-tested procedures that could survive the whims of an unstable regime. They were systematizers who made the administrative apparatus work. Their techniques of documentation had evolved from policies devised by secretaries during the ʿAbbāsid period centuries earlier. Yet their official responsibilities did not encompass the essential services they performed, either for their patrons or themselves. Bureaucrats sought to procure revenues, legally or illegally, on behalf of their Mamluk patrons, who in return guaranteed their clients' positions. This reciprocal relationship is critical to our understanding not only of civilian-militarist relations, but the quality of government itself during this era.

As the regime's tool, the administrative apparatus concentrated its innovative facilities on its primary, albeit clandestine, objective. Dīwān officials were accomplished masters in the fine arts of extortion, embezzlement, bribing, and forgery, which yielded reliable revenues, possibly in excess of those obtained through legitimate channels. Thus, the relationship between bureaucratic client and military patron was a symbiotic one, and although the bureaucrat's influence reached far, it was ephemeral. Without question, of the three occupational categories, the bureaucratic was the least autonomous.

In light of the demands it placed on the bureaucrats, the ruling elite sought to recruit particularly trustworthy personnel to staff its network of dīwāns. Relying on long-standing precedent, the Mamluks tended to appoint either Muslim clients of proven loyalty or members of a religious minority, both of whom could be subjected to a variety of pressures. The profile reported for bureaucrats as a whole reflected these recruitment procedures. Among those who manned the bureaus, two elements stood out: Syrian Muslims whose faith was undisputed, and Egyptian Copts who professed Islam but were regarded as suspect nonetheless. Both groups exhibited administrative sophistication and proven dependability. Both had received their training in major centers of government: the Syrians in the provincial capitals, the Copts in the imperial ministries of Cairo. These two elements contrasted sharply. On the one hand, few Coptic officials were accepted as genuine ʿulamaʾ because of their dubious credentials as Muslims. On the other hand, the Syrians were for the most part recognized as true believers, and their status as ʿulamaʾ was unquestioned; they managed to penetrate other professional fields more readily than their Coptic associates. Even so, the two elements were compelled to cooperate in pursuit of their objectives. Both depended on the ruling elite for their status; they rose or fell with their patrons. And both groups—along with their Muslim Egyptian colleagues—tended to restrict their careers to dīwān-related activities. Service as revenue procurers branded even persons of unquestioned faith as agents of the regime, and thus as unfit to interpret the Sharīʿa or to guide public worship. For their own part, many bureaucrats, regardless of their credentials as believers, resigned themselves to a client relationship with the military elite. Even if they had initially aspired to a legal, scholarly, or spiritual office, their career tracks often barred access to such positions. And in the final analysis, power was attractive, even if perilous. In Mamluk society, a civilian could pursue few alternative routes to gain it. For most bureaucrats, power and the wealth it generated compensated well enough for their unsavory image.

Unlike their counterparts in the dīwāns, jurist-scholars saw themselves as learned custodians of Sunna. They exercised their prerogatives as lawyers and educators on the grounds of their erudition in the Islamic sciences. In contrast to the bureaucrats, jurist-scholars wielded enormous moral authority unmatched by any real capacity to compel obedience. Their prestige resulted in large part from their credibility as guarantors of orthodoxy and communal probity in the face of adverse political circumstances. Viewed from this perspective, the dichotomy between their formal duties as jurisprudents and their parallel role as educators acquired a rationale based on practical experience.

As litigators, jurist-scholars were confined primarily to civil matters.

They influenced the affairs of state only in their subordinate capacity as advisors. But by guarding their exclusive control over Shārīʿ litigation, the jurist-scholars retained their authority to interpret divine law, which was the pillar of the Islamic community and superior to the state itself. As judges, the jurist-scholars were in practice dependent on the state to enforce their decisions. As scholar-interpreters, however, they commanded a sphere of independent action. They institutionalized their independence in an elaborate religio-academic network that they controlled by manipulating appointments and promotions. Although the regime supported this network financially through endowments, the jurist-scholars decided who among their number would fill its professorial chairs.

In this light, even the regime's prerogative to appoint judges was qualified by the jurist-scholars' regulation of their own infrastructure. In theory, the sultan determined who would receive major judgeships throughout the empire. He could thus place his own candidates, influence the implementation of formal litigation, and demand official justification for his arbitrary decisions. But in reality, the regime was obliged to select its candidates for the bench from a body of individuals highly conscious of their interests, who not only set the standards for official orthodoxy but designated the roster of personnel qualified to serve as jurisprudents at any given time. Consequently, even in the courts the regime's intrusion was curbed by the solidarity of the jurist-scholars. Every stage of the educational process helped shape the outlook of the future judge toward his vocation, and equipped him to deal with those who might compromise its autonomy.

The geographic composition of the jurist-scholars accorded with their formal duties and professional organization. The lawyer-teachers—and their upper echelons in particular—may be regarded as members of a truly international fraternity: the Sunnī ʿulamaʾ. In Cairo, their cosmopolitan qualities may be attributed in part to the maintenance by royal fiat of all four legal schools. Many, possibly a majority, of the individuals appointed to the three minority judgeships (Ḥanafīs, Mālikīs, and Ḥanbalīs) were born elsewhere. These qāḍīs heard fewer cases than their Shāfiʿī colleagues, but they maintained a living tradition of orthodox scholasticism in the colleges, where most held professorships in their respective madhhabs. A question emerges whether these judges formed interest groups centering around their legal affiliations, and whether such groups embraced foreigners in the city. So far, we have no hard evidence on this, although institutions noted for their emphasis on the minority schools of the Sharīʿa had concentrations of non-Egyptian scholars and students associated with them.

In any case, the issue of foreign interests relates directly to the larger problem of professional solidarity. Foreign and indigenous scholars alike appear to have shared attitudes toward their calling and the ruling authority. No statements appeared in the biographies of foreigners to set their views on these matters apart from those of the native majority. Whatever the nature of foreign interests in the capital, they were almost certainly integrated into the upper ranks of the religio-academic system. The jurist scholars, despite their diverse origins, thus shared a universal vision of their faith, a uniform scholastic method, a self-serving conception of recruitment, and a defensive attitude toward political authority. For these reasons, erudite foreigners blended quite easily with the local literati to form a close-knit professional class.

Turning from interpreters of Sharīʿa to religious practitioners, our perception of their contribution to society becomes clearer in light of the demonstrated correlation between their formal duties and practical services on the one hand and the patterns of their geographic origins on the other. In comparison with either the bureaucrats or jurist-scholars, religious functionaries wielded the least power. By virtue of their official duties, they stood aloof from the affairs of state, and accordingly had little or no say in the decisions that determined the political destiny of their community. But by setting moral standards through pious example, religious functionaries personified the ideals of the Prophet and his companions. These values were transmitted through the ages as their legacy. For the ordinary believer, such ideals were the essence of the faith. They were primarily communicated by those whom the local populace regarded as their own.

The holy person's manifestation of piety was, in most cases, tied to his long-term residence in the local region or neighborhood. Quite often he descended from a venerated lineage. His stature as an exemplar of morality was based on his personal contact with the people who revered him. The local divine's capacity to inspire his flock grew slowly from countless examples of his commitment to the faith and special services to his constituency. His pious aura was less transferable than the scholarly erudition that learned men attained the same way throughout the Muslim world. The cosmopolitanism of jurist-scholars and parochialism of religious functionaries therefore accorded with their respective vocations.

These were the three major occupational categories. I have summarized how cosmopolitanism and differentiation interacted in ways peculiar to each. The issues that remain are more speculative. They shift the discussion away from the realm of fact to the forum of hypothesis. Yet these questions merit consideration because they confront areas of controversy in the discipline more directly. These issues, as I see them, are as follows: the relationship between foreign and indigenous elements of the civilian elite, the curriculum pursued in the religio-academic network, and the interplay between intermediary status and autonomy. The first two questions lead into yet another: the place of orthodox doctrine in local tradition.

As striking as it was among more refined circles, cosmopolitanism was less noticeable throughout the lower levels of the civilian elite, regardless of category. We are left with an overall impression of foreign groups embedded within a regional learned class whose roots extended deep into the Cairo-Delta zone. More significantly, persons who moved to Cairo from abroad were attached to a limited number of prominent religio-academic institutions. This does not necessarily imply their social isolation, since the evidence suggested mutual association whenever contact between foreign and indigenous scholars took place. But the native ʿulamaʾ appeared as the medium that disseminated among the lower orders the universal Sunnī principles professed by more cosmopolitan figures. This pattern of intercommunication between foreigners and Egyptians at the elite level provides an insight into the capacity of Cairene society to maintain a genuine commitment to universal orthodoxy while remaining true to its own local traditions.

Contact between learned non-Egyptians and the masses thus seems to have been infrequent. Sporadic association certainly occurred, since specific instances of it were reported in the biographical sources. Yet there were few cases of foreigners contributing spiritual guidance to the community at large. The image that we have depicts them engaged in the litigation, scholarship, and mystic observances characteristic of other regions. There is no reason to assume that non-Egyptians surrendered their international identity after establishing themselves in the capital. As a body of scholars who were highly aware of their station, they continued to maintain ties with their peers abroad. They may have promoted their influence through circles of students and teachers from the same countries or factions based on the legal schools and Ṣūfī orders. None of these possibilities prohibited involvement with the local ʿulamaʾ. But whether foreigners were assimilated into the greater society is less clear.

One can speculate that this tendency prevailed widely in the Islamic world. It lends plausibility to the case for universal doctrine (high Islam) thriving in the context of regional, even syncretistic, beliefs held by the masses. The probable restriction of cosmopolitanism to a limited segment of society does not imply that the public was unaware of a foreign presence in their midst. Wide respect accrued to literati of non-Egyptian origin from both the indigenous ʿulamaʾ and the general populace. No disharmony was reported in the sources. Rather, this hypothesis suggests that universal theory was fused with local practice in such a way as to allow both dimensions of belief to coexist.

These observations presume close ties binding the civilian elite to an institutional network. What do these ties indicate about the second issue: the topics that were discussed in this network? The prominent colleges and shrines clearly supported a well-defined professional organization. A uniform curriculum was elaborated, expounded, and transmitted in them. Yet these core institutions formed only part of a larger whole. The famous houses trained a minority of those whom the biographers designated as ʿulamaʾ. What about the majority? Most must have received formal educations, for how else could they be classified as learned or qualify for positions requiring advanced training? Nevertheless, if this majority did pursue higher studies, the biographers rarely mentioned them.

Does this phenomenon accord with genuine fact or is it the consequence of the compilers' bias? Al-Sakhāwī in particular stressed the continuity of classical tradition. Did he disregard the curricula of all but eminent persons, those who made the most legitimate contributions to scholarship? Not entirely, since the studies completed by individuals of little importance were mentioned on occasion, if not elaborated on. But the pattern that emerged from the subjects and works that al-Sakhāwī listed clearly stressed orthodox consistency. Few deviations from the standard mold ever appeared, and we are left with few hints of doctrinal disparity. Was there a connection between uniformity of curriculum and the absence of references to persons studying in the majority of educational institutions? Al-Sakhāwī was disinclined to report any topics other than those that conformed with standardized courses in the elite colleges. Indeed, he regarded the revival of classical purity as his mission in life. He sought to inspire public confidence in orthodox solidarity by identifying individuals whose academic careers exemplified Sunnī ideals.

What, then, was taught in the other institutions? One is led to assume curricular uniformity throughout the central Islamic lands during this period. The scholars who composed the learned establishment were dedicated to teaching an extant, perfect, and complete corpus. Blatant defiance of the accepted disciplines and texts would be unthinkable, in any case, under the conditions of Egyptian society in the later Middle Ages. The Mamluk regime would tolerate no open break with established scholarly canons. And the judiciary, which pledged itself to uphold the unity of legal principle and to defend the integrity of the Sharīʿa, was distributed throughout the entire collegiate system, with several important district courts housed in otherwise undistinguished madrasas.

There is thus no cause to postulate radical deviation anywhere in the educational system. But since the courses taught in the majority of institutions cannot be traced, the possibility of local variation cannot be ruled out. We are only certain that the more visible colleges monopolized neither litigation nor scholarship. The prominent institutions seem to have dominated higher learning because the sources included only the topics that were expounded under their auspices. Nor did doctrinal conservatism automatically imply uniformity in pedagogical procedures. Al-Sakhāwī was preoccupied with alleged lapses of standards because he believed such lapses to be symptomatic of a greater danger: religious heterodoxy. His silence is suggestive in itself, because it could point to variations in local practice. This most informed of prosopographers may have been disinclined to record the studies undertaken by the majority of the persons he described for reasons other than their insignificance as scholars. He might have attempted to deemphasize any departure from orthodoxy by omitting references to it in his biographical compendium.

But even if open dissent from orthodoxy can be discounted on the grounds of the political and intellectual climate of the age, the potential for incomplete transmission may not. The incidence of sinecurism, which was widespread in many lesser institutions, lends credence to this possibility. Even if eminent scholars occupied chairs at lesser colleges, they did not necessarily focus their attention on students enrolled there. If we consider the educational background of those individuals who ascended to the top of the learned elite, their conspicuous absence as students from the less distinguished training centers may attest to both substandard programs and minimal opportunities for cementing ties with important colleagues at these houses.

These possibilities raise a host of intriguing questions. Institutions of secondary rank constituted the bulk of the religio-academic system. Yet in all likelihood, they were not as carefully monitored by either agents of the regime or theological purists among the ʿulamaʾ. Could unsanctioned disciplines be expounded there more openly? More significantly, could established canons within legitimate fields be criticized with less risk of detection or public outcry? In such settings, could local variants in Shāriʿ tradition be more expeditiously collated with formal belief? These questions cannot now be answered, but until they are, our understanding of scholasticism during the later medieval period will remain defective.

The final issue leads the investigator farther afield. What does the phenomenon of autonomy imply about the role of the civilian elite as intermediaries between the Mamluks and their subjects? At the very least, it qualifies the view of the ʿulama' as a category of persons who were equipped intellectually and psychologically to serve in many diverse capacities at the same time. The concept of mediation as a series of concrete vertical interactions within the social hierarchy is valid.[2] The argument here relates the issue of social solidarity in the face of political adversity to the occupational differentiation and variations in personnel observed in the three major categories. How did intermediary status and autonomy interact to distinguish each group from the others?

The activities of the bureaucrats demonstrated a systematic character as aspects of fiscal aggrandizement. Therefore, mediation in the case of dīwān officials fulfilled the wishes of the ruling elite rather than the needs of the masses who bore the burden of their demands. One can assume that the civil population reacted negatively to this type of service. It certainly cannot be termed advocacy. Because of their role as procurers, bureaucrats required a dependent, symbiotic relationship with their patrons. The conditions of their employment hardly encouraged them to develop positive strategies to resolve long-term flaws in the economy. The Mamluks themselves gave their clients little incentive for maintaining a positive attitude toward government. As argued in Chapter One, if an individual attempted to apply honest standards to his duties, he undermined his own career. Thus, the roots of the regime's fiscal dilemmas were in large measure instrinsic to the system itself.

As their biographies so vividly attested, most of the ʿulama' who suffered disparagement during their careers had elected to join the regime's service. Crossover between the bureaucracy and the other categories occurred, to be sure. Power and wealth could exert an irresistible attraction on the ambitious civilian. But the individuals who were coopted suffered a loss of personal prestige as guardians of correct belief since fiscal corruption was clearly a departure from the principles of the Sharīʿa. These people sacrificed their professional integrity by accepting a client's position and thereby reduced their credibility in the eyes of the community.

Credibility was at the heart of the status enjoyed by jurist-scholars. Their designation as mediators in the traditional sense of advocacy seems appropriate if we consider occasional reports of judges authorizing popular rebellions or interceding on behalf of persons subjected to gross injustice. Nevertheless, this interpretation is qualified by the limited reach of the qāḍīs' practical jurisdiction. Moral authority and social prestige were vital to the ʿalim's position as a respected pronouncer of legal opinions, but what powers did such authority grant him? Was self-interest compatible with the principle of spokesmanship in any case?

These queries point to the jurist-scholars' relationship with society and their own identity as a profession.

In Cairo, under the watchful eye of the sultan, the upper ranks of the juridical-scholarly establishment stood somewhat aloof from the problems of the masses. Although they were acknowledged by the common people as the leaders of the Muslim community, the impact of their litigation, especially on the lower orders, is difficult to assess. Moreover, the Sharīʿa courts could do little to mitigate the excesses from on high that ordinary people endured as a fact of life. But the jurist-scholars' perception of themselves as an interest group goes far to explain their approach to higher education. It also provides us with a model for analyzing their place in society.

The data patterns in Chapter Four depicted the network of religio-academic institutions as the training ground for the ʿulamaʾ, the young scholar's point of entry into a learned brotherhood. The formal purposes of the instruction he received in the colleges were sound interpretation of Sunna and the preparation of lawyer-teachers who were also of true faith. Its practical purpose, however, was to determine the membership of a profession. These three objectives were fully compatible. An aspiring student's primary goal was to build up the personal contacts necessary for his placement and subsequent promotion—either in the judiciary or the madrasas. He did not aspire to become an intellectual innovator, because this would have compromised his convictions as a devout Muslim. Rather, he devoted his creative energies to developing peer ties.

The peer bond grew from the student's association with his professors, who, after assessing his capacity to absorb the content and legitimate explication of a canonical text, formally certified his competence as a scholar. It was this act of certification, the ijāza, plus the professors' opinion that the novice had developed the proper conception of his calling, that admitted the student to the body of ʿulamaʾ. A beginner's success was therefore measured primarily by his ability to duplicate his superiors' work and follow in their footsteps. This definition of success posed no threat to the underriding scholastic charge of the ʿulamaʾ: to preserve a corpus of teachings intact for future generations. Such a charge might allow for local modifications, provided that they were neither openly acknowledged nor permitted to challenge central tenets of the faith. An educational process that emphasized rote memorization and personal contact with masters whose depth of conviction was unquestioned could accommodate minor variations with little threat to the principle of orthodoxy. An instructor's reputation may have taken precedence over the specific curriculum items he taught. Unbridled inquiry, however, was quite another matter. It might transform the latent question of heterodoxy implicit in local discrepancies into a burning public dispute. Thus, the lack of intellectual innovation in this system derived from the fact that it neither facilitated the formation of peer ties nor promoted a method of inquiry that tolerated local custom.

Returning to the broader question of the ʿalim's contribution to society, does the model of an interest group accommodate the principle of advocacy? This is unlikely under the conditions of the age. The ideal of custodianship must be weighed against the realities of the Mamluks' rule in the heart of their realm. Denied the capacity to enforce their will, jurist-scholars could rely only on their moral authority and professional integrity. They sought to secure both by maintaining their independent control over the religio-academic establishment. Their autonomy was thus effectively limited to their role as guardians of Sunna.[3] But this role should not be underestimated. The term "advocacy" and all that it connotes was unsuited to either the jurist-scholars' self-image or the options available to them. However, their capacity to defend their independence augmented their credibility in the eyes of the populace as guarantors of moral truths before a highly amoral regime. Jurist-scholars set an example for the faithful by demonstrating that their class could surmount the coercion of an autocracy that so flagrantly defied such truths.

To the religious functionaries, moral influence derived from pious example rather than learned erudition. Unlike the schoolmen, their multifaceted activities put them in touch with every echelon of Cairene society. From their career profiles, religious functionaries appeared as the most autonomous component of the civilian elite. Yet the highest of them associated closely with the members of the ruling regime. The intimate confessional relationships between imāms or khaṭībs on the one hand, and Mamluk amīrs on the other appeared repeatedly in their biographies. Did personal association with the military caste restrict an imām's utterances or censor a khaṭīb's opinions? We are not sure. But the almost total exclusion of Mamluks from religious fields, and their extraordinary respect for personal baraka suggest that venerated figures maintained their own autonomy even when they accepted a patron's support. The Mamluks themselves were not disposed to manipulate religious functionaries so long as the latter avoided open confrontation.

How then is the intermediary role of these figures to be defined? In their case the impact of arbitrary rule can be linked to the possibility of communal transcendance: the capacity of individuals to cope with inequity by rising above it as a group. The role of revered persons provides the clearest example of how a noncorporate society found cohesion in its faith and solace from its oppressors. A wide gulf separated a prayer leader in the imperial court or a Friday preacher in al-Azhar from a lowly mosque intendant or devout ascetic in a poor quarter. But their manifestation of piety joined them together and won them public esteem. Their life style persuaded others of its efficacy as well as its blessedness. Accordingly, devoutness was a vital stabilizing force in an otherwise unstable universe. The person endowed with baraka radiated security and self-confidence. At all levels of society, those who held religious offices embodied trusted values and continuity with the past. For this reason, the common people seem to have empathized more with them than with the jurisprudents or scholars. That revered figures commanded the respect, even awe, of the military caste added enormously to their stature.

On the basis of such unrivaled popular esteem, the religious functionaries may be seen as the symbolic legitimators of an entire confessional community. Once again, spokesmanship seems inappropriate to their situation. Direct intercession on behalf of the downtrodden rarely emerged as a tactic resorted to by civilians during this period. Rather, spiritual figures surrounded themselves with a revered aura. It was this that qualified them in the popular mind to promulgate the regime's edicts in the mosques without surrendering their autonomy to them or even condoning them. Religious functionaries, therefore, symbolized collectively the rectitude and permanence of the Muslim community. Drawn from all its social elements, they could deal with their overlords without being coopted by them. So long as their independence, granted by God himself, remained unchallenged, so could the greater community sustain its trust in His unfailing commitment to them—and the conviction that worldly power was peripheral to His ultimate plan.

In this way, symbolic legitimation contributed decisively to solidarity in the face of adversity. Unlike priests, Muslim religious functionaries radiated baraka without disassociating themselves from temporal affairs. The masses were able to identify with revered figures as an honored, yet approachable, dimension of themselves. Consequently, to the extent that they represented the whole community, their independence from the regime could be extended symbolically to all its members. Regardless of how onerous or disquieting the Mamluk presence might be, it could be endured if the community rested assured of its own permanency, which the regime could not threaten. The autonomy of religious functionaries, recruited from the most humble as well as the loftiest stations, demonstrated the validity of God's abiding promise to protect the Muslim community. The respect they received from the ruling elite, otherwise so impervious to civilian influence, was concrete proof that He would never abandon it.

Open challenges to the Mamluks' domination or intervention on behalf of their victims were inconsistent with the stance of the holy men who, rather, through their pious example, proved that they could transcend the sufferings of this life. They could not eliminate oppression itself because no civilian possessed the power to alter the political order in any fundamental way. But they could alleviate oppression by demonstrating how superficial it was in the divine scheme of things. This stance strikes the western observer as supremely conservative. And so it was. Continuity and stability were fundamental values in the political turbulence of the Muslim world during the later Middle Ages.[4] Yet from the perspective of these very values, the example set by religious functionaries meant a great deal to the common man or woman who possessed neither the education nor the outlook to indulge in abstract speculation on the conditions governing their lives.

Adroit procurers, learned custodians, pious legitimators—the civilian elite embraced them all. Their ties to the seat of power encompassed widely differing relationships according to the characteristics and options of each group. Their ultimate services were equally diverse: fiscal aggrandizement, guardianship of the law, communal transcendance. These contrasts are crucial to our understanding of a social system in which prerogatives were delegated from above but not surrendered. In Mamluk Egypt, as in its Muslim neighbors, final authority was vested at the top, never to be given away through charters. This concept of delegated authority encouraged the evolution of exceedingly subtle grades of subordination. These determined an individual's rank in the political hierarchy but not his standing in society. If authority was monopolized from on high, key civilian elements never relinquished their own prerogatives either, thereby coping quite imaginatively with the grim fact of their political inferiority.

This type of system differed sharply from the corporate approach to the distribution of power in western Europe. To be sure, Cairo during the fifteenth century did not encompass all aspects of social organization in premodern Islamic cities. Many distinct urban cultures flourished in the Muslim world, each exhibiting as many disparities as common traits. But the political order in a great metropolis like Cairo differed significantly from its counterpart in any European city. Since no Muslim society attributed corporate meaning to abstract institutions before the Ottoman period, the approach that evolved in Mamluk Cairo was consistent with the prevailing conditions of authority, while remaining consonant with the dictates of Islamic tradition.

In closing, I wish to offer a remark concerning the interpretation of sources. Medieval Islamic documents rarely spell out the questions raised during the course of this study. This is no small matter, for if we limit ourselves to the explicit in our documents, medieval Islamic historiography offers few prospects for progress beyond description. The lack of overt commentary may well have been due to the noncorporate nature of social institutions in the traditional Near East. It may also have reflected the hesitation of writers to lay bare their strategies for dealing with adversity. In other words, they may have deliberately obscured these devices to ensure their viability. Yet the Mamluks' toleration of certain forms of social dissidence, such as popular crime and sporadic violence, suggests that they were aware of their subjects' subtler maneuverings on occasion.[5] They may have recognized that their subordinates' strategies were difficult to eliminate but profitable to exploit. The Mamluks shared the concern of the civilian elite for preserving communal cohesion, if for no other reason than to simplify their own task. As a small minority, the Mamluks' effort in governing the empire was rendered less troublesome if key civilian elements helped quiet the masses, resigning them to the inertia of alien rule. But if the military elite tacitly acknowledged some of the strategies contrived by its subjects to mitigate its excesses, then the reason for their concealment is even more perplexing.

In the absence of explicit commentary, this and other paradoxes can be explored only after the investigator restructures his sources to discover hidden trends. A procedure of this type invariably runs the risk of distortion. But if the historian conducts his search in the tradition of Ibn Khaldūn, with an abiding commitment to accuracy of context, the rewards of his enterprise will outweigh its pitfalls.

Appendix I. A Survey of Major Institutions

The following institutions are described according to the groups they formed, which may be considered collegiate clusters. These were the sites most frequently mentioned in the sources, and were the centers of intellectual and spiritual life in Cairo during the fifteenth century. It is evident that none of these institutions functioned in isolation from one another, but were interrelated in a collegiate fashion. However, they were ranked at differing levels of prestige and reputation.

THE FESTIVAL GATE COLLEGIATE GROUP

The first cluster to be considered was located in the northeast district of the old Fāṭimid city, near the Festival Gate and Square (*Bāb al-ʿĪd*).

Saʿīd al-Suʿadāʾ (15)

This khānqāh,[1] the oldest in Egypt, was founded by Ṣalāḥ al-Dīn in 569/1173-1174. Its title derived from a laqab of an individual whose house Ṣalāḥ al-Dīn occupied as a base for his Kurdish troops. This was the eunuch (Ustādh) ʿAnbar, deceased in 544/1149-1150. Ṣalāḥ al-Dīn converted the house into a khānqāh "in support of the Ṣūfī poor newly arrived from remote lands."[2] The sultan endowed it with several waqfs based on an orchard near Elephant Lake, a bazaar (qayṣarīya) in the city, and two provincial towns: Nāḥīyat Dahmar and an unspecified site in Bahnasawīya province.[3] Ṣalāḥ al-Dīn specified that each Ṣūfī should receive foodstuffs, meat, and bread every day, and he had a bath built for the community.[4] Ultimately, this khānqāh was recognized as "the Ṣūfī house" because of its primacy. Its rector took the title of grand shaykh (shaykh al-shuyūkh). The khānqāh accumulated further endowments throughout the thirteenth and fourteenth centuries. Its grand shaykhs were drawn from men deeply involved in affairs of state.[5] It attracted many renowned scholars, and by A.D. 1400 it was regarded as housing the most illustrious assemblage of Ṣūfīs in the Mamluk empire. The social backgrounds of the residents now rarely corresponded to Ṣālāḥ al-Dīn's wish that the convent provide for poor mystics from abroad.

By the turn of the fifteenth century, the khānqāh was at the zenith of its wealth and prestige. Maqrīzī notes that during the reign of Barqūq some three hundred Ṣūfīs were resident. He provided rather specific details about their support. Every day each person received: three flat loaves to weigh three raṭls of bread, a portion of meat at one-third raṭl, and its accompanying broth. Every month each Ṣūfī received a portion of confections and soap, and every year clothing worth forty dirhams or its monetary equivalent.[6] However, during Barqūq's reign disputes erupted over disposition of the khānqāh's substantial waqf endowment.[7] Maqrīzī's description of these disputes and the resultant collusion of prominent grand amirs with the affected parties provides an example of the complex interrelationship between members of the military and civilian elites. The example clearly depicts the final authority of Mamluk amirs to decide between contending factions, even when a board of prominent jurists was appointed to reinterpret the waqf writ. Nonetheless, that a commission of inquiry was duly summoned by the sultan in response to complaints raised by the Ṣūfīs does suggest the extent of their influence over the military elite.

In the year 806/1403-1404, when Egypt suffered a severe famine, all waqf yields diminished and several entirely ceased to produce.[8] Throughout the fifteenth century, the khānqāh's prosperity rose and fell according to the varied currents of the Egyptian economy, but it retained its primacy among the monastic houses. A significant percentage of the scholarly and religious establishment of Cairo spent some time as members of its community.

Baybarsīya (13)

This khānqāh,[9] located a short distance north of Saʿīd al-Suʿadāʾ, was founded by the amir Rukn al-Dīn Baybars al-Jāshankīr in 706/1306-1307, prior to his enthronement. It was also referred to as al-Ruknīya after its founder's laqab. The institution consisted of the khānqāh itself, a hospice (ribāṭ), and the amir's tomb, all connected by a gallery along the street that contained several shabābīk for public recitation of the Koran. The complex covered one-and-one-third feddans of valuable city property. After Baybars several amirs contributed waqfs to the khānqāh, most of them drawn on shops in the Lance Dealers' bazaar and the Zuwayla quarter. Baybars spent an enormous sum of money on the interior decoration of the structure, and Maqrīzī considered it to be the most sumptuous khānqāh in Egypt. In 709/1309-1310 it maintained a community of four hundred Ṣūfīs, including those in both the cloister and the hospice. Of these, one hundred were former troopers (ajnād) and, therefore, apparently were retired Mamluks.[10] The Ṣūfīs received allotments of food like those provided in Saʿīd al-Suʿadāʾ. Maqrīzī also noted that Baybars established Ḥadīth specialists and Koran readers in his tomb to recite the Scriptures and Prophetic traditions over his grave. The waqfs for this were established in Damascus, Ḥamā, Minyat al-Makhlaṣ in Jīza, Upper Egypt, the Delta, and on several mercantile establishments and qayṣarīyas in Cairo.[11] After Baybars' deposition by al-Nāṣir Muḥammad's partisans in 708/1309, the khānqāh was closed for twenty years. It was then reopened with its waqfs restored. In 776/1374-1375, Sultan Shaʿbān II added to these endowments, providing every Ṣūfī with a monthly cash allowance of seven dirhams in place of certain food allotments. This was subsequently raised to ten dirhams. During the late fourteenth century, several famines diminished the waqf yields, and after 796/1393-1394 only jurists (fuqahāʾ) and troopers (ajnād) were to be admitted. Maqrīzī remarked that persons of humble origin were still living there in his day, but they had all entered prior to 796.[12] In other words, by A.D. 1400 the khānqāh functioned as a residence for both the learned and retired military elites, to the exclusion of the poor.

Jamālīya (16)

This third institution of the Festival Gate group was a madrasa founded by the amir Jamāl al-Dīn Yūsuf al-Ustādār in 810/1407.[13] The amir equipped his madrasa lavishly in the somewhat parasitic fashion of the period by purchasing a large collection of books assembled by Sultan Shaʿbān in the Citadel from Sultan Ḥajjī for 600 dīnārs. This raised a controversy, since many of these volumes had been copied under waqfs in support of other institutions that held a claim over them. A staff was appointed for the madrasa consisting of a Ṣūfī shaykh, professors in fiqh and Ḥadīth from the four legal schools (eight in all), and a professor of Koranic exegesis. Provisions were made to support their students, each of whom was to receive three raṭls of bread per day and thirty dirhams per month (with no mention of meat). Each professor was to receive 300 dirhams per month.[14] In addition, the madrasa supported an imām and his family, prayer callers, servants, and stewards.

Amir Jamāl al-Dīn took care to outfit the madrasa like a palace because he intended to retire in it. He set up waqfs from his own fief in Jīza so that his descendants would be the executors.[15] After his arrest and execution by Sultan Faraj in 812/1409-1410, these waqfs were confiscated by the crown, although the madrasa remained open. Only part of the book collection was returned to its original location. Amir Jamāl al-Dīn's son and his niece's husband were able to regain control of the waqfs and to restore them to the family after several years. Maqrīzī provides an outline of their manipulations that makes interesting reading.[16] The family held the office of nāẓir thereafter. Maqrīzī noted that Amir Jamāl al-Dīn spent 12,000 gold dīnārs on the construction of the madrasa.[17]

Qarāsanqurīya, Ḥijāzīya, Sābiqīya (14, 17, 18)

Three other madrasas were an integral part of the Festival Gate group, although they were not as prominent as the institutions discussed above. They were founded during the fourteenth century by Mamluks concerned both about providing for their descendants and about establishing a scholastic institution to their memory. The oldest of the three madrasas was founded by Amir Shams al-Dīn Qarāsanqur al-Manṣūrī, the viceroy, in the year 700/1300-1301.[18] The complex included the madrasa, a masjid, and a Koran school (maktab) for orphans. A professorship in fiqh was endowed in the madrasa, and the amir's own house was put in a waqf trust to support it. The waqf and office of nāẓir remained under the control of Qarāsanqur's descendants until 815/1412-1413, when the family died out.

The second of these institutions was established in 761/1359-1360 by a daughter of al-Nāṣir Muhammad, Khūnd Ṭaṭar al-Ḥijāzīya, wife of the amir Baktamur al-Ḥijāzī.[19] The princess established waqfs to support professorships in both Shāfiʿī and Malīkī jurisprudence. The first individual to hold the Shāfiʿī chair was Sirāj al-Dīn ʿUmar ibn Raslān al-Bulqīnī, noted previously. An imām and Koran readers were appointed, a library was collected, and a Koran school for orphans was founded with a post for the teacher. Maqrīzī supplied details on special gifts to the staff and students during festivals.[20]

The third of these institutions was built at the order of the eunuch amir Sābiq al-Dīn Mithqāl al-Anūkī, commander of the sultan's Mamluks, in 763/1361-1362.[21] This madrasa supported a professorship in Shāfiʿī jurisprudence. The first to hold the post was the eminent scholar Sirāj al-Dīn ʿUmar ibn ʿAlī al-Anṣārī, known as Ibn al-Mulaqqin, who taught many of the individuals surveyed in this study. A Koran reader was also appointed, a public fountain installed, and a library and an orphanage established. These three madrasas appear strikingly similar in terms of founders and range of provisions supported by waqfs. Their relatively small staffs did not reduce the quality of instruction, since famous scholars were attracted to the posts.

THE BAYN AL-QAṢRAYN COLLEGIATE GROUP

A group of extremely prestigious institutions was founded, starting in the late Ayyūbid period, on the site of the ceremonial square that once separated the two Fāṭimid palaces in the center of the rectangle. This collegiate cluster consisted of seven institutions devoted primarily to legal scholarship or public service. These seven stood at the zenith of the academic hierarchy of the Mamluk state. They were the forum of the most prominent and successful figures in Egyptian scholarly life during the later Middle Ages. Virtually every important scholar-teacher of the period studied or taught at at least one of them. Many did work in several. Four of these seven institutions were founded by Mamluk sultans, who were willing to allow the ʿulamaʾ relative independence in allocating the enormous endowments they provided to bring their foundations up to the level of the others in the group. The seven were located from north to south along the Bayn al-Qaṣrayn, as follows: the Kāmilīya, Barqūqīya, Nāṣirīya, and Manṣūrīya madrasas, and the Māristān al-Manṣūrī immediately behind Qalāʾūn's tomb—all on the west side of the street. On the east side, continuing south, were the Ẓāhirīya and Ṣāliḥīya madrasas. These seven are discussed in chronological order of their founding.

Kāmilīya (19)

This madrasa, known also as the Dār al-Ḥadīth al-Kāmilīya, was founded by Sultan al-Malik al-Kāmil in 626/1229.[22] It was established to train scholars primarily in Prophetic traditions and secondarily in jurisprudence. Property in several quarters of the Bayn al-Qaṣrayn district was placed in waqf trusts to maintain its activities. Until the turn of the fifteenth century this madrasa represented the most respected center of scholarship in Prophetic traditions in Egypt. After the famine of 806/1403-1404, however, it suffered a severe decrease in revenues and entered a prolonged decline. Most of the individuals appearing in the biographical sources who studied and taught there did so prior to this date.

Ṣāliḥīya (26)

This madrasa was the last major Ayyūbid contribution to the academic establishment in Egypt. It was founded by al-Malik al-Ṣāliḥ Najm al Dīn Ayyūb in

639/1241-1242 and was completed in 647-648/1249-1251. The madrasa formed a complex with the sultan's tomb, built by the famous Shajar al-Durr.[23] In 641/1243-1244, professorships in jurisprudence for each of the four schools were endowed. This marked the first time all four madhhabs were maintained in a single institution. The waqfs of the madrasa were increased by Sultan Aybak in 648/1250-1251, and again by Sultan Berke Khān ibn Baybars, who established waqfs on the Goldsmith's Bazaar adjacent to the complex, on other sites in Cairo, on the town of Al-Maḥallat al-Kubrā in Gharbīya, the Jazā'ir of Jīza province, and Aṭfīḥ province.[24] The professorships in the Ṣāliḥīya madrasa were thus among the most lucrative in Cairo, as were the stipends available to their students. In 730/1329-1330 Amir Jamāl al-Dīn Aqūsh al-Ghazāwī, viceroy of al-Karak, endowed a post for a khaṭīb in the Shāfiʿī īwān (hall) at fifty dirhams per month. Subsequently, the position of imām and prayer caller were established.[25] Maqrīzī stated that these munificent waqfs survived the depressions and political upheavals at the turn of the fifteenth century and rendered Ṣāliḥīya among the wealthiest madrasas of his day. The Koran readers of this institution were attached directly to the tomb itself, and were supported from waqfs set up on the estate of Shajar al-Durr.[26]

The Ṣāliḥīya madrasa also functioned as the supreme judicial tribunal of the state. In its portico īwān, the four chief justices heard cases referred to them from the lower courts. Since their decisions could be questioned, if not dismissed, by the sultan alone, this madrasa was the final civilian appelate court of the empire. The grand qāḍīs were, of course, served by a host of notaries, scribes, and jurisconsults. Therefore, al-Ṣāliḥīya was much more than a center of worship and scholarship. As the most prominent seat of civil litigation in Cairo, it was a forum of state politics and intrigue. Sultans monitored its activities to assess political sentiments of the ʿulamaʾ. No legal student aspiring to a judgeship could hope to locate himself more suitably than here to learn both the law and statecraft at first hand.

Ẓāhirīya (23)

Sultan al-Ẓāhir Baybars al-Bunduqdārī founded this madrasa in 660/1262 and witnessed its completion in 662/1263.[27] A vast waqf was established to support it, drawn on many properties in Syria. Professorships in both Shāfiʿī and Ḥanafī jurisprudence, Prophetic traditions, and Koranic readings were set up. A Koran school for orphans was established next to the madrasa. Baybars also granted a waqf on the Sultan's quarter (rubʿ) between Bāb Zuwayla and Bāb al-Kharq.[28] By A.D. 1400 this madrasa was one of the most respected in Egypt, and was considered to offer the most comprehensive instruction in Shāfiʿī and Ḥanafī jurisprudence in Egypt.[29]

Manṣūrīya (22)

This madrasa and tomb were located inside the main gate to the Manṣūrī hospital. They were built by Sultan al-Malik al-Manṣūr Qalāʾūn in 683-684/1284-1285.[30] Professorships in the jurisprudence of the four madhhabs and in medicine were established in the madrasa. In the tomb (qubba), professorships in the four schools, Prophetic traditions, Koranic exegesis, and textual drills and recitation were established on the basis of a waqf set up by a grandson of Qalā'ūn. This waqf encompassed the taxes from an entire village district, Dahmashat al-Ḥammām in Sharqīya province, and yielded 4,000 gold dīnārs a year.[31] Sultan Qalā'ūn himself endowed a major collection of books in the tomb, most of which were sumptuously bound. Maqrīzī remarked that both scholars and students were struck with awe at the imposing atmosphere of the tomb. No other academic institution was considered to provide an equivalent setting for study and contemplation.

Al-Māristān al-Manṣūrī (28)

The major hospital of Cairo was founded by Sultan Qalā'ūn in 683/1284 and completed the following year.[32] The sultan wished to establish an institution unparalleled in the Muslim world, and endowed the hospital with waqfs yielding about one million dirhams a year to cover its operations.[33] The hospital occupied the area behind the Manṣūrīya madrasa and tomb, extending back to the next street. It was built on the cruciform plan, with four central īwāns and numerous adjoining chambers and halls. The īwāns were each provided with fountains to guarantee a ready supply of clean water for consumption, treatment, and sanitation. The staff included both physicians and pharmacists (ʿaqāqīr) to treat patients and administer medicines to them; a host of special servants (farrāshūn), male and female, waited on patients.[34] Teachers (muʿallimūn) were appointed to train these servants, although we have no details as to what sort of training they received. The īwāns were equipped to handle specific disorders: one each for fevers, eye diseases, surgery, and dysentery; there was a separate hall for women.[35] There was also an area reserved for rheumatics and anemics (mabrūdūn), divided into male and female quarters with separate facilities for preparation of food. There were kitchens and areas for storage of foods, herbs, and medicines, and a treasury for receipts. Living quarters for the staff, headed by the chief physician, were provided in the hospital. If one considers the role of the māristān as a home for convalescents and the aged in addition to the array of functions and facilities mentioned above, it is possible to surmise the complexity of the Manṣūrī hospital.[36]

Nāṣirīya (21)

This madrasa constituted part of the vast building program undertaken by Qalā'ūn's son, al-Nāṣir Muḥammad.[37] The madrasa was actually founded by Sultan al-ʿĀdil Katbughā, but completed by al-Nāṣir Muḥammad in 703/1303-1304. The building was considered one of the most impressive in the city because of its interior. Its gate had been transferred from the Roman Cathedral in Akka, lending an incongruous touch of European Gothic to the madrasa. Al-Nāṣir Muḥammad established several waqfs on the Qayṣarīya of Amir ʿAlī in the shurbūsh[38] merchants' street in the Duhaysha quarter, and on shops of the Bāb al-Zuhūma section—both in Cairo—and on a property outside Damascus. Al-

Nāṣir buried his son, Anūk, in the madrasa tomb, and endowed a waqf to support Koran teachers there. Professorships in jurisprudence of the four madhhabs were established, and an imām was appointed for the mosque. A large library was installed in the madrasa. Maqrīzī noted that a special guard of eunuchs was posted in the foyer to prevent strangers from gaining access to the inner īwāns.[39] Every month students, readers, and faculty received an allotment of sugar, and every year the meat from the Sacrifice Festival was divided among them. Maqrīzī considered al-Nāṣirīya among the most significant madrasas of the city.

Barqūqīya (20)

This madrasa is the only institution of the Bayn al-Qaṣrayn cluster dating from the Circassian period. Sultan Barqūq founded it in 786/1384-1345, and established a khānqāh there as well.[40] Barqūq chose this site for his own pious contribution to Islamic society because he was keenly aware of the renown of the extant institutions along the Bayn al-Qaṣrayn. He was willing to acquire the site from descendants of Qalā'ūn at great expense in order to establish there the institution named for him. Since this madrasa played a role comparable to those of its sister schools, it is certain that Barqūq endowed it lavishly, and directed its scholars to form the curriculum based on jurisprudence in the four madhhabs and the related Islamic sciences. Barqūq took a personal interest in the construction of the madrasa, and visited it on occasion to view its progress and to attend prayer services in the completed sections.

The institutions discussed above formed the two major clusters discernible in the biographical sources. The other prominent institutions of the northeast and southeast districts did not have similar patterns. There were considerable differences between them in terms of relative wealth, reputation, numbers of students, and their backgrounds.

THE MOSQUE OF AL-ḤĀKIM AND THE BĀB AL-FUTŪḤ—BĀB AL-NAṢR AREA (3, 144, 146)

This immense structure is one of the most imposing monuments surviving from the Fāṭimid period.[41] Because of the controversial reign of its founder, the early history of the mosque has always been well known. Successive rulers continued to keep the mosque in good repair. After the earthquake of 702/1302-1303, much of the structure was rebuilt.[42] Sultan Baybars II al-Jāshankīr organized a madrasa based on waqfs drawn on properties in Jīza, Upper Egypt, and Alexandria.[43] The by-then standard policy of establishing a professorship in each of the four orthodox schools was followed here. Also, a professorship in Prophetic traditions was endowed. Maqrīzī noted that provisions were made to support a large number of students. The first appointee to the chair in Shāfiʿī jurisprudence was Badr al-Dīn Muḥammad ibn Jamāʿa, who became one of the most eminent lecturers in Cairo during the fourteenth century. A substantial library and school for orphans were founded, a host of Koran readers was appointed, and a large cistern fountain was built, drawing its water directly from the Nile. All told, Baybars invested about 40,000 dīnārs on the renovations and new endowments.[44] These endowments were maintained throughout the fourteenth and fifteenth centuries, and yet this institution cannot be said to have ranked with the great madrasas of the later Middle Ages in terms of students.

The north walls of this mosque belonged to the northern ramparts of the northeast rectangle, and separated the Victory and Succor Gates. The Victory Gate represented the terminus of the Main Avenue (Qaṣaba) (145), and led into the populous Ḥusaynīya suburb (142). The areas immediately north and south of it were important market centers. The Succor Gate led directly into the cemetery bearing its name. Many little zāwiyas were clustered about it, and one of the two funerary oratories of Cairo (4) was located here. The Succor Gate was considered a holy place imbued with baraka and spirits. Groups of pious ascetics tended to congregate in its vicinity.

AL-AZHAR AND ITS CHAPELS (34-37)

The foremost mosque of the Mamluk empire and one of the most illustrious of the Muslim world requires no general description.[45] During the Ayyūbid and Mamluk periods, successive sultans and amirs added façades, halls, chapels, and minarets to the original simple rectangular structure, until the present assemblage of different styles emerged. Maqrīzī tells us something about the quality of academic and spiritual life at al-Azhar while describing the disruptive actions of Amir Ṣūdūn al-Qāḍī, the grand chamberlain, who was appointed nāẓir in 818/1415.[46] This rapacious figure appeared on the scene at a time when the mosque had attained an extraordinary degree of wealth and influence. Maqrīzī stated that resident students, referred to as '"poor" or "indigent," alone totaled some 750 persons, drawn from Iran, Egypt, and the Maghrib. These students, organized into arwiqa or nations, enjoyed a level of popular support unequalled by their colleagues in other institutions of the city. The opportunity for plunder presented by charitable bounty accumulated over generations was not lost on Amir Ṣūdūn. He drove the students out of the compound and confiscated their possessions. Al-Azhar ceased temporarily to function as either a mosque or a madrasa. Ultimately, Amir Ṣūdūn, accompanied by a retinue of "servants, slaves, and riff-raff," set upon the remaining occupants of the mosque while they were at evening prayer, beating many and confiscating hoards of booty. Although the nāẓir was arrested some months later by the sultan and exiled to Damascus, his actions illustrate quite clearly that not even the most revered institution in Cairo was secure from Mamluk spoliation.

The biographical sources do not indicate that al-Azhar enjoyed scholastic primacy over comparable institutions. Rather, it seems to have combined a number of functions more varied than those of its contemporaries. In any case, al-Azhar never truly identified with either of the two collegiate clusters of the central city, and retained its own distinct character.

Two chapels, serving as collegiate hospices, were built into the Azhar complex.

The earliest of these was founded by Amir ʿAlāʾ al-Dīn Ṭaybars al-Khāzindārī in 709/1309-1310.[47] A Shāfiʿī professorship was established and a library assembled. Maqrīzī dwelled on the sumptuous furnishings of the chapel, particularly the carpets spread out for Friday prayer. The second chapel was commissioned by Amir ʿAlāʾ al-Dīn Aqbughā ʿAbd al-Wāḥid, an ustādār of Sultan al-Nāṣir Muḥammad. It was completed in 740/1339.[48] The institution was specifically reserved for Ṣūfīs and Koran readers, and a staff consisting of a shaykh, muʾadhdhin, imām, and servants was appointed. Aqbughā stipulated in his waqf endowment that the office of nāẓir go to the Shāfiʿī qāḍī of Cairo, and provided subsequently for the support of his own descendants. The waqf was established on shops in the "Below the Apartments" section (165) due west of the Bāb Zuwayla (167). Maqrīzī stated that these chapels were functioning in his own day and retained their separate identity.

ASHRAFĪYA (30)

The last two institutions considered here that were located in the Fāṭimid rectangle were both founded by Circassian sultans. Neither of them formed an element of a collegiate cluster; like al-Azhar they stood out as distinct institutions. What they lacked in age and in prestige of cumulative academic reputations they compensated for by wealth. Both institutions functioned as madrasas and as hospices for Ṣūfīs. The first was the work of Sultan al-Malik al-Ashraf Barsbāy, constructed between 826 and 827/1423-1424.[49] It was located immediately to the west of the Main Avenue, at the entrance to the Amber Dealers' bazaar.

Although Maqrīzī provided no information on the endowment program established to support the madrasa, the sultan's waqf testament gives the specific details. A scholar from each of the four madhhabs who specialized in Prophetic traditions and jurisprudence was to be maintained at the compensation of 3,000 specie dirhams per month (the equivalent of fifty silver dirhams) and six loaves of wheat bread per day. These four professors were to teach their disciplines according to a prescribed curriculum, with the books specified. The extent to which the sultan himself selected the works is uncertain. It is likely that he merely approved the decisions made by influential scholars he respected, who supervised the drawing up of the waqf testament. The number of students in all four madhhabs was not to exceed sixty-five at any one time. Sultan Barsbāy displayed the preference of his caste for the Ḥanafī affiliation by providing five Ḥanafī students with 1,500 specie dirhams per month and twenty students in the three other madhhabs with the same amount, to a total of 7,000 dirhams. Each student was to receive three loaves of bread per day. Two nāẓirs were appointed to administer the madrasa, one in charge of registration and student attendance, and the other of the budget. Each was to receive 100 dirhams per month and three loaves of bread per day. Positions for two librarians and one calligrapher were established, each to be compensated at 300 dirhams per month and three loaves per day. The relative salaries for these offices are noteworthy.

The two controllers were paid much less than any of the resident scholars, suggesting their lower rank and possible lack of formal education. Thus they might well have been prone to manipulating budgets and charging students special "fees" in order to narrow the gap between their salaries and those of the faculty.

An elementary school for thirty orphans was established for the purpose of their instruction in writing, recitation, Koran, and calligraphy. The orphans were to receive collectively 2,000 dirhams per month and ninety loaves a day. Individually, they were to receive two sets of clothing per year, one for winter and one for summer. The orphans were placed under the care of a teacher (mu'addib) who was paid 300 dirhams per month and the predictable three loaves a day. The level of his salary would indicate that he was a recognized faculty member of the madrasa.

Sultan Barsbāy maintained an active interest in the construction of his madrasa, and attended Friday prayer services even when the structure was only partially finished. He also buried his wife in the madrasa prior to its completion.[50] In general, the biographical sources indicated that this madrasa remained a major scholastic institution throughout the fifteenth century. Its faculty chairs offered attractive benefits to recognized scholars.

MU'AYYADĪYA (51)

The second of these institutions was founded by Sultan al-Mu'ayyad Shaykh in 819/1416.[51] It was located immediately north of the Bāb Zuwayla (167) on the west side of the Main Avenue, and occupied the sites of a former caravansaray and prison. The structure included the mosque-madrasa and the tomb of the sultan and his family.[52] Sultan al-Mu'ayyad spent 40,000 dīnārs on its construction. He inaugurated the core of a library by transferring a large collection of books from the Citadel to the madrasa. He had appointed his close associate and secretary of the chancellery, Qāḍī Nāṣir al-Dīn Muḥammad ibn al-Bārizī, khaṭīb and librarian of the madrasa, and the latter presented some five hundred volumes to the collection at a cost of 1,000 dīnārs.[53] Ibn al-Bārizī had personal reasons for investing in the library, since the two posts to which he was appointed were reserved for his descendants. Al-Mu'ayyad Shaykh was eager to seek out the most eminent scholars of the day to fill professorial chairs in his madrasa, and he succeeded in engaging the most famous specialist in Koranic exegesis in Egypt, Ibn Ḥajar al-ʿAsqalānī, who accepted the post of lecturer in Shāfiʿī jurisprudence. Chairs in the other three schools were occupied by men of similar fame.[54] A chair in Prophetic traditions was also established. A rector or shaykh of mystic principles to head the Ṣūfī community of the madrasa and an imām to lead public prayer were appointed, thus completing the basic staff. Throughout the remaining years of his life, al-Mu'ayyad Shaykh maintained a keen interest in his madrasa, attending services and lectures, and interring members of his family there. Due to his lavish endowments, the madrasa became one of the prominent academic institutions of the fifteenth century.

INSTITUTIONS OF THE SOUTHEAST SECTION

With a few exceptions, the religio-academic institutions of the zones between the northeast rectangle and the Citadel represented the efforts and aspirations of Mamluk sultans and amirs. Only the mosques of Ibn Ṭūlūn in the Qaṭāʾiʿ area and al-Ṣāliḥ Ṭalāʾiʿ (52) below the Zuwayla Gate were founded before the fourteenth century. The imprint of the expectations of the Mamluk elite may be detected intermittently throughout the scattered references in the sources to the institutions they founded.

Shaykhūnīya (83-84)

The most prominent of the institutions established in the southeast was the madrasa and khānqāh complex founded by Grand Amir Sayf al-Dīn Shaykhū al-Naṣīrī, ra's al-nawba, in 756/1355.[55] It was located on the Cross Street (173) between the Ṭūlūnid mosque and the Citadel Square. The complex, bisected by the street, occupied more than a feddan of properties purchased from merchants and householders of the Qaṭāʾiʿ district. Maqrīzī considered the complex to be one of the most important centers of learning in Egypt. Amir Shaykhū established professorships in the four madhhabs, Prophetic traditions, and Koranic readings. He placed control of the critical office of nāẓir al-awqāf for the khānqāh in the hands of its shaykh and rector, apparently aware that a member of his own caste would be certain to exploit the office to the detriment of the order.[56] Maqrīzī mentioned that positions for twenty Ṣūfīs were endowed in the madrasa, but did not provide a figure for the much larger khānqāh itself.[57] However, he stated that the waqfs set up to support both the madrasa and khānqāh were so vast as to cause widespread comment and to attract scholars and mystics from all over Egypt and the Muslim world. The institution retained its great wealth until the famine year of 806/1403-1404. Its holdings would have been enough to weather the crisis, but Sultan Faraj confiscated some of the waqfs, thus inaugurating a period of gradual decline throughout the fifteenth century. During its prosperous years, both staff and students enjoyed a high standard of living, virtually identical to the level provided by Saʿīd al-Suʿadāʾ, which Amir Shaykhū wished to emulate.

INSTITUTIONS OF THE CITADEL SQUARE AREA

The Maydān al-Rumayla or Citadel Square (171) was the focus of royal ceremonial activity in the capital. It was also the terminus of many important streets. To the immediate south, the Cemetery Gate (176) led into the vast Qarāfa mortuary zone (177) with its specialized population. The second funerary oratory of Cairo, al-Mu'minī (75), was located at the Qarāfa Gate. The entire square was surrounded with monuments, and the Chain Gate (Bāb al-Silsila) (133) on the east side of the square constituted the formal entrance to the imperial court. The largest of the royal mosques in Egypt was founded on the west side of the square by Sultan Ḥasan in 757/1356 (74).[58] The building has never ceased to inspire awe in those who view it, despite the vicissitudes it has experienced. Yet it did not play a significant role in the academic system during the fifteenth century.

Maqrīzī noted that the sultan spent 20,000 dirhams a day on its construction, which lasted three years. The total amounted to 1,000 mithqāls of gold. As a result of the collapse of its northern minaret in 762/1360-1361, 300 persons died. Many of these were orphans maintained in the mosque elementary school. This would suggest the large number of persons maintained in the institution. Sultan Ḥasan established waqfs in several cities both in Egypt and Syria, and confiscated the estates of many amirs to support the mosque. Yet this was not reflected in biographical references to academic activity during the fifteenth century. Quite possibly, the political embroilments of the later fourteenth century that engulfed the structure discouraged scholars from teaching there.

There were other madrasas around the square, but the only one meriting comment was built in the Citadel itself (68) by Sultan al-Nāṣir Muḥammad ibn Qalā'ūn in 718/1318.[59] It served as the mosque of the sultan and his family, and subsequently of the long line of Ottoman pasha governors and autonomous Shuyūkh al-Balad until Muḥammad ʿAlī erected his Byzantine edifice. Maqrīzī did not provide details about its staff or endowment, but a number of individuals in the biographical sources resided there. The mosque is important because members of the royal family received their educations in it. The office of khaṭīb in this royal mosque was reserved for the Shāfiʿī grand qāḍī, the civilian chief justice of Egypt.

THE AMIRATE MADRASAS

These institutions, which set the standard for the southeast sections of Cairo, shared several characteristics. All were founded (from A.D. 1300 into the fifteenth century) by Mamluk amirs who lavished enormous sums on their construction, regardless of the state of the economy or vitality of the regime. These institutions may be said to represent an expression of anxiety on the part of the amirs who sought to enshrine an aspect or memory of themselves in something permanent, even if they used extorted money to do so. They realized how transient and ephemeral their own careers were. Actually, several of these madrasas are noteworthy expressions of late medieval architecture, due primarily to the vision of the architects who were not obliged to spare in their efforts. Since these institutions had so many characteristics in common, a description of one of the most prominent will serve to illuminate the group.[60]

Ṣarghatmishīya (92)

The most eminent representative of the amirate colleges was founded by Sayf al-Dīn Ṣarghatmish al-Nāṣirī, ra's al-nawba, in 757/1356,[61] who purchased the site to the immediate east of the Ṭūlūnid mosque. Amir Ṣarghatmish endowed his madrasa with several waqfs established on sites in Egypt and Syria in support of higher studies of the Koran, Prophetic traditions, and Ḥanafī jurisprudence.

One senior and three junior (nā'ib) professorships were established, and all those appointed to them were to have demonstrated their scholarly erudition in Ḥanafī studies. The madrasa was to accommodate sixty students, who were to devote themselves exclusively to research in works by Ḥanafī scholars. The senior professor was to present a lecture on Ḥadīth and one on jurisprudence each working day. Members of the junior staff each gave three courses or recitation sessions in basic principles of Ḥanafī jurisprudence every working day. An orphanage school accommodating forty children directed by a teacher (*mu'allim*) and an assistant (*'ārif*) was established as an annex to the madrasa. The pupils were taught the Koran, calligraphy, and arithmetics. The dedication of the madrasa was a major event, attended by the four grand qāḍīs and many luminaries among the 'ulama'. The biographical sources indicated that the madrasa maintained a distinguished faculty during the fifteenth century. The unusually high percentage of foreign-born scholars who studied there was due partially to its exclusive concern for interpreting works of the Ḥanafī madhhab to students.

THE ṬŪLŪNID MOSQUE (91)

Another institution requiring no general description, the mosque built by Aḥmad ibn Ṭūlūn[62] in the ninth century A.D. to provide his Turkish and Nubian troops with a place for worship had a varied history. It had on occasion been used as a storehouse and hospital. Sultan al-Nāṣir Muḥammad ibn Qalā'ūn restored it to active prayer service, and endowed it with waqfs drawn on estates confiscated from several rebellious amirs in support of professorships in jurisprudence, Koranic exegesis, Prophetic traditions, and medicine. Provisions were also made for the appointment of a khaṭīb, imām, farrāshūn, and prayer callers. A library and elementary Koran school for orphans were established.[63] By the early fourteenth century, therefore, the Ṭūlūnid mosque was functioning as a madrasa with a substantial endowment. During the fifteenth century, it had a lowered status in terms of staff and students, even though its fame from earlier centuries was clearly recalled by contemporary historians.

INSTITUTIONS OF THE QARĀFA AND ṢAḤRĀ' (128, 200, 203)

Since these two districts were mortuary zones, the institutions located there were always associated with tombs. Only the great saints whose memories were evoked by the construction of chapels and hospices, or amirs and sultans who wished to embellish their tombs with learned and pious men left institutions capable of attracting members of the 'ulama'. The major mortuary complexes, as indicated in the biographical sources, are described here.

The Tomb of Imām al-Shāfi'ī (115)

The earliest of these was constructed around the tomb of Imām al-Shāfi'ī by Sultan al-Malik al-Kāmil in 608/1211.[64] The tomb of al-Shāfi'ī was and remains today the holiest Muslim shrine in the metropolis of Cairo. During the fifteenth century it was regarded as a source of healing emanations, of baraka. Pilgrims flocked there from all over the Muslim world to recite prayers while circumambulating the sarcophagus of the great legal doctor. The sick and infirm congregated there either to be cured or to die at the holy site. There were chapels and small schools attached to the tomb, but the complex never assumed the role of a true collegiate madrasa. Indeed, no major college mosque functioned in the Qarāfa area.

THE MAMLUK TOMBS

In the Ṣaḥrā' or Desert Plain due east of the city, several great Mamluks of the fourteenth and fifteenth centuries built their mausoleums. Six of these are cited in the biographical sources: the Mausoleum of Amir Tankiz-Bughā (120), completed in 764/1362,[65] the Mausoleum of Amir Yūnus al-Nawrūzī al-Dawādār (122), completed in 783/1382,[66] the joint Mausoleum of Sultans Barqūq and Faraj (123), completed in 810/1407,[67] the Mausoleum of Sultan Barsbāy, completed in 835/1432,[68] the Mausoleum of Sultan Īnāl (125), completed in 859/1456,[69] and the Mausoleum of Sultan Qāytbāy (121), completed in 879/1474.[70] Although several of these institutions are in a semiruined state today, they were all built on a grand scale. The obsession of the Mamluks to surround their graves with pious individuals drove them to establish lavish waqfs in support of their mortuary hospices and madrasas. However, the biographical sources indicated that these institutions never achieved a primary or even secondary rank in the intellectual establishment. Their relatively isolated location appears to have been a factor behind this phenomenon.

THE OLD CAIRO AREA

Although Old Cairo (Miṣr) and the Nile shore districts maintained numerous religio-academic institutions, only two appeared frequently in the biographical sources. These were the mosque of ʿAmr ibn al-ʿĀṣ (113)[71] and the Hospice of the Prophet's Relics (Ribāṭ al-Āthār al-Nabawīya) (114).[72] Both institutions dated from the first century of Islamic rule in Egypt, and were continually restored. Maqrīzī's discussion of the mosque of ʿAmr did not include details on new waqfs or staff during the Mamluk period. The evidence suggests, however, that the mosque remained an active madrasa of secondary rank throughout the fifteenth century. It definitely received endowments. The Ribāṭ al-Āthār functioned primarily as a hospice for pilgrims. Sultan al-Ashraf Shaʿbān established a lectureship in Shāfiʿī jurisprudence there and endowed the post and places for students with a waqf that was still yielding revenue during Barqūq's reign. Since the hospice was located on the east bank of the Nile, it was protected by a dyke, the maintenance of which was expressly provided for in the waqf writ. Even so, the hospice was damaged during the floods of 806/1403-1404, and required repairs.

SIRYĀQŪS (130)

The khānqāh at Siryāqūs[73] some twelve miles north of Cairo represented yet another aspect of the building program inaugurated by Sultan al-Nāṣir Muḥammad. It provided cells for one hundred Ṣūfīs to live in seclusion suitable for meditation. The first khaṭīb of the khānqāh, Badr al-Dīn ibn Jamāʿa, was also appointed the specialist in Prophetic traditions, and personally witnessed the recitation of twenty traditions by the sultan's son, ʿAbd al-ʿAzīz. Ibn al-Jamāʿa became rector of the khānqāh and received the title of grand shaykh (shaykh al-shuyūkh), the only individual so honored other than the rectors of Saʿīd al-Suʿadāʾ and al-Azhar. During the next half century a market town grew up around the khānqāh, which was extremely active on Fridays, when persons came from all over the countryside to deal there. Maqrīzī stated that the scholars attracted to the khānqāh were among the most eminent in Egypt because they were so luxuriously maintained. Daily, each Ṣūfī received a raṭl of mutton precooked in broth and four raṭls of fine (*naqqī*) bread. Every month he received forty silver dirhams worth two dīnārs, a raṭl of confections, two raṭls of olive oil, and two raṭls of soap. Every year new clothing was distributed, and special gifts were provided during the annual festivals.[74] The khānqāh maintained a resident physician, surgeon, and oculist to deal with medical problems. Personal drinking and washing vessels were distributed to each Ṣūfī every Ramaḍān. Al-Nāṣir Muḥammad had built a bath into the complex, and in 790/1388 a separate bath for women was added. Therefore, until 806/1403 the institution was extremely prosperous, supported by the waqfs al-Nāṣir Muḥammad established. After this year of famine and confiscation, its revenues were diminished but never eliminated. The khānqāh at Siryāqūs remained the most important religio-academic institution outside the city proper during the later Middle Ages.

Appendix II. Positions Held by Individuals Engaged in the Twenty-One Occupations of the Major Group, and by Ṣūfīs and Copts

Figures appearing in these lists constitute the basis for Table 11. Totals appearing in the table are derived from the totals of occupational categories in these lists. Definitions of terms appear in Appendix III.

Asterisks indicate the positions on the list against which all others are compared.

LIST 1. OCCUPATIONAL POSITIONS HELD BY KĀTIBS

Category I

shādd	1
amīr mashwara	1
ustādār	7
kāshif	1
muqaddam	1
nā'ib	1
naqīb	2
TOTAL	14

Category II

ṣāḥib dīwān jaysh	1
kātib	82*
kātib ʿalīq	1
kātib dukkān	1
kātib dīwān	1
kātib dīwān jaysh	1
kātib mamālīk	1
kātib muwaqqiʿ dast	1
kātib sifāra	1
kātib sirr	9
kātib khizāna	1
mushrif ḥawāṣil	1
mubāshir	5
mubāshir aqrabā'	1
mubāshir dīwān	1
mubāshir dīwān jaysh	1
mubāshir awqāf	1
milk umarā'	2
mustawfī	2
mustawfī dīwān mufrad	2
mustawfī khāṣṣ	2
muwaqqiʿ	5
muwaqqiʿ dast	2
muwaqqʿ dīwān inshā'	1
nā'ib mustawfī dawla	1
nā'ib kātib sirr	1
nāẓir	5
nāẓir iṣṭabl	4
nāẓir bandar	2
nāẓir dawla	4
nāẓir mufrad	7
nāẓir jaysh	12
nāẓir kiswa	1
nāẓir awqāf	1
nāẓir khāṣṣ	7
muḥaṣṣil	1
wazīr	13
TOTAL	185

Category III

shāhid	7
sharūṭī	1
shaykh	1
muḥtasib	1
nā'ib shaykh	1
nā'ib ḥukm	1
nā'ib qāḍī	6
qāḍī	1
qāḍī mālikī	1
mutaḥaddith	1
wakīl bayt māl	1
TOTAL	22

Category IV	
ṣanā'iʿī khaṭṭ	1
ḥarīrī	1
kaḥḥāl	1
nāsikh	1
mudhahhib	1
khādim	6
TOTAL	11

Category V	
shāʿir	2
muʿallim	1
muʿīd	1
mudarris	3
mukattib	1
muqri' bukhārī	1
muqri' maṣḥaf	2
mutaṣaddir taktīb	1
khāzin kutub	1
TOTAL	13

Category VI	
imām	4
muqri'	2
khaṭīb	1
TOTAL	7

LIST 2. OCCUPATIONAL POSITIONS HELD BY KĀTIBS AL-SIRR

Category I

shādd	1
amīr ʿashara	1
amīr rakb	1
ustādār	14
dawādār	2
ḥājib	1
kāshif	1
kāshif wajh qiblī	1
muqaddam	1
murattib	1
mu'tamin mamlaka	1
nā'ib	4
rasūl firanj	1
TOTAL	30

Category II

ṣāḥib dīwān inshā'	1
kātib	9
kātib ʿalāma	1
kātib umarā'	1
kātib inshā'	2
kātib dīwān inshā'	3
kātib sifāra	1
kātib sirr	100*
mubāshir	2
mubāshir dīwān inshā'	1
milk umarā'	2
muwaqqiʿ	17
muwaqqiʿ dast	5
muwaqqiʿ dīwān inshā'	2
muwaqqiʿ ḥukm	1
nā'ib kātib sirr	9
nā'ib nāẓir jaysh	1
nāẓir	12
nāẓir dhakhīra	1
nāẓir aḥbās	2
nāẓir iṣṭabl	5
nāẓir aswāq	1
nāẓir bandar	2
nāẓir dār ḍarb	2
nāẓir dīwān inshā'	1
nāẓir dīwān mufrad	1
nāẓir dīwān musta'jir	1
nāẓir dīwān khāṣṣ	1
nāẓir ḥaramayn	1
nāẓir jawālī	2
nāẓir jaysh	33
nāẓir kiswa	1
nāẓir mufrad	1
nāẓir maẓālim	1
nāẓir tawqīʿ	1
nāẓir awqāf	1
nāẓir khāṣṣ	8
wazīr	9
TOTAL	245

Category III

shāhid	1
shaykh	7
shaykh muwaqqiʿīn	1
shaykh khuddām	1
muftī dār ʿadl	1
muḥtasib	8
nā'ib shaykh	1
nā'ib ḥukm	1
nā'ib qāḍī	11
naqīb ashrāf	5
qāḍī	22
qāḍī shāfiʿī	5
qāḍī ḥanafī	5
qāḍī mālikī	7
qāḍī quḍāt	1
wakīl bayt māl	4
TOTAL	81

Category IV

ṭabīb	1
ra'īs ṭabīb	2
khaṭṭāṭ	1
khādim	6
khādim barīd	1
TOTAL	11

Category V

shā'ir	9
mu'īd	2
mudarris	11
mudarris fiqh	2
mudarris ḥadīth	1
mutaṣaddir	1
mutaṣaddir iqrā'	1
khāzin kutub	1
TOTAL	28

Category VI

imām	1
muqri'	1
khaṭīb	5
khalāwī	1
TOTAL	8

LIST 3. OCCUPATIONAL POSITIONS HELD BY MUBĀSHIRS

Category I

bardadār	1
murattib jawālī	1
wakīl	1
TOTAL	3

Category II

shāhid dīwān mufrad	1
shāhid awqāf	1
ṣayrafī	1
kātib	4
kātib ghayba	1
kātib sirr	1
mushrif	1
mubāshir	59*
mubāshir ḥammām	1
mubāshir dhakhīra	1
mubāshir mufrad	1
mubāshir ḥukm	1
mubāshir awqāf	3
muqassim	1
mustawfī	1
mustawfī mufrad	1
mutaṣarrif	1
mutakallim	5
mutakallim awqāf	1
muwaqqiʿ	3
muwaqqiʿ dast	1
nā'ib nāẓir awqāf	1
nāẓir	9
nāẓir iṣṭabl	1
nāẓir jaysh	1
nāẓir kiswa	2
nāẓir mufrad	1
nāẓir mukūs	1
nāẓir awqāf	2
nāẓir khāṣṣ	1
wazīr	2
TOTAL	111

Category III

ʿaqīd	1
shāhid	8
sharūṭī	1
shaykh	8
shaykh ṣūfī	1
amīn ḥukm	1
faqīh	1
muftī dār ʿadl	1
muḥtasib	3
nā'ib muḥtasib	1
nā'ib qāḍī	8
naqīb ashrāf	1
qāḍī	3
qāḍī ḥanbalī	1
qāḍī ḥanafī	1
qāḍī mālikī	1
wakīl bayt māl	2
wakīl kiswa	1
TOTAL	44

Category IV

bazzāz	1
tājir	2
tājir sukkar	1
ṭashshāt	1
khādim	6
TOTAL	11

Category V

shaykh taṣawwuf	1
ismāʿ	1
muʿallim	1
muʿīd	4
mudarris	10
mudarris shāfiʿī	1
mudarris fiqh	6
mudarris ḥadīth	3
mudarris taṣawwuf	1
muqriʾ aṭfāl	2
muqriʾ aytām	1
nāʾib mudarris	1
khāzin kutub	1
TOTAL	33

Category VI

imām	3
muʿtaqad	1
muqriʾ	4
muqriʾ ṭibāq	2
muqriʾ jawq	1
nāʾib imām	1
khaṭīb	13
TOTAL	25

LIST 4. OCCUPATIONAL POSITIONS HELD BY MUWAQQIʿS

Category I

ustādār	4
dawādār	2
nā'ib	2
nā'ib nuwwāb	1
naqīb	6
TOTAL	15

Category II

shāhid kiswa	1
shāhid awqāf	3
kātib	4
kātib inshā'	2
kātib dast	1
kātib dīwān jaysh	1
kātib mawākib turk	1
kātib sirr	17
kātib awqāf	1
kātib khizāna	1
mubāshir	3
mubāshir dīwān inshā'	1
mubāshir awqāf	2
mustawfī	2
mutakallim awqāf	1
muwaqqiʿ	116*
muwaqqiʿ inshā'	3
muwaqqiʿ darj	1
muwaqqiʿ dast	8
muwaqqiʿ ḥukm	1
muwaqqiʿ mufrad	1
nā'ib kātib sirr	4
nāẓir	9
nāẓir ashrāf	1
nāẓir aḥbās	3
nāẓir dār ḍarb	1
nāẓir dawla	2
nāẓir dīwān inshā'	2
nāẓir dīwān khuddām	1
nāẓir jawālī	3
nāẓir jaysh	3
nāẓir kiswa	1
nāẓir mufrad	2
nāẓir masjid	1
nāẓir mawārīth	2
nāẓir tawqīʿ	1
nāẓir awqāf	7
nāẓir khāṣṣ	3
wazīr	6
TOTAL	223

Category III

ʿaqīd	2
shāhid	23
sharūṭī	3
shaykh	2
amīn ḥukm	2
muftī	2
muftī dār ʿadl	1
muḥtasib	5
nā'ib ḥukm	9
nā'ib qāḍī	27
qāḍī	11
qāḍī shāfiʿī	1
qāḍī kabīr	1
qāḍī maḥmal	3
qāḍī quḍāt	1
qāḍī rakb	2
wakīl bayt māl	2
TOTAL	97

Category IV

ḥā'ik	1
ḥarīrī	1
nāsikh	4
tājir	2
khādim	2
TOTAL	10

Category V

shāʿir	7
shaykh taṣawwuf	2
adīb	1
muʿīd	2
mudarris	11
mudarris shāfiʿī	1
mudarris fiqh	2
mudarris ḥadīth	1
mudarris tafsīr	1
muḥaddith	2
mukattib	2
muqri' ḥadīth	2
mu'addib	1
mu'addib aṭfāl	1
mu'arrikh	1
mutaṣaddir	2
muwaththiq	1
khāzin kutub	1
TOTAL	41

Category VI

imām	9
muqri' jawq	2
nā'ib khaṭīb	2
wāʿiẓ	1
khaṭīb	9
TOTAL	23

LIST 5. OCCUPATIONAL POSITIONS HELD BY NĀẒIRS

Category I

shādd	5
amīr ʿishrīn	1
amīr ʿashara	3
amīr ṭabalkhāna	2
amīr ḥajj	1
amīr mashwara	1
amīr maḥmal	1
amīr khamsa	1
ustādār	3
ustādār dhakhīra	1
ustādār amlāk	1
ustādār khāṣṣ	1
atābek	2
dawādār	1
ḥājib	3
jundī	1
kāshif	1
lālā	1
mudabbir mamlaka	1
muqaddim	4
murattib	1
murattib jawālī	1
nā'ib	15
ra'īs nawba	1
sāqī	1
wakīl	2
wālī	1
khāṣṣakī	3
khāzindār	2
TOTAL	62

Category II

shāhid awqāf	2
ṣāḥib	1
muḥaṣṣil	1
kātib	4
kātib mamālīk	1
kātib sirr	9
kātib khizāna	1
mubāshir	7
mubāshir ḥammām	1
mubāshir aqribā'	1
mubāshir dīwān	1
mubāshir awqāf	2
muqassim	1
mustawfī	3
mutaṣarrif	2
mutaṣarrif ṣadaqāt rūmīya	1
mutakallim	5
mutakallim ʿamā'ir	1
muwaqqiʿ	7
muwaqqiʿ dast	2
nā'ib mustawfī dawla	1
nā'ib mutakallim	1
nā'ib nāẓir	2
nā'ib nāẓir jaysh	1
nā'ib nāẓir awqāf	2
nāẓir	169*
nāẓir ʿimāra	2
nāẓir aḥbās	7
nāẓir iṣṭabl	4
nāẓir awṣiyā'	1
nāẓir buyūt	1
nāẓir ṣadaqāt	1
nāẓir dār ḍarb	5
nāẓir dawla	2
nāẓir dīwān ashrāf	1
nāẓir dīwān mufrad	1
nāẓir dīwān khuddām	1
nāẓir ḥaramayn	1
nāẓir jawālī	6
nāẓir jaysh	15
nāẓir kiswa	7
nāẓir masjid	1
nāẓir matjar	1
nāẓir mawārīth	2
nāẓir awqāf	21
nāẓir awqāf ashrāf	1
nāẓir awqāf jārīya	1
nāẓir khāṣṣ	6
nāẓir khizāna	1
wazīr	4
TOTAL	322

Category III

shāhid	12
shaykh	38
shaykh ṣūfī	7
shaykh khuddām	1
amīn ḥukm	3
faqīh	5
muftī	5
muftī dār ʿadl	4
muḥtasib	12
nā'ib ʿaqīd	1
nā'ib shaykh	2
nā'ib ḥukm	6
nā'ib qāḍī	31
naqīb ashrāf	2
qāḍī	30
qāḍī ʿaskar	6
qāḍī shāfiʿī	8
qāḍī ḥanafī	7
qāḍī quḍāt	2
rasūl	3
wakīl bayt māl	10
wakīl kiswa	1
TOTAL	196

Category IV

ʿāmil sarāsīj	1
ʿāmil maqāṣṣ	1
bayyāʿ shirāʾ	1
bayyāʿ marathīyāt	1
ghassāl lazuward	1
ḥalwāʾī	1
nāsikh	3
naḥḥās	2
qaṣṣab sukkar	1
mudhahhib	1
tājir	7
khaṭṭāṭ	1
khādim	16
khādim dawāwīn	1
khawājā	1
zarrāʿ	1
TOTAL	40

Category V

shāʿir	7
shaykh taṣawwuf	6
ishtighāl	1
ismāʿ	2
muʿallim aṭfāl	1
muʿīd	12
mudarris	73
mudarris shāfiʿī	5
mudarris fiqh	32
mudarris ḥadīth	11
mudarris ḥanafī	1
mudarris kashshāf	1
mudarris mīʿād	3
mudarris qirāʾāt	2
mudarris taṣawwuf	1
mudarris tafsīr	10
muḥaddith	5
muqriʾ bukhārī	1
muqriʾ ṣaffa	1
muqriʾ ḥadīth	4
muqriʾ maṣḥaf	1
muʾarrikh	1
nāʾib mudarris	2
nāʾib mudarris fiqh	1
nāʾib mudarris ḥadīth	2
mutaṣaddir	4
mutaṣaddir ḥadīth	1
khāzin kutub	2
TOTAL	193

Category VI

imām	17
muqriʾ	7
muqriʾ ḥidāya	1
muqriʾ jawq	2
muqriʾ khuṭbat ʿīd	1
muʾadhdhin	1
mīqātī	1
nāʾib khaṭīb	3
wāʿiẓ	1
khaṭīb	24
TOTAL	59

LIST 6. OCCUPATIONAL POSITIONS HELD BY NĀẒIRS AWQĀF

Category I

shādd	1
amīr ʿashara	1
kāshif kanā'is	1
muqaddam	1
murattib	1
nā'ib	1
naqīb	1
khalīfa	1
TOTAL	8

Category II

shāhid ʿimāra	1
shāhid awqāf	1
kātib	1
kātib ʿalīq	1
kātib umarā'	1
kātib dīwān	1
kātib sirr	1
mubāshir	2
mubāshir awqāf	1
mustawfī khāṣṣ	1
muwaqqiʿ	6
muwaqqiʿ darj	1
muwaqqiʿ dast	2
muwaqqiʿ dast dīwān Inshā'	1
nā'ib kātib sirr	1
nā'ib nāẓir	1
nā'ib nāẓir awqāf	1
nāẓir	27
nāẓir ʿimāra	2
nāẓir aḥbās	7
nāẓir iṣṭabl	4
nāẓir buyūt	1
nāẓir ṣadaqāt	1
nāẓir dār ḍarb	1
nāẓir dawla	2
nāẓir dīwān	1
nāẓir dīwān mufrad	2
nāẓir jawālī	1
nāẓir jaysh	1
nāẓir kiswa	6
nāẓir masjid	1
nāẓir awqāf	52*
nāẓir khāṣṣ	2
TOTAL	135

Category III

shāhid	7
shaykh	6
shaykh ṣūfī	2
amīn ḥukm	3
muftī	3
muftī dār ʿadl	2
muḥtasib	8
nā'ib ḥukm	4
qāḍī	10
nā'ib qāḍī	10
qāḍī ʿaskar	3
qāḍī shāfiʿī	6
qāḍī ḥanafī	2
qāḍī mālikī	1
qāḍī quḍāt	3
rasūl	2
wakīl bayt māl	7
TOTAL	79

Category IV

tājir	2
khādim	6
khādim jawālī	1
zarrāʿ	1
TOTAL	10

Category V

shāʿir	1
shaykh taṣawwuf	1
ismāʿ	1
muʿallim aṭfāl	1
muʿīd	3
mudarris	18
mudarris shāfiʿī	3
mudarris āthār	1
mudarris fiqh	14
mudarris ḥadīth	9
mudarris tafsīr	5
muḥaddith	4
muqri' ṣaffa	1
mu'arrikh	2
na'ib mudarris fiqh	1
na'ib mudarris tafsīr	1
mutaṣaddir	2
mutaṣaddir ḥadīth	1
mutaṣaddir qirā'āt	2
khāzin kutub	1
TOTAL	72

Category VI

imām	5
muqri'	2
mu'adhdhin	1
nā'ib khaṭīb	1
khaṭīb	8
TOTAL	17

LIST 7. OCCUPATIONAL POSITIONS HELD BY SHAYKHS

Category I

amīr ʿashara	1
amīr shikār	1
dawādār	1
ḥājib	1
murattib	2
murattib dhakhīra	1
murattib maṭlūb	1
murattib ṣadaqa	1
murattib jawālī	2
murattib taṣawwufāt	1
nā'ib	2
nā'ib nuwwāb	1
rasūl firanj	1
rasūl mulūk atrāk	1
khāzindār	1
TOTAL	19

Category II

shāhid dīwān jawālī	1
shāhid kiswa	1
shāhid makhbaz	1
shāhid awqāf	3
ṣāḥib	1
kātib	1
kātib ʿalāma	1
kātib sirr	8
mubāshir	5
mubāshir awqāf	1
musta'jir awqāf	1
mutakallim	4
mutakallim awqāf	1
muwaqqiʿ	3
muwaqqiʿ dast	1
muwaqqiʿ dīwān inshā'	1
nā'ib nāẓir	2
nāẓir	40
nāẓir aḥbās	2
nāẓir buyūt	1
nāẓir dār ḍarb	1
nāẓir ḥaramayn	1
nāẓir jawālī	2
nāẓir jaysh	10
nāẓir kiswa	5
nāẓir mawārīth	1
nāẓir maẓālim	1
nāẓir awqāf	5
nāẓir awqāf jārīya	1
TOTAL	106

Category III

ʿaqīd ankiḥa	1
shāhid	18
shaykh	322*
shaykh shuyūkh	2
shaykh shāfiʿī	1
shaykh islām	1
shaykh ṣūfī	9
shaykh ḥanafī	1
amīn ḥukm	1
faqīh	10
faqīh aytām	1
muftī	9
muftī dār ʿadl	8
muḥtasib	19
nā'ib shaykh	4
nā'ib ḥukm	12
nā'ib muḥtasib	1
nā'ib qāḍī	44
qāḍī	34
qāḍī ʿaskar	7
qāḍī shāfiʿī	13
qāḍī ḥanafī	16
qāḍī mālikī	3
qāḍī maḥmal	1
qāḍī quḍāt	3
qāḍī rakb	1
mulaqqin	1
wakīl bayt māl	4
TOTAL	547

Category IV

ʿāmil maqāṣṣ	1
ʿāmil mirwāḥ	1
bayyāʿ ʿibar	1
bayyāʿ simsim	1
bayyāʿ waraq	1
bayyāʿ khayṭ	1
ṣanāʾiʿī ḥarīr	1
farrāsh	1
ghannām	1
ḥallāq	1
ḥabbāk	1
kutubī	1
nāsikh	3
naqqāsh	1
tājir	12
tājir burr	1
mukaffit	1
khādim	8
khādim barīd	1
khayyāṭ	2
zarrāʿ	1
TOTAL	42

Category V

shaṭranjī	1
shāʿir	10
shaykh fiqh	1
shaykh taṣawwuf	8
shaykh tadrīs	1
ishtighāl	1
ismāʿ	4
ismāʿ ḥadīth	2
muʿīd	14
muʿīd ḥanafī	2
mudarris	111
mudarris shāfiʿī	5
mudarris dār ḥadīth	1
mudarris fiqh	57
mudarris farāʾiḍ	2
mudarris ḥadīth	26
mudarris ḥanafī	3
mudarris kashshāf	1
mudarris mālikī	1
mudarris mīʿād	1
mudarris qirāʾāt	1
mudarris taṣawwuf	2
mudarris tafsīr	13
mudarris taqsīm	1
muḥaddith	8
mukattib	1
muqriʾ aṭfāl	4
muqriʾ ṣaffa	1
muqriʾ ṣaḥīḥ	1
muqriʾ farāʾiḍ	1
muqriʾ ḥadīth	2
muqriʾ mamālīk	1
mūsīqī	1
muʾaddib aṭfāl	2
nāʾib shaykh taṣawwuf	1
nāʾib mudarris	2
nāʾib mudarris ḥadīth	2
naḥwī	3
mutaṣaddir	7
mutaṣaddir amlāʾ	1
mutaṣaddir iqrāʾ	1
mutaṣaddir qirāʾāt	1
khāzin kutub	7
TOTAL	316

Category VI

Imām	27
Imām ribāṭ	1
āthārī	1
muʿtaqad	9
muqriʾ	16
muqriʾ ḥidāya	1
muʾadhdhin	3
mīqātī	1
nāʾib imām	2
nāʾib khaṭīb	2
wāʿiẓ	2
khaṭīb	30
khalāwī	1
TOTAL	96

LIST 8. OCCUPATIONAL POSITIONS HELD BY MUḤTASIBS

Category I

shādd	3
shādd ʿamāʾir sulṭān	1
amīr ʿashara	1
amīr ṭabalkhāna	1
amīr akhūr	1
amīr rakb	1
ustādār	8
ustādār dhakhīra	1
ustādār amlāk	1
ustādār ṣuḥba	2
ustādār khāṣṣ	1
dawādār	2
ḥājib	5
kāshif	1
mihmandār	1
nāʾib	1
naqīb	2
naqīb jaysh	2
sāqī	1
wālī	2
wakīl iṣṭabl	1
khāṣṣakī	4
TOTAL	43

Category II

shāhid awqāf	1
kātib	1
kātib sirr	8
mubāshir	5
mubāshir ʿimāra	1
mubāshir ḥukm	1
mubāshir awqāf	1
mutaṣarrif	1
mutakallim	3
muwaqqiʿ	4
muwaqqiʿ dīwān inshāʾ	1
muwaqqiʿ ḥukm	1
nāʾib kātib sirr	1
nāʾib nāẓir	1
nāẓir	11
nāẓir aḥbās	8
nāẓir aswāq	1
nāẓir buyūt	1
nāẓir dār ḍarb	2
nāẓir dīwān mufrad	1
nāẓir jawālī	2
nāẓir jaysh	8
nāẓir kiswa	7
nāẓir matjar	1
nāẓir mawārīth	1
nāẓir awqāf	1
nāẓir awqāf ʿāma	1
nāẓir khāṣṣ	9
wazīr	9
TOTAL	97

Category III

shāhid	6
shurṭa	1
shaykh	12
shaykh khuddām	1
amīn ḥukm	2
muftī dār ʿadl	1
muḥtasib	105*
nāʾib shaykh	1
nāʾib ḥukm	5
nāʾib qāḍī	9
naqīb ḥukm	1
qāḍī	13
qāḍī ʿaskar	3
qāḍī ḥanafī	5
qāḍī mālikī	1
rasūl	2
wakīl bayt māl	8
TOTAL	176

Category IV

ballān	1
kutubī	1
ʿāmil	1
sukkarī	1
tājir	4
khaṭṭāṭ	1
khādim	10
TOTAL	19

Category V

shāʿir	4
ismāʿ	1
muʿallim	1
mudarris	5
mudarris fiqh	6
mudarris ḥadīth	2
mudarris tafsīr	2
muḥaddith	1
mukattib	1
minhājī	1
muqriʾ ṣaffa	1
muʾaddib	1
muʾarrikh	4
TOTAL	30

Category VI

imām	5
muqriʾ	2
muqriʾ jawq	2
khaṭīb	5
TOTAL	14

LIST 9. OCCUPATIONAL POSITIONS HELD BY SHĀHIDS

Category I

amīr ʿishrīn	1
amīr ʿashara	1
amīr rakb	1
ustādār	3
dawādār	2
kāshif kanāʾis	1
murattib	2
murattib jawālī	1
nāʾib	6
naqīb	14
rasūl sulṭānī	1
safīr	1
wakīl	1
khāzin	2
TOTAL	37

Category II

shāhid ʿamāʾir awqāf	1
shāhid dīwān	1
shāhid kiswa	1
shāhid maḥmal	1
shāhid awqāf	3
shāhid khāṣṣ	2
ibṭāl awqāf	1
amr nafaqa	1
ṣayrafī	1
kātib	6
kātib amlāʾ	1
kātib inshāʾ	1
kātib ghayba	1
kātib qiṣaṣ	1
kātib sirr	1
mubāshir	9
mubāshir ʿimāra	1
mubāshir dīwān	4
mubāshir dīwān mamālīk	1
mubāshir taṣawwuf	1
mubāshir awqāf	4
mudīr	2
mustawfī	2
mutakallim	2
mutakallim ʿamāʾir	1
mutakallim awqāf	2
muwaqqiʿ	25
muwaqqiʿ umarāʾ	1
muwaqqiʿ inshāʾ	2
muwaqqiʿ darj	2
muwaqqiʿ dast	3
muwaqqiʿ dīwān	1
muwaqqiʿ dīwān inshāʾ	1
muwaqqiʿ ḥasharīya	1
muwaqqiʿ ḥukm	1
muwaqqiʿ mawārīth	1
muwaththiq	1
nāʾib nāẓir	2
nāʾib nāẓir bayt māl	1
nāʾib nāẓir ṣunduq	1
nāʾib nāẓir awqāf ḥanafīya	1
nāẓir	13
nāẓir iṣṭabl	1
nāẓir dīwān khuddān	1
nāẓir jawālī	4
nāẓir jaysh	1
nāẓir amlāk	1
nāẓir maqām	1
nāẓir mawārīth	1
nāẓir ḥasharīya	1
nāẓir awqāf	6
nāẓir khaṣṣ	4
muḥaṣṣil	1
wazīr	2
TOTAL	133

Category III

ʿādil	2
ʿādil majlis mālikī	1
ʿaqīd	7
ʿaqīd ankiḥa	2
shāhid	424*
shāhid jūra	3
sharūṭī	2
shaykh	19
shaykh ṣūfī	3
amīn ḥukm	5
faqīh	1
muftī	1
muḥtasib	5
nāʾib ʿaqīd	4
nāʾib ʿaqīd ankiḥa	1
nāʾib shaykh	2
nāʾib ḥukm	5
nāʾib ḥanafī	1
nāʾib jūra	1
nāʾib muḥtasib	3
nāʾib qāḍī	89
qāḍī	31
qāḍī ʿaskar	1
qāḍī shāfiʿī	3
qāḍī ḥanafī	1
qāḍī maḥmāl	4
qāḍī quḍāt	1
qāḍī rakb	3
wakīl bayt māl	2
wakīl kiswa	1
TOTAL	628

Category IV

ʿaṭṭār	1
ʿāmil mawāʿīd	1
ṭabbākh	1
ṭabīb	3
bayyāʿ quṭn	1
bazzāz	2
ṣanāʾiʿī khaṭṭ	1
ḥarīrī	3
kutubī	1
ʿāmil	2
mawardī	1
ghassāl	1
mujaddid	1
nāsikh	27
qazzāz	1
sukkarī	1
tājir	15
tājir shurb	1
tājir biṭāna	1
tājir baḥr	1
tājir burr	1
tājir ḥānūt	1
mujallid	1
warrāq	1
khashshāb	1
khādim	12
kharrāz	1
khayyāṭ	1
zarrāʿ	1
TOTAL	86

Category V

shāʿir	18
shaykh taṣawwuf	3
shaykh sabʿa	1
ismāʿ	1
muʿallim	1
muʿallim aṭfāl	2
muʿīd	8
mudarris	45
mudarris shāfiʿī	4
mudarris iqrāʾ	1
mudarris āthār	1
mudarris fiqh	17
mudarris ḥadīth	8
mudarris ḥanafī	2
mudarris kitāba	1
mudarris qirāʾāt	1
mudarris taṣawwuf	2
muḥaddith	4
minhājī	2
muqriʾ aṭfāl	8
muqriʾ ṣaffa	1
muqriʾ ḥadīth	9
muqriʾ mamālīk	1
muʾaddib aṭfāl	4
muʾarrikh	1
nāʾib khāzin kutub	1
nāẓim	2
naḥwī	1
mutaṣaddir	2
mutaṣaddir qirāʾāt	1
khāzin kutub	4
TOTAL	157

Category VI

imām	38
imām qaṣr	1
muʿtaqad	1
majdhūb	1
muqriʾ	19
muqriʾ tibāq	1
muqriʾ jawq	9
muʾadhdhin	1
muʾaqqit	1
mīqātī	2
nāʾib imām	3
nāʾib khaṭīb	7
wāʿiẓ	3
khaṭīb	55
TOTAL	142

LIST 10. OCCUPATIONAL POSITIONS HELD BY NĀ'IB QĀḌĪS

Category I

āghā	1
dawādār	1
murattib	3
murattib jawālī	3
nā'ib	6
nā'ib nuwwāb	2
naqīb	11
rasūl sulṭānī	1
safīr	2
khāzindār	1
TOTAL	31

Category II

shāhid aḥbās	1
shāhid iṣṭabl	2
shāhid ṣūfī	1
shāhid dīwān	1
shāhid dīwān jawālī	1
shāhid kiswa	1
shāhid makhbaz	1
shāhid awqāf	3
kātib	4
kātib amlā'	1
kātib sirr	8
kātib warrāqīn	1
mubāshir	8
mubāshir ḥukm	1
mubāshir taṣawwuf	1
mubāshir awqāf	6
mudīr dawālīb	1
mudīr maʿāṣir	1
makkās	1
mustawfī	1
mutakallim	6
mutakallim awqāf	2
muwaqqiʿ	26
muwaqqiʿ inshā'	2
muwaqqiʿ dast	3
muwaqqiʿ dīwān inshā'	1
muwaqqiʿ ḥukm	3
nā'ib nāẓir	4
nā'ib nāẓir awqāf	2
nāẓir	39
nāẓir ʿimāra	2
nāẓir aḥbās	3
nāẓir iṣṭabl	2
nāẓir aswāq	1
nāẓir buyūt	1
nāẓir ṣadaqāt	1
nāẓir dār ḍarb	2
nāẓir jawālī	1
nāẓir jaysh	7
nāẓir kiswa	1
nāẓir masjid	1
nāẓir qamḥīya	1
nāẓir awqāf	12
muḥaṣṣil	1
TOTAL	169

Category III

ʿaqīd	3
ʿaqīd ankiḥa	1
shāhid	81
shāriʿ	1
sharūṭī	1
shaykh	42
shaykh shuyūkh	1
shaykh ṣūfī	9
shaykh fuqarā'	1
shaykh khuddām	1
amīn ḥukm	13
faqīh	4
ḥākim	1
muftī	12
muftī dār ʿadl	14
muḥtasib	9
damīn	1
nā'ib ʿaqīd	2
nā'ib shaykh	2
nā'ib shaykh ṣūfī	1
nā'ib ḥukm	8*
nā'ib ḥanafī	1*
nā'ib muḥtasib	8
nā'ib qāḍī	461*
naqīb ashrāf	2
qāḍī	103
qāḍī ʿaskar	8
qāḍī shāfiʿī	3
qāḍī ḥanbalī	1
qāḍī ḥanafī	8
qāḍī kabīr	1
qāḍī maṭlūbīn	1
qāḍī mālikī	5
qāḍī maḥmal	11
qāḍī quḍāt	10
qāḍī rakb	2
rasūl	2
wakīl bayt māl	3
TOTAL	838

Category IV

ʿāmil	2
ʿāmil mawāʿīd	1
ṭabbākh	1
ṭabīb	1
bayyāʿ marathīyāt	1
bazzāz	2
ṣanāʾiʿī dahshāt	1
ṣanāʾiʿī maqāṭiʿ	1
ṣanāʾiʿī nafṭ	1
ḥarīrī	1
jabbān	1
jarrāḥ	1
jawharī	1
nāsikh	7
qazzāz	1
simsār	1
mudhahhib	1
tājir	12
tājir baḥr	1
tājir burr	1
mujallid	1
mutakassib ḥānūt	2
khādim	14
zayyāt	1
TOTAL	57

Category V

shaṭranjī	2
shāʿir	14
shaykh āthār	1
shaykh mīʿād	2
shaykh taṣawwuf	6
ismāʿ	4
ismāʿ ḥadīth	1
muʿallim aṭfāl	1
muʿīd	31
mudarris	144
mudarris ʿarabīya	1
mudarris shāfiʿī	3
mudarris ṭibb	2
mudarris ṭahawī	1
mudarris iʿāda	3
mudarris iqrāʾ	1
mudarris āthār	1
mudarris fiqh	68
mudarris farāʾiḍ	2
mudarris ḥadīth	22
mudarris ḥanbalī	2
mudarris ḥanafī	2
mudarris kashshāf	1
mudarris mālikī	7
mudarris mīʿād	5
mudarris qirāʾāt	3
mudarris taṣawwuf	2
mudarris tafsīr	11
mudarris taqsīm	1
muḥaddith	5
minhājī	1
muqriʾ aṭfāl	6
muqriʾ aytām	1
muqriʾ bukhārī	2
muqriʾ ṣaffa	1
muqriʾ ḥadīth	8
muqriʾ maṣḥaf	1
muʿaddib aṭfāl	1
muʾarrikh	3
nāʾib muʿallim	1
nāʾib mudarris	5
nāʾib mudarris fiqh	5
nāʾib mudarris ḥadīth	2
nāʾib mudarris taṣawwuf	1
nāẓim	2
mutaṣaddir	16
mutaṣaddir farāʾiḍ	1
mutaṣaddir ḥadīth	1
khāzin kutub	7
TOTAL	414

Category VI

imām	38
imām qaṣr	1
āthārī	1
muqriʾ	18
muqriʾ jawq	4
muqriʾ khuṭbat ʿīd	1
muʾaqqit	1
nāʾib khaṭīb	5
wāʿiẓ	4
khaṭīb	59
khalwāʾī	1
TOTAL	133

LIST 11. OCCUPATIONAL POSITIONS HELD BY QĀḌĪS

Category I

murattib	1
nāʾib	3
naqīb	1
TOTAL	5

Category II

shāhid makhbaz	1
shāhid awqāf	1
kātib	1
kātib sharʿ	1
kātib inshāʾ	1
kātib sirr	22
mubāshir	4
mubāshir awqāf	4
mudīr dawālīb	1
mudīr maʿāṣir	1
mustawfī	1
mutakallim	2
muwaqqiʿ	9
muwaqqiʿ inshāʾ	1
muwaqqiʿ dast	2
muwaqqiʿ ḥukm	1
nāʾib kātib sirr	1
nāʾib nāẓir	1
nāʾib nāẓir awqāf	1
nāẓir	26
nāẓir aḥbās	1
nāẓir aswāq	1
nāẓir buyūt	1
nāẓir dār ḍarb	1
nāẓir dīwān mufrad	1
nāẓir ḥaram sharīf	1
nāẓir jawālī	1
nāẓir jaysh	11
nāẓir kiswa	3
nāẓir awqāf	6
nāẓir awqāf jārīya	1
nāẓir khāṣṣ	2
TOTAL	112

Category III

ʿaqīd	3
shāhid	24
shāhid jūra	1
shāriʿ amlāʾ	1
shaykh	27
shaykh ṣūfī	2
shaykh khuddām	2
amīn ḥukm	1
faqīh	7
ḥākim	1
muftī	9
muftī dār ʿadl	8
muḥtasib	9
nāʿib ʿaqīd	1
nāʿib shaykh	1
nāʿib ḥukm	19
nāʿib muḥtasib	2
nāʿib qāḍī	91
naqīb ashrāf	1
qāḍī	250*
qāḍī ʿaskar	8
qāḍī shāfiʿī	7
qāḍī ḥanbalī	5
qāḍī ḥanafī	4
qāḍī maṭlūbīn	1
qāḍī mālikī	4
qāḍī maḥmal	3
qāḍī quḍāt	6
wakīl bayt māl	3
TOTAL	501

Category IV

ʿaṭṭār	1
ʿāmil mawāʿīd	1
bayyāʿ marathīyāt	1
ḥarīrī	1
maḥḥādh	1
nāsikh	2
raḥḥāl	1
tājir	11
tājir burr	1
tājir ṣābūn	1
ṭashshāt	1
mutakassib ḥānūt	1
warrād	1
khādim	6
khawājā	1
zarrāʿ	1
TOTAL	32

Category V

shaṭranjī	1
shāʿir	13
shaykh āthār	1
shaykh ḥadīth	1
shaykh taṣawwuf	4
ismāʿ	2
muʿīd	11
mudarris	82
mudarris shāfiʿī	3
mudarris fiqh	28
mudarris farā'iḍ	1
mudarris ḥadīth	10
mudarris ḥanbalī	1
mudarris ḥanafī	1
mudarris kashshāf	1
mudarris mālikī	1
mudarris mīʿād	1
mudarris qirā'āt	2
mudarris taṣawwuf	2
mudarris tafsīr	5
muḥaddith	6
muqri' aṭfāl	3
muqri' bukhārī	1
muqri' ṣaffa	1
muqri' ḥadīth	2
mu'addib aṭfāl	2
mu'arrikh	3
nā'ib mudarris	2
nā'ib mudarris fiqh	1
nāẓim	1
mutaṣaddir	5
mutaṣaddir farā'iḍ	1
mutaṣaddir ḥadīth	1
khāzin kutub	3
TOTAL	203

Category VI

imām	11
muqri'	3
muqri' ḥaram	1
muqri' khuṭba ʿīd	1
nā'ib khaṭīb	1
wāʿiẓ	1
khaṭīb	28
TOTAL	46

LIST 12. OCCUPATIONAL POSITIONS HELD BY QĀḌĪS AL-QUḌĀT

Category I

No positions reported

Category II

kātib sirr	4
muwaqqiʿ	2
muwaqqiʿ darj	1
muwaqqiʿ dast dīwān Inshāʾ	1
muwaqqiʿ ḥukm	1
nāẓir	6
nāẓir ʿimāra	2
nāẓir ṣadaqāt	1
nāẓir jaysh	1
nāẓir kiswa	1
nāẓir masjid	1
nāẓir awqāf	6
TOTAL	27

Category III

shāhid	1
shaykh	2
shaykh shuyūkh	1
shaykh islām	1
shaykh ṣūfī	1
amīn ḥukm	1
faqīh	1
muftī	5
muftī dār ʿadl	2
nāʾib ḥukm	7
nāʾib qāḍī	6
qāḍī	7
qāḍī ʿaskar	7
qāḍī ḥanbalī	1
qāḍī mālikī	1
qāḍī quḍāt	34*
rasūl	1
wakīl bayt māl	1
TOTAL	80

Category IV

No positions reported

Category V

shāʿir	2
shaykh taṣawwuf	1
muʿallim mīqāt	1
muʿīd	3
mudarris	11
mudarris shāfiʿī	2
mudarris iʿāda	1
mudarris fiqh	3
mudarris ḥadīth	6
mudarris mālikī	1
mudarris tafsīr	3
muḥaddith	2
nāʾib mudarris	3
nāʾib mudarris taṣawwuf	1
mutaṣaddir	2
TOTAL	42

Category VI

imām	1
muqriʾ	1
nāʾib khaṭīb	1
khaṭīb	5
TOTAL	8

LIST 13. OCCUPATIONAL POSITIONS HELD BY NĀSIKHS

Category I

murattib	1
nā'ib	4
khāṣṣakī	1
TOTAL	6

Category II

shāhid ḥānūt	1
amr naqafa	1
kātib	1
kātib dukkān	1
kātib dast	1
makkās	1
mustawfī	1
muwaqqiʿ	5
muwaqqiʿ darj	1
muwaqqiʿ dast	1
muwaqqiʿ ḥukm	1
nāẓir	3
TOTAL	18

Category III

ʿaqīd	3
shāhid	29
shaykh	3
shaykh ṣūfī	1
faqīh	2
muftī	1
nā'ib ʿaqīd ankiḥa	1
nā'ib ḥukm	4
nā'ib muḥtasib	1
nā'ib qāḍī	10
qāḍī	3
qāḍī ʿaskar	1
qāḍī farḍ	1
qāḍī ḥanbalī	1
qāḍī kabīr	1
TOTAL	62

Category IV

ʿaṭṭār	1
bazzāz	1
ṣanāʾiʿī kutub	1
ghassāl lazuward	1
ḥabbāk	1
jammād	1
kutubī	1
fannān	1
nāsikh	91*
qazzāz	1
mudhahhib	1
tājir	3
tājir bazz	1
warrāq	2
khādim	1
TOTAL	108

Category V

shāʿir	3
shāriḥ	1
shaykh taṣawwuf	1
muʿallim	1
muʿallim aṭfāl	4
muʿīd	7
mudarris	7
mudarris iqrāʾ	1
mudarris fiqh	2
mudarris ḥadīth	2
mudarris kitāba	1
mudarris qirāʾāt	1
mudarris taṣawwuf	2
muḥaddith	1
mukattib	3
muqriʾ aṭfāl	2
muqriʾ ḥadīth	5
muqriʾ mamālīk	2
muʾaddib	1
muʾaddib aṭfāl	4
nāʾib khāzin kutub	1
mutaṣaddir	1
khāzin kutub	4
TOTAL	57

Category VI

imām	11
imām jāmiʿ	1
muqriʾ	3
muqriʾ jawq	4
nāʾib imām	2
nāʾib khaṭīb	1
wāʿiẓ	1
khaṭīb	14
TOTAL	37

LIST 14. OCCUPATIONAL POSITIONS HELD BY TĀJIRS

Category I

shādd	2
bardadār	1
ḥājib	1
mudabbir mamlaka	1
murattib	2
murattib jawālī	1
mawlan	3
rasūl malik firanj	1
safīr	3
wakīl	2
TOTAL	17

Category II

shāhid kiswa	1
shāhid makhbaz	1
ṣāḥib	2
mushrif ʿamā'ir	1
mubāshir	2
mudīr ṭāhūn	1
mutaṣarrif	1
mutakallim	1
mutakallim awqāf	1
muwaqqiʿ	2
nā'ib nāẓir	1
nā'ib nāẓir jaysh	1
nāẓir	8
nāẓir aḥbās	1
nāẓir iṣṭabl	1
nāẓir jawālī	3
nāẓir jaysh	3
nāẓir kiswa	2
nāẓir awqāf	2
nāẓir khāṣṣ	4
qabbānī	2
muqaddir dār ḍarb	1
TOTAL	42

Category III

shāhid	16
sharūṭī	1
shaykh	13
shaykh shāfiʿī	1
shaykh islām	1
shaykh ṣūfī	1
amīn ḥukm	1
faqīh	2
muftī	1
muḥtasib	4
nā'ib shaykh	1
nā'ib ḥukm	2
nā'ib muḥtasib	3
nā'ib qāḍī	13
naqīb ḥukm	1
qāḍī	12
qāḍī shāfiʿī	7
qāḍī ḥanafī	1
qāḍī mālikī	1
qāḍī maḥmal	1
rasūl	1
mutaḥaddith matjar	1
wakīl bayt māl	3
TOTAL	88

Category IV

ʿaṭṭār	1
ṭabbākh sukkar	1
bawwāb	1
bayyāʿ qumash	1
bazzār	1
bazzāz	5
farrāsh	2
ghazzāl	1
ḥaddād	1
ḥarīrī	1
jammāl	1
jawharī	2
kārimī	8
kutubī	1
ʿāmil	2
ʿāmil azrār	1
ʿāmil malāʿiq	1
mallāḥ	1
nāsikh	3
naḥḥāl	1
naḥḥās	1
sukkarī	1
tājir	197*
tājir kabīr	1
tājir sulṭānī	1
mujallid	1
khādim	8
khādim fuqarāʾ	1
khawājā	11
zarrāʿ	2
TOTAL	260

Category V

shāʿir	6
shaykh taṣawwuf	1
shaykh sabʿa	1
ṣāḥib madrasa	1
muʿallim	1
muʿallim aṭfāl	1
mudarris	13
mudarris fiqh	4
mudarris ḥadīth	3
mudarris kashshāf	1
mudarris mīʿād	1
mudarris tafsīr	1
muḥaddith	1
minhājī	1
muqriʾ ḥadīth	1
muʾaddib aṭfāl	1
nāʾib mudarris fiqh	1
naḥwī	1
nāẓim	1
TOTAL	41

Category VI

imām	7
muʿtaqad	2
muqriʾ	4
muqriʾ jawq	3
muʾadhdhin	1
nāʾib imām	1
khaṭīb	5
TOTAL	23

LIST 15. OCCUPATIONAL POSITIONS HELD BY MUʿĪDS

Category I

dawādār	1
murattib	1
murattib jawālī	1
nā'ib	2
naqīb	1
TOTAL	6

Category II

shāhid ṣūfī	1
shāhid kiswa	1
shāhid mufrad	1
shāhid khāṣṣ	1
kātib	1
kātib sirr	2
mubāshir	3
mustawfī	1
muwaqqiʿ	3
muwaqqiʿ inshā'	1
muwaqqiʿ darj	1
muwaqqiʿ dast	3
muwaqqiʿ dast dīwān inshā'	1
muwaqqiʿ ḥukm	1
nā'ib nāẓir	3
nā'ib nāẓir awqāf	1
nāẓir	17
nāẓir jawālī	1
nāẓir jaysh	1
nāẓir kiswa	1
nāẓir masjid	1
nāẓir awqāf	5
TOTAL	51

Category III

ʿaqīd	3
shāhid	8
shaykh	15
shaykh ṣūfī	2
amīn ḥukm	2
faqīh	2
muftī	8
muftī dār ʿadl	3
nā'ib shaykh	1
nā'ib ḥukm	7
nā'ib qāḍī	32
qāḍī	13
qāḍī ʿaskar	4
qāḍī shāfiʿī	2
qāḍī ḥanbalī	1
qāḍī ḥanafī	2
qāḍī mālikī	1
qāḍī maḥmal	2
qāḍī quḍāt	7
TOTAL	115

Category IV

ʿāmil maqāṣṣ	1
bazzāz	1
nāsikh	6
khādim	2
khayyāṭ	1
TOTAL	11

Category V

shāʿir	1
shaykh ḥadīth	1
shaykh taṣawwuf	5
muʿīd	73*
muʿallim aṭfāl	1
mudarris	61
mudarris shāfiʿī	2
mudarris ṭahawī	1
mudarris dār ḥadīth	1
mudarris fiqh	21
mudarris ḥadīth	8
mudarris mālikī	1
mudarris mīʿād	2
mudarris qirāʾāt	1
mudarris taṣawwuf	1
mudarris tafsīr	3
muḥaddith	2
muqriʾ aṭfāl	1
muqriʾ bukhārī	1
muqriʾ ḥadīth	2
muʾaddib aṭfāl	1
nāʾib mudarris fiqh	1
nāʾib mudarris ḥadīth	1
mutaṣaddir	5
mutaṣaddir ḥadīth	1
khāzin kutub	2
TOTAL	200

Category VI

imām	10
muqriʾ	4
muqriʾ ḥidāya	1
muqriʾ khuṭbat ʿīd	1
muʾadhdhin	1
nāʾib khaṭīb	2
wāʿiẓ	5
khaṭīb	14
TOTAL	38

LIST 16. OCCUPATIONAL POSITIONS HELD BY MUDARRISES

Category I

amīr	1
dawādār	1
murattib	1
murattib jawālī	2
nā'ib	4
naqīb	1
rasūl firanj	1
rasūl mulūk atrāk	1
TOTAL	12

Category II

shāhid iṣṭabl	1
shāhid ṣūfī	1
shāhid dār tuffāḥ	1
shāhid kiswa	2
shāhid makhbaz	1
shāhid awqāf	2
kātib	3
kātib ʿalāma	1
kātib sharʿ	2
kātib sirr	8
mubāshir	5
mubāshir dīwān	2
mubāshir taṣawwuf	1
mubāshir awqāf	1
mudīr	1
mutakallim	4
muwaqqiʿ	10
muwaqqiʿ umarā'	1
muwaqqiʿ darj	1
muwaqqiʿ dast	2
muwaqqiʿ dast dīwān inshā'	1
muwaqqiʿ dīwān inshā'	2
nā'ib kātib sirr	1
nā'ib nāẓir	5
nā'ib nāẓir awqāf	1
nāẓir	54
nāẓir ʿimāra	2
nāẓir aḥbās	1
nāẓir bayt māl	1
nāẓir ṣadaqāt	1
nāẓir ḥaramayn	2
nāẓir jaysh	4
nāẓir kiswa	4
nāẓir masjid	1
nāẓir maẓālim	1
nāẓir awqāf	16
nāẓir awqāf jārīya	1
nāẓir khāṣṣ	1
TOTAL	149

Category III

ʿaqīd	1
ʿaqīd ankiḥa	1
shāhid	31
shaykh	96
shaykh shuyūkh	1
shaykh islām	1
shaykh ṣūfī	12
shaykh ḥanbalī	1
amīn ḥukm	3
faqīh	16
muftī	38
muftī dār ʿadl	17
muḥtasib	7
nā'ib shaykh	4
nā'ib shaykh ṣūfī	2
nā'ib ḥukm	39
nā'ib ḥanafī	1
nā'ib jūra	2
nā'ib muḥtasib	1
nā'ib qāḍī	110
naqīb ashrāf	1
qāḍī	78
qāḍī ʿaskar	14
qāḍī shāfiʿī	25
qāḍī ḥanbalī	3
qāḍī ḥanafī	13
qāḍī mālikī	7
qāḍī maḥmal	1
qāḍī quḍāt	12
wakīl bayt māl	5
TOTAL	543

Category IV

ʿāmil maqāṣṣ	1
ʿanbarī	1
ṭabbākh sukkar	1
ṭabīb	1
akkār	1
bayyāʿ marathīyāt	1
bazzāz	2
ṣanāʾiʿī dahshāt	1
ṣanāʾiʿī nafṭ	1
ghazzāl	1
ḥaddād	1
jammād	1
jawwāl	1
kaḥḥāl	1
kutubī	1
naqqāsh	1
nāsikh	5
simsār	1
tājir	10
tājir burr	1
tājir kutub	1
mutakassib ḥānūt	1
waqqād	3
warrāq	1
khādim	9
khayyāṭ	3
zarrāʿ	2
TOTAL	54

Category V

shaṭranjī	1
shāʿir	17
shāriḥ	1
shaykh ḥadīth	2
shaykh qirāʾāt	2
shaykh taṣawwuf	9
ishtighāl	1
ismāʿ	4
muʿallim	1
muʿallim ʿarabīya	1
muʿallim mīqāt	1
muʿīd	44
muʿīd ḥadīth	2
muʿīd ḥanafī	2
muṭāliʿ	1
maṭbaʿjī	1
mudarris	496*
mudarris shāfiʿī	8
mudarris ṭibb	2
mudarris ṭahawī	1
mudarris āthār	1
mudarris dār ḥadīth	1
mudarris fiqh	65
mudarris farāʾiḍ	2
mudarris ḥadīth	32
mudarris ḥanafī	2
mudarris kashshāf	2
mudarris mālikī	3
mudarris taṣawwuf	2
mudarris tafsīr	17
muḥaddith	9
muqriʾ aṭfāl	4
muqriʾ bukhārī	1
muqriʾ fiqh	1
muqriʾ ḥadīth	3
muqriʾ musnad	1
muʾaddib aṭfāl	2
muʾarrikh	2
nāʾib mudarris	5
nāʾib mudarris fiqh	5
nāʾib mudarris ḥadīth	4
naḥwī	3
mutaṣaddir	13
mutaṣaddir iqrāʾ	1
mutaṣaddir ḥadīth	1
mutaṣaddir qirāʾāt	1
khāzin kutub	11
TOTAL	796

Category VI

imām	28
muqriʾ	28
muqriʾ ḥidāya	1
muqriʾ jawq	1
muqriʾ khuṭbat ʿīd	1
muʾaqqit	2
mīqātī	2
nāʾib khaṭīb	5
wāʿiẓ	3
khaṭīb	51
TOTAL	122

LIST 17. OCCUPATIONAL POSITIONS HELD BY KHĀZINS AL-KUTUB

Category I	
murattib jawālī	1
khāṣṣakī	1
TOTAL	2

Category II	
kātib	1
kātib sirr	2
mubāshir	1
mubāshir dīwān	1
mutakallim	1
muwaqqiʿ	1
muwaqqiʿ dīwān inshāʾ	1
muwaqqiʿ dīwān wazīr	1
nāʾib nāẓir	2
nāẓir	2
nāẓir jaysh	1
nāẓir awqāf	1
TOTAL	15

Category III	
ʿaqīd	1
shāhid	4
shaykh	10
faqīh	2
muftī	1
muftī dār ʿadl	1
nāʾib ḥukm	1
nāʾib qāḍī	9
qāḍī	4
qāḍī shāfiʿī	2
TOTAL	35

Category IV

ṭabīb	1
ḥabbāk	1
nāsikh	4
khādim	1
TOTAL	7

Category V

shaṭranjī	1
shāʿir	1
shaykh taṣawwuf	1
ismāʿ	1
muʿallim kitāba	1
muʿīd	2
muʿīd ḥadīth	1
muʿīd ḥanafī	2
mudarris	16
mudarris shāfiʿi	2
mudarris iqrāʾ	1
mudarris fiqh	6
mudarris ḥadīth	3
mudarris ḥanafī	1
mudarris taṣawwuf	2
mudarris tafsīr	3
muḥaddith	1
muqriʾ aṭfāl	2
muqriʾ aytām	1
muqriʾ ḥadīth	2
muqriʾ aṭfāl	2
nāʾib mudarris ḥadīth	1
nāʾib khāzin kutub	1
naḥwī	1
mutaṣaddir	3
mutaṣaddir qirāʾāt	1
khāzin kutub	38*
TOTAL	97

Category VI

imām	9
muqriʾ	1
muqriʾ jawq	1
muqriʾ kutub	1
muʾaqqit	1
mīqātī	1
khaṭīb	10
TOTAL	24

LIST 18. OCCUPATIONAL POSITIONS HELD BY IMĀMS

Category I

murattib	1
murattib jawālī	1
nā'ib	1
nā'ib nuwwāb	2
safīr	2
TOTAL	7

Category II

shāhid awqāf	2
ṣāḥib	1
kātib	4
kātib amlā'	1
kātib sirr	1
jawālī	1
mubāshir	3
mubāshir saqī mā'	1
mubāshir taṣawwuf	1
mubāshir awqāf	1
mustawfī	1
mutakallim	1
mutakallim awqāf	2
muwaqqiʿ	10
muwaqqiʿ inshā'	1
muwaqqiʿ dast	1
muwaqqiʿ dīwān inshā'	1
muwaqqiʿ ḥukm	2
nā'ib nāẓir	2
nāẓir	23
nāẓir aḥbās	2
nāẓir dār ḍarb	1
nāẓir ḥaramayn	1
nāẓir jaysh	2
nāẓir kiswa	2
nāẓir masjid	1
nāẓir awqāf	7
qabbānī	1
TOTAL	77

Category III

ʿaqīd	2
shāhid	39
shāriʿ amlā'	1
sharūṭī	1
shaykh	33
shaykh shāfiʿī	1
shaykh ṣūfī	4
amīn ḥukm	2
faqīh	3
muftī	4
muftī dār ʿadl	2
muḥtasib	5
nā'ib ʿaqīd	1
nā'ib shaykh	3
nā'ib ḥukm	4
nā'ib qāḍī	42
qāḍī	11
qāḍī ʿaskar	2
qāḍī shāfiʿī	1
qāḍī ḥanbalī	1
qāḍī ḥanafī	4
qāḍī maḥmal	3
qāḍī quḍāt	1
qāḍī rakb	1
rasūl	2
wakīl bayt māl	1
TOTAL	174

Category IV

ʿāmil marāwīḥ	1
sharāʾibī	1
bayyāʿ quṭn	1
bazzāz	1
ṣanāʾiʿī dahshāt	1
ṣanāʾiʿī nafṭ	1
ghannām	1
ḥarīrī	2
jawwāl	1
kutubī	3
nāsikh	10
najjār	1
tājir	7
tājir burr	1
mutakassib ḥānūt	1
khaṭṭāṭ	1
khādim	11
khayyāṭ	3
TOTAL	48

Category V

shaṭranjī	1
shāʿir	12
shaykh qirāʾāt	3
shaykh taṣawwuf	9
shaykh sabʿa	1
adīb	1
muʿallim	1
muʿallim aṭfāl	3
muʿallim aytām	1
muʿallim kitāba	1
muʿīd	11
mudarris	39
mudarris shāfiʿī	2
mudarris ṭibb	2
mudarris iqrāʾ	1
mudarris fiqh	20
mudarris ḥadīth	10
mudarris ḥanafī	1
mudarris kitāba	1
mudarris qirāʾāt	5
mudarris taṣawwuf	2
mudarris tafsīr	4
muḥaddith	7
mukattib	3
muqriʾ aṭfāl	12
muqriʾ awlād	1
muqriʾ ḥadīth	10
muqriʾ maṣḥaf	1
muqriʾ mamālīk	2
muqriʾ sīra	1
muʾaddib	1
muʾaddib aṭfāl	3
muʾarrikh	1
nāʾib muʿīd	1
nāʾib mudarris	3
nāʾib mudarris fiqh	2
nāʾib mudarris ḥadīth	1
nāʾib mudarris tafsīr	1
nāʾib muqriʾ ḥadīth	1
nāʾib khāzin kutub	1
naḥwī	1
mutaṣaddir	5
mutaṣaddir qirāʾāt	1
khāzin kutub	7
TOTAL	200

Category VI

imām	238*
imām sulṭānī	1
muʿtaqad	1
muqriʾ	38
muqriʾ jawq	5
muʾadhdhin	6
muʾaqqit	1
mīqātī	1
nāʾib imām	4
nāʾib khaṭīb	7
wāʿiẓ	4
khaṭīb	60
khalāwī	1
TOTAL	367

LIST 19. OCCUPATIONAL POSITIONS HELD BY KHAṬĪBS

Category I

murattib	1
murattib jawālī	2
nā'ib	2
nā'ib nuwwāb	1
naqīb	3
safīr	1
wakīl	2
TOTAL	12

Category II

shāhid kiswa	1
shāhid awqāf	4
shāhid khāṣṣ	2
ṣayrafī	1
muḥaṣṣil	1
kātib	1
kātib ghayba	3
kātib sirr	7
mubāshir	11
mubāshir taṣawwuf	1
mubāshir awqāf	4
mudīr	1
makkās	1
mustawfī	1
mutakallim	1
mutakallim awqāf	2
muwaqqiʿ	7
muwaqqiʿ darj	1
muwaqqiʿ dast	1
muwaqqiʿ dast dīwān inshā'	1
muwaqqiʿ ḥukm	1
nā'ib kātib sirr	1
nāẓir	30
nāẓir aḥbās	1
nāẓir iṣṭabl	1
nāẓir ḥaramayn	1
nāẓir jawālī	1
nāẓir jaysh	4
nāẓir kiswa	2
nāẓir awqāf	9
qabbānī	1
TOTAL	104

Category III

ʿaqīd	2
shāhid	53
shāhid jūra	2
shāriʿ amlā'	1
sharūṭī	1
shaykh	37
shaykh ṣūfī	3
shaykh fuqarā'	1
amīn ḥukm	1
faqīh	8
muftī	7
muftī dār ʿadl	4
muḥtasib	5
nā'ib shaykh	2
nā'ib shaykh ṣūfī	1
nā'ib ḥukm	10
nā'ib jūra	1
nā'ib muḥtasib	2
nā'ib qāḍī	63
qāḍī	37
qāḍī ʿaskar	3
qāḍī shāfiʿī	7
qāḍī ḥanbalī	1
qāḍī ḥanafī	4
qāḍī quḍāt	6
qāḍī rakb	1
rasūl	2
mulaqqin	1
wakīl bayt māl	3
TOTAL	272

Category IV

ʿaṭṭār	1
bawwāb	2
bayyāʿ kutub	1
bazzāz	3
ḥalwāʾī	1
ḥarīrī	1
jawwāl	1
kutubī	2
mujaddid	1
makhbazī	1
nāsikh	15
nāsikh iṣlāḥ	1
naḥḥās	1
najjār	1
qaṣṣāb sukkar	1
tājir	5
tājir bazz	1
tājir jubna	1
tājir kutub	1
tājir zayt	1
warrāq	2
khashshāb	1
khādim	6
khayyāṭ	1
zarrāʿ	1
TOTAL	53

Category V

shaṭranjī	1
shāʿir	14
shaykh muḥaddithīn	1
shaykh mīʿād	1
shaykh qirāʾāt	1
shaykh taṣawwuf	6
ismāʿ	2
muʿallim aṭfāl	2
muʿallim kitāba	1
muʿallim mīqāt	1
muʿīd	13
muʿīd ḥadīth	2
mudarris	66
mudarris shāfiʿī	3
mudarris iʿāda	1
mudarris iqrāʾ	1
mudarris fiqh	35
mudarris ḥadīth	19
mudarris ḥanafī	1
mudarris mīʿād	2
mudarris qirāʾāt	3
mudarris taṣawwuf	1
mudarris tafsīr	6
mudarris taqsīm	1
muḥaddith	8
mukattib	1
muqriʾ aṭfāl	8
muqriʾ abnāʾ	1
muqriʾ bukhārī	1
muqriʾ ṣaffa	1
muqriʾ ḥadīth	10
muqriʾ mamālīk	1
muʾaddib aṭfāl	6
muʾarrikh	2
nāʾib mudarris fiqh	1
nāʾib mudarris ḥadīth	1
nāʾib mudarris taṣawwuf	1
nāʾib muqriʾ ḥadīth	1
riyāḍī	1
mutaṣaddir	9
mutaṣaddir qirāʾāt	1
khāzin kutub	8
TOTAL	246

Category VI

imām	53
imām mālikī	1
muqriʾ	19
muqriʾ jawq	3
muqriʾ khuṭbat ʿīd	1
muʿadhdhin	3
muʾaqqit	1
mīqātī	2
nāʾib imām	1
nāʾib khaṭīb	6
raʾīs mīqātī	1
wāʿiẓ	9
khaṭīb	279*
TOTAL	379

LIST 20. OCCUPATIONAL POSITIONS HELD BY MUQRI'S

Category I	
nā'ib	1
naqīb	1
safīr	1
TOTAL	3

Category II	
shāhid awqāf	1
kātib	2
kātib sirr	1
mubāshir	3
mubāshir awqāf	1
mutakallim	1
nāẓir	9
nāẓir ʿimāra	2
nāẓir ṣadaqāt	1
nāẓir jaysh	2
nāẓir kiswa	2
nāẓir awqāf	3
qabbānī	1
TOTAL	29

Category III	
shāhid	20
shaykh	19
shaykh ṣūfī	3
shaykh fuqarā'	1
shaykh khidma	1
faqīh	3
muftī	4
muḥtasib	4
nā'ib ʿaqīd ankiḥa	1
nā'ib ḥukm	5
nā'ib muḥtasib	1
nā'ib qāḍī	20
qāḍī	4
qāḍī ʿaskar	2
qāḍī ḥanbalī	1
qāḍī ḥanafī	2
qāḍī maḥmal	1
qāḍī quḍāt	1
wakīl bayt māl	2
TOTAL	95

Category IV

sharā'ibī	1
ṭabbākh sukkar	1
bawwāb	2
bazzāz	1
ḥarīrī	2
jawharī	1
jawwāl	1
nāsikh	3
tājir	4
tājir ḥānūt	1
mutakassib ḥānūt	1
warrāq	2
khādim	5
khabbāz	1
khayyāṭ	2
TOTAL	28

Category V

shāʿir	6
shaykh ismāʿ	1
shaykh muḥaddithīn	1
shaykh qirā'āt	5
shaykh taṣawwuf	3
shaykh sabʿa	1
adīb	1
muʿallim aytām	1
muʿīd	6
mudarris	37
mudarris ʿarabīya	1
mudarris fiqh	4
mudarris ḥadīth	5
mudarris mālikī	1
mudarris naḥw	1
mudarris qirā'āt	6
mudarris tafsīr	4
mudarris taqsīm	1
muḥaddith	2
muqri' aṭfāl	7
muqri' isbāʿa	1
muqri' awlād	1
muqri' ṣaffa	3
muqri' ḥadīth	3
mu'addib aṭfāl	2
mu'addib aytām	1
mu'arrikh	2
nā'ib muʿīd	1
nā'ib mudarris	2
nā'ib mudarris fiqh	6
nā'ib mudarris ḥadīth	1
nā'ib mudarris tafsīr	1
mutaṣaddir	3
khāzin kutub	1
TOTAL	123

Category VI

imām	38
imām qaṣr	1
muʿtaqad	6
muqri'	187*
muqri' jawq	9
nā'ib imām	1
nā'ib khaṭīb	4
ra'īs muqri' jawq	2
wāʿiẓ	2
khaṭīb	20
TOTAL	270

LIST 21. OCCUPATIONAL POSITIONS HELD BY MUʿTAQADS

Category I		*Category II*		*Category III*	
mamlūk sulṭānī	1	ṣāḥib	3	shāhid	1
murattib jawālī	1	mubāshir	1	shaykh	9
naqīb	1	mubāshir dīwān	1	shaykh fuqarāʾ	1
TOTAL	3	mutakallim	1	shaykh zuwwār	1
		taʿnān dūlāb	1	faqīh	4
		TOTAL	7	TOTAL	16

Category IV

abārīqī	1
bayyaʿ nashān	1
bayyaʿ sadarīya	1
ṣanāʾiʿī muʿjizāt	1
ṣanāʾiʿī qumāsh azraq	1
ṣanāʾiʿī sharīṭ	1
fawwāl	1
ghannām	1
ḥabbāk	1
rakkāb iṣṭabl sulṭānī	1
saddār	2
shaqqāʾ	1
sawwāq	2
suyūfī	1
tājir	2
tājir ghazl	1
warrāq	1
khādim	3
khādim maqām	1
kharīzātī	1
khawwāṣ	1
khayyāṭ	1
khudarī	1
sāqī qirba	1
sawwāq ghanam	1
zayyāt	1
TOTAL	31

Category V

shāʿir	2
adīb	1
muʿallim aṭfāl	1
mudarris mālikī	1
muqriʾ aṭfāl	2
muʾaddib aṭfāl	1
TOTAL	8

Category VI

imām	1
darwīsh	1
muʿtaqad	136*
majdhūb	16
muqriʾ	6
murabbiṭ	1
muʾadhdhin	2
suṭūhī	1
wāʿiẓ	4
TOTAL	168

LIST 22. OCCUPATIONAL POSITIONS HELD BY ṢŪFĪS

Category I

amīr	1
ustādār	1
jundī	2
murattib	1
murattib jawālī	2
mawlan	1
naqīb	2
ra'īs	1
zimām	1
TOTAL	12

Category II

shāhid ṣūfī	2
shāhid awqāf	2
shāhid khāṣṣ	1
amr nafaqa	1
ṣāḥib	1
ṣayrafī	2
jābī awqāf	1
kātib	2
kātib dīwān umarā'	1
kātib ghayba	1
kātib sirr	2
mubāshir	5
mubāshir dīwān	1
mubāshir riyāsa	1
makkās	1
musta'jir	1
mustawfī	1
mutakallim	2
mutakallim awqāf	2
muwaqqiʿ	10
muwaqqiʿ inshā'	1
muwaqqiʿ darj	2
muwaqqiʿ dast	3
muwaqqiʿ ḥukm	1
nāẓir	17
nāẓir ʿimāra	2
nāẓir dhakhīra	2
nāẓir aḥbās	3
nāẓir iṣṭabl	1
nāẓir buyūt	1
nāẓir ṣadaqāt	1
nāẓir dīwān musta'jirāt	1
nāẓir dīwān khāṣṣ	1
nāẓir jaysh	2
nāẓir kiswa	2
nāẓir masjid	1
nāẓir awqāf	6
qabbānī	5
wazzān	1
TOTAL	93

Category III

ʿaqīd	1
shāhid	45
shāhid ḥanbalī	1
shāhid jūra	1
sharūṭī	1
shaykh	42
shaykh shāfiʿī	1
shaykh ṣūfī	12
shaykh ḥanafī	1
shaykh muwaqqiʿīn	1
amīn ḥukm	1
faqīh	5
muftī	5
muftī dār ʿadl	2
muḥtasib	17
nā'ib ʿaqīd	1
nā'ib shaykh	3
nā'ib ḥukm	6
nā'ib qāḍī	34
qāḍī	14
qāḍī ʿaskar	2
qāḍī shāfiʿī	1
qāḍī farḍ	1
qāḍī ḥanbalī	1
qāḍī ḥanafī	9
qāḍī maḥmal	1
qāḍī quḍāt	3
rasūl	2
wakīl bayt māl	2
TOTAL	216

Category IV

ʿaṭṭār	1
ʿāmil sarasīj	1
ʿāmil malāʿiq	1
ʿāmil maqāṣṣ	1
ʿāmil azrār	1
sharāʾibī	1
ṭabbākh	1
ṭabbākh sukkar	1
ṭabīb	2
bawwāb	2
bayyāʿ shabbārī	1
bayyāʿ ʿibar	1
bayyāʿ fuqqāʿa	1
bayyāʿ samsīs	1
bayyāʿ ṣaqat	1
bayyāʿ waraq	1
bayyāʿ khayṭ	1
bazzāz	2
ṣanāʾiʿī tajlīd kutub	1
ṣanāʾiʿī qabbān	1
ṣanāʾiʿī ḥarīr	1
dallāl	2
farrāsh	1
ḥāris ḥammamāt	1
ḥammāmī	1
ḥarīrī	2
jarrāḥ	3
jawharī	1
jawwāl	1
kutubī	5
mallāḥ	1
nāsikh	15
naqqāsh	1
raʾīs jarrāḥīn	1
raʾīs mujabbirīn	1
simsār kutub	1
ṣaqaṭī	1
tājir	11
tājir bazz	1
tājir sukkar	1
mukaffit	1
mutakassib ḥānūt	3
warrāq	3
khādim	13
khayyāṭ	4
dūlāb ḥammamāt	1
zajjāj	1
zarrāʿ	1
zayyāt	1
TOTAL	103

Category V

shāʿir	20
shaykh āthār	1
shaykh ḥadīth	1
shaykh taṣawwuf	12
adīb	3
ismāʿ ḥadīth	1
muʿallim ʿilāj wa thaqāfa	1
muʿallim ʿarabīya	1
muʿallim aṭfāl	4
muʿallim arbāb ḥarb	1
muʿallim jarr qaws	1
muʿallim kitāba	1
muʿallim ramī	1
muʿīd	12
mudarris	39
mudarris shāfiʿī	2
mudarris iʿāda	1
mudarris aṭfāl	1
mudarris atrāk	1
mudarris fiqh	22
mudarris ḥadīth	12
mudarris ḥanbalī	1
mudarris ḥanafī	1
mudarris kitāba	1
mudarris mālikī	1
mudarris qirāʾāt	1
mudarris taṣawwuf	3
mudarris tafsīr	5
mudarris khuddām	1
muḥaddith	2
mukattib	1
muqriʾ aṭfāl	14
muqriʾ ṣaffa	4
muqriʾ fiqh	1
muqriʾ farāʾiḍ	1
muqriʾ ḥadīth	7
muqriʾ mamālīk	2
muqriʾ sīra	1
muthaqqif	1
muʾaddib	1
muʾaddib aṭfāl	1
muʾarrikh	2
nāʾib shaykh taṣawwuf	1
nāʾib mudarris	1
nāʾib mudarris fiqh	1
nāʾib mudarris taṣawwuf	1
nāʾib mudarris ḥadīth	1
nāʾib khāzin kutub	2
nāẓim	1
mutaṣaddir	4
mutaṣaddir qirāʾāt	1
khāzin kutub	5
TOTAL	208

Category VI

imām	39
imām ribāṭ	1
muʿtaqad	19
majdhūb	2
muqriʾ	30
muqriʾ shubbāk	1
muqriʾ ḥidāya	1
muqriʾ jawq	5
muqriʾ kutub	1
muʾadhdhin	5
mīqātī	3
nāʾib imām	1
nāʾib khaṭīb	4
raʾīs jawq	1
raʾīs ṣūfī	1
wāʿiẓ	5
khaṭīb	34
TOTAL	153

LIST 23. OCCUPATIONAL POSITIONS HELD BY COPTS (QIBṬĪS)

Category I		*Category II*		*Category III*
shādd	1	ʿāmil	1	No positions reported
shādd khāṣṣ	1	ʿāmil awqāf	1	
amīr	1	ṣāḥib dīwān	1	
amīr mashwara	1	ṣāḥib dīwān ashrāf	1	
amīr mīʾa	1	ṣāḥib dīwān jaysh	1	
ustādār	19	kātib	24	
ustādār dhakhāʾir	1	kātib umarāʾ	1	
ustādār amlāk	1	kātib dawālīb	1	
ustādār mustaʾjirāt	1	kātib dawāwīn	1	
ustādār awqāf	1	kātib dīwān	2	
dawādār	1	kātib dīwān jaysh	1	
kāshif	3	kātib dīwān mamālīk	1	
muqaddam	2	kātib dīwān murtajaʿāt	1	
nāʾib	1	kātib jaysh	1	
naqīb jaysh	3	kātib lālā	1	
wālī	2	kātib mufrad	1	
wakīl	2	kātib mamālīk	3	
TOTAL	42	kātib sirr	3	
		mubāshir	1	
		mubāshir istifāʾ mufrad	1	
		mubāshir dīwān	2	
		mubāshir dīwān jaysh	1	
		mubāshir khāṣṣ	1	
		milk umarāʾ	3	
		mustawfī	3	
		mustawfī dawla	2	
		mustawfī dīwān jaysh	1	
		muwaqqiʿ dīwān inshāʾ	1	
		mustawfī khāṣṣ	4	
		mustawfī khizāna	1	
		mutakallim dīwān	1	
		mutakallim mukūs	1	
		mutakallim awqāf	1	
		muwaqqiʿ	3	
		muwaqqiʿ dast	1	
		muwaqqiʿ dīwān inshāʾ	1	
		nāẓir	3	
		nāẓir iṣṭabl	9	
		nāẓir aswāq	1	
		nāẓir bandar	3	
		nāẓir dawla	18	
		nāẓir dīwān	3	
		nāẓir dīwān mufrad	10	
		nāẓir jaysh	15	
		nāẓir mufrad	8	
		nāẓir awqāf	1	
		nāẓir khāṣṣ	28	
		nāẓir khizāna	1	
		nāẓir khizāna kabīr	1	
		wazīr	49	
		TOTAL	228	

Category IV

bazzāz	1
tājir awlād	1
tājir firanj	1
khādim	11
khādim dawāwīn	1
khādim dīwān	2
khādim dīwān sulṭānī	1
TOTAL	18

Category V

shā'ir	4
adīb	1
mudarris taṣawwuf	1
muḥaddith	1
TOTAL	7

Category VI

muqri' shubbāk	1
TOTAL	1

Appendix III. Glossary of Occupational Terms

Definite articles of genitive constructs omitted.

abārīqī: pitcher and jug maker
adīb: literateur, man of letters
ʿadl, ʿādil: juristic adjunct assigned to a judge
ʿadl majlis al-Mālikī: adjunct of the Mālikī court
akkār: plowman
ʿāmil: worker, laborer; tax official
ʿāmil awqāf: tax official of pious trust foundations
ʿāmil azrār: button, tassel maker
ʿāmil malāʿiq: spoon maker
ʿāmil maqāṣṣ: sheers maker
ʿāmil mawāʿīd: time keeper, appointment fixer
ʿāmil mirwāḥ, marāwīḥ: fan maker
ʿāmil sarāsīj: saddler
amīn: trust officer
amīn ḥukm: trust officer of the judiciary
amīr: commander, Mamluk officer
amīr ʿashara: officer of ten Mamluk troopers: official military rank
amīr ḥājj: officer of the Pilgrimage
amīr ʿishrīn: officer of twenty Mamluk troopers: official military rank
amīr khamsa: officer of five Mamluk troopers: official military rank
amīr maḥmal: officer of the Pilgrimage caravan
amīr mashwara: officer of the (royal) consultation
amīr miʾa: officer of one hundred Mamluk troopers: official military rank
amīr rakb: officer of the royal escort during military campaigns
amīr shikār: officer of the hunt
amīr ṭabalkhāna: officer of forty Mamluk troopers: official military rank
amr nafaqa: bursar, treasurer of a bureau
ʿanbarī: ambergris perfume dealer
ʿaqīd: legal contract maker
ʿaqīd ankiḥa: marriage contract maker
atābek: second commander-in-chief of the armies (after *Atābek al-ʿAsākir*): official military rank
āthārī: custodian of religious relics
ʿaṭṭār: perfume, aromatics dealer

ballān: bathhouse attendant
bardadār: bailiff, court official
bawwāb: gatekeeper, doorman
bayyāʿ: seller, vendor

bayyāʿ fuqqāʿa: mushroom dealer, seller of dish prepared with the buri fish
bayyāʿ ʿibar, ʿabīr: seller of fragrances, perfumes
bayyāʿ khayṭ: seller of thread, twine, cord
bayyāʿ kutub: book dealer
bayyāʿ marathīyāt: seller of water-softened foods, such as dates or chick peas
bayyāʿ nishān: seller of emblems, decorations, bridal attire
bayyāʿ qumash: cloth dealer
bayyāʿ quṭn: cotton dealer
bayyāʿ sadarīya: seller of black velvet headgear
bayyāʿ samsīs: seller of spiced (ginger) bread covered with sesame seeds
bayyāʿ saqaṭ: junk dealer, rag man; seller of baskets
bayyāʿ shabbarī: dealer in camel litters and equipment
bayyāʿ shirāʿ: tent cloth dealer
bayyāʿ simsim: seller of sesame seed foods
bayyāʿ waraq: paper dealer
bazzār: seedsman
bazzāz: draper, cloth merchant

dallāl: auctioneer; broker, jobber
ḍamīn: bailsman, bondsman, guarantor
darwīsh: dervish, religious ascetic
dawādār: executive secretary of the imperial court
ḍawāhī: lamp maker
dūlāb ḥammāmāt: bath wardrobe attendant

fannān: artist
faqīh: legist, jurisprudent
faqīh aytām: instructor and interpretor of elementary principles of jurisprudence in an orphanage school
farrāsh: servant, attendant, one who spreads the carpets
fawwāl: seller of broad beans (*fūl*)

ghannām: shepherd, sheep dealer
ghassāl: washerman
ghassāl lazuward: worker in lapis-lazuli
ghazzāl: spinner of yarn

ḥabbāk: weaver
ḥaddād: ironsmith, blacksmith
ḥāʾik: weaver
ḥājib, hujjāb (pl.): chamberlain of the imperial court
ḥākim: governor, judge
ḥakīm: legal scholar, physician
ḥallāq: barber
ḥalwāʾī: confectioner, candy-pastry dealer
ḥammāmī: bath attendant

ḥarīrī: silk merchant
ḥāris ḥammāmāt: bathhouse guard, custodian

ibṭāl awqāf: validity inspector of pious trust foundations
imām: prayer leader
imām jāmiʿ: prayer leader of the mosque, usually referring to the Citadel mosque
imām mālikī: prayer leader of the Mālikī madhhab
imām qaṣr: prayer leader of the royal palace
imām ribāṭ: prayer leader of the Hospice (title undesignated)
ishtighāl: scholar
ismāʿ: professor, witness of formal textual recitation
ismāʿ ḥadīth: Witness of formal textual recitation from the Prophetic traditions

jāb: tax collector, revenue officer
jabbān: cheese merchant
jābī awqāf: collector of contributions for pious trust foundations
jālis: legal assistant in a civil court
jamdār: wardrobe keeper in the imperial court
jammād: plasterer, mortar mixer
jammāl: camel driver
jarrāḥ: surgeon
jawharī: jeweler
jawwāl: traveler, itinerant merchant
jundī: Mamluk trooper, official military rank
jūra: pertaining to a legal office in a local (neighborhood) court

kaḥḥāl: eye doctor, oculist
kārimī: spice merchant
kāshif: inspector, governor
kāshif kanāʾis: inspector of churches
kāshif wajh al-qiblī: inspector of Upper Egypt
kātib: secretary
kātib ʿalāma: secretary of the (royal) insignia
kātib ʿalīq: secretary in the royal provender (fodder) bureau
kātib amlāʿ: public secretary
kātib dast: secretary of the Royal Bench
kātib dawālīb: secretary in the bureau of the royal mills
kātib dīwān, dawāwīn: secretary in the financial bureaus
kātib dīwān al-jaysh: secretary in the army bureau
kātib dukkān: secretary in a shop, warehouse
kātib ghayba: interim secretary (during absence of the secretary of the chancellery or interim viceroy)
kātib inshāʾ, dīwān al-: secretary in the documents bureau (chancellery)
kātib khizānā: secretary in the royal depository of robes

kātib lālā: secretary to the lālā
kātib mamālīk: secretary to Mamluks or the barracks staff
kātib murtajaʿāt: secretary of reclaims
kātib muwākib al-Turk: secretary in the bureau of Mamluk ceremonials and pageants.
kātib muwaqqiʿ al-dast: secretary to the scribe of the royal bench in the Palace of Justice
kātib qiṣaṣ: secretary of accounts, accountant
kātib sharʿ: legal secretary
kātib sifāra: secretary to an officer's staff, or to a legation
kātib sirr, sirr khāṣṣ: secretary of the chancellery (lit., secretary of the confidence)
kātib umarāʾ: secretary to Mamluk amirs
kātib warraqīn: secretary to the stationers
khabbāz: baker
khādim: servant
khādim barīd: servant in the postal service
khādim dīwān, dawāwīn: servant in the financial bureaus
khādim dīwān al-sulṭānī: servant in the royal bureau
khādim jawālī: servant in the (minority) tax bureau
khādim maqām: servant in the holy sanctuary (Mekka)
khalāwī, khalāʾī, khalwāʾī: pious recluse, holy hermit
khalīfa: the caliph, formal head of government; in practice, subordinate to the sultan
kharizātī: Pearl stringer, borer of finework—precious metal and jewelry
kharrāz: shoemaker
khashshāb: lumber merchant
khāṣṣakī: an intimate or favorite amir, associate of the sultan
khaṭīb: preacher (esp. of the Friday prayer, invocation, and sermon)
khaṭṭāṭ: calligrapher
khawājā: royal merchant elevated to official standing in the imperial court, with executive responsibilities
khawwāṣ: basket maker, palm-leaf plaiter
khayyāṭ: tailor
khāzin: treasurer, royal wardrobe custodian
khāzin kutub: librarian
khāzindār: royal treasurer
khuḍarī: greengrocer
kutubī: book dealer

lālā: adjunct, instructor to a royal prince; court page

maḥḥādh, ḥadhdhāʾ: cobbler
majdhūb: holy or pious ecstatic, regarded by Ṣūfīs as the elect of God
makhbazī: proprietor of bakery, baker's assistant
makkās: tax collector

mallāḥ: salt merchant, mariner
mamlūk sulṭānī: A Mamluk purchased by a sultan preceding the incumbant ruler; transferred to the incumbent's service but identifying with his comrades purchased and trained at the same time
matbaʿjī: publisher, issuer of manuscripts; later a printer
mawardī: dealer in rosewater
mawlan: (royal) client, individual attached to service of the sultān; often a manumitted black slave.
mihmandār: royal host, official escort of visiting dignitaries to the imperial court
milk ashrāf: official concerned with properties belonging to the Prophet's descendants
milk umarā': Official concerned with property belonging to Mamluk amirs
minhājī: systematic scholar, writer of specific analyses of or commentaries on scholarly subject matter for use in curricula
mīqātī: time keeper, regulator of calendrical variations
mu'addib: elementary teacher in a Koran school
mu'addib aṭfāl: elementary teacher in a Koran school
mu'adhdhin: prayer caller
muʿallim: elementary or secondary teacher
muʿallim ʿarabīya: teacher of the Arabic language
muʿallim arbāb al-ḥarb: teacher of "the lords of war," i.e., Mamluk troopers
muʿallim aṭfāl: elementary or secondary teacher
muʿallim aytām: elementary teacher in an orphanage school
muʿallim ʿilāj wa thaqāfa: literally, teacher of "treatment and culture"
muʿallim jarr al-qaws: teacher of archery
muʿallim jawālī: teacher of tax auditing
muʿallim kitāba: teacher of writing
muʿallim mīqāt: teacher of time keeping and calendrical regulation
muʿallim ramī: teacher of lance casting
mu'aqqit, muwaqqit: time keeper
mu'arrikh: chronicler, historian
mubāshir: steward, intendant
mubāshir aqribā': steward of the (sword) sheaths
mubāshir awqāf: steward of pious trust foundations
mubāshir dhakhīra: steward of the sultan's treasures and munitions
mubāshir dīwān: steward of the financial bureau
mubāshir dīwān al-inshā': steward of the documents bureau, chancellery
mubāshir dīwān al-jaysh: steward of the army bureau
mubāshir dīwān al-khāṣṣ: steward in the bureau of privy funds
mubāshir dīwān al-mamālīk: steward in the bureau of troops
mubāshir ḥammām: steward of the bathhouse
mubāshir ḥukm: steward of a civil court
mubāshir ʿimāra: steward of the royal constructions
mubāshir istifā' al-mufrad: steward in the accounts department of the special bureau

mubāshir riyāsa: steward in service of the chief justice
mubāshir saqī al-mā': steward of the irrigation bureau
mubāshir taṣawwuf: steward of a mystic order
mudabbir mamlaka: director of the government, Mamluk official
mudarris: professor
mudarris ʿarabīya: professor of the Arabic language
mudarris aṭfāl: secondary instructor
mudarris āthār: professor of traditions, deeds, and utterances relating to the Prophet
mudarris atrāk: instructor of Mamluk troopers (lit. "Turks")
mudarris dār al-hadīth: professor of Prophetic traditions in the Dār al-Ḥadīth
mudarris farā'iḍ: professor of the law of descent and distribution of inherited property
mudarris fiqh: professor of jurisprudence
mudarris ḥadīth: professor of the science of Prophetic traditions
mudarris ḥanafī: professor of the Ḥanafī legal madhhab
mudarris ḥanbalī: professor of the Ḥanbalī legal madhhab
mudarris iʿāda: professor of repetitions, scholastic drill
mudarris iqrā': professor of the art of recitation
mudarris kashshāf: professor of elucidation of texts
mudarris khuddām: instructor of officials stationed in the sanctuary
mudarris kīmiyā': professor of chemistry, alchemy
mudarris kitāba: professor of writing
mudarris mālikī: professor of the Mālikī legal madhhab
mudarris miʿād: professor of religious lessons in Ṣūfī ceremonials
mudarris naḥw: professor of grammar
mudarris qirā'āt: professor of Koranic recitation, readings
mudarris shāfiʿī: professor of the Shāfiʿī legal madhhab
mudarris tafsīr: professor of Koranic exegesis
mudarris ṭahawī: professor of the works of al-Ṭahawī
mudarris taqsīm: professor of the law of property division and distribution, of arithmetic division
mudarris taṣawwuf: professor of mystic principles
mudarris ṭibb: professor of medicine
mudhahhib: gilder, inlayer
mudīr: director, supervisor
mudīr dawālīb: director of the royal irrigation mechanisms
mudīr maʿāṣīr: director of the royal cane and oil presses
mudīr ṭāḥūn: director of the royal mills
muftī: jurisconsult
muftī dār al-ʿadl: jurisconsult in the Palace of Justice
muḥaddith: transmittor of Prophetic traditions
muhandis: architect, engineer
muḥaṣṣil: tax collector
muḥtasib: market inspector
muʿīd: repetitor, drill instructor of textual recitation

mu'īd ḥanafī: repetitor of the Ḥanafī madhhab
mu'īd ḥadīth: repetitor of Prophetic traditions
mujabbir: bonesetter
mujaddid: renewer, rebuilder, repairman
mujallid: leather worker, book binder
mukaffit: inlayer, specialist in metal plating
mukattib: teacher of writing, librarian
mulaqqin: prompter, a faqīh
muqaddam: commander, an office restricted to the highest Mamluk amirs
muqaddir dār al-ḍarb: appraiser, assessor in the royal mint
muqassim: divider, distributer of property, cosmographer
muqri': Koran reader, reciter
muqri' abnā': Koran teacher and reader to children of Mamluks and high officials
muqri' aṭfāl: elementary Koran teacher
muqri' aytām: elementary Koran teacher in a Koran school
muqri' bukhārī: reader of the commentaries of al-Bukhārī
muqri' ḥadīth: reader of Prophetic traditions
muqri' hidāya: reader of the divine guidance, i.e., the Koran
muqri' isbā'a: reader of the seventh variant of the Koran
muqri' jawq: Koran reader in a choir that chants the scriptures
muqri' khuṭbat al-'īd: reader of the Friday sermon during the Great Festival
muqri' kutub: reader of the books, i.e., the 7 variants
muqri' mamālīk: Koran reader to Mamluk troopers
muqri' maṣḥaf: Koran reader
muqri' musnad: reader of the Islamic traditions
muqri' ṣaffa: Koran reader of a (Mamluk) military drill class
muqri' ṣaḥīḥ: reader of the *Ṣaḥīḥ* of al-Bukhārī
muqri' shubbāk: public Koran reader in a recitation gallery built into a major religio-academic institution
muqri' sīra: reader of the Prophet's biography
murābiṭ: marabout, individual endowed with divine emanation (baraka)
murattib: governor, salaried or pensioned executive official
murattib dhakhīra, murattib jawālī, murattib maṭlūb, murattib ṣadaqa, murattib taṣawwufāt: These terms represent sources of revenue—minority taxes, the sultan's treasures, claims and debts, the prescribed alms tax, and offerings presented to Ṣūfī communities. The office of *murattib* implied executive authority in the bureaus handling these revenues or that the official received his salary from them.
mushrif 'amā'ir: overseer of royal constructions
mushrif ḥawāṣil: overseer of tax receipts
mūsīqī: musician
musta'jir: leaseholder, official in bureau of leases
musta'jir awqāf: official in the bureau of leases based on pious trust foundations

mustawfī: accountant
mustawfī dawla: accountant of finances in the vizirate
mustawfī dīwān al-jaysh: accountant in the army bureau
mustawfī dīwān al-mufrad: accountant in the special bureau
mustawfī khāṣṣ: accountant in the bureau of privy funds
mustawfī khizāna: accountant in the royal wardrobe of the treasury
mutaḥaddith matjar: spokesman or agent of merchants
mutakallim: spokesman; Muslim theologian, scholastic
mutakallim ʿamāʾir: official in the bureau of royal constructions
mutakallim awqāf: official in the bureau of pious trust foundations
mutakallim dast: official of the royal bench in the Palace of Justice
mutakallim dīwān: official in the financial bureau
mutakallim mukūs: official in the bureau of tolls and imposts
mutakassib ḥānūt: proprietor of a shop
muṭalīʿ: reciter, public reader
muʾtamin mamlaka: security officer of the province
muʿtaqad: revered person, pious ascetic
mutaṣaddir: professor, instructor
mutaṣaddir amlāʾ: public or popular instructor
mutaṣaddir farāʾiḍ: professor of religious duties, esp. the law of descent and distribution
mutaṣaddir ḥadīth: professor of Prophetic traditions
mutaṣaddir iqrāʾ: professor of reading and recitation
mutaṣaddir qirāʾāt: professor of Koranic readings
mutaṣaddir taktīb: professor of writing
mutaṣarrif: administrator, particularly in the financial and taxation bureaus
mutaṣarrif ṣadaqāt al-rūmīya: administrator of obligatory alms revenues from Anatolia
muthaqqif: educated, cultured person
muwaqqiʿ: clerk, scribe
muwaqqiʿ darj: scribe of the scroll in the bureau of documents
muwaqqiʿ dast: scribe of the royal bench in the Palace of Justice
muwaqqiʿ dīwān: scribe in the financial bureau
muwaqqiʿ ḥashrīya: scribe in the bureau of escheats
muwaqqiʿ ḥukm: scribe in the civil courts
muwaqqiʿ inshāʾ, dīwān al-: scribe in the bureau of documents (chancellery)
muwaqqiʿ mawārīth: scribe in the bureau of escheats
muwaqqiʿ mufrad: scribe in the special bureau
muwaqqiʿ umarāʾ: scribe in the service of Mamluk amirs
muwaththiq: notary

nafaqa: expenses, budget, charitable gift to the poor
naḥḥāl: bee keeper
naḥḥās: coppersmith
naḥwī: grammarian

nā'ib, nuwwāb (pl.): viceroy (Mamluk official); deputy, assistant to an official
nā'ib jūra: deputy judge in a local (neighborhood) court
najjār: carpenter
naqīb: syndic, adjutant (military office)
naqīb ashrāf: syndic of the Prophet's descendants
naqīb ḥukm: sergeant of a civil court
naqīb jaysh: adjutant of the army (Mamluk officer)
naqqāsh: engraver, carver, sculptor
nāṣif: servant
nāsikh: copyist (of manuscripts)
nāẓim: poet, versifier
nāẓir: (financial) controller, supervisor
nāẓir aḥbās: controller of trust properties
nāẓir amlāk: controller of the sultan's estates
nāẓir ashrāf, dīwān al-: controller of properties and revenues held by the Prophet's descendants
nāẓir aswāq: controller of markets (horses and slaves)
nāẓir awqāf: controller of pious trust foundations
nāẓir awqāf ʿāmma: controller of general pious trust foundations
nāẓir awqāf al-ashrāf: controller of trust foundations endowed in support of the Prophet's descendants
nāẓir awqāf jarīya: controller of current, continuously yielding trust foundations
nāẓir awsiyā': controller of executors, trustees, and testators
nāẓir bandar: controller of the port
nāẓir buyūt: controller of the sultan's storehouses
nāẓir dawla: controller of the financial bureaus
nāẓir dhakhīra: controller of the sultan's treasures and munitions
nāẓir dīwān: controller of the financial bureaus
nāẓir dīwān al-khuddām: controller of the bureau of sanctuary officials
nāẓir dīwān musta'jir (āt): controller of leases and receipts
nāẓir ḥaram al-sharīf: controller of the sanctuary at Medina
nāẓir ḥaramayn: controller of the two sanctuaries (Mekka and Medina)
nāẓir ḥashrīya: controller of escheats
nāẓir ʿimāra: controller of royal constructions
nāẓir iṣṭabl: controller of the royal stables
nāẓir jawālī: controller of (minority) taxes
nāẓir jaysh: controller of the army
nāẓir khāṣṣ, dīwān al-: controller of the privy funds
nāẓir khizāna (al-kabīr): controller of the royal depository of robes
nāẓir kiswa: controller of the Kaʿba covering
nāẓir maqām: controller of the sanctuary (in Mekka)
nāẓir masjid: controller of the Kaʿba complex
nāẓir matjar: controller of commercial establishments
nāẓir mawārīth: controller of escheats

nāẓir maẓālim: reviewer of wrongs, injustices, complaints, petitions. Appelate judge who may call upon the authority of the sovereign to enforce a judgment
nāẓir mufrad, dīwān al-: controller of the special bureau
nāẓir mukūs: controller of tax, toll, and tariff receipts
nāẓir qamḥīya: controller of the granaries
nāẓir ṣadaqāt: controller of the obligatory alms tax
nāẓir tawqīʿ: controller of registration and documents

qabbānī: weigher
qāḍī: judge
qāḍī ʿaskar: military judge, judge of the army
qāḍī farḍ: judge of religious ordinances, specifically of inheritance cases
qāḍī ḥanafī: chief justice of the Ḥanafī legal madhhab
qāḍī ḥanbalī: chief justice of the Ḥanbalī legal madhhab
qāḍī kabīr: synonym for the qāḍī al-quḍāt
qāḍī maḥmal: judge of the pilgrimage caravan
qāḍī mālikī: chief justice of the Mālikī legal madhhab
qāḍī maṭlūbīn: judge of claims cases (debts and liabilities)
qāḍī quḍāt: chief justice of the Mamluk state
qāḍī rakb: civil judge of the sultan's military expeditions
qāḍī shāfiʿī: chief justice of the Shāfiʿī legal madhhab, usually synonomous with the qāḍī al-quḍāt
qassāb sukkar: sugar cane cutter
qazzāz: silk merchant, glazier

rabbāb iṣṭabl al-sulṭānī: controller of the royal stable
raḥḥāl: traveler, camel driver, caravaneer
ra'īs, rā's: chief, head of a profession or syndicate
ra'īs jawq: director of the scriptural choir
ra'īs mīqātī: chief timekeeper (to the imperial court)
ra'īs mujabbirīn: chief bonesetter (to the imperial court)
ra'īs muqri' al-jawq: director of the scriptural choir
ra'īs ṭabīb: chief physician (to the imperial court)
rā's nawba: chief guard (Mamluk official)
rasūl: ambassador, delegate
rasūl firanj: ambassador to the Franks (Europeans)
rasūl malik al-firanj: ambassador to a European monarch (not the Byzantine Emperor)
rasūl mulūk al-atrāk: ambassador to the kings of the Turks
rasūl sulṭānī: ambassador of the sultan
riyāḍi: mathematician; director of military exercises

saddār: maker of headgear and headcloths, caps
safīr: agent of a retinue, normally of a Mamluk amir or the imperial court

ṣāḥib dīwān al-inshā': intendant of the bureau of documents (chancellery)
ṣāḥib dīwān al-jaysh: intendant of the army bureau
ṣāḥib madrasa: intendant of a madrasa
ṣanā'i'ī: craftsman, manufacturer
ṣanā'i'ī dahshāt: magician
ṣanā'i'ī ḥarīr: silk producer
ṣanā'i'ī khaṭṭ: craftsman of the (royal) seal; geomancer
ṣanā'i'ī kutub: bookbinder
ṣanā'i'ī maqāṭi': manufacturer of cutting instruments
ṣanā'i'ī mu'jizāt: magician, performer of miracles
ṣanā'i'ī nafṭ: manufacturer of naphtha
ṣanā'i'ī qabbān: manufacturer of weight scales, steelyards
ṣanā'i'ī qumāsh azraq: manufacturer of blue cloth (for uniforms)
ṣanā'i'ī sharīṭ: manufacturer of ribbon, cord, string
ṣanā'i'ī tajlīd al-kutub: bookbinder
saqaṭī: trash, junk dealer
sāqī: cupbearer (in the imperial court)
sāqī qirba: water carrier
sawwāq: driver of animals
sawwāq ghanam: sheep driver
ṣayrafī: moneychanger
shādd: superintendant
shādd 'amā'ir al-sulṭān: superintendant of royal constructions
shādd khāṣṣ: superintendant of the privy funds
shāhid: notary of the judiciary and/or the bureaus
shāhid aḥbās: notary in the bureau of trust properties
shāhid 'āmā'ir awqāf: notary of constructions supported by trust foundations
shāhid awqāf: notary in the bureau of pious trust foundations
shāhid dār al-tuffāḥ: notary in the Dār al-Tuffāḥ
shāhid dīwān al-jawālī: notary in the bureau of (minority) tax receipts
shāhid ḥanbalī: court notary of the Ḥanbalī legal madhhab
shāhid ḥānūt: notary in a shop (ḥānūt)
shāhid 'imāra: notary in the bureau of the sultan's constructions
shāhid iṣṭabl: notary in the royal stables bureau
shāhid jūra: notary in the local (neighborhood) civil courts
shāhid kiswa: notary of the Ka'ba covering
shāhid makhbaz: notary of the royal bakery
shāhid mufrad, dīwān al-: notary in the special bureau
shāhid ṣūfī: ṣūfī notary
shā'ir: poet
shaqqā': woodcutter, lumber dealer
sharā'ibī: apothecary
sharārībī: tassel maker
shāriḥ: writer of expository textual commentaries
shāri': legal agent

shāriʿ amlāʾ: public legal agent
sharūṭī: contracts officer, policeman
shaṭranjī: chess player
shaykh: learned person; legal authority in a religious community or institution
shaykh āthār: shaykh of religious relics
shaykh fiqh: shaykh of jurisprudence
shaykh fuqarāʾ: shaykh of the poor and needy
shaykh ḥadīth: shaykh of Prophetic traditions
shaykh ḥanafī: shaykh of the Ḥanafī legal madhhab
shaykh islām, al-balad: shaykh of Islam, term applied to retired chief justices
shaykh khidma, khuddām: shaykh of the staff of the two sanctuaries
shaykh mīʿād: shaykh of religious lessons in Ṣūfī ceremonials
shaykh muḥaddithīn: shaykh of transmitters of Prophetic traditions
shaykh muwaqqiʿīn: shaykh of clerks, scribes
shaykh qirāʾāt: shaykh of Koranic readings and recitations
shaykh sabʿa: shaykh of the seven riwāyas (variants) of the Koran
shaykh shāfiʿī: shaykh of the Shāfiʿī legal madhhab
shaykh shuyūkh: grand shaykh, title applied to the rectors of Saʿīd al-Suʿadāʾ and Siryāqūs
shaykh ṣūfī: mystic shaykh
shaykh taṣawwuf: shaykh of mystic principles
shaykh zuwwār: shaykh of pilgrims (specifically to Medina)
simsār: broker, business agent, middleman
simsār kutub: book dealer
sukkarī: confectioner
suṭuḥī: (pious) resident of a religious institution (literally, a roof dweller)
suyūfī: sword maker

taʿnān dūlāb: caretaker of a mill, bureau
ṭabbākh: cook
ṭabbākh sukkar: worker in a sugar mill
ṭabīb: physician
tājir: merchant
tājir awlād: purchaser of Mamluks for the sultan
tājir baḥr: maritime merchant
tājir bazz: cloth merchant
tājir biṭāna: merchant of utensils (cooking ware, etc.); of a special sort of cloth
tājir burr: wheat merchant
tājir firanj: merchant dealing with the European import-export trade
tājir ghazl: merchant of thread, yarn
tājir ḥānūt: merchant of a shop, proprietor
tājir jubna: cheese merchant
tājir kabīr: merchant of recognized stature, not necessarily involved in the Mamluk bureaucracy
tājir mamālīk: purchaser of Mamluks for the sultan

tājir ṣābūn: soap merchant
tājir shurb: merchant of medicines, pharmacist
tājir sukkar: sugar merchant
tājir sulṭānī: royal merchant, involved in the Mamluk bureaucracy
tājir takfīt: merchant of inlaid work, engraved work, metal plate
tājir zayt: oil merchant
ṭashshāt: maker of bowls, basins

ustādār: major-domo (official in the imperial court)
ustādār amlāk: overseer of the sultan's estates
ustādār awqāf: overseer of pious trust foundations
ustādār dhakhīra, dhakhā'ir: overseer of the sultan's treasures and munitions
ustādār khāṣṣ: overseer of the privy funds
ustādār musta'jirāt: overseer of leases and reclaims
ustādār suḥba: chief steward of the imperial court

wā'iẓ: preacher
wakīl: commissioner, financial agent of the government
wakīl bayt al-māl: agent of the exchequer, treasury
wakīl iṣṭabl: commissioner of the royal stables
wakīl kiswa: commissioner of the Ka'ba covering
wālī: governor of a district
waqqād: stoker (in a bathhouse)
warrād: dealer in rose petals and other flower products for aromatics and dyes
warrāq: stationer, paper dealer
wazīr: vizier, prime minister
wazzān: weigher

zajjāj: glazier
zarrā': farmer
zayyāt: oil dealer
zimām: registrar, financial officer; chief eunuch in the imperial court

Notes

INTRODUCTION

1. The most significant recent contribution to the subject is Ira M. Lapidus' monograph, *Muslim Cities in the Later Middle Ages* (Cambridge, 1967). His analysis takes account of earlier studies by such figures as Brunschvig, Cahen, Gibb and Bowen, Marcais and Sauvaget, but then develops a new thesis based on the Mamluks' "privatization" of power and impact of this on the urban population. Richard W. Bulliet has produced the first systematic examination of the learned class in medieval Iran: *The Patricians of Nishapur* (Cambridge, 1972). His study focuses on genealogical ties and legal affiliations.

2. As argued by Lapidus, *Muslim Cities*, pp. 108-10. His interpretation is qualified by my findings, but remains an insightful portrayal of the diverse contacts between the civilian elite and other elements of society.

3. This argument is tempered by repeated instances of crossover between professional categories. With the exception of the military-executive, no occupational group was totally absent from any of these categories. All such groups included some individuals regarded as suitable for service in the legitimate spheres of ʿulamaʾ activity. The argument in this book is therefore based on variations in proportions between categories rather than complete exclusion of any group from them.

4. The most important work in the field of Mamluk studies has been done by Professor David Ayalon, whose series of articles explores several aspects of the military and social organization of the ruling elite.

5. H. Gibb, "Islamic Biographical Literature," in B. Lewis and P. Holt, eds., *Historians of the Middle East* (London, 1962), p. 54.

6. G. Levi Della Vida, "Sīra," *EI*[1] IV, 439-41. There is a little doubt that the *Sīra* that finally appeared in literary form incorporated apocryphal elements. The work of Ibn Isḥāq was completed more than a century after the Prophet's death. Indeed, one could argue that apocryphal additions were necessary in a biography of an individual whose life was regarded as a standard for personal conduct and yet was incompletely recorded. However, such additions were less justifiable for other persons who merely knew Muḥammad and served as transmitters of his utterances. Rather, the absence of information was tacitly acknowledged by omission rather than by speculation on the basis of hearsay or unsound isnāds (chain of authorities).

7. F. Rosenthal, *A History of Muslim Historiography* (Leiden, 1968), pp. 82-84; I. Hafsi, "Recherches sur le genre *Ṭabaqāt* dans la littérature arabe," *Arabica* XXIII (1976), esp. the section on traditionists, pp. 241-65.

8. Gibb, "Literature," p. 56.

9. *Ibid.*, p. 55.

10. Al-Dhahabī's *Ta'rīkh al-Islām* (History of Islam) (*GAL* II, 58-59, nos. 1-3, Suppl. II, 45-47) began from the death of the Prophet and proceeded up to the first decades of the eighth century A.H. The arrangement of its necrologies established a model followed by subsequent compilers.

11. Gibb, "Literature," pp. 56-57.

12. *Ibid.*, p. 56.

13. *GAL* II, 43, no. 1; Suppl. II, 31-32; in print, Ḥusām al-Dīn al-Qudsī, ed., 12 vols. (Cairo, 1353/1934). Al-Qudsī based his edition on the manuscripts held in the Egyptian National and al-Azhar libraries (Dār al-Kutub, Ta'rīkh: 675, 676, 887, 3270, 1510; al-Azhar, Ta'rīkh: 6547 [239], 52502 [3791], 52853 [3882], 52854 [3883]) and on the manuscripts held in Damascus (Ẓāhirīya, Ta'rīkh: 70) and Istanbul (Asafiya, I, 782) for the first volume.

14. *GAL* II, 52, no. 4. The first 220 biographies of this work have been printed in one volume: A. Y. Najatī, ed. (Cairo, 1956), based on several manuscripts (Dār al-Kutub, Ta'rīkh: 230, 1113, 2355; Ḥadīth: 11765, 13475, 1381, 13834; BN, f.a.: 2068-73). The Dār al-Kutub, Ta'rīkh 1113, and the BN manuscripts were consulted for the work as a whole. See also *Index* (in List of Abbreviations).

15. *Ḍaw'* VIII, p. 2, no. 1.

16. He expressed these views in a treatise on historical methods: *I'lān bi'l-Tawbīkh li-Man Dhamma Ahl al-Ta'rīkh* (The Open Denunciation of the Adverse Critics of the Historians), edited by F. Rosenthal (Baghdad, 1963); English translation in F. Rosenthal, *A History of Muslim Historiography* (Leiden, 1968), pp. 195-450. The work is important because it offers definitions and explains applications of historical terminology as well as cataloguing major types of historical works and their authors from the classical period to al-Sakhāwī's own day.

17. *Ḍaw'* 3245, X, p. 305, no. 1178. See also G. Wiet, "L'historien Abul-Maḥāsin," *BIE* XII (1930), 89-105.

18. A. Darrag, "La vie d'Abū'l-Maḥāsin ibn Taghrī-Birdī et son oeuvre," *AI* XI (1972), 165-67.

19. William Popper ("Sakhāwī's Criticism of Ibn Taghrī-Birdī," *SO*, pp. 371-89) rightly dismissed these as relatively minor. However, David Ayalon has noted this historian's occasional misinterpretation of both nomenclature and political terminology ("Names, Titles and 'Nisbas' of the Mamluks," *Israel Oriental Studies* V (1975), 202, 204-205). But, as Ayalon corroborates, Ibn Taghrī-Birdī's information on individuals involved in court circles was of great importance—and very accurate, especially concerning his own contemporaries.

20. The major sources are listed here. See bibliography for editions consulted by the author or noted in catalogues:

Al-'Aynī, *'Iqd al-Jumān fī Ta'rīkh Ahl al-Islām.*

Al-Biqā'ī, *'Anwān al-Zamān fī Tarājim al-Shuyūkh wa'l-Aqrān.*

Ibn Fahd al-Makkī (Taqī al-Dīn), *Laḥẓ al-Alḥāẓ bi-Dhayl Ṭabaqāt al-Ḥuffāẓ.*

Ibn Fahd al-Makkī (Najm al-Dīn), *Al-Mu'jam.*

———, *Dhayl al-Mu'jam.*

Ibn Fahd al-Makkī (ʿIzz al-Dīn), *Al-Kamīn bi-Dhayl al-ʿIqd al-Thamīn fī Taʾrīkh al-Balad al-Amīn* (continuation of al-Fāsī).
Al-Fāsī, *ʿIqd al-Thamīn fī Taʾrīkh al-Balad al-Amīn.*
———, *Shifāʾ al-Gharam bi-Akhbār al-Balad al-Ḥaram.*
Ibn Ḥajar al-ʿAsqalānī, *Inbāʾ al-Ghumr bi-Anbāʾ al-ʿUmr.*
———, *Rafʿ al-Iṣr ʿan Quḍāt Miṣr.*
———, *Al-Durar al-Kāmina fī Aʿyān al-Miʾa al-Thāmina.*
Ibn Khaṭīb al-Nāṣirīya, *Muntaqkhabāt min Kitāb al-Kawākib al-Wadīʾa fī Dhayl ʿalā Taʾrīkh Ibn Khaṭīb al-Nāṣirīya.*
Ibn Khaṭīb al-Nāṣirīya, *Al-Durr al-Muntakhib min Taʾrīkh Mamlakat Ḥalab.*
Al-Maqrīzī, *Kitāb al-Sulūk li-Maʿrifat al-Duwal waʾl-Mulūk.*
———, *Durar al-ʿUqūd al-Farīda.*
———, *Kitāb al-Muqaffa.*
Ibn Nāhiḍ, *Al-Sīrat al-Muʾayyadīya.*
Ibn Qāḍī Shuhba, *Ṭabaqāt al-Shāfiʿīya.*
———, *Al-Aʿlām bi-Taʾrīkh Ahl al-Islām.*
Al-Sakhāwī, *Al-Ṭibr al-Masbūk fī Dhayl al-Sulūk.*
———, *Dhayl ʿalā Rafʿ al-Iṣr.*
Ibn Taghrī-Birdī, *Al-Nujūm al-Zāhira fī Muluk Miṣr waʾl-Qāhira.*
———, *Al-Ḥawādith al-Duhūr fī Madā al-Ayyām waʾl-Shuhūr.*

CHAPTER I. THE FIFTEENTH CENTURY IN THE HISTORY OF CAIRO

1. Prior to the fifteenth century, the metropolitan area surrounding the walled city of Fāṭimid al-Qāhira itself had experienced occupation by foreign military forces, including the Franks in 1168-1169. During the termination of the Fāṭimid dynasty at the hands of Shirkūh and Ṣalāḥ al-Dīn, there was local rioting on various occasions, although no major disruptions or destruction of property took place within the city proper. These various incidents wrought damage but cannot compare with the ravages of a thorough pillage, such as befell Baghdād at the hands of the Mongols in 1258.

2. D. Ayalon, "Aspects of the Mamlūk Phenomenon—I," *Der Islam* LIII, no. 2 (1976), 196.

3. Ayalon summarizes the major regions or fronts adjoining the Dār al-Islām: the European zone, the Sudan and sub-Saharan Africa, the Indian Subcontinent, and Central Asia. This fourth zone constituted the great reservoir for manpower throughout the Middle Ages. Ayalon rightly stresses that the majority of those "entering Muslim territory or invading it from the fourth front almost always adopted Islam sooner or later, as far as they were pagans"; *ibid.*, p. 204. Although Turks were the most prominent element in the Mamluk corps of Egypt and elsewhere, slaves were also recruited from among Circassians, Greeks, other Europeans, Kurds, and Turcomans. See G. Wiet, *L'Egypte Arabe*, in Gabriel Hanotaux, ed., *Histoire de la nation égyptienne*, IV (Paris, 1937), 389.

4. Ayalon, "Aspects—I," p. 205; Wiet, *Egypte*, p. 387.

5. D. Ayalon, "Preliminary Remarks on the Mamluk Military Institution in Islam," in V. J. Parry and M. E. Yapp, eds., *War, Technology and Society in the Middle East* (Oxford, 1975), pp. 44-58; C. E. Bosworth, "Recruitment, Muster and Review in Medieval Islamic Armies," *ibid.*, pp. 59-77; and C. E. Bosworth, "Barbarian Invasions: The Coming of the Turks into the Islamic World," in D. S. Richards, ed., *Islamic Civilization, 950-1150* (Oxford, 1973), pp. 1-16.

6. Wiet, *Egypte*, p. 401.

7. On the iqṭāʿ system and its Egyptian variant, see C. Cahen, "L'évolution de l'iḳṭāʿ de IXᵉ au XIIIᵉ siècles," *Annales Economies, Sociétés, Civilisations* VIII (1953), 25-52; and his condensed statement in *EI*², III, 1088-90; see also A. N. Poliak, *Feudalism in Egypt, Syria, Palestine and the Lebanon, 1250-1900* (London, 1939); A. N. Poliak, "Some Notes on the Feudal System of the Mamluks," *JRAS* (1937), pp. 97-107; and D. Ayalon, "The System of Payment in Mamluk Military Society," *JESHO*, I, no. 1 (August 1957), 37-65, and no. 3 (October 1958), 257-96.

8. Wiet, *Egypte*, pp. 403-407. Aybak was killed on April 11, 1257, and Shajar al-Durr on the 15th.

9. *Ibid.*, pp. 410-38 for an outline of Baybars' career and legacy. See also R. Paret, "Sīrat Baybars," *EI*², I, 1126-27, for the popular literature on this figure.

10. Enforcement of this policy lapsed somewhat after the death of al-Nāṣir Muḥammad in 1340, especially in Upper Egypt. See Chapter II, note 20.

11. On the social implications of the Mamluk modification of the iqṭāʿ system, see J. Abu-Lughod, *Cairo, 1001 Years of the City Victorious* (Princeton, 1971), p. 31.

12. D. Ayalon, "The Circassians in the Mamluk Kingdom," *JAOS* LXIX (1949), 145.

13. *Ibid.*, pp. 141-42; Wiet, *Egypte*, pp. 521-22, 529-31, 538-40; A. Darraj, *L'Egypte sous la règne de Barsbay* (Damascus, 1961), pp. 58-59.

14. Ayalon, "Circassians," pp. 145-46.

15. D. Ayalon, "Studies on the Structure of the Mamluk Army—I," *BSOAS*, XV (1953), esp. pp. 208-11. Ayalon's series of articles on the organization of the Mamluk army provides a detailed analysis of the system that produced this condition. The Circassian attitude toward the throne intensified the existing problem of competition between differing factions of Mamluks. The reader is referred to these articles for an outline describing the specific ranks and designations used among the Mamluk military class itself.

16. W. Popper, *Egypt and Syria under the Circassian Sultans*, in University of California Publications in Semitic Philology XV (1955), 87-88.

17. Wiet, *Egypte*, pp. 401-402, 426-30, 456-58, 505-506.

18. Ayalon, "Studies—I," pp. 206-207; Popper, *Egypt and Syria*, pp. 87-88.

19. Ayalon, "Studies—I," pp. 217-19; Popper, *Egypt and Syria*, p. 88.

20. Ayalon, "Studies—I," pp. 209-10; Ayalon, "Circassians," p. 146.

21. C. E. Bosworth, *The Islamic Dynasties*, Vol. V of *Islamic Surveys*, edited

by M. M. Watt (Edinburgh, 1967), p. 64; S. Lane-Poole, *The Muḥammadan Dynasties* (London, 1894), pp. 80-83. These were:

al-Ẓāhir Barqūq, 784-791/1382-1389 and 792-801/1390-1399
al-Nāṣir Faraj, 801-808/1399-1409 and 808-815/1405-1412
al-Mu'ayyad Shaykh, 815-824/1412-1421
al-Ashraf Barsbāy, 825-841/1422-1437
al-Ẓāhir Jaqmaq, 842-857/1438-1453
al-Ashraf Īnāl, 857-865/1453-1461
al-Ẓāhir Khushqadam, 865-872/1461-1467
al-Ashraf Qāytbāy, 872-901/1468-1495

22. D. Ayalon, "Studies on the Structure of the Mamluk Army—II," *BSOAS* XV (1953), 459-61.

23. E. Ashtor, *Les métaux précieux et la balance des payements du proche-orient à la basse époque* (Paris, 1971), p. 88.

24. S. Labib, *Handelsgeschichte Ägyptens im Spätmittelalter (1171-1517)* (Wiesbaden, 1965), pp. 163-64. Barqūq proceeded to expand the offices of ustādār (major domo), nāzir al-khāṣṣ (controller of the special bureau), and nāẓir al-dawla (controller of the privy fund) in order to centralize the bureaucratic control over revenues under officials who were members of his personal staff.

25. Ashtor, "Balance," pp. 92-94.

26. *Ibid.*, pp. 402-403.

27. Darraj, *Barsbay*, pp. 40-42.

28. *Ibid.*, pp. 39-40.

29. Labib, *Handelsgeschichte*, pp. 409-10.

30. *Ibid.*, pp. 166-67, 410.

31. Popper, *Egypt and Syria*, pp. 95-96; D. Ayalon, "Studies on the Structure of the Mamluk Army—III," *BSOAS* XVI (1954), 60-61.

32. Popper, *Egypt and Syria*, pp. 102-103.

33. Darraj, *Barsbay*, pp. 63-64.

34. Labib, *Handelsgeschichte*, pp. 411-13; Darraj, *Barsbay*, pp. 110-19.

35. In addition to the influence of the sultan and amirs on the qāḍīs and, therefore, over the administration of the Sharīʿa, the military judges of the Mamluk state (quḍāt al-ʿaskar, ḥujjāb), who exercised jurisdiction in cases dealing with members of the military elite, functioned independently from the civil judiciary. A. N. Poliak went so far as to argue that they based their decisions in part on the Yāsa, the Mongol legal code, which was alien to the principles of the Sharīʿa. See Poliak, "The Influence of Chingiz Khan's Yāsa upon the General Organization of the Mamluk State," *BSOAS* X (1942), 863-76; and Poliak, "Le caractère colonial de l'état mamelouk dans ses rapports avec le horde d'or," *REI* IX (1935), 231-47. Ayalon has recently contested Poliak's conclusions concerning the Yāsa and its influence over Mamluk legal procedure, arguing that available textual evidence does little to support Poliak's arguments. See D. Ayalon, "The Great Yāsa of Chingiz Khan, A Re-Examination," *SI*,

XXXVI (1972), 136-56. In general, the military judges seem to have remained within the framework of the Sharīʿa, but were independent of the civil judges. They distinguished between Mamluk and civilian litigants, recognizing the legal prerogatives of the former.

36. Ayalon, "Payment," no. 3 (1958), pp. 291-92.

37. For example, al-Maqrīzī emphasized price inflation and debasement of coinage. He quoted prices at regular intervals in his chronicles not only to demonstrate the severity of the problem but also to show that it was measurable. For an analysis of al-Maqrīzī's data on prices and coinage, see J. Bacharach, "A Study of the Correlation between Textual Sources and Numismatic Evidence for Mamluk Egypt and Syria, A.H. 784-872/A.D.. 1382-1468," Ph.D. dissertation, Michigan, 1967.

38. Most recently discussed by A. Udovitch, "England to Egypt, 1350-1500: Long-term Trends and Long-distance Trade," in M. A. Cook, ed., *Studies in the Economic History of the Middle East* (London, 1970), pp. 115-28. See also E. Ashtor's summary in his *Social and Economic History of the Near East in the Middle Ages* (Berkeley and Los Angeles, 1976), pp. 319-31.

39. Ayalon, "Studies—I," pp. 209-10, 224-28.

40. D. Ayalon, "L'esclavage du mamlouk," *Oriental Notes and Studies*, Jerusalem Oriental Society, no. 1 (1951).

41. Wiet, *Egypte*, pp. 589, 606-607.

42. D. Ayalon, "Discharges from Service, Banishments and Imprisonments in Mamluk Society," *Israel Oriental Studies*, II (1972), 27-28; Labib, *Handelsgeschichte*, pp. 414-15. Note that this was distinct from the forms of payment to the Mamluks in active service. For details, see Ayalon, "Payment," pp. 37-65, 258-96.

43. Labib, *Handelsgeschichte*, p. 414; Ayalon, "Studies—III," pp. 76-77.

44. By the mid-fifteenth century, both royal and out-of-service Mamluks had organized themselves into gangs with lists of clients who paid them protection money to guarantee their own personal security and that of their businesses. This phenomenon reached its peak during the reigns of Jaqmaq and Khushqadam, and subsided somewhat during the reign of Qāytbāy. It seems that Jaqmaq encouraged the formation of such groups in order to relieve the pressure on him for payments. Later, he was obliged to encourage the organization of counter-gangs to combat the former groups. See Labib, *Handelsgeschichte*, p. 415.

45. Ayalon, "Payment," pp. 287-89.

46. Labib, *Handelsgeschichte*, p. 402; Ayalon, "Payment," p. 273-74. Note that Ayalon lists a figure of 7,165,000 dīnārs based on a statement by Ibn Iyās, in *Badāʾiʿ al-Zuhūr fī Waqāʾiʿ al-Duhūr*, edited by Muḥammad Mustapha (Cairo, 1963), III, 256, 317. This figure does not, however, include extraordinary payments that Labib includes, raising the total expenditures to eight million dīnārs.

47. Ayalon, "Payment," pp. 289-90.

48. Udovitch, "England to Egypt," pp. 115-16.

49. *Ibid.*, pp. 118-20. Plague epidemics struck Egypt every seven years on the average, and claimed especially children and the foreign-born. See D. Neustadt

(Ayalon), "The Plague and Its Effects upon the Mamluk Army," *JRAS* (April 1946), pp. 69-71; M. Dols, *The Black Death in the Middle East* (Princeton, 1976), ch. V, esp. pp. 185-93.

50. Udovitch, "England to Egypt," pp. 117-18.

51. That the Mamluk regime made no attempt to transfer and resettle the population underscores the lack of a pragmatic policy to cope with the agrarian decline. No consideration was given to the possibility of regrouping the peasant population in a more efficient pattern of distribution. The network of iqṭāʿs could have been reorganized, with certain provinces, especially in Upper Egypt, reserved for pastoral purposes (wool production, horse pasturage, and so forth). Whether the Mamluk regime could actually have carried out a population transfer, of course, or how effective it would have been is debatable.

52. For an analysis of medieval Muslim commercial practices and their relationship to the Sharīʿa, see A. L. Udovitch, *Partnership and Profit in Medieval Islam* (Princeton, 1970).

53. This is not to deny the impact of depressions, monetary crises, commercial failures, and natural disasters. However, these factors do not detract from the generally pragmatic attitude of the medieval Egyptian regimes up to the Circassian period. An exception may be the partial debasement of coinage inaugurated during the late Fāṭimid and early Ayyūbid periods to counteract the debasements of the Crusaders. Refer to A. Ehrenkreutz, *Saladin* (Albany, 1972), pp. 17-18; Ehrenkreutz, "The Standard of Fineness of Gold Coins Circulating in Egypt at the Time of the Crusaders," *JAOS* LXXIV (1954), 162-66; and Ehrenkreutz, "The Crisis of the 'Dīnār' in the Egypt of Saladin," *JAOS*, LXXVI (1956), 174-84.

54. Labib, *Handelsgeschichte*, p. 237; Wiet, *Egypte*, pp. 450-56, 489-90, 491-97.

55. Labib, *Handelsgeschichte*, p. 405.

56. Al-Qalqashandī, *Ṣubḥ al-Aʿshā fī Ṣināʿat al-Inshā* (Cairo, 1914-1928) VI, 32; W. Fischel, "The Spice Trade in Mamluk Egypt," *JESHO* I (1958), 162-64; G. Wiet, "Les marchands d'épices sous les sultans mamlouks," *CHE* VII (1955), 94.

57. Fischel, "Spice Trade," p. 164.

58. *Ibid.*, pp. 169-72; W. Fischel, "Über die Gruppe der Kārimī-Kaufleute," *Scripta Arabica, Annalecta Orientalia* (1937), 80-81; Wiet, "Marchands," p. 89.

59. Qalqashandī, *Ṣubḥ*, III, 464-66; Wiet, "Marchands," pp. 93-96; Fischel, "Spice Trade," pp. 167-68.

60. I. Lapidus, *Muslim Cities in the Later Middle Ages* (Cambridge, 1967), p. 89; Udovitch, "England to Egypt," p. 122.

61. Labib, *Handelsgeschichte*, pp. 355-56; Darraj, *Barsbay*, pp. 109-158.

62. Labib, *Handelsgeschichte*, pp. 402-408; Darraj, *Barsbay*, pp. 146-51, 195-237.

63. Labib, *Handelsgeschichte*, pp. 355-56, 372-73, 382-85, 402-404; Wiet, "Marchands," p. 103.

64. Labib, *Handelsgeschichte*, p. 403; Fischel, "Spice Trade," pp. 172-74. The

monopoly system was not enforced uniformly. After Barsbāy's death, the system lapsed temporarily—due, however, to bureaucratic difficulties rather than to recognition of its adverse effects. The system was renewed periodically, especially during the reigns of Qāytbāy and al-Ghawrī.

65. Darraj, *Barsbay*, pp. 159-237; Labib, *Handelsgeschichte*, pp. 373-82.

66. Labib, *Handelsgeschichte*, pp. 385-86, 388.

67. *Ibid.*, pp. 392-93.

68. *Ibid.*, pp. 337, 439.

69. *Ibid.*, pp. 403-404, 409.

70. The phenomenon of systematic confiscation as a policy mutually planned and anticipated by the sultan and his clients who bore the confiscations is a topic worthy of future study.

71. Labib, *Handelsgeschichte*, pp. 412-13.

72. *Ibid.*, p. 165.

73. *Ibid.*, p. 422; M. Sobernheim, "Das Zuckermonopol unter Sultan Barsbai," *ZA* XXVII (1912), 75-84.

74. Labib, *Handelsgeschichte*, pp. 420-21; Darraj, *Barsbay*, pp. 68-73.

75. Refer to Poliak, *Feudalism*; and Poliak, "Notes on the Feudal System," pp. 97-107.

76. Labib, *Handelsgeschichte*, pp. 338-39.

77. Ibn Khaldun, *Muqaddima*, translated and edited by Franz Rosenthal (New York, 1958) II, 93-96, 102-103, 124-28.

78. Darraj, *Barsbay*, pp. 59-66.

79. Labib, *Handelsgeschichte*, pp. 441-80. The European commercial revolution involves multiple causes, of course. It would have occurred regardless of the policies undertaken by regimes in the Near East, although these policies certainly influenced its timing. European interests in the region continued beyond the Mamluk period, as the capitulatory privileges granted to them by the Ottomans during the sixteenth and seventeenth centuries attest.

80. Ehrenkreutz, *Saladin*, pp. 233-38.

81. A. K. S. Lambton, *Landlord and Peasant in Iran* (London, 1953), p. 100; J. Aubin, "Comment Timur-Lenk prenait les villes," *SI* XIX (1963), 95-105; V. Minorsky, "The Aq-Qoyunlu and Land Reforms," *BSOAS* XVII:3 (1955), 449-62.

82. Lambton, *Landlord*, pp. 77-78, 80-83.

83. Marshall Hodgson provides a perceptive statement about social change following the Mongol invasions. See *The Venture of Islam* (Chicago, 1974), II, bk. IV, ch. 1, esp. pp. 391-410.

84. Walter Fischel, *Ibn Khaldun in Egypt* (Berkeley and Los Angeles, 1967), pp. 18-19, 20-22.

CHAPTER II. GEOGRAPHIC ORIGINS OF THE CIVILIAN ELITE

1. A unique body of source materials that do belong to this category is extant: the Cairo Geniza documents. Due primarily to the efforts of Solomon Goitein,

these varied materials, which bear upon many aspects of Egyptian and Mediterranean social and economic history during the central Middle Ages are in the process of publication and analysis. The Cairo Geniza documents were not an archive, but a random repository of documents bearing Hebrew characters, in a chamber belonging to a synagogue. See S. D. Goitein, *A Mediterranean Society, The Jewish Communities of the Arab World as Portrayed in the Documents of the Cairo Geniza* (Berkeley and Los Angeles, 1967), I, especially ch. 1 for details on the documents and their subject matter. See also S. Shaked, *A Tentative Bibliography of Geniza Documents* (Paris, 1964) for information as to location of current collections. The Geniza documents provide considerable information concerning geographic origins and travel patterns. However, it must be stressed that these documents apply to the Fāṭimid and early Ayyūbid periods rather than to the era under study here, the Circassian regime during the fifteenth century.

2. There was a qualifier inserted into the stream of nisbas by the biographers. They categorized nisbas as aṣl (ancestral site), thumma (intermediate site of residence), and the general nisba that usually included the final place of residence, if it was mentioned at all. Only 1,486 individuals of the 4,631 selected for this study actually bore the nisba "al-Qāhirī," even though all of them lived in Cairo.

3. Of 4,631 biographies, 1,286 listed birthplaces; some 4,074 biographies reported at least one geographic nisba. The two indicators must be compared together in order to depict a probable pattern of migration. There were 850 identifiable place names derived from the geographic nisbas, birthplaces, and references to travel. Of these, 433 were located within modern Egypt and 417 distributed unevenly throughout other regions of the Near East. This chapter does not include a survey of places of death outside Cairo, since the overwhelming majority of individuals died either in Cairo or in Makka or Madīna during a pilgrimage.

4. The actual percentage of foreign-born among the ʿulamaʾ was high during the fifteenth century. Of the birthplaces recorded by the compilers of the two sources, between one-half and two-thirds referred to Cairo and its environs, the remainder being located elsewhere in Egypt or in other states. This, plus the great range of nisbas relating to identifiable place names, would suggest a first-generation foreign-born percentage of about 30 to 40 percent among the ʿulamaʾ. Note that the overwhelming majority of all individuals in the biographical sources did identify with ancestral areas, and used such geographic nisbas as family surnames. However, those whose families had lived in Cairo for generations were distinguishable from those born elsewhere or from the children of recent immigrants.

5. Of the individuals who originated outside Cairo, about 40 percent of the total sample, some 60 percent came from the Egyptian districts between the Mediterranean ports and Aswān. Of these, in turn, the breakdown is roughly 65 to 35 percent (possibly 70 to 30 percent) for the Delta and the valley, respectively.

6. This is a general statement referring to a complex process. The critical

elements in the appointment procedure were the personal connections and relations the individual had established rather than rating of academic performance, which was only occasionally noted in the biographical accounts. It must be stressed that this pattern held true only for the individuals or families who were relocating in Cairo from places of origin *within* Egypt. The pattern of immigration from regions outside Egypt, with the possible exception of Syria-Palestine, was not supported by complete enough figures or by sufficient density of sites to establish our hypothesis.

7. There were 50 references to Alexandria in nisbas and 16 to it as a birthplace. There were 30 references to Damietta in nisbas and 11 to it as a birthplace.

8. Refer to Tables 1 through 6 for the Delta districts and towns, which compare data according to professional category with geographic sites.

9. This relationship was modified during the fifteenth century, since Alexandria suffered a gradual decline in terms of maintenance by the sultans and importance as an entrepôt of trade. The later Mamluk sultans actually transferred much of the commercial establishment of Alexandria to Cairo, primarily because of the dramatic increase in raids by European pirates against the city during the fifteenth century. By the time of the Ottoman conquest, Alexandria was already diminished to the level of a depressed semi-abandoned port town, and recovered little before the reign of Muḥammad ʿAlī.

10. During the Mamluk period Gharbīya included all of the territory between the Damietta and Rosetta branches of the Nile north of Minūfīya. The modern governorate of Kafr al-Shaykh therefore constituted a part of this district. The northernmost region of the district appears to have been relatively underdeveloped and unpopulated during the fifteenth century.

11. Al-Maḥallat al-Kubrā yielded 59 nisbas and 25 birthplaces. Minūf yielded 39 nisbas and 13 birthplaces.

12. Ibn al-Jīʿān, *Al-Tuḥfat al-Sanīya bi-Ismāʿ al-Bilād al-Miṣrīya* (Cairo, 1897), pp. 138-47; Popper, *Egypt and Syria under the Circassian Sultans* in University of California Publications in Semitic Philology XV-XVI, 99.

13. Given the skewing of data toward the second half of the century, the overall rate of migration would appear to have remained relatively constant. No radical shifts in the proportions of either nisbas or birthplaces were reported for any twenty-five-year period.

14. *Ḍaw'* 1547, V, p. 287, no. 975.

15. *Ḍaw'* 1704, VI, p. 85, no. 286.

16. *Ḍaw'* 170, I, p. 253, line 11.

17. For Asyūṭ there were 19 nisba references and 7 birthplaces.

18. This may be due to a degree of geographic ignorance on the part of al-Sakhāwī and Ibn Taghrī-Birdī, since the former was fairly familiar with the Delta but never mentioned traveling through Upper Egypt. Ibn Taghrī-Birdī was a Mamluk by class, and identified entirely with Cairo. He visited certain cities of the South during official expeditions of the sultan's bureaucracy, but did not reveal any detailed knowledge of Upper Egypt. Biographers such as al-Suyūṭī or al-Adfūwī might provide considerable information on clustering of Upper Egyptian villages and fill out this pattern of isolated centers.

19. J.-C. Garcin summarizes the social and political conditions contributing to this phenomenon. See "La méditerranéisation de l'empire mamelouk sous les Sultans Baḥrides," *RSO* XLVIII (1974), 109-16.

20. A comparison between the iqṭā' yields reported for the Delta and the upper valley districts based on the cadastre ordered by Sultan al-Nāṣir Muḥammad in 715/1315, and recomputed in 777/1376 during the reign of al-Ashraf Sha'bān, is provided by Ibn al-Jī'ān, *Tuḥfa*, pp. 3-5, and listed in detail subsequently. Note that on the average there were fewer individual holdings per district than in the Delta. However, the mean yield in dīnārs per fiscal unit (nāḥīya) was considerably larger in the upper valley (the overall mean yields were: 6554.3 DJ/unit for the upper valley, 3772.5 DJ/unit for the Delta). Nonetheless, since the Delta yielded nearly twice the revenue collected in the valley, it is more likely that even during the Baḥrī period Upper Egyptian infeudation embraced larger holdings of real estate which, however, produced less revenue per feddan than comparable units in the Delta. There is little evidence to suggest any reversal of this situation during the fifteenth century. Indeed, although there are no formal cadastres, other general demographic and economic trends imply a further decline of the area. See J.-C. Garcin, *Un centre musulman de la haute Egypte médiévale: Qūṣ* (Cairo, 1976), ch. V, esp. pp. 231-44 for the complex distribution and redistribution of iqṭā' units; ch. VIII, 453-59 for the enlargement of iqṭā's; pp. 499-506 for the agrarian decline; and ch. VII for the growing influence of Bedouin tribes. See also Darraj, *Barsbay*, 59-66.

21. Garcin has outlined a process of deurbanization accompanying the general demographic and agrarian decline. Given the primarily urban character of waqf-supported institutions in Egypt (cf. C. Cahen, "Reflexions sur le waqf ancien," *SI* XIV [1961], 54), the religio-academic establishment of the upper valley would reflect the effects of this process. See Garcin, *Qūṣ*, ch. V, esp. pp. 244-45; ch. VI, 287, 303, 343; ch. VIII, 445-52, 499-506.

22. J.-C. Garcin, "Le Caire et la province, constructions au Caire et à Qūṣ sous les Mamelouks Baḥrides," *AI* VIII (1969), 52-53; Garcin, *Qūṣ*, pp. 413-24.

23. G. Wiet, "Ḳibṭ," *EI*[1], II, 996-98; Garcin, *Qūṣ*, pp. 44-45, 57-59, 120-23, 169-70, 507-11.

24. *Ḍaw'* 705, IV, p. 65, no. 203.

25. *Ḍaw'* 705, XI, p. 72, no. 201. See also J.-C. Garcin, "Histoire, opposition politique et piétisme traditioniste dans le Ḥusn al-Muḥādarat de Suyūṭī," *AI* VII (1967), 32-35.

26. There were 127 nisbas and 41 birthplaces. This flow of individuals was reciprocal. A large number of Cairenes held a wide variety of posts in Damascus.

27. For information on the cultural milieu of Damascus during the later Middle Ages, refer to N. Elisséeff, "Dimashḳ," *EI*[2], 284-86; J. Sauvaget, "Esquisse d'une histoire de la ville de Damas," *REI* VIII (1934), 456-67; H. Sauvaire, *Description de Damas*, 2 vols. (Paris, 1895); K. Wulzinger and C. Watzinger, *Damaskus, Die Islamische Stadt* (Berlin, 1924); N. Ziadeh, *Damascus under the Mamluks* (Norman, 1964); and N. Ziadeh, *Urban Life in Syria under the Early Mamluks* (Beirut, 1953).

28. For a survey of the Mamluk elite in the major cities of Syria, see

I. Lapidus, *Muslim Cities in the Later Middle Ages* (Cambridge, 1966), esp. chs. 1 and 2.

29. *Ibid.*, pp. 116-42.

30. There were 95 references to nisbas, 36 to birthplaces.

31. Jean Sauvaget, *Alep, essai sur le développement d'une grande ville syrienne, des origines au milieu du XIXᵉ siècle* (Paris, 1941). Sauvaget's grasp of the impact of historical events on Aleppo and its society was profound. His analysis of the psychological reaction of the populace to repeated destruction and looting resulting from invading armies is basic to an understanding of the city's outlook during the late Mamluk period.

32. Aleppo province included less territory in modern Syria than in the Turkish Republic. The populations of this heterogeneous area spoke Turkish, Armenian, Kurdish, and Persian dialects as well as Arabic. Culturally, the region was highly developed and produced many individuals who became prominent in Cairo. The frontiers of this province extended, at their maximum, from roughly fifty miles west of Tarsus on the Mediterranean coast in a diagonal northeast to the Kizil and Qārā Sū rivers, then to the southeast into modern Iraq and the northwestern Euphrates Valley.

33. J. Mandaville discusses the importance of influential associates in the appointment process for the Damascus judiciary. See "The Muslim Judiciary of Damascus in the Late Mamlūk Period," Ph.D. dissertation, Princeton University, 1969, pp. 52-54.

34. *Ḍaw'* 2906, X, p. 3, no. 5.

35. Of 100 references to this position, 56 designated Syrians or Palestinians. Of the 48 references to birthplaces, 25 were located in Syria-Palestine. Other regions of the Near East contributed several of these ministers of state, (second only to the wazīr in rank and authority among civilian officials), making the Syrian preponderance more apparent.

36. *Ḍaw'* 3253, X, p. 318, no. 1196. See also Gaston Wiet, "Les Secrétaires de la chancellerie en Egypte, 784-922/1382-1517," *MRB*, I (1925), 291-92.

37. In such cases, successful avoidance of mulcting or confiscation usually suggested a payoff to the sultan or high officials on good terms with the sultan.

38. For example, the case of Abū ʿAbd-Allah Muḥammad ibn Salama al-Tawzarī al-Maghribī al-Karakī (*Ḍaw'* 2200, VII, p. 255, no. 640) who attached himself to Barqūq when the latter was imprisoned.

39. Damascus province included all of modern central and southern Syria from about thirty miles south of Ḥamā to and including most of modern Jordan, with the exception of the area east of the Dead Sea, which was administered by al-Karak, and all of modern Palestine-Israel from Ghazza east. This was an area of diverse regions, and several of the larger towns maintained their own courts and administered their hinterlands with considerable autonomy. Foreign, fiscal, and military policies were administered directly from Damascus, however, which was also the seat of the four chief justices for the province. Aleppo province was even more diverse than the area under Damascus' jurisdiction. Finally, the intermediate provinces of Ḥamā and Ṭarābulus included the west central regions of Syria and the modern north Lebanese and Syrian coasts, respectively.

40. The density of the clustering was, of course, significantly less for Syria-Palestine than for the Delta. Note that the scale of the maps of Egypt is four times that of the map of the eastern Mediterranean. But here we are interested in the pattern of clustering, suggesting secondary migration, rather than density. This phenomenon was similar to the configuration in the central Delta.

41. For example, al-Maqrīzī (*Ḍaw'* 338, II, p. 21, no. 66), the eminent historian, used his nisba as his shuhra or public title. This nisba was derived from a quarter in the ante-Lebanon town of Baʿlabakk, now famous for its ancient Roman monuments, but widely known in medieval times as a local center of scholarship. Al-Maqrīzī's family never abandoned its identification with its ancestral quarter.

42. Note that Beirut was comparatively insignificant, underscoring its relative underdevelopment during the Middle Ages and early modern period.

43. Lapidus, *Cities*, pp. 37-38.

44. The best brief account of the economic adjustments in Iran after the Mongol conquests is A.K.S. Lambton, *Landlord and Peasant in Iran* (London, 1953), ch. 4.

45. *Ibid.*, pp. 83-87. The Mongols seem to have envisaged a society and environment as ideal if they approximated the conditions of the Central Asian steppes: a vast region of semi-arid plains open to unhindered movement for thousands of miles, with few city-states to hinder pastoral activities. The Mongols were advanced pastoralists who sought to recreate this ideal environment in their conquered territories. Attempts to reproduce the topography of Central Asia in Iran were doomed, of course, to failure. The Mongols succeeded only in disrupting urban culture in several Iranian provinces.

46. J. Aubin, "Comment Tamerlan prenait les villes," *SI*, XIX (1963), 86-88, 90-91, 101-102, 121-22. Aubin has developed an interpretation of Timur's policies based on the Mongol "Weltanschauung." It sheds light on the enormity of the pillaging and devastation of the Mongols and their successors by explicating their attitudes as to what a society ought to be.

47. It is significant that the Aq-Qoyunlu dynasty initiated tax and land reforms in the tradition of the Ilkhānid ruler, Ghazan Khān, in order to stabilize the economic conditions they had inherited. See V. Minorsky, "The Aq-Qoyunlu and Land Reforms," *BSOAS* XVII (1955), 449-62; J. E. Woods, *The Aqquyunlu* (Chicago, 1976), pp. 121-22, 156-57, 169.

48. The sites located in Central Asia: Fārāb (123), Bukhāra (125), and Samarqānd (124), plus the Khwarazm steppe (116), were included in the Iranian region since their learned elites identified as Persians culturally.

49. Iṣfahān yielded only two nisba references and no birthplaces. This city had not yet attained the cultural status it was to achieve under the Safavids.

50. See H. Hookham, *Tamburlaine the Conqueror* (London, 1962), pp. viii-ix for a schematic map tracing the routes of Timur's campaigns. Hookham bases her routing of the invasions on the accounts of contemporary chroniclers, both in Timur's company and resident in the cities he pillaged.

51. *Ḍaw'* 4044, IX, p. 137, no. 315.

52. *Ḍaw'* 1358, V, p. 117, no. 417.

53. *Ḍaw'* 2419, VIII, p. 151, no. 359. See also Wiet, "Secrétaires," p. 202. There is no evidence that al-Hirawī was a Hindu or an Indian, although his family may have served in the Muslim royal courts of northern India.

54. *Ḍaw'* 3864, III, p. 168, no. 649; *Manhal* 426, I, f. 304b; *Index*, no. 637.

55. *Ḍaw'* 1174, VI, p. 165, no. 556. See also Wiet, "Secrétaires," pp. 281-86.

56. During the fifteenth century, Anatolia had not yet experienced total domination by the Ottomans. The Timurid invasions and disastrous rout of the Ottomans in 1402 at Ankara set back the course of Ottoman consolidation in Anatolia for several decades. Ironically, the Mamluks owed their final century of influence in southeastern Anatolia in large part to the devastations of their terrible enemy against the Ottomans, who at that time maintained cordial relations with Cairo

57. They owed their sustained rule also to the efforts and campaigning of Sultans al-Mu'ayyad Shaykh and Barsbāy, who sought to restore their Syrian and Anatolian dominions to the degree of control prevailing under Sultan Baybars. See Lapidus, *Cities*, p. 32.

58. Note that the circle in Map III-B located in the Armenian Knot indicating 21 nisba references applies to Kurdistān as a general area. No birthplaces were reported for Kurdistān alone, although the nisba Kurdī appeared quite frequently. This phenomenon implies that the majority of individuals who bore the nisba did not originate in Kurdistān.

59. *Ḍaw'* 3082, X, p. 131, no. 545.

60. This was a rationale behind all Mamluk regimes, of course. The elite troops were to remain alien in their adopted countries, and were to show loyalty only to themselves and their masters. Their sustained use of Turkish in Arabophonic Egypt posed a barrier between themselves and the mass of population that heightened their sense of separateness.

61. *Manhal* 44, I, p. 203, no. 110.

62. There were 17 nisbas and 4 birthplaces reported for Madīna, 58 nisbas and 28 birthplaces for Makka, and 20 nisbas, 12 birthplaces for Baghdād.

63. The references for the well-known North African sites were as follows:

	Nisbas	*Birthplaces*
Tūnis	15	6
Tawzar	3	0
Qusṭanṭīna	2	2
Bijāya	12	4
Tilimsān	3	0
Fās	7	2
Marrākish	2	0

64. *Ḍaw'* 768, IV, p. 144, no. 387; *Manhal*, II, f. 300a; *Index*, no. 1383.

65. *Ḍaw'* 182, I, p. 268, line 16. The birthdate is incorrectly given as 851/1447-1448.

66. *Ḍaw'* 2803, IX, p. 180, no. 466.

67. *Ḍaw'* 53, I, p. 12, line 20.

68. *Ḍaw'* 2604, VI, p. 288, no. 800. Ibrāhīm was the son of Muḥammad's father's paternal uncle.

69. *Ḍaw'* 2831, IX, p. 203, no. 499.

70. Refer to Chapter IV, section on the shāhids. The distinction between bureaucratic and legal functions was difficult to draw in the case of the notaries. Their pronounced localism would skew the representation of Cairo in either the bureaucratic or legal categories.

71. If the notaries indeed handled the majority of cases heard in the local courts, then their own backgrounds might suggest their primary reliance on local custom and tradition to decide cases. How the Sharīʿa would fit into this practice would depend in part on the legal affiliations of the notaries. The great majority were Shāfiʿis during this period. However, the upper levels of the judiciary were more evenly distributed among the four madhhabs and, moreover, these judges were often familiar with the tenets of the several schools. Thus, the majority of Cairo's population may have had relatively little contact with the more cosmopolitan elements of the court system.

CHAPTER III. RESIDENCE PATTERNS OF THE CIVILIAN ELITE

1. For a concise account in English of the history of al-Azhar and the scholars who have studied there, see B. Dodge, *Al-Azhar, A Millennium of Muslim Learning* (Washington, D.C., 1961). For bibliography see J. Jomier, "Al-Azhar," *EI*² I, 813-21.

2. Cf. Chapter IV, supported by Table 11, which compares positions held by individuals engaged in the twenty-one occupations of the major group.

3. Cf. Appendix II, list 22.

4. W. Popper, *Egypt and Syria under the Circassian Sultans*, vol. XV in University of California Publications in Semitic Philology (1955), 111-20; al-Qalqashandī, *Ṣubḥ al-Aʿshā fī Ṣināʿat al-Inshā* (Cairo, 1914-1928). Drawing upon his wide experience as a secretary in the royal chancellery during the first half of the fifteenth century, Qalqashandī compiled a monumental survey of scribal techniques as they had evolved in the central Islamic lands since the classical period. Many offices, particularly in the bureaucratic and legal categories, were described in detail. Qalqashandī often quoted directly from primary documents that were subsequently lost, thus providing us with invaluable glimpses into dīwān procedures and policy formation.

5. Only the term mudarris or professor was used for the maps. The patterns revealed by the professors were duplicated almost identically by the specialists in ḥadīth, tafsīr, fiqh, naḥw, maʿān, and bayān, and so on. These fields are discussed in relation to the general category of professors. The mudarrisūn represented the largest group of occupations reported by the biographical sources.

6. Popper, *Egypt and Syria*. Popper based his maps and notes on data provided by Ibn Taghrī-Birdī, Maqrīzī, and Qalqashandī; as well as the subsequent work of Herz and Creswell. K.A.C. Creswell, *Map of Cairo Showing Mohammedan Monuments* (Cairo, 1947, 1951). Max Herz et al., *Procès verbaux, Comité de conservation des monuments de l'art arabe* (Cairo, 1885-1913).

7. Al-Maqrīzī, *Al-Muwāʿiẓ wa'l-Iʿtibār bi-Dhikr al-Khiṭaṭ wa'l-Athār* (Cairo, 1853-1854), vol. II. Ibn Duqmāq, *Kitāb al-Intiṣār li-Wāsiṭat ʿIqd al-Amṣār* (Cairo, 1891-1892), vols. IV and V. ʿAlī Mubārak, *Al-Khiṭaṭ al-Tawfīqīya al-Jadīda li-Miṣr al-Qāhira*, 20 parts in 4 vols. (Cairo, 1888).

8. P. Ravaisse, "Essai sur l'histoire et sur la topographie du Caire d'après Maḳrīzī," *MMAFC* I (1887), fasc. 3, pp. 409-80; and III (1889), fasc. 3, pp. 31-115. P. Casanova, "Histoire et description de la citadelle du Caire," *MMAFC*, VI (1897), fasc. 4 and 5, pp. 509-781; P. Casanova, "Essai de réconstitution topographique de la ville d'al-Fousṭaṭ ou Miṣr," *MIFAO* XXXV, fasc. 1 and 2 (1913); fasc. 3 (1919). G. Salmon, "Etudes sur la topographie du Caire, la Ḳalʿat al-Ḳabch et la Birkat al-Fīl," *MIFAO* VII (1902), entire volume. M. Clerget, *Le Caire, étude de géographie urbaine et d'histoire économique* (Cairo, 1934).

9. K.A.C. Creswell, "A Brief Chronology of the Muḥammadan Monuments of Cairo to A.D. 1517," *BIFAO* XV (1918), 39-164; *The Muslim Architecture of Egypt* (Oxford, 1952, 1959).

10. J. L. Abu-Lughod, *Cairo, 1001 Years of the City Victorious* (Princeton, 1971); S. J. Staffa, *Conquest and Fusion, the Social Evolution of Cairo, A.D. 642-1850* (Leiden, 1977).

11. I. Salama, *Bibliographie analytique et critique touchant la question de l'enseignement en Egypte depuis la période des Mamlūks jusqu'à nos jours* (Cairo, 1938). See especially "Documents contemporaines à l'époque des Ayyubides et des Mamlūks," pp. 1-40, and "Documents recents concernant la période des Mamlūks," pp. 43-50.

12. Clerget, *Le Caire* I, 133-43. The Fāṭimid rectangle of Cairo could remain aloof to the mundane demands of commerce and economics because such activities were relegated to Fusṭāṭ, which was the center of trade and industry for the country, until its population was ordered out and the city was incinerated by Grand Vizier Shāwar, for reasons of defense, against the Crusaders.

13. Casanova, "Citadelle," pp. 510, 570-73, 591-601.

14. See Ravaisse, "Essai" I, 428-79. Ravaisse's objective was to reconstruct the Fāṭimid buildings, but in so doing, he described the districts and structures that replaced them. The maps accompanying his survey of the city's transformation superimpose the earlier Fāṭimid structures on the Mamluk-period topography still extant in part today.

15. Clerget, *Le Caire* I, 144-50. Clerget summarizes the basic topographical sources in detail.

16. *Ibid.*, pp. 150-53.

17. Abu-Lughod, *Cairo*, pp. 33-36.

18. S. Labib, *Handelsgeschichte Ägyptens im Spätmittelalter (1171-1517)* (Wiesbaden, 1965), p. 180.

19. Casanova, "Foustāt." References to the port, river front, and markets are scattered throughout all three fascicles.

20. Refer to George Makdisi, "Muslim Institutions of Learning in Eleventh-Century Baghdad," *BSOAS* XXIV (1961), 4-17 for a discussion of institutional types and their descriptive nomenclature. The variants treated here represent

the range of institutions in Cairo during the later Middle Ages and do not correspond in all respects to the religio-academic establishment of Baghdād during the eleventh century.

21. The early Fāṭimids were very interested in higher learning, but emphasized the elaboration of Shīʿī theology. Their academies (dār al-ʿilm) were designed primarily to train Ismāʿīlī missionaries or dāʿīs sent forth to convert the Dār al-Islām. By the twelfth century, the Fātimid network of academies had declined, and Ṣalāḥ al-Dīn encountered little resistance to his establishment of Sunnī religio-academic institutions.

22. The core of the curriculum always remained the Islamic sciences, which represented the essence of a genuine education. The product of such an education was, in theory, the pious scholar, sufficiently learned to adhere to God's ordinances through accurate interpretation of revealed scripture and law. Every madrasa offered variants of the Islamic sciences, but few maintained the expense of supporting several secular disciplines, which did not belong to the official curriculum.

23. The term "monastery" might be the most apt translation of the Muslim khānqāh, since the great majority (although not all) of its members were men, but the term "convent" appears in many secondary works. Here we retain the Arabic original, since neither translation seems quite appropriate.

24. The needs of individual Ṣūfīs were comfortably met in the great houses, and they received a monetary allowance per month. Such an allowance permitted a Ṣūfī to deal with the outside world and purchase personal possessions, in striking contrast to his monastic counterpart in Christian Europe. There are descriptions of specific khānqāhs in Appendix I.

25. This also is in striking contrast to the monasteries of Europe. The entire question of the role played by the urban khānqāhs of later Medieval Islam remains unstudied.

26. This was the khānqāh at Siryāqūs several miles north of Cairo (130).

27. It is not possible to deduce who actually paid fees for what services and to whom from the biographical sources.

28. The biographers were also discussing governmental activities well known to any literate person in Cairo. It would be unnecessary to provide detailed descriptions or locations. The religio-academic monuments are known to us because many survived into the modern period.

29. Occupations regarded by the biographers as unrelated to the ʿulamaʾ were mentioned only if an individual engaged in them prior to his learned career.

30. All information on instructors and curriculum items reported in the biographies has been filed for future analysis, and has not been examined at this stage.

31. Of 1,187 cases with birthplaces cited, some 700 referred to Cairo and its environs. The nisba count here would be misleading because a high percentage of the 4,631 individuals of the total sample would take the title "Qāhirī" once they were established there, regardless of their place of origin. For the survey of individuals from Cairo, therefore, only the birthplace count was used.

32. The general location of the major branches of the imperial bureaucracy during the Mamluk period is summarized by Popper, *Egypt and Syria*, pp. 81-100. The central bureaus were housed in the Citadel complex, but by no means all the myriad functions of even the major administrative-fiscal bureaus were confined to the Citadel area. Many offices, in fact, were not fixed at a specific site but moved about according to the type of service performed. The failure of the biographical compilers to designate the location of many administrative and legal offices stands as a serious defect in this type of source.

33. There were 23 cases of individuals born in Cairo for the Ẓāhirīya madrasa.

34. Note that the Citadel (*al-Qalʿa*) itself was reported, not the Citadel mosque founded by al-Nāṣir Muḥammad. The four individuals who form this group received their educations within the imperial court itself.

35. There were 26 nisba and 16 birthplace references for al-Azhar; 29 nisba and 7 birthplace references for Ẓāhirīya.

36. On the figures for birthplaces in Cairo, there were 9 for al-Azhar and 23 for Ẓāhirīya. Thus, there were more cases of individuals born in the Delta than in Cairo for al-Azhar, and the opposite for Ẓāhirīya. In both cases, the large contingent of Delta people may be noted.

37. References occurred as follows:

Festival Gate Group	*Nisbas*	*Birthplaces*
Saʿīd al-Suʿadāʾ	16	11
Sābiqīya	7	2
Ḥijāzīya	6	4
Jamālīya	13	5
Baybarsīya	17	7
Qarāsunqurīya	5	4
Bayn al-Qaṣrayn Group		
Kāmilīya	17	7
Barqūqīya	13	8
Nāṣirīya	7	4
Manṣūrīya	12	3
Māristān Manṣūrī	19	2
Ẓāhirīya	10	4
Ṣāliḥīya	10	3
al-Azhar	35	22
Ashrafīya	13	5
Muʾayyadīya	19	4

38. References are to:

	Nisbas	*Birthplaces*
Baybarsīya	32	10
Saʿīd al-Suʿadāʾ	51	21
al-Azhar	38	22

39. There were 19 nisba and 2 birthplace references cited. Note that this discrepancy in the ratio of nisbas to birthplaces held true for most citations of

Upper Egyptians in the biographical sources. The settlement of first-generation migrants seems to have been infrequent and irregular.

40. There were 10 nisba references and 3 birthplaces cited.

41. *Ḍaw'* 3144, X, pp. 186-87, no. 781.

42. There were 12 nisba references and 7 birthplaces cited.

43. Mu'ayyadīya had the second-highest concentration (after al-Azhar): 17 nisba and 7 birthplace references. Al-Mu'ayyad Shaykh's career in Syria and the many associates he cultivated there was reflected in this concentration. Shaykh also maintained an interest in scholars from Egypt, Syria, and elsewhere, and set a tradition for appointing a cosmopolitan group to staff his madrasa.

44. There were 18 nisba references and 5 birthplaces cited for Shaykhūnīya.

45. According to the biographical sources, the Iranians as a group were geographically mobile. Even in Iran, relatively few confined themselves to institutions of one city. Many of the prominent Iranian scholars had studied in Iran, Afghanistan, India, Syria, and even Anatolia before settling in one or more of the institutions in Cairo.

46. Note that there was only one reference to an actual birthplace reported for any Iranian in the education survey. This occurred at Ṭaybarsīya (37), *Ḍaw'* 1080, III, p. 139, no. 552 (Shīrāz). All other references were to nisbas.

47. The one exception was the khānqāh at Siryāqūs (130).

48. There were 14 nisba and 2 birthplace references.

49. Mamluk amirs who founded and maintained these madrasas, it should be pointed out, did not always determine appointments themselves. That they did so on occasion, however, was clearly indicated by the biographical sources. The question of Mamluk attitudes toward the Anatolians is complex, but the fragmentary and scattered evidence in the biographies suggests a special relationship.

50. Several years of surveying at the site would reveal several of these institutions, but people of this area are not receptive to foreigners conducting research. A survey of the Desert Plain, the Southern Cemetery, and the Bāb al-Naṣr Cemetery would uncover many of the zāwiyas or tombs mentioned in the medieval texts.

51. Individuals adhering to one legal school often studied with specialists in another, of course, especially at the advanced level. Many legal scholars had become familiar with the canons of all four.

52. Like other non-Egyptians, many North Africans completed most of their formal studies prior to their move to Cairo, and yet there were scattered references which suggests that many of them were students in Cairo. Research on the modern period also reveals a steady flow of North African students and scholars east to Egypt and beyond. Nevertheless, the biographical sources for the medieval period provided only a limited number of cases in which places of education were cited.

53. For the group distribution, there were 15 nisba and 4 birthplace references; for the residence pattern, 13 nisba references.

54. The formal educations of a large percentage of individuals described in the biographical sources were not mentioned. This tendency is emphasized among the less eminent individuals. The dictionaries, and particularly the *Ḍaw'*,

were remarkable for their thorough coverage, but they did not dwell on the studies (often rather modest, admittedly) of individuals who failed to gain much recognition in learned circles.

CHAPTER IV. OCCUPATIONAL PATTERNS OF THE CIVILIAN ELITE

1. Most succinctly stated by Ira Lapidus in *Muslim Cities*, pp. 108-109. Lapidus' assertion summarizes the established view, which is based upon the consistent appearance of multiple offices in contemporary biographical literature. Such occupational multiplicity has been largely accepted on face value, and has been assumed to have occurred at random, thereby supporting the image of the ʿulama' as an unspecialized, multicompetent elite.

2. These surviving structures are important because they suggest the quality of life enjoyed by the wealthiest classes. However, too few remain to provide information on the residence pattern of the class as a whole.

3. Al-Jāḥiẓ, cited by C. Pellat, *The Life and Works of Jāḥiẓ* (Berkeley and Los Angeles, 1969), p. 273.

4. F. Krenkow, "Kātib," *EI*[1] II, 819.

5. This statement must be qualified by a distinction between the two functional aspects of the office: the kātib al-inshā' (documents, archival secretary), and the kātib al-amwāl (fiscal secretary). The former clearly exhibited qualities of the ʿulama' class; its duties required broad learning as well as special skills; see Qalqashandī I, 13, 130-466 (a detailed, possibly idealized, survey of requisite knowledge). The kātib al-amwāl did not have equivalent characteristics: Qalqashandī I, 9, 54-56; II, 441-43; III, 150; V, 452; VI, 41. The biographers used the term "kātib" when referring to the latter function. In cases of the former, they used the appropriate terminology or, more frequently, designated such individuals as muwaqqiʿs or clerks. Because of this distinction in roles, clerks have been analyzed separately. For a recent analysis of the secretary-clerk issue, refer to J. Escovitz, "Vocational Patterns of the Scribes of the Mamlūk Chancery," *Arabica* XXIII (1976), 42-62.

6. Qalqashandī I, 50.

7. Qalqashandī comments on the advisability of requiring an established identification with Islam as a prerequisite for holding an archival or documentary post: I, 61-64, 89-91; V, 443.

8. *Ibid.*, I, 19; III, 487, 552; IV, 17, 44, 189, 196-97, 225-30, 238; XII, 89, 96, 160; XIII, 310 (for his special relationship with the sultan).

9. *Ibid.*, I, 104, 110, 137; IV, 19, 29-30; VI, 206-207; VII, 164; VIII, 214; XI, 114, 294. See also Labib, *Handelsgeshichte*, p. 166.

10. Qalqashandī IV, 59-60; VI, 209-14.

11. See *Manhal* 25, I, f. 23, *Index*, no. 47; G. Wiet, "Les Secrétaires de la chancellerie en Egypte sous les Mamlouks circassiens, 784-922/1382-1517," *MRB* I (1925), 277-83, no. VIII; *Ḍaw'* 1830, VI, p. 235, no. 812; Wiet, "Secrétaires," pp. 283-84, no. IX; *Ḍaw'* 920, IV, p. 313, no. 848; *Manhal* 332, II, f. 345; Wiet, "Secrétaires," pp. 296-99, no. XXI; *Index*, no. 1461.

12. See C. Petry, "Geographic Origins of Dīwān Officials in Cairo during the Fifteenth Century," *JESHO* XXI (1978), 171-77.

13. *Ḍaw'* 2751, IX, p. 137, no. 350; Wiet, "Secrétaires," pp. 286-88, no. XI.

14. *Ḍaw'* 2859, IX, p. 236, no. 583; Wiet, "Secrétaires," pp. 288-89, no. XII, pp. 299-300, no. XXII, p. 303, no. XXVII.

15. *Ḍaw'* 1652, VI, p. 51, no. 140.

16. *Ḍaw'* 235, I, p. 314, line 4; Wiet, "Secrétaires," p. 296, no. XX.

17. Only one concentration appeared, at the Baybarsīya khānqāh (13): four occupational references, and two for residence. Three of these occupational references named "secretaries of the absence" (kuttāb al-ghayba), or those with interim duties, while the nāẓir was away or otherwise preoccupied. There were eight other similar references to institutions in the northeast and other districts. There was only one reference to the Citadel complex (138). The residence pattern may be regarded as more indicative of where these people lived, but it did not approach a comprehensive survey. Saʿīd al-suʿadā' (15) was the only site having more than one person. Most of the references in the northeast were near the Festival Gate or the Bayn al-Qaṣrayn groups. In other districts, one area was worthy of mention: Raṭlī Lake, (183), which was surrounded by spacious houses and gardens inhabited primarily by wealthy amirs and officials. Three of the kātibs were reported in this vicinity, the only references to residences in this area in the entire survey. A private house in this district required a substantial income and also social acceptance by its dominant class, the Mamluks. The secretarial element appears to have been among the few groups who could qualify on both accounts. There were two cases of kātibs living in the tomb areas of the Desert Plain (120, 202). Both individuals had retired to a life of seclusion from temporal affairs.

18. Qalqashandī III, 451-54; IV, 466; VII, 201, 230.

19. There were five occupational references for each institution.

20. In addition, there were references to residence along the shores of the Elephant Lake (170), along the Būlāq road (185), and in the Nile port itself (190). These private homes were all owned by individuals who had attained more remunerative positions subsequent to their stewardships. For example, the individual in the Birkat al-Fīl district (*Ḍaw'* 43, I, p. 70, line 9) held nineteen positions during his career. He was Burhān Ibrahīm ibn ʿAbd al-Raḥmān al-Karakī, and was a Koran reader, imām, nāẓir, repetitor, faqīh, khaṭīb, Ḥanafī judge, shaykh, and professor.

21. C. E. Bosworth comments on the evolution of the term *tawqīʿ*, which denoted the editing and transcription of official correspondence. See his "Christian and Jewish Religious Dignataries in Mamlūk Egypt and Syria: Qalqashandī's Information on Their Hierarchy, Titulature and Appointment," *IJMES* III: 2 (1972), 199, note 1.

22. Qalqashandī refers to these officials as kātibs. However, al-Sakhāwī consistently chose variants on the term tawqīʿ to designate their positions. For the muwaqqiʿ (kātib) al-dast see Qalqashandī I, 103, 137; III, 486-87; IV, 30; V, 464; XI, 229, 333. For the muwaqqiʿ (kātib) al-darj see I, 104, 138; IV, 30, 193; V, 465. See also Popper, *Egypt and Syria*, p. 97.

23. There were 38 references to Coptic secretaries; only 5 to Coptic clerks. Yet the total number of secretaryships reported only exceeded the number of clerkships by roughly a third. There was clearly a greater percentage of Copts (including converts to Islam) in the secretarial class.

24. Qalqashandī V, 465; IX, 257-58; Popper, *Egypt and Syria*, pp. 117-18. See also Labib, *Handelsgeschichte*, pp. 164-68. Labib mentions the highest financial officers of the state, but the nature of their functions and social position as he described them characterized the entire occupational category during the Mamluk period.

25. Qalqashandī XI, 252; XII, 302 (refers to a letter of appointment to the controllership of the Umayyad mosque in Damascus).

26. For example, the case of Amir Ṣūdūn al-Qāḍī, appointed nāẓir of al-Azhar (cf. Appendix I, description of al-Azhar).

27. There were 42 references to these positions held by Mamluks, but the actual percentage of nāẓirs among the total group of Mamluks would be much higher than indicated by these figures, since the study considered only persons born in Egypt to a Mamluk parent or first-generation Mamluks with children.

28. Qalqashandī V, 465 (description of the office):

nāẓir al-jaysh (army) IV, 17, 30; (the office in Damascus) IV, 190; (titulary) VI, 61; (example of tawqīʿ of investiture) XI, 323-24, XII, 153-54;

nāẓir al-khāṣṣ (privy funds) IV, 30; (description of the office) VI, 44; (connections with other bureaus) VI, 216; (supplanting of wāzīr) VIII, 231;

nāẓir al-dawla (fiscal bureaus) XI, 117; (description of the office) IV, 29, XI, 316;

nāẓir bayt al-māl (treasury) IV, 31; (titulary) IX, 257;

nāẓir al-jāmiʿ (mosque) XI, 252; (example of tawqīʿ of investiture for the Umayyad mosque) XII, 302;

nāẓir al-bīmāristān (hospital) IV, 34, 38; (note references to special preference given to grand amirs) IX, 256; (refers to "notables" of the pen) IX, 256, XI, 117;

nāẓir al-aḥbās (trust properties) IV, 38;

nāẓir al-awqāf (pious trust foundations) IV, 220

29. From among the holders of 80 occupations, representing all six categories, the nāẓirs accounted for between 20 and 25 percent of those accused of a crime and suffering some form of arrest and punishment. Most of the crimes had to do with embezzlement, and the great majority of all references were to people in Category II.

30. There were 104 cases of these positions held by Copts. This figure must be compared with the 571 controllerships reported in the general occupation count. Only the offices of nāẓir and nāẓir awqāf were included in the major group. Also, the presence of Mamluks in this category must be weighed. Copts appeared frequently in controllerships of the special bureau (dīwān mufrad), privy funds (khāṣṣ), army (jaysh), and fiscal bureaus (dawla)—all dealing with manipulation of royal accounts and military pay.

31. *Ḍaw'* 1504, V, p. 252, no. 846.
32. *Ḍaw'* 44, I, p. 65, line 11.
33. *Manhal* 450, III, f. 120; *Index*, no. 2054.
34. *Ḍaw'* 1425, V, p. 184, no. 630.
35. There were 24 occupational references, but none for residence.
36. Qalqashandī VI, 17; A. Cour, "Shaikh," *EI*[1], IV, 275.
37. Placement of this office in the legal category was decided primarily on the grounds of function. References to shaykhs based in religio-academic institutions most often depict individuals serving as arbiters who guide their communities according to their recognized expertise in the Sharīʿa rather than serving as custodians of religious observance (Category VI). This occupational distribution supports the impression we have from random references to duties and prerogatives in the biographical accounts and narrative sources.
38. Qalqashandī (references to Ṣūfī shaykhs in various counseling capacities) VI, 18, 163, 165; IX, 264, 275; XI, 83-84; XII, 284; (references to rectorships) IV, 37-38; XI, 90, 98, 118, 121, 370; XII, 7; (references to titulary) VIII, 172, 175, 191, 198-212.
39. *Ibid.*, III, 277; VI, 57; VII, 239; VIII, 172; IX, 180; XIV, 204, 226, 228, 348. See also Popper, *Egypt and Syria*, p. 100; J. Kramers, "Shaikh al-Islam," *EI*[1] IV, 275-76.
40. The references to these occupations were as follows:

	Occupation	*Residence*
Baybarsīya	16	8
Saʿīd al-Suʿadā'	27	8
Jamālīya	6	2
Barqūqīya	8	3
Ẓāhirīya	6	4
Ashrafīya	7	3
Mu'ayyadīya	6	2
Fakhrīya	5	2
Bāsiṭīya	6	1
Shaykhūnīya	31	5
Siryāqūs	11	3

41. See R. Levy, "Muḥtasib," *EI*[1] III, 702-703; C. Cahen and M. Talbi, "Ḥisba," *EI*[2] III, 485-89; see A. ʿAbd ar-Rāziq, "La *ḥisba* et le *muḥtasib* en Egypte au temps des Mamlūks," *AI* XIII (1977), 115-78, and Labib, *Handelsgeschichte*, pp. 179-84 for the scope of the muḥtasib's office and occupations subject to his supervision.
42. Qalqashandī (description of the office) IV, 37; V, 451-52; X, 150; XI, 96, 209; (references to protocol in the Council of Justice) III, 483; IV, 45; (copy of tawqīʿ of investiture to the office in Damascus [al-Shām]) XII, 337.
43. However, 17 cases were reported of Ṣūfīs holding this office.
44. E. Tyan, "Le notariat et le régime de la preuve par écrit dans la pratique du droit musulman," *AFDSEB*, no. 2 (1959); Tyan, *Histoire de l'organisation judicaire en pays d'Islam* (Leiden, 1960), pp. 236-52; J. Schacht, *An Introduction*

to Islamic Law (Oxford, 1964), p. 82; T. de Juynboll, *Handbuch des Islamischen Gesetzes* (Leiden, 1910), pp. 315-21; W. Heffening, "Shāhid," *EI*[1] IV, 261-62. On their qualifications, see Qalqashandī IX, 311, 393-94; X, 270, 342, 355; XI, 194-95; XII, 47.

45. Qalqashandī, XI, 197, 201; XII, 47, 52; (for services rendered in court proceedings) X, 289; XI, 186, 192-93. The occupational pattern reported for notaries suggests a broad network of neighborhood and ward courts distributed according to local political configurations and concentrations of commercial activity. Most civil litigation may well have taken place in these courts. The biographical sources referred repeatedly to service in them. The pattern (Figs. 15-A, 15-B), widely scattered as it is, may be regarded as only a rough indication of the actual range of sites.

46. The shāhid, although trained in the law, performed a bureaucratic as well as a judicial role in the court. In both capacities, he processed evidence for a superior's judgment. See Qalqashandī V, 466; (service in Provincial administration) III, 451, 454; (taxation and escheats) III, 458, 460, 490; (office of controller of the army) IV, 31, 190; (treasury) IX, 257-58; (archival service) X, 188; (special bureau) XI, 229.

47. Although many of these occupations required considerable training they were not considered learned professions, like the other four categories (II, III, V, VI).

48. There were 6 references to each institution.

49. There were 25 references to the former, 24 to the latter.

50. The biographical sources reported 53 cases of Ṣūfīs who were also notaries, paralleling the concentrations in the khānqāhs.

51. The following basic works each contain a bibliography: Schacht, *Introduction*, esp. ch. 25; N. J. Coulson, *A History of Islamic Law* (Edinburgh, 1964); M. Khadduri and H. J. Liebesny, eds., *Law in the Middle East*, vol. I: *Origin and Development of Islamic Law* (Washington, D.C., 1955); T. de Juynboll, "Ḳāḍī," *EI*[1], II, 606-607; de Juynboll, *Handbuch*, pp. 309-15. For prerogatives of the judge, see Tyan, *Histoire*, esp. ch. 2.

52. J. Mandaville, "The Muslim Judiciary of Damascus in the Late Mamlūk Period," Ph.D. dissertation, Princeton, 1969, pp. 8-9.

53. Concentrations of occupational sites were reported for the Ṣāliḥīya madrasa (26), the seat of the high tribunal; for the Shā'rīya (143), Futūḥ (144), and Zuwayla (167) Gates; and for a relatively obscure institution, the Jāmiʿ al-Fākihīyīn (40) (*Khiṭaṭ*, II, 293; *Map*, sec. 5-G, no. 109; *Chronology*, p. 64). There were no details on the judicial role of this foundation. It apparently served as the seat of a local court, since three references were made to deputies appointed to it. In the southeast there was one concentration at the mosque of al-Ṣāliḥ Ṭalā'iʿ (52), seat of a court for the area below the Zuwayla Gate. Other than these, references were scattered throughout the northeast, especially in market districts. Outside the old city, there were references along the Cross Street: the Ṭūlūnid mosque (91), Ṣarghatmishīya (92), and Jāwalīya (94); to the northwest at al-Maqs (104); and to Siryāqūs (130). The sparse representation for both notaries and deputies at Būlāq (190) indicate that the Nile port was not a center

of Shāriʿ litigation. The lack of occupational sites in the two mortuary zones (Fig. 16-B) was consistent with their function.

54. The biographical accounts rarely elaborated on either salaries or prices. What an individual received either legitimately or illicitly from an office may therefore not be determined directly from them. However, the controllerships clearly represented a lucrative source of personal income for all who held them.

55. He was Zayn ʿAbd al-Raḥmān ibn Muḥammad al-Miṣrī (*Ḍaw'* 765, IV, p. 140, no. 370). He was also a professor and khaṭīb in the Ṭūlūnid mosque.

56. On the evolution of four chief justiceships in Cairo, one for each madhhab, see Qalqashandī I, 419; IV, 34-35; XI, 174; (for examples of tawqīʿ of investiture) XI, 177, 181, 196, 204; (for a reference to salary of 100 dīnārs per month) III, 522.

57. On court protocol and ceremonial duties, see *ibid.*, III, 260, 482, 496, 506, 515-16, 523-25.

58. *Ḍaw'* 1704, VI, p. 85, no. 286; *Manhal* 279, II, f. 473; *Index*, no. 1723.

59. *Ḍaw'* 170, I, p. 253, line 11.

60. *Ḍaw'* 2189, VII, p. 244, no. 596.

61. Analysis of the family fortunes after A.D. 1517 awaits examination of biographical sources compiled during the sixteenth century. Several branches had died out by the late fifteenth century, but the central line descending from ʿUmar was still flourishing.

62. *Manhal* 283, III, f. 230; *Index*, no. 2288.

63. *Ḍaw'* 739, IV, p. 106, no. 301; *Manhal* 282, II, f. 297b; *Index*, no. 1381.

64. *Ḍaw'* 1230, III, p. 312, no. 1199; *Manhal* 278, II, f. 210; *Index*, no. 1197.

65. *Ḍaw'* 2258, VII, p. 294, no. 762; *Manhal* 288, III, f. 176b; *Index*, no. 2180.

66. *Ḍaw'* 1798, VI, p. 181, no. 620; *Manhal* 284, III, f. 2; *Index*, no. 1807.

67. *Ḍaw'* 2788, IX, p. 171, no. 439; *Manhal* 285, III, f. 272; *Index*, no. 2350.

68. *Ḍaw'* 3308, XI, p. 8, no. 19; *Ḍaw'* 2222, VII, p. 268, no. 683.

69. *Ḍaw'* 2223, VII, p. 268, no. 684.

70. *Ḍaw'* 4005, XII, p. 14, no. 74.

71. *Ḍaw'* 3522, XI, p. 17, no. 90.

72. *Ḍaw'* 3506, XII, p. 7, no. 39.

73. *Ḍaw'* 524, II, p. 188, no. 519.

74. *Ḍaw'* 4015, XII, p. 38, no. 221.

75. *Ḍaw'* 3668, XII, p. 137, no. 847.

76. *Ḍaw'* 3543, XII, p. 31, no. 180.

77. *Ḍaw'* 569, V, p. 310, no. 1025.

78. *Ḍaw'* 3806, II, p. 119, no. 357.

79. *Ḍaw'* 2713, IX, p. 95, no. 260.

80. Concentrations appeared at the khānqāhs of Baybars (13) and Saʿīd al-Suʿadā' (15), and at the madrasas of Barqūqīya (20), Ashrafīya (30), al-Azhar (36), and Mu'ayyadīya (51). The clusterings emphasized the Festival Gate and Bayn al-Qaṣrayn groups and the Azhar quarter. Both references to Bahā' al-Dīn Street (149) involved members of the Bulqīnī family. These aggregates are further evidence of the prestige of these institutions. The paucity of sites in

other districts of the capital, with the exception of Ṣarghatmishīya, emphasized the tendency toward residential concentration within the judiciary.

81. The concentration at Ṣarghatmishīya was, in fact, the largest for the judges anywhere. There were seven cases reported, all of whom were of Syrian or Anatolian background.

82. The tendencies reflected in the residence pattern must be compared to positions held by Ṣūfīs regardless of residence. There were 47 positions for notaries (11 percent of 427 total), 40 for deputies (9 percent of 470), and 17 for judges and chief justices together (6 percent of 284). The level of active association with the Ṣūfī community implicit in the residence pattern thus sustains the trend toward diminishing identification as one proceeded up the scale.

83. These were Badr Ḥasan ibn Suwayd al-Miṣrī al-Qibṭī, a merchant in youths, that is, slaves (tājir awlād), *Ḍaw'* 1042, III, p. 101, no. 406; and Sa'd Ibrāhīm al-Nāṣirī al-Muslimī al-Qibṭī, *Ḍaw'* 103, I, p. 184, line 23, who held several bureau and tax controllerships in addition to being a royal merchant to the Franks (tājir firanj). A figure of 30,000 dīnārs income was mentioned for this position. This individual was married to the mother of the famous scholar, Zayn ibn Mazhar, and therefore provided one of the few cases of a Muslim Copt marrying into the 'ulama'.

84. He was Zayn 'Amrān ibn Ghazzī al-Maghribī al-Mālikī (*Ḍaw'* 1677, VI, p. 63, no. 216) who became a royal merchant (tājir sulṭānī) in the port of Alexandria. Al-Sakhāwī did not specify whether he was actually born in Morocco, but he became a prosperous merchant in Cairo prior to his appointment to the sultan's mercantile staff.

85. Qalqashandī VI, 13; XIII, 40 (example of tawqī' of investiture).

86. For examples of titles accruing to the tujjār al-khawājakīya, refer *ibid.*, VI, 10, 15, 30-31, 38-39, 41-42, 52, 55-57, 62, 68-69, 71, 165-66, 167-68. These titles designated persons exercising executive or administrative authority.

87. *Ibid.*, V, 464.

88. Marshall Hodgson provides a brief but perceptive statement about the role of education as cultural conservation in his *Venture of Islam*, II, 437-45.

89. Qalqashandī: (definition of the position) IV, 39; V, 464; IX, 256; XI, 97; (reference to the final authority of the chief justice over curriculum taught in madrasas) XII, 440; (titulary included in tawāqi' of investiture) XI, 122, 124, 227, 231; XII, 78.

90. The disciplines that were taught by large numbers of professors were: jurisprudence (with further specialization according to legal school, types of legal application, and so on), prophetic traditions, logic, grammar, the Arabic language, rhetoric, literature, Koranic recitations and readings, law of descent and distribution of inheritances, Koranic exegesis, calligraphy, medicine, and mystic principles (taṣawwuf).

91. He was Fakhr al-Dīn ibn Ghunnām al-Qibṭī al-Ṣūfī (*Ḍaw'* 3450, XI, p. 164, no. 520), who taught mystic principles at Sa'īd al-Su'adā' and Baybarsīya. He was also a Koran reader in the galleries (shabābīk) of both houses.

92. Several other madrasas of the northeast were mentioned frequently, in-

cluding the mosque of al-Ẓāhir Baybars (1), a vast but relatively obscure institution during the fifteenth century.

93. *Khiṭaṭ*, II, 426.

94. Of 496 individuals who held a professorship during their careers, 93 were identified as Ṣūfīs, of whom 23 were designated as either Shādhilīs or Qādirīs. Therefore, about 20 percent of the professors were mystics. In contrast with the 93 professorial positions, 53 notarial positions were held by Ṣūfīs.

95. These appeared at the mosque of al-Ḥākim (3), the Mankūtamurīya madrasa (6) on Bahā' al-Dīn Street; Sa'īd al-Su'adā' (15) in the Festival Gate group; Kāmilīya (19), Ẓāhirīya (23), and Ṣāliḥīya (26) colleges along the Bayn al-Qaṣrayn; al-Azhar (36); Ashrafīya (30), and Mu'ayyadīya (51); the Zaynī mosque (43) in the Bayn al-Surayn, and Shaykhūnīya (83) in the southeast.

96. Qalqashandī: (description of the office) IV, 39; V, 463; XI, 97; (examples of tawāqi' of investiture) XI, 70, 222; XII, 370, 440; (titulary) VI, 47; (rank) IX, 256. See also J. Pedersen, "Khaṭīb," *EI*[1] II, 927-29.

97. There were 19 references to the former, 20 to the latter.

98. *Khiṭaṭ*, II, 327; *Map*, sec. 3-F, no. 83; *Chronology*, p. 120.

99. *Khiṭaṭ*, II, 283.

100. Popper, *Egypt and Syria*, p. 34.

101. *Khiṭaṭ*, II, 312; *Map*, sec. 2-A, no. 341; *Chronology*, p. 98.

102. There were 15 positions held by khaṭībs who were Ṣūfīs.

103. Forty-eight individuals engaged in 30 occupations (64 positions) during their careers suffered from blindness and were designated as darīr. Of these 48, 11 were muqri's, about 22 percent of the total.

104. There were 15 positions as readers held by Mamluks or their descendants, in comparison with 3 executive positions held by muqri's. The implication is that these Mamluks themselves did not belong to the first-generation core of the elite that monopolized most executive offices.

105. *Ḍaw'* 3215, X, p. 263, no. 1051.

106. *Ḍaw'* 565, II, p. 233, no. 656.

107. *Ḍaw'* 1031, III, p. 94, no. 382.

108. *Ḍaw'* 2485, VIII, p. 195, no. 509.

109. *Ḍaw'* 1672, VI, p. 61, no. 194.

110. *Ḍaw'* 999, III, p. 67, no. 278.

111. *Khiṭaṭ*, II, 315.

112. There were 68 positions held by muqri's who were Ṣūfīs. This would include individuals who taught the Koran to children.

113. *Ḍaw'* 1508, V, p. 255, no. 857.

114. *Ḍaw'* 1311, III, p. 74, no. 272.

115. Of 96 prominent associates listed for the mu'taqads, 36 were Mamluks, or some 38 percent of the total—one of the higher percentages appearing among the major occupations. No other social group of such humble origins approached this level of association.

116. There were 19 cases of Ṣūfī mu'taqads reported. Not all of these resided in Sa'īd al-Su'adā', al-Azhar, or the Ḥusayn mosque.

117. Cf. H.A.R. Gibb, *Studies on the Civilization of Islam* (Boston, 1962), pp. 27-30, 217.

118. This phenomenon held only for individuals included in the two biographical dictionaries. The nature of Mamluk involvement with Ṣūfī orders is a broad question this study does not examine directly, since Mamluks were not its focus. Not all persons resident in the major hospices were necessarily civilians; see, for example, Maqrīzī's references to troopers (junūd, ajnād): Appendix I, description of Baybarsīya.

119. There were 54 references to Baybarsīya, 96 to Saʿīd al-Suʿadāʾ, 22 to Shaykhūnīya, and 8 to Siryāqūs.

120. There were 11 references to al-Azhar, 25 to Ashrafīya, and 19 to Muʿayyadīya.

121. Aside from the above-named institutions, there were very few references to residence and no clusters were reported in other districts. The paucity of references to either of the two mortuary zones suggests that few muʿtaqads who chose to live there were Ṣūfīs. The residence pattern for Ṣūfīs was based on the largest number of references to any specific group; their location in the city, of course, was not necessarily the same at the time of their professional activity.

122. See M. Perlmann, "Notes on Anti-Christian Propaganda in the Mamluk Empire," *BSOAS* X (1940-1942), 843-61; Perlmann, "Asnāwī's Tract against Christian Officials," *IGM* II, 172-208.

123. For the literature on the subject of deterioration of dhimmī status in Egypt during the Mamluk period, refer to G. Wiet, "Ḳibṭ," *EI*[1] II, 990-1003. See also Bosworth, *Christian and Jewish Dignataries*, III, no. 1 (1972), 66 for further bibliography; and particularly E. Ashtor-Strauss, "The Social Isolation of the Ahl al-Dhimma," *EMPH*, pp. 73-94.

124. *Ḍawʾ* 98, I, p. 183, line 11. He was Saʿd Ibrāhīm ibn Fakhr al-Dīn, known as Ibn al-Sukkar wa'l-Līmūn, whose father was noted previously as the husband of Khadīja, daughter of Taqī Muḥammad al-Bulqīnī. His father's faith in Islam was recognized as sufficient by the Bulqīnī family to permit his marriage to one of their own. We may assume that his economic assets contributed to his social recognition. Saʿd Ibrāhīm's family connections through his mother granted him a legitimate place in the learned elite. Few Muslim Copts shared his good fortune.

CHAPTER V. A TRIPARTITE ELITE: CONCLUSIONS AND HYPOTHESES

1. A fourth category, composed of artisans and merchants, was too diverse to provide clear trends. And in any case, the statistics for this group are questionable, since artisan-commercial positions appeared only in the accounts of individuals established in the first three fields.

2. Summarized by I. Lapidus, *Muslim Cities in the Later Middle Ages* (Cambridge, 1967), pp. 113-15, 141-42. In the chapters preceding these conclusions, he outlines the structure of urban society in the Mamluk state. My hypothesis speaks to a related but distinct issue that has yet to receive the attention it

warrants in the literature: the concept of advocacy, and whether it is appropriate to the political climate of Mamluk times.

3. The self-serving implications of such custodianship did not promote a closed system. Although the influence of prominent families pervaded the upper levels of the ʿulamaʾ hierarchy, mobility characterized the group as a whole. The jurist-scholars drew their members from many segments of society and denied access only to those whose faith was suspect. The ʿulamaʾ did not regard themselves as ethnically distinct from the greater community.

4. The perennial outbreak of violence in the cities of the Mamluk state cannot be ignored. The repeated flaring up of disorder in the form of demonstrations, riots, and assaults bespeaks unarticulated popular frustration over abuse from on high. Food shortages, erratic taxation, price fixing, and feuding between Mamluk factions were salient causes of unrest. In the absence of institutionalized means of adjudicating these sorts of grievances, the masses had no other outlet for venting their anger. But in Cairo, the presence of the largest garrison in the empire discouraged all-out revolt. For most of the time, the populace was resigned to its fate. It is in light of these circumstances that communal transcendance must be weighed. I submit that it is a more accurate term than fatalism.

5. Lapidus (*Muslim Cities*, pp. 159-61) makes a perceptive point when he notes how the amirs in Damascus were able to exploit these phenomena to suit their own interests. His observation could be applied to other social groups to broaden our understanding of Mamluk-civilian relations.

APPENDIX I. A SURVEY OF MAJOR INSTITUTIONS

1. *Khiṭaṭ*, II, 415; ʿAlī Mubārak, IV, 102-103; *Map*, sec. 4-H, no. 480.
2. *Khiṭaṭ*, II, 415, lines 8-9.
3. *Ibid.*, lines 9-10.
4. *Ibid.*, lines 11-12. The daily provisions are noteworthy. Meat was provided for each Ṣūfī every day, a luxury in a society in which meat was scarce and so expensive that the majority of the population purchased it only on feast days. The residents of the major houses were thus allowed to enjoy the standard of food reserved for the elite.
5. *Ibid.*, lines 14-16. Maqrīzī mentions that the khānqāh attracted notables from the highest military and civilian circles.
6. *Ibid.*, p. 416, lines 1-3. If the relative prices of bread, meat, confections, and soap could be ascertained, they and the cost of the clothing could be multiplied by the numbers of resident Ṣūfīs to determine how much money was actually required to support the community. Whatever the figure, it would be less than the total yield of the waqfs, since the khānqāh elite and other agents always appropriated some of the yield for personal expenses. In any case, since meat in particular was expensive, it is obvious that the khānqāh required substantial funds to maintain its community.
7. *Ibid.*, p. 415, lines 29-38; p. 416, lines 5-20. The grand amirs were: the viceroy, Ṣūdūn al-Shaykhūnī, who altered the allotment of revenues to favor

his civilian client, and Yalbughā al-Sālimī, appointed nāẓir of the khānqāh in order to supervise the inquiry proceedings resulting from the dispute. Sirāj al-Dīn al-Bulqīnī, the eminent judge, served on the board. It is possible that the involvement of Mamluks in this incident was motivated by personal greed, as suggested by the discovery of illicit patronage relationships.

8. *Ibid.*, p. 415, line 13.

9. *Ibid.*, p. 416; *Map*, sec. 4-H, no. 32; *Chronology*, pp. 86-87.

10. *Khiṭaṭ*, II, 417, lines 7-8.

11. *Ibid.*, p. 417, lines 10-11.

12. *Ibid.*, p. 417, lines 19-20.

13. *Ibid.*, pp. 401-403; ʿAlī Mubārak, V, 121; *Map*, sec. 4-H, no. 35; *Chronology*, p. 119.

14. *Khiṭaṭ*, II, 402, lines 6-7.

15. *Ibid.*, lines 19-29.

16. *Ibid.*, p. 403 entire.

17. *Ibid.*, p. 402, line 25.

18. *Ibid.*, II, 388; *Map*, sec. 4-H, no. 31; *Chronology*, p. 86.

19. *Khiṭaṭ*, II, 382; ʿAlī Mubārak, II, 77, vi, 6-24; *Map*, sec. 4-H, no. 36; *Chronology*, p. 110.

20. *Khiṭaṭ*, II, 38, lines 36-37.

21. *Ibid.*, p. 393; ʿAlī Mubārak, II, 13; *Map*, sec. 4-H, no. 45; *Chronology*, p. 110.

22. *Khiṭaṭ*, II, 375; ʿAlī Mubārak, II, 14; *Map*, sec. 4-H, no. 428; *Chronology*, p. 75. This individual was almost certainly a black, and would be termed a ḥabashī.

23. For the madrasa, see *Khiṭaṭ*, II, 374; ʿAlī Mubārak, VI, 9; *Map*, sec. 4-H, no. 38; *Chronology*, p. 76; and for the tomb, *Khiṭaṭ*, II, 374; *Map*, sec. 4-H, no. 38; *Chronology*, p. 77.

24. *Khiṭaṭ*, II, 374, lines 15-20.

25. *Ibid.*, lines 21-26.

26. *Ibid.*, p. 375, lines 3-7.

27. *Ibid.*, p. 378; *Map*, sec. 4-H, no. 37; *Chronology*, p. 78.

28. *Khiṭaṭ*, II, 379, lines 31-37.

29. It is significant that this madrasa, of which only remnants survive today, greatly surpassed the huge mosque Baybars built north of the rectangle (*ibid.*, p. 299; *Map*, sec. 1-H, no. 1; *Chronology*, pp. 79-80) in terms of reputation and numbers of students during the fifteenth century. No detailed discussion of the mosque is provided here, since it did not play any noteworthy role during our period.

30. For the madrasa see *Khiṭaṭ*, II, 379, 406; ʿAlī Mubārak, V, 99-100, vi, 15; *Map*, sec. 4-G, no. 43; *Chronology*, p. 82. For the tomb see *Khiṭaṭ*, II, 380, 406; *Chronology*, pp. 81-82.

31. *Khiṭaṭ*, II, 380, lines 23-27.

32. *Ibid.*, p. 406; *Map*, sec. 4-G, no. 43; *Chronology*, p. 81.

33. *Khiṭaṭ*, II, 406, lines 28-29.

34. *Ibid.*, line 32.

35. *Ibid.*, lines 33-37.

36. The Manṣūrī hospital remained the primary medical center of Cairo throughout the fifteenth century. Although there were several other hospitals in Cairo, and especially one founded by Sultan al-Mu'ayyad Shaykh, none equalled this institution. More important, the biographical sources referred specifically to the Manṣūrī hospital.

37. *Khiṭaṭ*, II, 382; *Map*, sec. 4-G, no. 44; *Chronology*, p. 85.

38. The shurbush was a triangular headdress worn in place of a turban by amirs and others permitted military garb. Men of law and scholarship could not wear it. See R. Dozy, *Supplément aux dictionnaires arabes*, II, 742.

39. *Khiṭaṭ*, II, 382, line 24.

40. *Ibid.*, p. 418; ʿAlī Mubārak, VI, 4. Maqrīzī referred only briefly to the khānqāh here. The absence of a description of the madrasa itself in his account prevents a discussion of the waqfs set up in support of the institution. See also Ibn Taghrī-Birdī, *Al-Nujūm al-Zāhira fī Mulūk Miṣr wa'l-Qāhira*, edited by W. Popper in University of California Publications in Semitic Philology, V, part 4 (1935), 378; English translation in same series, XIII, part 1 (1954), 12.

41. *Khiṭaṭ*, II, 277; *Map*, sec. 3-H, no. 15; *Chronology*, pp. 51-52.

42. *Khiṭaṭ*, II, 278, lines 10-20.

43. *Ibid.*, lines 21-22.

44. *Ibid.*, line 33.

45. *Ibid.*, p. 273; *Map*, sec. 5-H, no. 97; *Chronology*, pp. 49-51.

46. *Khiṭaṭ*, II, 276, lines 34-39; p. 277, lines 1-14. Maqrīzī did not list prominent figures resident in al-Azhar, as he did for other institutions.

47. *Ibid.*, p. 383; ʿAli Mubārak, VI, 9; *Chronology*, p. 87.

48. *Khiṭaṭ*, II, 383; ʿAli Mubārak, VI, 3; *Chronology*, p. 96.

49. *Khiṭaṭ*, II, 330; *Map*, sec. 4-G, no. 175; *Chronology*, p. 123; Salama, *Bibliographie analytique et critique touchant la question de l'enseignement en Egypt depuis la période des Mamlūks jusqu'à nos jours* (Cairo, 1938), pp. 35-36. See also A. Darraj, *L'acte de waqf de Barsbay* (Cairo, 1963), pp. 2-9, for information on the sources of the waqf endowments. The list of commercial establishments in Cairo and villages in the Delta and Jīza province gives an impression of the revenues tapped by the sultans to support their academic projects. The consistently large concentrations of scholars and Ṣūfis reported by the biographical sources coincided with the formidable list of revenue-producing sites. Since these waqfs were recently established, they were yielding their quotas of revenues throughout the fifteenth century. We may therefore assume that Ashrafīya was one of Cairo's wealthiest madrasas during our period.

50. Ibn Taghrī-Birdī, *Nujūm*, XVIII, part 4 (1958), 16-18, 20. An element of haste is implied here. The sultans of the Circassian period were anxious to prove their outward piety by worshiping in their monuments even before they were completed. These men realized that their power base was ephemeral and that they might be overthrown and executed at any time. Pressure was placed on the laborers to speed up construction so that the founders might personally

witness the dedication. Barsbāy could not have realized in 826/1423 that he would survive on the throne until his natural death in 841/1437.

51. *Khiṭaṭ*, II, 328; *Map*, sec. 5-G, no. 190; *Chronology*, pp. 120-21. Since Maqrīzī personally observed the construction of this mosque and madrasa, he reported many details about the stages of its construction. Some thirty architects and one hundred laborers were employed continuously.

52. The tomb is located to the immediate left of the entrance foyer. The approach to the massive domed chamber of the mausoleum and the subsequent exit into the mosque proper provides a dramatic visual experience. No other Mamluk structure gives this same effect.

53. *Khiṭaṭ*, II, 329, lines 10-12.

54. *Ibid.*, p. 330, lines 9-14. Maqrīzī described the khuṭba delivered by Ibn Ḥajar al-ʿAsqalānī during the dedication ceremony presided over by the sultan.

55. *Ibid.*, II, 313, 421; ʿAlī Mubārak, V, 35; *Map*, sec. 8-F, no. 152; *Chronology*, p. 106.

56. *Khiṭaṭ*, II, 421, line 13.

57. *Ibid.*, p. 313, line 31.

58. *Ibid.*, p. 316; ʿAlī Mubārak, IV, 83; *Map*, sec. 8-G, no. 133; *Chronology*, pp. 108-109; Salama, *Bibliographie*, pp. 34-35.

59. *Khiṭaṭ*, II, 325; *Map*, sec. 8-H, no. 143; *Chronology*, pp. 93-94.

60. Other important amirate madrasas and mosques in this area were:

Qajmāsīya (53): ʿAlī Mubārak, VI, 13; *Map*, sec. 6-G, no. 114; *Chronology*, p. 145.

The Mosque of Aṣlam (54): *Khiṭaṭ*, II, 309; *Map*, sec. 6-G, no. 112; *Chronology*, p. 101.

Maḥmūdīya (57): *Khiṭaṭ*, II, 395; ʿAlī Mubārak, II, 34; V, 109; VI, 14; *Map*, sec. 6-G, no. 117; *Chronology*, p. 117.

The Mosque of Īnāl al-Yūsufī al-Atābakī (58): *Khiṭaṭ*, II, 401; ʿAlī Mubārak, II, 34; *Map*, sec. 6-G, no. 118; *Chronology*, p. 117.

Mihmandārīya (55): *Khiṭaṭ*, II, 399; ʿAlī Mubārak, II, 101; *Map*, sec. 6-G, no. 115; *Chronology*, p. 95.

The Mosque of Alṭunbughā al-Māridānī (56): *Khiṭaṭ*, II, 308; *Map*, sec. 6-G, no. 120; *Chronology*, pp. 100-101.

Umm al-Sulṭān (60): *Khiṭaṭ*, II, 399; ʿAlī Mubārak, III, 102; IV, 60-61; VI, 3; *Map*, sec. 7-G, no. 125; *Chronology*, p. 112.

The Mosque of Qūṣūn (63): *Khiṭaṭ*, II, 307; *Map*, sec. 6-F, no. 202; *Chronology*, p. 95.

The Mosque of Aq Sunqur (61): *Khiṭaṭ*, II, 307; *Map*, sec. 6-F, no. 202; *Chronology*, pp. 102-104.

Aljayhīya (69): *Khiṭaṭ*, II, 399; *Map*, sec. 7-G, no. 131; *Chronology*, p. 113.

Aytmishīya (62): *Khiṭaṭ*, II, 400; ʿAlī Mubārak, II, 103; *Map*, sec. 7-H, no. 250; *Chronology*, p. 116.

Manjakīya (64): *Khiṭaṭ*, II, 320; *Map*, sec. 8-H, no. 138; *Chronology*, p. 105.

The Mosque of Almāṣ (88): *Khiṭaṭ*, II, 307; *Map*, sec. 7-F, no. 130; *Chronology*, p. 95.

Bunduqdārīya (87): *Khiṭaṭ*, II, 420; ʿAlī Mubārak, VI, 16; *Map*, sec. 8-F, no. 146; *Chronology*, p. 82.

The Mosque of Jawhar al-Julbānī (71): *Map*, sec. 8-G, no. 134; *Chronology*, pp. 124-25.

Qanibayhīya al-Maḥmūdīya (72): *Map*, sec. 8-G, no. 136; *Chronology*, p. 152.

Janibakīya (73): *Map*, sec. 6-G, no. 119; *Chronology*, p. 126.

Jāwalīya (94): *Khiṭaṭ*, II, 389; ʿAlī Mubārak, VI, 3-27; *Map*, sec. 8-E, no. 221; *Chronology*, p. 86.

61. *Khiṭaṭ*, II, 403; ʿAlī Mubārak, V, 38; VI, 9; *Map*, sec. 8-E, no. 218; *Chronology*, pp. 32-33.
62. *Khiṭaṭ*, II, 265; *Map*, sec. 9-E, no. 220; *Chronology*, pp. 44-48.
63. *Khiṭaṭ*, II, 268, lines 21-39.
64. *Ibid.*, p. 444; *Map*, sec. 12-G, no. 281; *Chronology*, pp. 74-75.
65. *Map*, sec. 7-K, no. 85; *Chronology*, pp. 110-11.
66. *Khiṭaṭ*, II, 426; *Map*, sec. 7-H, no. 139; *Chronology*, pp. 114-15.
67. *Map*, sec. 4-L, no. 149; *Chronology*, pp. 119-20.
68. *Map*, sec. 4-L, no. 121; *Chronology*, pp. 125-26.
69. *Map*, sec. 3-L, no. 158; *Chronology*, p. 134.
70. *Map*, sec. 5-K, no. 99; *Chronology*, pp. 138-39.
71. *Khiṭaṭ*, II, 246; *Map*, sec. 13-B, no. 319; *Chronology*, pp. 41-42.
72. *Khiṭaṭ*, II, 429.
73. *Ibid.*, p. 422.
74. *Ibid.*, lines 34-38.

Bibliography

CONTEMPORARY SOURCES

Biographical Works

al-Biqāʿī, *ʿAnwān al-Zamān fī Tarājim al-Shuyūkh wa'l-Aqrān.* ms. Dār al-Kutub, Ta'rīkh: 1001, Taymūrīya: 2255 (*GAL* II, 179, no. 6, note 9).

Ibn Ḥajar al-ʿAsqalānī. *Al-Durar al-Kāmina fī Aʿyān al-Mi'a al-Thāmina.* 4 vols. Hyderabad, 1348-1350/1929-1931. This work was referred to as the *Muʿjam* or Dictionary (*GAL* II, 83).

———. *Rafʿ al-Iṣr ʿan Quḍāt Miṣr.* Vols. I and II in print: Cairo, 1956, 1971; remainder in ms.: Dār al-Kutub, Ta'rīkh: 105; BN, f.a.: 2150 (*GAL* II, 83).

Ibn Qāḍī-Shuhba. *Ṭabaqat al-Shāfiʿīya.* ms.: Ahmad III: 2836; on film: Ms. Inst. of the Arab League: 312 (*GAL* II, 64).

Ibn Taghrī-Birdī. *Al-Manhal al-Ṣāfī wa'l-Mustawfī baʿd al-Wāfī.* Vol. I in print: Cairo, 1956; remainder in ms.: Dār al-Kutub, Ta'rikh: 1113; BN, f.a.: 2068-73 (*GAL* II, 52, no. 4). Summary of biographies provided by Gaston Wiet, "Les biographies du Manhal Safi," *MIE* XIX (1932).

al-Maqrīzī. *Durar al-ʿUqūd al-Farīda fī Tarājim al-Aʿyān al-Mufīda.* ms.: Mosul: 1264 (*GAL* II, 49; Suppl. II, 37).

———. *Kitāb al-Muqaffa.* ms.: Leiden, Or. 1366, 3015; BN, f.a.: 2144 (*GAL* II, 48).

al-Sakhāwī. *Al-Ḍaw' al-Lāmiʿ fī Aʿyān al-Qarn al-Tāsiʿ.* 12 vols. Cairo, 1353/1934 (*GAL* II, 43, no. 1; Suppl. II, 31-32).

———. *Dhayl ʿalā Rafʿ al-Iṣr ʿan Quḍāt Miṣr.* Cairo, 1969 (*GAL* II, 43).

al-Ṣafadī. *Al-Wāfī bi'l-Wafīyāt.* 8 vols. in print: Istanbul, 1949, 1953; Damascus, 1959; Wiesbaden, 1962-1974. Remainder of work in numerous ms. collections (*GAL* II, 31-32, no. 1; Suppl. II, 28, no. 1).

Geographical and Topographical Works

Ibn ʿAbd al-Ḥaqq. *Murāḍ al-Iṭlāʿ ʿalā Ismā' al-Amkina wa'l-Biqāʿ.* 3 vols. Cairo, 1954.

Ibn Duqmāq. *Kitāb al-Intiṣār li-Wāsiṭat ʿIqd al-Amṣār.* Vols. IV and V. Cairo, 1309/1891-1892.

Ibn al-Jīʿān. *Al-Tuḥfat al-Sanīya bi-Ismā' al-Bilād al-Miṣrīya.* Cairo, 1897.

al-Maqrīzī. *Al-Mawāʿiẓ wa'l-Iʿtibār bi-Dhikr al-Khiṭaṭ wa'l-Āthār.* 2 vols. Cairo, 1270/1853-1854.

al-Qalqashandī. *Ṣubḥ al-Aʿshā fī Ṣināʿat al-Inshā.* 14 vols. Cairo, 1914-1928.

Yāqūt. *Muʿjam al-Buldān.* Edited by F. Wüstenfeld. 6 vols. Leipzig, 1866-1870.

Historiographical and Narrative Works
(Several of the Latter Containing Necrologies)

al-ʿAynī. *ʿIqd al-Jumān fī Tāʾrīkh Ahl al-Islām.* ms. Dār al-Kutub, Taʾrīkh: 1044 (*GAL* II, 65; Suppl. II, 51).
al-Fāsī. *ʿIqd al-Thamīn fī Taʾrīkh al-Balad al-Amīn.* ms. Dār al-Kutub, Taʾrīkh: 178 (*GAL* II, 172-173; Suppl. II, 221).
———. *Shifāʾ al-Gharam bi-Akhbār al-Balad al-Ḥaram.* ms.: BN, f.a.: 1633; sections in print: F. Wüstenfeld, ed., *Die Chroniken der Stadt Mekka.* II. Leipzig, 1859, pp. 55-334 (*GAL* II, 172-173; Suppl. II, 222).
Ibn Fahd al-Makkī (ʿIzz al-Dīn). *Al-Kamīn bi-Dhayl al-ʿIqd fī Taʾrīkh al-Balad al-Amīn.* ms. Berlin: 9755; Rada Lampur: 3212, on film, Ms. Inst. of the Arab League: 3032 (*GAL* II, 224).
———. *Al-Nuzhat al-Sanīya fī-mā Yuṭlub min Akhbār al-Mulūk wa-Khulafāʾ al-Diyār al-Miṣrīya.* ms. Berlin: 9734.
Ibn Fahd al-Makkī (Najm al-Dīn). *Al-Muʿjam.* ms. Berlin: 10131 (*GAL* II, 225; Suppl. II, 225).
———. *Dhayl al-Muʿjam.* ms. Berlin: 10132 (*GAL* II, 225).
Ibn Fahd al-Makkī (Taqī al-Dīn). *Laḥẓ al-Alḥāẓ bi-Dhayl Ṭabaqāt al-Ḥuffāẓ.* Damascus, 1928-1929 (*GAL* II, 225; Suppl. II, 46, 225).
Ibn al-Furāt. *Taʾrīkh al-Duwal wa'l-Mulūk.* Vols. VIII and IX: C. Zurayk, ed. Beirut, 1936-1939 (*GAL* II, 49).
Ibn Hajar al-ʿAsqalānī. *Inbāʾ al-Ghumr bi-Anbāʾ al-ʿUmr.* Vols. I-III: Cairo, 1969-1972; remainder in ms: BN, f.a.: 1601-1604; Dār al-Kutub, Ta'rikh: 2476 (*GAL* II, 83).
Ibn Iyās, *Badāʾiʿ al-Zuhūr fī Waqāʾiʿ al-Duhūr.* P. Kahle, M. Sobernheim, M. Mustafa, H. Roemer, A. Dietrich, H. Ritter, eds. 5 vols. Istanbul, 1931-1945; Cairo and Wiesbaden, 1960-1963. French translation by G. Wiet. *Histoire des Mamlouks Circassiens.* Vol. II. Cairo, 1945; *Journal d'un Bourgeois du Caire.* 2 vols. Paris, 1954, 1960.
Ibn Khaldūn. *The Muqaddima.* Translated and edited by F. Rosenthal. 3 vols. New York, 1958.
———. *Al-Taʿrīf bi-Ibn Khaldūn, Riḥlatuhu Gharban wa Sharqan.* Cairo, 1951.
Ibn Khaṭīb al-Nāṣirīya. *Al-Durr al-Muntakhib min Taʾrīkh Mamlakat Ḥalab.* ms. Br. Mus., Or. 25 (*GAL* Suppl. 30).
———. *Muntakhabāt min Kitāb al-Kawākib al-Wadīʿa fī Dhayl ʿalā Taʾrīkh Ibn Khaṭīb al-Nāṣirīya.* ms. Alexandria, Taʾrīkh: 178 (*GAL* Suppl. II, 30).
Ibn Nāhid. *Al-Sīrat al-Muʾayyadīya.* This work is not extant. Refer to Berlin, 8645, 9a. See also F. Rosenthal. *A History of Muslim Historiography.* Leiden, 1968, p. 259.
Ibn Qāḍī-Shuhba. *Al-Aʿlām bi-Taʾrīkh Ahl al-Islām.* Vol. I (781-800/1379-1397) in print: A. Darwich, ed., Institut français, Damascus, 1977. Remainder in ms.: Dār al-Kutub, Taʾrīkh: 293; BN, f.a.: 1598-1600 (*GAL* II, 63; Suppl. II, 50).

Ibn Taghrī-Birdī. *Ḥawādith al-Duhūr fī Madā' al-Ayyām wa'l Shuhūr*. Edited by William Popper, in Vol. VII, nos. 1-4 of University of California Publications in Semitic Philology, 1930-1931 (*GAL* II, 52, no. 6).

———. *Al-Nujūm al-Zāhira fī Mulūk Miṣr wa'l-Qāhira*. Edited and translated by William Popper in Vols. V-VII, XII, XIV, XVII-XIX, XXII, of University of California Publications in Semitic Philology, Berkeley, 1915-1960 (*GAL* II, 51, no. 1).

al-Maqrīzī. *Kitāb al-Sulūk li-Maʿrifa Duwal al-Mulūk*. In print: 12 parts in 4 vols. Cairo, 1934-1973 (*GAL* II, 48; Suppl. II, 36-37).

al-Sakhāwī. *Al-Jawāhir wa'l-Durar fī Manāqib Shaykh al-Islām Ibn Ḥajar*. ms. BN, f.a.: 2105.

———. *Iʿlān bi'l-Tawbīkh li-Man Dhamma Ahl al-Tawarīkh*. F. Rosenthal, ed. Baghdad, 1963. English translation by F. Rosenthal. *A History of Muslim Historiography*. Leiden, 1968, pp. 195-450 (*GAL* II, 43, no. 5).

———. *Irshād al-Ghāwī bi'l-Isʿād al-Ṭālib wa'l-Rāwī li'l-Iʿlām bi-Tarjamāt al-Sakhāwī*. ms. Leiden: 1106 (*GAL* Suppl. II, 31, no. 9).

———. *Al-Ṭibr al-Masbūk fī Dhayl al-Sulūk*. Cairo, 1896-1897 (*GAL* II, 48, no. 3).

MODERN SOURCES

Historiographical Works

Ahlwardt, W. *Verzeichnis der arabischen Handschriften der Königliche Bibliothek* Vols. I-X. Berlin, 1887-1899.

Alam, M. "Ibn Khaldūn's Concept of the Origin, Growth and Decay of Cities." *IC* XXXIV (1960), 90-106.

Amar, E. "La valeur historique de l'ouvrage biographique intitulé Al-Manhal al-Ṣāfī par Abū-l-Maḥāsin ibn Taghrī-Birdī (MSS. 2068-2072 de la Bibliothèque Nationale)." *Mélanges Hartwig Derenbourg*. Paris, 1909, pp. 245-54.

Ashtor, E. "Some Unpublished Sources for the Baḥrī Period." *Studies in Islamic History and Civilization, Scripta Hierosolymitana* IX (1960), 11-30.

Bosworth, C. E. *The Islamic Dynasties*. Vol. V of *Islamic Surveys*, edited by M. M. Watt. Edinburgh, 1967.

Brockelmann, C. *Geschichte der Arabischen Litteratur*. 2 vols. Leiden, 1949. Three supplementary volumes. Leiden, 1936-1942.

Cahen, C. "Les chroniques arabes concernant la Syrie, l'Egypte et la Mésopotamie de la conquête arabe à la conquête ottomane dans les bibliothèques d'Istanbul." *REI* X (1936), 333-62.

Darrag, A. "La vie d'Abū'l-Maḥāsin ibn Taghrī-Birdī et son oeuvre." *AI* XI (1972), 163-81.

Fischel, W. "Ibn Khaldūn's Activities in Mamluk Egypt (1382-1406)." In *Semitic and Oriental Studies Presented to William Popper*. Berkeley, 1951, pp. 102-24.

———. "Ibn Khaldūn's *Autobiography* in the Light of External Arabic Sources." *SO* I, 287-308.
———. *Ibn Khaldūn in Egypt*. Berkeley and Los Angeles, 1967.
———. "Ibn Khaldūn's Sources for the History of Jenghiz Khān and the Tatars." *JAOS* LXXVI (1956), 91-99.
Gibb, H.A.R. "The Islamic Background of Ibn Khaldūn's Political Theory." *BSOAS* VII (1933-1935), 23-31.
———. "Islamic Biographical Literature." In B. Lewis and P. Holt, eds. *Historians of the Middle East*. London, 1962.
Hafsi, I. "Recherches sur le genre *Ṭabaqāt* dans la littérature arabe." *Arabica* XXIII (1976), 227-65; XXIV (1977), 1-41, 150-86.
Hamzah, ʿAbd al-Laṭīf. *Al-Ḥaraka al-Fikrīya fī Miṣr fī'l-ʿAṣrayn al-Ayyūbī wa'l-Mamlūkī al-Awwal*. Cairo, 1968.
———. *Al-Qalqashandī fī Kitābihi Ṣubḥ al-Aʿshā: ʿArḍ wa Taḥlīl*. Cairo, 1962.
Lane-Poole, S. *The Muḥammedan Dynasties*. London, 1894.
Levi Della Vida, G. "Sīra." *EI*[1]. IV, 439-41.
Little, D. P. *An Introduction to Mamlūk Historiography*. Vol. II in *Freiburger Islamstudien*. Wiesbaden, 1970.
Mahdi, M. *Ibn Khaldūn's Philosophy of History*. London, 1957.
Popper, W. "Sakhāwī's Criticism of Ibn Taghrī-Birdī." *SO* II, 371-89.
Rosenthal, F. *A History of Muslim Historiography*. Leiden, 1968.
Wiet, G. "L'historien Abul-Maḥāsin." *BIE* XII (1930), 89-105.
———. "Kindī et Makrīzī." *BIFAO* XII (1916), 61-73.
Ziyāda, M. M. *Al-Mu'arrikhūn fī Miṣr fī'l-Qarn al-Khāmis ʿAshar*. Cairo, 1954.

Geographical and Topographical Works

MAPS

Arabia. U.S. Geological Survey and the Arabian American Oil Co. Washington, D.C., 1963. Scale 1:2,000,000.
Cairo. Survey of Egypt, Great Britain 1936-1940. Scale 1:5,000.
Creswell, K.A.C. *Map of Cairo Showing Mohammedan Monuments*. Survey of Egypt. 2 sheets. Cairo, 1947, 1951. Scale 1:5,000.
Dardano, A. *Libia, Carta dimostrative fisico-politico*, Ministero Dell' Africa, Italiana Servizio Cartagrafico, No. 754. Rome, 1941—XIX. Scale 1:3,000,000.
Duraffourd, M. *Etats de Syrie et du Liban*. Travaux du Cadastre et d'Amélioration foncière. Paris, 1931. Scale 1:500,000.
Duran, F. S. *Türkiye*, Kanaat Kitabevi. Istanbul, 1953. Scale 1:2,000,000.
Egypt. Normal Series, Directorate of Military Survey. Great Britain, 1941. 62 sheets. Scale 1:100,000. *Index to Place Names Appearing on the Normal 1:100,000 Map Series of Egypt*. Ministry of Finance, Egypt. Cairo, 1932.
Französich-Nordafrika. Heersplankammer, Germany. Sonderausgabe, XI, 1941. Scale 1:2,000,000.

Kosack, W. *Historische Kartenwerk Ägyptens, Altägyptische Fundstellen, Mittelalterliches arabisches Ägypten, Koptische Kultur (Delta, Mittelägypten, Oberägypten).* 2 vols. Bonn, 1971.

The Middle East. John Bartholomew and Sons, The Geographical Institute. Edinburgh, 1956. Scale 1:4,000,000. (Map III)

Official Standard Names Gazeteers. U.S. Board on Geographic Names, Office of Geography, Department of the Interior. Washington, D.C.

———. Afghanistan. 1971.
———. Algeria. 1972.
No. 54. Arabian Peninsula. 1961.
No. 45. Egypt-Gaza Strip. 1959.
No. 19. Iran. 1956.
No. 37. Iraq. 1957.
No. 114. Israel. 1970.
———. Jordan. 1971.
No. 115. Lebanon. 1970.
———. Libya. 1973.
No. 112. Morocco. 1970.
No. 67. Pakistan. 1962.
No. 51. Spain-Andorra. 1961.
No. 68. Sudan. 1962.
No. 104. Syria. 1967.
No. 81. Tunisia. 1964.
No. 45. Turkey. 1960.
No. 42. U.S.S.R. 1970.

Rashdan, A. *Communication Map of U.A.R.* Cairo Drafting Office. Cairo, 1963. Scale 1:500,000. (Maps I and II)

Sahab Historical Map of Iran under the Safavi Dynasty in the 16th and 17th Centuries. No. 1002. Tehran, 1971. Scale 1:2,300,000.

World Outline Maps (Area Series). Army Map Service (AM), Corps of Engineers, U.S. Army. Washington, D.C., 1952. Sheet 13: Mediterranean Area (Map V); Sheet 13-A: Iran, Iraq, Arabian Peninsula (Map IV). Scale 1:10,000,000.

STUDIES

Ashtor-Strauss, E. "L'urbanisme syrien à la basse-époque." *RSO* XXXIII (1958), 181-209.

Brockelmann, C. "Al-Ḳalkashandī." *EI*[1]. II, 699-700.

Elisséeff, N. "Dimashḳ." *EI*[2]. II, 283-86.

Gaudefroy-Demombynes, M. *La Syrie à l'époque des Mamelouks.* Paris, 1923.

Golb, N. "The Topography of the Jews of Medieval Egypt, Inductive Studies based Primarily upon Documents of the Cairo Genizah." *JNES* XXIV (1965), 251-70.

Haartmann, R. "Politische Geographie des Mamlūkenreiches, Kapitel 5 und 6 des Staatshandbuchs Ibn Fadlallah al-ʿOmaris." *ZDMG* LXX (1916), 477-511.

Maspero, J. and G. Wiet. "Matériaux pour servir à la géographie de l'Egypte." *MIFAO* XXXVI (1914, 1916).

Petry, C. "Geographic Origins of Dīwān Officials in Cairo during the Fifteenth Century." *JESHO* XXI (1978), part II, 166-84.

———. "Geographic Origins of the Civil Judiciary of Cairo in the Fifteenth Century." *JESHO* XXI (1977), part I, 52-74.

Ramzī, M. *Al-Qāmūs al-Jughrāfī li'l-Bilād al-Miṣrīya min ʿuhud Qudamāʾ al-Miṣrīyīn ilā Sanat 1945*. 2 parts in 5 vols. Cairo, 1953-1963.

Sauvaget, J. "Esquisse d'une histoire de la ville de Damas." *REI* VIII (1934), 422-80.

———. *Alep, essai sur le développement d'une grande ville syrienne, des origines au milieu du XIXᵉ siècle*. Paris, 1941.

Sauvaire, H. *Description de Damas*. 2 vols. Paris, 1895.

Toussoun, O. "La géographie de l'Égypte." *MSRGE* VIII, parts 1-3, 1926.

Wulzinger, K. and C. Watzinger. *Damaskus, Die Islamische Stadt*. Berlin, 1924.

Wüstenfeld, F. "Calcashandis Geographie und Verwaltung von Ägypten." *Abhandlung der Gesellschaft der Wissenschaften zu Göttingen* XXV (1879).

Ziadeh, N. *Damascus under the Mamluks*. Norman, 1964.

———. *Urban Life in Syria under the Early Mamluks*. Beirut, 1953.

History and Topography of Cairo

Abu-Lughod, J. L. *Cairo, 1001 Years of the City Victorious*. Princeton, 1971.

Casanova, P. "Essai de reconstitution topographique de la ville d'al-Fousṭaṭ ou Miṣr." *MIFAO* XXXV (1913, 1919).

———. "Histoire et description de la citadelle du Caire." *MMAFC* VI (1897), 509-781.

Clerget, M. *Le Caire, étude de géographie urbaine et d'histoire économique*. 2 vols. Cairo, 1934.

Creswell, K.A.C. "A Brief Chronology of the Muḥammadan Monuments of Cairo to A.D. 1517." *BIFAO* XV (1918), 39-164.

———. *The Muslim Architecture of Egypt*. 2 vols. Oxford, 1952, 1959.

Garcin, J.-C. "Le Caire et la province: constructions au Caire et à Qūṣ sous les Mamelūks Baḥrides." *AI* VIII (1969), 47-62.

———. *Un centre musulman de la haute Egypte médiévale: Qūṣ*. Cairo, 1976.

———. "La méditerranéisation de l'empire mamelouk sous les Sultans Baḥrides." *RSO* XLVIII (1974), 109-16.

Herz, M. et al. *Procès verbaux, Comité de conservation des monuments de l'art arabe*. Cairo, 1885-1913.

Mayer, L. A. *The Buildings of Qaytbay*. London and Cairo, 1938.

Mubārak, ʿAlī. *Al-Khiṭāṭ al-Tawfīqīya al-Jadīda li-Miṣr al-Qāhira*. 20 parts in 4 vols. Cairo, 1888.

Popper, W. *Egypt and Syria under the Circassian Sultans*. Vols. XV-XVI of

University of California Publications in Semitic Philology. Berkeley, 1955-1957.

Ravaisse, P. "Essai sur l'histoire et sur la topographie du Caire d'après Maḳrīzī." *MMAFC* I, fasc. 3 (1887), 409-80; III, fasc. 3 (1889), 31-115.

Salmon, G. "Etudes sur la topographie du Caire, la Ḳalʿat al-Ḳabch et la Birkat al-Fīl." *MIFAO* VII (1902).

Staffa, S. *Conquest and Fusion, the Social Evolution of Cairo, A.D. 642-1850.* Leiden, 1977.

Zaki, Abdel Rahman. *A Bibliography of the Literature of the City of Cairo.* Cairo, 1964.

Mamluk History

Atiya, A. S. "An Unpublished XIVth Century *Fatwā* on the Status of Foreigners in Mamluk Egypt and Syria." In *Paul Kahle Festschrift, Studien zur Geschichte und Kultur des Nahen und Fernen Ostens.* Leiden, 1935, pp. 55-68.

Awad, M. "Sultan al-Ghawrī, His Place in Literature and Learning." *Actes du 20e Congrès Internationale des Orientalistes* (1938), 321-22.

Ayalon, D. "Aspects of the Mamlūk Phenomenon." *Der Islam.* Part I: LIII, no. 2 (1976), 196-225; part. II: LIV, no. 1 (1977), 1-32.

———. "The Circassians in the Mamluk Kingdom." *JAOS* LXIX (1949), 135-47.

———. "Discharges from Service, Banishments and Imprisonments in Mamluk Society." *Israel Oriental Studies* II (1972), 25-50.

———. "L'esclavage du mamelouk." *Oriental Notes and Studies,* Jerusalem Oriental Society, no. 1 (1951).

———. "The European-Asiatic Steppe: A Major Reservoir of Power for the Islamic World." *Acts of the 25th Congress of Orientalists, Moscow* II (1960), 47-52.

———. "The Great Yāsa of Chingiz Khan, a Re-Examination." *SI* XXXIII (1971), 97-140; XXXIV (1971), 151-80; XXXVI (1972), 113-58; XXXVIII (1973), 107-56.

———. *Gunpowder and Firearms in the Mamluk Kingdom.* London, 1956.

———. "The Mamlūks and Naval Power, a Phase of the Struggle between Islam and Christian Europe." *Proceedings of the Israel Academy of Sciences and the Humanities* I, no. 8 (1965).

———. "The Muslim City and the Mamlūk Military Aristocracy." *Proceedings of the Israel Academy of Sciences and the Humanities* II, no. 14 (1967).

———. "Names, Titles and 'Nisbas' of the Mamlūks." *Israel Oriental Studies* V (1975), 189-232.

———. "Notes on the Furūsiyya Exercises and Games in the Mamlūk Sultanate." *Studies in Islamic History and Civilization, Scripta Hierosolymitana* IX (1960), 31-62.

———. "The Plague and Its Effects upon the Mamlūk Army." *JRAS,* April, 1946, pp. 67-73.

———. "Preliminary Remarks on the Mamluk Military Institution in Islam." In V. J. Parry and M. E. Yapp, eds. *War, Technology and Society in the Middle East*. Oxford, 1975, pp. 44-58.

———. "Studies on the Structure of the Mamluk Army." *BSOAS* XV (1953), 203-38. 448-76; XVI (1954), 57-90.

———. "The System of Payment in Mamluk Military Society." *JESHO* I (August 1957), 37-65; I (October 1958), 257-96.

———. "The Wafidīa in the Mamlūk Kingdom." *IC* XXV (1951), 89-104.

Bosworth, C. E. "Barbarian Invasions: The Coming of the Turks into the Islamic World." In D. S. Richards, ed. *Islamic Civilization, 950-1150*. Oxford, 1973, pp. 1-16.

———. "Recruitment, Muster and Review in Medieval Islamic Armies." In V. J. Parry and M. E. Yapp, eds. *War, Technology and Society in the Middle East*. Oxford, 1975, pp. 59-77.

Darraj, A. *L'Egypte sous le règne de Barsbay*. Damascus, 1961.

Fischel, W. J. "Ascensus Barcoch." *Arabica* VI (1959), 57-74, 152-72.

Guémard, G. "De l'armement et de l'équipement des Mamelūks." *BIE* VIII (1926), 1-19.

Mayer, L. A. *Mamlūk Costume, A Survey*. Geneva, 1952.

———. *New Material for Mamlūk Heraldry*. Jerusalem, 1937.

Muir, W. *The Mameluke or Slave Dynasty of Egypt*. London, 1896.

Paret, R. "Sīrat Baybars." *EI*[2] I, 1126-27.

Poliak, A. N. "Le caractère colonial de l'état mamelouk dans ses rapports avec la horde d'or." *REI* IX (1935), 231-48.

———. "The Influence of Chingiz-Khān's Yāsa upon the General Organization of the Mamlūk State." *BSOAS* X (1940-1942), 862-76.

———. "Some Notes on the Feudal System of the Mamlūks." *JRAS* (1937), pp. 97-107.

Salīm, M. R. *ʿAṣr Ṣalāṭīn al-Mamālīk wa Nitājuhu al-ʿIlmī wa'l-Adabī*. 6 vols. to date; Cairo, 1946—

Sauvaget, J. "Noms et surnoms des Mamelouks." *Journal Asiatique* CCXXXVIII (1950), 31-58.

———. *La poste aux chevaux dans l'empire des Mamelouks*. Paris, 1941.

Tekindag, S. *Berkuk devrinde Memluk sultanligi*. Istanbul, 1961. Used for bibliography.

Wiet, G. *L'Egypte Arabe*. In Gabriel Hanotaux, ed. *Histoire de la Nation Egyptienne* IV (Paris, 1937).

———. "Un refugié mamlouk à la cour mongole de Perse." *Mélanges Henri Massé*. Tehran, 1963.

Iranian and Central Asian History

Aubin, J. "Comment Timur-Lenk prenait les villes." *SI* XIX (1963), 83-122.

Barthold, W. *Histoire des Turcs d'Asie Centrale*. Paris, 1945.

Fischel, W. J. *Ibn Khaldūn and Tamerlane: Their Historic Meeting in Damascus*. Berkeley and Los Angeles, 1952.

Fischel, W. J. "A New Later Source on Tamerlane's Conquest of Damascus (1400-1401)." *Oriens* (1956), pp. 201-32.

Hookham, H. *Tamburlaine the Conqueror*. London, 1962.

Lambton, A.K.S. *Landlord and Peasant in Persia*. London, 1953.

Minorsky, V. "The Aq-Qoyunlu and Land Reforms." *BSOAS* XVII:3 (1955), 449-62.

Spuler, B. *Die Mongolen in Iran*. Berlin, 1955.

Woods, J. E. *The Aqquyunlu; Clan, Confederation, Empire*. Chicago, 1976.

Economic History

Ashtor, E. "Le coût de la vie dans l'Egypte médiévale." *JESHO* III (1963), 150-89.

———. "Le coût de la vie dans la Syrie médiévale." *Arabica* VIII (1961), 59-73.

———. "Le coût de la vie en Palestine au moyen âge." *Eretz-Israel: Mayer Memorial Volume* VII (1963), 154-64.

———. "L'évolution des prix dans le proche-orient à la basse époque." *JESHO* IV (1961), 15-47.

———. "The Kārimī Merchants." *JRAS* (1956), 45-56.

———. "Matériaux pour l'histoire des prix dans l'Egypte médiévale." *JESHO* VI (1963), 158-69.

———. *Les métaux précieux et la balance des payements du proche-orient à la basse époque*. Paris, 1971.

———. "Migrations de l'Iraḳ vers les pays méditerranéens." *Annales Economies, Sociétés, Civilisations* XXVII, no. 1 (1972), 185-214.

———. "Prix et salaires à l'époque mamelouk." *REI* XV (1949), 49-94.

———. "Quelques indications sur les revenus dans l'orient musulman au haut moyen âge." *JESHO* II (1959), 262-80.

———. "Salaires dans l'orient médiéval à la basse époque." *REI* XXXIX (1971), 103-17.

———. *A Social and Economic History of the Near East in the Middle Ages*. Berkeley and Los Angeles, 1976.

Bacharach, Jere. "A Study of the Correlation between Textual Sources and Numismatic Evidence for Mamluk Egypt and Syria, A.H. 784-872/A.D. 1382-1468." Ph.D. dissertation, Michigan, 1967.

Cahen, C. "Contribution a l'étude des impôts dans l'Egypte médiévale." *JESHO* V (1962), 244-78.

———. "Douanes et commerce dans les ports méditerranéens de l'Egypte médiévale d'après le *Minhādj* d'al-Makhzūmī." *JESHO* VII (1964), 217-314.

———. "L'évolution de l'Iḳṭāʿ de IXᵉ au XIIIᵉ siècles." *Annales Economies, Sociétés, Civilisations* VIII (1953), 25-52.

———. "Iḳṭāʿ," *EI*² III, 1088-90.

Cohen, H. "The Economic Background and the Secular Occupations of Muslim Jurisprudents and Traditionists in the Classical Period of Islam." *JESHO* XIII, part 1 (1970), 16-61.

Darrāj, A. *Al-Mamālīk wa'l-Firanj fī'l-Qarn al-Tāsi' al-Hijrī, al-Khāmis 'ashr al-Mīladī*. Cairo, 1961.
———. "Les relations commerciales entre l'état Mamlouk et la France." *Bulletin of the Faculty of Arts, Cairo University* XXV (1963), 1-21.
Ehrenkreutz, A. S. "The Crisis of the 'Dīnār' in the Egypt of Saladin." *JAOS* LXXVI (1956), 178-84.
———. *Saladin*. Albany, 1972.
———. "The Standard of Fineness of Gold Coins Circulating in Egypt at the Time of the Crusaders." *JAOS* LXXIV (1954), 162-66.
Escovitz, J. H. "Vocational Patterns of the Scribes of the Mamlūk Chancery." *Arabica* XXIII (1976), 42-62.
Fischel, W. J. "The Spice Trade in Mamluk Egypt." *JESHO* I (1958), 157-74.
———. "Über die Gruppe der Kārimī-Kaufleute." *Studia Arabica, Analecta Orientalia* (Rome 1937), 65-82.
Gibb, H.A.R. *Studies on the Civilization of Islam*. Boston, 1962.
Labib, Subhi. "Geld und Kredit, Studien zur Wirtschafts-Geschichte Aegyptens im Mittelalter." *JESHO* II (1959), 225-46.
———. *Handelgeschichte Ägyptens im Spätmittelalter (1171-1517)*. Wiesbaden, 1965.
———. "Al-Tijāra al-kārimīyya wa'l-Tijārat Miṣr fī'l'Uṣūr al-Wusṭā." *Bulletin de la Société Egyptienne d'Etudes Historiques* IV (1952), 5-63.
Lapidus, I. "The Grain Economy of Mamlūk Egypt." *JESHO* XII (1969), 1-15.
Michel, B. "L'organisation financière de l'Egypte d'après Qalqachandi." *BIE* VII (1925), 127-47.
Rabie, H. M. *The Financial System of Egypt, A.H. 564-741 / A.D. 1169-1341*. Oxford, 1972.
Sobernheim, M. "Das Zuckermonopol unter Sultan Barsbai." *ZA* XXVII (1912), 75-84.
Toussoun, Omar. "Mémoire sur les finances de l'Egypte depuis les pharaons jusqu'à nos jours." *MIE* VI (1924).
Udovitch, A. L. "England to Egypt, 1350-1500: Long-term Trends and Long-Distance Trade." In M. A. Cook, ed. *Studies in the Economic History of the Middle East*. London, 1970, pp. 93-128.
———. *Partnership and Profit in Medieval Islam*. Princeton, 1970.
Wiet, G. "Les marchands d'épices sous les sultans mamlouks." *CHE* VII (1955), 81-147.

Institutional, Religious, and Social History

'Abd ar-Rāziq, A. "La *ḥisba* et le *muḥtasib* en Egypte au temps des Mamlūks." *AI* XIII (1977), 115-78.
———. "Un document concernant le mariage des esclaves au temps des Mamlūks." *JESHO* XIII (1970), 309-14.
Ashtor-Strauss, E. *See* Strauss, E.
'Āshūr, S. A. *Al-'Aṣr al-Mamālīk fī Miṣr wa'l-Shām*. Cairo, 1965.
———. *Miṣr fī 'Aṣr Dawlat al-Mamālīk fī Miṣr wa'l-Shām*. Cairo, 1959.
———. *Al-Mujtama' al-Miṣrī fī 'Aṣr Salāṭīn al-Mamālīk*. Cairo, 1962.

Björkman, W. "Beiträge zur Geschichte des Staatskanzlei im Islamischen Aegypten." *Hamburgische Universität, Abhandlungen aus dem Gebiet der Auslandskunde* XXVIII, Reihe B, Bd. 16 (1928).

Bosworth, C. E. "Christian and Jewish Religious Dignitaries in Mamlūk Egypt and Syria: Qalqashandī's Information on Their Hierarchy, Titulature and Appointment." *IJMES* III (1972), 59-74, 199-216.

———. "Some Historical Gleanings from the Section on Symbolic Actions in Qalqashandī's Subh al-A'shā." *Arabica* X (1963), 148-53.

Bulliet, R. W. "City Histories in Medieval Iran." *Bulletin of the Society for Iranian Studies* I (1968), 104-109.

———. *The Patricians of Nishapur.* Cambridge, 1972.

———. "A Quantitative Approach to Medieval Muslim Biographical Dictionaries." *JESHO* XIII (1970), 195-211.

Cahen, C. and M. Talbi. "Ḥisba." *EI*[2] III, 485-93.

Coulson, N. J. *A History of Islamic Law.* Edinburgh, 1964.

Cour, A. "Shaikh." *EI*[1] IV, 275.

Darraj, A. *L'acte de waqf de Barsbay.* Cairo, 1963.

Dodge, B. *Al-Azhar, A Millennium of Muslim Learning.* Washington, D.C., 1961.

———. *Muslim Education in Medieval Times.* Washington, D.C., 1962.

Dols, M. *The Black Death in the Middle East.* Princeton, 1976.

Fischel, W. J. "The City in Islam." *Middle East Affairs* VII (1956), 227-32.

Garcin, J.-C. "Histoire, opposition politique et piétisme traditioniste dans le Ḥusn al-Muḥādarat de Suyūṭī." *AI* VII (1967), 33-88.

Heffening, W. "Shāhid." *EI*[1] IV, 261-62.

Heyworth-Dunne, J. *An Introduction to the History of Education in Modern Egypt.* London, 1939; reprint 1968.

Hodgson, M.G.S. *The Venture of Islam.* 3 vols. Chicago, 1974.

Huart, C. "Imām." *EI*[1] II, 473-74.

Jomier, J. "Al-Azhar." *EI*[2] I, 813-21.

———. *Le mahmal et la caravane égyptienne des pèlerins de la Mecque, XIII*[e]*-XX*[e] *siècles.* Cairo, 1953.

Juynboll, T. de. *Handbuch des Islamischen Gesetzes.* Leiden, 1910.

———. "Ḳāḍī." *EI*[1] II, 606-607.

Khadduri, M. and H. Liebesny. *Law in the Middle East, I: Origin and Development of Islamic Law.* Washington, D.C., 1955.

Kramers, J. H. "Shaikh al-Islam." *EI*[1] IV, 275-79.

Krenkow, F. "Kātib." *EI*[1] II, 819.

Laoust, H. "Le ḥanbalisme sous les Mamlouks Baḥrides (685-784/1260-1382)." *REI* XXVIII (1960), 1-71.

Lapidus, I. *Muslim Cities in the Later Middle Ages.* Cambridge, 1967.

Levy, R. "Muḥtasib." *EI*[1] III, 702-703.

Madelung, W. "Imāma." *EI*[2] III, 1163-69.

Makdisi, G. "Muslim Institutions of Learning in Eleventh-Century Baghdad." *BSOAS* XXIV (1961), 1-56.

Mandaville, J. "The Muslim Judiciary of Damascus in the Late Mamlūk Period." Ph.D. dissertation, Princeton, 1969.
Pedersen, J. "Khaṭīb." *EI*[1] II, 927-29.
Pellat, C. *The Life and Works of Jāḥiẓ*. Berkeley and Los Angeles, 1969.
Perlmann, M. "Asnāwī's Tract against Christian Officials." *IGM* II 172-208.
———. "Notes on Anti-Christian Propaganda in the Mamluk Empire." *BSOAS* X (1940-1942), 843-61.
Poliak, A. *Feudalism in Egypt, Syria, Palestine and the Lebanon (1250-1900)*. London, 1939.
———. "Les révoltes populaires en Egypte à l'époque des Mamelouks et leurs causes économiques." *REI* VII (1934), 251-73.
Salama, I. *Bibliographie analytique et critique touchant la question de l'enseignement en Egypte depuis la période des Mamlūks jusqu'à nos jours*. Cairo, 1938.
Salibi, K. S. "The Banū Jamāʿa: A Dynasty of Shāfiʿite Jurists in the Mamluk Period." *SI* IX (1958), 97-109.
———. "Listes chronologiques des grands cadis de l'Egypte sous les Mamelouks." *REI* XXV (1957), 81-125.
———. "The Maronites of Lebanon under Frankish and Mamluk Rule (1099-1516)." *Arabica* IV (1957), 288-303.
Schacht, J. *An Introduction to Islamic Law*. Oxford, 1964.
Schimmel, A. "Kalif und Ḳāḍī im Spätmittelalterlichen Ägypten." *Die Welt des Islams* XXIV (1942), 1-128.
———. "Some Glimpses of Religious Life under the Late Mamlūks." *IC* IV (1965), 353-92.
———. "Sufismus und Heiligenverehrung im Spätmittelalterlichen Ägypten." In *Festschrift Werner Caskel*. Leiden, 1968, pp. 274-89.
Shalabi, A. *A History of Muslim Education*. Beirut, 1954.
Strauss, E. (Ashtor-). "L'inquisition dans l'état mamlouk." *RSO* XXV (1950), 11-26.
———. "The Social Isolation of the Ahl al-Dhimma." EMPH, pp. 73-94.
Tritton, A. S. *Materials on Muslim Education in the Middle Ages*. London, 1957.
———. "The Tribes of Syria in the Fourteenth and Fifteenth Centuries." *BSOAS* XII (1948), 567-73.
Tyan, E. *Histoire de l'organisation judicaire en pays d'Islam*. 2nd ed. Leiden, 1960.
———. "Le notariat et le régime de la preuve par écrit dans la pratique du droit musulman." AFDSEB. No. 2 (1945).
Wiet, G. "La grande peste noire en Syrie et en Egypte." *Etudes d'Orientalisme, Mémorial Lévi-Provençal* I (Paris, 1962), 367-84.
———. "Ḳibṭ." *EI*[1] II, 990-1003.
———. "Les secrétaires de la chancellerie (kuttab-el-sirr) en Egypte sous les Mamlouks circassiens (784-922/1382-1517)." *MRB* I (1925), 271-314.
———. "Le traité des famines de Maqrīzī, traduction française." *JESHO* V (1962), 1-90.

Index

ʿAbbāsid caliphate, in Cairo, 18
ʿAbbāsid empire, military slaves in, 15
ʿAbbāsid period, bureaucracy during, 313
ʿAbbāsids, served by Ibn Ṭūlūn, 17
Abū Bakrīya madrasa, Iranians in, 65, 155
Abu Lughod, J., topographical work of, 131
Abū Tīj, migration from, 48
academicians from Anatolia, 69
academies: of Fāṭimids, 419 n21; Ismāʿīlī teaching in, 138
accountants, Syrians as, 56
accounts, balancing of, 203
Adana, migration from, 68
Aden, migration from, 31
al-Adhraʿāt, migration from, 59
advocacy, feasibility of, 322
Afghanistan, migration from, 63
Africa: routes to, 74; sub-Saharan migration from, 77
agent of exchequer, nāẓir as, 217
agrarian economy, supervision of, 23
agrarian production, decrease in, 28
Aḥbās, controlled by Cairenes, 56
Ajlāb, 21
Akhmīm, migration from, 48
Akka, cathedral gate of, 332
alchemy: Iranian in, 65; in madrasas, 139
Aleppo: administrative center, 51; Anatolian in, 70; as buffer, 53; controller of army in, 208; data from, 9; devastation of, 53, 60; Ḥanafī judge from, 54; jurisdiction of, 59; kātib al-sirr in, 208-209; learned classes in, 54; Mālikī justice of, 208; professoriate in, 250; Shāfiʿī justice of, 207
Aleppo province: Anatolian portions of, 68; Maghribī in, 75; Turko-Arabic culture of, 69
Alexandria: administration of, 44; decline of, 412 n9; European merchants in, 31; exile to, 42; Maghribī in, 76; migration from, 41-42; muqriʾ in, 264; rivals Fusṭāṭ, 40; slave port, 27; tie to military elite, 42; trade in, 34, 245; waqfs in, 333
Alfīya of al-ʿIraqī, Maghribī studies, 76
algebra in madrasas, 139
Algeria, migration from, 75
ʿAlī al-Muqriʾ, 265
ʿalim, recognition as, 251
ʿalim status, attainment of, 160-61
Aljayhīya madrasa: Iranians in, 155; muʿīds in, 248; stewards in, 210
Amber Dealers' bazaar, waqfs on, 335
Amida, migration from, 68
amirate madrasas: cater to Mamluks, 252; Iranians in, 155; khaṭībs in, 261; librarians in, 255; location of, 338; Maghribīs in, 158; muʿīds in, 248; muqri's in, 266; professors in, 252; shaykhs in, 222
amir of forty, nāẓir as, 215
amirs: alliances of, 20; appoint muqriʾ, 263; attitude toward sultanate, 19; confiscations by, 25; employ ʿulamaʾ, 40; endowments of, 134-35, 139; foundations of, 150; reputations of, 141; in southeast, 133; staffs of, 53, 142; support muqri's, 262
—ties: to Bulqīnī, 236; to Damascenes, 52; to Delta Egyptians, 45; to Iranians, 66-67; to Maghribī, 274; to muqriʾ, 265; to muʿtaqads, 269; to religious functionaries, 322; to Syrians, 54; use of Copts, 273. *See also* Mamluks
ʿAmr ibn al-ʿĀṣ mosque: Anatolians in, 157; Cairenes in, 147; Delta Egyptian in, 46; description of, 340; khaṭībs in, 261; in later Middle Ages, 135; Maghribīs in, 159; nāẓirs in, 219; professors in, 253; shaykhs in, 223
ʿAmrān al-Maghribī, Zayn: tājir sulṭānī, 428 n84
Anatolia: adjacent to Iran, 63; artisans from, 72; data on, 144; individuals from in *Ḍaw'*, 9; khānqāhs in, 139; learned establishment in, 69; migration from, 68, 70; officials from, 72; Ottoman rule over, 68; political autonomy of, 416 n56; settlement in, 65. *See also* Asia Minor

Anatolians: assimilation of, 69; interest groups of, 161; distribution of, 164; militarists, 71; in mortuary zones, 147; origins of, 68. *See also* Rūmīs
anarchy, normative state of, 21
ʿAnbar, Ustādh, 327
ancient sciences, studies by Maghribī, 75
al-Andalus, Maghribīs from, 75-76. *See also* Spain
Anūk ibn al-Nāṣir Muḥammad, burial of, 333
ʿAqāqīr, *see* pharmacists
Aqbughā ʿAbd al-Wāḥid, ʿAlāʾ: founds hospice, 335
ʿaql, quality of, 225
Aqmar mosque, khaṭībs in, 261
Aqsarāy, migration from, 68
Aqūsh al-Ghazāwī, Jamāl: endowment of, 331
Arab conquest, urban growth after, 40
Arab lands, biographical sources in, 8
Arabia: individuals from in *Ḍawʾ*, 9; data on, 144; Ḥanafism in, 160
Arabian tribes, 73
Arabic, Anatolian's fluency in, 70
Arabic culture in holy cities, 73
Arabic grammar, Iranians in, 65
Ardabīl, migration from, 65
arithmetics in madrasas, 139
Armenian Knot: control of, 53, 68; pillaging in, 64; populations of, 63
artisan category: analysis of, 130; Anatolians in, 72
artisans: as judges, 231; as merchants, 244; as muʿīds, 248; as muʿtaqads, 268; as professors, 252; as shāhids, 226; as Ṣūfīs, 271; from Upper Egypt, 49; from Yemen, 73
arwiqa in al-Azhar, 334
Arzinkān (Erzinjan), migration from, 68
ascetics: analysis of, 130; from Delta, 150; Iranians as, 156; in khānqāhs, 139-40; near Bāb al-Naṣr, 334; as social type, 256; in tombs, 136, 141; Turkish-speaking, 70. *See also* muʿtaqads
Aṣḥāb: implementors of Muḥammad's memory, 5; reliability of, 6
al-Ashʿarī as nisba, 45
Ashrafīya madrasa: Anatolians in, 156; Delta Egyptians in, 45; description of, 335; imāms in, 259; khaṭībs in, 261; librarians in, 255; muʿīds in, 248; muqriʾs in, 266; nāẓirs in, 218; shaykhs in, 222; stewards in, 210; Ṣūfīs in, 272; Syrians in, 153-54; Upper Egyptians in, 151
Asia Minor, immigrants from, 72. *See also* Anatolia
Aṣlam mosque: Iranians in, 155; khaṭībs in, 261
Asnā, migration from, 48
ʿAsqalān, migration from, 59
astronomy in madrasas, 139
Asyūṭ: deputy judge in, 50; migration from, 48
Aswān, migration from, 47-48
Atabeks: attitude of, 19; in Aleppo, 208
Aṭfīḥīya: migration from, 48; waqfs in, 331
Atrāk, status of, 156. *See also* Turks
Aubin, J., on Mongol outlook, 415 n46
autonomy: of bureaucrats, 313; of imāms, 258; implications of, 319-20; of jurist-scholars, 315; of khānqāhs, 262
Ayalon, D.: on geographic zones, 405 n3; on Ibn Taghrī-Birdī's errors, 404 n19; on Mamluk ranking, 406 n15
aʿyan, interchanged with ʿulamaʾ, 4, 200
Aybak, al-Muʿizz: endowment of, 331, usurpation of, 18
ʿAydhāb, decline of, 49
al-ʿAynī, Badr, 69-70; as chief justice, 71, 231
ʿAyntāb: Maghribī in, 75; migration from, 68, 70
Aytmishīya madrasa: Anatolians in, 157; Iranians in, 65, 155; professors in, 252
Ayyūbid amirs, endowments of, 135
Ayyūbid period: al-Azhar during, 334; Fāṭimid city from, 160; foundations of, 132, 330; status of ʿulamaʾ during, 20; urban transformation during, 133
Ayyūbids: defenders of Sunnī Islam, 28; Mamluk institution under, 18; special payments by, 27
Azerbayjānī traditions in Iran, 63
al-Azhar: Arabians in, 159; Cairenes in, 146; as cathedral mosque, 138; copyists in, 242; cosmopolitanism of, 149-50;

Delta Egyptians in, 151; description of, 334; in Fāṭimid period, 132; imāms in, 259; Iranians in, 155; Iraqis in, 157; Ismāʿīlīs in, 139; khaṭībs in, 261-62; librarians in, 255; Maghribīs in; 75-76, 158, 161, 164; muʿīds in, 248; muqri's in, 262, 264-66; muʿtaqads in, 269; preacher in, 323; professors in, 253; stewards in, 210; study of, 128; Ṣūfīs in, 272; Syrian in, 154; Upper Egyptians in, 151-52

Bāb al-Futūḥ area, description of, 333-34
Bāb al-ʿĪd, *see* Festival Gate
Bāb al-Kharq, waqfs near, 331
Bāb al-Naṣr: description of, 333-34; district north of, 134
Bāb al-Silsila, *see* Chain Gate
Bāb al-Zuhūma, waqfs near, 332
Bāb Zuwayla: entrance to southeast, 133; madrasa near, 336; waqfs near, 331. *See also* Zuwayla Gate
al-Badawī, al-Sayyid: in Ṭanṭa, 44
Baghdād: in ʿAbbāsid period, 204; familial origins in, 207; migration from, 72-73, 78; muqri' from, 264; Niẓāmīya in, 138; in regional politics, 72
Bahā' al-Dīn quarter: Bulquīnī madrasa in, 233; al-Sakhāwī from, 8; shaykhs in, 223
Bahasna, migration from, 68
Bahnasawīya, migration from, 48; waqfs in, 327
Baḥrī period: building during, 132-33; commerce during, 29-30; equilibrium of, 21; Fāṭimid city during, 160; political developments of, 18; status of ʿulama' during, 20
Baḥrī sultans: defend Sunnī Islam, 28; inhibit rural aristocracy, 18; military and civilian spheres under, 19
baker as muqri', 265
Baktamur al-Ḥijāzī, wife of, 329
Balyanā, migration from, 48
Bām, migration from, 64
Banī Suwayf, migration from, 48
baraka: of buried saints, 141; efficacy of, 322-23; in holy cities, 58; of revered persons, 136, 267; in al-Shāfiʿī tomb, 340
al-Barantīshī, 75
Barqūq and Faraj, mausoleum of, 340
Barqūq, al-Ẓāhir: alters bureaucracy, 407 n24; appoints Iranian, 67; founds madrasa, 333; in al-Karak, 59; Saʿīd al-Suʿadā' under, 327; succession under, 19; urban recovery under, 134
—ties: to muqri', 264; to nāẓir, 215, to Syrians, 55, 57
Barqūqīya madrasa: Bulqīnī in, 239; Cairenes in, 146; Delta Egyptian in, 46; description of, 333; khaṭībs in, 261; muqri' in, 264; Syrians in, 154
barracks: muqri's in, 266; nāẓirs in, 219
Barsbāy, al-Ashraf: controls ports, 73; founds madrasa, 335; mausoleum of, 340; monopolies of, 30-31
—ties: to Anatolian, 71; to Iranian, 66; to Syrians, 56, 208-209
Bāsiṭīya area, merchants in, 245
Bāsiṭīya madrasa: Iranians in, 155; khaṭībs in, 261; librarians in, 255; shaykhs in, 222
Baṣra: in ʿAbbāsid period, 204; migration from, 73
baths: in biographies, 142; in khānqāhs, 140; in Siryāqūs, 341; supported by kārimīs, 30
bawwāb, *see* gatekeeper
Baybars al-Jashankīr, Rukn: endowment of, 333; founds khānqāh, 328
Baybars, al-Ẓāhir: architect of Mamluk state, 18; endowment of, 158; founds madrasa, 331; sultanate after, 19
Baybarsīya khānqāh: Bulqīnī in, 236, 238; Cairenes in, 146, 148, 161; copyists in, 242; Delta Egyptians in, 150; description of, 328; imāms in, 259; Iranians in, 154; judges in, 241; khaṭībs in, 262; muqri's in, 262, 265-66; shāhids in, 227; Ṣūfīs in, 271-72; Syrians in, 154
Bayn al-Qaṣrayn cluster: Anatolians in, 156; Bulqīnī in, 239; Cairenes in, 146; Delta Egyptians in, 149; exclusivity of, 146; institutions of, 330; Iraqis in, 157; khaṭībs in, 261; librarians in, 254-55; muʿīds in, 248; muqri's in, 265; professors in, 252; shāhids near, 227; stewards in, 210

Bayn al-Qaṣrayn district: location of, 131; madrasas in, 136; waqfs in, 330
Bayn al-Sūrayn, khaṭībs in, 261
bayt al-māl, *see* treasury
bazaars, foundation of, 133
bazzāz, *see* cloth merchant
bean seller, muʿtaqad as, 268
Bedouin forces of initial conquests, 15-16
Beneath the Apartments street: markets along, 245; waqfs in, 335
Berke Khān, al-Saʿīd: endowment of, 331
Beyliks of Anatolia, 69
Bijāya, migration from, 74-75
biographers: comprehensiveness of, 144; reliability of, 8; on religious functionaries, 256
biographical literature indigenous to Islamic community, 5
biographical sources: flaw in, 81; geographic origins in, 37; limitations of, 14; local institutions in, 162; objectives behind, 38; progression of, 6-7
Biography of the Prophet, motives behind, 5
Birkat al-Fīl, *see* Elephant Lake
birthdays, *see* mawlids
birthplaces: of Anatolians, 69; citations of, 419 n31; as geographic indicators, 411 n3; in Syria-Palestine, 58
Black Sea steppes, slaves from, 22, 27
Black Sheep Turcomans in Iran, 63
blindness of muqri's, 263-65
Book Dealers' market, merchants in, 245
Boujie, *see* Bijāya
Buḥayra, migration from, 41-43
building programs of Mamluks, 133
Bukhāra, migration from, 64
Būlāq: Cairenes in, 147; development of, 134-35; imāms in, 259; khaṭībs in, 261; litigation in, 230; markets in, 245; professors in, 253; stewards in, 211; in study, 4; Syrians in, 154; Upper Egyptians in, 151
Bulliet, R. M., biographical work of, 403 n1
Bulqīna in Gharbīya, 46, 233
al-Bulqīnī: Abū Bakr, descendants of, 232; ʿAlāʾ ʿAlī, 238; ʿAlam Ṣāliḥ, 233; as Shāfiʿī justice, 217; Alif, 237; Badr Abū'l-Saʿādāt, 239; Badr Muḥammad, 233; Bahāʾ Muḥammad, 237; Bilqīs, 237; Fatḥ Muḥammad, 237; Jalal ʿAbd al-Raḥmān, 46, 233; associate of nāẓir, 217; Iranian replaces, 66; Janna, 237; Khadīja, 238; Muẓaffar, descendants of, 232; Nāṣir Muḥammad, 233; Shihāb Aḥmad, 45-46, 232, 238; Sirāj ʿUmar, 45-46, 232; in Ḥijāzīya madrasa, 329; Tāj Muḥammad, 236; Taqī Muḥammad, 237; Umm Ḥasan, 238; Zayn Qāsim, 236; Walī Aḥmad, 237; Zuhūr, 237-38
Bulqīnī family: qualities of, 232, 239; avoids dīwān offices, 240
Bulqīnī women, marriage of, 240
bureaucracy: crisis in, 23; in hospitals, 141; of imperial court, 142; of Ottomans, 69; secretaries in, 204; Ṣūfīs in, 270. *See also* financial-secretarial professions
bureaucrats: access to information, 203; as fiscal agents, 320; functions of, 313; position of, 11, 220; as professional class, 312; regional distribution of, 79
bureaus: activities of, 227; muwaqqiʿs in, 212; nāẓirs of, 214; shāhids in, 225. *See also* dīwāns
burj, barracks of, 18
Burjīya, definition of, 18
Burnt Gate, prison of, 67
Burṣa, migration from, 68, 71
Būsh, migration from, 48
Buṣrā al-Shām, migration from, 59

Cairenes: in executive positions, 81; geographic data on, 144; at local level, 162; in southeast institutions, 147
Cairo: adaptation to, 38; contrast with European cities, 324-25; cosmopolitanism in, 79; craftsmen from, 79; deputy judge in, 50; elite in, 46; immigration from East to, 35; Iranians in, 63; Iraqis in, 73; migration to, 77; military occupation of, 405 n1; no academic cloister, 136; opportunities in, 35, 40; population of, 22; professoriate in, 250; religio-academic establishment of, 24, 128; religious functionaries from, 79; repository of Islamic culture, xxii; residence/

occupations in, 9; role under Mamluks, 15, 40; in scholarly works, xxii; security of, 35; Syrians in, 154; transfer to, 37, 40. *See also* al-Qāhira
Cairo-Delta group as model, 153
Cairo-Delta interest, 161
Cairo-Delta zone: as core area, 148; culture of, 164; individuals outside, 144-45; religious functionaries from, 256, 313; students/staff from, 161; ʿulamaʾ from, 317
Cairo families: in bureaucracy, 47
caliphs: use of Mamluks, 15; tie to bureaucrats, 209
calligraphers: in Ashrafīya, 335; Iranians as, 67
calligraphy: in madrasas, 139; nāsikhs study, 242
Cambridge, 132
caravan routes across Sahara, 74
caravansarays: in biographies, 142; foundation of, 133; kārimīs support, 30; in Upper Egypt, 49
Casanova, P., topographical works of, 131
Caspian Sea: migration from, 63; pillaging around, 64
categorization of occupations, 200
Caucasus: Mamluks from, 18, 22, 72; slaves from, 27
cemeteries, Iranians in, 156
Cemetery Gate, location of, 337
Central Arab lands, bureaucrats in, 79
Central Asia: Arab penetration of, 15; individuals from in *Ḍawʾ*, 9; Mongols from, 62; slave trade in, 27; source of Mamluks, 15, 22, 72; migration from, 77; Shamanism in, 268
Central Asian dialects spoken by Mamluks, 70
certification of jurist-scholars, 321
Chain Gate, entrance to Citadel, 337
Chamberlain, nāẓir as, 215
chancellery, urban personnel in, 313. *See also* dīwān al-inshāʾ
chemistry in madrasas, 139
chief justices: analysis of, 130; appointment of, 24; based in madrasas, 132; deputy judges become, 229; in Ṣāliḥīya madrasa, 331; shāhid as, 226; as shaykh al-Islām, 221; status of, 231-32; at Ẓāhirīya madrasa, 153. *See also* qāḍīs al-quḍāt
chief physician, Iranian as, 67
China, Kārimī knowledge of, 30
Christian officials of Syrian background, 56
Christian practices, retrogression to, 272
Christians, poll tax on, 264
chronometry in madrasas, 139
Circassian language, spoken by Mamluks, 70
Circassian madrasas: Cairenes in, 146-47; Iranians in, 155
Circassian period: building during, 133; cultivation during, 29; disequilibrium of, 21, 23; expenditures on Mamluks during, 22; intellectual life during, 25; judiciary during, 24; khānqāhs during, 140; monopolies during, 49; payment abuse during, 27; provincial neglect during, 43; status of ʿulamaʾ during, 20
Circassian regime: defends Sunnī Islam, 28; financial straits of, 26; foundations of, 335; succession under, 19
circumcisions, muqriʾs at, 262
Citadel: barracks of, 18; bureaucracy of, 150; Cairenes in, 146-47; construction of, 133; Delta Egyptian in, 46; dīwāns in, 142; funeral in, 71; government transferred to, 132; judges in, 240; Mamluks in, 202; nāẓirs in, 219; no Maghribīs in, 159. *See also* imperial court
Citadel area, basis of study, 136
Citadel mosque: description of, 338; imāms in, 258; Iranians in, 155; khaṭībs in, 261; muqriʾ in, 263. *See also* Naṣirī mosque
Citadel Square, institutions of, 337
cities under Ilkhānids, 62
civilian clients of military elite, 133
civilian elite: assimilation into, 162; autonomy, 4; bureaucrats from, 202; cohesion of, 325; cosmopolitanism of, 312, 317; distribution of, 128; in khānqāhs, 139, as mediators, 319-20; multicompetence of, 200-201; muʿtaqads in, 267; professional options of, 40; in religio-academic institutions,

civilian elite (*cont.*)
37; in religious service, 221-22; social position of, 3; Ṣūfīs in, 270-71; symbiosis with Mamluks, 20, 200-201; training of, 160
civilians: in biographies, 81; corruption of, 24; in executive category, 202
civil strife, absence of, 78
Clerget, M., topographical work of, 131
clerks: analysis of, 130; from Delta, 47; distinct from copyists, 242; imāms as, 258; merchants as, 244; as professors, 252; as professional class, 212; status of, 211; Syrians as, 56, 208. *See also* muwaqqiʿs
clients, Copts as, 274
cloth merchant as muqriʾ, 264
clustering: in Delta, 42; in Iran, 63-64; in Syria, 58, 415 n40
colleges: in Damascus, 52; dual function of, 229; ranking of, 318-19; shaykhs of, 25. *See also* madrasas
collegiate clusters: of Bayn al-Qaṣrayn, 330; Cairenes in, 146; Delta Egyptians in, 149; environment in, 136; Iranians in, 155; Maghribīs in, 158; prominence of, 160; shaykhs in, 222; Syrians in, 153; Upper Egyptians in, 151
collegiate mosque, definition of, 138
collegiate network monopolizes Islamic sciences, 251
collegiate system, coalescence of, 132
coinage, debasement of, 62, 409 n53
commerce, bureaucratization of, 32
commercial revolution, consequence of Renaissance, 33, 410 n79
communal transcendence of religious functionaries, 322-23
concentration coefficient, 110
Constantine, *see* Qusṭanṭīna
controller of army: civilian as, 214; Copt as, 216; in Damascus, 217; kātib al-sirr as, 208; Syrian as, 56; in Ṭarābulus, 56
controller of privy funds, Copt as, 216
controller of waqfs, Copt as, 273; in Ṣāliḥīya madrasa, 217. *See also* nāẓir al-awqāf
controllers: analysis of, 130; Bulqīnī as, 239; Copts as, 273; from Delta, 47; imāms as, 258; merchants as, 244; muqriʾ as, 265; professors as, 252; Syrians as, 55. *See also* nāẓirs
convent, *see* khānqāh
conversion from Judaism, 67
Copts: as ʿalim, 430 n124; as amirs, 273; in bureaucracy, 50, 314; as clerks, 211; as controllers, 215, 424 n30; converted to Islam, 81; dependence on Mamluks, 205; in Fusṭāṭ, 135; as kātibs al-sirr, 206; as merchants, 244; mobility of, 220; no muḥtasibs, 224; options of, 272-74; as professors, 252; in religio-academic institutions, 209; secretaries among, 204; as stewards, 210. *See also* qibṭ
Coptic lineages, descent from, 272
Coptic monasticism, 139
copyists: Anatolian as, 71; background of, 79; from Levant, 57; as muqriʾ, 264. *See also* nāsikhs
corruption by Syrians, 56
course in madrasa, 251
courts: autonomy of, 315; in Damascus, 52; imāms in, 259; limitations of, 321; location of, 132-33, 227-28; muwaqqiʿs in, 212; of Old Cairo, 135
cosmopolitan elements: influence of, 164
cosmopolitanism in Cairo, 79; extent of, 317-18; impact of, 142
craftsmen from Cairo, 79
Creswell, K.A.C.: maps and topographical works of, 131; homes located by, 202
crossover between occupations, 200, 403 n3
Cross Street: institutions of, 337; markets along, 245
Cross Street area: basis of study, 136; Iraqis in, 158; Mamluks in, 202
Crusader elements in Palestine, 18
curriculum: Islamic sciences in, 419 n22; jurisprudence in, 229; of madrasas, 138, 318; subjects outside, 250; uniformity of, 80; variation in, 162
custodians in mortuary zone, 136

Dahmashat al-Ḥammām, waqfs in, 332
Damascus: administrative center, 51; Bulqīnī in, 233; culture of, 52; data from, 9; Delta Egyptian in, 46; Ḥanafī

justice of, 55; judiciary in, 208, 228; jurisdiction of, 59; learned classes in, 54; Mālikī justice of, 208; Mamluks in, 52; muqri' in, 263; professoriate in, 250; qāḍīs from, 54; Shāfi'ī justice of, 217; viceroy of, 55; waqfs in, 328, 332
Damascus province, location of, 414 n39
Damietta: administration of, 44; migration from, 41-42; Shafi'i justice of, 208; slave port, 27; tie to military elite, 42; trade through, 34, 245
Damietta branch, focus for emigration, 42
Daqhiliya, migration from, 43
dār al-'ilm, *see* academies
dār al-Islām, threats to, 34
al-Darj, 211
dars, durūs, *see* course
al-Dast, 211
dates: occurrence of, 12; skewing factor in, 78, 84
David: temple of, 58; line of, 67
Ḍaw' al-Lāmi', centennial dictionary, 6; topics covered, 9
Delta: bureaucrats from, 46; concentrations in, 41; craftsmen and laborers from, 79; cultural conditions of, 43; migrations from, 42, 78; nisba-birthplace ratio, 48; pedagogues from, 80; religious functionaries from, 79; similarity to Cairo, 147, 149; variation in migration, 43; waqfs in, 328
Delta Egyptians: concentrations of, 162-63; dominate scholarship, 45; at local level, 162; marriage patterns of, 41; resettlement of, 41. *See also* Lower Eqyptians
Delta pattern, Iranian contrast with, 155
demographic factors, cause of decline, 29, 32
depressions in fourteenth century, 19; impact on southeast, 134
deputy judges: muqri's as, 263-64; shāhids as, 226. *See also* nā'ib qāḍīs
Desert Plain: cemetery of, 134-35; mu'taqads in, 269; shaykhs in, 222. *See also* Ṣaḥrā'
al-Dhahabī, biographical compiler, 6
Dimashqīs in Cairo, 54
Dīwān al-inshā': definition of, 204; head of, 205; in Syria, 208; Syrian controller of, 209. *See also* chancellery
dīwān offices: khaṭībs in, 261; given by Mamluks, 207
dīwān officials, revenue procurement by, 313
dīwāns: Copts in, 273-74; overlap of duties in, 212; personnel in, 313-14; of regime, 142; stewards in, 210. *See also* bureaus
Diyār Bakīr: migration from, 68
diyār al-'ilm, *see* academies
al-Diyār al-Miṣrīya, individuals from in *Ḍaw'*, 9
documents, processing of, 203
dower, 240
Duhaysha quarter, waqfs in, 332
Dumyāṭ, *see* Damietta
Dumyāṭīs, activities of, 42
al-Durar al-Kāmina, scope of, 9
Dutch, exploration by, 33

ecology in Iran, 63
economy, deterioration of, 25
education: in biographies, 12; of Coptic nāẓir, 217; elementary level of, 255-56; memorization in, 247; objectives of, 247
educational pattern of geographic groups, 160
educational sites, usage of, 144
educators in Damascus, 52
Egypt: economic decline of, 26, 28; famine in, 328; as imperial power, 19; in oriental trade, 29-30, 33; real estate in, 32
Egyptian merchants under monopoly, 31
Egyptian provinces, individuals from in *Ḍaw'*, 9
Egyptians in al-Azhar, 334
Elburz mountains, migration from, 63
Elephant Island tract in study, 4
Elephant Lake: Mamluks near, 202; settlement near, 133-34; waqfs near, 327
elite institutions: clientele of, 161; cosmopolitanism of, 144; functions of, 162; influence of, 164; Iranians in, 155; reputation of, 160
embezzlement by Syrians, 56
endowed chairs in Damascus, 52

England, exploration by, 33
ethno-geographic elements, interest groups of, 161, 164
Ethiopia, migration from, 77
eunuchs in Nāṣirīya madrasa, 333
Europe: commercial revolution of, 410 n79; Kārimī knowledge of, 30; trade to, 245
European merchants circumvent Near East, 33
European Renaissance, consequences of, 33
Europeans, Turkish-speaking, 72
Euphrates valley, migration from, 59
executive offices, Anatolians in, 72; Copts in, 273; secretaries in, 205-206

Fakhrī mosque, shaykhs in, 222
familial ties in biographies, 12
famine: as cause of decline, 29; in fourteenth century, 19; of 806/1403, 330, 341
Faraj, al-Nāṣir: arrest of amir by, 329; confiscation by, 337; Succession under, 19
—appointment: of Copt, 216; of judges, 55; of Syrian, 207
—ties: to Maghribī, 75; to nāẓir, 216; to Syrian, 54
farmer: Bulqīnī as, 233; as judge, 231
farrāshūn: in hospitals, 141, 332; in Ṭūlūnid mosque, 339
Fārs, migration from, 63-64
Fās (Fez), migration from, 74
Fāṭimid city, influence of, 131, 133, 160
Fāṭimid district: Bulqīnīs in, 233; collegiate clusters in, 327; Delta Egyptians in, 149; institutions of, 147, 335; Iranians in, 155; librarians in, 255; professors in, 252; al-Sakhāwī from, 8; shaykhs in, 222-23; Ṣūfīs in, 272; Syrians in, 153; as university town, 132. *See also* northeast district
Fāṭimid elite, location of, 131
Fāṭimid palaces, square between, 330
Fāṭimid period: Fusṭāṭ during, 135; Ismāʿīlism during, 139; monuments of, 333; southeast during, 133; trade during, 29, 49
Fāṭimid structures, disappearance of, 132
Fāṭimids: found Cairo, 40; Sunnī attitude toward, 132
fawwāl, *see* bean seller
Fayyūm, migration from, 48
fees in hospitals, 141
Festival Gate cluster: Anatolians in, 156; Delta Egyptians in, 149; exclusivity of, 146; institutions of, 327; Iraqis in, 157-58; khaṭībs in, 261; librarians in, 254; muʿīds in, 248; muqri's in, 265, stewards in, 210; Ṣūfīs in, 272; Syrians in, 152-53
festivals, muqri's at, 262. *See also* ʿids
field commanders, attitudes of, 19
fifteenth century, depression during, 22
Filasṭīn, *see* Palestine
financial-secretarial professions, analysis of, 130. *See also* bureaucracy
fiscal aggrandizement by bureaucrats, 203
fiscal matters, details on, 13
foreign consumers, conditions affecting, 29
foreigners: in Cairo, xxii; integration of, 316; occupational variations among, 312-13; role of, 317; in Ṣarghatmishīya, 339; among ʿulamaʾ, 411 n4
foreign suppliers, conditions affecting, 29
fountains: attached to madrasas, 139, 330; in Ḥākim mosque, 334; in khānqāhs, 140; supported by kārimīs
Franks, threat to Islam, 28
French, exploration by, 33
Friday prayer, function of, 138
Friday preacher, *see* khaṭībs
Friday sermon, delivery of, 260
funerals, muqri's at, 262
funerary oratory: near Bāb al-Naṣr, 334; of al-Muʾminī, 337
Fuqahāʾ in Baybarsīya khānqāh, 328
Fusṭāṭ: as commercial center, 135; as earliest city, 131; khaṭībs in, 261; location of , 40; in study, 4

galleries for Koran recitation, 140
garrisons: absent from Palestine, 57; in Aleppo, 53
gatekeeper as muqri', 264
gates: courts near, 228; shāhids near, 227

Gaziantep, *see* ʿAynṭāb
Geniza documents, 410-11 n1
gentry class, absence of, 18
geographic nisba, interpretation of, 38
geometry: in madrasas, 139; studied by Maghribī, 75
Gharbīya: administrative institutions in, 47; Bulqīnīs in, 232; location of, 412 n10; migration from, 41-42; religious functionaries from, 45; saints' zone, 44, 150; towns in, 48; waqfs in, 331
al-Ghawrī, al-Ashraf: Mamluks imported by, 26
Ghazān Khān, conversion of, 62
Ghazza: migration from, 59; nāẓir in, 216
Gibb, H.A.R.: on biographical literature, 6
Giza, *see* Jīza
Goitein, S.: on Geniza documents, 410-11 n1
gold enlayers, Upper Egyptians as, 49
goldsmiths' bazaar, waqfs on, 331
Gothic in Nāṣirīya gate
government, scholars in, 248
governors, duties of, 23
grammar in madrasas, 139
Granada, Maghribī from, 76
greengrocer, muʿtaqad as, 268
guest houses supported by kārimīs, 30

Ḥabashīs, 77
Ḥadīth: in Islamic law, 5-6; muqri's erudition in, 263; policy sanctioned from, 232; study of, 65. *See also* Prophetic traditions
Ḥadīth scholarship by al-Sakhāwī, 8
Ḥadīth specialists in khānqāhs, 328
Ḥadīth transmitters and spiritual conviction, 7
ḥajj, Maghribī on, 74
Ḥājjī, al-Ṣāliḥ: library of, 329
al-Ḥākim mosque: Bulqīnī in, 237; description of, 333-34; in Fāṭimid period, 132; khaṭībs in, 261; muʿīds in, 248; stewards in, 210
Ḥalab, *see* Aleppo
al-Ḥalabī, ʿAlāʾ, 208
al-Ḥalabī, Burhān, 208-209
Ḥalabīs in Cairo, 54
Ḥamā: administrative center, 51; bureaucrat from, 207; data from, 9; jurisdiction of, 59; kātib al-sirr in, 208; Mālikī justice of, 208; qāḍīs from, 54; waqfs in, 328
Hamadān, migration from, 64
Ḥanafī affiliation of Ashrafīya madrasa, 335
Ḥanafī judgeships, holders of, 54
Ḥanafī jurisprudence: in amirate madrasas, 163; in Ṣarghatmishīya, 338; Syrians in, 153; in Ẓāhirīya, 153, 158, 331
Ḥanafī justice: Anatolian as, 71; of Damascus, 55
Ḥanafī madhhab: Iranians in, 163; Mamluk emphasis on, 155; prominence in Arabia, 160; study in, 149
Ḥanafīs, role in Cairo, 315
Ḥanbalī justice, muqriʾ as, 264
Ḥanbalīs: role in Cairo, 315; in Ẓāhirīya, 158
handasa, *see* geometry
ḥānūt, ḥawānīt, *see* shops
harbor facilities supported by kārimīs, 30
harem, muqri's in, 266
Ḥasanīya, *see* Sultan Ḥasan mosque
Ḥātim al-Fāsī, 74
al-Ḥawādith al-Duhūr, 11
headmen of villages, 23
Hebron: exile to, 58; migration from, 59; patriarchal tombs in, 58; status of, 57
heresy during Circassian period, 25
Herz, M.: homes located by, 202; topographical works by, 131
heterodoxy, threat of, 319, 322
Ḥijāz: individuals from in *Ḍawʾ*, 9; Maghribī in, 74; in Mamluk period, 74; migration from, 78-79
Ḥijāzīya madrasa: description of, 329; khaṭībs in, 261
Ḥijāzīs in Cairo, 159
Ḥimṣ, administrative center, 51
Hirāt (Herat), migration from, 64, 66
al-Hirawī, Shihāb, 66
Ḥiṣn Kayfa, migration from, 68
history: instruction in, 250; in madrasas, 139
holy cities, inhabitants of, 73

holy hermits: Iranians as, 156; as mu'taqads, 269; in tombs, 136; from Upper Egypt, 152
holy men from Anatolia, 70
honorarium: imāmates as, 258; khaṭīb's office as, 262; librarianship as, 253
Hormūz, Straits of, migration from, 63
Hospice of Prophet's Relics: Bulqīnī in, 239; description of, 340; professors in, 253
hospices: parochialism at, 161; residence in, 164. *See also* khānqāhs
hospitals: controller of, 217; shaykhs of, 25; supported by kārimīs, 30. *See also* māristān
hostels attached to madrasas, 139
houses: of Mamluk amirs, 134; muqri' owns, 265; nāẓirs own, 220
Ḥusaynīya quarter: development of, 134; location of, 334
Ḥusayn mosque, mu'taqads in, 269

Ibn Abū Qāsim, 75
Ibn 'Aqīl, Bahā', 46
Ibn 'Arab, al-Burṣāwi, 71
Ibn al-Bārizī, Kamāl, 207-208
Ibn al-Bārizī, Nāṣir; 207; in Mu'ayyadīya, 336
Ibn Baṭṭūṭa, travels of, 37, 75
Ibn Duqmāq, topographical works of, 131
Ibn Fakhr al-Dīn, Sa'd, 430 n124
Ibn Ghurrāb, Sa'd, 216-17
Ibn Ḥajar al-'Asqalānī: influence on al-Sakhāwī, 9; in al-Mu'ayyadīya, 336; as Shāfi'ī justice, 217
—ties: to Bulqīnīs, 236, 238; to Maghribī, 75; to muqri', 264
Ibn Isḥāq, author of *Sīra*, 403 n6
Ibn Jamā'a, Badr: in Ḥākim mosque, 333; khaṭīb in Siryāqūs khānqāh, 341
Ibn Jubayr, travels of, 37
Ibn Khaldūn: accuracy of, 325; career of, 74; as chief justice, 231; patronage of, xxii; reaction to Cairo, xxi, 15, 35, 77
Ibn al-Kuwayz, 'Alam, 56
Ibn al-Mulaqqin, Sirāj: in Sābiqīya madrasa, 330
Ibn Naṣr-Allah, Muḥibb, 264
Ibn Qubbān, marriage to Bulqīnī, 238
Ibn al-Ṣābūnī, 'Alā', 217-218
Ibn Sharaf al-Dīn mosque: muqri' in, 264
Ibn al-Shiḥna, Muḥibb, 54
Ibn Suwayd al-Qibṭī, Badr: tājir awlād, 428 n83
Ibn Taghrī-Birdī: background of, 10; on Copts, 274; on imāms, 258; objectives of, 7, 11; methodology of, 12; omissions of, 13; tie to Anatolian, 71; tribute to Bulqīnī, 233
Ibn Ṭūlūn, Aḥmad: founds al-Qaṭā'i', 133; Mamluks under, 17; mosque of, 339
'īds in Delta, 44. *See also* festivals
'Īd al-Ṣaghīr, *see* Lesser Festival
Idfū, migration from, 48
Ifriqīya, migration from, 74
Īj, alchemist from, 65
ijāza, *see* certification
Ilkhānid chieftains, extortion by, 62
Ilkhānid period, ascetics during, 267
Ilkhānid regime, appointments of, 62; in Iran, 61
illiteracy of Mamluks, 266
Imām al-Shāfi'ī tomb: Anatolians in, 157; description of, 339-40; Iranians in, 156; mu'īds in, 248; nāẓirs in, 217, 219; professors in, 253; shaykhs in, 223
imāms: analysis of, 130; in Aqbughāwīya, 335; definition of, 258; distribution of, 259; in Ḥijāzīya, 329; Maghribī as, 76; in Mu'ayyadīya, 336; in Nāṣirīya, 333; as professors, 256; in Ṣāliḥīya, 331; in Ṭūlūnid mosque, 339; Upper Egyptians as, 50. *See also* prayer leaders
imperial court: Anatolians in, 157; chief justices in, 232; Copts in, 273; imāms in, 258; muqri's in, 266; mu'taqads in, 269; requirements of, 26. *See also* Citadel
Īnāl, al-Ashraf, mausoleum of, 340
India: individuals from in *Ḍaw'*, 9; migration from, 77; migration to, 63-64
Indian merchants under monopoly, 31
Indian Ocean: kārimīs in, 30; Portuguese in, 73
infeudation in Upper Egypt, 49

inflation during fifteen century, 26
inspectors, responsibilities of, 23
Institut français, associates of, 131
intellectual establishment, cosmopolitanism of, 144
interest groups: in religio-academic network, 161; in residence patterns, 164
invasion, absence of, 78
inns: supported by kārimīs, 30
Iqfahs: migration from, 48
iqṭāʿ holdings: administration of, 24; revenue from, 22; title to, 27; in Upper Egypt, 49; yields from, 22, 26, 413 n20
iqṭāʿ system: centralization of, 18; expansion of, 18; in Iran, 61; removal from, 240
Iran: adjacent to Anatolia, 68; data on, 144; government of, 61; individuals from in *Ḍaw* , 9; invasion of, 61, 63; khānqāhs in, 139; migration from, 64, 78-79; population concentration in, 63
Iranian elite under Timurids, 34
Iranian-Muslim culture after invasions, 63
Iranian Plateau, routes to, 64
Iranian sites, patterns of, 63
Iranians: in amirate madrasas, 153; in al-Azhar, 334; in executive category, 81; geographic mobility of, 421 n45; impact of invasions on, 61; integration of, 163; interest groups of, 161; occupations of, 65; preeminence of, 67; studies of, 154. *See also* Persians
Iraq: control over, 72; data on, 144; migration from, 79
Iraqis in Cairo, 72
al-ʿIraqī, Zayn, tomb of, 76
al-ʿIraqī, Walī: tie to Bulqīnī, 236
Iṣfahān, migration from, 64
al-Iskandarīya, *see* Alexandria
Islam, blasphemy against, 272
Islamic community, exclusion of Copts, 273
Islamic historiography, limitations of, 325
Islamic law: closed to Copts, 274; training in, 312
Islamic sciences: closed to Copts, 204, 274; in curriculum, 138-39, 247; erudition in, 314; instruction in, 41, 250; Iranians in, 65; khānqāhs involved in, 160; khaṭībs' erudition in, 260; and mysticism, 221; uniformity of, 80
Islamic societies: Sufism in, 270; uncorporate nature of, 203
Islamic tradition, dictates of, 325
ism, definiton of, 12
Ismāʿīlī dāʿīs: of Fāṭimids, 132, 419 n21; in al-Azhar, 139
Ismāʿīlī teaching in academies, 138
Istanbul: migration from, 68; supersedes Cairo, 38
Italian city-states, mercantile associations of, 33

al-Jaʿfarīya, migration from, 73
al-Jāhiẓ on bureaucrats, 204-205
Jamālīya madrasa: description of, 329; Iranians in, 154-55; muqriʾs in, 265; nāẓir in, 217; Syrian in, 55
jāmiʿ, jawāmiʿ, *see* mosque
Jannaq Lake, house near, 45
Jaqmaq, al-Ẓāhir: arrests nāẓir, 217; confiscation by, 45; palace of, 134
—ties: to Iranian, 66; to muqriʾ, 264; to Syrian, 208
Jazāʾir of Jīza, waqfs in, 331
al-Jazīra district, migration from, 60
Jazīrat al-Fīl, *see* Elephant Island tract
Jenghis Khān, career of, 34
Jerusalem: artisans from, 57; data from, 9; exile to, 58; Iranian in, 66; jursidiction of, 59; migration from, 59; status of, 57
jewelers, few Upper Egyptians as, 49
Jewish ancestry of Iranian, 67
Jews, poll tax on, 264
Jīʿānī mosque, khaṭībs in, 261
Jidda, transit station, 31
Jīlān, migration from, 63
Jirjā, migration from, 48
Jīza: Bulqīnī in, 237; professors in, 253; in study, 4; sultan's property, 43; waqfs in: 328-29, 333
Jordan river, east bank of, 59
Judaism, Iranian convert from, 67
judges: Bulqīnīs as, 239; in Damascus, 52; function of, 227-28; as imāms, 259; as jurist-scholars, 315; merchants as, 244; as nāẓirs, 214, 217; shāhids

judges (*cont.*)
as, 226; as shaykhs, 221. *See also* qāḍīs
judgeships in families, 230
al-Judhamī, 75
judicial establishment, entry into, 149
judicial fields: instruction in, 250-51; Syrians in, 54
judiciary: Bulqīnīs in, 240; closed to Copts, 274; composition of, 221; cosmopolitanism of, 80; in Damascus, 52; distinct from muḥtasibs, 224; imāms in, 259; kātibs al-sirr in, 207; location of, 132; in madrasas, 229; Maghribīs in, Mamluk influence on, 232; moral authority of, 228; orthodoxy in, 318; promotion within, 321; Ṣūfīs in, 227, 270
Julbān, 21
jundī, ajnād: in khānqāhs, 328; marriage to civilians, 238. *See also* trooper
jurisprudence: in curriculum, 138-39, 229; shāhids teach, 226
jurist-scholars: from Anatolia, 69; autonomy of, 315; custodians of Sunna, 314; definition of, 229; distribution of, 148; in elite institutions, 251; foundation of ʿulamaʾ class, 246; as interest group, 321; as khaṭībs, 261; mediation of, 320; moral authority of, 322; as professional category, 312; promotion by, 251; as religious functionaries, 256; trained in amirate madrasas, 252
Jurjān: migration from, 63
Justice Palace: Delta Egyptian in, 46
Juyūshī quarter: merchants in, 245; shaykhs in, 223

Kaʿba mantle, controller of, 216-17
Kafr al-Shaykh, migration from, 43
Kakhtā, migration from, 68
al-Kāmil, al-Malik: completes Citadel, 132; founds madrasa, 330; enlarges Shāfiʿī tomb complex, 339-40
Kāmilīya madrasa: Cairenes in, 146; description of, 330
al-Karak: administrative center: 51, 59; bureaucrat from, 56; exile to, 55, 216; jurisdiction of, 59
al-Karakī, Burhān, 423 n20
al-Karakī, Jamāl: 56, Iranian replaces, 66
al-Karakī, Mūsā, 56
Kārimī merchants: influence of, 29; under monopoly, 31; services of, 30
kāshif, kashafa, *see* inspectors
Katbughā, al-ʿAdīl: foundation of, 332
kātib al-amwāl, 422 n5
kātib al-inshāʾ, 422 n5
kātib al-sirr: analysis of, 130; definition of, 205-207; Syrians as, 206; tie to clerks, 211. *See also* secretary of chancellery
kātibs: analysis of, 130; as copyists, 212; from Delta, 47; distribution of, 209, 423 n17; pressures on, 212; as Ṣūfīs, 209. *See also* secretaries
Kawm al-Rīsh, in study, 4
khabbāz, *see* baker
al-Khalīl, *see* Hebron
khāns: in biographies, 142, foundation of, 133
al-Khānqāh, migration from, 42
khānqāhs: associated with tombs, 141; in Barqūqīya, 333; Cairenes in, 146; in central Delta, 150-51; copyists in, 242; definition of, 139-40; in education, 160; in elite group, 271; expenses of, 140; function of, 253; imāms in, 258-59; influence on Mamluks, 139; Iranians in, 155; judges in, 241; kātibs in, 209; khaṭībs in, 261-62; of later Mamluk period, 132; Maghribīs in, 158; muḥtasibs in, 225; muʿīds in, 248, 250; muqriʾs in, 264-66; muʿtaqads in, 269; muwaqqiʿs in, 213; nāẓirs in, 218-20; professors in, 253; regulations of, 270; residence in, 145, 164; shāhids in, 227; shaykhs of, 25, 221-23; in southeast, 134; Syrians in, 152-54; Upper Egyptians in, 152; usage of, 419 n23. *See also* hospices; monasteries, Ṣūfī hospices
Kharq Gate, markets around, 245
Kharūbīya madrasa, professors in, 253
khāṣṣakīya, 21
khaṭībs: analysis of, 130; in Citadel mosque, 338; definition of, 260; from Delta, 45; distribution of, 261; muqriʾ

as, 264, as professors, 256; in Ṣāli-ḥīya, 331; in Ṭūlūnid mosque, 339
Khaṭīrī mosque: khaṭībs in, 261; stewards in, 210-11
khaṭṭ, *see* calligraphy
khawājā: Anatolians as, 72; father of nāẓir, 217; merchants as, 245
khāzins al-kutub: analysis of, 130; definition of, 253-54; distribution of, 254-55. *See also* librarians
khubz, 27
Khurāsān, migration from, 63-64
khushdashīya, 21
Khushqadam, al-Ẓāhir: appoints nāẓir, 217
khuṭba, function of, 260
Khwarazm Steppe, migration from, 63
kimiyā', *see* alchemy
Kirmān, migration from, 64
kitchens in khānqāhs, 140
Koran: initial studies in, 41; memorization of, 46, 247, 265; muqri's' erudition in, 263; recitation of, 140, 262, 328; sanctions policy, 232
Koranic exegesis: in curriculum, 138-39; Iranians in, 65; Maghribī teaches, 75; professor of, 246; in Ṭūlūnid mosque, 339
Koranic recitation: Mamluk respect for, 266
Koran readers: in Aqbughāwīya, 335; from Delta, 45; in Ḥākim mosque, 333; in khānqāhs, 328; Maghribī as, 76; in madrasas, 329-30. *See also* muqri's.
Koran school in Qarāsanqurīya, 329. *See also* kuttābs
Kūfa, migration from, 73
kunya, definition of, 12
Kurdish traditions in Iran, 63
Kurdish troops of Ṣalāḥ al-Dīn, 327
Kurds: in Ayyūbid army, 18; east of Mamluk frontier, 68
kuttābs: bureaucrats in, 202; function of, 80. *See also* Koran school

laborers from Cairo, 79
al-Ladhqīya, migration from, 59
Lance Dealers' Bazaar, waqfs on, 328
Lapidus, I. M.: on investment, 60; on multicompetence, 422 n1; thesis of, 403 n1; on urban society, 430 n2
laqab, definition of, 12
Lebanon, sites in, 59
legal categories, kātibs al-sirr in, 206
legal families, influence of, 228
legal fields, secretaries in, 204
legal offices, merchants hold, 244
legal-scholarly professions, regional distribution of, 79-80
Lesser Festival, khuṭba of, 236
Levant: commerce in, 57; devastation of, 60; insecurity of, 53; organization of, 51; rate of migration of, 60
librarians: in Ashrafīya, 335; Syrians as, 208; as final position, 254. *See also* khāzins al-kutub
libraries: concentration of, 136; copyists in, 242; in Damascus, 52; in Delta, 44; in Ḥākim mosque, 333; in khānqāhs, 140; in madrasas, 329-30, 332-33, 336; supported by kārimīs, 30; in Ṭaybarsīya, 335; in Ṭūlūnid mosque, 339
literateurs, Iranians as, 67
literati in Cairo, xxii
literature in madrasas, 139
logic in madrasa curriculum, 138-39
Lower Egyptians: data on, 144; in khānqāhs, 148. *See also* Delta Egyptians

madhhabs: in Ashrafīya, 335; definition of, 12; in Ḥākim mosque, 333; in Manṣūrīya, 331; minority, 231; in Nāṣirīya, 333; in Ṣāliḥīya, 331; in Shaykhūnīya, 337
al-Madīna: al-Sakhāwī in, 9; migration from, 72, 78; as sanctuary, 73
Madīnans in Cairo, 73
madrasas: associated with tombs, 141; bureaucrats in, 202-203; Cairenes in, 146; courts in, 229; curriculum of, 161; deanships in, 46; definition of, 138; in Delta, 44; dominate education, 160; founded by Iranian, 66; imāms in, 258; khaṭībs in, 260; of later Mamluk period, 132; Maghribīs in, 158-59; as mosque, 139; muʿtaqads in, 269; parochialism in, 161; professors in,

madrasas (*cont.*)
253; promotions within, 321; proximity of, 136; repetitors in, 247; in southeast, 132; Ṣūfīs in, 272; in Upper Egypt, 49. *See also* colleges
al-Maghrib: ascetics in, 267; data on, 144; migration from, 74; *See also* North Africa
Maghribīs: in al-Azhar, 334; character of, 74; distribution of, 164; infrequency of, 76; interest groups of, 161; migration of, 421 n52; in Mālikī madhhab, 158; occupations of, 74; as travelers, 75. *See also* North Africans
Maḥallat Abū Haytham, Ṣūfī from, 45
al-Maḥallat al-Kubrā: Bulqīnīs in, 232; migration from, 41-42; muqri' from, 265; Shāfi'ī justice in, 46; waqfs in, 331
al-Maḥallī, Burhān: tie to Syrians, 56
Maḥmūdīya madrasa: Iranians in, 155; librarians in, 255
Main Avenue: location of, 131; markets along, 245; terminus of, 334. *See also* Qaṣaba
majdhūbs: Anatolians as, 157; mu'taqads as, 268; Syrians as, 154; Upper Egyptian as, 152
major-domo, nāẓir as, 216
Makhlaf, migration from, 73
Makka: data from, 9; migration from, 72, 78; al-Sakhāwī in, 9; as sanctuary, 73
Makkans, occupations of, 73
Malaga, Maghribī in, 76
Malaṭya, migration from, 68
Mālikī judgeships, held by kātibs al-sirr, 208
Mālikī jurisprudence at al-Azhar, 158
Mālikī madhhab, Maghribīs in, 74, 158
Mālikīs, role in Cairo of, 315
mamālīk al-salāṭīn al-mutaqaddima, 21
al-mamālīk al-sulṭānīya, 21
mamālīk al-'umarā', 21
Mamluk armies, successes, 16
Mamluk barracks, Cairenes in, 147
Mamluk Egypt: bureaucracy in, 204; distribution of power in, 324
Mamluk elite: demand for orthodoxy, 25; dependence on agriculture, 28; extravagance of, 32; favor Turkish speakers, 157; fiscal demands of, 26; individuals in, 11; influence of khānqāhs on, 139; investment by, 60; from Muslim periphery, 81; prerogatives of, 20; in provincial cities, 78; respect for Iranians, 155
—ties: to bureaucrats, 47; to Delta ports, 44
Mamluk empire; cities of, 313; elite institutions in, 132, 160; individuals from in *Ḍaw'*, 9; northern marches of, 53; regions outside, 81
Mamluk epoch: achievements of, 3; segments of, 18
Mamluk foundations: Cairenes in, 147; Iranians in, 163
Mamluk frontier: areas east of, 68; Iranians cross, 63
Mamluk governors, staffs of, 206
Mamluk houses, imāms in, 258
Mamluk institution: achievements/shortcomings of, 17; origin of, 15
Mamluk metropolis: Fāṭimid center of, 131
Mamluk period: al-Azhar during, 334; Cairo during, 131; Ḥijāz during, 73; judiciary during, 228-29; land reclamation during, 43; population during, 138; southeast during, 133
Mamluk regime: oppression of, 323; response to natural disasters, 29; slaves in, 245
Mamluk rulers, appointment of judges, 230
Mamluk sphere, exclusivity of, 230
Mamluk state: bureaucrats in, 47, 79; individuals from outside, 163; juridical study in, 153; prestige of, 34; professional activity in, 201; 'ulama' of, 206-207
Mamluk tombs: Anatolians in, 157; description of, 340
Mamluk trainees, isolation of, 16
Mamluk troops, payments to, 27
Mamluk zone, Syrians in, 153
Mamluks: as aliens, 16; appointment policies of, 314, 421 n49; in biographies, 81; coalitions of, 23; costs of, 22; in Damascus, 52; definition of, 15; discord among, 20, 24; dissidence under, 325;

economic policies of, 33, 320; endowments of, 138, 254; entitled shaykh, 222; in executive category, 202; favor Turkish speakers, 70; exile of, 58; fiscal insecurity of, 25; foundations of, 329; identity of, 21, 32; importation of, 26; influence judiciary, 232; investments of, 25; in khānqāhs, 328; litigation involving, 230; marriages of, 237-38, 240; as muḥtasibs, 224; as muqri'ṣ, 263; mutiny of, 22; as nāẓirs, 214, 219; neglect of duties, 23; in Nile valley, 17; out of service, 22, 223, 408 n44; privileged caste, 16; provincial decline under, 60; real estate of, 32; reject dynastic principle, 19; reliance on ʿulama', 52; revenues of, 26; rule in Anatolia, 68; source of intrigue, 21; in southeast, 154; spoliation of, 334; stress on orthodoxy, 318; support of, 28; symbiosis with civilian elite, 20; threat to sultan, 28; tombs of, 141; torture of, 22; vulnerability of, 17. *See also* amirs
—attitude: toward civilians, 136, 138, 155; toward Syria, 53
—respect: for clerks, 212; for Ṣūfīs, 270, 272
—ties: to ascetics, 71, 136; to Bulqīnīs, 233, 236, 239; to bureaucrats, 313; to civilians, 129, 201; to clients, 11, 207; to imāms, 258; to merchants, 245; to muqri's, 264-66; to muʿtaqads, 268; to religious functionaries, 322; to secretaries, 205; to Syrians, 153; to ʿulama', 4
—use: of Copts, 273-74; of foreign luxuries, 32
Mandaville, J. on judiciary, 228-29
Manfalūṭ, migration from, 48
al-Manhal al-Ṣāfī, 2
Manṣūrī hospital: description of, 332; nāẓir of, 215-17, 219; stewards in, 210
Manṣūrīya madrasa/tomb: Anatolians in, 156; description of, 331-32; Bulqīnīs in, 238-39; librarians in, 254; Maghribī in, 75; muqri' in, 264
maps, use of, 129
al-Maqrīzī: influences Ibn Taghrī-Birdī, 10; as muḥtasib, 224; rivals al-ʿAynī, 70; shuhra of, 415 n41; topographical works of, 131
—on: ʿAmr ibn al-ʿĀṣ mosque, 340; Ashrafīya, 335; al-Azhar, 334; Baybarsīya, 328; Citadel mosque, 338; commercial institutions, 142; Ḥākim mosque, 333; Ḥijāzīya, 329; inflation, 408 n37; Jamālīya, 329; libraries, 254-55; Manṣūrīya, 332; muqri's, 265; Nāṣirīya, 333; Saʿīd al-Suʿadā', 327; Ṣāliḥīya, 331; Shaykhūnīya, 337; Siryāqūs, 341; Sultan Ḥasan mosque, 338; Ṭaybarsīya, 335
al-Maqs mosque, khaṭībs in, 261
Marʿash, migration from, 68
Mardān, migration from, 64
Mardīn, migration, from, 68
māristān, definition of, 140-41. *See also* hospitals
market inspectors, analysis of, 130. *See also* muḥtasibs
markets: in biographies, 142; courts near, 228; of Old Cairo, 135; shāhids near, 227; spoliation of, 223
Marrākish, migration from, 74
marriages, muqri's at, 262
Mashhad, migration from, 64
masjid in Qarāsanqurīya, 329
Marw, migration from, 64
mathematics: instruction in, 250; in madrasas, 139
mawlids in Ṭanṭa, 44
Mawṣil (Mosul), migration from, 73
mediation: of civilian elite, 20, 231-32; of religious functionaries, 322-23
medicine: in madrasas, 139, 331; no Ṣaʿīdīs in, 49; studied by Maghribī, 75; in Ṭūlūnid mosque, 339
Medieval Europe, distribution of power in, 324
Medieval historians allusions to immigration, 37
mercantile systems under Mamluk rule, 29
merchants: Anatolians as, 72; background of, 79; Iranians as, 67; Maghribīs as, 75-76; in Mamluk service, 133; as nāẓir, 217; residence patterns of, 37; shāhids as, 226; in slave trade, 27; success of, 29; from Yemen, 73. *See*

merchants (*cont.*)
also state merchants; sulṭānī merchants; tājirs
Middle Ages: Sufism during, 270; travel during, 37
Middle East: social organization of, 201
Middle Egypt: Copts in, 50; migration from, 48; nisba-birthplace ratio, 48
migration: patterns of, 77-78; stimuli behind, 39; rate of, 60, 64, 78
militarists: in khānqāhs, 139-40; Turkish-speaking, 71
military campaigns, costs of, 26, 28
military elite: clients of, 314; ranking of, 20
military-executive category: analysis of, 130; regional distribution of, 80-81
military groups, residence patterns of, 37
military intelligence, secretaries in, 204
military judges: Bulqīnī as, 233, 236, 239; jurisdiction of, 407 n35; litigation of, 230
military slaves, cost of, 26. *See also* slaves
Minbaba in study, 4
ministries, *see* dīwāns
minority taxes: Bulqīnī controller of, 237; muqri' controller of, 264
mint, controlled by Cairenes, 56
Minṭāsh, tie to Iranian, 65
Minūfīya: administrative institutions in, 47; migration from, 41-42; religious functionaries from, 45; as saints' zone, 44, 150; towns in, 48
Minyat Banī Khasīb: migration from, 48; muʿtaqad from, 152
Minyat al-Makhlaṣ, waqfs in, 328
miscellaneous items in biographies, 13
Miṣr, *see* Old Cairo
Miṣr al-Qadīma, *see* Old Cairo
Mithqāl al-Anūkī, Sābiq: founds madrasa, 330
monasteries: in Damascus, 52; shaykhs of, 25. *See also* khānqāhs
monastic houses in Delta, 44
monastic institution at Siryāqūs, 42
monasticism in Egypt, 139
Mongol invasions: in Iran, 61, 155; in Iraq, 72; Mamluk reaction to, 53
Mongol-Turkic elite: in Iran, 61
Mongols: after conversion, 62; agriculture under, 61; environment of, 415 n45; as Mamluks, 18; routes used by, 64; threat to Islam, 28
monopolies of Mamluk regime, 30-32. *See also* spice monopoly
Morocco, migration from, 74
mortuary zones: Anatolians in, 157, 164; Arabians in, 159-60; Cairenes in, 147; class supported by, 135-36; Delta Egyptians in, 150; imāms in, 259; institutions of, 339; Iranians in, 156; Maghribīs in, 159; muʿīds in, 248; muqri's in, 266; muʿtaqads in, 269; nāẓirs in, 219; professors in, 253; shaykhs in, 223; in study, 4; Syrians in, 154; Upper Egyptians in, 151
mosques: definition of, 138; in Delta, 44-45; imāms in, 258; khaṭībs in, 261; of later Mamluk period, 132; muʿtaqads in, 269; supported by kārimīs, 30
muʿallim, distinct from muʿīd, 248. *See also* teachers
Mu'ayyadīya madrasa: Anatolians in, 156; Delta Egyptians in, 149; description of, 336; imāms in, 259; Iranians in, 155; khaṭībs in, 261; Maghribīs in, 76, 158; muʿīds in, 248; muqri's in, 264-66; nāẓirs in, 218; shaykhs in, 222; stewards in, 210; Ṣūfīs in, 272; Syrians in, 153-54, 208; Upper Egyptians in, 151
Mubārak, ʿAlī: topographical works of, 131
mubāshirs: analysis of, 130; definition of, 209-10; from Delta, 47; in hospitals, 140-41. *See also* stewards
mudarrises: analysis of, 130; definition of, 250; distribution of, 252. *See also* professors
mudarris tafsīr, function of, 246
Muḥammad: ascent from Jerusalem, 58; biography of, 403 n6; prototypic Muslim, 5
Muḥammad ʿAlī, mosque of, 338
Muḥammad, al-Nāṣir: buildings of, 133-34; daughter of, 329; founds khānqāh, 341; founds madrasa, 332; mosque of, 338; partisans of, 328; restores Ṭūlūnid mosque, 339; ustādār of, 335

Muḥammad ibn Manjak, Nāṣir: appoints muqri', 263
muḥtasibs: analysis of, 130; definition of, 223-24; distinct from judges, 224; in executive and fiscal offices, 205; nāẓir as, 215; of Old Cairo, 135. *See also* market inspectors
muʿīds: analysis of, 130; definition of, 246-47; distribution of, 248; function of, 80. *See also* repetitor
multicompetence of civilian elite, 312
multiple officeholding: of civilian elite, 201; among secretaries, 204
al-Mu'minī, funerary oratory of, 337
al-Muqaṭṭam: cemetery quality of, 134; Citadel near, 133; muʿtaqads in, 269; Upper Egyptian in, 152
al-Muqayrī, ʿImād: tie to Syrian, 56
muqri's: analysis of, 130; definition of, 262-63; distribution of, 265-66; families of, 263; patrons of, 263; as professors, 256. *See also* Koran readers
muqṭāʿs, 29
murattib, 27
murattib al-dhakhīra, Iranian receives, 66
mushtarawāt: definition of, 21; insecurity of, 22; shortage of, 27
Muslim calendar, festivals of, 262
Muslim community: jurist-scholars in, 321; rectitude of, 323
Muslim Copts, distinct from ʿulama', 274
Muslim historiography, origins, 6
Muslim institutions, closed to Copts, 273
Muslim regimes in India, 64
Muslims: clerks as, 211; of Coptic descent, 81
Muslim societies, revered persons in, 255
Muslim world: scholarly network of, 144; scholasticism in, 316; ʿulama' from, 150; values of, 324; view of Mamluk Egypt, 34; western reaches of, 35
al-Mustaʿīn, Caliph: appoints kātib al-sirr, 208; tie to Upper Egyptian, 50
al-Mustanjid Yūsuf, Caliph: marriage to Bulqīnī, 237
al-Mustanṣir mosque: muʿīd in, 264
muʿtaqads: analysis of, 130; from Anatolia, 70-71; 157; definition of, 267; in Delta, 44-45; distribution of, 269; professors as, 252; Syrians as, 154; from Upper Egypt, 152. *See also* ascetics
al-Muʿtaṣim, Caliph: reliance on Mamluks, 15
muwaqqiʿs: Copts as, 273; definition of, 211; distribution of, 212-13; secretaries as, 204; as ʿulama', 212. *See also* clerks
mystic principles, *see* taṣawwuf
mysticism and Islamic sciences, 221
mystics: Iranians as, 67; supported by kārimīs, 30; Upper Egyptians as, 152. *See also* Ṣūfīs

Naḥīyat Dahmar, waqfs in, 327
nā'ib muḥtasibs of districts, 23
nā'ib qāḍīs: analysis of, 130; definition of, 228; distribution of, 229, 426 n53; mobility of, 229. *See also* deputy judges
nāsikhs: analysis of, 130; definition of, 241-42; muwaqqiʿs as, 212. *See also* copyists
al-Nāṣirī al-Qibṭī, Saʿd: tājir firanj, 428 n83
Nāṣirī mosque, Cairenes in, 147. *See also* Citadel mosque
Nāṣirīya madrasa: Bulqīnī in, 237; Cairenes in, 146; description of, 332-33
natural sciences, Iranians in, 65
Nawrūz: ties to Iranians, 65-66; as viceroy, 55
Nāẓir al-awqāf: analysis of, 130; of Shaykhūnīya, 337. *See also* controller of waqfs
nāẓir al-jawālī, *see* minority taxes
nāẓir al-jaysh, *see* controller of army
nāẓir al-māristān, *see* controller of hospital
nāẓirs: in Ashrafīya, 335; definition of, 213; distribution of, 218; harassment of, 214; of hospital, 141; Mamluks as, 214; as muḥtasib, 224; pressures on, 212; as qāḍīs, 230-31; of royal bureaus, 205; secretaries as, 205; Syrians as, 56; waqf doner as, 329. *See also* controllers
Near East: bureaucracies of, 202; social institutions in, 325; urban institutions in, 78

necrologies in chronicles, 7
Nile: fortress on, 18; ports of, 134
Nile shore district: development of, 134; institutions of, 340; Mamluks in, 202; professors in, 253
Nile swamps, reclamation from, 134
Nile valley: depression of, 49; integrity of, 40; religious establishment in, 49; tie with North Africa, 74; upper reaches of, 77
nisbas: definiton of, 12; distinctions between, 411 n2; to distinguish persons, 38; as geographic indicator, 411 n3; sequences of in Syria, 58; as surname, 38
Nīshabūr, migration from, 64
Niẓām al-Mulk, founder of madrasa, 138
North Africa: ascetics from, 159; cultural backwater, 35, 76; immigration from, xxi; individuals from in *Ḍaw'*, 9; physicians from, 74; travel through, 74. *See also* al-Maghrib
North Africans: in al-Azhar, 158; culture of, 74; economic stature of, 75; in Festival Gate cluster, 158-59; proportions of, 159. *See also* Maghribīs
northeast district: Anatolians in, 156; Arabians in, 159; basis of study, 136; Delta Egyptians in, 150; development of, 131; dominance in education, 160; during Fāṭimid period, 132; imāms in, 259; Iranians in, 155; Iraqis in, 157; khaṭībs in, 261; librarians in, 255; Maghribīs in, 158; merchants in, 245; muʿīds in, 248; muqri' in, 265; Syrians in, 154; Upper Egyptians in, 151; zone of ʿulama', 240. *See also* Fāṭimid district
northwest district: Cairenes in, 147; development of, 134; Mamluks in, 202
notaries: from Delta, 47; distribution, 426 n45; function of, 417 n71; localism of, 80; merchants as, 244; no Copts as, 274; prerogatives of, 212; Syrians as, 56. *See also* shāhids
notaryship initiates career, 225
Nubia: individuals from in *Ḍaw'*, 9; migration from, 77
al-Nujūm al-Zāhira, 11
nuwwāb as subordinate faculty, 252
occupational categories: Iraqis in, 73; Makkans and Madīnans in, 73; selection of, 130
occupational pattern of geographic groups, 161-62
occupational sites: analysis of, 130; usage of, 144-45
occupations, regional variation in, 79
oculist in Siryāqūs khānqāh, 341
oil dealer, muʿtaqad as, 268
Old Cairo: Anatolians in, 157; Cairenes in, 147; development of, 135; as earliest center, 131; Ḥanafī qāḍī of, 55; imāms in, 259; institutions of, 340; khaṭībs in, 261; litigation in, 230; Maghribīs in, 159; nāẓirs in, 219; professors in, 253; Shāfiʿī chief justice of, 46; shaykhs in, 223; in study, 4
omissions by biographers, 13
ophthalmia of muqri', 264
oratories in khānqāhs, 140
orphanages: in khānqāhs, 140; in madrasas, 139, 330; shaykhs of, 25; supported by kārimīs, 30. *See also* schools for orphans
orthodoxy: under Mamluks, 35; al-Sakhāwī stresses, 318
Ottoman court, Iranian at, 66
Ottoman Pasha governors in Citadel, 338
Ottoman period, political order before, 324-25
Ottoman rule: in Cairo, 4; over Anatolia, 68-69
Ottoman state, growth of, 24
Ottoman sultans attract ʿulama', 69
Ottomans, trade under, 33
Oxford, 132

palace, muqri's in, 266
Palestine, artisans from, 57; Crusader elements in, 18; in Mamluk empire, 51; migration from, 59
pastoralism of Turcomans, 63
peasantry: economic decline of, 29; under Ilkhānids, 62
peer ties among jurist-scholars, 321
pensions for Mamluks, 27
Persian civilization, centered in Zagros, 63

Persian commercial classes under Ilkhānids, 62
Persian cultural sphere, 68
Persian Gulf, migration from, 63, 73
Persian intellectual tradition, 68
Persians: in India, 65; under Ilkhānids, 62. *See also* Iranians
pharmacists in Manṣūrī hospital, 332
philosophy: in madrasas, 139; studied by Maghribī, 75
physicians: background of, 79; in hospitals, 140; Iranians as, 67; Maghribīs as, 74; in Manṣūrī hospital, 332; in Siryāqūs khānqāh, 341
piety: parochialism of, 316; social function of, 255; and Sufism, 271
pious trust foundations, controller of, 217. *See also* waqfs
plague: cause of decline, 29, 32; in fourteenth century, 19; impact on southeast, 134
plantation setting of southeast, 134
poetics in madrasa, 139
poets: Iranians as, 67; supported by kārimīs, 30; Syrian as, 208
polarization between Mamluks and ʿulamaʾ, 155
Poliak, A. N.: on Yāsa, 407 n35
police networks, organization of, 23
polo fields of Mamluk amirs, 134
poor, exclusion from khānqāh, 328
poor houses attached to madrasas, 139
Popper, W.: on bureaucracy, 420 n32; maps of, 131; occupational classifications of, 129; on northwest-southwest districts, 134
ports, litigation in, 230
Portugal, exploration by, 33
Portuguese in Indian Ocean, 73
prayer callers: from Delta, 45; in Ṣāliḥīya, 331; in Ṭūlūnid mosque, 339
prayer leaders from Delta, 45. *See also* imāms
preacher, muqriʾ as, 263
prestige in religio-academic network, 163
principalities of Anatolia, 69
privy funds, control of, 56, 218
privy treasury, nāẓirs in, 219
professional activity of civilian elite, 201
professional appointments in biographies, 13
professional entry, elite institutions in, 160-61
professional solidarity, 316
professorial chairs, Bulqīnīs hold, 240
professors: in Ashrafīya, 335; Bulqīnīs as, 239; certification by, 251; deputy judges as, 229; in Ḥākim mosque, 333; in Ḥijāzīya madrasa, 329; imāms as, 259; in Jamālīya, 329; in Manṣūrīya, 331; merchants as, 244; in Muʾayyadīya, 336; muʿīds as, 248; muqriʾs as, 263-65; as muʿtaqad, 268; in Nāṣirīya, 333; as nāẓirs, 214, 217; religious functionaries as, 256; in Ṣāliḥīya, 331; in Ṣarghatmishīya, 339; shāhids as, 226; in Shaykhūnīya, 337; security of, 251; in Ṭaybarsīya, 334; in Ṭūlūnid mosque, 339; in Ẓāhirīya, 331. *See also* mudarrises
Prophet: cities of, 73; ideals of, 316
Prophet's life, model for behavior, 5
Prophetic traditions: Bulqīnī in, 239; in Kāmilīya madrasa, 330; in madrasa curriculum, 138-39; in Muʾayyadīya, 336; in Ṣarghatmishīya, 338; in Ṭūlūnid mosque, 339. *See also* Ḥadīth
prosopography as genre, 6

qāḍī al-ʿaskar, *see* military judge
Qādirī order in Cairo, 270
qāḍīs: analysis of, 130; definition of, 227-28, 230; distribution of, 240-41; of districts, 23; jurisdiction of, 320; as kātibs al-sirr, 206; in minority madhhabs, 315; pressures on, 24; from Syria, 54; testimony heard by, 225; ties to amirs, 54. *See also* judges
Qāḍīs al-quḍāt: analysis of, 130; definition of, 231. *See also* chief justices
al-Qāhira: usage of, 131, 133; khaṭībs in, 261. *See also* Cairo
Qalāʾūn, al-Manṣūr: descendants of, 333; endowment of, 219; founds madrasa, 331; founds hospital, 332; iqṭāʿ system under, 18; tomb of, 254
al-Qalqashandī: commentaries of, 129; manual of, 417 n4

Qalyūbīya: administrative institutions in, 47; migration from, 41-42
qanāt network in Iran, 62
Qarāfa: Cairenes in, 147; cemetery of, 135; Delta Egyptians in, 150; institutions of, 339; Iranians in, 156; location of, 337; muʿtaqads in, 269; nāẓirs in, 219; professors in, 253; in study, 4; Upper Egyptians in, 152
qarānīṣ, qarāniṣa, 21
Qarāsanqur al-Manṣūrī, Shams: founds madrasa, 329
Qarāsanqurīya madrasa, description of, 329
Qaṣaba, merchants in, 245. *See also* Main Avenue
Qaṣaba district, evolution of, 133
Qaṣr al-Kabsh district: Mamluks in, 202; settlement in, 133-34
Qaṭāʾiʿ district: settlement in, 133-34; institutions in, 337
Qaṭrān, migration from, 68
Qāy, migration from, 48
Qayṣarīya of Amir ʿAlī, waqfs on, 332
Qāytbāy, al-Ashraf: arrests nāẓir, 218; charisma of, 27; Mamluks imported by, 26; mausoleum of, 340; military expenses of, 28; reign of, 21; ties to Bulqīnī, 239; ties to Maghribī, 76
Qazvīn, migration from, 64
al-Qibābī, Muḥayy, 263-64
Qibṭ, usage of, 272. *See also* Copts
Qinā: decline of, 49; migration from, 48
Qipjak spoken by Mamluks, 70
Qipjak Turks as Mamluks, 18
Qubbat al-Naṣr, Iranians at, 67, 156
al-Quds, *see* Jerusalem
Qunīya (Konya), migration from, 68
Qūṣ: decline of, 49; migration from, 48
Quṣayr, decline of, 49
Qusṭanṭīna, physician from, 74

al-Rāʿī, 76
ramad, *see* ophthalmia
ra's al-nawba, civilian marries, 238
ra's nawbat al-nuwwāb, 23
Rashīd al-Dīn, reforms of, 62
rātib, 27
ratio, nisbas to birthplaces, 48
Raṭlī Lake area: Mamluks in, 202; merchants in, 245
Ravaisse, P. on topography, 131, 418 n14
Rawāḥīya madrasa, muqriʾ in, 263
Rawḍa Island: barracks on, 18; development of, 134
Rāy, migration from, 64
Raydānīya in study, 4
recitation: in madrasa curriculum, 138-39; muqri's' erudition in, 263
reconquista, threat to Muslim community, 35
rectors, *see* shaykhs
Red Sea: commodities from, 245; control of, 73; ports on, 31, 34, 49
regional traditions, transfer of, 81
religio-academic establishment: muḥtasibs in, 225; parochialism of, 161
religio-academic institutions: from Ayyūbid period, 132; in commercial setting, 142; Copt in, 273; elite group of, 160; foreigners in, 317; imāms in, 259; judges in, 240; khaṭībs in, 260; libraries in, 254; muqri's in, 262-63; muʿtaqads in, 268; nāẓirs of, 213-14; of North Africa, 77; of Ottomans, 69; shaykhs in, 221-22; in southeast, 134; Syrians in, 153; system of, 128; as training ground, 321; in urban context, 136
religio-academic network: interest groups in, 161; jurist-scholars in, 315; localism of, 144; ranking in, 319; shāhids in, 226; stewards in, 210
religious functionaries: analysis of, 130; autonomy of, 322; Iranians as, 154; as professional class, 312; shāhids as, 226; social role of, 316; as symbolic legitimators, 323
religious occupations: copyists in, 242; of Maghribī, 76; regional distribution of, 79; secretaries in, 204
renegades, Turkish-speaking, 71
repetitor: muqriʾ as, 263. *See also* muʿīds
residence pattern of geographic groups, 164
residential sites: analysis of, 130; usage of, 144-45

rest homes supported by kārimīs, 30
revenue, procurement of, 313
revered persons, *see* muʿtaqads
rhetoric in madrasas, 139
ribāṭ, *see* hospice
Ribāṭ al-Āthār al-Nabawīya, *see* Hospice of Prophet's Relics
royal mint, controller of, 216
royal stables, controller of, 217
Rūm, *see* Anatolia
al-Rumayla, Maydān, *see* Citadel Square
Rūmī, Jalāl al-Dīn, 65
Rūmīs: in Mamluk foundations, 157; status of, 72, 156; ties to royal family, 157; usage of, 68. *See also* Anatolians
rural population, reduction of, 29

Sābiqīya madrasa, description of, 329
Saburbāy, tie to Bulqīnī, 239
sacred fields in madrasa curriculum, 139
Ṣafad: administrative center, 51; jurisdiction of, 59; kātib al-sirr in, 208-209
al-Ṣafadī: compendium of, 8, 11
al-Safaṭī, Walī, 217-18
Safavids, 61
Sahara, routes across, 74
Ṣaḥrā': Arabians in, 159; Cairenes in, 147; Delta Egyptians in, 150; institutions of, 339; nāẓirs in, 219; in study, 4; Upper Egyptians in, 152. *See also* Desert Plain
al-Ṣaʿīd, artisans from, 49. *See also* Upper Egypt
Saʿīd al-Suʿadā' khānqāh: Arabians in, 159-60; Bulqīnī controller of, 239; Cairenes in, 146, 148; Cairo-Delta interest in, 161; copyists in, 242; Delta Egyptians in, 150; description of, 327; judges in, 241; imāms in, 259, khaṭībs in, 262; muqri' in, 264-66; muʿtaqads in, 269; professors in, 253; shāhids in, 227; Ṣūfīs in, 271-72; Syrians in, 154; Upper Egyptians in, 152
Ṣaʿīdīs: in al-Muqaṭṭam, 152; paucity of, 47. *See also* Upper Egyptians
saints, shrines of, 136, 223. *See also* sayyids
saints' zone in Delta, 44, 150
Sakhā, migration from, 9
al-Sakhāwī: attitude toward training, 7; background of, 8; on Bulqīnī marriages; 238; character of, 10; compiler of centennial dictionary, 6; comprehensiveness of, 144; on historical methods, 404 n16; methodology of, 12; objectives of, 9-10, 318-19; omissions of, 13; on Ibn Taghrī-Birdī, 11; tie to Maghribī, 75
Ṣalāḥ al-Dīn: activities in Egypt, 405 n1; image of, 132; khānqāh dates from, 139; founds khānqāh, 327; madrasa dates from, 138; Mamluk institution under, 18; nephew of, 132; sultanate after, 19
Ṣalāḥīya madrasa, Iranian at, 66
Salama, I., work of, 131
salaries for Mamluks, 27
Ṣāliḥīya madrasa: Cairenes in, 146; chief justices in, 153; copyists in, 242; description of, 330-31; as high court, 331; instruction in, 251; khaṭībs in, 261; nāẓir on faculty, 217; shāhids near, 227
al-Ṣāliḥ Najm al-Dīn Ayyūb: death of, 18; foundation of, 330-31
al-Ṣāliḥ Ṭalā'iʿ mosque: foundation of, 337; shāhids near, 227
Saljūq wazīr founds madrasa, 138
Salmon, G., topographical works of, 131
Samannūd, Bulqīnī in, 237
Samarqānd, migration from, 64
Samarrā, 17
Sanhūr, migration from, 265
al-Sanhūrī, Zayn, 265
Ṣarghatmish al-Nāṣirī, Sayf: founds madrasa, 338
Ṣarghatmishīya madrasa: Anatolians in, 157, cosmopolitanism of, 162; Delta Egyptians in, 150; description of, 338-39; in education, 160; Iranians in, 65, 155; judges in, 241; librarians in, 255; Maghribīs in, 159; muʿīds in, 248; professors in, 252; shaykhs in, 222; in southwest, 134, stewards in, 210; Syrians in, 152-53, 163; Syrian interest in, 161; Upper Egyptians in, 151
Ṣarūjā mosque, muqri' in, 265
Ṣarukhān, migration from, 68

Sauvaget, J., on Aleppo, 414 n31
sawākin, 31
sayyids in Delta, 44. *See also* saints
scholarly categories: kātibs al-sirr in, 206; secretaries in, 204
scholarly-educational professions, analysis of, 130
scholars: in Damascus, 52; Iranians as, 154; in khānqāhs, 139-40; library of, 254; regional background of, 80; supported by kārimīs, 30; ties to Maghribī, 74
schools for orphans: attached to madrasas, 329, 331, 336, 339; in mosques, 333, 338-39. *See also* orphanages
schools of law in Cairo, 315
scientists, Iranians as, 67
secretarial class: ranking of, 47; segregation from ʿulamaʾ, 209
secretaries: belittlement of, 204; contrast with kātib al-sirr, 204; Copts as, 273; distinct from copyists, 242; in executive and fiscal offices, 205; mobility of, 204-205; subordination of, 214. *See also* kātibs
secretary of chancellery: Copts as, 273; rarely from Delta, 47; Iranians as, 66-67; Syrians as, 55-56. *See also* kātib al-sirr
secular disciplines: instruction in, 250; in madrasas, 139
servants: in hospitals, 141; of military elite, 133; muʿtaqads as, 268
shabābīk, *see* galleries
Shaʿbān II, al-Ashraf: endowments of, 328, 340; library of, 329; tie to Syrian, 54
Shādhilī order in Cairo, 270
Shāfiʿī jurisprudence: nāẓir in, 217; in Ẓāhirīya, 153, 158, 331
Shāfiʿī justice: of Aleppo, 207; Bulqīnī as, 233; Cairenes as, 54; Delta Egyptian as, 46; Iranians as, 66; as khaṭīb in Citadel mosque, 338; as nāẓir, 217, 335
Shāfiʿī madhhab, Delta influence on, 149
Shāfiʿī qāḍī, *see* Shāfiʿī justice
al-Shāfiʿī tomb, *see* Imām al-Shāfiʿī tomb
shāhids: analysis of, 130; definition of, 225; distribution of, 227; residence of, 253; role of, 226. *See also* notaries
Shajar al-Durr: career of, 18; husband's tomb, 331
al-Shām, *see* Syria
shamanism, influence on Mamluks, 268
sharīʿa: centrality of, 221; on contracts, 29; contrast with applied law, 224; departure from, 320; influence on merchants, 244; integrity of, 318; interpreters of, 314; in litigation, 80, 229-30; minority schools of, 315; shāhids trained in, 274; sultan enforces, 216, 232; Syrians studying, 153; training in, 226; variants in, 319; violation of, 215
sharīʿa court system, autonomy of, 251
shāriʿ jurisprudence, maturation of, 7
shāriʿ legal system: chief justices in, 231; jurist-scholars dominate, 315
sharīfs in Delta, 44
Sharqīya: administrative institutions in, 47; migration from, 41-43; as saints' zone, 44; waqfs in, 332
Shaykh al-Islām as chief justice, 221
Shaykh, al-Muʾayyad: enthronement of, 67; favors foreign ʿulamaʾ, 156-57; founds madrasa, 336; patronage of Syrians, 57; title of, 222; as viceroy, 55
—ties: to Bulqīnī, 236; to Iranian, 66; to Syrians, 55-56: 153, 207-208
shaykhs, analysis of, 130; in Aqbughāwīya, 335; definition of, 221; distribution of, 222; fiscal oppression of, 25; imāms as, 259; in legal category, 425 n37; in Muʾayyadīya, 336; muʿtaqads as, 268; as nāẓirs, 214; overlap with other offices, 130; of Shaykhūnīya, 337; Ṣūfīs as, 270
Shaykh al-Shuyūkh: office of, 221; of Saʿīd al-Suʿadāʾ, 327; of Siryāqūs, 341
Shaykh al-Tāj al-ʿAjamī, 66
Shaykhū, Sayf: foundation of, 337; tie to Iranian, 67
Shaykhūnīya madrasa/khānqāh: Anatolians in, 71, 156; Cairenes in, 146-48; copyists in, 242; cosmopolitanism of, 162; Delta Egyptians in, 149-50; description of, 337; in education, 160;

Ḥanafī jurisprudence in, 149; imāms in, 259; Iranians in, 65, 155; librarians in, 255; Maghribīs in, 158-59; muqri's in, 264, 266; nāẓirs in, 219; professors in, 252; shaykhs in, 222; stewards in, 210; Syrian interest in, 161; Syrians in, 152-53, 163; Ṣūfīs in, 272; Upper Egyptians in, 50, 151-52
al-Shawbak, migration from, 59
Shīrāz, migration from, 64
Shirkūh, activities in Egypt, 405 n1
Shirwān, migration from, 65
al-Shirwānī, Jalāl, 65
shops: in biographies, 142; courts near, 228
shrines: of revered person, 141; shaykhs of, 25. *See also* zāwiyas
shuhra: definition of, 12; as family name, 38
Shurbūsh merchants' street, waqfs in, 332
Shuyūkh al-balad in Citadel, 338
silk merchants, Iranians as, 67
sinecurism: by civilian elite, 201; implications of, 319
Sinjār, migration from, 73
Sīra: definition of, 5; of Prophet, 403 n6
al-Sirāfa as staff, 56
Sīrat al-Nabī, 5
Siryāqūs khānqāh: Anatolians in, 156; Cairenes in, 148; Delta Egyptians in, 150; description of, 341; in education, 160; imāms in, 259; Iranians in, 155; judges in, 241; Maghribīs in, 159; Ṣūfīs in, 272
Siryāqūs village, migration from, 42
Sīwās, migration from, 68
Skandarīs, activities of, 42
skewing factor: of dates, 84; in migration rates, 78
slaves: dependence on purchasers, 16; for military service, 15; trade in, 27, 245. *See also* military slaves
slave traders, Anatolians as, 72
social unrest in fourteenth century, 19
Somalia, migration from, 77
sources used by biographers, 13
southeast district: Anatolians in, 156-57; Arabians in, 159; basis of study, 136; Cairenes in, 147; Delta Egyptians in, 149-50; development of, 133; institutions in, 337; Iranians in, 155; Iraqis in, 158; judges in, 240-41; khaṭībs in, 261; librarians in, 255; Maghribīs in, 158-59; muʿīds in, 248; muqri's in, 266; nāẓirs in, 219; professors in, 252; Ṣūfīs in, 272; Syrians in, 153-54; Upper Egyptians in, 151
southwest district: Cairenes in, 147; Delta Egyptians in, 150; development of, 134; khaṭībs in, 261; Mamluks in, 202; Upper Egyptians, 151
Spain: center of scholarship, 35; exploration by, 33. *See also* al-Andalus
special bureau, control of, 56
specialization in professions, 312
spice monopoly, outline of, 30. *See also* monopolies
spy networks, secretaries in, 204
stables of Mamluk amirs, 134
Staffa, S. J., topographical work of, 131
standard of living, decline in, 32
state control over applied law, 224
state merchants as bureaucrats, 31. *See also* merchants
stewards: Copts as, 274; duties of, 210; merchants as, 244; Muslims as, 252. *See also* mubāshirs; superintendants
storehouses, nāẓirs in, 219
streets, shāhids near, 227
Striped Palace, nāẓirs in, 219
students: contact with foreigners, 142; in hospitals, 140
student-teacher ties, function of, 229
Succor Dome, *see* Qubbat al-Naṣr
Sudan, individuals from in *Ḍaw'*, 9
Ṣūdūn al-Qāḍī, nāẓir of al-Azhar, 334
Ṣūdūn min Zāda madrasa: Iranians in, 155; professors in, 252
al-Ṣūfī, Shams, 264-65
Ṣūfī communities: residence in, 145; stewards in, 211
Ṣūfī hospices: Cairenes in, 146; nāẓirs in, 219. *See also* khānqāhs
Ṣūfī institutions: autonomy of, 214; Syrians in, 152
Ṣūfī orders: Delta Egyptians in, 45; foreigners in, 317; in judiciary, 227; membership in, 148; respect for ascetics by, 152

Ṣūfī shaykh in Jamālīya madrasa, 329
Ṣūfī theology studied by Maghribī, 75
Ṣūfīs: Anatolians as, 71, 156; in Aqbughāwīya, 335; Arabians as, 160; autonomy of, 270; in artisanship and commerce, 222; in al-Azhar, 151; Bulqīnī as, 238; copyists as, 242; deputy judges as, 230; distribution of, 271-72; hospices for, 150, 241, 335; imāms as, 259; Iranians as, 155; in khānqāhs, 140; as khaṭībs, 262; Maghribīs as, 159; merchants as, 246; in Mu'ayyadīya, 336; as muqri's, 266; mu'taqads as, 268-69; muwaqqi's as, 213; professors as, 253; shāhids as, 227, 253; shaykhs as, 221; in Shaykhūnīya, 337; support of, 327, 419 n24. *See also* mystics
Sufism: distribution of, 129; and public piety, 271; as social system, 221
sugar, monopoly over, 32
Sultan Ḥasan mosque: Cairenes in, 147; description of, 337-38; Iranians in, 155; khaṭībs in, 261; muqri' in, 263
sulṭānī merchant: in monopolies, 244; as nāẓir, 217. *See also* merchants; tujjār al-sulṭān
sultans: accept renegades, 71; appoint judges, 24, 228, 315; appointment policy of, 215; attitude toward controllers, 216; confiscation by, 240; demand for funds, 26; economic policies of, 33; encroachment on waqfs, 213; endowments of, 139, 433 n50; extortion by, 22; foundations of, 150, 330; monitor jurist-scholars, 321; peer status of, 19; purchase Mamluks, 22; reputations of, 141; response to unemployed Mamluks, 28; response to Ṣūfīs, 328; security of, 19; support muqri's, 262
—ties: to chief justices, 232; to imāms, 258; to kātib al-sirr, 47, 205; to mu'taqads, 268-69
sultan's agents, nāẓirs as, 213
sultan's household, opulence of, 32
sultan's palace, Anatolians in, 157
Sunna: custodians of, 7, 322; interpreted in colleges, 321
Sunnī ideals, exemplars of, 318
Sunnī learning in madrasas, 138
Sunnī religious service, Ṣūfīs in, 271
Sunnī scholarship, Ayyūbid centers of, 132
Sunnism, nature of, 164
superintendants: analysis of, 130; from Delta, 47. *See also* stewards
supervisor of waqf endowments, analysis of, 130
surgeon in Siryāqūs khānqāh, 341
al-Suyūṭī, Jalāl, 50; as polymath, 51, 239; status of, 151
symbiosis between bureaucrats and militarists, 81
Syria: in Mamluk empire, 51; kātibs al-sirr from, 206; Maghribī in, 75; migration within, 58; muqri' in, 264; provinces of, 414 n39; real estate in, 32; scholars from, 57; waqf in, 331
Syria-Palestine: as buffer zone, 53; bureaucrats from, 79; clustering in, 59; data on, 144; individuals from in *Ḍaw'*, 9; migration from, 78; nisba-birthplace ratio, 48; qāḍīs from, 54
Syrian cities, devastation of, 60
Syrian coast, sites along, 59
Syrian steppe, sites in, 59
Syrians: in bureaucracy, 47, 153-54, 314; in commerce, 57; distribution of, 163; in executive positions, 81; in intelligence, 206-207; interest groups of, 161; as jurist-scholars, 154; as religious functionaries, 57; from rural areas, 59; studies of, 152; in Ṣūfī institutions, 152; ties to patrons, 207; transfer to Cairo, 53

Ṭabalkhānah, *see* amir of forty
Ṭabaqāt, Ḥadīth referees in, 6
al-Ṭablāwī, 'Alā', 215-16
Tabrīz, migration from, 64, 67
al-Tabrīzī al-Isra'īlī, Fatḥ, 67
Ṭahṭā, migration from, 48
tājir awlād, Copt as, 428 n83
tājir firanj, Copt as, 428 n83
Tājir sulṭānī, Maghribī as, 428 n84
tājirs: analysis of, 130; definition, 242, 244; distribution of, 245. *See also* merchants
Takrīt, migration from, 73
Tanbadī, migration from, 48

Tankiz-Bughā, mausoleum of, 340
Ṭanṭa: mawlids in, 44; migration from, 264
al-Ṭanṭadā'ī, Badr, 264
Ṭarābulus: administrative center, 51; controller of army in, 56; data from, 9; jurisdiction of, 59; kātib al-sirr in, 208; migration from, 59
Ta'rīkh al-Islām, 404 n10
taṣawwuf, principles of, 150-51, 271
Ṭaṭar al-Ḥijāzīya, Khūnd: founds madrasa, 329
Ṭaṭar, al-Ẓāhir: appoints Bulqīnī, 236
taqqī': definition of, 423 nn21, 22; prerogative of, 213
taxation: control over, 214; under Ilkhānids, 62
tax base, capacity of, 22
taxes, returns from, 26
Ṭaybars al-Khāzindārī, 'Alā': founds hospice, 335
Ṭaybarsīya Chapel, Iranians in, 155
teachers: function of, 246; in Manṣūrī hospital, 332; supported by kārimīs, 30. *See also* mu'allim
textiles, monopoly over, 32
thaghr, definition of, 42
theology in madrasa curriculum, 138-39
throne, goal of amirs, 19
al-Ṭibnāwī, Nūr, 45
Tigris valley, migration from, 59
Tilimsān, migration from, 74-75
Timur Lenk: campaigns of, 60, 415 n50; knew of Ibn Khaldūn, 74; routes used by, 64; spoliations of, 34
Timurid conquest, impact of, 34
Timurid crisis, cause of migration, 67
Timurid invasions: into Anatolia, 69; end migration era, 34; into Iran and Iraq, 63-64, 79; Mamluk reaction to, 53; migration before, 65; against Ottomans, 24; stimulate migration, 60
Timurid period, ascetics during, 267
Timurids, support of 'ulama', 34
Tlemcen, *see* Tilimsān
tomb guards in mortuary zone, 136
tombs: in Delta, 44; fiscal benefits of, 142; in khānqāhs, 140; of Mamluks, 141; muqri's in, 266; mu'taqads in, 269; shaykhs in, 223
Tower, barracks of, 18
towns under provincial courts, 228
Transoxiana, migration from, 64, 77
treasury controlled by Cairenes, 56
Tripoli, *see* Ṭarābulus
trooper, attitude of, 19. *See also* jundī
trust properties controlled by Cairenes, 56
tujjār al-kārim, *see* kārimī merchants
tujjār al-sulṭān: under Barsbay, 31; Maghribīs as, 75. *See also* sulṭānī merchant
Ṭūkh, migration from, 42
Ṭūlūnid mosque: Bulqīnī in, 236-37; Cairenes in, 146-47; Delta Egyptians in, 150; description of, 339; khaṭībs in, 261; Maghribīs in, 158-59; mu'īds in, 248; muqri's in, 266; professors in, 252; in southwest, 134; stewards in, 210; Syrians in, 153
Tūnis: Ibn Khaldūn in, xxi, 75; physician from, 74
Tunisia, migration from, 74
Tūrān-Shāh, assassination of, 18
Turco-Persian elite of Iran, 62
Turcoman confederations: east of Mamluk frontier, 68; in Iran, 63; in Iraq, 72
Turkish; favored by Mamluks, 70; learned by nāẓir, 217
Turkish peoples, pagan culture of, 268
Turkish-speaking regions, mu'taqads from, 268
Turks, status of, 72. *See also* Atrāk
Two Shrines, Iranian controller of, 66

'ulama': admission to, 321; from Anatolia, 157; associated with tombs, 141; attitude toward controllership, 218; attitude toward Copts, 215, 273; attracted to Anatolia, 69; autonomy of, 251, 274; allocate Mamluk endowments, 330; artisan activities of, 241; in bureaucracy, 214; consensus among, 7; copyists as, 242; chief justices in, 231; cosmopolitanism of, 162, 315; from Cairo-Delta zone, 317; demoralization of, 24; exclude secretaries, 209; exposed to political tension, 20; of foreign background, 163; in hospitals, 140; hostility toward secretaries, 205; households of, 145; impact of invasions

ʿulamaʾ (*cont.*)
on, 62; interchanged with aʿyan, 4, 200; from Iran, 63, 155; jurists among, 319; legal function of, 220-21; mediation of, 201, 231-32; merchants as, 242, 244; migration by, 77; muḥtasibs as, 224; multicompetence of, 4, 320; muʿtaqads as, 267; muwaqqiʿs as, 212-13; as nāẓirs, 214; from North Africa, 77; political sentiments of, 331; prerogatives of, 20; in regime's service, 320; relationship with bureaucracy, 202-203; religious functionaries as, 255; self-reliance of, 60; separation from militarists, 258; shaykhs as, 223; in southeast, 134; status as, 252; stewards as, 210; Ṣūfīs as, 222, 271; in Syria, 54; Syrians as, 163, 314; training as, 80; Turkish-speaking, 70; under Timurids, 34; from Upper Egypt, 49, 151; urban background of, 77
ʿulamaʾ class: in Anatolia, 69; cosmopolitan elements of, 164; integration into, 162; judges in, 230; Shāhids in, 226
ʿulamaʾ families: deputy judges in, 229; judges in, 230; muqriʾs in, 263
ʿulūm qadīma, *see* ancient sciences
Umayyad mosque: Bulqīnī in, 237; khaṭīb in, 207-208
Umayyad period: use of Mamluks during, 15; fate of Aleppo from, 53; role of Damascus from, 52
Umm al-Sulṭān madrasa: Iranian at, 65; professors in, 252
Upper Egypt: commodities from, 245; Coptic establishment in, 50; data on, 144; depopulation of, 29, 48; deurbanization of, 413 n21; holy hermits from, 152; literati from, 50; migration from, 48; mystics from, 152; nisba-birthplace ratio in, 48; trade in, 49; waqfs in, 328, 333. *See also* al-Ṣaʿīd
Upper Egyptians: paucity of, 162-63; in ʿulamaʾ class, 151. *See also* Ṣaʿīdīs
urban centers in Muslim world, 324
Urmā (Urmia), migration from, 68
Ushmunayn district: migration from, 48; muʿtaqad from, 152
ustādār, nāẓir as, 216
vestibule area, nāẓirs in, 219
viceroys: of Aleppo, 54; attitude toward sultanate, 19; of Damascus, 55; staffs of, 206; ties to Iranian, 65
vizierate, Copt receives, 216
Vizier Gate, shaykhs at, 222
violence in cities, 431 n4

al-Wāfī bi'l-Wafīyat, 8, 11
wāʿiẓ, muqriʾ as, 263
wakīl bayt al-māl, *see* agent of exchequer
wālīs, *see* governors
waqf endowments: of later Mamluk peiod, 132; pressure on, 24
waqf funds: Bulqīnī controls, 236; of hospitals, 141
waqf properties: in Damascus, 52; revenues from, 433 n49; in Upper Egypt, 49
waqf supervisors from Delta, 47
waqf writ, librarianship in, 253
waqfs: controlled by Cairenes, 56; controllers of, 219; encroachment on, 213; of kārimī merchants, 30. *See also* pious trust foundations
warehouses supported by kārimīs, 30
warrior-nomads, Mongols as, 61
Wāsiṭ, migration from, 73
water carrier, muʿtaqad as, 268
wazīrs: pressures on, 212; secretaries as, 205; supplanted by kātib al-sirr, 205
White Sheep Turcomans in Iran, 63

Yamanīs in Cairo, 159
Yashbak min Mahdī, al-Dawādār: support of muqriʾ, 265
Yashbak, atābek: tie to Syrian, 208
Yashbak tomb: Iranians in, 156; nāẓirs in, 219
Yazd, migration from, 64
Yemen: Anatolian's ancestor from, 71; migration from, 73
Yūnus al-Nawrūzī, mausoleum of, 340
Yūsuf al-Ustādār, Jamāl: founds khānqāh, 329

Zagros mountains, population of, 63

al-Zāhid mosque, khaṭībs in, 261
Ẓāhirīya madrasa: Arabians in, 159-60; Cairenes in, 146; Delta Egyptians in, 149; description of, 331; instruction in, 251; Iranians in, 155; librarians in, 255; Maghribīs in, 158; prominence of, 160; Shāfiʿī and Ḥanafī jurisprudence in, 158; Syrians in, 153; Upper Egyptians in, 151
Zāwiyas: Anatolians in, 157; near Bāb al-Naṣr, 334; in Delta, 44-45, 150-51; in Damascus, 52; Iranian in, 67; muʿtaqads in, 268-69; persons supported in, 136; shaykhs in, 223; in Upper Egypt, 49. *See also* shrines
Zaynī mosque, khaṭībs in, 261
Zimāmīya madrasa, Bulqīnī in, 237
Zuwayla Gate: markets around, 245; shāhids near, 227. *See also* Bāb Zuwayla
Zuwayla quarter: shaykhs in, 223; waqfs on, 328

Library of Congress Cataloging in Publication Data

Petry, Carl F., 1943-
The civilian elite of Cairo in the later Middle Ages.

Bibliography: p.
Includes index.
1. Elite (Social sciences)—Egypt—Cairo—History—15th century. 2. Social classes—Egypt—History—15th century. 3. Professions—Egypt—History—15th century. I. Title.
HN786.C3P48 305.5′2 80-8570
ISBN 0-691-05329-4 AACR2